# The
# Confederate Soldiers
# of
# Hamilton County, Tennessee

AN ALPHABETICAL LISTING OF THE CONFEDERATE SOLDIERS
WHO LIVED AT ONE TIME IN HAMILTON COUNTY, TENNESSEE

*Nathaniel Cheairs Hughes, Junior*
*and John C. Wilson*

Heritage Books
2024

**HERITAGE BOOKS**

*AN IMPRINT OF HERITAGE BOOKS, INC.*

**Books, CDs, and more—Worldwide**

For our listing of thousands of titles see our website
at
www.HeritageBooks.com

Published 2024 by
HERITAGE BOOKS, INC.
Publishing Division
5810 Ruatan Street
Berwyn Heights, MD 20740

International Standard Book Number
Paperbound: 978-0-7884-8723-1

DEDICATED
WITH APPRECIATION AND ADMIRATION
TO
LIBRARIANS,
PARTICULARLY THOSE OF
HAMILTON COUNTY,

AND TO
THOSE UNHERALDED SOULS
WHO INDEX

# TABLE OF CONTENTS:

PREFACE

Chattanoogans have a happy impression of the history of their city and county. There were painful interludes, it is agreed--the agony of Cherokee removal and then, twenty years later, a period of occupation and military rule--two years under the Confederates, two years under the Federals. But things healed nicely and promptly as symbolized by the splendid statue of Billy Yank and Johnny Reb shaking hands atop Lookout Mountain.

Perhaps this is so, perhaps not. A great deal is known about the Union veterans of this county, particularly the men who came here as soldiers and remained, deciding to make Chattanooga their home. The John Wilders and Hiram Chamberlains and John E. MacGowans invested enormous energy and love in this strip of land along the Tennessee called Hamilton County. They shaped post-war Chattanooga. One hundred and fifty years later their descendants still are the propertied leaders of the community, devotedly keeping the memories of their ancestors bright and burnished, their names remembered and honored.

There were a few ex-Confederates of note, of course. David M. Key springs to mind. But after Key, one must scratch for names as though there had been a vacuum, as though many notables of 1860 had been transported. Considered as a group, these remaining Confederates, the ex-rebels of 1865-1876, seem to have had minimal impact upon post-war Chattanooga and Hamilton County. They were low-profile citizens, of humble station for the most part. These former soldiers did not own the banks or the newspapers or rule politically, at least not until after 1876 when a large influx of new citizens brought many former Confederates to town from all over the South. Some of these newcomers had money; some had valuable connections stretching across the South; some were determined to assert themselves economically and politically.

Who were the Confederates of Hamilton County, anyway, both the newcomers and those who ran out into the dusty streets waving a strange new flag in the spring of 1861. It is said the original Rebels were mostly city dwellers as opposed to those who lived on farms out in county, those who tended to be Unionists. Miss Zella Armstrong, historian of Hamilton County, left a list of about six hundred Confederates and hinted there might be more.

Curiosity led the authors to investigate. We began compiling names in the fall of 1994, using Miss Zella's list as the nucleus of our roster. We talked to everyone who would listen, we checked cemetery records and tombstones, we leafed through thirteen volumes of the minutes of the Nathan Bedford Forrest Camp, UCV, we read thousands of obituaries, we went through the compiled service records of the units raised in Hamilton County, and we read the censuses of the county, cross-checking them against the military records. The Confederate regimental records and rolls we often found disappointing--fragmentary, incomplete and sometimes carelessly prepared. One of the Hamilton County units--Osborne's Scouts--had no rolls, no official records at all.

The investigation grew wider. A doctor in Oklahoma sent us medical records of the 19th Tennessee Infantry which contained many Chattanoogans, a man in Illinois provided extensive information about the unfortunates imprisoned at Rock Island. The roster grew by leaps, especially when we determined to include both the residents of Hamilton County in 1860 and those who settled here after the war.

Many of the names proved bogus unfortunately. When, just after the turn of the century, the State of Tennessee decided to provide pensions to destitute veterans and their widows, Confederates popped up everywhere. Many of these had never worn the gray unfortunately, and many Confederate widows were so vague about their husband's service that their pension claims were dismissed out of hand.

Other problems confounded our search. Men from Catoosa and Walker County, Georgia, and northeast Alabama often mixed into Tennessee regiments and vice versus. Men jumped from unit to unit; units were disbanded; different units carried the same name; units split, combined or were absorbed. Many of our Hamilton County Confederates, for instance, rode with Colonel Carter. Which Colonel Carter? Col. Nathan W. Carter who commanded the 21st Tennessee Cavalry (known also as Carter's Scouts and as Wheeler's Scouts) or Col. James E. Carter who commanded one of the two regiments designated as the 1st Tennessee Cavalry. Our men served with both. What about the men of Co. H, 26th Tennessee Infantry who would be transformed into Co. I, 1st Confederate Infantry, a Georgia regiment. Then there was Capt. J. S. Tyner's Co. K, 1st Confederate Cavalry (a Tennessee unit) which also was called the Second Company K, 12th and 16th Confederate Cavalry, then became Tyner's Company of Sappers and Miners detached from the Army of Tennessee as an engineering unit working for General Wheeler. Wheeler's Engineers, in effect.

Was the farmer William Smith at Soddy in 1860 the same as the William Smith of Co. D, 1st Tennessee Cavalry, or was he William Smith of Co. K, 43d Tennessee Infantry, or was he some other man? Or both? How could one be sure about Franklin Jones? Was he listed as Frank or B. F. or B. or Franklin or Benjamin Franklin? Some Confederates, when captured, refused to give their captors accurate information about their place of residence or even their names or ranks. Some Hamilton County units proved extremely unstable with high desertion rates. Then there were the men of Cleveland and Dayton and Jasper and Ringgold who were in and out of Chattanooga so frequently, before and after the war. Many of them were members of the Forrest Camp and appeared at first glance to be Chattanoogans, but were not. Their names had to be deleted. What about Confederate enrolling officers? Many of them held no commission. Should they be given places on the roster? Members of the Home Guard? Should we include those women who organized themselves as scouts? What about nurses? What about the civilians who helped with the commissary, operated the ferries and the railroads? What about the unofficial black Confederates? We scratched our heads and did our best. We confess to having been quite arbitrary at times, purging our list again and again, although when in doubt we decided to err on the side of being inclusive. The individuals we removed, however, have been collected in Appendix 1. Some, undoubtedly, will be reinstated.

Then there were strange locations within Hamilton County, places that no longer exist. Nat Hughes, in his ignorance, immediately discounted any Confederates from Chickamauga and Rossville. Surely these could not be our men of Hamilton County. Sadly, after skipping over the service jackets of such soldiers, he came to realize that Rossville, Chickamauga Station and Graysville were also Tennessee names.

The result, however imperfect, is our roster of Hamilton County Confederates, a mass of about 2,500 individuals and we believe we have omitted several hundred. Abounding in mysteries and unresolved dilemmas, our mission must be considered preliminary, pointing the way for further research, a more complete, a more accurate second edition.

A word about the units is in order. There were an unusually high number for a county with a population of 13,258 (11,647 white, 1,419 slave, 192 free black). The Confederate cause was contagious, of course, and the majority of community leaders backed the cause with their money and their sons, but this is not sufficient reason. We believe Chattanooga's central location and being a rail center led many young men to town--many not only from Georgia and Alabama but from Rhea and Polk counties, from Jasper and Cleveland and Spring City. We did not count these men unless we found they made Hamilton County their home. A. P. Stewart did when he served on the Chickamauga and Chattanooga Battlefield Commission; so did Henry Watterson when he edited the Rebel. We claimed these two, and others.

Of the Confederate cavalry, Company B, 1st Tennessee Cavalry (Carter's) was raised here. So were Company H ("Lookout Rangers"), 2d Tennessee Cavalry (Ashby's); Company I, 5th Tennessee Cavalry; Second Company K, 1st Confederate Cavalry; Company H, 8th Tennessee Cavalry; Second Company A, 13th Tennessee Cavalry Battalion; Company A and I, 4th Tennessee Cavalry (Murray's) and Company F ("Bird Rangers"), Roger's East Tennessee Cavalry. Companies B and K of Avery's 4th Georgia Cavalry (also designated as 12th Georgia Cavalry) also were raised here. Along with these more "formal" units were J. W. Clark's Independent Cavalry Company, Snow's Scouts, Osborne's-Jenkins' Scouts and Company B, Carter's Battalion of Mounted Scouts.

Chattanooga boasted its own artillery battery--Barry's Battery or the "Lookout Battery," a large, proud unit organized and equipped by Dick Watkins and his friend Robert L. Barry. They and their men defended Chattanooga in 1862, fought in the Vicksburg debacle, the Atlanta Campaign and ended the war swimming for their lives at Spanish Fort in Mobile Bay.

As for infantry, there were Companies A and I of the 19th Tennessee Infantry; Companies

D and H, 37th Tennessee, and Companies H and K, 36th Tennessee which would be combined into Company L of the 35th (Many Hamilton Countians already were in Companies I and K of this same regiment). Company K, 43d Tennessee was solidly Chattanooga as were G and H of the 26th, a unit destined to be captured in its first battle at Fort Donelson and imprisoned at Fort Morton, Indiana. Many of these unfortunates would be exchanged only to be shot to pieces at Murfreesboro and recaptured at Vicksburg. Some of the remnants of the 26th would be reunited in the 63d Tennessee Mounted Infantry. Such were the infantry companies of Hamilton County

Hamilton County provided one general officer to the Confederacy--Francis Marion Walker, school-teacher and lawyer, the popular, widely respected leader of the "bloody 19th" who was killed at Atlanta the day before his commission arrived. Two other Confederate general officers lived here temporarily and deserve mention: Henry M. Ashby and Alexander P. Stewart.

Many people have encouraged us. First among them are Clara Swan and Jim Douthat who acted not only as cheerleaders but as wonderful resources. Indeed, our journey began with a conference with Clara, and Jim became not only our mentor but our publisher. Jim Ogden, historian at Chickamauga National Military Park, always could be counted on for help. Jim is a local treasure.

Benton McAdams, Loves Park, IL, provided extensive information on those unfortunate Hamilton County soldiers imprisoned at Rock Island. Bucky Hughes, Chattanooga, proof-read the entire manuscript. Jack D. Welsh, M.D., Oklahoma City, shared freely medical information and discoveries on his trips to the National Archives. Betty J. Broyles, Athens, TN, kindly read the manuscript and made a number of valuable recommendations. Other helpful individuals we must mention are: Bruce S. Allardice, Des Plaines, Ill.; Bruce W. Benton, Chattanooga; Tim Burgess, White House, TN; Carl E. Campbell, Chattanooga; C. Pat Cates, Woodstock, GA; Francine Cooper and Yvonne Crumpler, Birmingham Public Library; Robert S. Davis, Hanceville, AL; Nick Dobbs, Chattanooga; Malone Everett, Chattanooga; Keating Griffiss, Lookout Mountain, TN; Ron Hale, Chattanooga; Marylin Bell Hughes, Tenn. State Library and Archives; Weymouth T. Jordan, Jr., North Carolina Division of Archives and History; Sam B. Lowe, Lookout Mtn., GA; Helen Matthews, Atlanta History Center; Jim Tingen and Patrice H. Glass, Chattanooga Hamilton County Bi-Centennial Library; Jerry Witt, Springfield, VA; and Jerry Wormsley, Chattanooga. We appreciate them all.

# ABBREVIATIONS

| | |
|---|---|
| AAG | Assistant Adjutant General |
| ANV | Army of Northern Virginia |
| AOL | Absent without leave |
| Arty. | Artillery |
| BDTA | Biographical Directory of the Tenn. General Assembly |
| Bn. | Battalion |
| Brig. | Brigade |
| Btry. | Battery |
| Capt. | Captain |
| Cav. | Cavalry |
| CFP | Chattanooga Free Press |
| Chatt. | Chattanooga |
| Co. | County; Company |
| CN | Chattanooga News |
| CS | John Wilson, Chattanooga Story |
| CSA | Confederate States of America |
| CSR | Individual compiled military service record |
| CT | Chattanooga Times |
| CVQ | CSA Veteran's Questionaire |
| Dept. | Department |
| Disch. | Discharged |
| Div. | Division |
| 1870HC | 1870 Hamilton County, TN Census |
| Enl. | Enlisted |
| Exch. | Exchanged |
| FHR | Burial records of Forest Hills Cemetery |
| GHT | Goodspeed, History of Tennessee. |
| HC | Hamilton County |
| HH | Household |
| Hosp. | Hospitalized |
| Imp. | Imprisoned |
| JW | John Wilson's Family History column |
| Lindsley | Lindsley, Annals of the Army of Tennessee |
| MCCD | Diary of Thomas H. McCallie, Chattanooga Bi-Centennial Library |
| MI | Mounted Infantry |
| MR | Memorial Resolutions of Chattanooga Bar Association |
| MSR | Military Service Record |
| NBFM3 | Nathan B. Forrest Camp Minute Book #3, Bi-Centennial Library |
| Prom. | Promoted |
| QM | Quartermaster |
| RI ledger | Ledger of Rock Island Prison |
| Regt. | Regiment; regimental |
| Res. | Resided |
| SAACH | Soldier's Applications for Admission to Confederate Home, Nashville |
| TCVQ | Tennessee Veteran's Questionaire |
| TCSH | Inmate Tenn. Confed. Soldiers' Home, Nov. 17, 1902. |
| TP | Tennessee Confederate veteran pension application |
| Transf. | Transferred |
| TWP | Sherrill, Tennessee's Confederate Widows |
| WF | McGehee, "Wake of the Flood" |
| Z | Armstrong, History of Hamilton County and Chattanooga |

# A

ABERNATHY, John Clayton
     Born 30 March 1824 d. 20 March 1911 and is buried in the Rhea Springs Cem. Nancy A. Bidnell, wife 1829-1904. Retired physician res. with son Young L. on Forest Ave. [1910HC][RCCR1]

ABERNATHY, Young L. B.     Co. E, 3TN Cav. Bn.; Co. D, 1TN Cav. (Carter's)
     Born May 21, 1846 in Madisonville, son of Dr. John C. (CSA surgeon) and Nancy A. Bicknell Abernathy of Rhea Co., he entered the army in 1861 at 16. Fought at Fishing Creek and at Perryville. Discharged fall, 1862, being under age. Upon close of war he entered medical school and after receiving his medical training, he practiced several years at Decatur in Meigs Co. Returned to Rhea Co. to practice with his father. In 1871 in Rhea Co., he married Emma H. Day, daughter of Maj. John Day. After having lived in Rhea Springs and Rockwood, the Abernathys moved to Hill City in 1888 along with another Rhea Co. doctor, R. W. Colville, to take part in the new suburb of Hill City. One of its streets was named for Dr. Abernathy. For a time he was head of the medical division of Univ. of Chattanooga. Methodist. Died April 2, 1928 at res. at Boynton Terrace and buried at White Oak Cem. (Chattanooga Memorial Park). [Campbell, Records of Rhea; CS; CT, May 19, 1897, April 3, 1928; TWP, 257; NBFM2,8;TP16,107]

ACREE, Dr.
     Seriously ill in 1888. Was a CSA soldier. [NBFM1]

ADAMS,
     In 1902 shown as 80 years old, "sick in Hill City." [NBFM3]

ADAMS, A. R.
     Born 1845 GA. Res. 1910 on 18th St. with wife Eliza and one grown daughter. [1910HC]

ADAMS, Asa     Co. B, 1TN Cav. (Carter's)
     Born c1842, son of Elizabeth Adams, he was a farm laborer at Ooltewah at the start of the war. Enl. Aug. 7, 1861, Cleveland. His grandfather, Asa Adams, a NC native, also lived at Ooltewah. Killed at Piedmont, Va., June 5, 1864.

ADAMS, Charles     Co. E, 29NC
     Born 1843 in Clay or Cherokee Co., NC. Enl. Aug. 17, 1861. Wounded in hand, Murfreesboro, Dec. 31,

1862; deserted and took USA oath. [1890VetCensus]

ADAMS, Hamilton     Co. G, 63TN
     Born 1821, TN. Farmer at Harrison with wife Susan Hixson. Conscripted by CSA but enroute to Knoxville deserted. [Jerry Wormsley to author, Nov. 19, 1996; 1860HC]

ADAMS, James     Snow's Co. B, 1TN Cav. (Carter's)
     He joined along with his older brother, Asa Adams, Aug. 7, 1861, at Cleveland. Born c1845 and lived at Ooltewah.

ADAMS, William Charles     3TN Cav.
     Born 1838 in Polk Co., he enl. in Chattanooga, was captured at Vicksburg, paroled and remained north of the Ohio River. He married (1865) in Warrick Co., IN, Elizabeth Robinett. He died Oct. 16, 1892 at Fairmount in HC. [TWP3307]

ADCOCK, EDMOND     Co. A, 19TN
     Born c1842 in NC. Res. Chattanooga, 1860 with mother Elizabeth and two sisters. Moulder in Chattanooga when enl. May 10, 1862, Corinth. Captured Sept. 10, 1863 near Chattanooga and listed as deserter. Took USA oath. Member of NBF Camp, 1891-95. Moved away and "supposed to have perished" in Galveston, TX in Nov., 1891. Been missing ever since. [NBFM2]

AIKEN  (see EAKIN)

AIKEN, Capt. Jasper Newton     Co. K, 43TN
     Born c1833 in TN. Lawyer in Chattanooga, 1860. Enl. Oct. 17, 1861 at Ooltewah; elected captain Dec. 14, 1861; captured at Vicksburg, July 4, 1863; paroled. During Early's Valley campaign in the summer and fall of 1864, Aiken, as senior captain commanded the regiment which served as cavalry.

AIKEN, Thomas     Co. F, 3TN
     Born Aug. 15, 1842, Monroe Co., TN. Enl. 1863. Captured at Vicksburg. Methodist. Res. of Chattanooga, 1908, "decrepit and needy." Was night watchman when he could get work. Applied to TN Soldiers Home, 1912. [TP10,686]

ALDEHOFF, Henry W.
     Born 1819 in Prussia. Teacher in Chattanooga with wife Raena and six children. "A 'most enthusiastic reb,' according to a visitor." [WF]

ALEXANDER, Gideon  "Gid"     4TN Cav.
     Enl. 4TN Cav. June 6, 1861 at the age of twelve in his father's Company [Capt. David Alexander].

Salesman in Chattanooga 1891 when he joined NBF Camp. [NBFM2][UDC]

ALEXANDER, James M.     2nd Co. K, 1st CSA Cav.
        Born c1842 in TN. Enl. Sept. 1, 1862 in HC. Served as surgeon F&S, 33rd Tennessee Inf. surgeon of Gen. Thrall Brig. in the 83rd Inf., Cheatham's Division. Hospitalized March, 1865 with acute diarrhea. Res. 1870 with wife Margaret at North Chickamauga. [UDC1]

ALEXANDER, T. J.       1Lt. Co. E., 1TN Cav.
        Born Jan. 15, 1839 in Maury Co., TN. Enl. April 1, 1861 in Co. C, 1TN Cav. Dry goods clerk in Chattanooga and member of NBF Camp, 1895. [NBFM2]

ALEXANDER, William M.   Co. A, 4TN Cav. Bn.
        Born June 9, 1845 in Rutherford Co., TN. Enl. Aug. 1, 1862 near Sparta. Perryville, Murfreesboro, Chickamauga, Atlanta Camp, and opposed Sherman's March to the Sea. Col. Baxter Smith: "a first class soldier." Paroled May 5, 1865. To TX 1884 and returned 1888. Manufacturer and gen'l. dealer in lumber in Chattanooga Baptist. NBF Camp, 1895; Died in Cincinnati. July 5, 1920 and buried Forest Hills Cemetery. [FHR; CT July 1920; NBFM2:8,15,022]

ALEXANDER, William Thomas   Co. B, 30AL
        Born at Jacksonville, AL, June 23, 1847, son of Robert Alexander, he began his service as a member of the Calhoun Guards at Ft. Morgan. He then enl. in Co. B, 30AL at Tazewell, TN, Port Gibson and Baker's Creek, MS. After his exchange rejoined Army of TN at Missionary Ridge and during Atlanta campaign, he was wounded at Jonesboro and hospitalized at Macon and Montgomery where he ended the war as a clerk in the medical department. He surrendered at Talladega, AL and became express agent, then postmaster at Jacksonville. He moved to Chattanooga in 1896, 26 years after his marriage to Jennie Frank. Traveling salesman for Thacher Medicine Co. Died at res. on Battery Place, Dec. 7, 1926 and buried in Citizens Cem. [NBFM2: TP15,796]

ALFORD, Sgt. Alexander W.      Co. A, 2TN Cav. (Ashby's)
        Born 1843 in Roane Co. and grew up in Sweetwater. Enl. 1861. Fishing Creek, Murfreesboro, Somerset, KY, Chickamauga, Atlanta Campaign. A comrade described him as "a good Christian, a reliable soldier, and I believe he was as brave a man and as daring a scout as there was in the Confederate army." Married (1865) Sarah E. Neil. To TN 1907. Res. 1910 near Rossville. Died 1911 in HC. [TWP, p. 113; TP11,766; 1910HC]

ALFORD, Thomas A.  Co. C, 41TN
        Enl. Feb. 16. 1863, Fayetteville, TN. Died at his home near Tyner May 14, 1920, age 74, and buried in family cem. [CT May 25, 1920]

ALLEN, 1Lt. Andrew J.     Co. C, 2TN (Robison's)
        Born in Davidson Co., TN. Enl. May, 1861. Captured and imprisoned at Johnson's Island. Stonecutter in Chattanooga. Moved away in 1889. [NBFM2]

ALLEN, Isaac David    Co. G, 9GA Cav.; Co. F, 4GA Cav. (Avery's)
        Born May 2, 1829 in Rutherford Co., NC. Enl. May, 1861. ANV. Resigned as 1Lt, July, 1862 and joined 4GA Cav. becoming Lt. once again. Captured 1864 and imprisoned at Johnson's Island till end of war. Married (at Lafayette, GA) Elizabeth Vickery, a native of Habersham Co., GA. Member of Chickamauga-Chattanooga Nat'l Park Comm., 1894. NBF Camp. Res. of Chattanooga in 1903. Died Nov. 26, 1910 in Chattanooga and buried Forest Hills Cemetery. [FHR; CT Nov. 27, 1910; NBFM2; TP5335; TWP3491; 1890VetCensus]

ALLEN, James Alfred G.      Co. A, 16LA
        Born Jan. 16, 1833 at Columbus, KY, son of Louis and Lucy Feltz Allen, he was raised in East Feliciana Parish, LA. He married Mrs. Mary Josephine Travis (Travers?) in 1852. He was employed as an overseer until Sept. 29, 1861 when he enl. in Co. A, 16LA; to Chattanooga in 1862 where he was hospitalized. Later assigned duty there as a mechanic in the Government Works Shop until summer of 1863. In 1865, soon after the close of the war, he returned to Chattanooga and became a carpenter. Served as city jailer for short while, then was elected Chattanooga's first Chief of Police in 1883. Congregationalist. Allen resided in East Lake where he died 29 Jan. 1906. He was buried in CSA Cem.[CT Jan. 31, 1906; GHT, pp. 904-05; NBFM2, 4; Lusk, FH]

ALLEN, John Benton     Co. E, 37TN; Co. H, 2TN Cav. (Ashby's)
        Born 1844 in Jefferson Co. The family moved to Bradley Co. His father, John Allen, died when John Benton Allen was four. His grandfather was Benton Allen of New Market, TN. His mother was Mary Ann White, daughter of Thomas White of HC. As a boy, he went to live with a foster father, Absalom Sivley of King's Point. Enl. at Ooltewah on Oct. 31, 1861. Later he joined Ashby's Cavalry. Captured at Lancaster, KY, on July 31, 1863, and taken to Camp Chase, OH. He went from there to the prison at Fort Delaware and was not released until June 20, 1865.   After the war he was a clerk, then a carpenter, at Chattanooga. [JW; TWP]

ALLEN, Thomas Benton    Co. I, 3TN
Born Sept 12, 1842 in Meigs Co., TN. Enl. May 2, 1861 in Knoxville. Wounded at Vicksburg. Moved away, then returned and became a farmer. Res. of Hill City in 1902. Died in Chattanooga July 6, 1920. Buried in Cottonport Cem, Meigs County. [CT July 7, 1920; NBFM2; TP4512]

ALLISON, Albert J.    Co. E 39th GA Inf.
Born 15 November 1842 in Tennessee a son of William P. Allison, enlisted 4 Mar 1862 in Lafayette, GA. Captured at Vicksburg, MS 4 July 1863 and held as prisoner of war. In 1869 married Martha Long. Died 7 July 1902 in Walker Co., GA. [cf. Kay Allison Dobbs]

ALLISON, Jesse B.
Born c1826. Provost Marshal of Chattanooga Steamboat pilot at Chattanooga in 1870, age 43. Owned and operated steamboats on Tennessee River for many years. Wife Eliza A. was active at Centenary Methodist Church. Died Mar. 21, 1905 and buried Forest Hills Cemetery. [JW; 1870, 1880 Census]

ALLISON, John L.
He and his brothers W.F. and Albert J. were in CSA. Died Lafayette, GA about Nov., 20, 1918. John L. was born in 1837 in Tennessee the son of William P. Allison and married Elizabeth Long on 4 Aug 1857 [she was sister to Martha, wife of Albert J. Allison] [CT Nov. 25, 1918: Kay Allison Dobbs]

ALLISON, William F.  Co. A, 3GA Mtd Inf., Co. "3", 3TN Cav. - Captain. Son of William P. Allison, born in Tennessee. Served with brothers John L. and Albert J. [cf. Kay Allison Dobbs]
Born Feb. 19, 1832 in Monroe Co., TN; he enl. Oct. 7, 1862. Fought at Murfreesboro, the Tullahoma campaign, at Chickamauga and under Longstreet at Knoxville. He served in the Atlanta campaign and against Sherman in the Carolinas, ending his service at Bentonville. Paroled at Greensboro Apr. 26, 1865. Following the war he farmed and sold agricultural equipment, residing at Eagle Cliff, GA, a "suburb" of Chattanooga. He married Minerva J. Scarborough. Died near Flintstone, GA, Mar. 29, 1907 and buried Eagle Cliff. [CT, March 30, 1907; NBFM7]

ALLRED, BLACKSTONE W.    Co. H, 26TN
Born Nov. 5, 1826, in Overton County, TN. Enl. Aug. 5, 1861 at Livingston, TN. He married (1877 in HC) Lou Frank Sparks. Farmer and member of the Christian Church. Died at his res. in St. Elmo, June 22, 1901 and buried CSA Cem. [TWP, p. 161; NBM2,3; CT June 25, 1901]

AMMONS, Washington H.    Co. C, 12GA Cav.
Born Macon Co., NC, 15 April 1832. Enl. 1862. Shiloh, 2nd Manassas, Chickamauga, Franklin, Nashville. Paroled May 12, 1865 at Kingston, GA. Res. TN 1885, Hill City in 1905. Died 28 Spetember 1916 in Searis, AL, married Elizabeth M. Rickets on 28 July 1865. She was born in 1835 and died in 1912. [TP7016] [UDC2]

ANDERSON, Allen L.    2d Co. K, 35TN
Born 1834 in TN. Farmer at Chattanooga

ANDERSON, Isaac W.
Born Winchester, VA, but spent most of his life in Pridgeport, AL. Captain in CSA assigned to railroad duty. May have been in Co. A, IGA State Line. For 53 years and employee of the Nc&St.L. Railroad. Died in Chattanooga March 14, 1913 and buried in Forest Hills Cemetery.

ANDERSON, James C. 1Lt.    2nd Co. K, 1st CSA Cav.
Born Feb. 3, 1834 in McMinn Co. Enl. July 14, 1862 at Tyner's Station. In winter, 1863 assigned adj. and inspector genl. of Gen. W. W. Allen's Brigade, serving until July 1864. Detailed in the Engineering Dept. of Wheelers Corps and served as scout within Federal lines. Wounded at Buzzard Roost and Resaca. Paroled May 3, 1865 in Charlotte, NC as a Lieut. After the war gained fame as tunnel builder, engineer. For a time was chief engineer for E. TN, VA & GA (Southern RR). "His experience was valuable while the county's highway tunnel through Missionary Ridge was being constructed and it was he who first convinced engineers of that project." Died Sept. 13, 1920 at home on Cleveland Pike, 86 yrs., and buried at Concord Cem. [CSR; NBFM2; CT Sept. 14-15, 1920]

ANDERSON, Jefferson Campbell  Tyner's scouts
Born 1844 in HC, son of William Walker and Louisa Penelope Campbell Smith Walker. Named for his mother's father. J.C. Anderson. Married Mary Ellen Burton. Died in HC and buried Concord Cem. [JW;TWP, p. 80; 1880HC]

ANDERSON, John    Co F, 35th TN
Age 24 in December, 1863; born in SC; coal miner in HC; enl. Oct. 11, 1862.

ANDERSON, Sgt. Maj. John C.    Barry's Batry.
Enl. 4 April 1862 at Chattanooga. Paid bounty of $50.00; promoted to Orderly Sgt. 1 Dec 1863; at Spanish Fort he led 30 men swimming "eight miles to Blakely, got skiffs there, and rowed across the bay to Mobile next day." Paroled at Meridian, MS 11 May

1865. [Barry, "Lookout Battery."]

ANDERSON, John Henry
      Born Oct. 6, 1848 in McMinn Co. Came to
Soddy when a boy. Mason, Presby. Died May 5, 1931
and buried Presbyterian Cem., Soddy [CT May 6, 1931]

ANDERSON, Sgt. William Walker Jr.    Barry's Btry.
      He wanted to join Frank Walker's company at
the start of the war, but the health of his wife was bad so
he stayed with her. Son of the Chattanooga pioneers,
William Walker Anderson and Elizabeth McChesney, he
had married Lydia Cravens in 1859. He spent the first
portion of the war manufacturing saltpeter in a furnace
at the mouth of the cave on the side of Lookout Mountain
opposite Moccasin Bend. This was in conjunction with
his father-in-law, Robert Cravens. He also "explored the
caves in that section and along Walden's Ridge for dirt,
cut forest of blackjack timber for ashes, and had boxwood
for making powder." He joined the Lookout Artillery in
Knoxville on Sept. 2, 1862.
      Anderson was in camp at Pollard, AL, when he
received word that his wife was quite sick. He said
Captain Robert L. Barry, "willingly gave me leave of
absence and told me to write it myself, for I had never
missed a roll call." He was discharged April 3, 1863, and
found that his wife had arranged for a substitute to take
his place. Afterward, he shipped coal and coke to
Confederate authorities at Memphis. He and his
brother-in-law, James Cravens, leased mines from Robert
Cravens, built a higher tram-road, and were getting out
the first carload of coal when Yankee guns began
bombarding Chattanooga.
      The Andersons, along with his parents, hauled
their movable possessions in wagons to Chickamauga
Station and went by rail to Adairsville, GA. Later they
went to Dawson, GA. Mrs. W.W. Anderson Sr. died
there on Jan. 6, 1864, and Lydia Cravens Anderson died
three months later. W.W. Anderson Jr. settled at
Forsythe, Ga. Born about 1837, he lived until 1926. His
second wife was Louisa Estelle Sharp. The Andersons
originally were from Rockbridge County, VA. [JW;
W.W. Anderson letter in Anderson family clipping file
at Chattanooga Library]

ANDREWS, Lt. Col. J. Garnett                1GA
      Born in Washington, GA in 1837, son of Judge
Garnett and Annulet Ball Andrews, he was educated at
the Washington Male Academy and the U of GA. He had
just begun the study of law when GA seceded. He became
a 1Lt. in the 1GA Regulars, then AAG to Gen. Henry R.
Jackson. In 1862 he joined Cutt's Btry. and soon became
Capt. He next became AAG to Gen. Arnold Elzey and
helped organized local defense troops. He participated as
a member of the 15GA in the Wilderness, Cold Harbor,

South Anna and Petersburg, ending the war as Lt. Col.
of the 8th Bn., CSA infantry, consisting of 600 foreigners
enl. from the Federal army with whom he defended
against Stoneman's 1865 raid. After the war he practiced
law and edited newspaper at Yazoo City, MS, served in
the legislature, and compiled "Andrews Digest of
Mississippi Decisions." In 1881 he moved to
Chattanooga where he practiced law, dealt in real estate
and became mayor (1891-93). Active in NBF Camp.
Married (1867) Rosalie Champe Beirne. Mason.
Episcopalian. He died at res. on Georgia Ave., May 6,
1903 and was buried at Washington, GA. [CT May 7,
1903; Hist. of St. Paul's, 171-72; NBFM7]

ANDREWS, Robert W.    Co. G, 6TN; Co. B, 3d CSA
Engineers
      Born Maury Co., TN. Enl. May 15, 1861 at
Jackson Co., TN. in Co. G, 6TN and remained with them
until transferred Co. B, 3d Engineers in June, 1863.
Paroled at Catawba Bridge, SC May 5, 1865. After war
made home at Jackson until coming to Chattanooga in
1883. Married Parmelia R. (1830-1915). Died Jan. 30,
1925 and buried Forest Hills Cemetery. [NBFM2;
TP12,466]

ARENZ (ARENS), C. H.          Co. H, 1LA
      Not found, however, in Booth, LA Troops.
[NBFM2]

ARMOR, George W.          Co. K, 43TN
      Age 19 in 1861, he enl. Oct., 1861, at Ooltewah.
He was brigade forage master. He was captured at
Vicksburg July 4, 1863, and was paroled at Talledega,
AL, on May 16, 1865. At the start of the war, he and his
older brother, Robert C. Armor, were laborers on the
extensive farm of B.R. Scott near Chattanooga. The
Armor brothers were born in Alabama.

ARMOUR, Joseph T.    Co. G, 26TN; 2nd Co. I
                                        1CSA (GA)
      Enl. Feb. 5, 1863 in Ringgold, GA. Wounded
Sept. 1, 1864 and sent to Ocmulgee Hospital, Macon,
GA. Returned to duty Nov. 19, 1864. Paroled at
Greensboro, NC, May 1, 1865.

ARMOR, Robert Cowden          Co. K, 43TN
      Born 1840 Habersham Co., GA. He was 21
when he enl. Oct. 17, 1861, at Ooltewah. He was
captured along with his brother at Vicksburg on July 4,
1863. Married (1866) Mary Elizabeth Augusta Patterson.
Died 1890 in HC. [TWP; 1880 Census]

ARMISTEAD, Robert A.  2nd Co., Washington Arty. of
NC
      Born in Dinwiddie Co., VA, Sept. 2, 1844. Enl.

at Petersburg 1864. Captured April 10, 1865. In 1901 resided in Chattanooga, occupation clerk in Southern Express Co. Living in Memphis prior to death there Feb. 2, 1909. [NBFM2,4,7]

ARMSTRONG, Capt. John MacMillan    Barry's Btry.
A Knoxville native, born Nov. 20, 1828, he was the son of Addison Wear and Nancy Jane McMillan Armstrong. He attended Maryville College, then he spent five years in Abbeville District, SC, and five years in Knox Co. before coming to Chattanooga in 1858. When the war broke out, he was a clerk, working at the hardware company of Richard L. Watkins. Enl. May 15, 1862, at Chattanoogain Lookout Battery, Col. William's Regt., TN Art. Later he transferred to Lt. Col. S.C. Williams' Arty. Bn. where he was promoted from Lt. to Capt. (ordnance officer). He was paroled May 11, 1865 at Meridian, MS.
Armstrong returned to Chattanooga after the war and worked for J.H. Warner Hardware Company and held the city street sprinkling contract. Married 1867 Martha J. Turnley, native of AL born 1849 died 1925 in Chattanooga. John was 6', blue eyes, fair complexion, a Presbyterian and father of Chattanooga historian Zella Armstrong. He died Feb. 28, 1897 in Chattanooga and was buried Forest Hills Cemetery. [FHR; CT Feb. 28, 1897, July 1, 1903; NBFM2; TWP 6297; UDC1&2]

ARMSTRONG, Martin Van Buren    Co. C, 5TN Cav.
Born 4 March 1844 in Meigs Co. and married (1887) Ada Atchley [1857-1930]. Martin's brother, William Clayton Armstrong [1851-1837] also seved in Co C, 5th TN. After war Martin and Ada resided in Meigs and Rhea counties before coming to Chattanooga. Mason. Died at his home in East End July 2, 1912 and buried CSA Cem. [CT July 3.1912; TWP, p. 129; UDC2]

ARNETT, Luke        2nd Co. K, 1st CSA Cav.
Enl. Aug. 1, 1862, then captured at Chicka-mauga. He and his brother-in-law, William C. Douglas, were released from jail at Chattanooga upon the entreaty of the Rev. Hiram Douglas to Gen. George Thomas. War records say Arnett deserted on Jan. 6, 1864. Born about 1847, he was the son of George W. Arnett. The family lived in the Savannah Valley near Ooltewah, but they moved to AR after the war. [JW]

ARNETT, William  2nd Co. K, 1st CSA Cav.
He enl. Aug. 1, 1862 and was killed in action near Loudon, TN, on May 12, 1863, while trying to make his way through the Union lines to join his company. He was the oldest son of George W. Arnett, who resided in the Savannah Valley near Ooltewah. He was about 19 when he died. The family later recovered his uniform showing the hole where the bullet tore through the breast

of the coat and left blood stains. [JW]

ASHBY, Brig. Gen. Henry Marshall
Born Fauquier Co., VA, 1836, the son of Marshall and Lucinda Cocke Ashby, he had moved to Chattanooga by 1860 and was living in the home of his uncle, Daniel F. Cocke. He gave his age as 22 and his profession as "trading." He married Laura Purse. Ashby enl. as a Pvt in Co. A, 4TN Cav. Bn. in Knoxville, then was elected Capt. of Co. G in 5TN Cav Bn. When the 4th and 5th TN Cav. Bns. merged to form 2TN Cav., he became Col. of the regiment. After the battle of Murphy he was commissioned Brig. Gen. Wounded June, 1863.
Ashby and his men operated in E. TN during most of 1862, then participated in the Battle of Murfreesboro, John S. Scott's East KY Raid, Joe Wheeler's Sequatchie Valley Raid, and ended the war with a splendid charge at the Battle of Bentonville, March 21, 1865. After the war Ashby returned to Knoxville to meet his death at the hands of an ardent Unionist, E. C. Camp, on July 10, 1868, and was buried in Old Gray Cem., Knoxville. [1860HC]

ASHFORD, Robert J.   Fraser's GA Btry  "Pulaski Lt. Arty" Co A 4th GA Inf.
Born 1848, Watkinsville, GA, son of William Henry Ashford, enl. in the GA State troops in July, 1864, and fought in the battles around Atlanta. He then went to VA as a member of the Pulaski Artillery and served at Petersburg. He moved to Chattanooga in 1883 and engaged in the wholesale produce trade. Left Chattanooga in 1902 and died 2 Jan 1925. [NBFM2,3; CSA Mil. Hist., pp. 361-62]

ASHLEY, George Reese        Co. L, 36TN
Born Oct. 17, 1839, son of Joseph and Mary Ashley. Married Mary Sue Kirklen Colquitt. Enl. Jan. 9, 1862 in Chattanooga. Died Feb. 22, 1919. Buried Ashley Cem. on Lake Resort Dr. [1880 HC Census]

ASHLEY, James H.        Co. L, 36TN
Born c1837, son of Joseph and Mary Ashley. Enl. Dec. 16, 1861, Cleveland. Re-enl. Jan. 9, 1863, Chattanooga. Listed as absent without leave.

ATCHLEY, Calvin A.        F&S, 63TN
Born c1827. Physician; res. near Ooltewah with wife Martha, 1860. Asst. Surgeon with 63TN.

ATCHLEY, Daniel        Co. A, 26TN
Born c1835 in TN. Res. 1860 in household. of Posey Moon in Long Savannah. [1860HC]

ATCHLEY, James M.        Co. A, 26TN
Born 1842 in Meigs Co., he married (1865)

Eliz. Francis Earley. He died 1906 in HC. [TWP, p. 52]

AUSBURN [OSUBURN], Capt. H. M.     Co. L, 36TN
     He enl. Jan. 9, 1862 at Chattanooga. A native of NC, he and his wife, Mary J., had a farm at Harrison prior to the start of the war. He was born about 1830. [1860HC]

AUSTIN, James R.      Co. B, 5TN Cav. Bn.
     Enl. at Chattanooga on Aug. 11, 1861. Wounded at Winchester, TN. According to Mrs. Williams (nee Shelton) of Athens, AL, who nursed CSA sick and wounded, JRA died in Corinth, MS in 1864.

AUSTIN, Levi     Co. H, 4TN Cav., Co. B, 5TN Cav. Bn.
     He was 22 years old and was a farm laborer living near Chattanooga when the war broke out. Enl. Aug. 11, 1861. Color bearer. He died as a prisoner of war in Chattanooga, Feb., 1862.

AVERY, Henry C.      Co. A, 19TN
     Born 1844 in GA, son of John and Susannah. Enl. July 22, 1861, Cumberland Gap. Charged with desertion, Jan., 1864. Res. Hixson, 1870, with wife Louisa A. Cut and corded wood.

# B

BABRY, Thomas Milligan
     Born Franklin Co., GA. Married (1866) Adenia (Adini) Mason Miller. Died 1908 in HC. [TWP, p. 143]

BACHMAN, Capt. Jonathan Waverley     Co. G, 19TN
     Born Oct. 9, 1837 in Kingsport, TN, son of Jonathan, he was educated at Emory and Henry and was enrolled as a divinity student in New York City when war came. Enl. as pvt. and soon became chief clerk of the 1st TN Brigade which he accompanied to Virginia, fighting at Cheat Mountain and in the Romney expedition. Helped organized the 60TN, becoming captain of Co. G. Served at Vicksburg and after Champion's Hill became senior officer in the regiment. Following his exchange he resigned his commission in Oct., 1864 and became chaplain of the 60th, serving the remainder of the war in east TN and southwest VA. He was with Gen. John Hunt Morgan when the latter was killed and NBF Camp records show that he served on staff of S. D. Lee. Following the war he resumed his theological studies and in 1873 came to Chattanooga as pastor of the First Presbyterian Church which he served

enthusiastically until 1923. He died at his residence on McCallie Ave., Sept. 26, 1924 and buried Forest Hills Cemetery. He was honored by giving his name to the chapter of the Children of the Confederacy (affiliated with Missionary Ridge Chapter #1777) the Jonathan Waverley Bachman Chapter. [JW; CT Sept. 27, 1924; CV 21:281 (CSA photo); CSA Military History (Expanded) 10:364-365]

BAGGETT, Jackson A.     Co. D, 37TN
     Born c1844 in TN, son of William and Alias. Enl. Sept. 1, 1861 in Knoxville. Hospitalized May 5, 1862. Sent to Corinth, Okolona, MS. Deserted Sept. 7, 1863 at Ooltewah.

BAGGETT, William     Co. D, 37TN
     Born 1809. Farm laborer at Chattanooga when he and son Jackson enl. Hospital Aug. 1862. in Chattanooga Still sick in Chattanooga in 1863. Deserted and dropped from rolls.

BAILEY, C. Leon     Co. I, 10MS; Madison Lt. Arty.
     Born June 9, 1844, Madison Co., MS, son of William Stewart and Maria Scott (Field) Bailey. Enl. Canton, MS, June, 1861 in 10MS. Trans. to Madison Light Arty. Poague's Arty. Bn. ANV, from May, 1862 to end of war. Wounded at Petersburg. Paroled Apr., 1865. Came to Chattanooga, 1893, with Southern Express Co. for whom he worked over 40 years as clerk. Moved back to Canton a number of years before his death. Married (1872) Ida Pace who died about 1927. Died in Canton, MS, Nov. 13, 1928 and buried there. [NBFM2,7; 1910HC; CT Nov. 14, 1928]

BAILEY, E. Volney (Vardell) "Vod"     Co. C, 40GA
     Born Dec. 27, 1829 in SC, he had brother Jordan Bailey. Sharpshooter who was wounded at Vicksburg, losing two fingers. "Had to carry his hand on a board for over six months." To Chattanooga about 1868. Died June 17, 1912, at res. on East Main and buried CSA Cem. His wife was Mary Jane Tate. [CT June 18, 1912; Jan. 14, 1914; TWP, p. 127; TP1289; NBFM7; 1880HC; 1890VetCensus]

BAILEY, Jonathan     Co. B, 5TN Cav. Bn.; Co. L, 35TN; Co. H, 4TN Cav.
     He was farming and residing with his young wife, Malinda, and daughter, Martha, when the war started. Bailey was then 32 years old. Enl. at Chattanooga, Aug. 11, 1861. Bailey traveled with the unit to KY, but ruled to have a physical disability in December of 1861 while at Mill Springs. Paid $116.06 and released from further service. He re-enl. on Jan. 22, 1863, in 35TN at Chattanooga. Captured at Neill's Gap, Ga., on Aug. 7, 1864, and died in prison at Camp Chase,

CONFEDERATE SOLDIERS OF HAMILTON COUNTY, TENNESSEE

7
\*\*\*\*\*\*\*\*\*\*\*\*\*\*\*\*\*\*\*\*\*\*\*\*\*\*\*\*\*\*\*\*\*\*\*\*\*\*\*\*\*\*\*\*\*\*\*\*\*\*\*\*\*\*\*\*\*\*\*\*\*\*\*\*\*\*\*\*\*\*\*\*\*\*\*\*\*\*\*\*\*\*

and released from further service. He re-enl. on Jan. 22, 1863, in 35TN at Chattanooga. Captured at Neill's Gap, Ga., on Aug. 7, 1864, and died in prison at Camp Chase, Ohio. He was 6'1" tall, had dark complexion, gray eyes and brown hair. [1860HC]

BAILEY, Thomas J.     23GA
          After joining this Georgia unit, he served with Lee in the Army of Northern Virginia. He was born at Calhoun, Ga., in 1831. Bailey lived for many years at Avondale. He died Feb. 25, 1904, and buried CSA Cem. [CT Feb. 26, 1904]

BAIRD, Lemuel Moore     Co. C, 45TN
          Born Jan. 12, 1843 in Rutherford Co., TN; Married (1867) Martha Catherine Nevills. Res. 1605 Dodson Ave. Died Dec. 16, 1918 in Chattanooga and buried in Citizens Cem. [TWP, 202; CT Dec. 17, 1918]

BAIRD, W. T.     10TN Cav.
          Born Gibson Co., TN, Feb. 16, 1843 and spent much of his life in that portion of the state. Enl. 1862 in Forrest's Cav. Married Mary C. Presbyterian. Died May 31, 1924 at res. in Mineral Park, TX and buried CSA Cem. in Chattanooga. [CT June 2, 1924]

BAKER, Jacob     Co. H, 1TN Cav. (Carter's)
          Born c1841 in TN. 1860 res. in household of Nancy Baker in Birchwood. [1860HC]

BALDWIN, Sgt. Isaac M.     Co. D, 37TN
          Enl. Sept. 1, 1861, at Knoxville and rose to 1st Sgt in June, 1863; wounded at Chickamauga. He deserted and took the USA oath of allegiance on Feb. 14, 1864. He was 5'tall, had light complexion, gray eyes and light hair.
          Baldwin was a son of Isaac Baldwin, one of the pioneer settlers at Ross's Landing. His mother, Crissa Baldwin, was a NC native. The Baldwins were originally from Jefferson Co., TN. Isaac M. Baldwin was born in 1838 and died at Tunnel Hill, GA, Feb. 14, 1922. [CT Feb. 15, 1922; J. W. Frist Fam.]

BALDWIN, William L.     Co. D, 37TN; Co. D, 4th (12th) Georgia Cav.
          Born c1830, son of the Ross's Landing pioneers Isaac and Crissa Baldwin. Drayman. Enl. Sept. 1, 1861 at Knoxville. "Charged with desertion but did not desert." Sick at Chattanooga Aug. 21, 1863. Enl. in Capt. William J. Rogers' unit recruited in Lookout Valley. William Baldwin was killed in 1887 "in an altercation. He was said to have been defending his home." [1860HC; J. W. Frist Fam.]

BALLEW, Thomas P.     2d Co. I, 26TN; 2d Co.I, 1CSA

(GA)
          Born c1840, South Carolina. Enl. Feb. 16, 1863 in Ringgold, GA. Farm laborer for Winston Pollard at Ooltewah, 1870.

BANKS, Hugh R.     1st SC Rifles
          Born Sept. 27, 1843 in Charleston, SC, his college education was interrupted by the war. Enl. 1861 in 1st SC Rifles then became a CSA paymaster in the Department of NC, SC, and GA. Went to TX after the war and married (1873) Ella Hammond. He remained until 1878 when he returned to Charleston. He came to Chattanooga in 1884 and entered the real estate business. Died Nov. 5, 1894 and buried Forest Hills Cemetery. [FHR; GHT, p. 907; NBFM2,7]

BANKSTON, John Henry     Co. A, 1st TN (Rock City Guards)
          Born in Nashville in 1843. Married (1867) Sarah Jane Powers. To Chattanooga in 1872 to join firm of Tom Snow Heating and Roofing. NBF Camp, 1885-96. Methodist. Died here Jan. 4, 1915 and buried Forest Hills Cemetery. [CT Jan. May 1915; FHR; TWP, p. 165]

BARBEE, George W.     Co. C, 3rd TN (Vaughn's); 31st TN
          Born in Jefferson Co., TN, he was a farmer near Dandridge. Enl. May 15, 1861. After fighting at First Manassas, transferred to 31st TN. Wounded at Shiloh and fought at Jackson and Vicksburg. Married Maria E. Died in Chattanooga, Jan. 14, 1890, and buried in CSA Cem. [NBFM1, 7]

BARBER, Henry     Co. I, 19th TN
          Born c1844, son of Joseph (railrroad laborer at Chattanooga) and Alsa Barber. Enl. May 20, 1861, Knoxville. Deserted Feb. 1862, re-enl. Aug. 1, 1863, deserted again Sept. 1863. Res. Carroll Co., TN, 1870.

BARBER, Joseph     Co. B, 5th TN Cav.
          Enl. at Chattanooga on Aug. 11, 1861. Farmer and railroad laborer. He and his wife, Alsa, had moved to Chattanooga from their native GA several years prior to the war. Disch. March, 1862 and given pay of $158. His age then was listed at 52. He was 6'1" tall with dark hair; and gray eyes. Res. Rutherford Co., TN, 1870.

BAREFIELD, Wheeler S. Co. A, 38th AL; Co. K, 43rd TN
          Born Feb. 24, 1842 in Clarke Co., AL. Enl. Oct. 17, 1861 at Ooltewah; enl. March, 1862 in Clarke Co., 38th AL. Captured at Missionary Ridge and imprisoned at Rock Island where he remained until June, 1865. Lived in Chattanooga since 1905. Married Mary K. (1845-1915). Methodist. Died Feb. 6, 1914 at res. 24

Battery Place and buried Forest Hills Cemetery. [CT Feb. 7, 1914; NBFM2,7; CSR; FHR; Lindsley, 528]

BARLEY, Joseph W.          Co. K, 4th AL
          Born March 10, 1836 in Madison Co., AL. Enl. in Huntsville. Wounded at Fort Donelson. and captured at Jackson Co., AL Nov., 1863. Released from Rock Island Prison April, 1865. [NBFM2; TP6299]

BARNES, John          Barry's Btry.
          Born 1840 in TN, son of M. L. and Allice. 1860 farm laborer with wife Sarah. [1860HC]

BARNES, Silas          Co. F, 35thTN
          Died Feb. 28, 1863 [Lindsley]; killed in action [z].

BARRY, Robert L., Captain          Barry's Btry.
          Born March, 1834 in Lumpkin Co., GA, and raised there. Son of Dr. Andrew L. and Margaret McDowell Barry. At outbreak of the war, Barry was a clerk for the dry goods firm of Moore and Marsh at Chattanooga where he enl. May 15, 1862. He was paroled May 15, 1865, at Meridian, MS. Located in Atlanta, July, 1865. Rejoined as clerk, then salesman, Moore and Marsh which also had relocated there. He lived in Atlanta with wife Laura and children Robert E. and Maggie E. until c1885 when he moved to Decatur. Applied for pension, 1910 listing his only property as 8 shares Realty Trust Co.; Supt., Conf. Soldiers Home, Atlanta, 1909-10. Presbyterian. Died in Decatur, Nov. 30, 1918, at home of son Robert with whom he had made his home since death of wife in 1907. "A man of strong and rugged character." Buried Decatur Cem. [NBFM4; 1870, 1900 GA Census; Garrett Necrology]

BARTON, Robert McKinney, Sr.
          Born July 20, 1820 in Grainger Co., TN, he was son of Isaac and Jane Barton. Practiced law in Morgan and Greene Cos. and eventually settled in Hamblen Co. He married Hannah E. McFarland in 1848. Although an active Whig, he was appointed judge by his close friend Andrew Johnson who was disappointed to see his anti-secessionist friend become a supporter of the Confederacy. He represented Hancock, Hawkins and Jefferson cos. in General Assembly (Confederate), 1861-63. Barton also was put in charge of the rolling stock and managed the vital and vulnerable E TN, VA and GA RR throughout the war. He was captured at Saltville, VA in April, 1865. He came to Chattanooga in 1876 and resumed the practice of law. Presbyterian. He died here Feb. 18, 1896 and was buried in Chattanooga Memorial Park. [CT July 1, 1903; BDTA, 2:44]

BASSETT, William H. (M.)          Co. B, 1TN Cav. (Carter's)
          Born c1828, son of Hugh and Joanne Bassett, early Hamilton County settlers. Died April 8, 1865 in Chattanooga of diarrhea. His widow was Martha A. Bassett.

BATES, Levi M.
          Member of Chattanooga Police Dept. and resided on Cedar St. NBF Camp. "Died suddenly while on duty at Mountain City Stove Co.," Nov. 24, 1904 and buried in Forest Hills Cemetery. [FHR; CT Nov. 26, 1904; NBFM7]

BATES, Robert B. (H.)     1st Co. H, 24TN
          Born 1845, GA. Farmer in James Co., TN 1910 with daughter Nannie F. Methodist. Died April 14, 1917 at his home in Apison.[1910 James Co.; CT April, 16, 1917]

BATSON, Madison F. Nathan W. Carter's Scouts (Co. A, 21 TN Cav.)
          Born Davidson Co., 1833. Enl. Oct., 1862. Murfreesboro, Sublett's Creek (wounded and discharged); A farmer, 5'10" tall, blue eyes, sandy hair, fair complexion. Res. in St. Elmo, 1907. [TP9412]

BAXTER, 1st Sgt. John Lafayette
          Co. H, 1st TN (Turney's)
          Born Feb. 24, 1844 in Murray Co., GA. Enl. April, 1861 at Knoxville. Wounded at Chancellorsville, Wilderness and Gettysburg. Captured Petersburg, April 2, 1865 and released June  10, 1865. Res. East Chattanooga, 1888. [NBFM2; TP14,212]

BEAN, James     Co. D, 4th (12th) GA Cav.
          Enl. Oct. 2, 1863, with Capt. William J. Rogers. He was a son of E. G. and Jane Bean of Lookout Valley. He was born about 1846.

BEAN, John W.          Co. K, 43TN
          Born 1834, VA. Enl. Dec. 1, 1861 at Ooltewah. Res. 1910 in household of brother-in-law Robert W. Bolton in HC. [1901Vet Census; 1910HC]

BEAN, Wesley Co. D, 4th (12th) Georgia Cav.
          Enl. Oct. 4, 1862 and was discharged with a medical disability on July 27, 1863. Born c1829 in SC, he was a miller living in Lookout Valley at the start of the war. He lived in Alabama prior to moving to Hamilton County.

BEAN, Sgt. William     Co. B, 1st TN Cav. (Carter's)
          Born about 1838, he lived on a farm at Birchwood before the war. His mother was Mary. Enl.

Aug. 7, 1861, Cleveland. He became an officer and was captured in Hamilton County. He was sent to Louisville, KY, on Christmas Day, 1863 and took USA oath two days later and was listed on CSA rolls as a deserter. Bean was released upon the condition that he stay north of the Ohio River. He had a sallow complexion, dark hair, gray eyes and was 5'8" tall. [1860HC]

BEAN, William    Co. D, 4th (12th) Georgia Cav.
    He enl. Oct. 2, 1863, in Lookout Valley by Capt. William J. Rogers. He was taken prisoner and sent to Louisville, KY, on Dec. 12, 1863. He took the oath of allegiance and was paroled north of the Ohio River. He had a dark complexion, dark hair, hazel eyes and was 6' tall.

BEARDEN, William M.    Co. C, 8th GA
    Enl. in Macon, GA May 16, 1861. Elected 2Lt., Co. D, 39NC, Oct. 28, 1861. Wounded at 1st Manassas on 21st birthday. Enl. as pvt., Co. D, 1VA Cav, Aug. 1, 1864. Came to Chattanooga 1888 and founded with J.B. Pound the *Chattanooga News*. Sold out to Pound after a few years. Joined NBF Camp in 1891. Died Dec. 26, 1925 and buried Macon, GA. [BBFM7; Henderson 1:935; CTDec. 28, 1925]

BEASLEY (see BEAZLEY)

BEASON, Abel B.
    Born 1822 in NC, he emigrated to Chattanooga c1840 and served for nearly 15 years as a sheriff's deputy. In 1852 Beason acquired a large tract of land on the north side of river, part of which became Hill City. There he owned and operated a ferry. Openly supporting the Confederacy, he was "shot by one of Wilder's soldiers and driven from his home into Georgia." Abel Beason married Penelope Stringer, daughter of Capt. William Stringer. Beason died in the winter of 1882 after he went out in search of wood and the wagon turned over on him. [JW; 1860HC]

BEASON, William  Co. I, 19th TN
    Born c1850, son of Abel and Penelope Stringer Beason. Enl. March 8, 1863, Knoxville. Absent sick July and dropped from rolls as deserter in Sept. He was never married and died in 1879. [1860HC; JW]

BEATTY, W. H.
    [NBFM1]

BEAVER, Alfred C.    Co. G, 65th GA
    Born Cherokee Co., NC, 1840. "Deserted at Loudon, TN, April 3, 1863. To TN, 1906". [TP12,500]

BEAVER, Hiram Oliver    Co. I, 5th TN (McKenzie's)
    Born June 14, 1846 in Monroe Co., TN and enl. July 18, 1864 [If this date is correct, then he could not have been in the battles of Chickamauga and Gettysburg.], McMinn Co. "In charge at Gettysburg." Chickamauga, Atlanta Campaign. (wounded at Jonesboro), Bentonville. "Smallest man of his company, but about the best soldier of the regiment." Paroled Charlotte, NC, May 4, 1865. Farmer. Methodist 40 years. Died near Dayton, TN, Oct. 20, 1929 and buried CSA Cem. [NBFM2, 6; Pension Application #5244; CT Oct 21, 1929; 1910HC.]

BEAZLEY, John J.    Co. C, 3rd GA
    Born May 21, 1821 at Spottsylvania Co., VA. Mexican War vet. Enl. at Pinfield, Green Co., VA in 1861. Wounded at Battle of Seven Pines. Paroled in Apr., 1865 as major and settled in Gordon Springs, GA. Later Res. at St. Elmo. Died Sept. 23, 1904 and buried Dalton, GA. [NBFM2]

BECTON, Benjamin May    Co. H, 47th TN INF
    Enl. Dec. 31, 1861, Camp Trenton. Placed on detached service with Pioneer Corps. Assigned to take care of pontoon bridge at Kelly's Ferry, 1863. Married Sara. [TWP9209][UDC1]

BEENE, J. C.    Co A 4th TN (Cheatham's Div.)
    Three of his daughters joined the UDC from Marion County. [NBFM1][UDC1:30]

BEENE, L. J.    Co A 4th TN
    Three of his grand daughters from South Pittsburg joined the UDC on him. [UDC1:30]

BEGGS [see Biggs]

BELL, Calvin C.        53rd TN
                [TP15,688]

BELL, George
    Died Aug. 25, 1915 at his home in St. Elmo. Res. Chattanooga 27 years. [CT Aug. 26, 1915]

BELL, Cpl. Martin Van Buren    Co. A, 4th TN Cav. Bn.; Co. H, 2nd TN Cav. (Ashby's)
    Born 1840 in northern AL, he enl. June 17, 1861 at Knoxville; Captured March 30, 1863 at Somerset, KY; paroled Charlotte, NC, May 3, 1865; He had fair complexion; light hair; gray eyes; and was 5'9" tall. Married Sarah A. came to Chattanooga with his family in 1879 and in 1886 became a member of the police force, "never missed a day's service" until three weeks before his death Jan 6, 1901 in Chattanooga. Buried Citizens Cemetery. and moved to CSA Cem. [CT Jan. 7, 1901; NBFM4; TWP4764]

BELL, Samuel H.      Co. F, 35th TN
Born 1842 in TN, son of John W. and E. S. of Ooltewah. Enl. Nov. 1, 1862 at Chattanooga; died Dec. 16, 1862. He had dark hair, fair complexion, blue eyes, and was 5'8" tall. [1860HC]

BELL, William S.      Surgeon
Mexican War; Mayor of Chattanooga (1858); physician and owned Bell's Distillery. Helped organize the Provisional Army of Tennessee in the summer and fall of 1861, filling positions as surgeon of artillery, purveyor, division medical director, surgeon to the general hospital (all without official rank) and also on staffs of TN generals G.J. Pillow and J.P. McCown. Finally, at the request of Leonidas Polk, he became Medical Director of the Army of the Mississippi in early 1862. In the defense of New Madrid, MO, Bell had "both legs shot off" on March 13, 1862, dying that night as the town was being evacuated. His wife was Elizabeth Keith. [CSR; OR, 8:128, 778, 781, 786]

BELL, M. V.      Co H 2nd TN CAV.
Born 9 Sept. 1846 and married a woman by the name of Sallie H. [UDC1:31]

BELL, William Van Buren
Born 1840 in Marshal Co., AL, married (1888 in Hamilton County) Sallie Ann Mitchell Orr, and died 1891 in HC. [TWP, p. 134]

BELLAH, William Parks  Co. B, Cobb's Legion, GA Inf.
Born March 17 1832, Barnesville Blues, GA, son of Rev. Morgan and Melvina Price Bellah. Enl. July 20, 1861, Bowdon, GA under Gen. Bragg. He was wounded at Perryville, and captured. Taken to Baltimore to prison. He was admitted to Chimborazo Hospital, Richmond, May 20, 1862 and returned to duty June 3, 1862. Resigned Jan. 8, 1864 because of Perryville wound. Married (Oct. 25, 1864) Sarah Amelia Hardaway in Barnesville. Died Dec. 17, 1897, Chattanooga. [1890VetCensus; CSA Patriot]

BENNETT, James      Co. H, 4th TN Cav.
Born 1835 in IL, son of Mary. Farm laborer. Enl. Aug. 11, 1861. Killed at Cedartown, GA. [1860HC]

BENNETT, Cpl. John P.  Co. B, 1st TN (Turney's); 2nd KY Cav.
Enl. Apr. 5, 1861. Later joined Morgan's command and was captured at Mt. Sterling, KY, June 9, 1864. Exchanged at Richmond, VA, March 23, 1865. Liquor dealer in Chattanooga. Joined NBF Camp in 1891. Moved to Nashville. [NBFM2]

BENNETT, Moses      Co. L, 36th TN; Co. L, 35thTN
Born 1842 in IL, son of Mary. Enl. Jan. 9, 1862 in Co. L, 36th TN at Chattanooga; transferred to Co. L, 35th TN, then to Stone's Cavalry. Killed Chickamauga, 1863. [1860HC]

BENNETT, William T.      Co. H, 4th TN Cav.
Born 1842 in IL, son of Mary. He joined Wharton's Brigade in Wheeler's Div. Farm laborer. [1860HC][UDC1:32]

BENTON, Little Page Sims  Co. B, 5TN Cav.
Born 1843, son of Edmond Harley and Zillah Sherrill Benton. Res. Catoosa Co., GA. Enl. Aug. 24, 1861 at Knoxville. Sergeant, in charge of caissons at Missionary Ridge. Deserted Feb. 1, 1864 and took USA oath. He had dark complexion, dark hair, hazel eyes, and was 5'11"tall; married (1869) in Hamilton County Margaret Sivley. Died July 20, 1895 in HC and buried Concord Cem. [TWP, p. 84; CMSR; Bruce W. Benton info.; TWP2976; 1880HC Census]

BERRY, Capt. Thomas  1st Lt Co A 31st AL Inf. and Capt. Co A 51st Talledega, AL
As the son of Chattanooga's first mayor, James Enfield Berry, he lived in Chattanooga several years just after the Indian removal. Thomas Berry had been born in Rockridge Co., VA on 21 Sept. 1820, and he went to work at age 13 when his father met financial misfortune. Thomas in 1840 moved to the cotton center at Rome, GA, and developed a thriving plantation, Oak Hill. He married Margaret Frances Rhea on 10 April 1860 in DeKalb Co., AL. Berry fought at Vera Cruz in the Mexican War and rose to the rank of captain. When the Civil War broke out, he formed a Confederate company that fought at Vicksburg and elsewhere. During Sherman's march to the sea, the soldiers invaded Oak Hill and took the chickens and livestock. Much of the place was burned, but the white-columned mansion survived. After the war, Berry borrowed $50,000 from Northern investors and rebuilt his plantation. A daughter, Martha, was born in 1866 and she started a renowned school at Oak Hill that later became known as Berry College. Thomas Berry died in 3 Jan 1887. [JW; Inez Henry, Miracle in the Mountains.][UDC1; UDC2]

BETTERTON, Elijah R.  Co. I, 11th VA
Born May 6, 1846 in Falling Mills, Campbell Co., VA, son of Thomas Betterton. Enl. in the Lynchburg home guard in the spring of 1862 and participated in several "expeditions" in 1863-1864. Then in fall, 1864 he enl. in Co. I, 11VA, fought at Five Forks, was captured and imprisoned at Point Lookout, MD. In 1870 he moved to Chattanooga and engaged in the wholesale liquor trade. He married (1865) Delilah Whitlow. Universalist. Died at home on Missionary Ridge May 14, 1922 and

buried Forest Hills Cemetery. [FHR; NBFM2; CN May 15, 1922; 1910HC]

BETTIS, Bradley (Braley)    Co. H, 1st TN Cav. (Carter's); Co. G, Walker's Bn., Thomas Legion (NC Inf.)

Born 1837 in Jefferson Co. 1860 res. Birchwood with wife Martha in household of Caleb Bettis. Enl. Thomas' NC Legion, Sept., 1862. [1860HC]

BICE, Asberry (Alvey, Alvara, Albery)  Co. D, 37TN
Born c1838. Day laborer with wife Jane. Enl. Sept. 1, 1861 at Knoxville; charged with stealing bacon and jailed in Chattanooga June 30, 1862. Escaped. Captured at Chickamauga, Sept. 15, 1863 and took USA oath Oct. 14, 1863 and enl. in 11KY Cav., n.d. He was 5'9" tall, with gray eyes, brown. hair; fair. complexion. [1860 HC census]

BICE, Amos Naman    Co.B, 7th AL; Barry's Btry.
Born Feb. 15, 1845 in Spartanburg Dist., SC. Enl. at Stevenson, AL, March 1, 1861 and transferred to Barry's Btry May 5, 1862 in Chattanooga. He fell off caisson on retreat from Jackson, MS and "broke my jaw bone which was taken out." Rejoined his unit and was captured Sept. 10, 1864 on retreat from Atlanta. Wounded in leg at Spanish Fort. Paroled May 11, 1865 in Meridian, MS. Employed by Chattanooga Plow. Died at his home on Whiteside St., Aug. 3, 1908 and buried Forest Hills Cemetery. [Brown Diary; NBFM2, 7; TP6471]

BICE, John Garner    Co. H, 4th TN Cav.; Co. B, 5th Cav. Bn.
Born in NC and brought to Hamilton County as a child. Enl. Aug. 11, 1861 and promoted to Sgt. for gallantry at Murfreesboro. Married (1867) Mary J. Burnett and resided 315 Montgomery Ave. (Main St.). Died Nov. 2, 1904 in Chattanooga and buried Forest Hills Cemetery. [TWP, p. 13; CT Nov. 3, 1904]

BICE, O. M.
His wife died at age 72 yrs. on Nov. 15, 1918 and was buried in CSA Cemetery. [CT Nov. 16, 1918]

BICE, William Wallace    Co. G, 9th GA
Born June 30, 1839 in Calhoun, AL. Enl. Apr., 1861 in LaFayette, GA. Wounded and Captured Gettysburg and imprisoned at Fort Delaware and Point Lookout until end of war. Married (1870) O. M. D. Beasley, died Feb. 27, 1913 at his home in St. Elmo and buried CSA Cemetery. [CT March 11, 1913; TWP, p. 135; NBFM2; TP5245]

BIGGERS, Lorenzo Joseph (also Joseph L.) Pemberton's

Co., GA Home Guards
Born Muscogee Co., GA, July 18, 1847. Enl. June, 1864. To TN, 1910. Res. 1912 in St. Elmo. Wife was J. Frances "Fannie" (m. 1876). Died c1927. Buried in Sawyer Cem. HC. [TP12467; 1910HC]

BIGGS, Hamilton L.    Ironmaster    Ordnance
A native of Liverpool, England, born March 8, 1830, Biggs was educated there and learned the trade of foundry man. He settled in Chattanooga in 1860 after working several years in VA where he married Susan Dunavant in 1855. He built and operated a foundry in Chattanooga with his brother James. They manufactured cannon, solid shot and shell for the Provisional Army of Tennessee until the city fell in August, 1863, at which time Hamilton Biggs went to Selma, Alabama, where he was employed at the Shelby Iron Works producing armor for CSA gunboats. Paroled at Selma in 1865, Biggs moved to Birmingham where he opened the new city's first foundry and machine shop. He also owned a stove factory in Birmingham. [Evans, CSA 8:480-81; WF, p. 89]

BILLINGS, Amos    Co. L, 35th TN
Born SC, he was a farmer in Hamilton County who enl. Oct. 16, 1862 at Chattanooga and deserted Sept. 8, 1863 at Lee and Gordon's Mills. Black eyes, dark hair, fair complexion, 6' 1 1/2" tall.

BISPLINGHOFF, Henry    Co. H, 2TN Cav. (Ashby's)
Born c1822 Waltrous, Prussia. Emigrated to NY, then lived at a German colony in Roane Co., TN, before coming to Chattanooga by steamboat in 1859. Bisplinghoff was chief cooper at Bell's Distillery before the war. Enl. June 17, 1861 at Knoxville. Staff bugler until disch. Sept. 15, 1862 as overage. Then became member of the Chattanooga Home Guard. His wife, Sybilla Witte Bisplinghoff, and his mother, Hellena Bisplinghoff, were nurses at the hospitals in Chattanooga during the war. He stayed on in Chattanooga after the war and died about 1880. [JW]

BLACKWELL, Capt. John Lindsay  Co. A, 1TN Cav; promoted to Major, 5th TN Cav. (McKenzie's)
His parents, William and Rebecca Lindsay Blackwell, were among the first settlers in East Brainerd, owning a large farm at Graysville. He was born Jan. 1, 1817, when the family was in Franklin Co., GA. Res. Chickamauga, TN, 1860 and owned one slave. He enl. Aug. 24, 1861, at Camp Cummings and was promoted to captain the following Jan. 7. He was first with Co. A of the 3TN Cav. and later Co. E of the 5TN Cav. and was under Gen. Forrest in many campaigns. He was home sick on furlough in June, 1862. He rejoined the cavalry and was elevated to 1Lt., then Major. Blackwell was in

Bragg's invasion of KY, in Middle TN, and the battles around Chattanooga, including Chickamauga and Missionary Ridge. However, his right hand was wounded by a pistol shot and his left hand suffered an accidental injury and then was frost bitten, causing one finger to stiffen. Unable to use a pistol or saber, Major Blackwell submitted his resignation on Dec. 1, 1863. He married Mary Floyd, who died in 1873. Blackwell moved to TX in the 1880s and died there about 1893. [JW]

BLACKWELL, Sgt. William Jackson     5th TN Cav.; 1st FL Reserves   Sgt.
          Born c1821 in GA, William Jackson was a younger brother of John Lindsay Blackwell, W.J. Blackwell joined the 5th TN Cav. at Chattanooga in 1863 and later was with the 1st FL Reserves and held the rank of Sgt. He was paroled at Madison, FL, on May 15, 1865, and took the USA oath in Worth Co., GA, Sept. 22, 1865. He bought a horse in Atlanta and rode it back to his East Brainerd farm near Graysville, GA. He married Sarah Ann Carter, then Elmira E. Morgan. He died Aug. 18, 1890, at age 69 and is buried in the Blackwell Cem. at the present Council Fire development. [JW; information supplied by Dr. Anthony Hodges; 1860HC.]

BLAIR, Dr. D. Y.          Surgeon, 60th TN MI
          Born c1834 and res. with minister J.N. Bradshaw, 1860. Enl. Nov. 7, 1862, Haynesville. Asst. Surgeon and later Surgeon (Dec. 3, 1862). [1860HC]

BLALOCK, Joseph G.     Co. E, 11th GA
          Pvt. March 1, 1862. Absent without leave April, 1, 1864. Died Dec. 15, 1914, age 82, at res. on High St. and buried Menlo, GA.

BLANTON, J. A.     Phillips Ga. Legion
          Born in NC c1836. Enl. Aug. 1861 in Phillips Ga. Legion. Contractor in Chattanooga who moved to Dalton. Died 1903. [NBFM2, 7]

BLEDSOE, Anthony Street   2Lt., Co. I, 17th TN; Co. D, 33rd AL
          Born Sept. 25, 1837[24 Feb 1825] in Franklin Co., TN. Enl. May 11, 1861. Wounded Chickamauga. Married (1885) Lee Greer. Brothers William and James also CSA. Manual laborer. Married Lee Greer on 6 June 1883 in Franklin Co., TN. She was born 15 May 1845. Died at res. on Colville St., Nov. 16, 1917 and buried in Citizens Cem. [TWP, 214; CT Mar. 11, 1917; TP7468][UDC2]

BLEVINS, Jehu H. P. [Joseph High]     3rd TN
          Born 11 March 1840. Enlisted with his two brothers John W. and Lysurgus R. (killed in Norton, VA). Jehu married Sarah E. Campbell on 31 Dec. 1867

in Meigs Co. She was born 11 Dec 1838 and died 9 July 1901. Jehu died Feb. 19, 1917 in Chattanooga and buried in Decatur, TN, "his old home." 75 yrs. Mason. [CT Feb. 20, 1917]

BLEVINS, Jonathan B.     Co. D, 37th TN
          Born Oct. 15, 1824 in Marion Co., TN. He was a blacksmith who enl. Sept. 1, 1861 at Knoxville; conscript; absent sick May 15, 1863-May, 1864. He resided at 1315 Whiteside St. (Broad St.). Blevins died Aug. 6, 1900, and was buried in the CSA Cem. Member NBF Camp, 1895-96. [CT Aug. 7, 1900; NBFM2]

BOLTON, Hiram B.  Co. D, 4th (12th) GA Cav.
          Enl. Oct. 4, 1862, at Chattanooga under Capt. William J. Rogers. Born c1839, he was a son of Solomon Bolton, a tenant on the Henry Simmerman farm at Moccasin Bend. The Boltons were Melungeons, who earlier lived in SC. Married Caroline. [JW]

BOND, Bartlett W.  Co. A,          1st TN (Turney's)
          Born 1834 in Bradley Co. and married (1857) Jemima E. Walker. Died in HC. [TWP, p. 62]

BOOTH, William C.     Barry's Btry.
          Born May 2, 1829 in Madison Co., GA. Enl. July 14, 1862 at Chattanooga in Barry's Btry; Rec'd $50.00 bounty for enlistment. Served as nurse in CSA hospital Aug.-Nov., 1863; disabled for field duty because of tumor, present at Spanish Fort, however. Res. given as Dade Co., GA, although does not appear in 1860 nor 1870 census. He was 5'7" in height, with blue eyes, light complexion, and light. hair. Married (1866) Lettie J. Howard. Living in Chattanooga in 1905 and died that year, Oct. 28. Buried Brown Gap Cem., Dade Co., GA. [TWP, p. 60; TP 6931]

BOTT, W. L.          Co. A, 9th VA
          Born March 25, 1843, Dinwiddie Co., VA. Enl. Spring, 1862. Drewry's Bluff (wounded). Captured April 1, 1865 and imprisoned at Pt. Lookout until July, 1865. To TN in 1871and Res. Chattanooga, 1907. Died at home of daughter, Mrs. F.H. Gross, 2103 Vine, March 29, 1913. Buried Citizens Cem. [TP9703; CT March 30, 1913]

BOURGES, James F.
          Charter member NBF Camp, 1885.

BOWERS, Anthony     Co. E, 39th NC
          Born Oct. 8, 1835, Yancy Co., NC. [obit: born 1838 in Marsh Creek, SC.] Res. in Clay Co., NC where he enl. Nov. 6, 1861. Brothers James C. and Thomas. J. in same company. Murfreesboro, Chickamauga, Atlanta Campaign. Paroled Meridian, MS, May 9, 1865. Married

(1866) Mary "Polly" Fowler. To TN, 1886. Res. Chattanooga, 1910. Died April 18, 1917 in Chattanooga [TWP, p. 196; CTApril, 19, 1917; TP11,823]

BOWMAN, Benjamin T.     Co. H, 18th TN
Born June 20, 1841, Rutherford Co., TN. Enl. July 10, 1861, Camp Trousdale. Captured at Ft. Donelson and imp. Camp Butler. After exchange fought at Murfreesboro, Chickamauga, Resaca. Recaptured July 30, 1864 at Atlanta and imprisoned Camp Chase. Carpenter. Res. household of son Robert Bowman on Long St., 1910. [NBFM1; TP10791; 1910HC]

BOWMAN, Daniel     Co. D, 4th AL Bn.
Born 1830 in Cherokee, AL, he fought at Shiloh, Port Hudson and Missionary Ridge. Captured Sept. 13, 1863 near Chickamauga, he was imprisoned at Camp Chase. Married Martha. [TP5724]

BOYCE, James P.          SC
Became a distinguished Baptist divine after his war service with a South Carolina regiment. His father, Ker Boyce, was a wealthy Charleston businessman, who was one of the early investors in Chattanooga property. The Boyces had a farm in East Chattanooga. JPB used part of the family fortune to endow Furman Univeristy at Greenville, SC. He died in 1888. [JW]

BOYD, Alexander H.     Co. B, 1st TN Cav. (Carter's)
The Boyds were residing at Ooltewah in 1860. Enl. Aug. 7, 1861 in Cleveland. Born c1839, son of John Hodge Boyd and Mahala Bush. Martha's address is given in the war records as Graysville, Catoosa Co., GA. He died Dec. 27, 1861, from a wound he received at Mill Springs, KY. [1860HC]

BOYD, Francis Marion     Co. K, 43rd TN
Born c1836, son of John Hodge and Mahala Bush Boyd. FMB was farmer at Ooltewah prior to war. Enl. Nov. 11, 1862, Ooltewah. Captured at Vicksburg. Justice of peace after the war. [1860HC]

BOYD, Hugh A.     Bird's Rangers (Co. F, Roger's East TN Cav.); Co. F, 35TN
Born Atlanta, GA, Aug. 24, 1830, son of Hugh and Mary Boyd who moved to HC c1836. HAB was constable at Harrison prior to war. Enl. Oct. 18, 1862, Varnell Station, GA in 35TN, transferring from cav. Sick in hospital at Ringgold, April, 1863 and still reported absent sick when unit in camp near Tyner Station, July 13, 1863. Mason. Living at home of dau., Mrs. T.R. Standifer in James Co. when he died Aug. 7, 1909 in Chattanooga Married Sarah A. His sons were Joseph W. of Highland Park and Walter of Ridgedale. [CT Aug. 8, 1909]

BOYD, James T.     Co. G, 1GA
Born Feb. 25, 1845, Daugharty Co., GA. Enl. 1862, Millen's Stat; transferred to 1GA. Several slight wounds. Paroled Hamburg, SC. To TN c1915. 1917 applied from HC for admission to TN Soldiers' Home. Res., 1917 East Lake [SAACH]

BOYD, John Hodge, Jr.     Co. K, 43rd TN
Born 1841, TN, son of John Hodge (veteran of Seminole War) and Mahala Bush Boyd of Ooltewah. Enl. Nov. 10, 1862 at Ooltewah; captured at Vicksburg, July 4, 1863. Took oath of allegiance at Ooltewah, 1864. Res. James Co., 1909. Married Rebecca Rogers (1866) and res. Ooltewah. 1910 widower res. with two grown daughters on farm in James Co. [1910 James Co.]

BOYD, John W.          Pvt. Co F 5th TN Inf
He was born in 1829c in Monroe Co., TN and died 18 April 1863 near Tullahoma in Coffee Co., TN. He had married on 22 April 1852 in Monroe Co. to Flora Jane Cagle (b. 1833c and died in 1924 in Rhea Co.). He enlisted at Chattanooga 6 Jan 1863. [UDC3:34]

BOYD, John William     Co. F, 35th TN
Born 1826, son of Hugh and Mary Boyd who moved from GA to HC c1836. J.W. Boyd married Mary Ann Acuff (1848). They had three daughters and five sons. Enl. Jan. 6, 1863, Chattanooga. [Lindsley]

BOYDSTON, Asa Conner 2Lt     Co. H, 36th TN; Co. C, 1st TN & Ala. Cav.
Born 1833, TN, son of John and Sara Lee Condry Boydston. Married Jane Blevins, 1855. 1860 farmer at Chattanooga with wife Jane and two children. [1860HC]

BOYDSTON, George A.     Co. D, 4th (12th) GA Cav.
Enl. Oct. 4, 1862, with Capt. William J. Rogers. He obtained a medical disability on Nov. 1, 1862. He was one of the sons of Cavanaugh and Polly Boydston of Lookout Valley. He had married Ann Williams in 1856. [JW]

BOYDSTON, Lt. James Madison "Jimmy"     Co. D, 4th (12th) GA Cav.
Born Dec. 31, 1828 in HC, one of the sons of Cavanaugh and Polly Boydston of Lookout Valley. Enl. Oct. 2, 1862, and was a scout. He was later captured and placed in a Union prison. Paroled as 1st LT in May, 1865. He married Rachel Hood, then Martha (Mattie) Hood. Blind last 12 years of life, he died Nov. 21, 1911, in the house in which he had been born in Wauhatchie. [JW; TP5363; CT Nov. 22, 1911; 1910HC]

BOYDSTON (BOYDSON) 1Sgt., 1Lt. Thomas    Co. I, 19th TN

Born 1820, son of Cavanaugh and Polly Slape Boydston of Lookout Valley. Clerk for atty. Richard Henderson just before enl. May 20, 1861, Knoxville. Served in QM Dept. but discharged overage. Died 1886. [JW]

BOYDSTON, William    3rd Lt, Co. F, 35th TN

Born 1833 in TN, son of Cavanaugh and Polly Slape Boydston of Lookout Valley. Married Jane White, 1855. 1860 Farmer at Chattanooga with wife Jane and two children. Enl. Oct. 1, 1862., Chattanooga Sick in hospital, Chattanooga, April, 1863 and at Ringgold, May, 1863. Severely wounded Chickamauga, Sept. 20, 1863 and sent back to hospital Prom. to 3Lt but resigned Sept. 8, 1864, doing so because the regt. had grown so small with about 100 men and 30 officers. [JW]

BRACKEN, Archie L.    Co. H, 4th TN Cav. (Starnes)

Born June 9, 1845 in Marion Co. Enl. April, 1863. Fought at Chickamauga, Knoxville. Married (1874 in Marion) Laura A. Chadoin. Farmer. Died in HC, Oct. 6, 1915 and buried Citizens Cem. [TWP, p. 177; TP8289]

BRACKETT, John    Co. B, 5th TN Cav.

BRACKETT, Rufus    Co. B, 5th TN Cav.

Born 1844 in TN. Res. 1860 in house hold of Elijah Mayfield in Chattanooga [1860HC]

BRADEN, O.    Barry's Btry.

Deserted [Brown's Diary].

BRADFORD, Col. William M.    31st TN MI
F&S 39th MI, TN

Born Feb. 14, 1827 in what is now Polk Co., TN, son of Henry and Rachel McFarland Bradford. Attended school and practiced law in Athens. Practiced also in Dandridge (Jefferson Co.) and Chattanooga. Married at Dandridge (1846) Elizabeth K. Inman. Surveyor of Polk Co. and postmaster of Columbus. Clerk and Master of Jefferson Co., 1851-54. TN Gen'l Assembly, 1859-61. Organized the 39th (31st) Tennessee Infantry which later became a mounted command. Served in East TN and KY under Kirby Smith, fought and was captured at Vicksburg and when exchanged served as a subordinate commander for John C. Vaughn, sometimes commanding a brigade. Refused to surrender when news of Lee's surrender reached the brigade and Bradford took his men to NC to join President Davis whom they escorted into Georgia. Paroled at Washington, GA. NBF Camp. Wife Elizabeth K. wrote the history of the 31st Regiment in Lindsley's Annals, pp.

463-469. Presbyterian. Mason. Died June 11, 1895 in Chattanooga and buried in Citizens Cem. [1890VetCensus; NBFM2; BDTA, 1:69-70]

BRADLEY, Andrew A.    Co. B, 1st CSA (GA) (Villepigue's)

Born Oct. 24, 1838 in Greenville Co., SC. Enl. at Ringgold April 1, 1861. Santa Rosa Island; wounded at Kennesaw Mountain; Decatur, GA; Jonesboro, GA and on retreat from Nashville. Never captured. Paroled at Greensboro, NC, having served four years under Capt. James C. Gordon. To TN, 1902. Farmer in Rossville (HC). Res. 1910 in household with grown son and dau. Died March 8, 1914 and buried at Chickamauga, GA. At time of death res. 1207 47th St., Rossville. [NBFM2; TP9940; 1910HC; CT Nov. 6, 1914]

BRADLEY, Andrew Alexander    Wood's Regt., MS Cav.

From the DAR records, he never lived in Hamilton County. [UDC2P59] [TP9871]

BRADSHAW, George H.

Born April 23, 1844 in Maury Co. Enl. He fought at Chickamauga and Chattanooga. He died at his res. on West 9th St. March 29, 1906 and was buried in Forest Hills Cemetery. [CT Mar. 30, 1906]

BRADSHAW, John D.    Co. K, 49GA

Born 1835 in Lincoln Co. and married (12 Jan. 1862 in Bartow Co., GA) Mary Pinion born 8 March 1844 in North Carolina. "Detailed by the Confederate Government to the Cooper Iron works, later Quemby & Robinson of Etowah, GA, making cannon balls, cannon and arms for the CSA army.    Taken prisoner by Sherman's army on 20 May 1864. Paroled from Rock Island Federal prison when the war ended." [UDC2:60] Appt. Regt. musician, Nov. 1, 1864; Surr. Appomatox CH, April. 9, 1865. To Chattanooga in 1869. Steel expert. --a "puddler." Died at res. on Boyce St. Nov. 17, 1911. [TWP, 299; CT Nov. 18, 1911.]

BRADT, Morris

Had just brought his bride to Chattanooga when the war broke out. He served in the Home Guard. Born in Prussia in 1831, he had come to America as a young man. He was married at Macon, Ga., in 1860, and he and his wife, Julia, then came to Chattanooga, where he sold real estate. The Bradts stayed on after the war. They had a fine home and a vineyard on Cameron Hill.

BRADY, Benjamin    Co. D, 37th TN

Born c1815 in NC. Farm laborer. Enl. Sept. 1, 1861 at Knoxville. Died Oct. 10, 1861 of measles at Knoxville; apparently married twice: Matilda and later

Arva M.

BRADY, James W.     Co. I, 19th TN

     Born 1827 in GA, son of Benjamin (farm laborer from NC) and Matilda. Res. in Chattanooga, 1860. Enl. May 20, 1861, Knoxville. Slightly wounded at Murfreesboro, Dec. 31, 1862, and severely wounded at Missionary Ridge. Died from wounds at Fairground Hospital, Atlanta, Dec. 31, 1863. QM given money he possessed at time: $17.50. [1860HC]

BRADY, Owen R.     Co. K, 43rd TN

BRAMER, D. B.
     Res. of Hamilton County in 1901.

BRANDON, Phillip A.     Co. E, 12th AL
     Born Colnsia, Cherokee Co., AL, Aug. 18, 1836. Enl. May 5, 1861 in 12th AL. Army of Northern Virginia: South Mountain., Sharpsburg, Fredericksburg, Chancellorsville (wounded), Gettysburg. Wounded three other times and disch. Aug. 25, 1863. To TN, 1887. Res. Vaughn St. 1893, 1899. [NBFM2; TP10,187]

BRANHAM, Capt. Isham R.     Co B 2nd GA Bn
     AAG, staff of Alfred Iverson, Oct. 24, 1863; AG Dept.; on Gen. Cobb's staff; adjt. to Gen. Iverson and was enrolling officer of Bibb Co., GA. He became preacher after war; daughter, Adela. [UDC1]

BRANHAM, James     Co. L, 36th TN
     Enl. Jan. 9, 1862 at Chattanooga.

BRANSON (BRONSON), John Rufus     Co. C, 41st TN; Co. C, 8th TN
     Born Feb. 9, 1840 in Lincoln Co., son of John and Cynthia Branson. Several of his brothers joined the CSA army and one was captured at Fort Donelson and died in prison. J.R. Branson enlisted Nov. 4, 1861, Camp Trousdale. Sent home on sick furlough Dec. 15, 1861. Enl. 8th TN, April 24, 1862. Ordered by Col. R.W. Smith, military governor of Corinth, to report to Col. Fulton for duty at Tupelo, MS. With 8th TN, Jan 1864. Married (1869) Elizabeth Rodgers. Res. of Chattanooga, 1903. Res. 2217 Sidney St. at time of his death, Feb. 28, 1924. [TWP, 229; TP5358; CT Feb. 29, 1924; 1910HC]

BRECKINRIDGE, Stanhope Preston     Asst. Surgeon.
     Born April 20, 1841 in Louisville, KY, he graduated from Centre College and entered the Confederate army as asst. surgeon, 4KY, then on staff of J.S. Marmaduke, then was surgeon of 2KY Mounted Volunteers and fought with them at Murfreesboro. He was "assigned to [5th Company, Washington Artillery of New Orleans] Battery in Oct[31,] 1863 in Camp at Missionary Ridge. Present with Battery at Battle of Missionary Ridge" where he remained with the wounded and was captured. Exchanged Jan. 31, 1864 and sent to Genl. Hospital Sick Hdq., A of TN, Dalton. That spring he reported to Director of Hospitals, S. H. Stout. Later he was transferred to Richmond, VA and put in charge of one of the principal hospitals. "After the war he practiced his profession in LA and MS until his health was broken down. He then came to Chattanooga to recuperate and died here March 14, 1887. He was buried in Louisville. [NBF Minutes]

BRENNAN, Richard V.
     Born in London, England, Sept. 26, 1822, he lived a sea-faring life as a young man before settling in Lexington, KY. Sympathetic with the South, he was instrumental in getting weapons from the armory of the Kentucky State Militia and supplying them to the Confederate forces. He fled before being arrested and eventually settled in Chattanooga in 1870, dying here May 16, 1902.

BRENT, N. H.
     [NBFM1]

BREWER, Clark H.     Co. I, 19th TN
     Born in VA in 1843; wounded in battles of Shiloh and Murfreesboro. Joined Henderson's Scouts but captured at Vicksburg. A Chattanoogan, but residing in Memphis Nov. 1, 1889. Personal friend of F.M. Walker. [CV 15:240; CT Nov. 1, 1889]

BREWER, James M.
     Born 1847, TN. Res. with wife Juliete in Soddy, 1910. Laborer, odd jobs. [1910HC]

BREWSTER, J. R.     Co. K, 43th TN
     Enl. Nov. 10, 1862 at Ooltewah; Captured Vicksburg, July 4, 1863.

BRIDGES, John F.     Co. K, 43th TN
     Enl. Oct. 17, 1861; deserted Nov. 3, 1862.

BRISON, William C.
     Born c1841, NC. Farmer in HC, 1910, wife Liddie. [1910HC]

BROCK, David     Co. G, 3rd TN Mtd. Inf.
     Born May 4, 1827 in McMinn Co., he enl. in March, 1862 in Calhoun, TN. Captured at Vicksburg July 4, 1863. Living in HC, 1870; Rossville, GA, Jan., 1900. [UCV applications, NBF Camp]

BROCK, John     Co. H, 26th TN; 2d Co. I, 1st CSA (GA)

Enl. July 8, 1861, Knoxville. Wounded in head and sent off from Fort Donelson, Feb. 12, 1862. Transferred to 1st CSA, Nov. 8, 1862. Absent, in Bradshaw's Cav., Dec. 31, 1862. Captured Calhoun, GA, May 25, 1864 and imp. Rock Island, IL (Deserter-- refused to take oath") where he died of disease Aug. 16, 1864 and was buried there.

BROCK, Younger    Co. H, 26th TN; Barry's Btry.
Enl. Sept. 6, 1861, Knoxville. While wounded himself, he was sent as nurse with wounded from Fort Donelson, Feb. 15, 1862. Joined Barry's Btry.


BRONSON (See BRANSON)

BROOKS, David        Co. C, 26th TN
Born 1827 in TN. Farm laborer at Chattanooga with wife Eliza. [1860HC]

BROOKS, Levi      Co. L, 1st TN Cav. (Carter's)
Born 1842 in TN, son of Gideon and Winny of Long Savannah. Captured July 22, 1864, Claiborne Co., TN and sent to Chattanooga Paroled May 2, 1865, Claiborne Co., TN

BROOKS, Preston      Co. F, 35th TN
Age 17 in 1862, he enl. Dec. 16, 1862 at Chattanooga. He was the son of Gideon and Winny Brooks, who had a farm at Long Savannah near Ooltewah. He was 5'6" tall with a fair complexion. Deserted at Chattanooga, Dec. 20, 1862.

BROOKS, William Huston      Co. E, 16th TN
Born June 9, 1837 in Warren Co., TN. Enl. at McMinnville, May 14, 1861 in Co. A (E), 16TN. Captured at Lookout Mountain. and escaped. Paroled at Washington, GA in 1865. Became night watchman in Chattanooga for Electric Light Co. Married Margaret Rhea. Res. of Ridgedale c1895. Died at Ft. Cheatham, suburb of Chattanooga, May 29, 1911, and buried CSA Cem. [TWP, p. 115; NBFM2]

BROWN, Alexander F.      Co. A, 17th TX Inf.
Walker's Division
Born in Pike Co., GA, April 16, 1845. Enl. at Natchitoches, TX, Apr., 1861. Paroled at Henderson, TX. Iron agent in Chattanooga c1896. Lived at 12 Fleming Row. Died at home in Ridgedale, Nov. 5, 1911. Had lived in Chattanooga for 35 yrs. and was in insurance business 20 yrs. Wife Margaret. Married 1866. Buried CSA Cem. [NBFM2; TP7181; CT Nov. 6, 1911; 1910HC; UDC1:50]

BROWN, George E.

Master mechanic and supt. of construction of CSA railroad shops.

BROWN, George Washington    Co. H, 2nd TN Cav; Barry's Btry.
Born July 10, 1842 in Blount Co. and was brought to Chattanooga at age five. Enl. Sept 27, 1862 in Ragsdale's Cav. Co. Transferred to Barry's Btry; Captured at Spanish Fort. Carpenter. Married Mary K. (1842-1915). Died Jan. 16, 1912 in Chattanooga and buried White Oak Cem. [NBFM2,4,7; CT Jan. 18, 1912]

BROWN, H. J.            Barry's Btry.
Enl. at Chattanooga Jan. 27, 1863; transferred to Winston's Btry., March 15, 1863.

BROWN, Hira[sic]      Co. H, 4th TN Cav.

BROWN, J. C.    Co. C, 7th GA
Died 1912; buried CSA Cem.

BROWN, J. D.  Co. F, 39th TN
Born 1840, GA. Farmer at Tyner with wife Catherine, 1860. [Henderson, 301; 1860HC]

BROWN, Cpl. J. W.    Co. L, 35th TN
Enl. Sept. 17, 1862 at Chattanooga. Drummer.

BROWN, James  Bugler, Co. A (Ragsdale's), 4TN Cav.

BROWN, James
Born 1840, S.C. Res. 1910 on Forest Ave. with wife Ella. Janitor for apartments. African-American. [1910HC]

BROWN, James B.    Barry's Btry.
Born Cleveland, TN. Enl. April 4, 1862 at Chattanooga; paroled May 11, 1865 in Meridian, MS. Married Elzanie (Murray Co., GA, 1887). Died in Murray Co., 1903. [TWP9717]

BROWN, James B.
Born 13 July 1835 in TN. Farmer near Harrison with wife Rhoda J. Died, age 84, Jan. 6, 1920 at his home in Brown's Chapel neighborhood where he is buried. [CT Jan. 7, 1920; 1860HC]

BROWN, James E.
Married Elizabeth E. [TWP2095]

BROWN, James F.  Co. D, 1st TN Cav.
Born April 10, 1835 in Bledsoe Co., TN. Farmer in TN and TX. Methodist. Died Aug. 12, 1927 at res. in Ft. Payne, AL. Buried beside wife in CSA Cem. [NBFM7; CT Aug. 14, 1927]

BROWN, James G.
Born 1841, GA., of C.N. Brown was his father and S.C. his mother. 1910 machinist res. in boarding house on Carter St. Widower. [1910HC]

BROWN, James S.
Born 1835, TN, of TN parents. 1910 res. Houston St. with wife Hattie whom he married 1860. [1910HC]

BROWN, James W. (G. D.)   2 GA Bn.; Co. C, 17GA
Born Sept. 26, 1844 in Bibb Co., GA, he enl. at Columbus April 19, 1861, in Co. A, 2GA Bn., then Co. C, 17GA. In Jan., 1862, however, he was detailed to work in arsenal in Richmond where he remained until Aug., 1863 when to was transferred to the arsenal in Augusta, GA. Eventually he ended up in the navy yards in Mobile. In Chattanooga after the war he was an ice machine engineer. NBF Camp. He died Feb. 19, 1921 in HC and buried CSA Cem. [TP12,456; NBFM7; CT Feb. 20-21, 1921]

BROWN, John Hardin   Co. H, 4th TN Cav
Born 1838 in Blount Co. Enl. Aug. 11, 1861. Perryville, Murfreesboro. Captured May, 1863 at Trousdale's Ferry. Paroled 1865 in Charlotte, NC. Married (1866 in HC) Dolly D. Davis. Plasterer and day laborer who died at res. in East Lake Feb. 23, 1910 and buried CSA Cem. [CT Feb. 24, 1910; NBFM2,7; TP7910]

BROWN, John J.   Co. C, Wheeler's Scouts
Born July 3, 1847, Athens GA. Enl. Jan., 1864. Captured at Columbus, GA and paroled at Macon in 1865. Merchant in Chattanooga. Died April 19, 1909 at home on East 8th and buried Forest Hills Cemetery. [FHR; NBFM2]

BROWN, John L. "Doc" Co. C, 20th TN
Black soldier born Oct. 25, 1839, Davidson Co., TN. Slave of Morgan W. Brown. Joined May 20, 1861 with Lt. John C. Thompson at Nashville. Young master killed at Fort Pickens and Brown wounded. "He bore dispatches to Felix Zollicoffer and performed many other duties of service and responsibility." Disch. Corinth, May 22, 1862. "He has married a middle aged colored woman who is trying to run him off from home. We are perfectly willing to take care of him at Silverdale, but he refuses to go to the poor house. He wants to go to the Old Soldiers Home." Res. East 12th St., 1924. [TP186]

BROWN, John S.   Co. D, 1st TN Cav (Carter's); Co. D, Douglas's - Bn., 21st TNCav.
Born Bledsoe Co., TN, April 10, 1835. Enl. Spring, 1862. Severe attack of typhoid during Chickamauga campaign. 1909 res. Chamberlain Ave., "doing little jobs in garden and about the store." Buried CSA Cem. [TP11,730]

BROWN, Joseph H.   Co. H, 4th TN Cav.
Enl. July 11, 1861 in Chattanooga. Plasterer in Chattanooga in 1887. Died Feb. 23, 1910 at his home in East Lake. NBF Camp. Buried in CSA Cem., Chattanooga. [CT Feb. 24, 1910]

BROWN, 2 Lt. Lafayette   Co. F, 39th GA
Pvt., May 1, 1862. 2Lt., Jan. 20, 1863. Resigned March 20, 1864. [Henderson, 301; 1890VetCensus]

BROWN, Ridley S.   Co. F, 17th TN
Born Bedford Co., TN, May 12, 1838. Wife was Martha W. Fought at Barboursville, Loudon, and wounded and captured at Wildcat, KY. Became forage master for Bushrod Johnson's brigade. Hoover's Gap. Took USA oath at Lawrenceburg 1864 to avoid prison. Captured 1865 at Lawrenceburg with scouts. Carpenter in Chattanooga, 1910. Married Martha Jones of Shelbyville. Res. Chattanooga, 1921. Methodist. Died June 16, 1923 at home of daughter on Beck Ave. in Hill City and buried Red Bank Cem. [TP15:534, CT June 17, 1923; 1910HC]

BROWN, William A.   Co. L, 35th TN
Deserted at Salisbury, NC, March 15, 1865.

BROWN, Sgt. William C.   Barry's Btry.
Commissary Sgt. for btry. Active member at least throughout 1864-65; Captured at Spanish Fort evening of April 8, 1865. Died 1905 and buried CSA Cem. CW Diary at Chattanooga Bi-Centennial Library.

BROWNING, George W.   Co. A, 19th TN
Born c1847 in AL, son of I.J. (Justice of Peace from VA) and Caroline Browning. Enl. May 10, 1862, Corinth, MS. Elected Cpl. Severely wounded at Murfreesboro and sent home. Captured Missionary Ridge, Nov. 25, 1863 and imprisoned Rock Island, IL. [1860HC]

BROYLES, A. Horton   Co. G, 36th GA
Previously lived in Washington Co., TN with wife Sarah. Died Jan. 22, 1917 in Chattanooga and buried Forest Hills Cemetery. [CT Jan. 23, 1917]

BROYLES, Charles E.   Co. G, 36th GA
NBF Camp. [NBFM2]

BRUCE, William M.   Co. H, 26th TN; 2d Co. I, 1st CSA

Enl. Aug. 6, 1861, Knoxville. Left sick Bowling Green, KY, Jan. 23, 1862. Transferred to 2nd Co. I, 1st CSA, Nov. 8, 1862. Deserted 1863. Released by Fed. authorities after taking USA oath, Dec. 23, 1863 and sent north of Ohio River.

BRUDER, J. M.    Co. A, 19th TN
Enl. at Knoxville on May 20, 1861. He was with the troops near Shelbyville in May of 1863. He was captured at Missionary Ridge and died in prison. [CSR]

BRUMBY, Dr. Ephraim R.    Co. I, 7th GA Cav.
Born in Tuscaloosa, AL, Aug. 23, 1845, he attended Georgia Military Academy at Marietta. He was the son of Professor Richard T. and Mary Brevard Brumby. Enl. April, 1863 at Marietta in 7GA Cav. and at one time during the war served as a "courier for Wade Hampton." Afterwards he was engaged in the drug business in Athens, GA and beginning in 1903 in Chattanooga. He married (1870) Mamie McPherson. Presbyterian. He died in Chattanooga Feb. 12, 1918 and was buried in Athens. [CT Feb. 13, 1918; NBFM2; TP15,211]

BRUMMETT, John W.    Co. H, 3rd KY; Co. C, Cons. 3rd TN
Born Nov. 20, 1839 and spent most of life in KY. Wounded twice, once at Chickamauga. Lived in Chattanooga 15 years. Died at res. in Avondale Feb. 9, 1920 and buried Somerset, KY. [CT Feb. 10, 1920]

BRYAN, Daniel Gideon    Co. A, 24th Sharpshooter Bn.
He was the son of Josiah Jackson Bryan, an early commission merchant at Chattanooga. Daniel G. Bryan was born in 1847 when the family was living at Hamburg, SC. He married Carrie Burg.

BRYAN, Josiah Jackson, who was one of the merchants along the river front at Chattanooga prior to the war, served as a guard at Andersonville Prison. He was born in Cocke County, TN, in 1820, the son of Josiah Jackson Bryan Sr. He married Julianna Hull of Hamburg, SC. The family moved to Chattanooga in September, 1849. Mrs. Bryan helped make the flag for William Ragsdale's Co. A, 4th TN Cav. (Branner's). It was made out of pieces of silk dresses from Chattanooga ladies. A Democrat, J.J. Bryan was alderman and then mayor of Chattanooga after the war. When he died in 1883, he was buried in the Citizens Cemetery.

BRYANT, James P.    Co. K, 43th TN
Age 39 in 1864 (1860 census has him 34 in 1860), he enl. Oct. 17, 1861. He was captured at Vicksburg on July 4, 1863, and exchanged. Bryant was captured again on Sept. 2, 1864, near Martinsburg, VA.

He was imprisoned at Fort Delaware. He had dark complexion, gray eyes and brown hair and was 5'8" tall. Prior to the war, he was a day laborer living with his wife, Margaret, at Chattanooga. He was a native of South Carolina. The family lived in GA prior to moving to Chattanooga several years before the war.

BRYSON, Fletcher
CSA. Res. in GA in 1864. After war moved to Chattanooga and was a clerk at the Old Crutchfield House. [Wells, Rems]

BUCKLAND, H.    Clark's Independent Cav. Co.
Enl. Aug. 31, 1862 at Chattanooga; deserted Dec. 1, 1863 in East TN.

BUCKLAND, James L.    Clark's Independent Cav. Co.
"Enl. Aug. 31, 1862 at Chattanooga; deserted Feb. 15, 1864 in East TN. He was 5'9"tall, fair complexion, brown eyes, black hair; signs by mark."

BUCKNER, Levi
Born 1833, NC. 1910 res household daughter Margaret Foster on Lightfoot Mill Rd. Farm laborer. [1910HC]

BUFF, James M.    Co. G, 26th TN; Barry's Btry.
Born c1833 in TN. Farm laborer at Chickamauga with wife Mary A. Enl. Sept. 8, 1861, Knoxville. Disch. Nov. 19, 1861. Re-enl. May 12, 1862, at Chattanooga in Barry's Battery, and did duty as a blacksmith. He was captured at Spanish Fort on April 8, 1865 and imprisoned at Ship Island, MS.

BULLOCK, Cabell B.    Co. B, 1st KY
Born Frankfort, KY. Enl. 1861 in Co. B, 1KY. Surrendered at Augusta, GA May, 1865. Lived in Lexington, KY. Fire Insurance. [NBFM2]

BULLON, James    Clark's Independent Cav. Co.
Enl. Aug. 31, 1862 at Chattanooga; deserted Sept. 8, 1863.

BUNCH, Benjamin F.    Co. B, 1st TN Cav (Carter's)
Served in 26th TN, then 2nd TN Cav. Died Nov. 14, 1910, age 82, at res. on Whiteside St. and buried CSA Cem. [CT Nov. 16, 1910; TP8399]

BUNCH, William F.    26th TN; Co. D, 1st TN Cav. (Carter's)
Born Jefferson Co., TN, Sept., 1830. Enl. fall, 1861. Fort Donelson; joined Carter's Cav. Wounded in leg and captured at Harrodburg, KY, Oct. 5, 1862. Res. on Whiteside St. in 1906. [TP8399]

BUNN, T. H.     Co. B, 7th TN Cav.
     Died at Fincastle, VA, Aug. 28, 1862.

BURCH, Col. John Christopher
     In the opinion of Henry Watterson, he "had a great big intellect." He had never known a man of "finer political judgment." Burch was born in Jefferson Co., GA, Oct. 17, 1827, the son of Morton Newman Burch and Mary Ballard. He ventured north to receive his undergraduate education at Yale, then returned to GA and began the practice of law in Murray Co. In 1852, Burch moved to Chattanooga where he continued his law practice. He represented HC in the TN General Assembly, 1855-57, then entered the Senate in 1857 representing Hamilton, Rhea, Bradley, Bledsoe and Marion cos. In 1859 he moved to Nashville where he became editor of the powerful Democratic paper the Nashville Union and American. Although a close friend of Andrew Johnson, he broke political ties with him and supported John C. Breckinridge in the presidential election of 1860.
     During the war Burch helped Gideon Pillow organize the Provisional Army of TN and served as his chief of staff. During the winter of 1861-62 he provided indispensable help for prominent East TN Unionists, representing them in court and making a direct appeal on their behalf to Richmond. Burch participated in the Fort Donelson debacle in Feb., 1862, escaping with Pillow rather than surrendering, and when Pillow was "suspended," Burch joined Forrest as a staff officer. Unsuccessful in obtaining an appointment to Brig. Gen., although strongly supported by TN generals Cheatham and McCown, he resigned for "personal affairs problems," but quickly returned to help Pillow. In 1863-1864 Burch displayed great energy and initiative, creating and coordinating a network of conscript and deserter camps, thereby helping to replenish the manpower of the Army of TN. He also served on the staffs of N. B. Forrest, Jones M. Withers, S. R. Anderson, and was an aide to Gov. Isham G. Harris.
     In 1869, he purchased controlling interest in the Union andAmerican and continued as editor until 1873 when he became Comptroller of TN. In 1879 he went to Washington where he was elected secretary of the U. S. Senate. He died there July 28, 1881. His wife was Lucy Newell. [CSR]

BURGESS, Martin L.     Co. G, 26th TN
     Born c1837 in TN. Farmer at Tynersville with wife Rachel. Enl. July 8, 1861, Knoxville and detailed as wagoner. Captured near Chattanooga, Sept. 11, 1863, took USA oath and enl. 11th KY Cav. (USA). He had light complexion, light brown hair, blue eyes, was 5'4 ½" tall.

BURGINS, Thomas     Barry's Btry
     Enl. June 28, 1862; Transf. "back to Capt. Harvey" by Maj. Gen. J.P. McCown.

BURK, George W.     Co. K, 43rd TN
     Enl. Nov. 10, 1862 at Ootewah, TN; captured at Vicksburg, July 4, 1863; with light complexion, dark hair, black eyes, and 5'10 ½" tall.

BURK, J. W.     2nd Co. K, 1st CSA Cav.
     Enl. Aug. 1, 1862. Deserted Nov. 5, 1862 at Chattanooga. Then rejoined and hospitalized. Appears to have deserted after Missionary Ridge.

BURK, Sgt. James A.     Co. K, 43rd TN
     Born c1842. Living south of Ooltewah with his mother, Nancy, prior to enlistment.

BURKE, John F.     Co. H, 26th TN
     Enl. July 8, 1861, Knoxville. Captured at Fort Donelson. Left sick Montgomery, AL, Sept. 30, 1862.

BURK, William Albie     Co. K, 43rd TN
     Born 18 Jan 1844. Enl. May 10, 1862, at Ooltewah. He also served in Co K 12 Reg. Captured at Vicksburg. Burk was living prior to the start of the war with his mother, Nancy Burk, and his brothers and sisters. They were at Zion Hill south of Ooltewah.He married Nannie Bradley on 5 Sept 1871. She was born in 1844 and died in 1922. He died 17 June 1891.
     [UDC2:79]

BURKHART, George, Jr.     Co. G, 21st TN Cav. (Carter's)
     Born 1845, son of George Washington and Celia Burkhart of Chattanooga.

BURKHART, George Washington     Co. G, 21st TN Cav. (Carter's)
     Born 1814 in TN. Farm laborer at Chattanooga with wife Celia.

BURKHART (BURKHALTER), William Carroll Co. L, 35th TN
     Born HC, 1840, son of George W. and Celia Burkhart. Enl. Jan. 9, 1862 in Co. L, 36th TN at Chattanooga; transferred to Co. L, 35th TN; in battle of Murfreesboro, Chickamauga; paroled May 1, 1865 at Greensboro, NC. He had fair complexion, dark hair, blue eyes, and was 5'8" tall. Married Louisa Jane. 1906, prosperous farmer near Hixson. Died June 1, 1922 and buried in Hixson Cem. [1880 HC Census] [TP7783; CT6.2.1922]

BURKHEART [BURKHEAD], William  Co. A, 19th TN

He was killed at Murfreesboro on Dec. 31, 1862. [CSR]

BURKS, William P.     23AL

Born near Atlanta in 1834, he moved as a boy to Pike Co., AL. During the Civil War he served as a private in the 23rd Alabama Infantry, fighting at Chickamauga and Missionary Ridge. Following the war, he located at Montgomery, AL, then moved to Chattanooga where he became manager of the Mutual Loan and Insurance Company. Although a much younger man, Burks became a friend of Jefferson Davis and was an honorary pallbearer at the latter's funeral. He died Feb. 25, 1905 in Chattanooga and was buried in Montgomery, Alabama. His wife's maiden name was Ledbetter. [CT, Feb. 26, 1905.]

BURNS, Allen Crockett   45th VA

He was involved in banking in Chattanooga prior to the war and enl. in 45VA, becoming adjutant. He was taken prisoner at Cloyd's Mountain near Dublin, VA, in 1864, and spent the last months of the war in the prison at Camp Chase, OH.

He was born in Wythe Co., VA, in 1840, son of James and Eleanor Burns. He was cashier of the Discount and Deposit Bank after it was organized in 1867. Allen married Ellen N. Bell, daughter of David Newton Bell, in 1869 and the young couple lived on McCallie Ave. He served as a Chattanooga alderman and died here Dec. 24, 1880. [CT, July 1, 1903]

BURNS, George Henderson     Co. K, 43[th] TN

Born May 28, 1832 in Monroe Co. Enl. July 31, 1863 at Ooltewah. Married (1860 in Bradley Co.) Nancy Lewis of HC. Died at Riceville, TN. [TWP4147]

BURROUGHS, H. G.     Co. L, 35th TN

Enl. Jan. 9, 1862 at Chattanooga; killed at Chickamauga, Sept. 19, 1863.

BURROUGHS [BURROW], Nicholas Phillip
Co. B, 17th TN

Born 3 Feb 1841 in Bedford Co., TN. He took part "in all the battles around Chattanooga. Prior to his death on July 11, 1900, he resided in South Chattanooga for 20 years and was in the grocery business. He married Edmonia Pond on 19 Sept. 1878 at Tullahoma, TN. She was born in 1860 and died in 1886. Died July 11, 1900 and buried Forest Hills Cemetery. [CT July 12, 1900; Lusk, FH]

BURROUGHS, William H.     Co. L, 35th TN

Enl. July 4, 1862 at Dalton; deserted at Salisbury, NC, March 15, 1865, took USA oath and sent to Chattanooga; with fair complexion, dark hair, blue

eyes, and was 6'2" tall.

BURT, Mason

Born 1839, MS. Res. 1910 on Ford St. with wife Mary and 7 children. African-American Baptist preacher. [1910HC]

BURT, Nash H.     Co. G, 1st TN (Turney's)

Born in NC c1832 and probably raised in Franklin Co., TN. He became a lawyer in Shelbyville, TN, then moved his practice to Columbia where he also became one of the incorporators of the Columbia Gas Co. in 1860. He served as acting counsel at St. Thomas in the West Indies. During the Civil War he enl. initially in 1TN, then served as private secretary to Gov. Isham G. Harris with the rank of Lt. Col. Coming to Chattanooga in 1866, he became a law partner of former Union officer G. A. Wood. Burt would reside in Chattanooga until 1901 and become known as a "hero in the yellow fever epidemic of 1878." He died in Birmingham, July 31, 1903. [1860 Maury Co., TN census, p. 81; CT Aug. 1, 1903]

BURTON, Robert     Co. L, 36th TN

Enl. Jan. 9, 1862 at Chattanooga.

BUSTER, Marshall   Co. H, 37th TN

Born 1844 in TN, son of Matilda. Farm laborer at Ooltewah in 1860. [1860 HC census]

BUTLER, Cpl. Asher

Enl. Sept. 1, 1861. in Co. D, 37th TN; teamster; deserted Sept. 15, 1863 at LaFayette, GA; wounded May 25, 1864; took USA oath July 8, 1864; and was 5'9" tall, with dark complexion; dark hair; and blue eyes.

BUTLER, J. W.     Co. F, 12th MS Cav.

Born in Lawrenceville, GA in 1844, he fought in the Confederate army as a young man then farmed after the war before moving to Chattanooga and becoming a merchant. Charter member of NBF Camp, 1885 and in 1888 he became associated with the Chattanooga Plow Co. He married Carolyn Thompkins. Butler died in Leesburg, FL April 16, 1918 and was buried in Forest Hills Cemetery.     [CTApril, 18, 1918; FHR]

BUTLER, John E.

Born 1846, VA. Res. 1910 on Park Dr. with wife Maloda. House carpenter. [1910HC]

BUTLER, Thomas F.     Co A GA Inf. Volunteers, transferred to Co. C, 1st GA; Chatham's Artillery and then to Medical Purseyers Department

Born VA. Trans. to Claghorn's Co., Chatham

Seige Arty, March 4, 1862; to medical dept., July 1, 1864. Appt. hospital steward, July 4, 1863. Became head of the general office of the Southern Express Co. when it moved its headquarters to Chattanooga. He married a woman named Nannie M. who was born 1 Jan 1841. Died April 9, 1908 at his home in St. Elmo. [CTApril 10, 1908; UDC1:63]

BUTLER, Troup   Co. E, 17th GA
Born in Statesboro, GA. 1st Lt., Aug. 8, 1861; Resigned April, 2, 1863 and ordered to report to Commandant of Camp of Instruction, Calhoun, GA, Sept. 25, 1862. Appt. Captain and AQM. Served at Macon and later assigned duty with 1st GA Cav, Reserves, Feb. 18, 1865. Brother-in-law of Garnet Andrews. Died Oct. 25, 1909 in Chattanooga and buried in Washington, GA. [CT Oct. 26, 1909]

BYNINGTON, Charles W.   Barry's Btry.
Enl. July 26, 1864 at Atlanta; paroled May 11, 1865 in Meridian, MS.

BYRNES (BURNS), Joseph   Co. L, 36th TN; Co. L, 35TN
Enl. Jan. 9, 1862, Chattanooga; transf. to 35th TN. On detached duty at Dalton, Nov.-Dec., 1862 rolls.

BYRUM, F. A.
Born upper East TN. Baptist and ordained minister, serving churches in KY and TN. Died at res. on Holly St. Feb. 26, 1920 and buried CSA Cem. [CT Feb. 27, 1920]

BYRUM (BYRAM), S. Alexander   Co. G, 43th TN
Born c1843. Enl. Nov. 20, 1861. Disch. March 6, 1862.[TP 13,481]

# C

CAIN, I Lt. James M.   Co. D, 37TN; Co. F, 2TN Cav. (Ashby's); 4th GA Cav.
Born 1831 in GA. 1860 barkeeper res. house hold of G.W. Sivley in Chattanooga; became officer but resigned when company strength dropped so low and enl. in Avery's Cav. joining his brother.

CAIN, Peter   Co. F, 35TN

Enl. Oct. 1, 1862 at Chattanooga; sick in hospital, Aug., 1863. Deserted from hospital, Sept. 7, 1863. Paroled at Greensboro, NC, May 1, 1865.

CALDWELL, Cpl. Isaac Anderson   Co. E, 1TN (Turney's)
Wife was Mary Carolina. [TWP801]

CALDWELL, James   Co. I, 19TN.
Mortally wounded at Murfreesboro, Jan. 1, 1863; died in Chattanooga, May 11, 1863, and buried CSA Cem.

CALDWELL, James A.   3TN; Co. E, 59TN
Born Sept. 1, 1842 in Catoosa Co. (then Walker), GA, son of O. H. P. and Jane Johnston Caldwell, he became a student at Stewart College, Clarksville, TN, but abandoned his studies to enlist in Vaughn's 3TN. After service in VA, he became ill and re-enl. in Co. E, 59TN. He fought at Perryville and Champion's Hill. Captured at Vicksburg, he was exchanged in time to participate in Longstreet's Knoxville campaign. In 1864 he fought under Early in the Shenadoah, at Martinsburg, Winchester and Fisher's Hill. Making his way to TX, he was captured and paroled at Macon, GA. He entered the U of VA where he studied law. He located in Chattanooga in 1867 and practiced until 1870 when he became clerk and master of chancery. He married (1873) Elizabeth Stephenson Gillespie. For over 30 years he served as president of the Chattanooga Gas Light Company. Presbyterian. NBF Camp. Died June 20, 1920 at res. at corner of McCallie and Lindsay and buried Forest Hills Cemetery. [FHR; GHT, pp. 920-21; CT June 21, 1920]

CALDWELL, Leonidas M.   Co. F, 35TN
Born April 19, 1830, Monroe County, TN and was a farmer in HC before the war with wife Mary and two children born in GA. Enl. Sept. 20, 1862 at Chattanooga. He had dark eyes, dark hair, dark complexion, and was 6 feet tall. Died Jan. 11, 1911 and buried in Forest Hills Cemetery.

CALDWELL, Monroe M.   Co. C, 23TN
Born May 17, 1836; Died Oct. 31, 1906 and buried Forest Hills Cemetery.

CALVERT, James J.   Co. C, 39AL
Born 1829. Res. Chattanooga, 1890 [1890Vet Census]

CAMBY (CARNBY), D. C.
Born 1844. Farmer on Mtn. Creek Pike, 1910 with wife E. F. [1910HC]

CAMP, William E.     Co. K, 43TN; Co. F, 39GA
        Born in Walker Co., GA, he was 16 years old and a farmer when he enl. Oct. 17, 1861 at Ooltewah; discharged Nov. 5, 1862 for being under age; gray eyes, fair complexion, black hair. Enl. as pvt. in 39GA, Sept. 26, 1863. Wounded 1864 and hospitalized Ocmulgee Hospital, Macon, GA where he died Oct. 10, 1864. [Henderson, 301]

CAMPBELL, Cpl. Amos Alexander     Co. B, 20NC
        Born Jan. 9, 1839 in Carbarrus Co., NC, he was a 24-year-old farmer when he enl. April 18, 1861. Promoted to musician and transferred to the regimental band in Sept., 1861. Served through Dec., 1864 with the Army of Northern Virginia. Married Mary C. Died in Chattanooga March 17, 1909 and buried in CSA Cem. [CT March 19, 1909; Oct. 24, 1910; TP 6952, 10,803]

CAMPBELL, David               Barry's Btry.
        Enl. Sept. 16, 1862 at Chattanooga; hospitalized in Newton, MS, Sept., 1863; deserted Dec. 21, 1863; Brown's Diary: "got furlough at hospital and got caught by Yankees. He was 5'8" tall, fair complex., light hair, blue eyes.

CAMPBELL, Henry C. (E.)    Barry's Btry.
        Enl. May. 15, 1862 at Chattanooga; $50 bounty; Nov., 1863 was hospital nurse; hosptialized in Atlanta, July 4, 1864; Captured April 8, 1865 at Spanish Fort; imprisoned at Ship Island, MS. Res. Dallas (HC), 1870.

CAMPBELL, J. M.   Co. L, 36TN
        Enl. Jan. 9, 1862 at Chattanooga.

CAMPBELL, Jesse        2NC
        Born Eagle, NC in 1824 and resided there most of his life. He came to Chattanooga in 1906 and died here Jan. 3, 1911. Buried in CSA Cem. [CT Jan. 24, 1911]

CAMPBELL, Capt. John P.      36TN
        Assistant Commissary of Subsistence, June 3, 1862.

CAMPBELL, William C.  Co. K, 43TN
 Enl. Oct. 17, 1861 at Ooltewah; transferred May 1, 1862 to Snow's Company.

CANNON, Sgt. B. J.  Co. L, 36TN; Co. L, 35TN
        1860 farm laborer in household of Wm. Caruthers, Ooltewah. Enl. Jan. 9, 1862 in 36TN at Chattanooga; transferred to 35TN; elected 3rd Sgt.; fought in the Battle of Murfreesboro, then deserted at Tunnel Hill Feb. 20, 1864. Evidently returned to the Confederate army, for he was paroled in Augusta, GA,

May 18, 1865.

CANNON, George W. C.     Co. A, 19TN
        Born 1829, TN Farmer at Ooltewah with wife Martha and three sons. Enl. Aug. 4, 1863, Chattanooga In hospital at Charleston, TN, Dec., 1863. Captured Calhoun, GA, May 16, 1864 and sent to Louisville, then Alton, IL. Volunteered for US Navy but rejected.

CANNON, Robert M.     Co. F, 5TN Cav.
        Born 1842, TN, he lived with his mother, Hester Cannon, and his two younger brothers and sisters. His mother was a domestic worker, and he was a day laborer. The family had lived in GA prior to moving to HC.    Ik died at home in Chickamauga, TN, on Oct. 5, 1862.

CANTRELL, Jesse Cleveland     Co. F, 4GA
        Born Oct. 30, 1835 in Calhoun, GA. Enl. April 28, 1861 at Calhoun, GA. Army of Northern Virginia: Seven Days, Chancellorsville, Sharpsburg, Spottsylvania, Wilderness, Gettysburg, Winchester, and commanded sharpshooters at Petersburg. Wounded Shepardstown. Paroled at Appomattox. Married Jennie Crow (1867) and moved to Chattanooga. Engineer. Baptist. NBF Camp. Died Jan. 30, 1930 in Chattanooga; buried Forest Hills Cemetery. [NBFM2; TP 13,504; 1880 HC Census; CT Jan. 31, 1930; UDC1]

CANTRELL, L. A.     Co. I, 6SC; 5SC Cav.
        Born March 24, 1842, Spartanburg Dist., SC. Wounded Seven Pines,
        May 31, 1862. Imprisoned Elmira, NY and remained until after war. To Chattanooga, 1868 and became Supt. coking operations, Milne Chair Factory, Chattanooga. Applied to TN Soldiers Home from HC, 1920. Died after Aug., 1920. [SAACH]

CANTRELL, Samuel B.     Barry's Btry.
        Enl. May 1, 1862 at Chattanooga; received $50 bounty but deserted same month.

CAPE, William    Co. D, 37TN
        Born c1842 in TN. Day laborer living in house hold of Crissa Baldwin in Chattanooga, 1860. Enl. Sept. 1, 1861 at Knoxville. Died May 17, 1862, at Corinth, MS. [1860 HC census]

CAPEHART, Sgt. William E.     Co. I, 19TN
        Born c1843 in GA, son of Joseph (hotelkeeper, born NC) and Elizabeth Capehart (born SC). WEC was railroad laborer in 1860.

CARD, William H.     Co. A, 19TN
        Enl. May 20, 1861, Knoxville. Deserted.

CARDEN, ALEXANDER    2nd Co. K, 1st CSA Cav.
Born NY, 1840. Enl. Aug. 1, 1862 in HC. Deserted Aug. 25, 1863. 1910 res. Sale Creek with wife Lucy A. and 8 children. Farmer. [1910HC]

CARDEN, William Crawford    Co. A, Bn. of
GA State Cadets
Born Feb. 13, 1846 in Bradley Co., son of Leonard and Talitha Hale Carden. At GA Mil. Inst. when war broke out. Enl. at Marietta, May 15, 1864 and fought throughout Atlanta Campaign. Returned to school after war and licensed to preach Nov. 6, 1869. Married (1875) Mattie Stewart. Became a Methodist minister. Secty. of Holston Conf. many years. Commander of NBF Camp and res. Alton Park when he died May 19, 1924 and buried Forest Hills Cemetery. [NBFM2; TWP, 231; TP 15,164; CT May 20, 1924; UDC2pg 92]

CARLOCK, 3 Lt. George Washington    Co. H, 26TN;
2d Co. I, 1CSA (GA)
Born 1835. Enl. July 8, 1861, Knoxville. Resigned as 3Lt., Nov. 6, 1861, but on rolls of 1CSA May 1, 1864.

CARLOCK, J. M.    2nd Co. I, 26TN; 2d Co. I, 1th CSA (GA)
Enl. Aug. 10, 1862 in Chattanooga. Transf. by order of Gen. Hardee, May 1, 1863. Absent without leave after Aug. 23, 1863.

CARLOCK (CORLOCK), James S.    Co. H, 26TN
Enl. July 8, 1861, Knoxville; captured at Fort Donelson, Feb. 16, 1862; imprisoned at Camp Douglas where he died March 16, 1862.

CARLOCK, W. H.    Co. H, 26TN
Enl. Aug. 6, 1861 at Knoxville; sick, honorably discharged Oct. 13, 1862.

CARMACK, Isaac    Co. A, 19TN
Enl. at Knoxville on May 20, 1861. He served at Cumberland Gap, then went on furlough. He was killed in the battle at Fishing Creek on Jan. 19, 1862. [CSR]

CARMACK, J. L.    Co. L, 35TN
Enl. Jan. 9, 1862; wounded in thigh at Murfreesboro, Dec. 31, 1862 and was unable to return to duty.

CARNES, Eli    Co. I, 19TN
Born c1806 in SC. Farm laborer at Chattanooga with wife Clarisa (born SC). Enl. May 20, 1861, Knoxville. Disch. medical disability. [1860HC]

CARNES, Richard J.    Co. B, 5TN Cav. Bn.
Born Ala., c1840, apparently son of Eli and Clarissa Carnes, he was a farm laborer living with his wife, Caroline, at the start of the war. She was from GA. He was discharged on July 31, 1862, and took the oath of allegiance on March 24, 1864. He had dark complexion, brown hair, gray eyes, and stood 5'11" tall.

CARNEY, Alfred    Co. F, 19TN
Born 1829 in Cocke Co. In 1893 res. in Soddy where he hauled wood and was a preacher. [TP1356]

CARNEY, 2Lt. Thomas    Co. A, 19TN
Born March 5, 1835 in Spartanburg Dist., SC., he fought in the Mexican War before coming to Chattanooga in 1852. He was engine driver in Chattanooga's first Fire Department. Enl. April 23, 1861 in Co. A. became 2Lt. and fought at Shiloh, Corinth, and was wounded at Jonesboro. He was captured, but escaped at Nashville, and surrendered in NC. He returned to Chattanooga and rejoined the Fire Dept. Drayman, 1870. Member NBF Camp, 1895-96. He died at his res. on Cedar St. Oct. 2, 1906 and was buried in CSA Cem. [CT Oct. 3-4, 1906; NBFM2]

CARPENTER, James    Co. H, 4th TN Cav.
Killed Jan. 1, 1863, in Battle of Murfreesboro. He was about 25. A native of NC, he was living prior to the war on a farm at Sale Creek with his mother, Jane Carpenter, and younger brothers Samuel and David.

CARPER, Joseph H.    2nd Co. K, 1CSA Cav.
Son of William Foster and Elizabeth Spicer Carper of Silverdale section of Tyner. Enl. Sept. 24, 1862 in HC. Deserted Sept. 12, 1863. Married Sallie and was living in HC in 1880. Lawyer. [JW Carper Fam.]

CARR (see DARR)

CARRIER, 1 Lt. William B.    Co. K, 26TN
Born 1836, TN. Res. Anderson Pike, 1910 with wife Mary E. [1910HC]

CARROLL, Abner C.    Co. F, 35TN
Before the war, he was a prosperous farmer living across the river from Chattanooga. His worth in 1860 is given as $11,000. He had married (1852) Mary Williams, a daughter of Samuel Williams. Age 36 in 1862, Carroll was born in Washington Co., TN. Enl. as a substitute for Frederick Hanshield in Co. F of the 35TN. He had blue eyes, auburn hair, a fair complexion and stood 5'8" tall. Died Dec. 10, 1872. [CT April 19, 1908]

CARRUTH, Leroy    Co. A, 19TN

Enl. May 20, 1861 and assigned as gunsmith. Captured near Chattahoochie, July 4, 1864 and imp. Camp Morton, IN. Took USA oath, Nov. 17, 1864.

CARSON, James W.    Co. H, 26TN; 2d Co. I, 1CSA (GA)
Enl. July 8, 1861; left with wagon master Feb. 19, 1862, Clarksville; enl. June 8, 1862 in Barry's Btry. at Chattanooga and on rolls of Lookout Btry., Dec. 31, 1862. Paroled May 11, 1865 at Meridian, MS.

CARSON, John M.    Co. I, 31TN
Born Nov. 13, 1842 in Jefferson Co., TN. Enl. March, 1862. Wounded and Captured at Vicksburg July 4, 1863 and paroled July 15, 1863. Became real estate dealer in Chattanooga but moved to Atlanta and died there after 1890. [1890VetCensus; NBFM 7]

CARTER, James    Co. D, 4(12)GA Cav.
He enl. Oct. 4, 1862. He was reported absent and was believed to be in the hands of the enemy.

CARTER, William    Co. D, 4(12)GA Cav.
He enl. Aug. 1, 1863, at Chattanooga in Capt. William J. Rogers' company. In March of 1864, he was in the Ocmulgee Hospital at Macon, GA. He was captured in April of 1865 and took the oath of allegiance. He had a dark complexion, gray hair, hazel eyes, and was 5'11" tall.

CARUTHERS, Andrew Jackson    2nd Co. D, 1CSA (GA)
Enl. May 1, 1862 in Ringgold, GA. Sick during fall, 1862. Promoted to Cpl., then Sgt. in 1864. Captured at Nashville and imprisoned at Camp Douglas until end of war. Married Mary Elizabeth Oct. 4, 1869. Died Dec. 4, 1914.

CARRUTHERS, Benjamin Newton    2nd Co. K, 1CSA Cav.
Born Feb. 8, 1834, probably son of William and Rachel Moore Carruthers. Farmer at Ooltewah with wife Elizabeth, daughter of Wm. Snow. Enl. in HC, July 19, 1862. Although rolls state he deserted Feb. 14, 1863, he was imprisoned and his health long affected by his confinement. Farming in Ooltewah, 1870. He and family moved to Wise Co., TX where he died Jan. 10, 1890 and was buried at Paradise, TX. [Dickey, Waller, A Family History]

CARUTHERS, Lt. Christopher C.    2nd Co. D, 1CSA(GA)
Enl. May 1, 1862 in Ringgold, GA. Promoted to 2Lt. Nov. 18, 1862, 1Lt, Sept. 2, 1863. Hospitalized in Jan., 1865.

CARRUTHERS(CARETHERS, CAROTHERS), John H.    2nd Co. K, 1CSA Cav.
Enl. in HC, July 14, 1862. Captured Jan 6, 1864 at Charleston, TN and imp. at Rock Island, IL where he died Feb. 21, 1864 of rubeola and was buried. [CSR; RI ledger]

CARRUTHERS (CARUTHERS), Sgt. S. D.    nd Co. K, 1CSA Cav.
Enl. in HC, July 14, 1862. Deserted Feb. 5, 1863 at Shelbyville, TN.

CARSON, 2Lt. James M.    Co. I, 31TN
Enl. March, 1862 in Chattanooga Captured Vicksbug. Real estate dealer in Chattanooga in 1890. Moved to Atlanta and died there. [NBFM1,7]

CARSON, James W.
Enl. July 8, 1861 in Co. H, 26TN; also served in 2nd Co. I, 1GA CSA; enl. June 8, 1862 in Barry's Btry. at Chattanooga; paroled May 11, 1865 at Meridian, MS.

CARSON, W. A.    Barry's Btry.
Enl. May 1, 1862 at Dalton; died June 19, 1863 in hospital in Greenville, AL.

CASEY, A. S.    Co. K, 59TN Mtd. Inf.
Born 1837; married Julia. Presbyterian. Died July 18, 1924 and buried Forest Hills Cemetery. [CT July 19, 1924]

CASEY, Henry    Co. H, 1TN Cav. (Carter's); Co. G, Walker's Bn., Thomas' NC Legion
Born 1837 in Clark Co., TN. 1860 farmer at Chattanooga with wife Sarah and two children. [1860HC]

CASH, James A.
Sgt. Maj., NBF Camp, 1912.

CASSON, S. E.    34VA Cav. Bn.
[TP 12,873]

CASTEEL, Benjamin F.    Co. H, 43TN
Born c1843, son of Daniel and Abigail of Chattanooga. Enl. Nov. 16, 1861, Riceville, TN. Prom. 1Cpl. May 10, 1862. Died July 15, 1863, Vicksburg.

CASTEEL, Daniel    Co. H, 43TN
Born c1822, he was railroad brakeman living in Chattanooga with wife Abigail prior to enl. Feb. 12, 1862, Knoxville. Prom. to Sgt., April 9, 1862. Captured Vicksburg, July 4, 1863 and paroled. Among sick and wounded parolees sent by boat to Mobile via New Orleans.

CATE, Alfred M.　Co. D, 43TN
　　　　Born 1830, farmer in Ooltewah. Wife was E.J. [1860 HC Census]

CATE, Greenbury
　　　　Born Oct. 31, 1831 in Sevier Co., TN. Enrolling officer in Bradley Co., 1862-63. "Home was burned and a lot of his personal property destroyed." Res. Chattanooga, 1911. [TP12,365]

CATE, Capt. Henry Glaze　Co C 36 TN Inf.
　　　　Born 22 Dec 1836 in McMinn Co., TN. Served as Asst. Quartermaster. 1870, McMinn Co., age 36. He died April 1907 in Calhoun, TN and was married to Tennie Miller. [TWP2630; UDC2 pg 100]

CATE (CATES), John　Co. L, 35TN
　　　　Enl. Feb. 23, 1862 at Chattanooga.

CATE, Capt. William L.　Co. C, 36TN; Co. C, 35TN
　　　　Born 1830. Farm laborer near Ooltewah, 1860. Married Malissa. [1860 HC Census]

CATES, Felix Grundy　Co. L, 36TN
　　　　Enl. Jan. 9, 1862 at Chattanooga. 1870, Gibson Co., TN.

CATES, R. L.　Barry's Btry.
　　　　Deserted [Brown's Diary]. Died Camp Morton, IN Prison, July 17, 1864. Buried Greenlawn Cem., Camp Morton. [CV (Jan., 1914)]

CATHEY, Samuel C.　Freeman's Btry.
　　　　Born March 26, 1846 in Cannon Co., TN. Enl. Resaca, GA, May, 1863 in 6TN Arty. (Freeman's Btry.), Dibbrell's Brig. Captured near Columbia, TN, Aug., 1864 and paroled Apr., 1865. Shoemaker in Chattanooga about 20 years. NBF Camp. Died Sept. 18, 1906 at his res. on Louisa St. and buried CSA Cem. [CT Sept. 19, 1906; NBFM2]

CATRON, Lt. George A. (Alfred G.?)　Co. K, 1VA
　　　　Born near Wytheville, VA, Sept. 1, 1826, and enl. in 1VA. Discharged from service Dec. 23, 1863 to serve as civil officer of CSA. He moved to Chattanooga in 1872 and became real estate salesman. Married Evaline P. Ewing, Oct. 8, 1845 in VA. Died in Chattanooga March 11, 1901 and buried in Citizens Cem. PHOTO in CT. [CT, March 12, 1901; NBFM2]

CAVENDER, Benjamin Franklin　Co. B, 1TN Cav. (Carter's)
　　　　Born 1839 in TN, son of Henry Cavender. Farmer in Ooltewah. [1860 HC Census]

CAVENDER, G. A.　Co. M, 1TN Cav. (Carter's)

CHAMBERS, Andrew J.　Co. G, 26TN; 2d Co. K, 1CSA (GA)
　　　　Enl. July 8, 1861., Knoxville. Dark complexion, black hair, hazel eyes, and 6' tall; Captured Fort Donelson, Feb. 16, 1862. Pvt. 1CSA, Dec. 26, 1863, Dalton. Took USA oath, Jan. 10, 1864 at Nashville.

CHAMBERS, A. L.　Barry's Btry.
　　　　Lost in Feb. on retreat. [Brown's Diary]

CHAMBERS, Henry Alexander　Co. C, 4NC; Co. C, 49NC
　　　　Born Iredell Co., NC, May 17, 1841, son of Joseph and Ellen Cashion Chambers. Student at Davidson College at outbreak of war. Enl. at Statesville, NC June 7, 1861. Promoted Capt. Dec. 3, 1862. Became senior Capt. and sometimes cmdg. regt. Fought at Fredericksburg, New Bern, Drewry's Bluff, Bermuda Hundred, the Crater, and siege of Petersburg. Was in command of regt. at Five Forks when he was wounded and hauled in ambulance to Appomattox where he surrendered with remnant of the army. Taught school and read law at Morgantown, NC, 1865-66. Married in 1867 to Laura Lenoir. Made his home successively at Madisonville, Loudon and Chattanooga Represented Monroe Co. in TN legislature, 1870-72 and then state senator from that district in 1877. Presbyterian. Mason. Married (2) in 1877, Lizzie Welcker Turner. Lawyer in Chattanooga, US postage agent, 1877, and in 1878 assigned to New Orleans as agent over TX, LA, and southern MS. To Chattanooga, 1888, and on City Council four terms. Historian of NBF Camp. Lived at 511 Poplar St.; died here Nov. 18, 1925 and buried Forest Hills Cemetery. [NBFM2,10; Biog. BDTA; Diary (1863) at Chattanooga Bi-Cent. Lib.; CT Nov. 19, 1925; UDC1]

CHAMBLISS, John Alexander　Chaplain, SC Troops
　　　　Born 1840. Married Mary Mauldin, Greenville, SC. Noted Baptist preacher. Professor of Classics at Maryland College. Died 1916 and buried Forest Hills Cemetery.

CHAMLEE, T. A.　Co. F, 39TN Mounted Inf. (Lillard's)
　　　　Res. 1912 James Co. [TP13,712]

CHAMPION, Lt. Charles B.　Co. H, 36TN
　　　　Born 1831 in Franklin Co., TN, son of William and Adoline Champion of Ooltewah. He had a farm at Harrison prior to the war. Enl. Aug. 7, 1861 in Cleveland and served, Feb. 1-May 13, 1862. Elected sheriff of HC, 1874-78. His wife was Jane E. Smith. Died June 1, 1908

on his Harrison Road farm and was buried at family burial ground. The body was later moved to Bartlebaugh Baptist Church. [JW, Champion family; CN, June 1, 1908; CT June 2, 1908; 1860HC]

CHAMPION, William Coke       Co. B, 1TN Cav. (Carter's)
Born 1837, son of William and Adoline Champion, brother of Charles B. At the start of the war, he was living at Ooltewah with T.W. Spicer, justice of the peace. Enl. Aug. 7, 1861 at Cleveland. He was assigned to guard commissary stores. He served at Cumberland Gap and in the Battle of Murfreesboro before deserting Dec. 14, 1864, in Washington Co., TN, and taking the oath of allegiance. He was released at Knoxville. Married (1865) Matilda B. He died HC, 1884. [TWP, p. 109; JW, Champion family; 1860HC]

CHAMPION, W. E.
From Harrison, TN. Asst. Surgeon, CSAS. [Proceedings of Medical Board of the Provisional A of TN, p. 123]

CHAPMAN, Henry Z.       Co. F, 20SC
Born 1829. Married Emeline Hoadley. Died 1911 and buried Forest Hills Cemetery.

CHEEK, James Marion  Co. H, 2TN Cav. (Smith's)
Born c1841. Methodist. Died at res. on Clio St. and buried Oak Hill. [CT Jan. 7, 1929]

CHEEK, Thomas H.
Born Oct. 30, 1836 in Rappahannock Co., VA, son of Elijah and Mary Holtzman Cheek. He went to Memphis about 1850, where he became engineer, captain and owner of several steamboats and married (1859) Mary M. Reid (Reed) and Lizzie Gillespie. He enl. as a cavalryman under Forrest, then was at once transferred to the ordnance department at Columbus, MS, then Selma, AL. He established four saw-mills to manufacture lumber for the AL and TN RR. Subsequently he operated the grist mill at Marietta, GA, then moved it to Macon. Following the war, Cheek engaged in operating the Kennesaw Mills in Marietta until 1887 when he moved to Chattanooga where he owned and operated grain warehouses and elevators, and was a member of 1st Presbyterian Church. NBF Camp. He died at res. on McCallie Ave. March 28, 1906 and was buried in Marietta. [CT March 29, 1906; GHT, p. 923]

CHENEY, Robert Dee
Born June 20, 1840 in Murfreesboro, TN, he moved to AR and joined CSA, serving as member of P. R. Cleburne's staff. Wounded at Shiloh, Richmond, Murfreesboro and Franklin. Married (1865) Martha Florence Sharp. Died Nov. 19, 1917 in Chattanooga and buried Forest Hills Cemetery. [CT Nov. 20, 1917; TWP, 302]

CHESHIRE, Calaway (Calvin)       Co. D, 37TN
Born c1848 in TN, son of Eliza. Enl. March 18, 1863 in Catoosa Co. Entitled to bounty being under 18 yrs. Deserted at Missionary Ridge Dec. 10, 1863. Captured Graysville, Nov. 27, 1863 and imp. Rock Island. Joined US Navy, Jan. 25, 1864. [1860HC]

CHESHIRE, James T.       Co. D, 37TN
Born 1832 in SC. Day laborer at Chattanooga Married Margaret. Enl. Sept. 1, 1861 at Knoxville. Disch. July 1, 1862 for disability.

CHILDERS, James C.   Co. A, 5th TN Cav. (McKenzie's)
Born c1831. Enl. Jan. 14, 1861, at Knoxville. Home sick March, 1863. Paroled as POW July 29, 1863 at McMinnville. Age 35 on March 11, 1864 roll. Deserted March 11, 1864 at Tunnel Hill. Farming Ooltewah, 1870, with wife Rebecca. [1860, 1870HC]

CHILDERS, John       Co. L, 36TN; Co. L, 35TN
Enl. Jan. 9, 1862 at Chattanooga; transferred to Co. L, 35TN; fought in battle of Murfreesboro.

CHILDRESS, David M.,   Co. A, 19TN
Enl. May, 1861 and fought in the battles at Fishing Creek and Shiloh, then was killed at Murfreesboro on Dec. 31, 1862. His father, David Childress, was paid $37.54 on a war claim that his son was owed. [CSR; Warner, Personal Glimpses]

CHRISTIAN, John L.       First Co. E, 42TN; Co. F, 55AL
Born March 17, 1845 in Jackson Co., AL. Enl. Oct. 31, 1861 but missed Fort Donelson because detached to bury brother. Never served in battle and remained in occupied part of TN. To TN in 1912; res. in Memphis in 1916, Chattanooga in 1920. [TP 14,889]

CHUMLEY, William T.       3d Co. F, 35TN
Born c1842 in Halifax Co., VA, son of William F. Chumley and Eliza. Day laborer on father's farm near Chattanooga. Family had moved from VA to TN in late 1840s. Enl. Jan. 9, 1862. Wounded Chickamauga. Gray eyes, light hair, fair complexion, and 5'5" tall. [1860 HC]

CHURCH, F. G.   Co. C, 22GA Bn. Heavy Arty.
Born Jan. 1, 1846 in Hardin Co. near Savannah, son of R. S. Church. Joined the army just after Chickamauga. He was in fighting at Calhoun, GA, to Atlanta and then Savannah, where he was left in a

hospital at the time of Sherman's invasion. He was sent to Guyton Hospital and was paroled at Atlanta three days after Johnston's surrender. Moved to Chattanooga in 1920. Married (1899, in Chattanooga) Eva Sanders. Methodist. Died July 18, 1931 at Shepherd, TN and buried CSA Cem. [TP16,175; TWP294; 10,338; CT July 18-19, 1931]

CLAGUE, William C.
Born 1848, TN. 1910 res. in household of nephew Martin Ford in Chattanooga. [1910HC]

CLARK, Sgt. A. A.     Co. C, 64GA
Born March 2, 1845 in Abbevillle Dist., SC. Enl. Sept. 15, 1862. Wounded once. Captured and paroled at Appomattox. [NBFM2]

CLARK, Sgt. Carroll     5th TN Commanded by Col. Ben J. Hill
Born in Warren Co. and married Margaret Johnson. Died in HC. [TWP, p. 91; UDC1 pg 81]

CLARK, Charles Dickens     Co. A, 13TN Cav.
Born on a farm in Van Buren Co., TN, Oct 7, 1847, son of John S. Attending Burritt College when war broke out. Enl. at 16 yrs. On staff of Gen. Dibrell. After the war completed studies at Burritt and studied law at Cumberland Univ. Graduated 1874 at the head of class; to Chattanooga 1882; second federal judge from Chattanooga, 1894. Married: Georgiana Hickman, Lucy Dumas and Willie Kimbrough. Died March 16, 1908 [CT March 16, 1908]

CLARK, George M.     Co. E, 1NC State Troops (6NC)
Born July 28, 1845 in Haywood Co., NC. Enl. at Haynesville April 4, 1861. Wounded at Malvern Hill. Captured near Jonesboro, TN, Nov., 1863. Paroled as captain in April 1865. 1900 res. in Chattanooga, occupation carpenter, living on Whiteside St. Died at res. on Elizabeth St., March 11, 1905 and buried in CSA Cem. [NBFM3, 7]

CLARK, Capt. J. W.     Co. L, 36TN; Clark's Indep. Cav. Co.
Enl. as private, Jan. 9, 1862 at Chattanooga. Commanded independent cavalry company that acted principally as escort and couriers for Gen. S.B. Buckner and occasionally for Gens. W.J. Hardee and Bushrod Johnson. Picket duty in Middle TN in 1863. Clark's Co. was absorbed into Capt. John B. Dortch's 2KY Cav. Bn. in 1864. (Perhaps same as Capt. Jimmie Clark in Josephine Hooke Diary)

CLARK, Riley C.     Co. H, 4TN Cav.; Co. F, 39GA

Pvt., Feb. 14, 1864. Captured Resaca, May 16, 1864 and imp. Camp Morton, IN. Released May 18, 1865. [Henderson, 301]

CLAY, J. M.     Co. D, 42GA
Born Sept. 3, 1845 in DeKalb Co., GA. Enl. Sept. 7, 1862. Afterwards served in Stovall's Brigade. Paroled April, 1865. Carpenter in Chattanooga in 1891. [NBFM2]

CLEAGE, Thomas A., Sr.
Born Athens, TN Aug. 24, 1835. Banker in Athens prior to war: Planters Bank and T.A. Cleage & Co. Cashier of State Bank of TN. Married Penelope Van Dyke ( Sept. 15, 1856). During the war his wife was arrested by order of Gen. Sherman at her home in Athens for feeding Confederate soldiers. She and her children were sent through the line near Bristol. Presbyterian. When CSA forces evacuated East TN, he carried bank's funds to Augusta, GA where he remained throughout war. Returned unused funds to State of TN. Moved to Quincy, IL and entered milling business, returned to Athens and became successful contractor, building McMinn Co. courthouse. Res. Chattanooga a number of years, but returned to Athens 1898. Died Dec. 11, 1900 in St. Elmo of cancer and buried Forest Hills Cemetery. Thomas was the grandfather of historian Penelope Johnson Allen. [CT Dec. 12, 1900; UDC1 pg 84]

CLEM, Samuel     Barry's Btry.
Enl. Jan. 27, 1863 in Chattanooga. Transferred March 15, 1863 to Winston's Btry.

CLIFT, Capt. James Warren     Co. H, 36TN
Born 1838 in Soddy, he was one of the two sons of William and Nancy A. Clift of Soddy who fought for the Confederacy. Two other sons, Joseph Clift and Robert Brooks Clift, joined their father in going with the Union. J.W. Clift at age 17 volunteered for Mexican War service and because of his fluency in Spanish served as an interpreter. At the outbreak of the Civil War he raised Co. H and was elected Capt. Later he would serve on the regimental staff. On Aug. 31, 1862, he enl. in Clark's Independent Cav. Co. at Chattanooga. Married Mary Jane McKenzie. After the war he returned home and farmed, but eventually became involved in management of the Soddy Coal Company and served in the Tennessee legislature. Presbyterian. Married (1) Miss McKenzie (1849), (2) Tipton Bradford (1875). Clift died March 8, 1910 at his home in Soddy. [JW, Clift family; CT 9 March 1910; Armstrong, Ham. Co., 2:293; GHT, pp. 924-25]

CLIFT, Moses Haney     Co. H, 36TN; 4TN Cav. (Starnes)

Born Aug. 25, 1836 in Soddy, his mother was Nancy Arwin Brooks, daughter of Gen. Moses Brooks of Knox County, a Revolutionary soldier. Moses Clift at the age of 22 was reading law in household of John L. Hopkins, in Chattanooga. He had gained his law license just as the war began. Though his father, William Clift, was a rabid Unionist, M.H. Clift raised Co. H of the 36TN, but seven months later he transferred to the 4TN Cav., James W. Starnes-William S. McLemore's Reg. He served with this unit until the battle of Fort Donelson. Afterwards he was promoted to Captain on the staff of Col. Starnes, and he was with him until Starnes was killed at Tullahoma in June, 1863. Then Moses Clift served under Gen. G. G. Dibrell. Clift was promoted to Major at the battle of Kennesaw Mountain and to Colonel at the Battle of Bentonville, N.C., in the closing months of the war. Clift was wounded three times and fought in 23 battles, including Chickamauga. After that battle, he spent several hours in his home territory inside the Federal lines gaining valuable information. Before the fighting at Tunnel Hill, he again was within the Federal lines for three weeks, including two days at home at Soddy with his father. "Bears the distinction of having captured his own father." Although great admirer of Forrest, believed that his commander Wheeler "efficient," "the finest scout and obtainer of information."

Clift was a prominent attorney at Chattanooga after the war, and he also had considerable business and real estate interests. He was one of the commissioners for Chickamauga Park. He first married (1867) Ataline Cooke, and later married (1883) Florence V. Parrott of Cartersville, Ga. One of his descendants was Montgomery Clift, the famed actor. Moses Clift died Dec. 3, 1911 in Nashville and was buried in Citizens Cem. [JW, Clift family; 1860HC; GHT, 925; CT Dec. 4, 1911; Ridley, Battles and Sketches, pp. 159-161; UDC1 pg 85; UDC2 pg 109]

CLIFT, Lt. Col. William Joseph (Joe)    5TN Cav.
    Born Feb. 14, 1838 in Soddy, he was one of the divided Clifts who chose to go with the Confederacy, serving a short while as company commander with the 36TN, then becoming Lt. Col. of the 5TN Cav. He was the son of James Clift, a minister who at one time was the county court clerk for HC. James Clift was a brother of William Clift of Soddy. William Joseph Clift practiced law after the war at McMinnville, then at Chattanooga. He was a leading criminal attorney, and it was said he defended over 200 cases in several states and "cleared over 75 percent of them and never had a man hung." He had the "grand distinction of being a member of the Sons of CV and the GAR. Died March 12, 1901 and was buried in McMinnville. [CT March 13, 1901; JW, Clift family]

CLINE, David  Co. A, 19TN
    Born c1807, PA. Stonemason in Chattanooga with wife Nancy A., also born PA. Their sons David and William B. born in MD, then family moved to Chattanooga. Enl. May 20, 1861, Knoxville. Disch. with medical disability.

CLINE, R.    Clark's Independent Cav. Co.
    Enl. Aug. 31, 1862 at Chattanooga; deserted Nov. 25, 1863 near Chattanooga.

CLINE, William B.  Co. A, 19TN
    Born c1840 in MD, son of David and Nancy Cline of Chattanooga. Enl. May 10, 1862 at Corinth. Assigned to hospital duty. Reported sick and absent, May 1864.

CLINTON, 1 Lt. George W.    Co. C, 1CSA (GA)
    Born Campbell Co., GA, Oct. 6, 1840. Enl. in independent company of CSA cavalry, March 4, 1861. Co. A, 1GA Inf. Worked in Wariton, FL navy yard. In battles of Ft. McRee, Ft. Pickens, Santa Rosa Island and Chickamauga (wounded) and, New Hope Church (wounded). Paroled Greensboro, NC, April, 1865. To TN in 1881. Owned meat market on Whiteside St. for 30 years. Died at res. in Chattanooga Jan. 24, 1907. Buried Citizens Cem. [CT, Jan. 25, 1907; NBFM2; TP 8114]

CLINTON, H.    Barry's Btry.
    Deserted. [Brown's Diary]

CLOUD, F. M.    Co. H, 26TN
    Enl. July 8, 1861, Knoxville. Honorably disch. Dec. 6, 1861.

CLOUD, George W.    Clark's Independent Cav. Co.
    Enl. Aug. 31, 1862 at Chattanooga; re-enl. Feb. 18, 1863, Knoxville by W. P. Wood for war; deserted Sept. 10, 1863; POW March 26, 1864. Took oath at Chattanooga as rebel deserter.

CLOUD, Robert    Co. H, 26TN
    Enl. July 8, 1861, Knoxville. Wounded and Captured Fort Donelson, Feb. 16, 1862. Died at Camp Douglas, July 1, 1862.

CLOUSE, James P.(T.?)    Co. G, 3CSA Cav.
    Born Shellmound, TN. Fought as cavalryman under Wheeler at Chickamauga and Missionary Ridge. Married (1879) Menervy Cary. Died May 26, 1914 at home on East 16th St. and buried at Shellmound. [TWP, p. 156; CT May 27, 1914]

CLOUTS, Capt. M. L.    Co. G, 6GA Cav.
    Res. of James Co., 1905. [TP353]

COATS, Lemuel "Lem"      Co.D, 37TN
Born 1843 in AL, son of Thompson and Caroline of Chattanooga. Enl. Sept. 1, 1861, Knoxville; wounded Chickamauga and hospitalized Macon where he deserted. Captured at Chattanooga and sent to Rock Island where he enl. in the US Navy. [1860HC]

COBB, William J.      Co. A, 19TN
Born Dec. 18, 1839 in Buncombe Co., NC; enl. June 3, 1861 at Knoxville and accompanied the regiment to Cumberland Gap where he became sick. He was with the troops near Shelbyville and then at Corinth, where he again became ill. Cobb transferred April 11, 1864 to Co. B, 65GA. Captured and imprisoned at Camp Chase. Took USA oath March, 1865 "they were starving us and I promised not to come south until after the war." Living in HC, April, 1908. Moulder in foundry. Res. 1910 on Winden St. with wife Martha (married 1870). Member of NBF Camp. Died at home in East Lake, June 4, 1910 and buried CSA Cem. [CSR; TP7961; CT June 6, 1910; NBFM2; 1910HC]

COCHRAN, George W.      Asst. Surgeon, 3CSA Cav. (Col. W. N. Estes)
Born Iredell Co., NC, 1835. Enl. Oct., 1862. Murfreesboro, Fort Donelson, Chickamauga. Captured Sept 21, 1864, Camp Hampton, VA and imp. Johnson's Island, Ohio. Paroled near Hillsboro, NC, May, 1865. [TP12,885]

COCHRAN, James. H.      2d Co. K, 26TN; 2d Co. K, 1CSA(GA)
Enl. July 8, 1861 in Co. G, 26TN at Knoxville; captured at Fort Donelson, Feb. 16, 1862; imprisoned at Camp Morton, IN. Deserted or recaptured at Stevenson, AL, Sept. 23, 1863. Probably same as James Cochrane (Co. H, 26TN) who was captured and died in prison in Indianapolis, IN.

COCKE, Maj. Daniel F.  Asst. Commissary Genl.; 1TN Bn.
Born 1816, Fauquier Co., VA, son of Washington and Sarah Floweree Cocke. To Bledsoe Co., TN, as a young man and made fortune in stock raising and other businesses. Married Augusta Roberson. Moved to Chattanooga Creek about 1855, building mansion "Oakland" on Clifton Hill. Farmer with wife Margaret and 8 children and 44 slaves, 1860. Uncle of Henry M. Ashby who came to live at Oakland. Appt. Asst. Comm. Gen. in Provisional Army of TN, May 9, 1861, then served on staff of Gen. S.B. Anderson, July 9, 1861. To VA where he is said to have served in 1TN Bn. while children placed in school in Richmond. Sold Oakland for $20,000 in 1862 and fled south. After the war resided in Franklin, TN where he died March 14, 1885. Buried Rest Haven Cem., Franklin. [1860HC; CSA Staff Officers, p. 6, J.W. Cocke family]

COCKE, John LaFayette
Born April 18, 1848, son of Daniel F. and Margaret A.R. Cocke. Family moved from Bledsoe Co. to farm along Chattanooga Creek in mid-1850's. Only 14, J.L. Cocke entered army and was on Morgan's Ohio Raid. Escaped capture by swimming the river on his horse. Served remainder of the war. Afterwards, he was businessman in Memphis. Married Adelaide Sledge of MS. Died at Memphis, July 24, 1913.

COFFEE, A. A.      Co. F, 52GA
Born 1841 in Wilkes Co., NC. Enl. March 4, 1862 in Clayton, GA. Retired from service because of disability, 1863. To TN, 1873. Res. Montgomery St. in 1906. [TP6227]

COGBURN, Cpl. John      Co. K, 43TN
He was living on a farm at Zion Hill south of Ooltewah before the war, son of William and Isabella Cogburn. Enl. Oct. 17, 1861.

COGGINS, A. H.
Enl. Jan. 9, 1862 in Co. L, 36TN at Chattanooga, later transf. to Co. L, 35TN.

COGGINS, James A.      Co. L, 35TN
Enl. Sept. 23, 1862, Jasper, TN.

COKER, L. F.    Co. G, 26TN; 2d Co. K, 1CSA (GA)
Born c1833. Enl. July 8, 1861, Knoxville. Captured Fort Donelson. On roll of 1CSA, Aug. 31, 1863. Died Sept. 4, 1925 and buried Rock Spring Cem. [CT, Sept. 5, 1925]

COLEMAN, William Dallas      Co. E, 4TN Cav
Born Cannon Co., TN, Jan. 16, 1845. Enl. Sept. 27, 1862, Munfordsville, Ky. Deserted and took USA oath, April 9, 1864, Chattanooga. "Made a crop for my father in Cannon County, 1865." Then to Rome, GA and returned to TN, 1887. 1910 dry goods, grocer. Res. Sale Creek, 1915. Buried Sale Creek Cem. [SAACH; 1910HC]

COLINS, J. K.      Co. L, 36TN
Enl. Jan. 9, 1862 at Chattanooga.

COLLINS, D.      Clark's Independent Cav. Co.
Enl. Aug. 31, 1862, Chattanooga; captured June 27, 1863 at Manchester, TN. Paroled Cumberland Gap. April, 29, 1865.

COLLINS, D.  Co. B, 1TN Cav. (Carter's)

Captured and paroled at Cumberland Gap, KY., April 29, 1865, remarks mention Grainger Co., TN.

COLLINS, Jesse R.   Co. G, 63TN
    Born c1830. Blacksmith at Long Savannah with wife Susan M., 1860. Enl. April, 21, 1863, Knoxville. Placed in QM Dept. Wounded in left thigh at Drewry's Bluff, May 16, 1864, and sent to Chimborazo Hospital in Richmond, where he died June 26, 1864.

COLLINS, Newton Jasper   Co. L, 35TN
    Born April 29, 1833 in Gwinette Co., GA. Enl. at Calhoun, GA in 1863. Dark complexion, brown hair, hazel eyes, 5'11" tall. In 1870 he was in Wauhatchie as a laborer in tanyard, wife Sarah. Married (1882) Mary Jane. 1900 res. Albion View on Walden's Ridge, HC. Occupation farmer. Died July 21, 1909 in Chattanooga and buried CSA Cem. "UDC conferred Cross of Honor on this soldier." [CT July 22, 1909; TWP, p. 139; NBFM2; 1860 HC census]

COLVILLE, Mary Louise Paine - Rhea Co. Girls Company.
    Born 1842 in Rhea County, TN, married 21 Oct. 1869 to Dr. Richard Waterhouse Colville. She died in Hill City on 25 Nov 1896 and is buried in the Chattanooga Memorial Park. [White Oak Cem.]

COLVILLE, Richard Waterhouse   Co. D, 19TN;
    Co. H, Cons. 3TN
    Born in Warren Co., TN, March 12, 1843, son of Captain Warner E. & Vesta Waterhouse Colville. Student at University of East Tennessee and May, 1861. Enl. as pvt. in Co. D, 19TN. Wounded at Murfreesboro (finger shot off) and promoted to 1Lt. Sept. 1, 1863. Took command of company when Capt. S. J. A. Frazier was wounded and captured at Chickamauga and retained it until surrender at Greensboro, fighting at Shiloh, Baton Rouge, Chickamauga, Missionary Ridge and Atlanta Campaign. Wounded again at Atlanta. Hospitalized at the School for Blind until after Tennessee Campaign. After war received M.D. from Nashville Medical College in 1868 and practiced 19 years at Washington [Rhea Co.], TN. His company surrendered at Bentonville and was paroled in Charlotte, NC from where he and six others from Rhea Co. walked home. Married Mary Louise Paine. Clerk & Master of Rhea County in the Chancery Court from 1875-1887. Moved in 1887 to Hill City where he and Captain Samuel J. A. Frazier purchased land and developed Hill City. In 1918, Dr. Colville returned to Rhea County and lived with his sister, Mrs. C. R. Robinson. It was in her home that he died on Dec. 181923 and was interred in Chattanooga Memorial cemetery beside his wife. [CSR; Stout Papers, Austin; CSA Mil. Hist. Ex., 10:427-28; CT Dec.

18.1923; NBFM2; 1910HC; Rhea County History]

COMBS, Daniel C.   Co. K, 5KY MI
    Born Perry Co., KY, 1844. Enl. Dec. 29, 1861. Captured April 25, 1863 in Breathitt Co., KY and imprisoned Camp Chase. Captured again and imprisoned at Lexington, KY. Paroled at Lex., 1865. To TN, 1887. Res. Hill City, 1911. Later res. Glendale Comm. Died Feb. 5, 1920 and buried Sively Cem. [TP13,051;CT Feb. 7, 1920]

COMBS, Richard Dempsey "Dempsey"   Barry's Btry.
    Born Oct. 27, 1846 in Catoosa Co., GA, a son of Judge J.M. Combs. Resided in Ringgold. Enl. in Barry's Btry. May 1, 1863 [Sept. 1, 1864] at Atlanta. Wounded at Spring "Ball". Paroled at Meridian, MS, May, 1865. In early 1870's was member of wholesale grain, hay, bacon and provision firm of Anderson, Combs & Co. Baptist. Died Sept. 30, 1930 at Soldiers Home in Atlanta and buried Adairsville. [NBFM6]

CONDRA, George Washington   Co. A, 3CSA Cav.(?)
    Born 1839, TN of NC parents. Res. Payne St., 1910 with wife Mary (m. 1862). Retail merchant. Ruling elder in Cumberland Presbyterian Church. Died of typhoid at res. on Payne St., April 10, 1911. [1910HC; CTApril 11, 1911]

CONDRA, Israel Alonzo   Co. F, 35TN
    Born during 1844 in HC the son of Sterling & Martha Condra. He was a farmer until he enl. Feb. 9, 1863. He served as a carpenter in the regiment and was wounded at Chickamauga, following which he recuperated at the res. of William Fitzgerald, then Lawrence Gardenhire. Blue eyes, black hair, dark complexion, 6'1" tall.

CONLEY, James F.   Barry's Btry.
    Born 1838, TN. Farm laborer in household of mother Sarah at Harrison, 1860. Paroled May 11, 1865 in Meridian, MS. Methodist. Died at his home in Rock Springs at age 90. He had lived in same house 80 years. [CT May 25, 1917; 1860HC]

CONNELLY, Ephraim H.   Co. A, 1TN
    Born Nashville June 21, 1837; fought in eleven battles in Army of Northern Virginia; after war estab. painting firm Connelly and Taylor here. Member, NBF Camp, 1896. Died Aug. 5, 1911 in Chattanooga and buried Forest Hills Cemetery. [CT Aug. 6, 1911; FHR; NBFM2]

CONNER, A. B.   Co. H, 45TN
    Born 1824 in TN, prob. son of Mary. Farmer in Chattanooga. Wife was Elizabeth. [1860HC]

CONNER, Dauswell "Daus"
     He joined the Confederate army in 1864. He was a son of James Crutchfield Conner and brother of James A. He married Lottie Barker, and they moved to Texas.

CONNER, George Cooper
     Born Oct. 9, 1834 in Ireland and emigrated to Canada in 1848. To Chattanooga in 1871 in service of Western and Atlantic RR. Editor of short-lived Confederate Democrat. Died in Chattanooga March 9, 1894. [CT July 1, 1903]

CONNER (CONNOR), James Alfred     Co. F, 35TN
     Born in HC in 1846, he farmed here until enlisting Jan. 7, 1863. He had black eyes, light hair, fair complexion, and was 5'10" tall. Conner was the son of James Crutchfield Conner, who was HC sheriff before and after the war. J.C. Connor and his sons, Alfred and Dauswell, were on their way home from their farm at the foot of Walden's Ridge when they were captured by Union scouts. They were kept as prisoners in a stable near Valdeau. Later they were kept prisoners in their home at the top of the Anderson Pike on Walden's Ridge, where the Conners had a toll house. James Alfred Conner was only 17 when he enl. Later, he was persuaded to join the Federal army, "which greatly grieved his mother and family." He married Amanda Vandergriff.
     Died July 20, 1920, age 77, at home near Red Bank and buried Red Bank Cem. [CT July 21-22, 1920]

CONNER, James Madison     Co. C, 3TN Cav. Bn.; Co. B, 1TN Cav. (Carter's)
     Born 1841, son of Maxmilian Haney and Martha Palmer Conner of the Salem community, HC. Enl. Aug. 7, 1861 in Cleveland. Married Eliza J. Bare. Moved to MO about 1878. Res. Alfalfa, OK, 1912. [Roark, Hardtack and Hardship; 1860HC]

CONNER, Samuel H.     Co. F, 35TN
     Born in Warren Co., TN, 1823, son of Mary, he farmed in HC. Wife was Sarah. Enl. Sept. 5, 1862. Sick most of 1862-1863, he was discharged Nov. 11, 1863 for disabilities.

CONNER, William Franklin     Co. B, 1TN Cav. (Carter's)
     Born 1845 in HC, son of M. H. and Martha P. Conner, and married (1880 in Dade) Laura Adelaide McGill. Died 1898 in HC. [TWP, 208; 1860HC]

CONNER, Wilson B.     Co. F, 35TN
     Born in HC in 1836, he farmed here until enlisting Feb. 6, 1862. He was captured while on scouting duty on Aug. 20, 1863, and took the USA oath

on Nov. 5, 1863. He suffered a leg wound during the war and afterwards walked with a cane. He was a half-brother of James Crutchfield Conner. The pair computed their losses to Union confiscations at $2,200. [TP500; Adams, Mountain Melody, pp. 37-46]

CONNOLLY (CONNALLY), Thomas          Clark's Independent Cav. Co.
     Enl. Aug. 31, 1862 at Chattanooga; deserted Dec. 22, 1863 at Morristown, TN. Took USA oath, Jan. 18, 1864.

CONRY, Peter
     Born 1830 in Ireland. Married (1860 in HC) Mary Cox. Died 1872 in HC. [TWP, p. 193]

COOK, George     Barry's Btry.

COOK, John M.     Barry's Btry.
     Enl. June 2, 1862 at Chattanooga; blacksmith; paroled May 11, 1865 after surrender with battery at Citronelle, AL on May 4, 1865.

COOKE, Col. James Burch,     59TN; Barry's Btry.
     Born April 1, 1819 near Greenville, SC, son of William Henry and Mary Cantrell Cooke. Moved as child to McMinn Co. and attended East TN Univ. Lawyer. Married 31 Jan. 1850 in Tellico Palins, TN Dolly Penelope McDermott bor 2 April 1830 at Tellico Plains and died 25 December 1875 in Chattanooga. Practiced law in Athens and represented the county in TN Assembly, 1851-55. Moved to Chattanooga, then to Huntsville. Commanded Co A 59TN, 1861-1863. Resigned because of health in March, 1863. After war to Huntsville, AL, then to Chattanooga in 1867 where he practiced law. Served short time on Tennessee Supreme Court, 1884. Baptist. Mason. Died here April 19, 1899 and buried CSA Cem. [CT July 1, 1903; BDTA, 1:161-62; CT April 20, 1899; UDC2 pg 117.]

COOK, John Burch, Jr.     Barry's Btry.
     This son of John, Sr., enl. May 4, 1862 at Chattanooga and was wounded at Resaca. Died in Atlanta June 12, 1864, leaving wife Magdalana and minor child. [Brown's Diary]

COOKSTON, Isaac     Co. I, 5TN Cav.
     Born Dec. 19, 1826 in HC, son of Joseph and Christina Vandergriff Cookston. Lived mainly in Meigs Co. before enl. in Feb. 10, 1863. He was with a scouting party at Boston, KY, enroute to Williamsburg, KY when his horse stumbled crossing the Cumberland River. He was thrown on the horn of his saddle, rupturing the stomach and was discharged. Married six times and had 16 children. His last wife was Mary Burk (1897), widow

of William Dunlap. He moved to Chattanooga in early 1900's and died June 22, 1912 at res. on Stewart St. and buried Greenwood Cem. [TWP, p. 127; 1910HC; CT June 23, 1912]

COOLEY, Larance C.          Co. D, 37TN
          Enl. Dec. 1, 1861 at Knoxville. deserted Feb. 21, 1864 at Dalton, GA; took USA oath March 9, 1864; Dark complexion, Light hair, blue eyes, 5'7" tall.

COON, John          Co. D, 37TN
          He enl. Nov. 14, 1862, at Knoxville. He was killed while on picket duty at Jonesboro, GA, on Sept. 3, 1864. Prior to the war, he lived at Chattanooga with his mother, Mary Coon, and his four younger sisters. The family was from SC.

COOPER, Alexander          Co. D, 4th (12th) GA Cav.
          He enl. Nov. 1, 1863, under Capt. William J. Rogers. The son of Benjamin and Mary Sarah Cooper, he was born about 1843.

COOPER, Erby     Co. A, 19TN
          Born c1839 in TN, son of Cannon (farm laborer from SC) and Malinda. Res. in Harrison in 1860. Enl. May 20, 1861, Knoxville. Sick at Ocmulgee Hospital, Macon, GA, Sept. 1864.

COOPER, QM Sgt. Gabriel "Gabe'     Barry's Btry.
          Born May 19, 1834, in NC. To Chattanooga when 10yrs. Enl. April 4, 1862 at Chattanooga; deserted Nov. 17, 1863 at Canton, MS; Deserted. Retail grocer in Chattanooga, 1870, wife Mary. Successful merchant in Chattanooga, 1885, but later lost most of his fortune. Died March 8, 1900 and buried Forest Hills Cemetery. [Brown's Diary; FHR; NBFM7; CT obit March 9, 1900]

COOPER, J. B.          Barry's Btry.
          Wounded at Resaca.

COOPER, James G.          Co E 60 GA
          Born 27 April 1845, Murray Co., GA. 1910 farmer in James Co. Married Irene Earnest 27 Dec 1873 in Whitfield Co. GA, she was born 9 September 1842 in Walker Co., GA and died 31 Oct. 1928 in Ringgold, GA. He died Sept. 6, 1921 in Ringgold. [1910 James Co.; CT Sept. 7, 1921; UDC 2 pg 118.]

COOPER, John A.          Co. F, 35TN
          Born May 27, 1843 in HC [Marion Co.?]. Enl. Sept. 6, 1861, McMinnville. Re-enl. at Chattanooga, Nov. 16, 1862. Wounded at Chickamauga. Prom. 4th Cpl. Captured at Jonesboro but exchanged and paroled Greensboro, NC, May 1, 1865. Died Sept 21, 1903 at res.

on Cowart St. and buried Forest Hills Cemetery. [NBFM2; TP5324; CT Sept. 22, 1903; 1890 Vet Census]

COOPER, Joseph          Co. G, 17 (7th?) KY Cav.
          Born in Ireland, June, 1827. Imprisoned at Rock Island when war ended. He married July, 1885, in Meigs Co. to Edith E. "Bettie" Richard, former wife of A.A. Hicks. Joseph died Feb. 23, 1914, age 87, at res. on Wilson Ave. Buried CSA Cemetery. [CT Feb 24, 1914]

COOVER, George D.          Co. D, 37TN
          Born Franklin Co., TN. Enl. May 27, 1863 at Chattanooga; died Jan. 20, 1864 at hospital in Marietta, GA.

CORBITT, Colonel W.          Co. H, 29GA
          Born 1834 in HC, son of Elisha and Mary Gann Corbitt. Family moved to south GA in early 1850's. Enl. Sept. 1, 1861, Savannah, in Alapaha Guards. Prom. 2Lt. May 7, 1862. At Atlanta, Aug., 1864 and slightly wounded in arm at Jonesboro, Sept. 1, 1864. Remained with unit until end of war. Married (1866) Roxy Summerlin and (1882) Mary Ann Roberts, having 6 children by first wife and 10 by second. Active Methodist. Died Feb. 27, 1915, Atkinson Co., GA.

CORBITT, Monroe L.          Co. H, 29GA
          Born HC, 1838, son of Elisha and Mary Gann Corbitt. Family moved to south GA in early 1850's. Enl. Sept. 1, 1861 at Savannah, Ga. in Alapaha Guards. Rose to Sgt. In Ocmulgee Hospital at Macon with diarrhea, June, 1864. Captured Dec. 7, 1864 at Stones River. Sent to Nashville, then Louisville, then Camp Chase. Paroled May 2, 1865. Married Sophonia Summerlin. Died at home of son, Lamar, in Atkinson Co., Ga., Aug. 12, 1921.

CORDELL, Andrew     Co. D, 4th (12th) GA Cav.
          He enl. Aug. 15, 1863, under Capt. William J. Rogers. He was absent in September of 1863 and was believed to be in the hands of the enemy. He took the oath of allegiance on Sept. 28, 1863. The Union listed him as a conscript who gave himself up at Chattanooga. He had a fair complexion, brown hair, blue eyes and was 5'6" tall. He was living in Lookout Valley at the start of the war with his wife, Maria. He was born about 1823.

CORDELL, Wiley          Co. A, 3CSA Cav.
          Born 1831. Married (1867) Susan Emeline Isbill. Died 1899 in HC. [TWP, p. 65.]

COREY, Cpl. Samuel H.          Co. H, LA Crescent Regt.
          Born in New England, he became brother-in-law of William Crutchfield. Enl. March 5, 1862 in New Orleans. Clerk to Maj. Gen. Sam Jones. After CSA

service, he became a merchant in Chattanooga. Died Feb. 24, 1879. [CT03S]

CORNELL, Mordica     Barry's Btry.
Enl. Sept. 18, 1862 at Chattanooga.

CORNUTT, J. M.     Clark's Independent Cav. Co.
Enl. Aug. 31, 1862 at Chattanooga. At Buckner's Hdq. April, 20, 1864. Also in Dortch's KY Cav. Bn.

CORRELL, Cpl. Christian     Co. A, 4TN Cav. Bn.
He was an officer briefly, however, he resigned on July 12, 1861, and became a wagon master.

COSBY, Capt. Williamson Marion     J. W. Starnes' TN Cav. (8TN Cav. Bn., 4TN Cav.)
Born 1835 in Williamson Co. and married (1883) Ella Bush. Contractor in HC for 20 years. Died at res. in East Lake, Dec. 4, 1905 and buried CSA Cem. [TWP, 281; CT Dec. 5, 1905]

COUCH (COUTCH), D. J. (R.)     Co. B, 4TN Cav. (McLemore's)
Born 1846, TN. Butcher boarding in home on Cowart Street in Chattanooga. [TP8468; 1910HC]

COUGHLAN, Peter "Pete"     Co. A, 19TN
Enl. at Corinth, MS May 10, 1862. Elected 3d Sgt. and promoted to 2d Sgt., May 1, 1864. Wounded at Franklin, Nov. 30, 1864 and captured there on Dec. 17, 1864, and not released until June 16, 1865. Then he returned to Chattanooga. Coughlan had dark complexion, dark hair and eyes, and stood only 5'3" tall. [CSR; Worsham, 150.]

COULTER, Adolph Johnson     C Co., 16TN Cav. Bn.
Born 1845 in Rhea Co. Enl. April 22, 1863. Pea Vine Ridge, Chickamauga, Morristown. Paroled Athens, GA, May, 1865. Farmer in Sale Creek, 1915. [TP10,171; 14,461]

COULTER, Alexander A.     Co. D, 1TN Cav. (Carter's)
He enl. Aug. 7, 1861, at Cleveland, TN. He died the following April 12 at his home in Sale Creek. He was about 19 years old and was the son of James Park Coulter and Mary Ann McDonald Coulter.

COUNTRYMAN, James A.     Co. H, 26TN; 2d Co. I, 1CSA (GA)
Enl. July 8, 1861, Knoxville. Captured Fort Donelson. Light complexion, light hair, blue eyes, 6'4" tall; Exch. Nov. 10, 1862. Deserted May 1, 1864. Took USA oath at Chattanooga, May 27, 1864.

COWAN, Lt. Col. John C.     19KY
With Jere Boyle, Cowan organized the 19KY and became its Lt. Col. He was wounded at Vicksburg and again at Sabine Cross Roads. He became an attorney in Chattanooga after the war, living with the A. C. Downs family on Vine St. He also practiced law in Keokuk, IA and in Danville, KY where he died Feb. 19, 1911 and was buried. [CT Feb. 20, 1911]

COWART, John     Co. B, 21TN Cav. (Carter's Mounted Scouts)
He was only 12 years old when he ran away from home and joined the Confederate troops. He served on the staff of Gen. John Morgan. Both he and his older brother, Thomas Cowart, were imprisoned at Camp Chase, OH, in 1864.
Cowart was one of the sons of John and Cynthia Pack Cowart. John Cowart Sr. served in the Mexican War, but he died at the time of the start of the Civil War. Cynthia Pack Cowart was the daughter of William Shorey Pack and Elizabeth Lowrey Pack. Her grandfather was Col. John Lowrey, a trader and leading Cherokee chief who owned a ferry at the mouth of Battle Creek near Jasper, TN. The Cowarts had a farm on the north bank of the Tennessee River across from Chattanooga. They operated a ferry across to town. John Cowart Jr. died in 1873, leaving a widow, Fannie. Their daughter, Osceoloa Cowart, died as an infant.

COWART, Thomas F.     Co. B, 21TN (Carter's Mounted Scouts)
The son of Maj. John Cowart and Cynthia Pack, he was born Sept. 17, 1847 in Hill City and always expressed pride in his Cherokee blood. At 15 he joined Co. B, but was captured in 1864 and imprisoned at Camp Chase, OH. After his exchange he went to the home of a brother in GA before returning to Chattanooga. He never recovered from his harrowing prison experiences, and he suffered from rheumatism and other ailments for the rest of his life, becoming "a mere wreck of the stalwart youth who marched away to battle at the opening of the Civil War."
Thomas Cowart was a "born politician," and served as justice of the peace for Hill City (North Chattanooga) on the Quarterly Court for several decades. He was chairman of the commission that built the tunnel through Stringer's Ridge, he was a Methodist and a member of NBF Camp. He was still living on a portion of the family farm in North Chattanooga when he died May 7, 1911. He was buried in White Oak Cem. Married (1880) Jennie A. Day. His daughter, Miss Nita Cowart, was HC school superintendent in 1907. [CT May 8, 1911; TWP, p. 159]

COWDEN, George W.     Co. L, 36TN

Enl. Jan. 9, 1862 at Chattanooga.

COX, John M.          Co. L, 2KY Cav. (Duke's)
Born June 5, 1845, in TN of parents born in VA and served throughout war in Morgan's Cav. Mason. Retail grocery merchant. Died at his home in St. Elmo, Oct. 22, 1915 and buried in Jonesboro, GA. [1910HC; CT Oct. 22, 1915]

CRAIG, A. R.          Co. H, 4TN Cav.
"Shot through both knees by his friend old Jess Pickett."

CRAIG, H. L. W.          Co. A, 19TN
Born c1840, he was living prior to war with father, R. W. Craig; operated a boarding house in Chattanooga. Enl. May 10, 1862, Corinth. Surgeon at Yandell Hospital, Columbus, MS, pronounced him unfit for duty and hospital 1863. Became a nurse and druggist at Fair Ground Hospital No. 1, Atlanta.

CRAIN, Henry Stratton          Co. H, 31TN
Born Oct. 8, 1840 in Chattanooga. Married (Dec., 1864) Mary Frances Taylor in Evansville, IN. Died April 3, 1913 in Clifton, TN. [TWP5211]

CRANE (CRAYNE), J. P.          2nd Co. K, 1st CSA Cav.
Enl. Sept. 20, 1862 in HC Captured near Jasper, TN., Oct. 8, 1863. Imp. at Camp Morton, IN where he died of pneumonia Jan. 10, 1864 and was buried.

CRANFIELD, William C.          Co. K, 43TN

CRAVENS, Capt. James Reagan
Was a son of Robert Cravens, whose home was the centerpiece of the "Battle Above the Clouds" on the side of Lookout Mountain. He joined the Confederate army and rose to the rank of captain. He married Harriet Newell Rogers and then Mary D. Lyle. He eventually went to medical school and moved to Texas to set up his practice. His father was a prominent iron master and was the first year-round resident of Lookout Mtn. His mother was Catherine Roddye of Rhea Co. The Cravens home "Alta Vista" is today a part of Chickamauga and Chattanooga National Military Park.

CRAVENS, Cpl. Jesse Roddy          Co. H, 2TN Cav. (Ashby's)
Born 1842, son of Robert and Catherine Roddy Cravens, he joined his older brother, James Reagan Cravens, in the Confederate army, though he was just 18 when the war started. Absent sick at Chattanooga from Nov. 28, 1861. After the war he married Mary Ella Brown and then Ida Holcomb. At the time of

Chattanooga's first city directory in 1871, he was a merchant living at Fourth and Walnut streets. He later was an insurance official and lived at Thomson, GA. Jesse Cravens died at his home near Thomson, GA, Aug. 16, 1917. [CT Aug. 20, 1917]

CRAVENS, Robert
Born May 5, 1805. Wife Caroline Cunningham. Died Dec. 3, 1886 and buried Forest Hills Cemetery. Contracted with TN Mil. & Financial Board to supply 20,000 lb. of saltpetre, May, 1861.

CRAWFORD, Banks          Co. A, 19GA
Born Atlanta, GA. Enl. July, 1861 at Lynchburg, VA. RR man in Chattanooga in 1888. Moved away c1894. [NBFM2,7]

CRAWFORD, Cpl. Elisha D.          Co. A, 19th TN; Co. H, Cons. 3TN
Born Feb. 9, 1834 in McMinn Co. TN. He enl. May 21, 1861 (with $50.00 bounty) and was wounded at Shiloh and hospitalized fifteen months. Afterwards he was promoted to 4th Cpl. Then he was a nurse at Hospital Academy at Marietta, GA. Then wounded at Atlanta. He was later listed as sick and absent without leave. A native of GA, Crawford was a carpenter at Chattanooga prior to the war. Member, NBF Camp. Residing on Frazier Ave. in Hill City when he died Sept. 8, 1902. Buried CSA Cem. [CSR; TP3400; Knoxville Daily Register, April 19, 1862; CT Sept. 7, 1902; NBFM2]

CRAWFORD, Erby G.          Barry's Btry.
Born c1832, he was painter in Chattanooga with wife Elizabeth prior to war. Apparently served as 1Lt. in Co. H, 36TN prior to enl., May 27, 1862, Chattanooga Paroled May 11, 1865 at Meridian, MS. Returned to Chattanooga after war.

CRAWFORD, E. W.          Barry's Btry.

CRAWFORD, James S. A.
Born 1836 in Augusta Co., VA, married (1865) Jemima Frances Hunt and died in HC. [TWP, p. 114]

CRAWFORD, Capt. John, Jr.          Co. E, 26TN
Died in prison at Camp Morton, IN, April 9, 1862.

CRAWFORD, John Tyler          Co. E, 26TN; Co. D, 5TN Cav. (McKenzie's)
Born Dec. 31, 1844 in Rhea Co., son of John and Martha Griffith Crawford. Attended common school and Washington Acad. (age 14-16). Enl. with brothers James Riley, Henry A. and Thomas H. Missed Fort

Donelson because he was in the hospital in Bowling Green with mumps. Enl. Jan. 12, 1863 in 5TN Cav. (McKenzie's). Chickamauga, Missionary Ridge, Atlanta Camp. Paroled May 3, 1865, Charlotte, NC. After war was worked on steamboats ---"floated up Market to 5th Street in great flood of 1867." Clerk, master and pilot on Cherokee, Resaca, and Last Chance. Died May 19, 1935 at home in Pampa, Gray Co., TX. [CT 22May1935; NBFM6; TVQ]

CRAWFORD, Sgt. William C.        Co. K, 43TN
        Born c1836, he enl. Dec. 1, 1861, at Ooltewah. Prior to the war, he was a farm laborer living at Harrison with his mother, Elizabeth Crawford, and his sister. [1860 HC]

CREW, Benjamin B.        4TN Cav.
        Born in Chattanooga Oct. 23, 1844, he was the son of Pleasant Crew. After receiving his education in Chattanooga, he joined the staff of the Chattanooga Daily Rebel and went to Marietta when the city was evacuated in September, 1863. When Marietta was threatened by Sherman, Crew left the paper and enl. in the 4TN Cav. He also served as a courier for Gen. W.J. Hardee. He returned to Chattanooga after being paroled, then moved to Atlanta where he eventually established Phillips and Crew, a company dealing in pianos and organs. He also published sheet music and Scott's Literary Magazine. He married Tillie Maffitt in 1872, and after her death, Virginia Fowler.

CREWS, George W.        Co. K, 43TN
        Born c1842, he enl. Oct. 17, 1861, at Ooltewah, and he died at Vicksburg on June 24, 1863. He was one of the sons of Abraham and Delila Crews. Abraham Crews was a carpenter living at Harrison prior to the war. The Crews family was originally from GA. [Lindsley, 528; 1860HC]

CREWS (CRUSE), Henry R.    Co. A, 5th (McKenzie's) TN Cav.
        He enl. Aug. 24, 1861, at Camp Cumming. He was one of the sons of Abraham and Delila Crews of Harrison. Age 25 on March 11, 1864 roll. Captured at Wallace's Crossroads July 15, 1862. Paroled at Cumberland Gap July 25, 1862, but detained at Knoxville. On rolls present Sept., 1862-Dec., 1864. Paroled May 3, 1865 at Charlotte, NC. Returned to HC and living there 1880 with wife Rebecca. [1860 HC]

CREWS (CRUSE), Thomas W.    5th (McKenzie's) TN Cav.
        Born c1837 in GA. Enl. March 25, 1863 at Whitley Co. KY. Captured April 25, 1864 and took USA oath May 3, 1864. 1870, locomotive engineer, with wife

Sophronia.

CRUSE, William (AKA Cruse, W. M.; Cruse, William M.)
        Enl. Jan. 14, 1863 at Knoxville, age 37 on March 11, 1864 roll, in Co. A, 5TN Cav. Present Aug. 31, 1862-April, 1863. Deserted Aug. 13, 1863.

CRUSE, William        Co. K, 5TN Cav.
        Enl. Sept. 24, 1862 at Maryville for 3 yrs. Present on rolls for Nov.-Dec., 1862. Absent sick Jan. 1, 1863. Reported absent without leave April 1, 1863. Jan. 10, 1864, took USA oath.

CREWS (CRUISE, CRUSE) William M.  Co. K, 43TN
        He enl. Oct. 17, 1861 at Ooltewah, and he was captured at Vicksburg on July 4, 1863. He was one of the sons of Abraham and Delila Crews of Harrison, born about 1844.

CROCKETT, Capt. Edward T.        Co. A, 30TN
        Buried CSA Cem.

CROFF, R. C.
        [NBFM1]

CROFFORD, George
    Enl. Jan. 9, 1862 in Co. L, 36TN at Chattanooga, then transferred to Co. L, 35TN Inf.

CROSS, Cpl. Absalom Looney        Co. A, 4Tn Cav.
        Absalom Looney Cross lived in Meigs Co. but came to Hamilton Co. to enlist in a company because none was being organized at the time in Meigs or Rhea Co.  He won promotion to cpl. in July of 1861, apparently taking the place of Christian Correll, who resigned. 1870 res. Scott Co.
        A. L. Cross was born in 1820 in Sullivan Co., TN and died in 1897 in Arkansas. He was 5'10" tall, fair complexion, gray eyes, and by profession a steamboat Pilot. During the war he was shot in the ankle. [Broyles]

CROSS, 1Lt. Robert Collop        Adjutant 44TN; 48TN
        Born April 7, 1833, Axminister, England. Emigrated a few years before the war becoming a bookkeeper in Nashville. Joined 55TN, then 44TN which he served as adjutant at Shiloh, Perryville, Murfreesboro, Chickamauga and Petersburg. Wounded at Ft. Sanders and Drewry's Bluff. Following war he operated a woolen mill in Fayetteville. His wife was Jennie, age 26, born in TN. In 1870, however, he is a resident of Bradley Co. with a wife named Margaret E., age 29. His occupation was carriage maker. Nevertheless Cross "lived in Chattanooga many years" before moving to Rome, GA where he worked for "a long time" in the business office

of the Rome Tribune. He also had an interest in mining operations nearby. He died in Rome Nov. 5, 1906. Buried at Forest Hills Cemetery. [FHR; NBFM2,4,7; CT Nov. 6, 1906; 1860 Davidson Co., and 1870 Bradley Co. Census]

CROUCH, D. I.          Co. B, 4TN Cav. (Starnes)
          Born Davidson Co., May 11, 1846. Murfreesboro, Missionary Ridge, Bentonville. Paroled Washington, GA, May, 1865. res. Chattanooga, 1906. [TP8468]

CROUCH, 3d Lt. Hickman H.      Co. B, 5TN Cav. Bn.; Co. H, 4TN Cav.
     Enl. Aug. 11, 1861 at Chattanooga; wounded at Newnan, GA, July 30, 1864.

CROW, Christopher Columbus    Co. F, 43TN
          He was from McMinn Co. Served in CSA army through Vicksburg where he was captured, then paroled. Wife was Sarah L. He died at Rossville, TN, Nov. 21, 1903. [TWP2941]

CROW, Finn M.
          Born c1844 in GA. Enl. Jan. 9, 1862 in Co. L, 36TN at Chattanooga, transferred to Co. L, 35TN. Deserted Dec. 24, 1863 at Tunnel Hill. Dark complexion, black hair, gray eyes, 5'10" tall. 1870 farming in Chattanooga, wife Rebecca. [TP12 786]

CROW, Sgt. Isaac L.        Co. F, 35TN
          Born c1837, Lumpkin Co., GA, he moved to HC where he was a farmer. He enl. Jan. 9, 1862, at age 27. Blue eyes, dark hair, fair complexion, 6'2" tall. 1870 at Chattanooga, wife Rebecca. [TWP]

CROW, Thomas        Co. L, 35TN
          Born 1825 in TN. Wagon maker in Harrison. Resided with wife Eleanor in household of Jackson Flippo. Enl. Jan. 9, 1862; he fought at Murfreesboro and was appointed drummer Oct. 1, 1863. He was paroled at Kingston, GA May 12, 1865. Fair complexion, light hair, blue eyes, 5'10" tall.

CROW, William M.
          Born c1823. Enl. Jan. 9, 1862 in Co. L, 36TN at Chattanooga and transferred to Co. L, 35TN; he fought at Murfreesboro but deserted Dec. 24, 1863 at Tunnel Hill, GA. Dark complexion, dark hair, blue eyes, 6' tall. 1870 millwright, Chattanooga, wife Martha A.

CROW, William P.       Railroad Conductor
          Crow was born on a farm in Henderson Co., NC, on Dec. 21, 1830. His parents were NC pioneers who moved to Dahlonega, GA, when he was in his teens. The Crows owned extensive property in the gold-mining region, and W.P. Crow was a miner before he went into railroading. He had many interesting war experiences while operating an engine for the Western and Atlantic RR between Atlanta and Chattanooga. For a price of several hundred dollars, he moved the equipment of the Chattanooga Daily Rebel out of Chattanooga after the town was shelled and a 12-pounder had hit the newspaper building on Market Street near Sixth. In 1864, he was captured by the Federal Army and imprisoned at Atlanta for the remainder of the war.
          Crow came to Chattanooga in 1865 at the close of the war and became master mechanic for the W&A. He left the railroad to go into business in 1873. He acquired considerable property and was worth $100,000 at one time, though he later suffered reverses. He had five children. Married Sarah G. Crow, he died April 20, 1898. [CT April 21, 1898; CT03S]

CROWE, 1Lt. James R.        Co. F, 35TN
          Born in Pulaski, TN, he enl. April 21, 1861 in Marion Co., AL.

CRUDUP, 1Lt Dempsey G.      Co. H, 7TN
          Born in Wilson Co. 1845ca., TN. Enl. May 20, 1861 in 7TN and afterwards was in Forrest's Cav. RR contractor and dealer in iron and iron ore in Chattanooga [NBFM2]

CRUISE, J. W.        Co. K, 43TN
          Died at Vicksburg, June 7, 1863. [Brooks, p. 101]

CRUMBLESS, JOHN
          Member of NBF Camp who died in 1890.

CRUMLEY, John        Co. I, 7GA
          Enl. Marietta, GA in 1862 Army Northern Virginia. With Longstreet at Chickamauga and during East TN Campaign, fall, 1863. Wounded at Lenoir, TN and discharged for disability. Died Nov. 6, 1890 and buried CSA Cem. [NBFM1,2,7]

CUETON, James (AKA F. A. Cueton)    Co. G, 5TN Cav.
          Enl. March 16, 1862 at Knoxville by W. P. Wood for 12 months in Jones Co. Transferred. to Lt. Willet's Co., 1TN Cav.

CULVER, James Jasper   Co. C "Jackson Lions," 31AL; Co. C, 49AL
          Born Aug. 7, 1843, Jackson Co., AL. Shiloh, Corinth, Baker's Creek, Baton Rouge (wounded). Captured at Port Hudson and paroled July 9, 1863. Went home to Stevenson, AL and stayed rest of war. To TN, 1875. Drayman. Married Laura Belle. 1909 res. HC.

[TP11,481; 1910HC]

CUMMINGS, Greenberry    Co. D, 4th (12th) GA Cav.
He enl. Aug. 1, 1863, under Capt. William J. Rogers. He was absent due to sickness, then he was captured along with his son, John Cummings, at Missionary Ridge on Nov. 25, 1863. Born c1822, he was a son of Thomas Cummings. Married Elizabeth. Farmer at Harrison, 1860. He died in 1892. [J. Wilson Cummings family]

CUMMINGS, John    Co. D, 4th (12th) GA Cav.
Born 1844 in HC, son of Greenbury and Elizabeth. Enl. Oct. 4, 1862. He was captured at Missionary Ridge on Nov. 25, 1863, along with his father, Greenberry Cummings. The family was from Lookout Valley. Married (1874 in Wauhatchie) Mary Elizabeth Boydston. Died 1905 in Wauhatchie. [J. Wilson Cummings family; TWP, p. 168]

CUMMINGS, W. F.    Barry's Btry.
Lost in Feb. on retreat. [Brown's Diary]

CUNNINGHAM, Hugh    2nd Co. K, 1st CSA Cavalry
Enl. July 14, 1862 in HC. Deserted Dec. 28, 1862 at Shelbyville, TN. Arrested and returned to regiment. Captured near Chickamauga and imp. Rock Island, IL. Transferred to USN and sent to rendezvous at Camp Douglas, May 23, 1864. [RI ledger]

CUNNINGHAM, Miles C.    Co. G, 26TN; Bradshaw's Cav. Squadron; 2d Co. K, 1CSA (GA)
Born 1842, TN. Enl. July 8, 1861, Knoxville. Detached to a company of arty. In Bradshaw's Squadron, Dec. 31, 1862; absent without leave 1863. Res. Chattanooga, 1910 in household of nephew C. C. Cunningham. Nailer in box factory. [1910HC]

CUNNINGHAM, William M.    Co. G, 26TN; 2d Co. K, 1CSA (GA)
Enl. July 8, 1861, Knoxville. Detached to arty., Dec. 4, 1861. Absent without leave from 1CSA, June 30, 1863.

CUON, Con    Co. A, 19TN
Enl. May 10, 1862, Corinth. Killed at Murfreesboro, Dec. 31, 1862.

CUPP, Dock    Co. H, 4TN Cav.
Died in Chattanooga 1862.

CUPP, William    Co. H, 4TN Cav.
Enl. April 23, 1863, in Chattanooga. Absent sick later in 1863.

CURD, Richard D.    Co. K, 12TN    1st Sgt.
Born c1843 Lebanon, TN. Enl. Apr 20, 1861. Surrendered at Greensboro, NC. Real estate agent in Chattanooga in 1893. Founded Paris Milling Co., Paris, TN. Died cJan. 15, 1903, Salisbury, NC. [NBFM2; CT Jan. 18, 1903]

CURRAN, O. S.    Co. A, 19TN
Killed in action in Murfreesboro. [Worsham, p. 74]

CURRY, George Washington    Surgeon
Son of Robert Brownlee and Jane Gray Owen Curry. Married Emily Donelson Martin. CSA Surgeon in hospitals in Memphis and Ringgold.

CUSTER, James M.    Co. I, 41TN
Born April 7, 1844, Franklin Co., TN. Enl. Feb. 10, 1862. Captured Fort Donelson. Carpenter in Chattanooga, 1897, "I have no family." "He is in very hard circumstances, indeed, he has no money, no friends, and is sick and nearly dead from the want of shelter and food." 1897 applied for admission to TN Soldiers Home from HC. [SAACH]

# D

DALTON, Lee Andrew    Co. E, 17TN
Born Livingston Co., Ky, Nov. 9, 1836. To Franklin Co., TN from KY when 13. Enl. Marvel Hill, TN. Fishing Creek, Murfreesboro. Evidently quit army and worked on farm in Bedford Co., TN, 1864-65. To Chattanooga 1871 and settled here permanently, 1884. Methodist. Res. Frazier Ave, 1920. Died Sept. 28, 1922 at res. 201 Frazier Ave. and buried Citizens Cem. [CT Sept 29, 1922; TP15,664]

DANGEY, Harry    Co. H, 2TN Cav.
Charter member of NBF Camp. Died in TX, 1886. [NBFM7]

DANIEL, David    Co. H, 26TN
Enl. July 8, 1861, Knoxville. Captured Fort Donelson and imp. Camp Douglas where hospitalized. Exchanged and left at Chattanooga, Oct. 5, 1862.

DANIEL, J. B.    Barry's Btry

DANIEL, R. P.
Born in GA. Died Nov. 21, 1908 in Chattanooga and buried Cinteth, GA. [CT Nov. 22, 1908]

DANIEL, William    Co. H, 26TN
Enl. July 8, 1861. Died in hospital, Bowling Green, KY, Dec. 13, 1861.

DARR, Samuel Curtis          Co. D, 5AR
          Born Shelby Co., TN, 1835. Enl. June, 1861 at Gainesville, AR. Fought at Belmont, Springfield, MO, Shiloh, Murfreesboro (wounded). Teamster. Married (1863) Maggie Elizabeth O'Neal. Died at res. on Long St., May 11, 1918 and buried Forest Hills Cemetery. [TWP, 199; TP8400; CT May 12, 1918]

DARRELL, John A,          Co. D, 15/37TN
          Born 1842. Enl. Sept. 1, 1861 at Knoxville. Company drummer. Wounded at Chickamauga. Promo. Cpl. Apr., 1864. Captured on picket June 10, 1864 near Pine Mountain out of Big Shanty, GA and imprisoned Rock Island. 20 years old from Chattanooga. [Rudd, "City's Rufus Tankesley."]

DAVIDSON, Jasper J.          Co. A, 5TN Cav. (McKenzie's)
          Born c1839 in GA. He enl. Aug. 24, 1861 at Camp Cummings. At hospital Aug. 10, 1862 and home sick during fall, 1862. Deserted March 11, 1864. Age 22 on March 11, 1864 roll. 1870 farmer in Ooltewah, wife Sarah J.

DAVIES, David J.
          Born Feb. 21, 1827 in Carmarthershire, Wales, he emigrated to the US at the age of 18 and learned the peddler's trade. He married Sarah Belle Ballard of Princeton, KY in 1857. A "strong Confederate," he did not serve in army but was "impressed" into the iron industry where he worked throughout the war. Afterwards he was employed by the Roane Iron Co. here and in Birmingham. Old and thrown out of work by the Panic of 1892, he traded his Chattanooga home for farmland near Valley Head, AL. Perfect teeth and "as if to confound and confuse the diet seekers after longevity, he was always a hearty eater, eating everything and anything." He also began smoking at age 88. He was Senior Warden at Thankful Memorial in St. Elmo. Died in St. Elmo, March 24, 1917 and buried in Forest Hills Cemetery. [CT March 3, 1917; FHR]

DAVIS, Albert
          Born 1849, GA. 1910 house carpenter boarding in household of Lulu McGaka. [1910HC]

DAVIS, Alfred A.          Co. H, 4TN Cav.

DAVIS, David
          Born 1832 in Wythe Co., VA and married (1856 in Giles Co., VA) Rachel A. French. Died 1910 in HC. [TWP, p. 88]

DAVIS, Decatur          Co. B, 1TN Cav. (Carter's)
          Enl. Aug. 7, 1861 in Cleveland. Became

teamster. Not found in 1860 HC.

DAVIS, Harvey L.          Co. A, 5NC Cav. Bn.; Co. I, 6NC Cav.
          Born Buncombe Co., NC, May 18, 1841. Enl. May 14, 1862 in Madison Co., NC; Winchester, KY, Kinston, NC, Goldsboro, NC. Paroled Raleigh, NC, April 26, 1865. Wife was Mahalie. To TN 1888. Res. 1913 in Chattanooga, 301 College St. Baptist. Odd Fellow. For 35 years worked at shops of Cincinnati, New Orleans and Texas RR. Died March 11, 1920 and buried Forest Hills Cemetery. [TP14,133; CT March 20, 1920]

DAVIS, Henry M.          Co. C, 2GA
          Born Sept. 21, 1845 in Macon Co., AL. Enl. Kingston, GA July 1, 1863 in 2GA. Died March 1, 1920; buried CSA Cem. [NBFM2; CT March 3, 1920]

DAVIS, J. W.          Co. H, 26TN; 2d Co. I, 1CSA (GA)
          Enl. July 8, 1861, Knoxville. Wounded and captured Fort Donelson, Feb. 15, 1862. Fair complexion, blue eyes, 5'9" tall. Trans. to 2d Co. I, Nov., 1862. In Buckner Guards Cav., Dec. 31, 1862. Sgt., June 30, 1864. Captured July 22, 1864 and imprisoned Camp Chase. Disch. and returned to duty, Oct. 18, 1864.

DAVIS, James Mack          Co. H, 4TN Cav.
          Enl. Aug. 11, 1861 at Chattanooga Bugler.

DAVIS, Jerry          Co. H, 4TN Cav.

DAVIS, John          Co. H, 4TN Cav.
          Born 1836 in TN, son of Hiram and Lucinda. Farm laborer with wife Mary and one child.

DAVIS, M. T.          Co. D, 37TN; Huggins Arty. Btry.
          Born c1844. Enl. Sept. 1, 1861 at Knoxville. Detached to arty. service, April, 1, 1862.

DAVIS, Robin E.          Co. H, 4TN Cav.

DAVIS, Samuel          Co. A, 19TN; Co. K, 43TN
          Enl. Dec. 1, 1863, Dalton. Deserted March 3, 1864 and took USA oath following day. He made detailed report to Union officers on whereabouts of CSA troops around Dalton. He told of seeing Gen. Johnston "as I got off the train." Had three brothers in Union Army. [z]

DAVIS, Thomas Pinkney          Co. A, 14GA
          Born Oct. 8, 1842 in Monroe Co., GA. Enl. at Forsyth July, 1861. Wounded June 28, 1862 in Seven Days Battle and in Chancellorsville. Captured and released from service, March, 1864, because of wound in

head which broke his skull. Wife was Sarah Elizabeth White. Tenant farmer. Res. St. Elmo. Died March 22, 1911 at Tyner's and buried at Peavine Cem., 4 mi. east of Chickamauga Nat'l Park. [NBFM2; TWP4816; 1910HC]

DAVIS, W. Scott          Co. H, 4TN Cav.

DAVIS, William M.          Co. H, 26TN
Son of Jehu R. Davis of Catoosa Co., GA, he enlisted July 14, 1861 at Knoxville; captured at Fort Donelson, Feb. 16, 1862; imp. Camp Douglas where he died March 7, 1862.

DAVIS, William P.
Born 1835, Smith Co., VA but spent most of life in TN. 2d cousin to Jefferson Davis. Methodist. Died Feb. 26, 1907 and buried Ooltewah. [CT Feb. 27, 1907]

DAWN, Ferdinand F.          Co. K, 43TN
Enl. Dec. 1, 1861 at Ooltewah. 1870 res. Unicoi County, Tennessee.

DAWSON, W. D.          Co. G, 19VA
Res. (1902) on Montgomery Ave. Died 1903 and buried CSA Cem.

DAY, Edwin F.          Barry's Btry.
Enl. Oct. 1, 1862 at Knoxville; Dec. 1862-Aug. 1863 on detached duty at Chattanooga; paroled May 11, 1865 at Meridian, MS; Res., Atlanta.

DAY, Sgt. George M.          Co. D, 37TN (Tankesley's Company)
Born c1843 in MA and came to Chattanooga as a child with father. Printer in Chattanooga after 1848, "pioneer printer." Enl. Sept. 1, 1861 at Knoxville; wounded in leg at Murfreesboro, Dec. 31, 1862; deserted Sept. 7, 1863 at Ooltewah. Married Amanda. Considered "original printer" of Times, also worked with S. A. Cunningham, editor of the *Confederate Veteran*. Died March 5, 1907 in Chattanooga (65 years old). Buried Forest Hills Cem. [CT, March 6, 1907]

DAY, John          Co. D, 37TN
Enl. April, 2, 1863 at Chattanooga as substitute for M. Pope. Deserted Jan. 2, 1863 at Tullahoma, TN.

DAY, Dr. Sam Houston          F&S, Pvt Co C 5TN Cav.
He was born Sept. 10, 1839 in Bradley Co., TN and died March 31, 1896 in Cleveland. Surgeon in Wheeler's Cav. Res. Bradley, 1870. Married April 26, 1879 to Mary Mee who died July 26, 1915 in Chattanooga, age 72yrs. [CT July 27,1915; TWP1208; UDC 2 pg 143.]

DEADERICK, 1st Lt. William Wallace          Co. F, 37TN
Born Aug. 4, 1842 in Boyle Co., KY, he was son of Chief Justice James W. Deaderick. One of six brothers in CSA, he enl. on his birthday in 1861 at Knoxville. He fought at Murfreesboro, Chickamauga and Missionary Ridge. Wounded at Perryville and at Murfreesboro. Paroled as 1Lt. at Augusta, GA in May, 1865. He died in Chattanooga March 10, 1913 and was buried in CSA Cemetery. [CT March 11, 1913; NBFM2]

DEAKINS, Absoleus L. "Ab"          Co. H, 35TN
Born 1836, TN Res. 1910 with wife Edna in household of son J.V. Deakins on Montague Ave. Died July 18, 1913 at Cedar Springs, TN (prob. long time resident). [1910HC; CT July 20, 1913]

DEAKINS, Frank
Born 1837 in Marion Co., TN. Married (1858) Mary D. (B.) Jones in Sequatchie Co. Enl. Sept. 5, 1861. Perryville. While home on furlough was captured and took oath of allegiance. Died Feb. 2, 1900 in Chattanooga. [TWP2324]

DEAKINS, Samuel D.          Co. H, 4TN Cav.
Died Oct. 6, 1900 in Jasper, TN and buried there. [NBFM7]

DEAKINS, William Rogers "Frank"          Co. H, 35TN
Born 1837 in Meigs Co. Married (1865) Mary E. Carney. Died 1879 in HC. [TWP, p.65]

DEAN, J. R. M.          Co. E, 11SC
1901 res. of HC. [TP3541]

DEANE, James          Co. I, 19TN

DEAN, John Robert          Co. A, 17TN
Born June 15, 1840 in Bedford Co., TN. He studied law then became superintendent of schools in Bedford. Enl. April 27, 1861. Captured at Petersburg. Following the war he came to Chattanooga in 1880 and opened a law practice. Married (1884 in HC) Clara Stahlschmidt. NBF Camp. Died at res. on Douglas St. March 5, 1906 and buried CSA Cem. [CT March 6, 1906]. His two daughters, Mary Clair and Daisy Roberta were both members of the U.D.C.. Applications for NBF Camp; TWP, 239; NBFM2,7; UDC2 pg 144.]

DEAN, Cpl. Robert          Co. K, 43TN
Born in Cocke County, TN, he was a 45 year-old farmer residing at Sale Creek when he enl. Oct. 17, 1861, at Ooltewah. He was discharged Nov. 5, 1862. He had a fair complexion, gray eyes, and was 5'10" tall.

DEATON, Charles A.

Born 1841, VA, of VA parents. 1910 res. Harrison and Georgetown Rd., James Co., with wife Rebecca (m. 1884). Manager of flour mill. [1910 James Co.]

DEBARDELEBEN, Daniel H.          Co. A, 8AL Cav.
Born Autauga Co. AL, 1845. Enl. 1862. Served four years in Confederate Army. Married Ethel. Died in Chattanooga Jan. 19, 1909, age 63. He was buried in Montgomery, AL. [CT Jan. 20, 1909; TP8712]

DECOSTA, Aaron Canady          Co. D, 18SC Reserve
Born Dec. 30, 1849 in Valdosta, GA (Charles-ton, SC). Enl. in 1864 in Co. D, 18SC Reserve. Married Sept. 7, 1873 in HC to Julia Adeline Milliken b. April 7, 1858. Railway Postal Clerk in Chattanooga in 1887. Died at res. on Bailey Ave, Jan. 11, 1921 and buried Forest Hills Cemetery. [FHR; TWP, 295; NBFM2; 1910HC]

DEDMON, Joseph
Railroad crossing watchman, age 70 when he died Nov. 27, 1906. He was buried in Ringgold, GA. [CT Nov. 28, 1906]

DEFRESE, R. H.[DEPRISE, R.H.]          Co. E, 16VA
Born in 1845 in VA. Enl. at Abington, VA in 1863. Wounded at Saltville. Paroled April 1865. In 1901 employed by Fite Music Store in Chattanooga. Res. Chattanooga c1901. Member NBF Camp, 1915. Died March 31, 1915 at Bristol, VA and buried there. [NBFM2,4,7]

DEGALLEFORD, John
Born c1826 in KY. Res. St. Elmo, 1910 with wife Elizabeth (m. 1893). Mechanical engineer. [1910HC]

DEMENT, Thomas J.          6VA Cav.
Born Washington, D.C. in 1838. Prior to war was clerk in Treasury Dept. Enl. April 1, 1861 in the Beauregard Rifles, then transferred to the 6VA Cav. and was wounded at Cedar Run, VA. He had the "physique of Joe Wheeler." To Chattanooga from Athens in early 1880's. Member of firm of Dement, Baird & Co. which sold farm implements and seeds. Appointed postmaster by President Cleveland. Exec. Comm., NBF Camp, 1894. Died Sept. 19, 1915 at his home on Wyatt St. and buried CSA Cem. [CT Sept. 20, 1915; NBFM2,7]

DEMPSEY, William L. Co. K, 4th GA Cav.
(Avery's) [TP8060]

DENNIS, John          Co. D, 43TN
Born in McMinn Co., c1840, son of James (German) and Matilda (Irish) Dennis. Attended school "about ten years." "Plowed and hoed and general farm work." Enl. April, 1862 in Meigs Co. Discharged July 12, 1863 at Vicksburg. Missionary Baptist. Farmer in Soddy in Sept., 1922. Died 2 April 1924, age 81. Active Baptist 58 years. [TVQ; CT April 3, 1924]

DENNISON, Barney          Barry's Btry.
Enl. June 22, 1862 at Chattanooga.

DENT, Charles J.          Co. H, 2TN Cav. (Ashby's)
The eldest son of Col. Jarrett Gray Dent, he ran away to join the Confederate army. He was 16 at the time the war started. Inseparable from his first cousin Lewis Shepherd, Dent also attended Aldehoff's School and enl. at age 15 in a Texas cavalry regiment. Placed on detached duty as Q.M. Sgt. Aug. 1, 1861, but returned to 2TN Cav. Aug. 12, 1862 and disch. underage Sept. 15, 1862. Long after the war he was in charge of a saw mill at Kinder, LA and died Aug. 25, 1910 in Alexandria. [CT Aug. 30, 1910]

DENT, Jarrett Gray          Co. A, 4TN Cav.
He cast his lot with the Confederacy "at the first tap of the drum." He enl. along with other recruits of Capt. William Ragsdale on Aug. 1, 1861, at Knoxville. He was named as asst. Q.M. for 4TN Cav. Bn. He was still serving as Q.M. and as paymaster the following August when he resigned from the army. He said he was doing so because he and others "recently contracted to make salt for the people of this state." Dent, before the war, was a railroad contractor who came to HC in the late 1840s to build the Western and Atlantic Railroad into town. Later, he helped construct the East TN and GA Railroad. After his first wife died, he married Mary Donahoo, sister of the wife of Col. Lewis Shepherd. In 1854, the Dents built a stately two-story home with a tall portico in front on his 250-acre "Bonny Oaks" farm near Tyner. After the war, he built levees on the Mississippi River and eventually moved to Dallas, TX, where he erected the Main Street Railroad. He died at Dallas in 1880.

DENTON, Isaac J.          Co. C, 26TN; 2d Co. D, 1CSA (GA)
Enl. Feb. 2, 1863, Ringgold, GA. Transf. Claimed by 80 TN as deserter, April 1, 1863.

DENTON, James R.    2nd Co. K, 1st CSA Cav.
Enl. July 14, 1862 in HC. Captured at Parker's Gap, Nov. 27, 1863 and imprisoned at Rock Island, IL. Enl. for USA frontier service, Oct. 17, 1864. [RI ledger]

**DENTON, William L.   2nd Co. K, 1st CSA Cav.**
Born c1818, TN. Enl. June 30, 1862 in HC. In 1870 was farming in Ooltewah with wife Martha. In 1910 was res. of Flat Woods Rd. in household of dau., Caldonia Ledford. [1910HC]

**DESHA, Hamilton          4GA Cav**
Born in Richland District, SC June 30, 1848. Enl. 1864 with twin brother Hampton in Murray Co., GA. Baptist. Married (1933) in HC Edith Louise Royal King. Church of Christ. Died Oct. 1, 1935 at res. on Roanoke Ave. and buried CSA Cem. [NBFM2; TWP, 311; CT Oct. 2-3, 1935]

**DESHA, Alexander Hampton          4GA Cav**
Born in Richland District, SC June 30, 1848. Enl. 1864 in Murray Co., GA. Surr. Kingston GA, 1865. To Chattanooga soon after. Baptist. Died Nov. 26, 1933 and buried CSA Cem. [CT Nov. 27, 1933]

**DEVALCOURT, Alex          2nd Co., Washington Artillery of New Orleans.**
Born and raised in New Orleans, he was a 20 year-old clerk when he enl. March 10, 1862. He was detailed to the battalion ordnance train June 20, 1863 and paroled in May, 1865. He moved to Chattanooga after the war where he was a barber and sometime bookkeeper. Member of NBF Camp, 1895-96. Died April 14, 1914 in Birmingham, AL and buried in LA. [NBFM2,4]

**DEVIN, Charles**
Died Nov. 10, 1918 in Chattanooga [NBFM7]

**DEVOTI, John C.   Co C, 2nd KY Cav.**
Clark's Independent Cavalry Co.
Born June 18, 1841 at Geneva [sic], Italy, son of Dumam and Catharine Devoti of Sardinia, Italy. His father was a merchant at Chattanooga prior to the war. Enl. Aug. 31, 1862 at Chattanooga. Orderly for Gen. S.B. Buckner and dispatch bearer at Chickamauga. Captured Dec. 13, 1864 in fight with Stoneman at Kingsport and imp. at Camp Chase. Released May 13, 1865. Awarded Cross of Honor by Gen. A.P. Stewart Chapter, UDC. Died May 9, 1922 at his home on Missionary Ridge. Bachelor. [NBFM2,7; CT May 10, 1922]

**DEWITT, William Henry          Co. I, 28TN**
Born Oct. 24, 1827 in Smith Co., TN, the son of the Rev. Samuel Dewitt and a Mary McWhirter. A school teacher in Macon and Jackson Counties, he studied law and practiced in Carthage. He became a member of the General Assembly, 1855-57 and he served in the Con-federate Congress, 1861-62. Moved to Chattanooga in 1875 where he died April 11, 1896. Married (1847) Emelia Price b. Nov. 18, 1827 and died in 1861 as did two of their children. He married again in 1867 to Elizabeth Wilson in Smith Co. Buried Forest Hills Cemetery. [McBride, TN Gen Assemb.; CT April 12, 1896; GHT, 931-32]

**DIAL, Jonathan Jackson          Co. G, 35GA**
Born at Walton Co., GA, 1845. Married (Milton Co., GA). Wife was Martha C. Yeargin. Enl. Feb. 27, 1862 and badly wounded near Hanover Junction, VA, May 22, 1864. He was an ambulance driver in early 1865 and captured at Amelia Courthouse, April 5, 1865. Released from Point Lookout, June 26, 1865. He died in North Chattanooga, Oct. 6, 1920 and, buried in Tullahoma. [TWP7487; CT Oct 7, 1920]

**DICKERSON, Arthur C. "Jack"   Co. B, 1AL Rifles**
Born in GA, 41yrs. old when enlisting on Feb. 17, 1861 in Eufaula Rifles. Carriage trimmer in Chattanooga in 1887. Married (1888, in Chattanooga) Martha Emeline Burk who had been previously married. Sent to Soldiers Home at Nashville, where he died, Oct. 23, 1912. [NBFM2; TCSH; TWP 5884]

**DICKEY, John P.          Co. G, 43TN; Co. G, 2TN (Ashby's) Cav.**
Born Jan 1, 1844 in Monroe Co., TN. Enl. June, 1862 at Charleston, TN. Afterwards joined Co. G, 2TN (Ashby's) Cav. Captured Aug. 3, 1863 at Danville, KY. Released from prison at close of war. Married Adelia Bates, sister of Creed Bates. Teacher and Methodist minister in Chattanooga for nearly 50 years. Died at Los Angeles. [NBFM2; CT Feb. 28, 1912]

**DICKINSON, Laurence Thomsen   Co. A, 2VA (1MD) Cav.**
Born June 21, 1843 in Cumberland Co., MD, son of William T. and Laetitia Jones Dickinson, he enl. Aug. 25, 1862. After Sharpsburg, his company became part of a MD cav. battalion and served as scouts and couriers for Gen. Richard S. Ewell in the Gettysburg campaign. He was wounded at Morton's Ford, Oct. 11, 1863 and captured at Brandy Station. He was imprisoned at the Old Capitol prison and at Point Lookout. Upon his exchange, he rejoined the MD cav. bn. and saw constant duty from Beaver Dam to Yellow Tavern. He participated in Early's invasion of MD and was severely wounded in right shoulder at Frederick July 7, 1864 and captured again while in hospital and imprisoned at Point Lookout. He was exchanged again at Savannah in Dec., 1864, returned to Richmond, but was too ill for field service. Finally had minnie ball removed eighteen months after war.

After the war (Oct. 15, 1867) he married Mamie Hill Tidball and engaged in leather manufacturing. They moved to Chattanooga in 1881 where he became supt. of the United States Leather Co. and president of the Board of Education. Episcopalian. Member of NBF Camp, 1895-96. Died March 31, 1923 in Keokuk, IA and buried CSA Cem. [CT Aug. 1, 1916; CV 2:207; NBFM4,7; Hist. St. Paul's, 173]

DICKS, Joseph          Co. A, 1SC
          Born Apr. 22, 1845 in Barnwell Dist., SC. Enl. Feb., 1862 in Co. A, 1SC. Army of Northern Virginia . Wounded at Sharpsburg and Gettysburg. Captured at Gettysburg. Released Sept. 1, 1863. Surr. Appomatox April 9, 1865. Married (1866) Emma I. Eubanks. Methodist and lived for some time in Williston, SC. Carpenter in St. Elmo. He died March 27, 1901 at res. on East 4th St. and buried CSA Cem. [TWP3492; CT March 28, 1901; NBFM2]

DICKSON, Cpl. Mike     Clark's Independent Cav. Co.
          Enl. Aug. 31, 1862 at Chattanooga. Aug. 31, 1863 reduced from Cpl. to sentinel by order Capt. Clark.

DICKSON, Richard West     Co. E, 35AL; Co. H, 31TN Mounted Inf.
          Born Greenville, TN, Nov. 28, 1843, and raised there. Fought in 12 battles including the siege of Port Hudson and Baker's Creek. Captured in Sept., 1864 following the Battle of Piedmont and imp. Fort Delaware. Unmarried. Presbyterian. Lived at Tunnel Hill, GA, then moved to Chattanooga in 1876, but "has never been able since the war to make a support." Died May 29, 1920 and buried White Oak Cem. [CT May 30, 1920; TP10,393]

DICKSON, Thomas     Clark's Independent Cav. Co.
          Enl. April 1, 1862 at Bridgeport, AL. Appt. 4th Cpl., June, 1862. Transf. to Clark's Co., Oct. 7, 1863. Roll for April 30, 1864 shows him present. [Henderson, p. 302]

DIE, Joseph          Co. L, 35TN
          Enl. Jan. 9, 1862 at Chattanooga.

DIETZ, OSWALD
          Born Wiesbaden, Germany, May 27, 1822, he studied at Karlsruhe, Munich and Berlin. Left Germany in 1848. Became an engineer in CSA army. Lived in AL, 1868-70, then to Chattanooga where he became City Engineer, 1876-80. Moved to Cincinnati in 1881 where he died March 9, 1898. [CT03S]

DILL, John Calvin "Cal"     Co. E, 62TN
          Born Polk Co., Jan. 13, 1839. Enl. Aug., 1862.

Vicksburg, Snyder's Bluff, Big Black. Captured at Vicksburg., paroled and exchanged but never returned to duty. Took USA oath, March 8, 1864. Res. in Harrison. Farmer, 1910 James Co., with wife Narcissus (m. 1861). Died March 12, 1928 at home of son J.D. Dill, near Harrison and buried McDonald Cem. [TP14,598; CT March 13, 1928]

DILL, Thomas H.          G Co., 3d TN Mounted Inf. (Lillard's)
          Born Athens, TN c1844. Enl. Nov. 20, 1861. Engineeer in Chattanooga. Moved to Dalton in 1891. [NBFM2,7]

DILLAHUNTY, James          Co. B, 1TN Cav. (Carter's)
          Killed in action Sept., 1862.

DILLARD, James M.          5TN Cav.
          Died Nov. 12, 1912 at his res. on Fort St. and buried Forest Hills Cemetery. [CT Nov. 13, 1912]

DILLARD, John          19TN
          Died July 12, 1913 and buried CSA Cem. [NBFM7; CT July 13, 1897]

DIVINE, Charles W.          Co. B, 2AR
          Born Montreal, Can. Jan. 1, 1849. Fought at Lookout Mtn. and Missionary Ridge. Carpenter in Chattanooga. Died Nov. 10, 1918 in Chattanooga and buried in CSA Cem. [CT Nov. 11, 1918; NBFM2]

DIVINE, John Lowry
          Employed by the CSA as guide and purchasing agent, he was captured after the battle of Missionary Ridge and placed in the prison at Fourth and Market. Later, he was released on parole through the influence of his former neighbor, William Crutchfield. Divine was a pioneer settler at Ross's Landing. Born in 1818 at Maryville, he was the son of Irish immigrants, Patrick and Mary O'Connor Divine. He married Elizabeth Williams first and then Rachel James. His widow Rachel V. Divine b. Oct. 7, 1841 was a member of the U.D.C. and stated that their "house was home for all passing soldiers." He built up a substantial fortune in real estate, livestock trading and a flouring mill. The Divine home was on West Ninth St. [UDC1 pg 114]

DOAK, John Valentine
          Died during war.

DOBBINS, Robert A.     2nd Co. K, 1st CSA Cav.
          Enl. Sept. 24, 1862 in HC. Captured near Graysville, GA in March, 1864 on scouting mission within Federal lines. Took USA oath, March 15, 1864. He resided in HC and had a light complexion, light hair,

blue eyes, and was 5'11" tall.

DOBBINS, William - Co. A, 5th (McKenzie's) TN Cav.
Enl. Aug. 24, 1861 at Camp Cumming. Age 25 on March 11, 1864 roll. Served throughout war and paroled May 3, 1865 at Charlotte, NC.

DOBBS, James M.          Co. H, 2TN Cav. (Ashby's)
Born c1822 in GA, son of David and Elizabeth McMullen Dobbs who moved from Elbert Co., GA to Cobb Co., GA before coming to TN. Married Maria Stanley. Major, Cobb's Co., Georgia Rangers, Mexican War. Conductor on first Western and Atlantic Railroad train that arrived in Chattanooga, Dec., 1849. Dobbs had farm and estate with a value of $48,000 at Chattanooga (near Rossville), 1860. Enl. Feb. 11, 1861 at Chattanooga. Died Sept. 10, 1869. [Goodspeed, HC, p. 933]

DOBBS, Sgt. Joseph D. Co. H, 2TN Cav. (Ashby's);
Co. A, 4TN Cav.
Born Feb. 2, 1840 in Cobb Co. GA, son of James M. and Maria Stanley Dobbs. Educated at the military school in Marietta, GA and Burrett College. Married (1858) Nancy Roberts, and was farm laborer, 1860. Enl. June 17, 1861 at Knoxville. Member of County Court, 1882-1894 and chairman of workhouse commission. Built first pike road with convicts. Under his prodding, roads built on Walden's Ridge and to Rossville. 1910 res. in household of son-in-law Albert Gifford. Unemployed. Died May 29, 1911. [GHT, 933; 1860HC; 1910HC; CT May 30, 1911]

DOBBS, Reuben T.
Born c1817 in SC. 1870 Chattanooga policeman, wife Jane. Died Jan. 9, 1899 [CT Jan 10, 1899]

DOBSON, E. J.          Co K, 22NC
Born 1836. Paroled at Appomattox. Died at res. on Gillespie St., March 5, 1903. Buried CSA Cem. [NBFM7]

DODD, Henry Clay "Clay"     Co. C, 23TN
Born July 31, 1843 near Liberty, DeKalb Co., GA. Attended Mt. Vernon College in Wilson Co. Enl. Aug. 4, 1861 at Camp Trousdale. Shiloh, Corinth. Discharged 1862 underage. Married (1866) Aratia Missie Griffith. Presbyterian. Res. on 14th St. in 1928. Died in Chattanooga May 29, 1928 and buried Forest Hills Cemetery. [TWP, 259; TP6103; CT May 30, 1928]

DODD, James W.          Co. K, 31TN
Born Anderson Dist. SC, Nov. 9, 1823. Enl. March 2, 1862. Disabled from typhoid and disch. March

20, 1863. Took USA oath because his section near Athens under martial law. In 1900 lived in HC near Dayton, an invalid, almost blind, supported by children. He died 20 March 1914 and is buried in the Salem Baptist Church Cemetery in Rhea County, TN. His wife Mary was born March 19, 1825 and died Sept. 18, 1897. In the 1880 Rhea Co. Census he is listed with six children varying in ages from 14 to 33 years of age. [TP2909]

DODGE, ALVIN
Died Dec. 11, 1907, age 71, in Chattanooga and buried Forest Hills Cem. [CT, Dec. 14, 1907]

DODSON, Maj. Elijah Mosely     2d Co. D, 1CSA (GA)
Co. B, 36GA       (Villepigue's)
Born in Dekalb Co., GA, Feb. 20, 1835, son of Samuel and Rebecca Gardner Dodson, he was in the thick of the fighting at Snodgrass Hill and Missionary Ridge. "Shot through the head just below the brain at Missionary Ridge." Wounded and permanently disabled at Kennesaw Mountain, June 19, 1864. After the war he practiced law in Ringgold, GA, and served in the GA Legislature. In 1871, he moved his law practice to Chattanooga. He was one of the founders of the Central Baptist Church. Dodson helped develop Sherman Heights in East Chattanooga, and Dodson Avenue was named for him. He was active in the early years of the Chickamauga and Chattanooga National Military Park. Married Frances Garmany, June, 1866. He died April 21, 1904 in Chattanooga, and was buried Forest Hills Cemetery. [J. Wilson Chattanooga's Story, CT April 22, 1904; FHR; NBFM4]

DONALDSON, William E.     Co. F, 1TN (Turney's)
Born Aug. 25, 1842 in Franklin Co., TN. Grew up on farm near Belvedere. Enl. at Winchester Apr. 11, 1861. Wounded four times including Gaines Mill and Fredericksburg. Captured at close of war. Studied law and practiced Winchester (1870), then Scottsboro, AL, then Jasper (1877). Elected dist. atty for 6th Judicial Circuit, 1896 and served until 1902. Married Nannie Graham, sister-in-law of Peter Turney. Invalid last 15 years of life from war wounds. Member NBF Camp, 1896. Died in Chattanooga Apr. 20, 1919 and buried in Jasper. [NBFM2; CT Jan. 21, 1919]

DONOHOO, Joseph     Co. H, 2TN Cav. (Ashby's)
Died Aug., 1862 [Lindsley]

DOOLEY, Martin V.     2d Co. K, 1CSA (GA)
Disch. since last muster, Knoxville by order Gen. Sam Jones. Enl. July 31, 1863, Chattanooga. Captured Nov. 25, 1863 at Missionary Ridge and imp. Rock Island. Enl. USN and transferred to Naval resid. at

Camp Douglas, Jan. 25, 1864. May have been in 37TN.

DORRIS, William Willis     22TN Cav. (Nixon's)
        Born Benton Co., TN, Feb. 14, 1843, he enl. spring, 1862 in Napier's Bn. which became Williams Co., Col. Nixon's regiment. In battle of Murfreesboro and was captured at Moulton, AL, April, 1864 and imprisoned at Rock Island for nine months. Immediately after war "made a crop" then entered mercantile business. Married (1868) Susan Ellen Allen. With Singer Sewing Machine Co. for over 30 years. Presbyterian. Died May 23, 1935 in Chattanooga and buried Chattanooga Memorial Park. [NBFM2; TWP, 310; CT May 24-25, 1935]

DORSEY, John R.  Co. F, 4GA
        Born May 11, 1839 in Bartow Co. GA. Wounded in Wilderness, May 5, 1864. Presbyterian. Merchant in Chattanooga in 1888. Died Jan. 2, 1917 at res. (home for 34 years) on Bessie St. and buried Forest Hills Cemetery. [CT Jan. 3, 1917; FHR; NBFM2,7]

DOUGLAS, Charles M.  Co. H, 4TN Cav; 2TN Cav.

DOUGLAS (DOUGLASS), Cpl. James K. P.    Barry's Btry.
        Enl. March 6, 1863 at Pollard, AL; paroled May 11, 1865; res, Banks Co., GA. [Brown's Diary]

DOUGLAS, Silas M.        Co. H, 4TN Cav.
        Died 1864.

DOUGLAS, William C.      2nd Co. K, 1st CSA Cav.
        Born 1844 in TN, he enl. July 14, 1862, then was captured at Chickamauga. His father, the Rev. Hiram Douglas of Ooltewah, was a prominent Unionist. He went to Gen. George Thomas in Chattanooga and was able to gain the release of William C. Douglas as well as Luke Arnett, who had married a daughter of Rev. Douglas. War records say that W. C. Douglas deserted in Ooltewah Valley on Sept. 26, 1863 and took USA oath. His mother was Caroline Warnock. The Douglas family sold their 200 acre farm at Ooltewah and moved to Arkansas along with the Arnetts after the war. [J. Wilson Douglas family; 1860 HC Census]

DOUTHIT, Anthony "Tony" C.      Barry's Btry.
        He was born in c1839 in Lincoln Co., TN and enl. April 25, 1862 at Chattanooga in Co G AL Inf.; captured at Atlanta on Sept. 2, 1864, and imprisoned at Camp Douglas, IL. On March 26, 1865, he enl. in Co. F of the Sixth USA Volunteers and in Dec. 1865 was sent to Bridger, Utah, but deserted. In 1892, he filed for a pension but was denied due to desertion. His father, Ira Ellis Douthit, was a Baptist minister at Chattanooga

prior to the war. His mother was Nancy Crofford Douthit. He was about 22 when he joined Barry's Battery, and was involved in railroading prior to the war. He married Emmily C. Sheppard in 1882 in Obion Co., TN.

DOUTHIT, James H. S.            Barry's Btry.
        Enl. Feb. 1, 1864 at Morton, MS; paroled May Nov.11, 1865 at Meridian, MS. He was another of the sons of Ira Ellis and Nancy Crofford Douthit born on 12 Feb 1846 in Lincoln Co., now Moore Co., TN. He filed for a pension in 1907 in Sequatchie Co. TN.

DOWLING, William       Co. A, 16MS
        Ran away from home in Queen's Co., Ireland at age 13 and outbreak of war found him in MS. Following the war he came to Chattanooga and was employed by the US govt., then erected the first brick kiln in the city. Became a contractor and built the old courthouse, the auditorium for the University of Chattanooga, and the first three-story building in the city. He married (1867) Mary Sullivan (1848-1925). Catholic. Died March 4, 1916, age 76, at res. on West 3rd St. and buried at Mt. Olivet. [CT March 5, 1916]

DOWNING, John S.       Co. K, 43TN
        Captured at Winchester, TN Aug. 9, 1863; imprisoned at Camp Chase.

DOWNS, Thomas J.  Co. B, 1TN Cav. (Carter's)
        Enl. Aug. 7, 1861 in Cleveland.

DOYAL, J. H.           53GA
        Born Sept., 1836 in Walton Co., GA and enl. at Griffin, GA, April, 1862. Wounded at Gettysburg on July 2, 1863 and captured. Released March, 1864. Died March 31, 1917 at Glass St. and buried in Hooker, GA. [CT April, 1, 1917; NBFM2; TP6420]

DOYLE (DOIL), John     Co. D, 37TN
        Enl. Sept. 1, 1862 and was transferred the following July to a dismounted cavalry unit. Records show he deserted Oct. 19, 1863, at Missionary Ridge.

DOYLE, Cpl. John Charles  Co. H, 2TN Cav. (Ashby's)
        Born Dec. 19, 1836, son of James P. and Mahala Childress Doyle, he moved with his family to Ringgold in 1845 and in 1856 to Kansas. There Doyle's father and two brothers were murdered by John Brown and when Brown was to be hanged in 1859, Gov. Wyse of VA gave him the privilege of springing the trap of the gallows which Doyle declined.
        *To John Brown the Commander of the Army of Harper's Ferry, Charlestown, Jefferson Co., VA, Care of Jailor, Charlestown.*

*Chattanooga, Tenn., Nov. 20, 1859.  John Brown - Sir: Although vengeance is not mine, I confess that I do feel gratified to hear that you were stopped in your fiendish career at Harper's Ferry, with the loss of your two sons. You can no appreciate my distress in Kansas, when you then and there entered my house at midnight and arrested my husband and two boys, and took them out of the yard, and in cold blood shot them dead in my hearing. · You can't say you done it to free our slaves; we had none and never expected to own one, but has only made me a poor disconsolate widow, with helpless children. While I feel for your folly, I do hope and trust you will meet your just reward. Oh! How it pained my poor heart to hear the dying groans of my husband and children. If this scrawl gives you any consolation, you are welcome to it.*

*Mahala Doyle*

*N.B. My son John Doyle, whose life I begged of you, is now grown up, and is very desirous to be at Charlestown on the day of your execution; would certainly be there if his means would permit, that he might adjust the rope around your neck, If Gov. Wise would permit.  M.D.*

*(A party of gentlemen at once subscribed the amount, but the letter being detained, it was ascertained young Doyle could not arrive in time.)*

Doyle enl. June 17, 1861 at Knoxville. He was detailed as a teamster at one time and at another was sick in the hospital. Paroled April 1865. After serving four years under Wheeler and Ashby, Doyle located in Rome, GA and married (1867) Cleopatra Ann Clowdis. They moved to Chattanooga in 1896. He died at res. on E. 10th St., Dec. 29, 1922 and was buried CSA Cem. [TWP, 223; CT Dec. 30, 1922; TP8499]

DRAKE, George M.
Described by Chattanooga historian Charles McGuffey as a "practical printer, careful scholar, forceful and eccentric man, with strong convictions," he worked for the Chattanooga Commercial, then was in journalism in Knoxville. He worked in the Post Office in Washington, DC, then retired on Lookout Mtn. He married Mary Clarke (1860, Union Springs, AL). Mrs. Drake was born in AL and buried Forest Hills Cemetery. [CT July 26, 1915; CT July 30, 1933]

DRAKE, George W.        Co. E, 4VA Cav.
Born April 4, 1842 in Powhatan Co., VA, son of Samuel B. and Sarah J. Ball Drake. Attended Richmond College and joined Powhatan Troop, Stuart's Cavalry with which he fought at Bull Run and until he was badly wounded near Spottsylvania. After war studied medicine at Vanderbilt, graduating in 1876, after which he practiced in Chattanooga and was President, TN

Medical Society, 1896. Married (1) Elmira Wood, (2) Laura Whitehead. Mason. Surgeon, NBF Camp, 1894. Moved to FL, then to Kansas City where he died Nov. 3, 1916. [CT April 16, 1896, Nov. 4, 1916; GHT 934; NBFM7]

DRAKE, James A.        McClung's Lt. Arty. Btry.
Born Iron City, TN, 1837. 1910 res. in house hold of son John H. on Evans St. Died May 9, 1914 in HC and buried CSA Cem. [CT May 10, 1914; 1910HC]

DUCKWORTH, D. Frank        Co. B, 5TN (McKenzie's) Cav.
Born March 10, 1849 in Rhea Co., son of John and Rebecca Snow Duckworth enl. Aug. 1, 1861 in Knoxville. Fishing Creek, wounded at Chickamauga, Wheeler's TN Raids. Atlanta Campaign, Carolinas Campaign, paroled at Charlotte, NC, May 3, 1865. To TX immediately after war and picked cotton and drove cattle before returning to TN, 1868. Common laborer. Died March 6, 1924 in Chattanooga and buried CSA Cem. [TP14318; NBFM2]

DUDLEY, Christopher Columbus "Chris"    Co. K, 4TN
Born 1844 in Jackson Co., AL. Wounded at Murfreesboro and captured on retreat out of TN, 1863. Imp. at Rock Island till end of war. Married (1874) Catherine Gullatt. Also married Nannie M. Died 1908 in HC. [TWP, p. 66; TP5837]

DUDLEY, 2Lt. J. R.        Clark's Independent Cav. Co.
Enl. July 16, 1861 at Camp Boone, TN. Deserted Nov. 25, 1863 near Chattanooga.

DUGGER, Benjamin Franklin        Co. G, 21TN Cav. (Carter's)
Born 1825 in NC. Farmer at Harrison with wife Jane H. and four children. [1860HC]

DUGGER, J. A.
Born 1845, GA. Res. 1910 a liverlyman in Soddy with wife M. L. [1910HC]

DUITT, Thomas        Co. A, 19TN
Killed in front of Atlanta, 1864.

DUNCAN, C. H.        Co. H, 26TN; 2d Co. I, 1CSA (GA)
Enl. July 25, 1861, Knoxville. Left sick at Cumberland City, Feb. 12, 1862. Absent without leave July 29-Aug. 3, 1863. Hospitalized Sept. 15, 1863. Absent sick, June 30, 1864; deserted hospital, Aug. 31, 1864.

DUNCAN, Daniel Lewis        Co E Wise's Legion,

59VA Inf. and Dunn's Bn.
        Born Dec. 22, 1834 in Amherst Co., VA. Attended UVA. Teaching at Allegheny College, Blue Springs, VA when war broke out and enl. there. Fought at Sewell Mtn., Kanawha Valley, Cotton Hill, Meadow Bluff, Lewisburg, Jackson's River, Giles Courthouse, Newburg, Jonesville and Fulton's Depot. To Barboursville, Cabell Co., VA [now WV], where he married in 1870 Ida J. McCorkle, born 1855. Lived in WV, KY, MS, MS, LA, AL before moving to TN in 1885. Baptist. Contractor for coal, coke and iron in Chattanooga Baptist. Died Jan. 7, 1929 at res. on N. Boynton and buried Forest Hills Cemetery. [NBFM4,8; TWP9408; CT Jan. 8, 1929; UCD1]

DUNCAN, Isaac N.      1st Co. H, 26TN; 2d Co. I, 1GA CSA (GA)
        Pvt. Feb. 16, 1863. Served under Bragg in operations around Chattanooga. Deserted, 1863 and took USA oath at Louisville, Dec. 16, 1863. and released. Light complexion, brown hair, grey eyes, 5'1 ½ tall" Name appears on USA oath, March 10, 1864, Chattanooga Baptist. Resided in Walker Co. Died March 9, 1920 at home near Chickamauga, GA and buried Chickamauga Cem. [CT March 10, 1920]

DUNCAN, John E. "Red John"    Co. F, 3TN Mtd. Inf. (Lillard's)
        Born 1835, Blount Co. Wounded Wautauga River near Carter's Station. Paroled Kingston, GA, 1865. Wife was Martha Elizabeth. To Chattanooga in 1903. [TP7494]

DUNCAN, Joshua        Co. H, 26TN
        Enl. July 14, 1861, Knoxville. Left sick at Cumberland City, TN, Feb. 12, 1862.

DUNCAN, Robert        Co. H, 26TN
        Enl. Sept. 8, 1861, Knoxville. Left sick Nashville, 1861.

DUNCAN, Thomas A.      Barry's Btry.
        Enl. April 4, 1862 at Chattanooga; captured Spanish Fort, April 8 1865; imp. Ship Island, MS.

DUNGEY, Henry (Harry)    Co. H, 2TN Cav. (Ashby's)
        Enl. June 17, 1861 at Knoxville. Was farrier for William Ragsdale's Company, then detailed as a butcher. Captured Somerset, KY March 30, 1863 and imp. at Louisville, then sent to City Point for exchange. Age listed as 50 in 1864. Paroled April, 1865. Died in TX, 1886, and buried CSA Cem.[NBFM2]

DUNLAP, William A.      Co. A, 19TN
        Enl. May 20, 1861 in Knoxville. He was killed at Fishing Creek on Jan. 19, 1862.

DUNN, William W.      Co. B, Cobb's Legion
        Born in NC in 1831, he enl. Sept. 1, 1861 at Atlanta. Wounded at Culpeper Court House and captured at Salisury, NC. Disch. at Camp Chase, June, 1865. Married (1865) Martha J. Stowers. A tailor in Chattanooga in 1886, William died Oct. 22, 1905 at the age of 73 and was buried in CSA Cem. Member of NBF Camp, 1895-96.[CT Oct. 23, 1905; June 10, 1920; NBFM2]

DURHAM, Arch D.      Co. H, 4TN Cav.
        Died in GA, 1864.

DURHAM, Sgt. James      Co. I, 26TN
        His daughter Dixie D. Kelley was born March 30, 1881 in Roane Co., TN. [UDC1 pg 123]

DURHAM, John      Co. D, 4GA Cav.; 12GA Cav.
        Member of Ervin Durham family of Crown Point, Marion Co. Brothers Archibald and Daniel also CSA but believed to have lived in Marion. Durham was buried at Suck Creek Cem. [J. Wormsley info]

DUTTON, T. A.      Co. A, 21VA; 1AL
        Born June 30, 1848; died Nov. 25, 1933.

DYER, D. W.    Co. G, 26TN; 2d Co. K, 1CSA (GA)
        Enl. July 8, 1861, Knoxville. Captured Fort Donelson and imp. Camp Morton, IN. Exchanged and disch. Oct. 13, 1862. Enl. May 1, 1863, Tullahoma, TN. Captured Sept. 11, 1863 near Chattanooga "Desires to be released at Nashville. Has taken Oath of Allegiance."

DYER, John C.    Clark's Independent Cav. Co.
        Enl. Aug. 31, 1862 at Chattanooga; farrier.

DYER, John (James) J.      11KY Cav.; Clark's Independent Cav. Co.
        Born in Walker Co., GA, Sept. 28, 1846, and enl. Aug. 20, 1863 at Knoxville in Co. C, 2Bn., 11 KY Cav. Also served in Clark's Independent Cav. Co. Captured May 12, 1865 at Macon, GA. Blacksmith in Chattanooga [NBFM2]

DYER, 2Lt. Spill B.      Co. H, 37TN
        Born Feb. 4, 1828, Rhea Co., TN; probably was a son of R. H. and Caron Dyer of Chattanooga; married March 6, 1850 to Pellina Ellender Parker at Lytel, GA. She was born Feb. 10, 1833 in Meigs Co., and died Oct. 15, 1903 at Chickamauga, GA. He enl. Sept. 17, 1861 at Knoxville; enl. Jan. 25, 1863 in Clark's Independent Cav. Co. at Tullahoma, TN. Wife Ellen and 6 children. He died March 10, 1905, Chickamauga, GA [1860HC;

CSA Patriot Index; UCD2 pg 159]

DYSMANY, 3d Lt. John       Co. H, 4TN Cav.
    Enl. Aug. 11, 1861 at Chattanooga.

# E

EAKIN, Albert       Co. F, 41TN
    Born July 13, 1843 in Bedford Co., son of John and Lucretia Pearson Eakin. Educated at Yale and came home to enlist. Captured at Fort Donelson and when exchanged became commissary in Wheeler's cavalry command. Married (1865) Cyrena Buford and in 1868 entered grain business in Shelbyville. He went to Nashville in 1881, after the death of his wife and married Laura Dayton born 19 May 1845. They came to Chattanooga in 1882 and established a grain company and elevator. Died Chattanooga, July 6, 1891 and buried Forest Hills Cemetery. [GHT, 937; UDC1 pg 124.]

EAKIN, Alexander L. (1860 census says Aiken)       Co. K, 43TN
    He was a laborer on the Baker farm at Zion Hill south of Ooltewah prior to enlisting Oct. 17, 1861. He enl. at Ooltewah. He was born c1834.

EAKIN (AIKEN), Col. William Lyle       1st (Eakins) East TN Cav. Bn., 59TN Mounted Inf.
    Born in Blount Co., Jan. 25, 1824, he attended Hiwassee College, then practiced law in Madisonville prior to the war. Married (1854) Jane Vaughn Dyer, sister of Gen. John C. Vaughn. Engaged in April, 1862, as commander of Eakins Bn. with instructions "to arrest all Union leaders who circulate exaggerated reports of the military draft, thereby inducing ignorant men to fly their homes to Kentucky." He and Col. J.B. Cooke organized the 59TN in May, 1862. Part of A. W. Reynolds' Brigade in Oct., 1862. Captured at Vicksburg. Captured at Battle of Piedmont, June 5, 1864, he was imprisoned over a year at Johnson's Island. Came to Chattanooga from Madisonville in 1866 and became a judge. Died Oct. 19, 1908 at his home on McCallie Ave. and buried Forest Hills Cemetery. [FHR; CT Sept. 26, 1904; Jan. 13, 1908; Oct. 20, 1908; Nov. 6, 1910; 1890VetCensus]

EARP, S. Wesley
    Enl. May 20, 1862 in Barry's Btry. at Chattanooga; deserted Feb. 6, 1863. [Brown's Diary]

EAST, A. J.
    Served under Stonewall Jackson and was captured at the Wilderness. Resident of Chattanooga

about 25 yrs., woodworker for Chattanooga Coffin Co. Died June 2, 1915 at his home on Missionary Ridge and buried in Rockville, IN. [CT June 3, 1915]

EAVES, C. R.

EAVES, John F.       Co. C, 8GA BN
    Born June 29, 1845 in Union Dist., SC and enl. at Cass Station, GA, Jan. 1, 1862. Paroled May, 1865 at Kingston, GA. Merchant res. in St. Elmo in 1888. Died Dec. 25, 1909 at his home at Jessup, GA. Body returned to Chattanooga by train for burial CSA Cem. Survived by second wife and nine children. [NBFM2; TP5859; CT Dec. 27, 1909]

EBLIN, J.       Barry's Btry.
    Deserted. [Brown's Diary]

ECKLES, John T.       11GA; 5GA Cav.
    Born Social Circle, Walton Co., GA. c1840. Enl. June, 1861 in 11GA, contracting rheumatism during Chickmauga camp. Which led to his discharge. Re-enl. in 5GA Cav (Avery's) in Forrest's command. Traveling salesman for Chattanooga Plow. Married (1863) Susan Zuber. Died March 8, 1899 and buried Forest Hills Cemetery. [FHR; CT Mar. 9, 1899; NBFM2; 1890VetCensus]

EDGEMAN, Bart       Clark's Independent Cav. Co.
    Born 1847, TN. Enl. Nov. 25, 1863 at Charleston, TN. Courier for Gen. Buckner. Farmer in James Co., 1910 with wife Malinda P.

EDMONDS, M. A.(J.)       Co. B, 1TN Cav. (Carter's)
    Enl. Sulphur Springs, in Rhea Co. TN, April 15, 1862 in Capt. Burton Leuty's Co. [Allen 1995:9]

EDWARDS, Benson L.       Co. F, 35TN
    Born c1821 in NC, he was a farmer living near Tyner at the start of the war. His children were Delia, Priscilla, Thomas, David, Noah, Temperance and Leatha. The family first lived in GA after leaving NC about 1850. He enl. Aug. 10, 1863, at Tyner's Station and was killed at Chickamauga on Sept. 20, 1863.

EDWARDS, Clayborne       Barry's Btry.
    Enl. June 27, 1863 at Bate's Bluff, MS; deserted Feb. 3, 1864 near Demopolis, AL. [Brown's Diary]

EDWARDS, J. B.       Co. B, 1TN Cav. (Carter's)
    Born c1840 in TN, he was a blacksmith at Ooltewah before the war, and was used by the army for blacksmithing. Enl. Aug. 7, 1861 in Cleveland, he was court martialed on Jan. 24, 1863. His wife, Easter J., was from Indiana. [1860 HC Census]

EDWARDS, James L.          Co. K, 43TN
          Enl. Oct. 17, 1861 at Ooltewah.

EDWARDS, Lt. James S.    Co. A, 4TN Cav.
          He was one of the Chattanooga merchants who
joined the unit of fellow storeowner William Ragsdale.
He also served as a lieutenant in the 19TN Infantry. Born
in VA in 1815, he had come to Chattanooga (then Ross's
Landing) in 1835 in a wagon train from Leesburg. One
of his ventures was Edwards Pills "for the relief of chills
and fever." He was a Chattanooga alderman on several
occasions prior to the war. He lost much of his estate due
to the war. Edwards died June 10, 1897 at the home of
his son-in-law, William Lauter, at Bluff View. Burial
was in Citizens Cem. [CT June 11, 1897]

EDWARDS, Robert D.          2nd Co. K, 1st CSA Cav.
          Born 1834, SC. Merchant at Chattanooga, 1860,
with wife Martha. $2,400/4,000 assets. Enl. Aug. 15,
1862 in HC. [1860HC]

EIDSON, Edward          Co. D, 4th (12th) GA Cav.
          He enl. Oct. 4, 1862. He was absent at the end
of Nov., 1863 and was believed to be in the hands of the
enemy. An engineer, he was born about 1833 in Georgia.
He and his wife, Elizabeth, were living in Chattanooga
at the start of the war and was a machinists at
Wauhatchie, 1870.

ELDER, Samuel Houston          2nd Co. K, 1st CSA Cav.
          Born c1838, son of Robert S. and Matilda Elder
of Limestone. He married Sarah H. White. Enl. Sept. 23,
1862 in HC. He and brother Robert had store boat that
made calls at various river landings as well as general
store at Snow Hill. Postmaster of Long Savannah. Died
March 19, 1910 of heart attack while walking from
Avondale to Snow Hill. Found dead on country road
March 19, 1910 near Harrison by farmer. Mason. Buried
Forest Hills Cemetery. At time of death living with dau.
Mrs. A.E. Smith in Highland Park. [CT Mar 21, 1910;
1860HC]

ELDRIDGE, G. C.
          Died about July 3, 1888 in Chattanooga,
destitute. Former CSA soldier.

ELKINS, William J. H.          Barry's Btry.
          Enl. May 7, 1862 at Chattanooga; $50 bonus;
lost in Feb. on retreat. [Brown's Diary]

ELLEDGE, William Jarrett
          Enl. Jan. 9, 1862 in Co. L, 36TN at
Chattanooga; transferred to 35TN. In battle of
Murfreesboro, but deserted July 4, 1863 and took USA
oath.

ELLEN, G. H.          24GA
          [TP15,000]

ELLER, Columbus C.    Clark's Independent Cav. Co.;
Co. I, 19TN
          Enl. Aug. 31, 1862 at Chattanooga, TN. Courier
for Gen. B.R. Johnson, April 25, 1864.

ELLER, Hampton          Co. H, 4TN Cav.

ELLIS, David Judson          26TN; Co. A, 5TN Cav.
(McKenzie's)
          He was living prior to the war near Tyner with
his mother, Catharine Ellis, and his four brothers and
one sister. The family was living in York District SC
when he was born 12 Sept. 1837. They lived in GA prior
to moving to HC in the late 1840s. Catharine Ellis
operated a farm herself for many years prior to the war.
Judson Ellis and his older brother, John Ellis, were
merchants. David married 10 Nov. 1867 in Hamilton Co.
Josie G. Smith who was born 27 Nov 1844 in Hamilton
Co., and died 24 Feb. 1911 in Decherd, TN.
          His daughter Katherine Ellis [Mrs. W. J. Hines]
states "...that her father enlisted 24 Aug. 1861 at Camp
Cummings, and was discharged 1 Sept. 1862 with a
certificate of disability. Discharged at Knoxville because
of frequent attacks of hoemoptist. He served as a body
guard to Gen. Joe Wheeler at the Battle of Missionary
Ridge." [UDC2 pg 165]

ELLIS, D. M.          1CSA Cav.
          Born in York Dist., SC c1845. Merchant in
Chattanooga Enl 1CSA Cav. [NBFM2] [Probably the
same as David Judson above.]

ELLIS, 2nd Lt. I. D.,    HC Home Guard, April 29, 1861

ELLIS, John E.    Co. H, 2TN Cav. (Ashby's); Co. A,
4TN Cav.
          Born c1837, SC, son of Catherine Ellis of
Tyner's Station; merchant before the war. Enl. June 17,
1861 at Knoxville. Captured Oct. 7, 1863 near
Shelbyville, TN and sent to Louisville, then to Camp
Morton, IN, then to Fort Delaware. Exch. Oct. 14, 1864
and paroled April 1865.

ELLIS, Lorenzo D.          Co. I, 19TN
          Born 1837. Miner in house hold of Jos. Johnson,
Soddy. Enl. May 20, 1861. Deserted May, 1862.

ELLIS, Samuel M.          2d Co. K, 1CSA Cav.
          Born about 1839, he enl. July 14, 1862 in HC in
2nd Co. K, 1CSA Cavalry and was paroled May 3, 1865
in Charlotte, NC. He was one of the sons of G.W. Ellis,
a farm laborer near Chattanooga. After the war became

a prominent merchant at Chickamauga (now Shepherd, TN) and later a merchant in Chattanooga. Member of NBF Camp, 1895-96. Died June 27, 1918 in Chattanooga and buried at Concord Church.

ELLIS, William A.    2nd Co. K, 1st CSA Cav.;
Co. A, 5TN Cav.
Born July 19, 1841 in York Dist, SC. He enl. at Oxford, AL in 1862 and transferred to 5TN Cav. July 1, 1864 in Cobb Co., GA. Paroled May 3, 1865 in Charlotte, NC. He was one of the sons of Catharine Ellis. Member of NBF Camp, 1895-96. Grocery merchant in Chattanooga. Died July 24, 1925 and buried Concord Cem. [NBFM2]

ELLISON, William    Clark's Independent Cav. Co.
Enl. Aug. 31, 1862 at Chattanooga, TN; captured June 27, 1863 at Manchester, TN.

ELY, John Alexander    Co. E, 4KY Cav.
Born Nov. 21, 1844 in Trimble Co., KY. Enl. Sept. 10, 1862 in Trimble Co. Was wounded in Greenville, TN at time Gen. Morgan was killed. Married Ruth Prigmore. Res. Hill City. Truck farmer. Died Jan. 11, 1915 and buried in Red Bank Cem. [NBFM2,4,7; TP 9 Sept. 1927]

EMERSON, James W.    Co. K, 43TN
He enl. Dec. 22, 1861, at Ooltewah. He was among those captured at Vicksburg, MS on July 4, 1863. Prior to the war, he was a farm laborer living at Zion Hill south of Ooltewah. He was born in Georgia c1828. His wife was Sarah.

EMORY, John    Co. A, 4TN Cav. (Murray's)
Born 1815 in TN, son of William and Nancy of Soddy. Farmer at Double Branch. Res. Soddy with wife Nancy, 1860. Enl. June 14, 1863, Chattanooga. Prom. to sgt. [1860, 1870HC]

EMORY, WILLIAM    Co. A, 4TN Cav. (Murray's)
Born 1825 in TN, son of William and Nancy of Soddy.

EPPINS, T. P.    Co. D, 37TN
Died March 26, 1863.

ERWIN, Andrew Jackson    Co. A, 1TN Cav. (Carter's)
Enl. Oct. 5, 1862 at Sulphur Springs, Rhea Co., TN. Married Ella. [TWP1389]

ERWIN, George W.    Barry's Btry
Born 1845, son of William and Saline of Zion Hill. Deserted June-July, 1864. [Brown Diary]

ERWIN, J. B.    Co. A, 2TN Cav. Bn.
Killed in action Dec. 7, 1864.

ERWIN, James C.    Co. H, 2TN Cav. (Ashby's)
Enl. July 18, 1861 at Big Creek. Paroled April, 1865.

ERWIN, Cpl. James L. M.    Barry's Btry.
Enl. Sept. 24, 1862 at Chattanooga. Paroled May 11, 1865 in Meridian, MS. Res. 1910 of Soldiers Home, Atlanta, GA.

ERWIN, William O.    Co. A, 4TN Cav.
Enl. June 17, 1861, when he was 22. He was killed in action on Feb. 20, 1862. He was the son of William and Saline Erwin. The family lived on a farm at Ooltewah.

ESBY, Albert M.    22AL
[TP9174]

ETTER, 3rd Lt. Leonard L.    C Co., 63TN
Born 1828. School teacher res. 1860 in house hold of Michael Marbett.

EVANS, James    Co. A, 19TN
Born 1839 in NC. Res. 1860 in Harrison with wife Mary. [1860HC]

EVANS, Lan
Born 1848, TN. Res. 1910 with wife Nan (married 1872). Blacksmith. [1910HC]

EVANS, Peter Solomon    Co. C, 26TN
Son of Augustus and Mary Ann Sivley Evans. Enl. Oct. 18, 1862 at Taylorsburg.

EVITT, Charles W.    Co. K, 43TN; Co. B, 1TN Cav. (Carter's)
Enl. Oct. 17, 1861, at Ooltewah. Transferred to Co. B, 1TN Cav., June 1, 1862. He was the son of William and Rebecca Evitt. The family had a farm at Ooltewah. William Evitt was from Virginia. Charles and his older brother, Nehemiah Evitt, were blacksmiths. Charles W. Evitt was born about 1839.

EVITT, Sgt. Nehemiah    Co. B, 1TN Cav. (Carter's)
Born c1837. A blacksmith, he enl. Aug. 7, 1861 in Cleveland. Hospitalized at Charlottesville, VA, June, 1864. Married Emiline Andrews Baird. Moved to Walker Co., GA after war where he was blacksmith, merchant and a Baptist preacher. Brutally attacked by Roscoe Marable, an ex-convict, Jan. 17, 1891, and died next day. Marable found guilty of first-degree murder and hanged in Walker Co. [Heritage of Walker Co.]

EWING, 1st Lt. Calvin J.          Co. K, 43TN
In the retreat from Port Gibson across Black River, Capt. J.N. Aikens reported that Ewing, "who was in command of a small company of sappers and miners, in the face of a terrific fire from the advance guard of the enemy, cut up and destroyed the pontoon bridge upon which our army had just crossed the river. It was a daring act, gallantly performed." Before the war, he lived on a farm at Zion Hill south of Ooltewah with his wife Jane, their sons, John and Albert, and daughter, Mary. He had a worth of $10,000 in 1860. He was born about 1821.

# F

FACKLER, Charles W.     Co. K, 4AL Cav., Forrest's
Regt.; Co. F, 3rd TN Cav.
Born Aug. 8, 1836 in Huntsville, Madison Co., AL. Fought in Forrest's Cav. under Cols. Russell and Holman. Captured near Huntsville, AL, in Sept. 1863 and released Feb. 1865. Bill clerk in Chattanooga for Alabama Great Southern RR until moved to watchman on King Street crossing due to poor health. Member NBF Camp, 1895-96. Died Apr. 1, 1900 and buried in Huntsville. [NBFM2; CT April 2, 1900]

FAIDLEY, Archibald

FAIDLEY, Charles Fenton        Co. F, 7 TN Cav. Bn.
Barteau's 2nd TN & Morton's Battery,
Forrest's Cav.
He wrote his wife, Susan Fothergill Faidley, from near Sparta when he joined the Confederate troops, "Take good care of yourself and Annie and hope for the best. I know you have a hard time and so do I, but I will not be gone always. The parting with you and Annie was a hard one with me. I could hardly keep from shedding tears, but you know I never do cry - even if I want to. I think of you and Annie every minute in the day and I know very well that you think of me all the time. When I am at home with you I may appear cold and gloomy, but it is not because I love you less than I always did. For no earthly objects were ever loved better than my wife and child are by me. So you must put your trust in God and hope that we may live a happy and better life yet."
Charles F. Faidley survived the war and returned to his wife and Annie. They later had Dora, Rose and Arch. The Charles Faidleys moved to Walden's Ridge after refugeeing there during the Yellow Fever epidemic of 1878. Charles F. Faidley died several years after this epidemic. [UDC1 pg 134]

FAIDLEY, Edward          Co. C, 7TN Inf.
Son of Archibald and Rosanna Young Faidley. He was only 19 when he enl. Later he was listed on the rolls as a deserter.

FAIDLEY, Henry
He married Matilda Lynch in May, 1863 when he was 23, but then he marched away to war. Four months later, he was among the casualties on the bloody fields of Chickamauga. He was a son of Archibald Faidley, a Virginian who was an early printer at Chattanooga. His mother was Rosanna Young.

FAIDLEY, 2nd Lt. Joseph Gailes - Co. C, 36 TX Cav.
Born in Chattanooga, son of Archibald and Rosanna Young Faidley, he spent his early manhood in TX. Inmate TN Confed. Soldiers' Home, Nov. 17, 1902 and died there in Nashville, Nov. 15, 1917. [CT Nov. 18.17; TCSH]

FAIRBANKS, Richard          Co. F, 35TN
Born in HC c1845, he lived at Snow Hill prior to the war. He was apparently the son of David and Nancy Fairbanks. David Fairbanks, a native of MD, was age 73 in the 1860 census. Nancy Fairbanks, a native of VA, was 56 on the 1860 census. Richard Fairbanks enl. Oct. 19, 1862. He had blue eyes, light hair, fair complexion and was 6' tall.

FARMER, John O.          Barry's Btry.
Born Dec. 7, 1827, SC. Day laborer at Chattanooga, 1860, wife Sarah. Express office worker and watchman, 1870. Wife Sarah and three children. Died July 29, 1879 and buried in Citizens Cem. [1860, 1870HC]

FARMER, Shadrick     Co. H, 26TN; Barry's Btry.
Enl. July 8, 1861, Knoxville; left btry. near Demopolis "before we crossed river." [Brown's Diary]

FARRIS, Charles Ambrose Driscoll     Co. D, 11TN Cav.
Born 1846 in Rutherford Co., TN, son of the Rev. Charles B. Farris. He married (1902) Mary Hubbard and moved to Chattanooga from South Pittsburg where he had been in lumber business for 25 yrs. Methodist. Died Oct. 31, 1923 at res. on Vine St. and buried Murfreesboro, TN. [TWP, 227; CT Nov. 1, 1923]

FARRIS, Hugh Francis "Frank"     Co. E, 26TN
Born Meigs Co., Sept. 2, 1842. His ancestry is said to date back to his great-great-grandfather, Matthew Norman, a lifelong friend of George Washington. Enl. "as a mere boy." Served throughout war (Fort Donelson, Murfreesboro, Chickamauga, Missionary Ridge, Atlanta

Camp., Franklin) and only received slight flesh wound. Captured following Franklin and imp. at Camp Morton. Released at the close of the war, he stopped for water at the home of a widow of a Union veteran who had been killed at Resaca. After speaking with Cynthia A. Maddux Daughtery, he told her he would come back some day and marry her. He did so. Methodist. Mason. Res. Harrison. Died Nov. 12, 1912, age 70, and buried at McCaleb (Maddux) Cem. [CT Nov. 13, 1912; TP13,584]

FARRIS, J. L.          Co. F, 39GA
         Pvt. May 1, 1862. Appt. 1st Cpl. June, 1862. Deserted near Dalton, March 10, 1864. Took USA oath at Chattanooga and releasesd, Mar. 14, 1864. [Henderson, 302]

FARRIS, Jasper          Co. H, 63TN
         Born 1836, TN. Farmer at Long Savannah with wife Elizabeth, 1860. [1860HC]

FAXON, John Wellington          Co. A, 14 TN Inf.
         Born in Buffalo, NY, May 24, 1840, he became a clerk in CSA Treasury for one year, then joined 14TN, serving in this unit until the surrender. Married 22 Dec. 1866 Florence Herring born 28 Nov. 1840 in Clarksville, TN and died 7 Mar. 1920 in Chattanooga. For nearly 18 years on staff of Louisville Courier Journal as Clarksville, TN correspondent. Moved to Chattanooga in 1890. Member of NBF Camp, 1895-96. Employed by First National Bank in Chattanooga and president of Chattanooga Chamber of Commerce. Died in Chattanooga Aug. 22, 1917 and buried in Forest Hills Cem. [CT Aug. 23.1917; FHR; Armstrong, HC; Mickle, Well Known Confederates, p. 38; NBFM2]

FEATHERS, Sgt. Alvin Marion          Co. F, 63TN
         Married Nannie Salena. In Obion Co., 1870. [TWP1977]

FELKINS, Logan          2nd Co. K, 1st CSA Cav.
         Enl. Aug. 13, 1862 in HC. Deserted at Shelbyville, TN, Dec. 10, 1862.

FELKINS, Presley L.          Barry's Btry.
         Enl. at Chattanooga March 16, 1862 and was paroled April 11, 1865, at Meridian, MS. He lived at Tynersville with his wife, Mararitha, and son, Henry, prior to the war.

FELKINS, William L.          Barry's Btry.
         Enl. March 11, 1863 at Chattanooga; Aug.-Oct., 1864 in Ocmulgee Hospital, Macon, GA.

FERGUSON, Sgt. Benjamin H.          Co. F, 35TN
         Age 21 in 1862, he was born in Knox Co. before

moving to Chattanooga where he enl., Oct. 1, 1862. Severely wounded at Chickamauga, he deserted at Tunnel Hill Jan. 19, 1864. Blue eyes, light hair, fair complexion, 5'6" tall. Charter member First Christian Church. Retail grocer, 1870, with wife Dorinda and 4 children. In 1881, he was an engineer on the steamer *Dugger* under Captain Joe F. Thompson, Colin Dugger and Thomas D. Wilkey. They transported iron ore up and down the Tennessee River. At time of death he was the oldest steamboat captain on TN River. Died on his boat and buried Citizens Cem. [CT April 26, 1921]

FERGUSON, James A.          32TN
         Born May 2, 1837 in Warren Co., TN, he enl. July, 1861 in Pulaski, TN. He became a scout for Wheeler and was wounded near Franklin and Columbia and captured at Franklin. He was a boot and shoe maker in Hill City in 1901. Died Aug. 4, 1904. [UCV applications for NBF Camp; CT Aug. 5, 1904]

FERGUSON, Samuel H.          Co. A, 4VA
         Born June 4, 1842 Bedford City, VA. Wounded at 1st and 2d Manassas. Resident of Chattanooga 25 yrs., West 4th St. Real estate dealer. Died Dec. 4, 1917 in Chattanooga and buried Citizens Cem. Wife was Bettie M. (1847-1932) whom he married 1870. [1910HC]

FIELDING, Sgt. Isaac N.          Co. A, 8FL
         Born 1833. Enl. April 1, 1862, Columbia, FL and was reduced soon after enlisting. Slightly wounded Dec. 11, 1862, Fredericksburg and taken to Richmond. Captured July 17, 1863 near Hagerstown, MD and imp. Ft. McHenry. Exch. March 17, 1864. Deserted to USA Aug. 17, 1864 and was sent to Philadelphia, PA. Found dead in his home at Long & Montgomery Sts., Chattanooga, April 12, 1906. [NBFM7]

FIELDING, Thomas J.          Co. F, 14TN
                              [NBFM2]

FIELDS, Sgt. Cornelius          2nd Co. K, 1st CSA Cav.
         Born 1832 in TN. Farm laborer with wife Mary and one child. Enl. Sept. 23, 1862 in HC. Paroled May 3, 1865 in Charlotte, NC. Living on farm at Stringer's Ridge, 1870 with wife Mary and dau. Mary.

FIELDS, John          Co. H, 4TN Cav.
         Born HC 1829, son of Willis Fields. He enl. 1861 and surrendered at Charlotte, in April, 1865. In 1902 res. Hill City, indigent. [TP4458]

FIELDS, John          Co. B, 5TN Cav.
         Born c1838, he was a son of Willis Fields. Enl. Aug. 11, 1861.

FIELDS, 2Lt. Richard     Co. H, 4TN Cav.
Enl. Aug. 11, 1861 at Chattanooga, son of Willis Fields.

FIELDS, Lt. William     Co. H, 4TN Cav.

FILBY, R. R.     Co. H, 26TN; 2d Co. I, 1CSA (GA)
Enl. July 8, 1861, Knoxville. Captured Fort Donelson and imp. Camp Douglas. Trans. 1CSA Nov. 8, 1862; deserted at Chattanooga, Aug. 24, 1863. Captured Chickamauga, Sept. 20, 1863. Took USA oath and released Oct. 16, 1863. Enl. in Union army.

FINE, John A. (TYNE)     Co. F, 3TN Mounted Inf. (Lillard's)
Born Cocke Co., TN, 1838. Captured Vicksburg. Res. Chattanooga in 1907. [TP9026]

FINLEY, WILLIAM     Bird Rangers
Son of Joseph W. Finley who lived near Chickamauga Station. Enl. in 1861 (widower with three small children) and "perished during the war." Sister Nan died in Chattanooga Aug. 6, 1909. [CT Aug. 8, 1909]

FIRSTE (FOSTER), W. H.     Co. F, 39TN
Res. James Co., 1912.

FISCHER, William F.
Born Mecklenburg, Germany, Aug. 19, 1846. Boyhood at Dalton, then joined CSA. To Chattanooga in 1867 and founded W.F. Fischer & Brother Jewelers. Presbyterian. Died June 23, 1909 and buried Forest Hills Cemetery. [CT June 24, 1909]

FISHER, Andrew J.     Co. K, 3TN Mounted Inf. (Lillard's)
Born Monroe Co., TN, July 12, 1837. Enl. March, 1862. Vicksburg (captured). Res. in Chattanooga, 1908. [TP10,150]

FISHER, Ireneaus (Irineus) F.     Co. B, 16TN Cav. Bn.
Born Knox Co., TN, May 9, 1843. Served "under Gen. Pegram in all his engagements" and Jubal Early. Paroled Washington, GA, May 1, 1865. Married Anna E. Wilson. Minister as local deacon at Zion Hill Methodist Episcopal Church 50 years. In 1909 res. Apison, James Co. Died Aug. 3, 1935 and buried Plowman Cem. [TP11,664; CT Aug. 4, 1935]

FITZGERALD, Coleman     Co. B, 1TN Cav. (Carter's)
Born 1846 in TN, son of Nasa and Mary Fitzgerald. Probably the C. B. Fitzgerald res. in Roane Co., 1870. Sulphur, OK, 1912. [1860 HC census]

FITZGERALD, William     Co. F, 35TN
Born 1843 in TN, son of Nasa and Mary Fitzgerald. [1860 HC census]

FITZGERALD, Woodson     Co. F, 35TN
He enl. Jan. 7, 1863, at Chattanooga On the second day of the Battle of Chickamauga, Sept. 20, 1863, he was hit with a minie ball that passed through the upper part of his right leg, shattering two bones. His wife Nancy was able to reach him at Green's Lake and take him in an ox cart to their home at Ooltewah. He was captured while recuperating and took the oath of allegiance on Dec. 11, 1863. He had dark complexion, black hair, black eyes, and was 5'11" tall. Woodson Fitzgerald was born in Franklin Co., GA, in 1827, the son of William Fitzgerald. He married Nancy Denny and died in 1896. [JWilson: Fitzgerald family; TP795]

FLEMING, J. W.     Co. I, 5AL
Born Oct. 12, 1840 Clarke Co., AL. Enl. at Grove Hill, AL. Apr. 27, 1861. Wounded twice in battle of Spottsylvania. Farmer in Highland Park. Mason. Died Dec. 15, 1910 in Chattanooga. Buried Forest Hills Cem. [FHR; CT Dec. 17, 1910; NBFM2]

FLEMING, William White     Co. F, 43TN
Born 1844 Iredell Co., NC. Enl. Nov. 9, 1861. Perryville, Baker's Creek, Raymond, Vicksburg. Married 7 March 1866 in Roane Co. to Sarah Martha Davis. Former sheriff of Graham Co., NC and member of NC Legislature. Deputy sheriff, 1910. He died in Chattanooga Jan. 21, 1918 and was buried in Forest Hills Cem. [CT Jan. 22, 1918; TWP, 199; 1910HC]

FLETCHER, J. E. (C.?)     Co. H, 26TN
Enl. July 8, 1861 at Knoxville; drummer; died Dec. 5, 1861 in hospital in Bowling Green, KY.

FLINN/FLYNN, Benjamin F.     Co. K, 36TN
Died in service ca. Aug., 1862 at the age of 19; unmarried. Before the war he was living with his mother Rachael R. Flynn at Harrison.

FLINN, William Griffith     Co. I, 26TN; 39TN Mounted Inf.
Born Oct. 1, 1823, Carter Co., TN; enl. July 3, 1861; soldier was severely wounded at Murfreesboro and was given an honorable discharge in 1863. He re-enlisted in the 2nd Engineers and served to the close of the war. Res. Chattanooga, 1893 where he was carpenter with "infrequent work." Married Candace Anne McCall, born 11 Aug. 1839 in Roane Co. He died March 22, 1898

and buried Citizens Cem. Member of NBF Camp, 1895-96. [TP1701; UDC2 pg 179]

FLORA, Theodore F. H.          Co. L, 36TN; Co. L, 35TN

Born c1846 in Hawkins Co., son of Emaline who was a washer-woman in Chattanooga. He had four younger brothers and sisters. Enl. Jan. 9, 1862, at Chattanooga in Co. L, 36TN and was transf. to Co. L of the 35TN. He was in the battle of Murfreesboro and was paroled on May 1, 1865, at Greensboro, NC. Married Mary Ann Morgan (1885). Mason. Baptist. Died June 5, 1923 in North Chattanooga and buried in Citizens Cem. [TWP, 225; CT June 6, 1923]

FLORA, William          Co. F, 35TN

Born c1833 in HC, son of Jacob and Mary. He farmed here until enlisting Oct. 1, 1862 at Chattanooga Dark eyes, dark hair, dark complexion, 5'4" tall. In HC with wife and four children, 1870, 1880.

FLORANCE, W. E.          2d Co., Washington Artillery

Born LA. Occup. clerk when enl. April 29, 1861 in New Orleans. At 23 yrs he was unmarried, residing in New Orleans. After war he became a bookkeeper in Chattanooga. Member of NBF Camp, 1885. [NBFM2]

FLYNN, George Washington          Co. I, 26TN; Co. K, 43TN

Born c1840. He was a farm laborer living with his mother, Rachael Flynn, at Harrison prior to the war. After enrolling in Co. I, 26TN, he re-enl. at Ooltewah, 43TN, on Oct. 12, 1862. Apparently also served with 3d Regt. of Engineers. NBF Camp, 1894. Died March 22, 1898 and buried CSA Cem. [NBFM2,7]

FOARD (FORD), J. H.          2nd Co. K, 1CSA Cav.

Enl. Sept. 20, 1862 in HC. Scouted behind Federal lines and never returned.

FORD, James Henry          Co. B, 1TN Cav. (Carter's).

Born c1843 in TN, son of William Daniel Ford. Enl. Aug. 7, 1861 at Cleveland. Hospitalized May, 1862. He deserted and took the oath at Chattanooga on April 20, 1865. Farmer at Birchwood with his wife, Mary, before the war. Light complexion, brown hair, blue eyes, and was 5'9" tall. [1860HC]

FORD, James H.          Co. K, 1CSA

Born Sullivan Co., TN, March 24, 1835, son of Benjamin and Pensacola Hawley Ford. Family moved to Chattanooga when he was a young boy. Afterward he returned to Chattanooga and became a clerk. Married

(1875) Rhoda Thomison. First wife Elizabeth Martin had died. For a while served as a member of the County Court. He died at his home on Dry Valley Rd. Jan. 20, 1913. [1910HC; CT Jan. 21, 1913].

FORD, 1st Lt. Nathan C.          Co. A, 21VA

Born Campbell Co., VA, March 6, 1833. Enl. June 20, 1861. Not re-elected 1st Lt. so transferred to Stuart's horse arty. Fought in most of important battles of ANV. Came to Chattanooga from Knoxville in 1870. He had married Mary S. Anthony Hancock in 1868. He was in the wholesale liquor business, then in wholesale tobacco, in Chattanooga and was one of the first police commissioners under appointment from Gov. William Bate. Died at res. on Walnut St., July 6, 1903 and buried Forest Hills Cemetery. [CT July 7, 1903; FHR]

FORD, Rhoda Thomison (Mrs. James H.)

Born near Washington in Rhea Co. Nov. 10, 1842 the daughter of William P. and Nancy (Smith) Thomison. Rhoda was elected 3d Lt. in cav. company organized by young ladies around Washington in Rhea County to carry clothing, food and "such other necessities and delicacies as able to procure" to nearby CSA camps. Arrested and "marched, a foot, in front of an armed guard of soldiers to Dayton, a distance of five miles, and from there to Bell's Landing" on TN River. There the 16 young ladies placed aboard US army cattle boat, the Chicken Thief, and brought to Chattanooga where Gen. Steedman ordered their release after they all signed the oath of allegiance. Married J.H. Ford on 20 Nov. 1873. Cumberland Presbyterian. Died at her home on Dry Valley Road Dec. 8, 1918 and buried White Oak Cem. [CT Dec. 9, 1918]

FORD, Cpl. Thomas J.          Barry's Btry.

The son of newspaper editor John W. Ford, he was a printer at Chattanooga when the war broke out. He enl. April 25, 1862, and died in Knoxville on Nov. 9, 1862, of pneumonia. A native of HC, he was 31 yrs. He had a light complexion and gray eyes and was 5'11" tall. His wife was Hetty Ford.

FORD, William B.          4AL Cav

Enl. Sept., 1862. Married (1879) Mary Golden Tate. Episcopalian. Real estate in Chattanooga, 1889. Died Oct. 27, 1922 at res. on Lindsay St. and buried White Oak Cem. [CT Oct. 13, 1908; NBFM7]

FORT, Capt. Tomlinson   Co. H, 1st GA Regulars.

Born in Milledgeville, GA, April 26, 1839, son of Dr. Tomlinson and Martha Low Fannin Fort, he graduated from Oglethorpe Univversity in 1857 and began the practice of law in Baldwin Co., GA. Enl. Feb. 12, 1861 and elected Lt. Became Capt. of Co. L in May,

1862, and fought in VA, being wounded twice at Malvern Hill and once at Second Manassas. He was again wounded on John's Island, SC July 7, 1864. Captured late 1864 and remained imprisoned until the surrender. His brother John Porter Fort was adjutant of the 1st GA. His other brother in the service was Dr. George N. Fort, Surgeon in 28th GA Regt. In Oct., 1865 Tomlison opened a law office in Chattanooga He served as mayor, 1875-76. Died Dec. 7, 1910 at Res. on Chester St. and buried in Milledgeville, GA. [CWTI Collection, USAMHI; NBFM2,7: UDC1 pg 144]

**FORTNER, Wiley**          Barry's Btry.
Enl. Oct. 4, 1862 at Chattanooga; wounded at Jackson, MS; captured at Spanish Fort, April 8, 1865; imprisoned at Ship Island, MS.

**FORTUNE, John W.**          Co. D, 21GA
Born Dec. 15, 1824 in Oglethorpe Co., GA. Enl. May, 1861. To TN, 1903. In 1909 res. E. 10th St., Chattanooga. [TP11,068]

**FOSTER, A. D.**
Born 1830, GA. Res. W. 7th St., 1910, in daughter's household. [1910HC]

**FOSTER, A. H.**          Co. G, 26TN; 2d Co. K, 1CSA (GA)
Born c1809. Enl. July 8, 1861, Knoxville. Commissioned 1Lt., July 8, 1861. Captured Fort Donelson and imp. Johnson's Island. Exch. Vicksburg, Sept. 1862. After his capture at Richmond, KY, Oct. 1862, he resigned his commission on the 29th of that month.

**FOSTER, A. S.**          2nd Co. K, 1CSA Cav. (GA)
Enl. Sept. 23, 1862 in HC. Detached by order Maj. Gen. Sam Jones at Chattanooga. Deserted Nov. 28, 1863.

**FOSTER, A. T.**          Co. A, 19TN
Died just after leaving Vicksburg.

**FOSTER, F. G.**
Born Liverpool, England. Enl. Nov. 1861 in Bragg's escort. Carpenter in Chattanooga c1895. [NBFM2]

**FOSTER, J. C.**  Co. G, 26TN; 2d Co. K, 1CSA (GA)
Enl. Aug. 28, 1861, Knoxville. Captured Fort Donelson and imp. Camp Morton. Cpl., Oct. 13, 1862. Killed at Peachtree Creek, July 20, 1864.

**FOSTER, J. D.**
Died April 30, 1914 and buried Forest Hills

Cem. [NBFM7]

**FOSTER, James**          Co. B, 1TN Cav. (Carter's).
Before the war, he lived at Birchwood with his parents, John C. and Malinda Foster. John C. Foster was a brick mason. The Fosters were from VA. James Foster was born c1843.

**FOSTER, James Daniel**          Co. E, 33rd AL
Born March 28, 1830 in Wilkes Co., GA. Enl. at Greenville, AL in spring of 1862. Served at Pensacola, Battle of Corinth. Because of disability assigned to Arsenal at Montgomery.   Lock and gunsmith in Chattanooga. Died Apr. 30, 1914 in HC and buried in Forest Hills Cem. [CT May 1, 1914, FHR; NBFM2; TP 4517]

**FOSTER, James R.**          2d Co. K, 1CSA (GA)
Enl. Aug. 3, 1863, Chattanooga. Deserted Aug. 16, 1864 at Atlanta and took the USA oath at Chattanooga, Aug. 23, 1864.

**FOSTER, John**          Barry's Btry.
Enl. Sept. 27, 1862 in Chattanooga

**FOSTER, John A.**          Co. I, 19TN
1903 res, HC. [TP2517]

**FOUST, Addison Taylor**          Co. A, 19TN
Born c1843, son of John and Matilda Hawley Foust. Enl. at Cumberland Gap. Died at Vicksburg. [CSR; Worsham; Lindsley, Military Annals of TN]

**FOUST, 1st Lt. Francis Marion Hawley**          Co. A, 19TN
Born Nov. 10, 1837, he was a son of John and Matilda Hawley Foust. The Foust family came to HC from Sullivan Co. by flatboat in 1843. He was sent out for recruiting services when the unit was at Corinth, MS, and he later was detached for special service with Gen. Bragg. Beginning in February of 1863, he was responsible for securing quarters and accumulating fuel for the soldiers around Chattanooga. He stayed in Chattanooga until early September when the Federal army arrived. At the battle of Franklin, he was wounded in the face. Died Mar. 8, 1888. [CSR; 1860HC]

**FOUST, Nathan Polk**          Co. A, 19TN; 2nd Co. K, 1CSA Cav.
Enl. May 21, 1861 at Knoxville in Co. A, 19TN, then on Sept. 20, 1862, joined in HC the 2nd Co. K, 1CSA Cav. He was discharged in 1863, but re-enl. again, being paroled May 3, 1865 in Charlotte, NC. The son of John and Matilda Foust, "Polk" Foust was born July 11, 1842. A bachelor, he left Chattanooga in 1878 to move to AR. He died at Winthrop, AR, in June, 1903. His

remains were brought back to the old Foust burial ground at Morrison Springs in Hamilton County. [CT June 12, 1903]

FOUST, William Henry
Like three of his brothers, fought with Co. A, 19TN. He also enl. Sept. 20, 1862 in the 2nd Co. K, 1CSA Cav. with his brother "Polk." He enl. just after he had married (1861) Elizabeth A. Wisdom, daughter of Abner Wisdom. Foust was born Dec 18, 1829 in Sullivan Co. and settled in Morrison Springs in 1843. After the war Foust lived in HC until moving to a farm near Charleston in Bradley Co. in 1883. He died there Dec. 15, 1903. [CT, Dec. 16, 1903]

FOUTS, Oliver Perry
He was the clerk at the Crutchfield House when the famed encounter between Jefferson Davis and William Crutchfield occurred in the hotel lobby. Fouts later joined the employ of the Confederate government during the war.
The Fouts family was originally from Fincastle, VA. He was the son of John R. Fouts and Lucinda Stever. O.P. Fouts was born in 1813 and named for the famous naval commander. After the war, Fouts helped operate the Stanton House and was a partner in a stockyard with A.J. Wisdom. A bachelor, he built up a sizable fortune. His home was at 508 West Ninth Street where he died March 9, 1899. [CT March 10, 1899; NBFM2]

FOWLER, Eliga W.          Co. E, 5TN
Fought at Missionary Ridge, Resaca, Franklin. Member of Cumberland Presbyterian Chruch. Resident in 1890 of Brittsville, TN. Died at 72 years old at his home in East Chattanooga, Aug. 26, 1915. [CT Aug. 27, 1915]

FOWLER, Sgt. J. M.          Clark's Independent Cav. Co.
Enl. Aug. 31, 1862 at Chattanooga, TN.

FOX, Cornelius R.          36GA
Born Murray Co., GA, July 5, 1847. Enl. Feb. 12, 1864. To TN, 1901. Wife was Beckie. Res. Long St., 1926. [TP16,053]

FOX, David          Co. D, 4th (12th) GA Cav.
He enl. Oct. 4, 1862 but disappeared from the unit about the time of the Battle of Missionary Ridge, Nov. 25, 1863. He took the USA oath of allegiance in Jan. of 1864. He had a dark complexion, black hair, gray eyes, and was 5'7" tall.

FOX, John B.          Co. B, 5TN Cav.

Born c1834, he was a farmer living with his wife, Martha, near Chattanooga prior to the war. Enl. Aug. 11, 1861, at Chattanooga.

FRAKER, William M.          Co. C, 39GA
Born Washington Co., TN, Dec. 22, 1841. Wounded Baker's Creek. Captured Sept 5, 1864 at McDonough, GA and imp. Camp Douglas until June 21, 1865. To TN 1884. With Queen and Crescent Railroad 31 yrs. Elder in Park Place Presbyterian Church. Res. 225 Magnolia St. Died June 26, 1914. [TP12,492; CT June 27, 1914]

FRANCIS, Eldridge G.          Co. I, 19TN
Born c1842, son of William and Mary Francis. William was a miller who died in 1850's. Enl. May 10, 1861. Hospitalized. Captured at Missionary Ridge, took USA oath and put to work at depot, Stevenson, AL. Married (1865) Elizabeth Jane Denton. Living on farm near Williams Island with Eliza Jane and two children, 1870.

FRANCISCO, H. C.          Co. A, 36TN
Born 1847, in TN. In 1910 farmer in HC with wife Matilda. [1910HC]

FRANKLIN, Bennett J.          Co. A, 1TN Cav. (Carter's)
Married Salena E. [TWP1400]

FRANKLIN, Jake
Born 1846, GA. Res. Glass St. with wife Mary. [1910HC]

FRAZIER, Capt. Samuel Josiah Abner    Co. D, 19TN
Born 29 Jan. 1840 at Rhea Co., Frazier was the son of a prominent lawyer and attorney general Samuel and Ruth Clawson Frazier. He graduated from East TN Univ. at Knoxville just prior to the war. He enl. April 6, 1861, at Knoxville and was elected captain May 29, 1861. He saw service at Cumberland and Big Creek gaps in KY, then at Fishing Creek. The unit was at Corinth, MS, then fought at Shiloh. They fought at Baton Rouge, LA, then returned to TN for the Battle of Murfreesboro. At Vicksburg, his regiment "has the unique experience of charging one of the enemy's gunboats." At Chickamauga, Frazier was seriously wounded by a shot through the windpipe. Two of his comrades were shot as they attempted to carry him off the field, and he suffered two more wounds as he lay on the ground. He was captured by the enemy and taken to Chattanooga, where he stayed some weeks at the home of the Rev. T. H. McCallie. He later was imprisoned at Camp Chase, OH, and Johnson's Island. While in the latter prison, he continued his study of law by paying 50 cents a week for an old edition of Blackstone. He earned the money by

making gutta percha rings for visitors.

Frazier moved to Chattanooga in 1882 and began the Hill City real estate development. He gave $10,000 toward the Walnut Street Bridge that connected Hill City with Chattanooga. He married (1871) Anna Keith. Died Dec. 11, 1921 and buried CSA Cem. [CSA Hist, v. 10, 480-81; Worsham, 215; TCWVQ, 2:851; GHT, 942; NBFM7; 1910HC]

FREEMAN, Drewry Hutchinson "Hutch"     Co. E, 2SC Rifles

Born 1838 in Pickens Dist., SC. Enl. 1862. Disabled by scurvy but still with army in VA at close of war. Married (1891, Walker Co.) Julie C. Carter. To Chattanooga in 1902. Died at his res. in East Lake, Feb. 24, 1912 and buried CSA Cem. [TWP, 7850; CT Feb. 26, 1912; TP6183]

FREEMAN, Joseph     Co. L, 36TN; Co. L, 35TN

Born c1822 in VA. Enl. Jan. 9, 1862 at Chattanooga. Transf. to Co. L of the 35TN. He fought at Murfreesboro. He was discharged on May 1, 1863 as "non-conscript." Prior to the war, he was a farm laborer living at Soddy, with his wife, Thursey (native of VA). In HC, 1870, with wife Thursey, 6 children. Farm laborer.

FRENCH, Bryon Brownlow     Co. C, 15AR

Born 1834, son of Joseph Harvey and Nancy Benson French. Died soon after Chickamauga from wounds he received there (or at Chattanooga immediately after the war from illness contracted in service). He was a nephew of the Chattanooga merchant John L. M. French.

FRENCH, Joseph Harrison     Co. H, 2TN Cav. (Ashby's)

Born 1840, son of Joseph Harvey and Nancy Benson French. His mother died in the 1840's and his father in 1850's so Mr. French and his 3 brothers came to Chattanooga by 1860 to live with their uncle, merchant John Lee McCarty French. Enl. Oct. 1, 1861 at Post Oak Spring. Promoted to Sgt. May 27, 1862. Killed at Chickamauga. [1860HC; JW, French Family]

FRENCH, Timothy Allen

Son of Joseph Harvey and Nancy Benson French. Killed at Chickamauga and buried in the Confederate Cem.

FRICKS, 2nd Lt. Flavius J.     Co. E, 39GA

Born 1829, Walker Co., GA, son of John and Sarah Dixon Fricks, pioneers in Walker Co. Captured Vicksburg, July 4, 1863 and paroled there July 8, 1863. Deserted while on furlough Oct. 1, 1863. Wife was

Sally M. Methodist. Mason. 1910 farmer res. in house hold of nephew on Dodds Ave. Died July 9, 1923 and buried Forest Hills Cem. [1910HC; CT July 10, 1923]

FRICKS, William Henry Harrison     Co. H, 26TN; Co. E, 39GA

Enl. July 8, 1861, Knoxville. Transferred to 39GA, Nov. 11, 1862. Appt. Cpl. Nov. 11, 1862; Sgt., Sept., 1863. Killed Missionary Ridge, Nov. 25, 1863.

FRIERSON, Capt. Thomas A.     Co. K, 23SC

Born Dec. 24, 1845 in Sumter, SC. Enl. Nov., 1861. Captured Chattanooga. Associated in law practice with N. L. Mayes, his brother-in-law. Real estate auctioneer during Boom of 1887-90 in Chattanooga. Member, NBF Camp, 1895-96. Died June 28, 1912 in Atlanta. [CT Aug. 3, 1912; NBFM7; NBFM2]

FRIST, Jacob Chester

Born Jan. 27, 1817, New Castle Co., DE. Carpenter. CSA. Died March 18, 1879 in Chattanooga and buried Citizens Cem. Married (2) Mary Ann Elizabeth Baldwin. Great Grandfather of Tennessee Senator Bill Frist. [CT Feb. 22, 1920]

FRIST, Robert Harris  Co. B, 4TN Cav. (McLemore's)

Born 1847, son of Jacob Chester and Mary Baldwin Frist. Enl. April 1, 1862, Chattanooga Detailed with Lt. Havron for scout duty. Paid $24.40 extra duty pay for use of horse. Clothes receipt for May 4, 1864. He died 1903.

FRITTS, Thomas W.

Born c1850, TN. Retail merchant in hardware, 1910. Res. household of son-in-law Leon Bailey. [1910HC]

FRY, Capt. George Thompson   Co. H, 37TN; Col., 7th CSA

Born Nov. 12, 1843 in Jefferson Co., TN, son of Henry H. and Elizabeth Peck Fry. Enl. March, 1861 in Co. C, 37TN. Switched from Co. G to Co. H at Shiloh. At the Battle of Stone's River, Fry fought with his feet tied up in sacks because someone had stolen his shoes while he was asleep resting from his march from Nashville to Murfreesboro, TN. At chickamauga he was severely wounded and left on the field for dead. A Roman Catholic priest discovered him to be alive and dragged him from the field ten minutes before the enemy burned the field which was covered with dry sedge grass. He recovered from his wounds and after a furlough he returned to the fight. He fought all the battles against Sherman in his march through Georgia. Wounded again at the Battle fo Jonesboro, GA in August 1864 and carried from the field by Rufus Tankesley. Following recovery he was elected to Colonel in command of the 37th. Took leave, went to VA and married 4 Apr. 1864 Mary A. Conley. After four days honeymoon returned to Army of Tennessee; wounded at Jonesboro. Studied law in VA, then moved to Atlanta, 1867. Gen. Mgr. of RR between Atlanta and Savannah. Resid. 1900 in Chattanooga. Occupation of lawyer. Member First Baptist. Died May 30, 1897 and buried Forest Hills Cemetery. [FHR; CV; TWP, p. 171; NBFM2; CT May 30, 1897; UDC1; UDC2]

FRY, Houston Greenberry
Born 1836 in Polk Co. and married (1856) Telitha Bidwell. He died 1891 in HC. [TWP, p. 18]

FRY, Hugh Lawson          Co. G, 59MS
Born Union Co., TN, Jan. 9, 1833. Enl. Mar. 2, 1862. Res. TN all his life except three years in Walker Co., GA. Married Elizabeth E. Res. Chickamauga, TN in 1901. In 1901, he applied for admission to TN Soldiers Home from HC. [TWP2688; SAACH]

FRY, Martin Monroe   Co. B, 3TN Cav.; 2TN Cav.
Born Aug. 19, 1844 in Giles Co., TN, son of Martin Fry. He enl. in spring, 1861 at Lynnville. Transferred early 1862 to Co. H, 1 Middle TN Cav. and fought at Shiloh, Farmington, Iuka and Corinth and cavalry fights at Coldwater and Coffeeville, MS. He also fought under Van Dorn at Thompson's Station and Forrest, at Chickamauga and Sweetwater and under Wheeler on the latter's middle TN raid. He served under Henry Ashby in the Atlanta campaign. Again under Forrest he fought at Athens and Sulphur Trestle, AL and once again under Wheeler opposing Sherman's March to the Sea and Carolina Campaign. Accused of burning a bridge and killing a negro and held prisoner until Oct., 1865. Sentenced to be hanged but pardoned by Pres. Johnson. Farmer and contractor. He moved to Chattanooga about 1880 as a railroad contractor and lived in St. Elmo. Baptist. Died June 8, 1926 and buried CSA Cem. in joint funeral at Alton Methodist Church with his friend Alexander Manning. [NBFM2,7; CT June 10, 1926]

FRYAR (FRYOR), Franklin (Frank)      Co. I, 19TN; Barry's Btry.
Enl. May 7, 1862, at Chattanooga. He was hospitalized at Atlanta in July, 1864 and was paroled in May 11, 1865 at Meridian, MS. Born in 1833, he was a son of Jeremiah Fryar Jr.

FRYAR, Jeremiah "Jerry" Co. H, 2TN Cav. (Ashby's)
Born 1836 in TN, son of John and Elizabeth of

Lookout Valley. Enl. June 17, 1861. at Knoxville. Wounded and absent, Oct. 7, 1863. Paroled April, 1865. Killed by a kinsman Jan. 11, 1868. He left a daughter, Mary, and sons Sevier and William.

FRYAR, Sevier          Co. H, 2TN Cav. (Ashby's)
Born 1839 in TN, son of John and Elizabeth of Lookout Valley and younger brother of Jeremiah. Enl. June 17, 1861 at Knoxville. Captured Aug. 31, 1862. Exchanged Sept. 4, 1862 at Cumberland Gap. Later listed as being home suffering from wounds at Stone's River. Picked up in HC and sent to Louisville. Took USA oath and disch. July 16, 1864 to remain north of Ohio River. Married Julia Lovelady and, after her death, married her younger sister, Milly Lovelady. Died Dec. 31, 1897 and is buried in private cem. on Snow Hill Rd.

FRYAR, William          Co. H, 2TN Cav. (Ashby's)
Born 1830 in TN, son of John and Elizabeth of Lookout Valley. Farmer at Harrison with wife Delila and three children. Enl. Oct. 4, 1862 at Chattanooga. Paroled April, 1865. Married Delilah Rogers.

FUELL, James          Barry's Btry.
Enl. July 11, 1862 at Chattanooga

FUGATE (FUGATT, FUGITT), Elias   Co. G, 26TN; 2d Co. K, 1CSA(GA); Barry's Btry.
Enl. July 8, 1861 in Co. G, 26TN at Knoxville; teamster; transferred May 31, 1862 to Barry's Btry. at Chattanooga; paroled May 11, 1865 at Meridian, MS. In Hancock Co. before and after war.

FULLALOVE (FULLILOVE), J. H.      Clark's Independent Cav. Co.
Enl. Aug. 31, 1862 at Chattanooga. Absent sick in Marietta, GA after Nov., 1863.

FULLALOVE (FULLILOVE), W. E.      Clark's Independent Cav. Co.
Enl. Aug. 12, 1863 at Knoxville, TN. Sent to Provost Marshal, Atlanta, Sept. 16, 1863. Charge murder.

FULTON, James Henderson     Gartrell's Command
Born Aug. 31, 1846, Dade Co., GA, son of William Douglas and Sarah M. J. Henderson Fulton. Student at Univ. of GA when war began. Married Mary Morrow, dau. of John and Sarah J. Gilliam Morrow. Mr. Fulton lived in Williamson Co., TN after war. Died April 14, 1914.

FULTON, William Douglass (1820-1882)
Born Athens, GA, Nov. 17, 1820, son of James and Mary Epsey Fulton. Practiced law in GA and was

Mexican War veteran. Located in Atlanta where he became superintedent of Georgia State Railroad. Came to Chattanooga in 1852 and was elected mayor in 1857; founded and operated Bank of Chattanooga until Federals occupied the city. Disappears until 1867 when he is found superintending the construction of the Maxwell House. Married Sarah M. J. Henderson. Moved to Williamson Co. in 1869 where he died Nov. 15, 1882. Represented Williamson and Maury cos. in TN Gen'l Assembly, 1877-79. [BDTA]

# G

GABBERT, OTIS T.
Enl. Jan. 9, 1862 in Co. L, 36TN at Chattanooga; transf. to Co. L, 35TN; fought at Murfreesboro. Postmaster and merchant at McDonald. Died Dec. 22, 1907 (65 years old). [CT Dec. 24, 1907]

GABBERT, W. G.  -  Co. B, 1TN Cav. (Carter's)
Not in 1860 HC. He was detailed in govt. tanning business in Oct. 1864.

GADBY, Sgt. G. P.          Co. A, 19TN
Killed at Shiloh. [Knoxville Daily Register, April, 19, 1862]

GADD, John          Co. G, 37TN
Born 1846 in TN, son of William and Rebecca.

GAFFNEY, James Matthew          Co. K, 13GA
Born in Ireland, 1836. Married Mary Kate Nance in Troup Co., GA. Enl. spring, 1861 at LaGrange, GA. Captured at Fisher Hill, VA, 1864 and imprisoned at Point Lookout, MD. Farmed after war, living in Whitfield Co., GA, then moved to East Chattanooga He died Feb. 9, 1910 at Waring, GA. [TWP8595]

GAINES, John Henry          Co. B, 38GA
Born 1838 in Cherokee Co., GA and married (1858) Julia Ann Davis [TWP: m. Elizabeth Ann Holcombe, Nov. 30, 1858 in Milton Co.,GA]. Enl. Feb. 24, 1862. Smashed hand in fall from RR car and disch. as disabled at Fredericksburg, VA, 1863. For 14 years was an employee of H. K. Judd. Died at res. in Sherman Heights Feb. 15, 1907, age 65 and buried in Gordon Co., GA. [CT Feb. 16, 1907; TWP3142; TP6686]

GALLAHER, 2Lt. John F.          Co. F, 2TN Cav.
(Ashby's)

Born in TN in November, 1843, he enl. Cavalry at Big Creek Gap. Commanded Co. F, May 3, 1865 in Charlotte, NC. After the war he settled in Kingston, TN and married Maggie P. about 1872. By 1880 he had made Chattanooga his home and had become a real estate agent. In the 1900 census, however, he is found to be a resident of Bryantsville, KY.

GALLAHER, Pleasant P.          Co. B, 5TN Cav.
(McKenzie's)
Born McMinn Co., 1843. "Cut off from the army at Benton, TN, near Hiawassee River, 1864." Absent without leave thereafter. 1906 res. of Red Bank, "invalided from chronic rheumatism" contracted during service. 1910 widowed farmhand res. O'Kean St. with three grown children. [TP2654; 1910HC]

GAMBLE, Charles Preston          Co. D, 4th (12th) GA Cav.
Born c1824, he hired a substitute, Isaac Goolsby, to take his place in the unit captained by William J. Rogers (Gamble's brother-in-law). Gamble was married to Susan Emmeline Rogers. The Gambles lived for several years after the Civil War at Harrison, then they moved to TX. [J. Wilson Gamble family; 1860HC]

GAMBLE, Thomas J.          Co. D, 4GA Cav.
He was in the unit that his father, Charles Preston Gamble, also joined, athough his father hired a substitute.

GAMBLE, Samuel H.          Co. K, 43TN
Enl. Dec. 2, 1861 at Ooltewah. Deserted Dec. 10, 1861.

GAMBLIN, George Washington          Co. D, 37TN
Born Dec. 17, 1840 in HC, son of Joseph. Enl. June 1, 1861 at Knoxville. Wounded at Nashville. Married Mary L. (1863 in Ringgold). Paroled May 4, 1865 at Greensboro, NC. Railroader in St. Elmo (Lookout Incline). Moved to Menlo, GA. Died Feb. 27, 1917. [TWP 6670; NBFM2,7]

GAMBLIN, Joshua          Co. H, 26TN
Enl. July 14, 1861, Knoxville. Detailed for arty. service Oct. 13, 1862.

GAMBLIN, W. G.          Co. G, 26TN
Enl. Aug. 28, 1861, Knoxville. Captured Ft. Donelson and imp. Camp Morton.

GANN, Andrew "Andy"          Co. G, 1CSA Cav.
Born 1839 in TN, son of Mary. Farm laborer at Soddy. Captured and imprisoned at Rock Island.

GANN, Daniel          Co. G, 1CSA Cav.
　　　Captured and imprisoned at Rock Island.

GANN, John Wesley
　　　Brother of Andrew and Daniel Gann.

GANNAWAY, Thomas Cotlett          Co. C, 16TN
　　　　　　Cav. BN
　　　Was born 1832 and died 7 Feb. 1879. He was
married 2 Dec. 1852 to Mary A. Rector who was born
July 1831. They are buried at Rector Cemetery in
Evansville, Rhea Co. [TP1454]

GANT, 2d Sgt. William          Co. H, 5TN Cav.
　　　Enl. Aug. 11, 1861 at Chattanooga Elected 2d
Lt. in 1862. Killed near Cedartown, GA, 1864.

GARDENHIRE, 1Lt. Francis Marion "Franz"   Co. B,
　　　　　　1TN Cav. (Carter's)
　　　Born at Loudon, TN, Sept. 10, 1836, he was
a grandson of William Gardenhire, a pioneer who lived
at Citico near Ross's Landing. His parents were George
W. Gardenhire and Polly Bottoms. Enl. during August,
1861, at Snow Hill. He was "a brave soldier and won
distinction for his gallantry in many engagements."
Wounded at the Battle of Cumberland Gap, he was
captured at Piedmont, VA on June 5, 1864. 5'11", dark
hair, grey eyes, light. complexion. After his capture, he
spent a year and nine months at Johnson's Island where
he made friends with the prison commander, who at the
end of the war outfitted him with clothes and provided
him first-class transportation back to HC.
　　　After the war, he managed the extensive family
property at Chattanooga and was a cattle dealer. He
married Leona Rogers in 1868. Their home was on East
Third Street, where Chattanooga High School was later
built. He was a member of First Presbyterian Church
and died at his res. on Harrison Ave., Sept. 29, 1905
and buried in Forest Hills Cemetery. She died 19 June
1927 in Chattanooga. [CT, Sept. 30, 1905; FHR;
1860HC]

GARDENHIRE, James T. "Judge"
　　　Captured at Ooltewah, Jan., 1864; accused of
being spy. Married Sarah, daughter of the Cherokee
Pathkiller.

GARDENHIRE, William Columbus
　　　Born in HC Feb., 1832, son of George W.
Gardenhire. In youth joined party of gold seekers and
sailed around Cape Horn to San Francisco. Later in Fiji
Islands he bought 2 "savages" and brought them to
America and sold them to P. T. Barnum for $10,000.
Moved to Dayton, TN c1875. Married Anna Grady of
Clearwater, FL. Died Oct. 24, 1915 in Clearwater.

Buried in Citizens Cem. with father and grandfather.
[CT Aug. 27, 1915]

GARNER, Irvin Clark          Co. C, 1TN (Turney's)
　　　Born 1837 in Franklin Co., he married (1866)
Mary Catherine Pryor, born 29 Sept. 1854. He died Nov.,
1899 on Leonard St. and buried at his old home in
Winchester. [TWP, p. 14; NBFM3; UDC1 pg 153.]

GARNER, William
　　　Born c1843 in SC of parents born in SC. In
1910 res. in town of Lookout Mountain with wife Julia
whom he married in 1903. No occupation listed athough
wife was laundress. [1910 HC]

GARNER, William H. H.          Barry's Btry.
　　　Enl. May 14, 1862 at Chattanooga; served three
years.

GARNER, William L.          Co. F, 3TN Cav.
　　　Born near Huntsville, AL in 1824, he spent his
early days there and received his education there. He
fought with Gen. Nathan B. Forrest "from the outset,
serving with gallantry and honor at Fort Donelson, Iuka,
Shiloh, Corinth and the assault on Fort Pillow." He came
to Chattanooga in 1887 and operated the Garner House
upstairs at 715 Walnut St. for 10 years. He died May 26,
1900 and was buried at Cartersville, GA. [CT May 28,
1900]

GARRETT, Sgt. Benjamin M.          Co. H, 26TN; 2d Co.
I, 1CSA (GA)
　　　Born 1838, GA of SC parents. Enl. July 8, 1861,
Knoxville. Captured Fort Donelson and imp. Camp
Douglas. Fair complexion, sandy hair, blue eyes, 6'1"
tall; deserted March 24, 1864. USA oath and sent north
Dec. 27, 1864. 1910 res., Read Ave. with wife Sarah E.
(married 1867). [1910HC]

GARRETT, John          Co. H, 26TN
　　　Enl. July 8, 1861, Knoxville. Missing in Battle
of Fort Donelson.

GARRETT, John Leander - Co. A, T. R. Freeman's
　　　　　　MO Cav.
　　　Born Cherokee Co. (later Etowah Co.), AL,
1845. Enl. May, 1864: Iron Mtn., Boonville, near Kansas
City, Price's 1864 Missouri Raid. Surrendered June 5,
1865 at Jacksonport, Jackson Co., AR. To TN, 1901.
Wife was Nancy C. (m. 1881). Res. 1911, East End, HC.
Janitor, public school. Died Aug. 28, 1911 at Rossville
and buried at Chickamauga. [TP12,578; 1910HC]

GARRETT, Rapley (Ralph)          Co. H, 26TN; 2d Co. I,
1CSA (GA)

Enl. July 8, 1861, Knoxville; left sick at Russellville, KY, Feb. 9, 1862; also served in 1CSA GA; enl. July 29, 1862 in Barry's Btry. at Chattanooga.

GASKILL, Varney A.   -   4th Brigade - QM Gen'l.
          State of GA
          Born Sept. 21, 1824 at North Clarendon, VT, son of Thos. Gaskill. Graduated from Middlebury College in 1846 and moved to GA where he became teacher, then a Baptist minister and a lawyer. Practiced law in Atlanta and served in the GA House and Senate. Became Quartermaster General of GA and paymaster, 4th Brigade, GA Volunteers. Lawyer in Chattanooga 1871-79 and served as alderman. Married four times, including Harriet Whiteside, widow of Col. J.A. Whiteside. Died Feb. 9, 1898 at Rutland, VT of Bright's disease. [CT03S; CT Feb., 11, 1898; UDC1 pg 154.]

GAULT, Lt. Samuel B.          Huggins Arty. Co.
          Born Oct. 22, 1841 in Lincoln Co., TN. Enl. at Sulphur Springs, TN, Apr., 1862 in Ramsey's Regt. Afterwards in Freeman's Batt., Forrest's Cav., and after Chickamauga in Dibrell's command. Res. of Chattanooga in 1893. [NBFM2]

GAUT, Lt. William          Co. H, 4TN Cav.
          He was killed in a battle at Cedartown, GA. Prior to the war, he was a farm laborer living near Moccasin Bend. He was a native of KY.

GAUT, Sgt. William          Co. B, 5TN Cav.
          Enl. Aug. 11, 1861.

GENNOE, Calvin          Co. D, 43TN
          Born Meigs Co., 1830, brother of David. Enl. 1862. Fought at Morristown, Vicksburg (captured and paroled). Captured again in Jefferson Co., TN, Oct. 28, 1864, and imprisoned at Camp Douglas. Released May, 1865. Res. of Hill City, 1907. Died Jan. 1, 1916, age 85, and buried Citizens Cem. [CT Jan. 2, 1916; TP8734; 1910HC]

GENSEL, N.S.          Co. D, 37TN
          Born c1821, SC. Watchman res. HC, 1860, with wife Martha and 7 children. Enl. Sept. 1, 1861 at Knoxville. Sent to Chattanooga sick, Aug. 1, 1862. Deserted Sept. 7, 1863 at Ooltewah.

GENTRY, John W.          Co. A, 8GA Cav. Bn.
          Born Spartanburg Dist., SC, 1838. Enl. 1861 at Savannah. Kennesaw Mountain, Franklin, Nashville. Res. of Sale Creek, 1908. Wife Ellen Jane. 1910 garden laborer. Buried Sale Creek Cem. [TP10,171; 1910HC]

GERALD, John          Co. H, 43TN

Born 1843 in TN, son of Samuel T. and Nancy Gerald of Ooltewah. [1860 HC Census]

GERHEART, George W.          Barry's Btry.
          Enl. July 18, 1862 at Chattanooga; paroled May 11, 1865.

GERMAN, Andy
          Born 1845, TN. 1910 servant in household of lawyer Bancroft Murray.

GERVIN, E. H.          Co. G, 26TN
          Enl. July 8, 1861, Knoxville. Captured Fort Donelson and imp. Camp Douglas where he died July 18, 1862.

GHOLSON, William
          Born 1841 in HC. Married (1876) Celia Francis McAdoo. Died 1893 in Obion Co. [TWP, p. 145]

GHORMLEY, William Henderson     4TN Cav;
          afterwards Co. C, 2TN Cav.
          Born Aug. 27, 1839 in Monroe Co., TN. Enl. June 29, 1861. After war to Chattanooga where he was a night watchman. He married on 12 June 1883 at Madisonville, Tn to Lida L. Hicks, his second wife. She was born 1860 and died March 1929 in Fayetteville, NC. Died Dec. 2, 1907 at res. on Catherine St. and buried CSA Cem. [CT, Dec. 3, 1907; NBFM2; UDC2 pg 195.]

GIBBS, Charles N.
          Born March 27, 1828 in Nashville, son of George W. and Lee Ann Dibrell Gibbs. Educated at Dresden Academy and Jackson, TN College. Mayor of Jackson, District Attny. for Western District of TN. In 1859 was member of TN Constit. Convention. Volunteer ADC to Forrest during war. 1873-81 was TN Secretary of State. To Chattanooga in 1881. Married Matilda Fenner Vaulx. Episcopalian. Died Jan. 11, 1920 at res. on Lindsay St. [CT Jan. 12, 1920]

GIBSON, David          Co. D, 37TN
          Born 1819 in SC. Farmer at Chattanooga with wife Rebecca and 7 sons. Enl. Sept, 1, 1861 at Knoxville. Disch. Aug. 15, 1862, disability. 5'10", dark complexion, black eyes.

GIBSON [GIPSON], Lt. H.          Barry's Btry.
          [Brown's Diary]

GIBSON, James H.          Co. K, 43TN
          Born c1835, TN. Farm laborer at Zion Hill, 1860 with wife Lornida and three children. Enl. Oct. 17, 1861 at Ooltewah.

GIBSON, Jeremiah "Jerry"     Co. D, 57NC Inf
Born June 19, 1844 in Winston-Salem, NC; resident of HC since 1886. Night jailer in charge when mob lynched Ed Johnson and was indicted. Married in 1889 to Lou Hixon. Color Sgt., NBF Camp, 1894. 1910 res. Wialingen Ave. with wife Lou. Died March 20, 1917 in Chattanooga and buried Citizens Cem. [TWP, 285; 1910HC]

GIBSON, John C.          Co. B, 2TN Cav. (Ashby's)
Born c1828, a bark grinder res. in household of Jemima Weace in 1860. Member of Wheeler's Cavalry, he lived in East Lake where he died Sept. 27, 1903 and was buried Forest Hills Cemetery. [CT Sept. 28, 1903]

GIBSON, Jordan          Co. F, 14AR; Co. B, 21AR
Musician.

GIBSON, Joseph W.          Barry's Btry.
He enl. April 4, 1862 at Chattanooga and he was hospitalized at Pollard, AL, from December, 1863 to April, 1864. He was captured at Cotton Gin, MS, on Jan. 1, 1865. Then he was held in the prisons at Louisville, KY, and at Camp Chase, OH. Prior to the war, he was living on the farm of his father, farm laborer Thomas Gibson, at Tynerville. The father was from SC, while the mother, Keziah Gibson, was from VA. Joseph Gibson was born about 1844. He was 5'5" tall with dark complexion, dark hair, and dark eyes.

GILBERT, Charles H.          Co. A, 1LA Cav.
Died in Chattanooga April 21, 1909. [CT April 22, 1909]

GILBERT, Isaac N.          Co. A, 1NC  Cpl.
Buried at Forest Hills Cemetery. [FHR]

GILBERT, L. V.     Co. A, 20AL Cav., Lee's Co.
Died July 20, 1903, age 63, at res. on Cowart St.; and buried at Steele, AL on AL & GA RR. [NBFM2, 7; CT July 21, 1903]

GILBERT, Stephen M.          Co. G, 7VA Cav.
Born 1840 in Berkeley Co., VA and enl. May 17, 1861 at Charleston, Jefferson Co., VA. Captured three times: Orange CH, Gettysburg, and near Harper's Ferry (1862). Paroled at Ft. McHenry at Baltimore. Married Sallie Finney. Res. Chatt; occup. merchant. In grocery business on Leonard St. Died June 15, 1905, age 65 years old at his res. on Early St., and buried Middleway, WVA. (FH?) [CT June 16, 1905; NBFM2; TWP6661]

GILBREATH (GILBRETH), Cpl. Evander          Co. F,

35TN
Born in Bledsoe Co., TN in 1823, he farmed in HC until enlisting, Oct. 1, 1862.

GILLBRIDE, Barney          Co. F, 35TN
Born in Taunaner, Ireland, 56 year old Gillbride (born 1806) became a coal miner in HC until he enl., Oct. 20, 1862 at Knoxville. Gray eyes, light hair, fair complexion, 5'3" tall. Buried in CSA Cem.

GILLESPIE, Maj. George L., Jr.
He was in business in Nashville when the war broke out, but quickly became captain of the HC Home Guard organized at Chickamauga on April 29, 1861. He joined the Tulloss Rangers (Co. C, 4TN Cav?), in May. This was a Sequatchie Valley unit that was outfitted by James A. Tulloss of Pikeville. Gillespie was later transferred to the commissary department where he served under Gen. Ben Alston until after the KY campaign of 1862. Then he was assigned to the staff of Maj. Gen. Carter L. Stevenson and later to that of Stephen D. Lee. He was in MS during the Chickasaw Bayou campaign of December, 1862, and fought at Champion's Hill against Grant in the siege of Vicksburg.
Gillespie was among those surrendered with the army of Pemberton in July, 1863. After he was exchanged, he rejoined the army and took part in battles at Lookout Mtn. and Missionary Ridge. During the Dalton-Atlanta campaign, Gillespie suffered a wound at Resaca, but returned to the AofTN and was with it at the surrender at Greensboro, N. C., April 26, 1865.
Born in Rhea Co. in 1836, he was the son of William N. Gillespie and Sidney Ann Leuty. He was a merchant and later a contractor at Chattanooga after the war. He married on Aug. 12, 1863 Victoria Brown, daughter of Thomas A. Brown of Roane Co. They lived on Walnut St. and attended First Presbyterian Church. He died in Atlanta on Feb. 22, 1923 and was buried in Forest Hills Cemetery. [NBFM2]

GILLESPIE, George S.  Co. E, 5TN Cav. Bn.;
          Sgt. Co. K, 2d TN Cav.     (Ashby)

GILLESPIE, James F.   Co. I, 2TN Cav. (Ashby's); Co. E, 4TN Cav.          Bn.
Born 1842 in TN, son of Mark and Eliza Jane Simpson Gillespie. Moved to TX after war. [1860HC]

GILLESPIE, James Wendell          Co. K, 43TN
Born Aug. 9, 1819, son of George and Anna Neilson Gillespie of Rhea Co. Studied medicine in Nashville and was practicing at Tynersville, 1860, with wife Nancy and one child. Represented Rhea, Bledsoe, Hamilton, Marion and Meigs cos. in TN Senate, 1849-53, and Rhea, Bledsoe and Hamilton in Genl. Assembly,

1859-61. Married Nancy S. Brazelton, 1854. In addition to practicing medicine, he operated a general store and traded in livestock. Trustee of Mars Hill Academy in Rhea Co. Captured in Mexican War. Although he opposed secession, he enl. 5th East TN Vols., Oct. 17, 1861, then recruited what became the 43TN Inf. Elected Col. Dec. 14, 1861. Captured in Vicksburg, July 4, 1863 and paroled July 9, 1863. Rejoined army and was one of escort for Jefferson Davis in Washington, GA. With the regt. when it surrendered, 1865. "A very handsome man, an ideal commander and a splendid soldier. He was in numerous hard battles, the siege of Vicksburg among them." After the war lived at Washington in Rhea Co. where he died Oct. 10, 1874 and was buried Mynatt Cem., a mile south of Washington. Camp #9 ov the U.C.V in Dayton was named for him. [Application for pardon from Former Confederates, 1865; J. Wilson, Gillespie Family; Campbell, Records of Rhea; Biog. Directory of TN Gen. Assembly; UDC1 pg 157.]

GILLESPIE, John M.          Co. F, 35TN; Co. B, 43TN
          Born May 20, 1836 in Kingston, TN, he came to Chattanooga in 1857. He joined the 35TN Inf. on Nov. 18, 1862, then transferred to Co. B of the 43TN on Feb. 5, 1863. He was a son of George Lewis Gillespie and Margaret Alice McEwen. He married Amelia King, a daughter of John King. Their son was John King Gillespie. He had blue eyes, dark hair and a fair complexion and was 5'10" tall. He became a merchant in Chattanooga where he died April 19, 1888; buried Forest Hills Cemetery. [CT 03S]

GILLESPIE, Dr. Joseph Strong
          Born in Rhea Co. March 18, 1821, he came to Chattanooga when it was Ross' Landing. This Chattanooga surgeon was loyal to the Southern cause. He had suffered a severe fall while sleepwalking and was unable to fight in the war. Dr. Gillespie was so outspoken for the Confederacy that he was arrested by Union troops, but was released on parole to treat wounded soldiers.
          He was one of the sons of George Gillespie, who had a large plantation in Rhea Co. His mother was Anna Neilson. Dr. Joseph S. Gillespie set up a medical practice at Chattanooga after completing the Louisville Medical College. He was Chattanooga's fourth mayor. In 1848, he married Penelope Whiteside, daughter of Col. James A. Whiteside. Dr. Gillespie resided at his farm "Canachee" east of Missionary Ridge after the war. He died March 28, 1896. [CT03S]

GILLESPIE, William M.    Co. A, 5TN Cav.; Co. D, 4(12) GA Cav.
          Born June, 1841 in Knox Co., TN, son of Marcus and Eliza Jane Simpson Gillespie. To HC at

very early age and helped father with farm until war broke out when he enl. in Co. A, 5TN Cav., remaining until death of father. Re-enl. Oct. 4, 1862 in Co. D, 4(12)GA Cav. and became Sgt. Returned to HC after the war and resumed farming. Married (1885) Maggie Castle. He became road commissioner of his district and member of County Court. Married (2) Tennie Davis. Died Jan. 31, 1915 at his home in Sunnyside, east of Missionary Ridge. Also shown as William A. and William J. [CT Feb. 1, 1915; GHT, 944]

GILLESPIE, William Stanton          Co. A, 4TN Cav.
          Born Nov. 28, 1850,          TN, son of Robert N. and Hannah Leuty Gillespie [Robert and Hannah were brother and sister to William and Sidna]. He married Clara Chadick in Chattanooga She died and William married Maud Gardner of Gatesville, TX, June 1, 1885.

GILLESPIE, William Stanton Leuty
          Born 1838, in TN, son of William N. Gillespie and Sidney Ann Leuty and brother of George L. Gillespie. For part of the war, he was sent out on "detached duty." Lived in TX before returning to Chattanooga Died at his home east of Missionary Ridge, Jan. 31, 1915. 1910 farmer res. on Ringgold Rd. with three children less than 16 years of age. [NBFM7; CT Feb. 1, 1915; 1910HC]

GIRVIN [GIVENS], Ebenezer H.          Co. G, 26TN; 2d
          Co. K, 1CSA (GA); Co. I, 16NC
          Enl. July 8, 1861, Knoxville. Captured; in prison at Camp Douglas, Chicago. Transf. to 16NC March 10, 1863. Wounded Gettysburg. Returned to duty and wounded again at Spotsylvania May 21, 1864. Returned to duty and wounded yet again at Reams Station. Returned to duty until hospitalized for gunshot wound to head, April 19, 1865. In hospital at Farmville through May 14, 1865.

GLADDIS, Thomas          2nd Co. K, 1CSA Cav.
          Enl. Sept. 20, 1862 in HC. Deserted at Shelbyville, TN, Jan 25, 1863.

GLADISH, William James          Co. I, 26LA
          Born June 30, 1838, Limestone Co., AL, son of Rev. William James Gladish of Petersburg, VA, who in 1834 married Anna May Van Hook shortly after she came from Amsterdam, Holland. She was from a wealthy family and she and her husband moved near Huntsville, AL where they operated a plantation with many slaves. Mrs. G spoke 5 languages fluently and taught school on the plantation including son W.J. who was first of seven children. After her death Rev. WJG moved with two of his sisters to the home of his aunt, Mrs Mary Balleau, at New Orleans. WJG was overseer on her plantation until

he enl. March 15, 1862 at Thibodaux. Chickasaw Bayou, Baton Rouge. Captured Vicksburg, paroled and returned to father's farm in Madison Co. where a "band of yankey soldiers come there and took me prisoner . . . Had to take the oath or go to prison." Became machinist after war and invented a self-feeding nail machine. However, it became worthless a short time later when the wire nail was invented. Married (Dec. 12, 1871) Lillian Curtis of Madison. To TN, Jan, 1881. Designed motorboats and called father of motor boating on TN River. Boarder on Walnut St., 1910 with wife Martha, born NJ. Agent for gasoline engine co., 1910. Res. 1918 on Broad St. Died Jan. 23, 1919 at home of son at 406 Pine St. Buried Forest Hills Cemetery. [Booth; TP15,384; 1910HC; CT Jan. 24-26, 1919]

GLASS, William J.      Co. H, 26TN; 2d Co. I, 1CSA (GA)
Enl. July 8, 1861, Knoxville. Capt. Ft. Donelson and imp. Camp Douglas. Light complexion, light hair, blue eyes, 5'11" tall. Deserted near Atlanta, Aug. 13, 1864. He took the USA oath, Aug. 22, 1864, Chattanooga Res. Walker Co.

GLOVER, Augustus C.      1st. Co. H, 7SC; Co. C, 48GA
Born May 22, 1845, Richmond, GA. Enl. Apr., 1861, 7SC, then 48GA. Wounded three times: Malvern Hill, on skirmish line and at Orange C.H. School teacher and farmer in HC. 1892 applied from HC for admission to TN Soldiers Home. [SAACH]

GLOVER, Daniel      Co. K, 43TN
Born c1842 in TN. Res. in household of Edmond Smith, 1860. Enl. Oct. 10, 1862 at Ooltewah; deserted Nov. 7, 1862. [1860HC]

GLOVER, Granderson F.      Co. A, 4TN Cav. Bn.
Enl. Sept. 6, 1861. at Big Creek. Sick at Chattanooga April, 30, 1862. Disch. overage Oct. 20, 1862. Re-enl. at Knox. Feb. 11, 1863 as a substitute. Deserted.

GLOVER, Richard      Co. H, 26TN ; 2d Co. I, 1CSA (GA)
Enl. July 8, 1861, Knoxville. Left sick Chattanooga, Oct. 5, 1861. Captured Fort Donelson and imp. Camp Douglas. Absent sick, Feb. 29, 1864. On daily duty as ambulance driver, Aug. 31, 1864. Paroled Greensboro, May 1, 1865.

GLOVER, Capt. Samuel H.      Co. H, 4TN Cav.
Enl. Aug. 11, 1861 at Chattanooga Wounded at Morristown Station, TN, Aug. 16, 1862. Raised Co. B, Carter's Mounted Scouts. Captured Jan., 1865 and

imprisoned at Camp Chase. [Z]

GLOVER, Thomas      Co. H, 4TN Cav.

GLOVER, Capt. William Culford   Co. H, 4TN Cav.
He was born Dec 1827 and died 20 July 1903, married Rebecca Williamson, who was born 4 Feb. 1850 and died 30 March 1929. [UDC2 pg 201]

GOAD, William C.      Co. H, 4TN Cav.
Died in prison, 1863.

GOBER, Dempsey M. Conner      Co. E, 66GA
Born 1822 in Newton Co., GA and married (1858) Elizabeth Louisa Patterson. Died 1882 in HC. [TWP, p. 265.]

GODHELP, Sigmond      Co. A, 19TN
Born c1836, Germany, and was clerk in Chattanooga. Enl. May 20, 1862, Corinth. Deserted near Chattanooga, Sept. 10, 1863., and he took the USA oath at Chattanooga and released at Nashville.

GODSEY, John P. -   Co. D, 4th (12th) GA Cav.
Enl. Oct. 4, 1862. A carpenter, he was assigned to a steam saw mill near Chattanooga the following day. He was born in VA about 1824. He and his wife, Hannah, a GA native, were living near Moccasin Bend at the start of the war.

GODSEY, Peter      Co. H, 4TN Cav.

GODSEY, Sgt. Thomas H.      Co. H, 4TN Cav.; Co. B, 5TN Cav.
Born about 1842, he was a farm laborer living with his wife, Altha, near Chattanooga at the start of the war. He enl. Aug. 11, 1861. He took the USA oath of allegiance on March 26, 1864, and was released at Chattanooga. He had a light complexion, sandy hair and blue eyes and was 5'8" tall.

GODSEY, William      Co. A, 19TN
Born c1830. Sawyer, res. Chattanooga with wife Mary. Enl. May 20, 1861, Knoxville. Disch. July 22, 1862.

GOFORTH, Daniel Boone      Co. B, 29TN
Born HC, Feb. 9, 1835. Married Nancy Carline [sic]. Res. 1903 in Archville, Polk Co., TN where he died March 9, 1911. [TP5717]

GOINS (GOEN, GOIN, GOANS), Charles      Co. K, 43TN
Age 18 in 1861, he enl. Oct. 17, 1861 at Ooltewah; captured at Vicksburg, July 4, 1863.

GOANS, Henry          Co. G, 37TN
Born 1842 in GA. Res. 1860 with father Jack and brothers Nathan and Richard. [1860HC]

GOANS, John          Co. E, 35TN
Born 1820 in TN. Farm laborer at Soddy with wife Louisa and five children.

GOANS, Nathan          Co. E, 35TN
Born 1823 in TN. Farm laborer at Soddy with wife Mary and two children. [1860HC]

GOANS, Richard B.  Co. G. 21TN Cav. (Carter's)

GOINS, Oscar Claiborne      Co. B, 19TN
Born in Grainger Co., TN, Feb. 24, 1830, son of Nancy Biby Goins. His parents moved to HC in 1833 and settled on a farm among the Cherokees. At 16 he clerked in a mercantile house and married (1) in 1853 Nancy Florence Potter but they separated. In 1858 he married (2) Esther Reynolds. At the beginning of the war he joined Co. B, 19TN with the rank of Lt. He fought at Fishing Creek and Shiloh, then returned to Chattanooga to help raise the Lookout Battery with Capt. R. L. Barry in which he served as farrier. He fought with the battery at Baker's Creek and at Jackson under W.W. Loring. During the winter of 1863-64 he was taken sick and returned home, settling in Chattanooga broken in health and fortune.
After the war he became a traveling salesman and in 1873 settled in Murray Co., GA, occupying the home built by Joe Vann, a prominent Cherokee. Goins died 1903 in Bradley Co., TN. [Memories of Georgia; JWGoins family]

GOINS, William A.          Co. A, 19TN
Enl. May 20, 1861 in Knoxville and apparently transferred to Co. C, 43TN. He was captured May 4, 1863 at Grand Gulf, MS and taken to Alton, IL prison where he died July 2, 1864 of chronic diarrhea. Probably brother of O.C. Goins. [Louise Richardson to Dr. Jack D. Welsh, June 3, 1995; CSR]

GOODE, William H.          Co. K, 43TN
Born 1831 in Greenville, TN. Enl. Dec. 12, 1861 at Ooltewah; captured at Vicksburg, July 4, 1863. Suffered measles at Vicksburg and could hardly see. "Has lost his eyesight and is in destitute condition." (March, 1887). Res. on Missionary Ridge in 1893. Still in HC in 1903. [NBFM2; NBFM1; TP497]

GOODEN, Joseph  -   Co. B, 1TN Cav. (Carter's).
Enl. Aug. 7, 1861, Cleveland. Captured Wartburg, TN, June 18, 1863. He was listed as absent without leave in the valley of VA in October of 1864. Before the war, he was a farm laborer residing with Dr. J.H. Locke at Ooltewah. He was born about 1841.

GOODRICH, George Washington          Co. B, 1TN (Maney's) ANV.
Born 27 Nov.1831, Greenup Co., KY and married (1879) Tennessee White Darwin, who was born 6 June 1857 and died 25 Aug. 1917. He was a book-keeper in Chatt in 1905. Died June 14, 1905 at res. on West 7th and buried in the Buttram Cem. in Dayton, TN. [TWP, p. 109; CT June 15, 1915; NBFM2, 7; RCCR2.]

GOODSON, Seybourne          Co. I, 5LA
Born Monroe Co., TN, 1839. Enl. May 22, 1861 in New Orleans. Present on roster through Feb., 1862. To TN, 1874. Res. Hill City, 1911. [Booth; TP12,487]

GOODWIN, Cpl. Joseph A. Co. B, 1TN Cav. (Carter's); Co. K, 43TN
He enl. Dec. 1, 1861, in the 43TN after first serving under Capt. Snow. He was captured at Vicksburg on July 4, 1863. He was detached Nov. 6, 1863, to bring in absentees from HC. Before the war, he lived on the farm of his parents, Thomas H. and Mary Goodwin, at Ooltewah. He was born about 1841. [1860 HC]

GOODWIN, Meredith F.      Co. K, 43TN
Age 16, he enl. March 24, 1862, at Ooltewah. He was discharged March 26, 1863, for being underage. He had fair complexion, dark eyes, dark hair and was 5'8" tall. He was the son of Thomas and Mary Goodwin of Ooltewah. [1860 HC]

GOOLSBY, Isaac C.          Co. D, 4th (12th) GA Cav.
He went into the unit on Oct. 4, 1862, as a substitute for Charles P. Gamble. He later was absent and presumed to be within enemy lines.

GORDON, Capt. James Clark    Co. H, 26TN; 2d Co. I, 1CSA (GA)
Born c1835, GA; and a rock mason in Chattanooga when he enl. July 8, 1861, Knoxville. Captured at Fort Donelson, Feb. 16, 1862, and imp. Johnson's Island; exch. Nov. 8, 1862; prom. to Lt. Col. Sept. 2, 1863. Rec. for promotion to Col. by Gen. H.D. Clayton, Mar. 3, 1865. Cmdg. 2d Bn, 1CSA, Oct. 31, 1863. Wounded in thigh at Kennesaw Mtn, June 17, 1864. Foard Hosp, Camp Marietta, June 20, 1864. Applied for a KY pension, 1912. He had a brother Cicero Gordon in the same unit.

GOSSITT, Richard

[NBFM1]

GOTCHER, John S.    2nd Co. K, 1st CSA Cav.
    Born c1838, son of Henry and Margaret Gotcher. Farmer at Tynersville, 1860, with wife Nancy and two young children born Arkansas. Enl. Sept. 23, 1862 in HC. Captured near Ooltewah Dec. 1, 1863 and imprisoned at Rock Island, IL where he died Feb. 19, 1864 and was buried. [CSR; RI Ledger]

GOTHARD, Gustavus Augustus Henry   Co. C, 16TN
                Cav. Bn.; Co. A, 4TN Cav.
    The Gothards were originally from Pendleton District, S.C., and they moved to Rhea Co., TN, in 1810. His parents were M. Larkin and Louise Taylor Gothard. Louise Taylor was the daughter of Robert and Katie Sevier Taylor, who lived at Watauga in the Washington District prior to moving to Rhea Co. Born April 10, 1844 at Sale Creek, he ran away from home to enlist at Knoxville, June 16, 1861. Later he transferred to Rucker's Legion, 16TN Cav. Bn., to serve alongside his father, Larkin Gothard. He fought at Fishing Creek, Perryville, and Chickamauga, and was wounded at Philadelphia, TN, then captured and held at Chattanooga until the surrender. Henry Gothard often served as a scout and, if apprehended, he was still so youthful that he could say he was out looking for the family cows. He actually had been sent away after the cows when he first ran off to the army. At Philadelphia, TN, Oct., 1863, Henry Gothard was severely wounded when he was hit in the head with artillery shrapnel and bled profusely. He was left for dead on the battlefield, but he was rescued by two young women. He was nursed in nearby homes and by slaves in the woods, then a silver piece was inserted in the back of his head where a bone had been shot away. He rejoined the army and fought with Vaughn's Brigade in the Shenandoah campaign, at Cedar Creek and New Market. In early 1865, Gothard was given permission along with two companions to deliver the unit's mail back to Rhea Co. His boat overturned on the Clinch River, and he was captured and imprisoned at Chattanooga. A family historian said he "was falsely accused, along with others, of the murder of the Federal provost marshal at Athens, TN." He was also falsely told that Gen. Lee had already surrendered. He was given a choice of taking the oath to the United States or hanging immediately for the murder. He had no way of knowing that Lee had not yet surrendered, but he knew he was innocent of the murder (Records show that he had not been near Athens in many months). So he took the oath on March 2 and walked to his home in Rhea Co. Because of the bitter feeling against ex-Confederates, Gothard went west and spent several years in MO, GA and TX before returning to HC where he married Nancy Louisa McKeown. They

resided for many years in St. Elmo, where he was the gatekeeper at Forest Hills Cemetery. He died Oct. 7, 1932 and was buried at Forest Hills. [Unpublished Gothard family history by Judy Kellerhals Boyles, Katherine Kellerhals Boyles and Betty McDaniel Kellerhals; CT May 3, 1931, Oct. 8, 1932; FHR; NBFM2; TP 2220]

GOTHARD, Elias    Co. D, 1TN Cav. (Carter's)
    He enl. at Knoxville on Aug. 5, 1861. He went over to the Union army, however, joining Co. D of the 12TN Cav. USA at Nashville on Nov. 10, 1863. He gave service as a blacksmith and also did scouting in Hickman Co. He was appointed a sergeant in January of 1864. He was mustered out at Fort Leavenworth on Oct. 7, 1865. He was a son of Allen and Mariah Gothard. Elias Gothard and his wife, Elizabeth, were living at Sale Creek just before the war. The Gothards were in Rhea Co. earlier and were originally from Newberry Co., SC. [JW]

GOTHARD, Larkin    Co. C, 16TN Cav. Bn.
    He was born 6 Apr.1807 when the family was still in Pendleton, SC. The Gothards were at Rhea Co. prior to moving to HC. He married (1830) Louise Taylor, born 10 Feb 1809 and died 1872 in Rhea. He farmed and tended a grist mill at Soddy. By 1860, however, Larkin and Louisa had moved back to Rhea where he died at home of dau. Elizabeth. According to his son Augustus, Gothard was 70 when he rode with Rucker's Legion.

GOTTSCHALK, James    CSN
    Born in Cologne, Germany, he emigrated in 1848 and joined the Confederate Navy where he was engaged in blockade running. He came to Chattanooga in 1866 and engaged in manufacturing and the mercantile trade. A member of Mizpah Temple, he died Dec. 2, 1898. [CT: 1903S]

GOULDING, Benjamin Lloyd    Co. C, 61NC; Co.
                B, 1GA
    Born Feb. 19, 1844 in Bath (Richmond Co.), GA. Enl. Nov. 12, 1861 in GA Militia and served in Signal Corps. Fought throughout Atlanta campaign. Captured at Ft. McAllister, fall, 1864, and imprisoned Point Lookout. Principal Rossville Academy, 1867. Organized and took charge of Chattanooga Weather Bureau when it was located in the courthouse, 1878-1885. Took charge of public library then on Market St. Assisted in organization of Chamber of Commerce; Secretary (1888-93). For number of years was state coal and oil inspector following death of J.F. Shipp. Presbyterian. Died March 20, 1934 in Chattanooga [A. Hodges info to Free Press, May 22, 1895; NBFM2,8; CT, May 5, 1904; Oct. 4, 1906; March 21, 1934; CV, Sept., 1915, p. 427]

GRAHAM, John Alexander          8TN Cav.
Born Jan. 27, 1838 in Warren Co., KY at Bowlilng Green. Enl. at Murfreesboro, TN in 1862. Afterwards Commissary Dept. of Cheatham's Div. Captured Huntsville, AL and paroled as captured after surrender. Married Carrie Almira Hollowell at Murfreesboro. She was born 12 Aug 1840 and died 29 April 1922. Resident of Chattanooga 24 years and worked as plasterer and for Chattanooga Life Ins. Died at res. on Douglas St., Nov. 18, 1907 and buried Forest Hills Cemetery. [CT, Nov. 19, 1907; FHR; NBFM2; TWP6719; UDC2 pg. 206]

GRANT, Capt. Ambrose Child          Co. H, 4TN Cav.
Born 1842 in Bangor, ME, he moved to Shellmound, TN in 1856 with his father. Resigning his position as a conductor on the Memphis and Charleston RR, he enl. in Co. H, 4TN Cav., fought at Mill Springs, then transferred to the QM Department. With the 4TN he took part in the actions at Murfreesboro and Munfordville and Bardstown. He was captured at Perryville. Upon his exchange he contracted typhoid and when he recovered he was assigned duty with the hospital as "special traveling agent." He returned to railroad work after the war, lost a leg in 1866 as a conductor on the NC & St. L., and was employed as chief claims clerk. Grant married Bessie Pride at Iuka, MS. They lived in Chattanooga on the East Terrace of Cameron Hill. Episcopalian. Died Feb. 1, 1902, age 63, and was buried at Citizens Cem. [CT Feb. 2, 1902; Hist. St. Paul's, 172; NBFM7]

GRANT, R. R.
Inmate TN Confed. Soldiers' Home, Nov. 17, 1902. [TCSH; NBFM3]

GRANT, T. J., Jr.          Co. E, 17TN
Born 1840 in Franklin Co. Enl. in May, 1861 and was disabled by a musket ball which struck his ankle during the battle of Murfreesboro. Res. Chattanooga in 1904. [TP6418]

GRAY, Fielding Wells   Co. E, 3CSA Cav.;
Barry's Btry.
Before the war, he resided near Tyner with his wife, Martha, and their son and daughter. A native of Virginia, he was born about 1833 and moved with his family first to Smith Co., then to the Worley District of HC about 1845. His father, L.E. Gray, was also from VA and lived beside Wells Gray at the war's start. F.W. Gray enl. Sept. 18, 1862 at Chattanooga; paroled May 11, 1865 in Meridian, MS. Martha Gray was from Alabama. F. Wells Gray was a carpenter, a Mason, and a Baptist. Died May 30, 1916, "age 84," at Whorley, TN and buried at Concord Baptist Church. [CT May 31,

1916; NBFM7]

GRAY, Henry Anderson          Co. A, 19TN
Born Hall Co., GA in 1822. Enl. Nov. 16, 1862, Chattanooga. Shot through the left knee at Murfreesboro, Dec. 31, 1862 and sent home. In 1893, he res. near Bunch P.O. and in 1901 near Stephenson, HC, unemployed; destitute. [TP583]

GRAY, James M.          Barry's Btry.
Enl. July 15, 1862 at Chattanooga; $50 bonus; Dec. 1862 on duty as hospital steward; captured near Jonesboro, GA Sept. 3, 1864; imprisoned at Camp Douglas; 5'8" tall; blue eyes; dark complexion; gray hair. [verified by Brown Diary]

GRAY, Cpl. Robert L.          2nd Co. K, 1st CSA Cav.
Enl. Sept. 20, 1862 in HC. Detached as wagoner Aug. 31, 1863 at division (Dibrell's) Hdq.

GRAY, Samuel M.          Co. H, 2TN Cav. (Ashby's)
Born 1836 in TN, son of Mary. Farmer at Harrison.

GRAY, William          Co. B, 33TN
Born Jan. 29, 1842 in Dade Co. GA. Enl. June 10, 1861 at Caperson Ferry, AL. Farmer at Chattanooga after war. Died Nov. 3, 1908 and buried Forest Hills Cemetery. [FHR; NBFM2]

GRAY, William A.   "MACK"          Barry's Btry.
Born Jan. 3, 1844 in Smith Co., TN. Farmer at Soddy with wife Margaret. Enl. April 4, 1862, at Chattanooga. His older brother, F. Wells Gray, was also in the unit. William A. Gray was hospitalized July-September of 1864. He was paroled May 11, 1865, at Meridian, MS. His father was L.E. Gray. Gray became Chief Inspector of the Southern RR and was killed in the yards near Union Depot, April 23, 1895. He was buried at Concord Cem. Member of NBF Camp. [CT April, 24, 1895; NBFM2]

GRAY, William R.          Co. C, 60GA
Born Walker Co., GA in 1844. Enl. July, 1861. Served in ANV: Seven Days, Chancellorsville, Winchester. Captured Spotsylvania Courthouse and imp. Fort Delaware. Tenant farmer, 1910. To TN in 1866. Minister for 20 yrs. and member of Greenwood Baptist Church. Died July 11, 1926 at his home in Harrison and buried McDonald Cem. [TP8079; 1910HC; CT July 12, 1926]

GREEN, Capt. Allen Baird          Co. B, 5TN Cav.
Brother of O.S. Green. Came to Chattanooga in 1852 with his family. He enl. Aug. 11, 1861, at

Chattanooga Baird's rise to captured came after the unit's initial Capt., C.C. Spiller, was promoted to Lt. Col. Green was killed in the fighting at Murfreesboro, being struck by a cannonball that also killed his horse and destroyed his saddle. "Sitting on his horse while the company was dismounted pulling down a fence, he was pierced with a bullet near the heart." Green's "brother shot and kill him [the Federal who shot A.B. Green]. Green's widow, Rhoda J. Green, applied for payment, listing the horse as worth $200 and the saddle $50. Buried at Murfreesboro during war. According to Brooks, p. 101, B.A. Green died at "home," Aug. 5, 1863. [CT Mar. 10, 1912]

GREEN, Edward        Co. L, 36TN
    Enl. Jan. 9, 1862 at Chattanooga.

GREEN, E. N.        Co. A, 35TN

GREEN, Enzor J.        Co. H, 4TN Cav.

GREEN, J. P.        Co. L, 36TN
    Enl. Jan. 9, 1862 at Chattanooga.

GREEN, Dr. Lapsley Yantis - 43TN Inf.  Surgeon
    Born at Perryville, KY, 10 May 1828. He was the son of Wilson Green and Elizabeth Walker. He married Caroline (Callie) Walker in KY. After gaining his medical training at the University of Louisville, he practiced in MS for four years prior to moving to Chattanooga in 1855. The Green's frame home was at Seventh and Chestnut. He volunteered as surgeon in the 43d Inf. which had been recruited largely by his kinsman Francis Marion Walker. Dr. Green was at Camp Key near Knoxville, where his duties included ordering cords of wood as fuel for the camp hospital. Due to ill health, he was transferred to hospital duty on June 1, 1862, by order of the Surgeon General. Meanwhile Caroline Walker Green was a nurse to wounded soldiers at Chattanooga Dr. Green continued his medical practice after the war from an office on the Chestnut St. property. His wife died 10 June 1903 and he died 21 June 1906 on Lookout Mountain. [CT June 22, 1906; Lindsley, p. 522]

GREEN, 1st Sgt. Morris        Co. F, 35TN
    Born in New Orleans in 1842, he became a merchant in Chattanooga before enl. Oct. 1, 1862. Died Tullahoma, TN April 23, 1863.

GREEN, Oliver Shuford    Co. H, 4TN Cav.; Co. B, 5th TN    Cav. Bn.
    Born Sept. 9, 1832 in SC and came to Chattanooga in 1852. "Shoof" was a farmer near Chattanooga, living with his wife, Rebecca, and their

two sons and daughter. Enl. Aug., 1861. During fighting in which his own brother Baird was killed, "a brother of Benton McMillan, later governor of Tennessee, was shot down in this battle and left to die. Green ran to his rescue and brought McMillan back to the lines, where he was later nursed to life."
    After the war he returned to Chattanooga and in 1880 moved to another part of the state, returning soon after. He became watchman at the car barns of the Chattanooga Railroad and Light Co. Later he was put in charge of the Walden Ridge Tunnel. Mason. NBF Camp. Died March 9, 1912 and buried White Oak Cem. [CT March 10, 1912; NBFM7]

GREEN, Robert A.        Co. K, 43TN
    He enl. Oct. 17, 1861, at Ooltewah. He was captured at Vicksburg on July 4, 1863. He died at his home on Aug. 5, 1863, when he was about 15 years old. The family lived at Zion Hill south of Ooltewah. His parents were John and Elizabeth Green. John Green was from GA and Elizabeth Green from NC. The family was living in GA when Robert A. Green was born and until several years before the war. [Lindsley, 528]

GREEN, Samuel E.        8TX Cav.
    Born Pikeville, TN, 1850. Brother of W. Taylor Green. Enl. at Kennesaw, 1864 in 8TX. Merchant in Chattanooga. Married Maryland Jenkins. Died here July 27, 1921 and buried Forest Hills Cemetery. [NBFM2,7; CT July 28, 1921]

GREGORY, James L.        Co. A, 62TN
    Born McMinn Co., 1845. Enl. Oct., 1862. Wounded at Big Black, May 17, 1863. 1903 res. East End. [TP5266]

GRIFFIN (GRIFFITH), Manassa (Manassas)    Barry's Btry.
    Enl. May 20, 1862 at Chattanooga; killed in action on Chattahoochee River (north side), July 7, 1864. [Brown's Diary]

GRIFFIN, Samuel Columbus [Cobben?]        Co. G, 66NC
    Born Davie Co., NC. Enl. Sept. 1, 1862 at Salisbury. Married Mary Elizabeth Cheek in Concord, NC, 1866 and lived at Mocksville, NC several years, coming to Chattanooga about 1891. Carpenter. [TWP2685]

GRIFFISS, John Carroll        1MD Inf.; Co. G, 13VA
    Born Oct. 4, 1844, in Baltimore. Married Penelope Adelaide (Nellie) Hooke 3 April 1866. She was born 3 April 1847 and died 4 March 1880. Worked for the Express Company in Chattanooga after war, then

wholesale grain, then Chattanooga Plow Co. He read law with D. M. Key and was admitted to bar but never practiced. 1st Presbyterian Church. Mason. Developed Caldwell-Griffiss block downtown and became director of 1st Nat'l Bank. Exec. Comm, NBF Camp, 1894. Died June 18, 1924 at his home on Walden's Ridge and buried Forest Hills Cemetery. [CT June 19, 1918; UDC2 pg 212.]

GRIGSBY, John    Co. G, 26TN; 2d Co. K, 1CSA (GA)
Born 1845 in TN, son of Thomas and Eliza. Res. of Harrison. Enl. 15 July 1861, Knoxville. Sick at Bowling Green, Jan. 23, 1862. In Howard's Bn., AL Cav., Dec. 31, 1862-Feb. 28, 1863.

GRISHAM (GRISSAM), Edmund D. (J.?)    Co. K, 43TN
Enl. Nov. 15, 1862 at Ooltewah; captured at Vicksburg, July 4, 1863; took USA oath, Dec. 11, 1863; dark complexion, black hair, and hazel eyes.

GRISHAM (GRISSAM), H. J.    Co. K, 43TN
Enl. Oct. 17, 1861 at Ooltewah.

GRISHAM, J. D.    43TN
In 1905 he applied from James Co. for admission to TN Soldiers Home.

GRISHAM, Jesse M.    Co. K, 43rd TN
He enl. Dec. 15, 1862, at Ooltewah. He was captured at the battle of Baker's Creek on May 16, 1863. He was imprisoned at Fort Delaware, where he died July 12, 1864. He was buried on the Jersey shore. Prior to the war, he was living on the farm of his father, Jesse Grisham, at Ooltewah. His mother was Levina Grisham. Jesse M. Grisham was born about 1845.

GRISHAM (GRISSAM), John    Co. K, 43TN
Enl. Oct. 12, 1861 at Ooltewah; captured at Vicksburg, July 4, 1863; took USA oath, Dec. 11, 1863; dark complexion, dark hair, black eyes, 5'8" tall. Died Finn's Point Prison, July 12, 1864 and buried in National Cem.

GRISTE, Allen    Washington Grays, 61NC
Born Aug. 14, 1838 in Beauford Co., NC. Enl. May 12, 1861. Paroled May, 1865. Hotel keeper in Chattanooga. At storming of Ft. Hutson was one of 12 men who volunteered to carry powder over to the fort. Was detailed to lead charge for Capt. of his company. Left Chattanooga. He died in 1918 at Tunnel Hill, GA. [NBFM2]

GRIZZLE, John H. - TN Conscript, Camp of Instruction
Enl. Sept. 18, 1862, Knoxville. Captured Sept.

9, 1863, Cumberland Gap. Imp. Camp Douglas, IL. Said he had been conscripted and took USA oath, April, 1864. Enl. in US Navy.

GRIZZLE [GRIZZELL], William
Born c1828, TN. Fireman in Chattanooga, 1860, with wife Elizabeth and two children. Enl. Oct. 19, 1862, Knoxville. Captured Sept. 9, 1863, Cumberland Gap. Imp. Camp Douglas, IL. Said he had been conscripted and took the USA oath, April, 1864. Applied for USN but rejected physical reasons.

GROSS, George    Co. H, 26TN
Unmarried son of William Gross, he enl. July 14, 1861, at Knoxville; killed in battle of Fort Donelson, Feb. 15, 1862.

GROSS, RICHARD    2nd Co. K, 1st CSA Cav.
Born 1836 in TN. 1860 farm laborer at Chattanooga with wife Elizabeth. Enl. Sept. 20, 1862 in HC. Deserted July 20, 1863.

GRUBB, A. J.    Co. G, 5TN
Of Meigs Co. Died Dec. 25, 1917 in Chattanooga; buried Beason's Cem. [CT Dec. 26, 1917]

GUERRA, Masalena    Barry's Btry.
Deserted June-July, 1864. [Brown's Diary]

GUIRE, G. W.    Co. G, 26TN; 2nd Co. K, 1CSA (GA)
Enl. July 9, 1861., Knoxville. Captured Fort Donelson and imp. Camp Morton. In Academy Hospital, Chattanooga, May 9, 1863. On hospital duty, July 1863-Sept. 1864.

GUIRE, J. C.    Co. G, 26TN
Enl. Aug. 25, 1861, Knoxville. Captured Fort Donelson and imp. Camp Morton.

GUIRE, James H.    Co. G, 26TN; 2nd Co. K, 1CSA (GA)
Enl. in 26TN Aug. 28, 1861 in Knoxville. Hospitalized most of 1863 and early 1864. Took USA oath, Nov., 1864 at Nashville. Res. in HC. Light complexion., sandy hair, blue eyes, and 5'8" tall.

GUIRE, Nathaniel    Co. G, 26TN; 2nd Co. K, 1CSA (GA)
Enl. in 26TN Nov. 27, 1861 in Knoxville. Hospitalized most of 1863 and early 1864. Took USA oath, Nov., 1864 at Nashville. Res. in HC.

GUTHRIE, David Martiel    Co. E, 3CSA Cav.
Born April 19, 1846 in Walker Co., GA. Enl. at Tunnel Hill, GA, Apr., 1863. Paroled May 12, 1865.

1901 farmer in St. Elmo. Baptist. 1910 real estate collection agent. Died April 23, 1919 in St. Elmo and buried Coulter's Cem., Cooper Heights. [TP5267; CT April 24, 1919; 1910HC]

GUTHRIE, James          Co. I, 19TN; Co. H, 19LA
          Transferred Feb. 1, 1864 from 19TN to 19LA. Hospitalized, order of Dr. Philson, May 8, 1864. Died of wounds in hospital, Vilner, GA, Sept. 9, 1864. [Booth]

GUTHRIE, James A. P.      Co. I, 19TN; Co. H, 19LA
          Born c1824 HC. Res. Harrison. Enl. May 20, 1861, Knoxville. On detached service as cook for sick at hospital at Camp Cummings. Justice of the Peace in HC during 1870's and lived until 1896.

GUTHRIE, J. Fred       Co. C, 61NC
          Born Jan 11, 1840 in Carteret Co., NC. Enl. Jan 14, 1862. Wounded at Kingston. Confectioner and Restauranteur in Chattanooga. Moved away several years later. [NBFM2]

GUTHRIE, J. S.          6GA
          Born in North GA, he came to Chattanooga after the war. Died Oct. 9, 1906 in Conway, AR where he had gone three months before for his health. Buried Forest Hills Cemetery. [CT Oct. 11, 1906]

GUTHRIE, Maj. Lawson        Co. K, 43TN
          Born in 1826, he was a veteran of the Mexican War, serving as Capt. of the Fifth Company, Fourth Regiment, of TN Volunteers and won a brevet promotion "for gallantry" at the battle of Cerro Gordo. He enl. in the Confederate army Oct. 17, 1861, at Ooltewah, becoming captain of the HC company of 43TN of which he was elected Major, Dec. 14, 1861. He was wounded in the thigh at Vicksburg, captured and later exchanged. His wound disabled him, however, and he resigned Jan. 22, 1864. The examining physician cited chronic bronchitis and hepatitis as aggravating factors.
          He was the son of Thomas Guthrie and Mary Canterbury, and he was born while the family was still in KY. The family moved to the King's Point area at Toqua about 1839, but they later moved north of Harrison. Lawson Guthrie married Narcissa Smith. [1860 Hamilton Co., TN Census]

GWINN, Alemiel
          Born 1845, Ky. Laborer in HC, 1910. [1910HC]

# H

HACKETT, Sgt. Albert Torrence        Barry's Btry.
          Born 30 June 1829 at Lawrenceville, GA. Enl. Oct., 1862 at Knoxville; paroled May 11, 1865 at Meridian, MS; res. of Barnesville, GA. He married twice, 1st Jane Payne on 27 Sept. 1854. She was born 30 Oct 1834 and died 9 Oct. 1860 in Ringgold. Second, he married Adelia McConnell. He lived the last 50 years of his life in Ringgold (prominent atty, solicitor general for district), but died in Chattanooga March 20, 1911 at the home of his grandson, J. Roy Johnson and buried in Ringgold. [Brown's Diary; CT March 21, 1911; UDC2 pg 216.]

HACKETT, Wright Smith 1Lt.      Co. C, 16TN
          Born 1834, he was son of Samuel H. Hackett of Greene Co. Educated at Harvard and Tusculum colleges, he became a lawyer prior to the war. He served in Savage's 16TN and was killed at Atlanta, July 22, 1864. He was buried at Griffin, GA, then re-interred at Forest Hills Cemetery, Oct. 31, 1899, the same day as F.M. Walker. Also shown as buried in CSA Cem. [CDT, Nov. 1, 1899]

HADDOCK, W. C.          Winston's Lt. Arty.
          Born 1839 in AL. Lived in GA before moving to HC where in 1860 he was farm laborer with wife Elizabeth J. Enl. Dec. 14, 1862. Sick in hospital at Chattanooga, Dec. 1862 and deserted Dec. 21, 1862.

HADDOX, David C.  Co. D, 37TN
          Born 1845 in GA, son of David and Lydia of Zion Hill. Enl. Sept. 1, 1861 at Knoxville.

HAFLEY, Winston C.      Co. C, Walker's Bn., Thomas Legion (NC Inf.)
          Born 1848, Athens, TN. Res. Blount Co., TN. Enl. 1862. Reported present Sept.-Oct 1862 and Jan.-April 1863; absent without leave May-June 1863; present Sept.-Oct. 1863; deserted Dec. 6, 1863; took USA oath at Knoxville, Dec. 16, 1863. Dealer in music in Chattanooga c1895. Poet and song-writer. Died in Atlanta, GA. May 9, 1904 and buried there. [NBFM2]

HAGAN, Richard Wallace        4TN Cav. (Murray's)
          Born Nov. 25, 1845 in Baltimore and came to Chattanooga as child with his family. Enl. Aug., 1862 in 4TN Cav. (Carter's); lost his horse at Perryville and rode out of KY on limber of White's TN Btry, which he proceeded to join. Fought at Murfreesboro, Chickamauga, Atlanta Camp. Res. of Hill City. Merchant. Member of NBF Camp, 1895-96. Died at

home on 312 Forest Ave, April 10, 1930 and buried Chattanooga Mem. Park. [NBFM2, 6; CT April 11, 1930]

HAGGARD, John T.      Co. D, 17TN (Newman's)
        Born Bedford Co., TN, 1836. Enl. July 16, 1862 at Estill Springs. Wounded at Franklin. Surrendered at Greensboro, NC, May, 1865. Res. of Chattanooga in 1903 but had become "peevish, fitful, cross." By 1910 "living on charity of friends." A burden to his children with whom he lived, when his welcome was worn out in Chattanooga he would go to Aubrey, TX for a few months, then return. [TP 5815]

HAGGARD, William H. Sgt.      Co. B, 5TN Cav.
        Born 1829 in TN. 1860 farmer at Chattanooga with wife Lorena and six children. [1860HC}

HAIR, Larkin      Home Guards
        Born Dec. 6, 1812; died Jan. 8, 1897. Wife was Cynthia L. Buried in Citizens Cem.

HALE, Benjamin M.      Co. D, 36TN
        Born 1827 in VA; blacksmith in Ooltewah. Married S.J. [1860 HC Census]

HALE, Bill      Co. C, 3TN Cav. Bn.; Co. B,
                1TN Cav. (Carter's)
        From Grasshopper Creek area, HC. [Roark, Hardtack and Hardship]

HALE, Cpl. Claiborne D.      Co. I, 19TN
        Born 1839 in TN, son of Elijah. Farmer at Harrison. Enl. May 20, 1861., Knoxville. Prom. to a Cpl. Deserted Dec. 28, 1862. [1860HC]

HALE, Madison      Co. C., 31TN
        Born July 16, 1827 in Washington Co., TN and moved as small boy to Jefferson Co. where he became a farmer. Married (1846) Nellie J. Bryson. Enl. Dec. 1862 but his health was frail, and he was discharged Jan. 8, 1863. Res. 1895 Chattanooga. Invalid. Member of NBF Camp who died July 31, 1891 and was buried in CSA Cem. [NBFM2, 7]

HALE, Lt. William M.      Co. I, 19TN
        Born about 1840, son of Elijah Hale, at Harrison. Farmer. Enl. May 20, 1861, Knoxville. Wounded at Shiloh. Prom. to 2nd Lt., May 10, 1862. Slightly wounded, Murfreesboro, Dec. 31, 1862; Jan. 8, 1864, absent on special recruiting duty. Deserted and took USA Oath, Dec. 27, 1863, HC. To remain north of Ohio River.

HALEY, James      Co. L, 35TN

Fifty-four years old in 1862, he enl. at Chattanooga, but was discharged not long afterwards as a "non conscript."

HALEY, 1st Sgt. Joel Thomas .      Co. B, 3GA Bn.
        Born Nov. 9, 1836 in Danielsville, GA. Was wounded at the battle of Jonesboro, and when he re-enlisted, he started his own company. Married 11 Oct. 1866 to Cornelia Cornelia Jones in Franklin Co., TN. She was born 14 Nov 1845 in Hart Co., GA and died 20 July 1926 in Atlanta, GA. He died Jan. 14, 1894 in HC. Buried Forest Hills Cemetery. [TWP, p. 145; UDC2 pg 218.]

HALEY (Hailey), John Cloud      Co. L, 36TN; Co. L, 35TN; Co. A,      4TN Cav.; Co. B, 2TN Cav.
        Born April 12, 1844 in Roane Co., he was son of William B. Haley. Enl. May, 1861 in the Indian Territory in Co. H, 2TN Cav. (Ashby's Brigade). Enl. Jan. 9, 1862 at Chattanooga, Co. L, 36TN; moved on to Co. L, 35TN, then in July, 1862, to Rice's Cavalry. Wounded four times. Captured in battle of Somerset, KY, Mar. 29, 1863; imprisoned at Johnson's Island and later Point Lookout, MD. Came to Chattanooga after war and became a river boat pilot in 1867. Was mate or captain on "nearly every boat that ran on the TN, including the M.H. Clift which blew up, injuring him severely. Resided in Hill City, 1910. Member of NBF Camp, 1895. He married Mary Jane Montgomery, born 13 Oct 1848 and died 31 May 1906. Moved to family farm in Roane Co., 1913. Died at Eureka, TN, Jan. 19, 1915 and buried there. [1910HC; CT Jan. 20, 1915; NBFM2; UDC1 pg 173]

HALL, Alexander      Co. L, 36TN; Co. L, 35TN
        Born c1830 in NC and farm laborer in household of C.B. Champion, 1860. Enl. Jan. 9, 1862 in Co. L, 36TN at Chattanooga; transferred to Co. L, 35TN; fought at Murfreesboro and was paroled at Greensboro, NC, May 1, 1865.

HALL, Isam P.      2d Co. B, 15TX
        Born 1846, Ga. 1910 stacker for lumber co. Res. Cross St. with wife Maudie (m. 1865) in household of son Jeff. [1910HC]

HALL, J. P.      Co. A, 1GA Cav.
        Born Lumpkin Co., GA. Enl. April, 1863. Lost eye from explosion of shell. Surrendered May 12, 1865 at Kingston, GA. To TN in 1868. Laborer in brickyard. Wife was M. Jane. Res. of Chattanooga in 1915. [TP 14,741]

HALL, J. T.      Co. H, 26TN
        Born c1842. Enl. July 8, 1861, Knoxville;

Captured Fort Donelson, Feb. 16, 1862, and imp. Camp Douglas.

HALL, John A.          Co. H, 26TN
        Born c1842. Enl. Aug. 6, 1861, Knoxville. Honorably disch. Dec. 6, 1861., Bowling Green.

HALL, John C.          Co. H, 26TN
        Born c1843. Enl. Aug. 6, 1861, Knoxville; Captured Fort Donelson, Feb. 16, 1862 and imp. Camp Douglas.

HALL, John M.          Co. I, 19TN
        Enl. Sept. 5, 1861 at Cumberland Gap, TN. He died in April, 1862. [Worsham, p. 49 says died in May, 1862 in Corinth.]

HALL, Thomas H.          Co. I, 19TN

HALL, William          Co. I, 19TN
        Enl. Aug. 15, 1861, Cumberland Gap. Deserted May, 1862.

HALL, William          2nd Co. K, 1st CSA Cav.
        Enl. Sept. 20, 1862. "Deserted."

HALLMAN, T. C.
        [NBFM3]

HAMILL, Daniel H.          Co. H, 2TN Cav. (Ashby's)
        Born in 1823, son of Samuel Hamill and Catherine Best. Married Mary Jones in 1849. Enl. Feb. 3, 1863 at Chattanooga and detailed as a teamster. He fought with the Confederate forces along with his brother, Elijah W. Hamill; another brother, John F. Hamill, joined the Federal forces. Daniel's household paroled April, 1865. He died in 1874. [UDC2 pg 221.]

HAMILL, Elijah W.          Co. L, 36TN
        Enl. Jan. Sept. 1862, at Chattanooga, and fought at Murfreesboro. He deserted Sept. 15, 1863, just before the fighting at Chickamauga and took USA "non com" parole. He was born in 1833 and was one of the sons of Samuel Hamill and Catherine Best. [1860HC]

HAMILTON, A. C.          Co. H, 26TN
        Born c1802. Enl. Aug. 6, 1861, Knoxville; disch. June 3, 1862.

HAMILTON, John M. - Co. H, 26TN; 2d Co. I, 1CSA
        Born c1839; enl. July 8, 1861, Knoxville with rank of 2d Cpl. Captured Fort Donelson, Feb. 16, 1862 and imprisoned Camp Douglas; transferred to 1CSA Nov. 8, 1862; Captured in Walker Co., GA, 1863 and took USA oath at

Nashville and released Dec. 24, 1863. Took oath again at Louisville, KY and released, Dec. 27, 1863, to stay north of Ohio during war.

HAMILTON, John R.          Co. H, 26TN
        Born c1840. Enl. July 8, 1861, Knoxville; Captured Fort Donelson, Feb. 16, 1862 and imprisoned Camp Douglas. Exchanged and "left at Chattanooga Oct. 5, 1862."

HAMILTON, Richard          Co. H, 26TN
        Born c1843. Enl. July 8, 1861, Knoxville; Captured Fort Donelson and imp. Camp Douglas.

HAMMONDS, J. M.          Co. L, 36TN
        Enl. Jan. 9, 1862 at Chattanooga.

HANCOCK, Harrison
        Born 1815, Chesterfield Co., VA and came to HC c1844. Married Jemima Gotcher and they lived at Tyner. Worked for CSA Govt. Died March 27, 1901 and buried at family burial grounds. Mason, Baptist.

HANCOCK, Henry Crawford    Co. E, 3GA or Co. C, 27GA or Co. B, 11GA
        Born Sept. 16, 1846, Hall Co., GA and married (1868) Nora Smith, born 27 Aug. 1849 in Hall Co., GA. Died Oct. 3, 1891 in HC and buried Forest Hills Cemetery. [TWP, 205; 1890 VetCensus]

HANCOCK, Cpl. Josiah          Co. G, 26TN
        Enl. July 8, 1861, Knoxville. Killed at Fort Donelson, Feb. 15, 1862. Widow Catherine Ann received his pay and effects. Res. Ringgold, GA.

HAND, J. C.          Co. H, 26TN
        Born c1842. Enl. July 8, 1861, Knoxville. Left sick at Bowling Green, Jan. 23, 1862.

HANEY, J. J.          4TN Cav.
        Born June 23, 1833 in Frederick Co., VA. Enl. June, 1861 in Gen. Sterling Price's escort as 1LT. Afterwards on Van Dorn's staff. Then served in 4TN Cav. until end of war. Wounded at Chickamauga. To Chattanooga, 1871 and lived here thereafter except 7 1/2 years in Atlanta. Centenary Methodist. Died at res. 17 Oak St., Dec. 20, 1898 and buried CSA Cem. [NBFM2; CT Dec. 21, 1898]

HANKINS, James C.          Co. B, 5TN Cav.
        Born about 1822, he was a farm laborer at Tyner prior to the start of the war. Enl. Aug. 11, 1861. His wife, Sarah, was a native of NC.

HANKINS, J. M.          Barry's Btry.

Enl. April, 4, 1862, at Chattanooga.

HANKINS, John C.          Co. A, 19TN
        Born c1822, TN, and res. Tyner where he was farm laborer with wife Sarah (born NC). Enl. May 1861, Knoxville. Detached to cut logs at Chattanooga, July, 1863. 1890, Lt. police in Chattanooga. Alive in 1903 although may be res. of Whitfield Co., GA by then. [TP2517]

HANN (see HORN)

HANNAH, Ezekiel "Zeke"          Barry's Btry.
        Enl. July 12, 1862. at Chattanooga; hospitalized Feb., 1863 in Canton, MS; paroled May 11, 1865 at Meridian, MS.

HANSHIELD (HOUSHIELD, HOUTSHIELD), Frederick     Co. F, 35TN
        Enl. Dec. 8, 1862 at Chattanooga; wounded at Chickamauga.

HARBIN, William John          Co. B, Palmetto SS
        Born 1842 in Oconee Co., SC and married (1868) Nannie M. Kidd. Died 1893 in HC and buried CSA Cem. [TWP;NBFM7]

HARDIN, Francis Marion          Co. M, 1TN Cav. (Carter's)
        Born 1843 in TN, son of Gilbert and Rebecca Hardin. Res. 1860 with parents in Birchwood. [1860HC]

HARDIN, Solomon "Sol"  Co. B, 1TN Cav. (Carter's); Barry's Btry.
        A native of KY, he was born about 1826, moved to TN and had a farm at Birchwood. His wife's name was Mary. He appears to have enl. in the 1TN Cav. (Carter's), then transferred, April 4, 1862, to Barry's Battery at Chattanooga. He was paroled on May 11, 1865, at Meridian, MS. Res. in HC in 1906.

HARDIN, William          Barry's Btry.
        Either born 1820 in KY with wife Mary at Birchwood. Prob. brother of Solomon. Or William born 1844 in TN, son of Gilbert and Rebecca. Both Wm Hardins living in Birchwood in 1860 [1860HC]

HARDING, Solomon
        Born 1852 in Bradley Co. and married (1866 in James Co.) Isadore Beloin[?]. Died 1922 in HC. [TWP, 223]

HARE (HAIR), Capt. Richard B.          Co. B, 45TN
        Born c1824, Bowling Green, KY. Enl. Jan,

1861 at Lebanon. Merchant, tailor in Chattanooga c1890. Died at res. on E. 5th St. Oct. 3, 1898 and buried Forest Hills Cemetery. [CT Oct. 4, 1898; NBFM2; 1890Vet Census]

HARGIS, Rufus          Co. H, 4TN Cav.
        Died 1862.

HARGIS, J. R.          Co. H, 4TN Cav.
        Born 1844, near Jasper. Enl. at Chattanooga Co. B, 3TN. Trans. to Co. H, 4TN Cav. Captured May, 1863 and imprisoned Camp Chase and Rock Island. Paroled March, 1865. Was in battles of Fort Donelson, East Ky., Murfreesboro, West Tenn Campaign, Franklin. Res. Taylor, TX, 1911. [Yeary, Rems. of Boys in Gray, p. 309, 349]

HARGRAVE, J. L.          Co. G, 26TN
        Enl. July 8, 1861, Knoxville. 1st Sgt.; Captured Ft. Donelson, Feb. 16, 1862 and imprisoned Camp Morton. Killed at Chickamauga.

HARGRAVE, 2Lt. William H.     Co. G, 26TN; 2d Co. K, 1CSA(GA)
        Enl. summer, 1861. Re-enl. Feb. 17, 1863 in Mobile, AL. Res. of Social Circle, GA. Age 17, fair complexion, dark hair, blue eyes, 5'7" tall. Promoted to Sgt., Feb. 29, 1864 and 2Lt. March 17, 1864. Wounded at Chickamauga, Sept., 1863, and Atlanta, July 22, 1864. Captured at Nashville, Dec. 16, 1864 and imprisoned at Johnson's Island. Was Lt. at time of his release, June, 1865. J. L. Hargrave probably brother. W.H.H. died May 9, 1909 at res. in Highland Park, age 66, and buried Chickamauga. [CT May 10, 1909; NBFM7]

HARKINS, William Wesley     Co. H, 3GA Mtd. Inf.
        Born 1845 near Asheville, NC, son of Thomas and Mary Harkins. He moved with his parents to Rome, GA where he enl. He participated in Bragg's KY Campaign, was captured and imprisoned at Louisville until exchanged. At a fight at Eagleville, TN, April 1, 1863, he was wounded, but recovered in time to fight at Chickamauga. Wounded again at McMinnville while serving under Wheeler. Captured at Mill Creek, Oct. 3, 1863 and imprisoned at Rock Island, IL where he remained until March 20, 1865. After the war he went to Cleveland, TN where he eventually engaged in railroading, becoming an inspector for the N. C. & St. L. RR. Moved to Chattanooga about 1894. Officer of the day, NBF Camp, 1894. His wife was Mattie J. Blalock, born 26 June 1848. Res. 1910 on Prospect St. with wife Martha. Foreman, RR depot. Died Jan. 29, 1918 and buried in Calhoun, GA. [NBFM2,7; UDC1 pg 179.]

HARRALL (HARRELL, HARRILL), Sgt. James. A. L. (B.) Barry's Btry.
Enl. Oct. 4, 1862. at Knox.; paroled May 5, 1865. at Meridian, MS; res. of West Point, GA.

HARRALSON (HARALSON), J. H. Sgt.   2nd Co. K, 1st CSA Cav.
Enl. Sept. 24, 1862 in HC. Promoted to 4th Sgt., March 1, 1863. Paroled May 3, 1865 in Charlotte, NC.

HARRALSON (HARALSON), H. C.       2nd Co. K, 1st CSA Cav.
Enl. March 3, 1864 in Whitfield Co., GA. Hospitalized at Atlanta June 9, 1864. Paroled May 3, 1865 in Charlotte, NC.

HARRALSON (HARALSON), T. M.  Bvt. 2Lt. 2nd Co. K, 1st CSA Cav.
Enl. Sept. 24, 1862 in HC. Wounded June 20, 1864 and hospitalized in Atlanta. Paroled May 3, 1865 in Charlotte, NC.

HARRINGTON, A. P.  Crescent Regt. of New Orleans
Born Dec. 11, 1839 in Tuscaloosa, AL. Enl. in New Orleans, March 4, 1862. Afterwards served in Co. G, 13LA. Shiloh. Captured at Perryville. Released Jan. 8, 1863. At close of war was ordnance Sgt. on duty at Augusta, GA. Living on Market St. above Greves Drug Store. Died in Chattanooga Sept. 17, 1902 and buried CSA Cem. [NBFM2,3]

HARRINGTON, Capt. Michael
Organized and commanded Chattanooga Home Guards.

HARRIS, Gilford Parkes   Co. H, 26TN; 2d Co. I, 1CSA; Co. F, 39GA
4th Cpl., Sept. 6, 1861. Transferred to 1CSA, Nov. 8, 1862; Aug. 31, 1864 roll shows him present; transferred to 39GA; surrendered Greensboro, NC, April, 26, 1865. [Henderson, 4:303]

HARRIS, J. W. - Co. C, 1MS&AL Cav. Bn.; 8CSA Cav.
Born May 20, 1845 in Lowdnes Co., MS. Enl. at Columbus, MS in 1861 in Co. C, 1MS&AL Bn of Cav.; afterwards in 8CSA Cav. Paroled as Capt. at Columbus MS. Became lumber merchant in Chattanooga. [NBFM2]

HARRIS, Jackson "Jack"   Wheeler's Cav.
Born 1823, TN. Farm laborer at Snow Hill, 1860 with wife Rutha. Died in Chickamauga. Member of 1st Universalist Church in Chattanooga. [CT Feb. 11, 1915]

HARRIS, Jesse J.       Co. G, 26TN; 2d Co. K, 1CSA (GA)
Enl. Aug. 28, 1861, Knoxville. Chaplain. Captured at Fort Donelson, Feb. 16, 1862, and imprisoned in Camp Morton.

HARRIS, John A. [See John L. and John S.]
Born 1835, Ireland. Married (1880) Ella Fulet. Buried CSA Cem. Died 1910. [1910HC]

HARRIS, John L.      Co. A, 10AL or Co. F, 2AL Bn. Lt. Arty.
Born Bambridge Co., Ireland Jan. 27, 1843. Enl. in AL. Settled in Chattanooga after war. Died at home on Dodson Ave. July 31, 1910 and buried CSA Cem.

HARRIS, John S.         Co. E, 20AL
Born County Down, Ireland. Enl. April 1, 1862, Greene Co., AL. Detailed in Nitre Bureau, near Larkinville, AL, and was there when war ended. He married Ella, born 1 May 1854 in Keroy, Ireland daughter of Welliemae & Mamie E. Res. East Chattanooga, 1906 but mind affected reports wife. Catholic. 1906 applied from HC for admission to TN Soldiers Home. [SAACH]

HARRIS, L.          Clark's Indep. Cav. Co.
Enl. Sept. 9, 1863 in Walker Co., GA. Deserted April 9, 1864 near Carnsville, GA.

HARRIS, M. B.  Co. G, 26TN; 2d Co. K, 1CSA (GA)
Enl. July 8, 1861; captured at Fort Donelson, Feb. 16, 1862 and imprisoned in Camp Morton. Absent recruiting duty, Feb. 28, 1863. Present Sept. 16, 1864.

HARRIS, Reuben L.      Co. G, 26TN; 2d Co. K, 1CSA (GA)
Enl. Aug. 28, 1861, Knoxville. Left sick at Bowling Green, Jan. 23, 1862. Also in 39GA, July 8-Dec. 31, 1862. Deserted and received at Louisville, Feb 13, 1865, took USA oath and released to remain north of the OH. [Henderson, 303]

HARRIS, T. C.
Vet. elected to NBF Camp in 1899.

HARRIS, Thomas R.            Barry's Btry.
He and his older brother, James C. Harris, had Unionist sympathies, but Thomas joined Barry's Battery, apparently unwillingly, in Knoxville on Oct. 3, 1862. He was in a hospital at Canton, MS, and was among those "caught by Yankees" at Missionary Ridge on Nov. 23,

1863. He was sent to Nashville, then to Louisville, KY, and finally to Rock Island prison in IL. Shortly after his release on Dec. 16, 1863, he joined the U.S. Navy. He was on board the U.S.S. Massachusetts, serving until August of 1865. His brother, James, was killed while fighting for the Union with the 4th East TN Cav. The Harris brothers were sons of Robert M. Harris and Lucinda Maupin, who were originally from Albemarle Co., VA. The family settled at an early date in the vicinity of Lookout Mtn. Thomas Harris married Catherine Tennessee Hamill on Sept. 2, 1862, just before he joined Barry's Battery. The couple lived in the vicinity of St. Elmo until 1891 when they moved to Sequatchie, TN. Harris died there in Oct. 1918 at the age of 76. [Brown's Diary; CT Oct. 7, 1918]

HARRIS, W. W.          Clark's Independent Cav. Co.
          Enl. Aug. 31, 1862 at Chattanooga; captured June 27, 1863 at Manchester, TN.

HARRIS, William Henderson H.   Co. K, 21TN; 1Cav. (Carter's)
          Born Dec. 23, 1846 in Marshall Co., TN. Enl. at Chapel Hill, TN July, 1864. Cut off by enemy in Lincoln Co., TN in Dec., 1864 and about 80 including Harris escaped South and were assigned to Nixon's TN Regt, Maj. Houston Dudley as Capt. Paroled at Gainesville, AL, May 9, 1865. Married 3 Oct. 1881 in Bedford Co., TN to Fannie A. Marsh, born 3 Juen 1861 in Bedford Co, TN and died 12 June 1916 in Chattanooga. They came to Chattanooga from Marshall Co. TN c1900. NBF. Died July 30, 1910. at res. on Houston St. July 30, 1910., age 64, and bur. CSA Cem. [CT July 31, 1910; NBFM2; TP 3930; UDC2 pg 231.]

HART, William          Clark's Independent Cav. Co.
          Enl. Dec. 9, 1862 at Triune, TN.

HART, William     Co. H, 26TN; 3CSA Cav.; 2d Co. I, 1CSA (GA)
          Born c1835. Enl. Aug. 6, 1861, Knoxville. Left at Chattanooga. Captured Fort Donelson, Feb. 16, 1862 and imprisoned Camp Douglas. Exchanged and left sick at Chattanooga, Oct. 5, 1862 and deserted.

HARTLINE, Henry Sims     Co. G, 19AL
          Born May, 1834 in Cherokee Co., AL. Enl. Sept., 1861, Huntsville, AL. Received "severe wound (at Shiloh, April 6, 1862) from which he never fully recovered." Captured April 7, 1862. NBF Camp. Died June 25, 1912 in Cohutta, GA and buried Forest Hills Cemetery. [CT June 26-27, 1912; NBFM4]

HARVY, Sgt. G. B. (P.)     Barry's Btry.
     Enl. April 20, 1862. at Cleveland; in arrest at Pollard,

AL, Nov., 1862-Apr., 1863; deserted May 1, 1863. [Brown's Diary]

HARVY, Samuel A.          Barry's Btry.
          Enl. April 15, 1862 at Chattanooga; deserted Dec. 11, 1862. [Brown's Diary]

HARVEY, William A.          Co. K, 43TN
          Born 1844 in GA. Res, 1860, in household of Thomas Love in Chattanooga Enl. Dec. 10, 1861 at Ooltewah; deserted March 31, 1862.

HASLET (HASLIT), William M. (W.)     Co. B, 1TN Cav. (Carter's)
          Captured Cumberland Gap, Sept. 9, 1863 and imprisoned Fort Delaware where he died (April 14, 1864) and was buried.

HATCH, James M.          Co. D, 61NC
          Died March 1919, 3130 Avenue J in East Lake and buried CSA Cem. [CT March 15, 1919]

HATFIELD, Franklin Miller     Co. K, 5TN; 35TN
          Born Dec. 27, 1837 in Bledsoe Co., TN. Enl. near McMinnville, Sept. 6, 1861 as 2nd Cpl., Co. K, 5TN. After Shiloh transferred to 35TN. Res. Fairmont, HC. Married Malvina. Farmer. Member of County Court. Died Feb. 14, 1904 near Calhoun, GA and buried in Daisy. [NBFM2,4; TWP619; CT Feb. 16, 1904]

HATFIELD, William M.          Co. K, 43TN
          Enl. Oct. 10, 1861 at Ooltewah; captured at Vicksburg, July 4, 1863 and paroled.

HATFIELD, William P.          16GA
          Born at Fairview, KY, 1836, he enl. in June, 1863 at Cedar Grove, GA. He was in the fighting at Chickamauga, captured and imprisoned at Cannelton, IN. He later lived at East Lake. [TP 16,640]

HATSON, Isaac          26TN; 2d Co. K, 1CSA (GA)
          No enlistment info. Disch. Nov. 8, 1862.

HAWKINS, J. C.          Co. H, 26TN; Co. A, 19TN
          Born c1842. Enl. Aug. 6, 1861., Knoxville. Captured at Fort Donelson, Feb. 16, 1862. and imprisoned in Camp Douglas. Left sick at Chattanooga, Oct. 5, 1862; Member NBF Camp, 1896.

HAWKINS, J. M.- Co. H, 26TN; 2d Co. I, 1CSA (GA)
          Enl. Sept. 17, 1861, Knoxville. Captured at Fort Donelson, Feb. 16, 1862 and imprisoned in Camp Douglas. Absent sick, sent to hospital in Chattanooga, Aug. 24, 1863. Detached as wagoner, June 30-Aug. 31, 1864.

HAWKINS, James E.   Co. H, 26TN; 1CSA Cav;
                              2d Co. 1, 1CSA (GA)
        Born c1842, SC. Farm laborer res. household of C.C. Lynes at Zion Hill, 1860. Enl. Sept. 17, 1861, Knoxville; left sick, Nashville, 1861.
        In Howard's AL Cav., Dec. 31, 1862. Transferred 1CSA, March 15, 1863. Admitted to Empire Hospital, May 24, 1864. Killed Kennesaw Mtn. Buried Oakland Cem., May 25, 1864. Block D, Row 6, Grave 14.

HAWKINS, Moses          Co. H, 26TN
        Born c1840. Enl. July 8, 1861, Knoxville. Died at Bowling Green, Dec. 3, 1861.

HAWKINS, Thomas H.          Barry's Btry.
        Enl. May 9, 1862 at Chattanooga; deserted April, 31, 1862 at Chattanooga; joined cav. organization; captured on retreat from Atlanta, Sept. 10, 1864. [Brown Diary]

HAWKINS, William A.          Co. G, 26TN; 2d Co. K,
                              1CSA (GA)
        Enl. July 12, 1861, Knoxville. Captured at Fort Donelson, Feb. 16, 1861 and imprisoned Camp Douglas. Sgt., June 30, 1863. Paroled at Greensboro, May 1, 1865.

HAYS (HAYES), David     2nd Co. K, 1st CSA Cav.
        Enl. July 14, 1862 in HC. Captured at home inside Federal lines Nov. 27, 1863 and imprisoned at Rock Island, IL until his release Oct. 27, 1863. Res of Walker Co., GA.

HAYS, Thomas          Co. A, 19TN
        Res. of Chattanooga. Enl. May 10, 1862, Corinth. Hospitalized, then deserted at Chattanooga, Sept. 7, 1863. Took USA oath and to be released north of Ohio River.

HAZLEHURST, George H.          CSA Engineers
Capt.
        Born in Brunswick, GA in 1824. Lived some years in Philadelphia where he was civil engineer and contractor. Served in Hardee's Engineer Corps. 1st Presbyterian Church. Died in Chattanooga Nov. 25, 1883.

HAZLETT, William M.          Co. B, 1TN Cav.
(Carter's)
        Not found in 1860 HC, his horse was killed in action in 1862, captured at Cumberland Gap, KY, on Sept. 9, 1863, sent to Camp Morton from Louisville, KY in January of 1864, sent to Fort Delaware on March 19, 1864, died there April 14, 1864 of inflammation of the lungs, buried on the Jersey shore opposite the post.

HEADERICK, Lewis B. - 64NC; Co. H, 5TN Cav.
        Born Greene Co., TN June, 1836 and practiced law in Greeneville. Enl. in 64NC, then re-enl. in Co. H, 5TN Cav. Also served as commissary. Taught school, entered merchandising business in Tunnel Hill, GA and then moved to Chattanooga, Feb., 1873. Practiced law in Chattanooga, was County Surveyor, 1880-1882 and represented HC in the TN Gen'l Assembly, 1882. Married 25 July 1896 to Margaret Jane Dickson. Mason. Died here April 16, 1899 and buried in White Oak Cem. Charter member of NBF Camp. [CTS; BDTA; UDC1 pg 189]

HEADRICK, James M.          Co. C, 23GA
        Born Paulding Co., GA, 1833. Seven Pines, $2^{nd}$ Manassas, South Mountain, Sharpsburg, Wilderness, Cold Harbor, Petersburg, and Ocean Pond, FL. Surrendered at Kingston, GA, May, 1865. Wife was Mary G. In TN 1898 and in 1911 res. Shepherd, James Co. [TP13,386]

HEARN (see Herron)

HEATON, James          Co. K, 43TN
        He enl. Dec. 2, 1861, at Ooltewah. He was discharged Jan. 14, 1862. Prior to the war, he was living at Limestone north of Harrison with his wife, Nancy, and daughter, Mary J. James was born about 1833, was a farm laborer.

HEATON (HETON), Cpl. Sidney R.          Co. K, 43TN
        Enl. Oct. 17, 1861 at Ooltewah.

HEDGES, Nathaniel
        1830-1863. Buried in CSA Cem. [John S. Sins]

HEFFLIN, J. M.          Co. A, 19TN
        Wounded at Murfreesboro. In May, 1863, it was reported that he had been furloughed and had "since died."

HEINECKE, E.          Co. F, 35TN
        Born 1841 in Prussia, he moved to Chattanooga where he enl., Oct. 6, 1862.

HELTON, E. R.,- Co. G, 26TN; 2d Co. K, 1CSA (GA)
        Enl. July 12, 1861, Knoxville. Captured Fort Donelson and imprisoned Camp Morton. At home on sick furlough Catoosa Co., Dec. 31, 1862. Disch. disability, May 17, 1863.

HELTON, John          Co. H, 4TN Cav.
        Died 1862.

HEMBREE, Andrew J.          Co. H, 4TN Cav.

HEMBREE, Isaac          Co. H, 4TN Cav.
          Died 1862.

HEMPFIELD, Havner          5TN Cav.
          Deserted. Took the USA oath of allegiance on Sept. 23, 1864. He had dark complexion, brown hair, blue eyes, and was 5'9" tall.

HENDERSON, A. A.          Co. I, 43TN
          Born c1843. Died East Chattanooga June 20, 1915 and buried in Charleston, TN. [CT June 20, 1915]

HENDERSON, Alfred M.          Co. C, 13TX
          Born Oct. 11, 1845 in Johnson Co., AR. Enl. Sept. 21, 1861 in Columbus, TX. Wounded at Valasco, TX in 1864. Wife was Nancy Turney. To Chattanooga about 1908 where he became hotel keeper. Died Nov. 26, 1924 and buried CSA Cem. [NBFM2; CT Nov. 27, 1924]

HENDERSON, Ezekiel Thomas          Co. B, Phillips GA Legion
          Born Jan. 31, 1838 in Cass Co., GA and enl. Feb. 7, 1862. Fought in ANV. Fredericksburg. Paroled, 1865. Came to Chattanooga from Bartow Co., GA and spent last 25 years of life here. Coal dealer. Married Mary Isabella Jones on 5 June 1868 at Montecelo, AR. She was born 15 Dec 1844 in Summerville, NC and died 21 Aug. 1903 in Chattanooga. Ezekiel died Nov. 6, 1908 in Chattanooga and bur. Forest Hills Cemetery. Ancestor of Bob Steel, Signal Mtn. [FHR; NBFM2; CT Nov. 8, 1908; UDC2 pg 242.]

HENDERSON, J. S.          2nd Co. K, 1st CSA Cav.
          Enl. July 14, 1862 in HC. Paroled May 3, 1865 in Charlotte, NC. Res of HC.

HENDERSON, JAMES F.          2nd Co. K, 1st CSA Cav.
          Enl. July 14, 1862 in HC. Deserted Nov. 28, 1863. Took USA oath Dec. 11, 1863. Res of HC.

HENDERSON, James Woods Cozby
          Born Oct. 20, 1823 in TN. Resided in Retro, near Sale Creek with wife Mary Ann and five sons. Captured at Missionary Ridge and imprisoned at Rock Island where he remained until after the war. Died Sept. 28, 1909 and buried in Soddy. [CT Sept. 29, 1909; RI ledger; 1860HC]

HENDERSON, Jerome Bonaparte          Co. H, 26TN
          Born 4 March 1840 in McMinn Co., TN. Enl. July 8, 1861, Knoxville. Captured Fort Donelson, Feb.

16, 1862 and imprisoned Camp Douglas where he died Mar. 4, 1862.

HENDERSON, John B.          Co. D, 1CSA (GA)
          Born Nov. 15 or 25, 1843 in Greene Co., TN, son of W. A. and Elizabeth Glascock Henderson. Farmer, manufacturer, banker. Enl. May 1, 1862, Ringgold. Sick in quarters Oct. 31, 1862. Detailed on Signal Corps, Fort Gaines, Dec. 31, 1862. Sick in quarters, Aug. 31, 1863. On 40 day furlough, Feb. 12, 1864. Fought at Chickamauga and Missionary Ridge. Lived 34 years in Catoosa Co., GA and 25 years in Rossville, HC, 1911. Helped build first cotton mill in Walker Co., GA. Also helped rebuild Lee & Gordon's Mill. Established first bank at Rossville. Universalist. Married Cornelia Hunt. Prominent citizen and served as mayor of Rossville. Died July 6, 1931 and buried at Chickamauga, GA. [NBFM 7; TP 14,282; CT July 7, 1931]

HENDERSON, Levi M.          Co. F, 35TN
          Enl. Oct. 21, 1862 at Chattanooga; died in hospital in Tullahoma, TN, Feb. 5, 1863.

HENDERSON, Richard
          Leader in Home Guard "Vigilance Committee," 1861.

HENDRIX (HENDRICKS), 2Lt. Blackstone          Co. H, 26TN; 2d Co. I, 1CSA (GA)
          Enl. July 8, 1861 at Knoxville; captured at Fort Donelson, Feb. 16, 1862 and imprisoned at Johnson's Island. Prom. 1Lt., Nov. 19, 1862. Deserted on or about Dec. 30, 1863 and dropped from rolls, Jan. 25, 1864. Also shown as deserted March 24, 1864.

HENDRICKS, J. M.
          Born 1846 in GA. 1910 res. on Rossville Rd. with wife R. V., his second wife whom he married 1885. [1910HC]

HENRY, R. S.          Co. D, 19TN
          Born March, 1837 in Rhea Co. Long time resident of Chattanooga. Died May 30, 1914 in Memphis and buried CSA Cem. [CT June 1, 1914]

HENRY, Samuel          Co. D, 1TN Cav. (Carter's)
          Born 1839 in TN, son of Elizabeth of Harrison. Farm laborer. Enl. Aug. 5, 1861, Knoxville. Captured Piedmont, VA, June 21, 1864; imprisoned Camp Morton; 5'10" tall, dark complexion, black hair, dark eyes.

HENRY, William          Co. K, 43TN
          He enl. Feb. 19, 1862, at Ooltewah. He deserted April 29, 1862. Before the war, he was a farm laborer

living at Long Savannah with his wife, Margaret, and daughter and two sons.

HENSLEY, B.          Barry's Btry.
Captured on retreat from Atlanta, Sept. 10, 1864. [Brown Diary]

HENSON, William Worthington     Co. D, 39TN MI
Res. of Bledsoe Co. until after 1870. As member of Tulloss Rangers captured and imprisoned "where he remained for a long time." Married Mary Painter of Pikeville. [NBFM1]

HERRON, James      Co. H, 2TN Cav. (Ashby's)
Enl. Aug. 1, 1863. Detached as teamster. Listed absent without leave Nov. 8, 1864. Surrendered May 19, 1865 at Chattanooga and took USA oath.

HERRON (HERIN, HERRIN, HEARN), Jesse J.   Co. L, 35TN
Enl. Sept. 23, 1862 at Dalton, GA. He became regimental fifer but deserted at Salisbury, NC, March 15, 1865. Dark complexion, dark hair, blue eyes, 5'10" tall.

HERVEY, Frank A.          Co. G, 14LA
Born Jan. 26, 1842 in Muscoza Co., GA. Enl. in Co. G, 14LA and transferred by order Gen. Bragg to Gen. Baylor's Brigade and made Chief of Arty. with rank of Captain. Wounded at Drainsville, VA, Franklin, LA and at mouth of Rio Grande. Captured crossing MS River carrying dispatches in 1863. Disch. June 14, 1865. Real estate dealer in Chattanooga. Died Mobile, AL, 1910. [NBFM2,7]

HESLIP, Lt. J. A.          4AL Btry.
Lived at Harrison; captured at Fort Pillow, June 8, 1863.

HEWLETT, John      Clark's Independent Cav. Co.
Enl. Aug. 31, 1862 at Chattanooga; captured near Knoxville, Dec. 1, 1863.

HEWITT, Austin
Born 1847, CT. 1910 res. Prospect St. in house hold of niece Emma Guedron who was born in GA. [1910HC]

HIBBLER, J. E.          Co. G, 1st MS Cav.
Born Sept. 20, 1847 in Sumter Co., AL. Enl. Jan 15, 1864 at Tupelo, MS. Paroled May 1, 1865. Employed at Big Spring Ice Co. in Chattanooga in 1893. Moved to Cookville, MS and died Feb. 25, 1921 in a sanitarium at West Point, MS. [NBFM2; CT Feb. 27,1921]

HIBBLER, Robert      Co. G, 1st MS Cav.
Born in Sumter Co., AL. Enl. Jan, 1862 in Co. G, 1MS Cav. After war was in real estate business in Chattanooga. Member, NBF Camp, 1896, but moved away. Died Feb. 25, 1921. [NBFM2,7]

HICKMAN, Elias      Co. K, 43TN
Enl. at Ooltewah on Oct. 17, 1861. He deserted June 5, 1862. Before the war, he was living on his father's farm at Sale Creek. He was the son of William and Elizabeth Hickman. Res., 1910 in household of daughter, Maggie Poe. [1910 VetCensus]

HICKMAN, John P.      Co. C, 7TN Cav. Bn.
Born Davidson Co. Enl. Sept. 20, 1862. Paroled May 26, 1865. Lawyer in Nashville after war. [NBFM2]

HICKS, Alexander      Co. L, 36TN
Enl. Jan. 9, 1862 at Chattanooga; transferred to Co. L, 35TN; fought at Murfreesboro; paroled May 1, 1865, Greensboro, NC.

HICKS, Elijah M.      Co. H, 4TN Cav.
Born July 10, 1838 in Marion Co., TN. Enl. at Jasper as pvt. in Capt. Peter Rankin's Co., Smith's Regt. which became Co. H, 4TN Cav. (Starnes). Paroled at Nashville at close of war. Blacksmith and farmer. Married Elizabeth(1). Shown with wife (2) Sarah E. and three grown children in his household, 1910. Mason. NBF Camp. Died at res. on William St. Nov. 17, 1915 in Chattanooga and buried in Whitwell, TN. [CT Nov. 18, 1915; NBFM2;TP 9928; 1910HC]

HICKS, Harrison      Co. L, 36TN
Enl. Jan. 9, 1862 at Chattanooga.

HICKS (HIX), James C.      Co. I, 35GA
Born Jan. 7, 1842, Chattooga Co. GA. Enl. Feb. 22, 1862. Seven Pines, Wilderness. Served under Stonewall Jackson and heard the shot that ended his life. Imprisoned 3 1/2 yrs Ft. Delaware, 16 months at Fort Lookout. Paroled May 1, 1865, Augusta, GA. Married (1870) Mary E. Harris, and after her death (1888) Mary Lucia Sams. Served two or three terms as city treasurer for Ringgold and was postmaster there for 4 years, and 16 years in Catoosa Co. GA. Ordinary, but "for a long number of years a resident of Chattanooga." Methodist. Died at res. on E. 19th St., Jan. 3, 1923, and buried in CSA Cem. [TWP, 234; CT Jan. 4, 1923; TP 15,682]

HICKS, Stephen J.      Co. G, 7TN
[NBFM4]

HIGGINS, Absalom H. - Co. L, 36TN; Co. L, 35TN
He enl. Jan. 9, 1862, at Chattanooga in Co. L of

the 36TN and soon transferred to Co. L, 35TN. He was wounded in the neck at Murfreesboro on Dec. 31, 1862. He deserted Jan. 24, 1864, at Tunnel Hill. Prior to the war, he had a farm near Chattanooga. He had dark complexion, dark hair and blue eyes and was 5'10" tall. "Died without knowledge of camp." 1920. [NBFM7]

HIGGINS, James H.  -  Co. L, 36TN; Co. L, 35TN
        Enl. Jan. 9, 1862 in Chattanooga; transferred to Co. L, 35TN; deserted July, 1863. Co. D, 1st TN-AL. Vidette Cav. 22 years old.

HIGGINS, Moses          Co. D, 37TN
        Born 1826 in GA. Farm laborer in Harrison and neighbor of Rubin Tankestly. Wife Martha. Enl. Mar. 10, 1863 at Chattanooga (conscript). Deserted July 9, 1863 and took USA oath. Detailed as Provost Guard, Brigade Hdq.

HIGHTOWER, Daniel Newton          Co. C, 6GA
        Born June 26, 1835 near Thomaston, GA. Enl. 6GA and wounded at 1st Bethel. Left army in 1863 and was president of GA State Relief Soc. to close of war. To Chattanooga soon after war. Charter member of Trinity Methodist. Sexton at Citizens' Cem., 1896. Died at his home on E. 11th. Buried Forest Hills Cemetery. [NBFM3; CT April 15,16, 1908]

HIGHTOWER, Thomas Hodge          Lynch's Btry.; Co. C, 31TN
        Born Jan. 15, 1844 at New Market in Jefferson Co., TN, he enl. Nov., 1861 at New Market, TN in Lynch's Btry., then Co. C, 31TN. Wounded Rogersville, TN. Captured March, 1863 at Jackson, MS. Rejoined Lynch's Btry about a year later and served out war. Married April 1867 Mattie Moore born 20 June 1846 in Grayson Co., VA and died 3 Sept. 1933 in Chattanooga. He was a farmer in Grayson, VA until 1911 when he came to Chattanooga. Methodist. Died April 28, 1932 at res. on Spears Ave. and buried CSA Cem. [NBFM2,8; TWP, 300]

HILDERBRAND, J. W.          Co. K, 43TN
        Enl. Dec. 1, 1861 at Ooltewah; deserted.

HILDERBRAND, W. A.          Co. K, 43TN
        Enl. Dec. 1, 1861 at Ooltewah; deserted.

HILL, Henry S.          Co. A, 19TN
        Born in AL c1834. Half-brother of John L. Hopkins with whom he read law. Practiced law in Chattanooga and was co-editor, Chattanooga Advertiser, c1858-62. TN Gen'l Assesmbly (Confederate), 1861-63. Enl. March 15, 1862. Paroled

at Greensboro, NC, May 1, 1865. [BDTA, 2:417]

HILL, J. F.          Co. G, 26TN; 2d Co. K, 1CSA(GA)
        Enl. July 8, 1861, Knoxville. Captured Fort Donelson, Feb. 16, 1862 and imprisoned Camp Morton. Exch. and at home sick, Oct. 14, 1862.

HILL, J. T.
        Old and destitute when he died in Nov., 1891. Buried CSA Cem. [NBFM1,7]

HILL, Jesse Thomas
        Born 1850 near Nashville and came to Chattanooga at age 18. Too young to fight, but ardent supporter of all CSA organizations and insured that textbooks of city schools should deal in a manner he considered proper with the South's cause in the civil conflict. Brother of Thomas and Samuel. J.T.Hill became a hero in the relief effort during yellow fever epidemic of 1878 and later was mayor of Chattanooga [NBFM7; CT March 8, 1938]

HILL, John R.          Co. E, 20TN
        Died May 29, 1903, age 70, at his home at 437 Oak St. Formerly of Clarksdale, MS. Buried Lavergne, TN. [TP 4995; CT May 30, 1903]

HILL, 1Lt. Thomas          McClung's Btry; Co. A, 1TN Lt. Arty
        Born May 7, 1846 at Nashville, TN, son of Robert T. Hill, he enl. Oct., 1861 as a private and was soon promoted to 1Lt. He fought at Fishing Creek, KY and at Shiloh (where he was wounded), Baton Rouge, and Port Hudson. Afterwards he and his battery fought in East TN at Greeneville, Carter's Depot, Saltville and Morristown. Captured in the Morristown fight and imprisoned Camp Douglas. After living several years in Nashville, he moved about 1876 to Chattanooga where he engaged in real estate. Won acclaim for his role in the yellow fever epidemic. NBF Camp. Inmate TN Confederate Soldiers' Home, Nov. 17, 1902 and died there Aug. 17, 1910. Buried in CSA Cem. near the home in Nashville. [CT Aug. 19, 1910; NBFM2; TCSH]

HILL, W. T. "Tom"          Co. D, 24GA
        Born 1834 in Haywood Co., NC. Veteran of most of Army of Northern Virginia battles: Seven Days, Antietam, Chancellorsville (where he was badly stunned and hospitalized), Gettysburg. "A private soldier of sterling worth." Contracted typhoid and permanently disabled. Res. of Alton Park in 1904. 1906 applied from HC for admission to TN Soldiers Home. [TP5934]

HILL, William Hinton          Co. E, 1GA

Born June 20, 1845 in Pea Vine, Catoosa Co., GA. Enl. July, 1863 at Bridgeport, AL. Fought at Chickamauga. Wounded at Peach Tree, Jonesboro and Franklin. Captured at Nashville Dec. 16, 1864 and imprisoned Camp Douglas until June, 1865. After the war, he married Alice Anderson. Moved to Chatt in 1886 and married (1890) Sarah Francis Trundle. In employ of Chattanooga Lumber Co. for 20 years as foreman of planing mill. Died at home in East Lake, July 8, 1922 and buried in Forest Hills Cemetery. [FHR; TWP, 221; CT July 9, 1922; NBFM2; TP 10,172; 1910HC]

HILTON, John B.          Co. H, 4TN Cav.
     Died in prison, 1864.

HISE, W. M.
     Born 1841, GA. Res in 1910 as a farmer on Rossville Rd. with wife C.C., his second wife whom he married 1880. [1910HC]

HIX (HICKS)

HIXSON, James - Co. H, 26TN; 2d Co. I, 1CSA (GA)
     Enl. Sept. 16, 1861, Knoxville. Captured Fort Donelson, Feb. 16, 1862, and imprisoned Camp Douglas. Disch. at Mobile, AL, by providing a substitute, Nov. 16, 1862.

HIXON, John          Co. B, 1TN Cav. (Carter's)
     Born 1836 in Bledsoe Co., son of John and Esther Hixson. Enl. fall, 1862. Fought at Murfreesboro, Cumberland Gap. Leg smashed when mount ran against tree. Captured following Missionary Ridge and chose to go across the Ohio River. Died near Birchwood, James Co., Feb. 22, 1908 and buried on farm of S.A. Smith. [TP 6046; TWP 10,606]

HIXON, John
     Born 1837, TN, son of TN parents. 1910 farmer in James Co. with wife Charity (m 1869).

HIXON, John David          Walker's 10th TN Cav.
     "Soldier lived on Lookout Mountain, close to the Tennessee line. He was killed isn the war about 1863. Frances Myer Hixon, soldier's mother, drew a pension for many years from the Government. She lived in Walker Co., GA." [UDC2 pg 252]

HIXSON, Timothy          Co. B, 1TN Cav. (Carter's)
     Born c1834 in GA, son of John and Cynthia Smith Hixson of Long Savannah. Married (1865) Mary Ann Smith. [1860HC]

HIXSON, William "Billie"          Co. B, 5TN Cav.

Born c1833 in Wauhatchie, son of William and Esther Hixson. He lived in Lookout Valley with his wife, Evaline. Enl. Aug. 11, 1861. Died in Chattanooga Dec. 9, 1907. [CT Dec. 10, 1907; TWP 10,606; 1860HC]

HIXSON, William          Co. H, 26TN; 2d Co. I, 1CSA (GA)
     Born c1840, son of John and Cynthia Smith Hixson. Enl. July 8, 1861, Knoxville. Captured Fort Donelson, Feb. 16, 1862 and imprisoned Camp Douglas. Sgt., Dec. 31, 1862. Deserted at Tunnel Hill, April 19, 1863. Married Rhoda Killian.

HIXSON, Wilson          Co. B, 1TN Cav. (Carter's)
     Born c1837 in GA, son of John and Cynthia Smith Hixson. Married (in James Co., 1881) Caldona Beavers. Res. 1910 in James County with wife Caldona and six grown children. Died 1924 in HC. [TWP, 297; TP 6047; 1860HC]

HODGE, Robert Jackson          Co. B, 54NC
     Born Jan. 4, 1844 in Burke Co., NC, and was farmer in Burke when he enl. April 28, 1862. Captured at Rappahannoch Sta., VA, Nov. 7, 1863 and imprisoned at Point Lookout. Exchanged and captured again at Petersburg. Prisoner at Hart's Island, NY until June 17, 1865. Married (1881) Mary Emma Sarena Hughes. Stone-cutter in Chattanooga. Died March 9, 1906 in HC. [TWP, 222; NBFM2; Manarin, NC Troops, 13:264]

HODGES, George W.
     Born 1840 in GA. Res. 1910 on Magnolia St. in household of son Olander. Wife was Maggie. [1910HC]

HODGES, John B.          Co. H, 4TN Cav.
     Died in prison, 1864.

HODGES, John Pettus          Co. A, 4TN Cav.
     Born 1831 in Greenville, SC., Hodges became a clerk for merchant A. D. Taylor in Chattanooga After becoming a Confederate he fought at Fishing Creek in KY lost his horse at Beech Grove in the retreat. He "bought one immediately after." Detached as commissary clerk, June 24, 1861. Captured near Kingston, GA, May 28, 1864 and imprisoned at Rock Island. Exchanged Mar. 13, 1865. Paroled Macon, GA. on April 26, 1865. Res. Jefferson Co., KY before returning to Chattanooga and re-entering mercantile business as Wornacut and Hodges. Hodges married (1853) Sidney A. P. Glass (died Jan. 25, 1908), daughter of John G. Glass, another Chattanooga storekeeper. The Hodges family lived at Park Place east of town. John Hodges died in HC in 1874. [TWP 355; [CT Jan. 26, 1908; 1860HC]

HODGES, Rufus          Co. H, 4TN Cav. Bn.
Died Jasper, TN, 1862.

HOLCOMB, G. L.          Co. B, 38GA
Res. Chattanooga, 1905. [NBFM7]

HOLDEN, Dennis M.          Co. D, 45TN
Born Rutherford Co.,TN. Wounded and disabled at Bentonville. Res. Chattanooga, 1907. [TP 8714]

HOLDER, Jesse          Co. K, 43TN
Born March 8, 1843 near Harrison. 1860 census lists him as 14. Shown as 18 when he enl. April 26, 1862, at Ooltewah. He deserted Nov. 19, 1862. His father, H.H. Holder, was a shoemaker residing at Snow Hill. His mother was Elizabeth Holder. Baptist. Died Jan. 31, 1906 at his home near Tyner and apparently became Union soldier as he was buried in National Cem. [CT Feb. 1, 1906]

HOLLAND, Benjamin F.          Co. D, 37TN
Born Oct. 9, 1843 in Monroe Co., TN. Enl. Sept. 1, 1861 at Knoxville. Fought at Mill Springs, Shiloh, Murfreesboro, and captured at Missionary Ridge. On list of deserters who took oath and released at Nashville, Oct., 1863. Res. Falling Water (HC) in 1907. [TP 8778]

HOLLAND, J. C.          Co. K, 4GA
Born Dec. 7, 1845 in Coweta Co. GA. Enl. at Vicksburg, MS, Feb. 10, 1863. Wounded in skirmish below Chickamauga. Captured at Vicksburg, July 4, 1863 and paroled July 8, 1863. 1900 res. St. Elmo, carpenter. [NBFM2]

HOLLAND, John          Co. D, 37TN
Born 1832 in SC. Farmer at Chattanooga in 1860. Enl. Mar. 3, 1863 at Chattanooga (conscript). Deserted Sept. 7, 1863 at Ooltewah and took USA oath.

HOLLAND, William A.
Born c1831, TN. Res. in household of son Wm. P. Holland, 1910. [1910HC]

HOLLINS, Robert Henderson   Co. A, 1TN
Born Nov. 30, 1840, Coffee Co., TN, son of Elbridge Jackson and Ann McGowen Hollins. Married (1860) Lucie A. Dumas [1841-1890]. Enl. Aug. 27, 1861, Camp Jones; paroled May 2, 1865, Farmville, VA. Died 1880 in AL. [CSA Patriot; UDC3:116]

HOLLIS, George E.          Co. H, 19AL
Born April 8, 1838 Fairfield Dist., SC. Enl. July 15, 1861 at Centre, AL. Wounded at Chickamauga;

captured at Atlanta July 28, 1864 and imprisoned at Camp Chase till end of war. Married (1868) Julia C. C. Wisdom. Died at age 70 on Aug. 19, 1908 and buried in Forest Hills Cemetery. [FHR; CT Aug. 22, 1908; TWP, p. 157; NBFM2]

HOLLOWAY, Jerry          Barry's Btry.; Co. A, 19TN
Enl. April 26, 1862 at Chattanooga; deserted April 31, 1862 at Chattanooga. Re-enl. April 21, 1863., Chattanooga as conscript. Deserted. Living in FL, 1900-1929, then returned to Chattanooga. [NBFM6]

HOLMAN, Thomas Christopher   Co. K, 41GA
Born Newnan, GA, Dec. 7, 1845. Enl. Feb., 1863 at Vicksburg and captured there. Wounded at Chickamauga Station on W&A railroad shortly after Chickamauga by accidental discharge from one of our men. Disabled and discharged. To Chattanooga in 1882. Carpenter and farmer but moved away. Methodist. Returned to Chattanooga in 1929 "after twenty five year absence." Died Aug. 17, 1932 at res. in East Lake; bur. CSA Cem. [CT May 3, 1931; NBFM7, 10; TP 13,206]

HOLMES, Henry Fernandez   Co. B, 12GA Bn. of Arty
Born Gwinett Co., GA, May 14, 1846. Oct. 1861-April 1862 served as corporal and QM in 3GA State Troops; enl. DeKalb Co., GA, May, 1862 in Co. C, 13GA Inf. Bn. Discharged March 31, 1863. Fought in battles and skirmishes in E. TN and KY. At Nashville at time of surrender. He married Susan Adeline [1845-1918] in 1864. After the war he was a stone mason in Nashville, Louisville and Indianapolis before coming to Chattanooga Superintended construction of north wall of CSA Cem. built by A.P. Stewart chapter, UDC. Chattanooga F&AM, Knight's Templar, Alhambra Shrine, Elks. Universalist. Home 608 Boynton Terr. Died Sept. 24, 1932 in Chattanooga and buried Forest Hills Cemetery. [NBFM2,6,8; TP 13,102; CT Sept. 25, 1932; UDC2 pg 258]

HOLMES, John J.          Co. I, 4TN Cav. (Starnes)
Born March 31, 1833 in Morrison, TN (Coffee Co.) and raised there. Enl. 1861: Fort Donelson, Straight's Raid. Deserted Aug. 30, 1863 and took oath Feb. 7, 1865. Wife was Emma. Baptist. Died Aug. 1, 1915 in Chattanooga and buried in Forest Hills Cem. [CT Aug. 2, 1915; TP13,636]

HOLMES (HOLMS), William H.          Barry's Btry.
Enl. Sept. 26, 1862. at Chattanooga; captured July 3, 1864 at Kennesaw Mountain.; deserted June-July, 1864; imprisoned at Camp Douglas, IL; enl. Mar. 25, 1865 Co. E, 6USA. [Brown's Diary]

HOLT, 2nd Lt. Alford (Albert) B.   2LT.   2nd Co. K,

ICSA Cav.
Son of R. A. Holt of Chattanooga He enl. July 14, 1862 in HC. Captured at Linden, TN, May 12, 1863. Imprisoned at Alton, IL.

HOLT, Caleb - Co. B, 5TN Cav.(McKenzie's)
Born Cocke Co., TN, Dec. 24, 1841. Wounded at Shiloh and at Allatoona where he lost an eye. Maj. A. L. Mims, however, reported, "Never at Shiloh; never belonged to Mims' Company--is a fraud." [TP1892; NBFM3]

HOLT, Henry H. Co. D, 37TN
Born 1841 in TN, son of Eliphas and Emaline. Farm laborer at Sale Creek, 1860. Enl. Sept. 1, 1861 at Knoxville. Detached to Provost duty in Sept., 1862 and also served as pioneer. Deserted Sept. 7, 1863 at Ooltewah and took USA oath, but reenlisted and re-captured in Giles Co., TN, April, 19, 1864 and sent to Camp Morton.

HOLT, Thomas J. Co. H, 2TN Cav. (Ashby's)
Born c1816. Enl. at Chattanooga Feb. 1, 1863. Deserted. Took USA oath of allegiance Oct. 26, 1864.

HOLTON, —?— Barry's Btry.
Deserted. [Brown's Diary]

HOLTZCLAW, Jesse Asbury Jackson's GA Arty.; Massenbury's GA Btry.
Born Feb. 28, 1836, Greene Co., GA, son of John G. and Lucy Newsome Holtzclaw. Grad. Mercer Univ., 1856, and read law under Judge Weaver of Greensboro, GA, and admitted to GA bar, 1858. Practiced law in Perry, GA, after war and in 1869 appointed internal revenue collector by Pres. Grant. Moved to Dalton and then to Chattanooga where he practiced law and served as judge. Married Sarah Edna Cooper (1860). Died July 13, 1898 at his home on Walnut St. and buried Forest Hills Cem. [CT July 14, 1898; Hale, TN, 8:2578-79]

HOOD, George W. Co. G, 26TN; 2d Co. K, ICSA (GA); Co. F, 39GA
Enl. July 8, 1861, Knoxville. Left sick at Bowling Green, Jan. 23, 1862. In 39GA, Dec. 31, 1862. Captured Vicksburg, July 4, 1863.

HOOKE, Albert McCallie Co. A, 19TN
Born July 15, 1847, son of Robert M. and Mary K. Rawlings Hooke. Married Mary Richardson. Paroled May 18, 1865, Albany, GA. Died Oct. 11, 1868.

HOOKE, James Granville Co. A, 19TN
Born July 16, 1840, son of Robert M. and Mary

K. Rawlings Hooke. Married Clara Oakman. Died Feb. 18, 1883 in Chattanooga

HOOKE, James Hervey Barry's Btry.
Born 1842 in TN, son of pioneer Chattanooga residents John Alexander and Mary L. [Long] Hooke. Enl. in Knoxville in 1862 and served until the end of the war. He was with the unit as it sought unsuccessfully to reinforce Pemberton at Vicksburg and had engagements near Jackson, MS. In the fierce fighting between Resaca, GA, and Atlanta, a shell exploded near Hooke. It left him with partial deafness that worsened in later years. During the war he "made an enviable record. He was well-liked by his comrades and was greatly respected for his bravery." JHH lived all his life, except for the Civil War years, in the same house. He was born in Chattanooga in 1842 and died there on Georgia Avenue, Nov. 30, 1898. He was buried in Citizens Cem. James H. Hooke never married. [CT Dec. 1, 1898; J Wilson - Hooke family; CTS; 1850HC]

HOOKE, Rezin Littletone "Reece"
Born Dec. 30, 1833, son of Robert M. and Mary K. Rawlings Hooke. Married Mary S. Walker, sister of Gen. F. M. Walker. Clerk in 1860. Died May 14, 1883.

HOOKE, Robert Alexander
Born March 24, 1845 in TN, son of Robert M. and Mary K. Rawlings Hooke. Physician. Married Mary A. Gill. Died March, 1875 in Washington Co., VA.

HOOKE, Robert McGinley
Born 1807 in Blount Co., TN, son of Robert and Abigail Alexander Hooke. Robert was an lawyer in Alabama, judge and served twice in the state senate. Married Mary Kennedy Rawlings. He was prominent in the TN railroad world, helping to construct the Nashville and Chattanooga line. Built home "Oakwood" on Broad St. Leader in Home Guard "Vigilance Committee," 1861 and served as supervisor of CSA enlistment. "Price put on his head by Union officers." Died in Chattanooga Oct. 17, 1883. [CTS; WF]

HOOKE, Robert N. W. Co. E, 19TN
Enl. June 4, 1861, Knoxville. Disch. under conscript law, July 21, 1862.

HOOKE, Robert R. Cpl. Co. A, 19TN
Born 1843 in TN, son of Samuel A.B. and Elizabeth C. Rawlings Hooke. Clerk in depot in 1860. Enl. May 20, 1861, Knoxville. Re-enl. May 10, 1862, Corinth. Present through June, 1864. [1860HC]

HOOKE, William Alexander

Born c1845, son of John A. and Mary L. Long Hooke, he died Jan. 2, 1916, age 71, and was buried in Forest Hills Cem. [CT Jan. 3, 1816]

HOOKE, William Romney "Rom"    Co. D, 19TN
Son of Samuel A.B. and Elizabeth Chilton Rawlings Hooke. Clerk in depot in 1860. Captured near Nashville, Dec. 16, 1864; forwarded to Louisville, KY, Jan. 1, 1865; imprisoned Camp Douglas, Jan. 2, 1865; transferred Chicago, IL, March 20, 1865. [1860HC]

HOOPER, Lt. Warren Franklin    Co. I, 19TN
Born c1835. Born Columbus, GA, 1839. At the opening of the war was reading law under Francis M. Walker. Married Mary Pocahontas Halliburton [14 Aug. 1840 - 28 June 1927], 15 Dec. 1857 in Murfreesboro. Enl. May 20, 1861 in Knoxville. Captured at Nashville, Dec. 16, 1864 and imprisoned for eight months at Johnson's Island, Dec. 20, 1864. Released June 16, 1865. He was one of the few Marsh Blues who returned to Chattanooga alive. Died at Murfreesboro in 1880 and buried Citizens Cem. [TWP 1669]

HOPE, William B.
Born Feb. 11, 1820 in Roane Co., TN, he was engaged in business in Chattanooga before the war. He was also a planter and slave owner. During the war "he served as an enrolling officer with the rank and title of colonel." He moved to Lenoir City after the war, dying there March 1, 1905. [CT, March 2, 1905]

HOPKINS, Surgeon Baird S."Bart"    36TN

HOPKINS, Lt. John Livingston    36TN
Born c1830, he had been law partner of David M. Key, then became city attorney of Chattanooga in 1853 and alderman in 1858. During the first half of 1862 he served as adjutant of the 36TN Inf., but poor health required him to abandon field duty and in 1863 he took his wife Mary E. Cooke Hopkins south to Water Valley, GA. Following the war they lived in Atlanta where Hopkins became a prominent superior court judge. Married Mary Cooke, daughter of Dr. Robert Cooke. She died at their home in Atlanta March 4, 1910. JLH living there in 1911. [CT Mar.5, 1910]

HANN (HORN, HAM, HAND), James C.  Co. H,
    26TN; Barry's Btry.; 2d Co. I, 1CSA (GA)
Enl. July 8, 1861 at Knoxville; left sick at Bowling Green, KY, Jan. 23, 1862; transferred May 30, 1862 to Barry's Btry. at Chattanooga; paroled May 11, 1865 at Meridian, MS; res. of Walker Co., GA.

HORN, William
Transferred from 36TN to Co. K, 43TN at

Ooltewah, Dec. 1, 1861.

HORNE, Cpl. William    Co. H, 37TN
Born HC, TN 1842 or 1843; enl. Sept. 17, 1861 at Knoxville; died Nov. 11, 1862 at Lauderdale Springs, MS; unmarried.

HORTON, Samuel Virgil    31AL
Born 1843 in Shelby Co., AL. Married (1860) Martha Ann Duncan. Died Nov. 17, 1914 and buried CSA Cem. [TWP, p. 171; CT Nov. 19, 1914]

HORTON, William Andrew    Co. K, 43TN
Born Sept. 16, 1845, Lumpkin Co., GA, son of Steven Horton, a farmer who was born at Monticello, Jasper Co, Ga., and afterwards lived at Dahlonega. His mother was Nancy Ann Cauley, daughter of Robert and Mary Cauley of Dahlonega. Enl. Oct. 17, 1861 (Horton in his veteran's questionaire says July, 1862) at Ooltewah. KY Campaign; Vicksburg (captured July 4, 1863). Paroled and sent to Dalton, GA., where he was exchanged. At the time of the surrender in 1865, he was in VA. He was married in HC where he bought an 80 acre farm after the war. Baptist. Shown in 1900 as a farmer at Chattanooga. Res. Dodds Ave. Died in Brainerd July 22, 1930 and buried Chickamauga. [NBFM2, 6,8; TP 15,663; TVQ]

HORTTIM, H. S.    Co. G, 19AL
Born May 24, 1834 in Cherokee Co., AL and enl. in Huntsville, Sept., 1861. Wounded and captured at Shiloh. Paroled May, 1865. Res. in 1900 on Montgomery Ave., Chattanooga. Occup. farmer. Died June 27, 1912 in Chattanooga. [NBFM2]

HOUSE, Charles F.    Barry's Btry.
Enl. April 30, 1862, at Chattanooga He was paroled May 11, 1865, at Meridian, MS. Prior to the war, he lived on a farm at Tyner. His father, G.W. House, was from VA, and his mother, Nancy House, from SC. He was born about 1839.

HOUSE, Hartwell "Harlie"  Co. E, 4TN Cav. (Starnes?
    McLemore's?)
Born 1841, Rutherford Co., TN; enl. Oct. 8, 1862: Lavergne, Parker's Cross Roads, Dover, Thompson's Station, Chickamauga (wounded), Atlanta Camp., Resaca (wounded) also. Married (1866) Mary E.; 1909 res. Highland Park. House painter. Died July 16, 1910 in Chattanooga and buried CSA Cem. [CT July 18, 1910; TP11461; 1910HC]

HOUSE, James M.    Barry's Btry.
Born 1847 in TN, son of G.W. and Nancy. Enl. April 30, 1862, at Chattanooga along with his older

brother, Charles. He was paroled May 11, 1865, at Meridian, MS.

HOUSHIELD (HOUTSHIELD): see HANSHIELD

HOUSELEY, James M.     Co. G, 63TN
    Born c1840. Farm laborer at Harrison with wife Amanda. Had served in cav. prior to enl. Nov. 12, 1861, Cleveland. At Charleston, TN, May, 1862. Captured near Petersburg, VA, June 12, 1864 and sent to Point Lookout, MD. Transferred to Elmira, Feb. 25, 1865 and released at Chattanooga, Mar. 1865.

HOUSLEY, William F.     3TN Cav. Bn.; Co. B,
                 1st TN Cav.
    Born in HC in 1841, he enl. first in the 3TN Cav. Bn., then transferred to the 1TN Cav. He served throughout the war, the last year as acting company commander, fighting at Fishing Creek, Cumberland Gap, and Murfreesboro. Also particiapated in raids with Morgan and Wheeler. Paroled near Dalton, spring, 1865, and soon moved to Cedar Glade, AR, where he was a merchant for ten years. In 1875 he relocated in Hot Springs where he became sheriff of Garland Co. and postmaster. Director of Soldiers Home in Little Rock. [Evans, CSA History, 14:511-12]

HOUSTON, Joseph H.     Co. B, 5TN Cav.
    Born in NC c1825, he was a farm laborer living at Harrison at the start of the war. His wife, Elizabeth, was also from NC. He enl. at Chattanooga Aug. 11, 1861. [1860HC]

HOWARD, Sgt. J. W.     Barry's Btry.
    Enl. April 4, 1862 at Chattanooga; "Was arrested and put in jail for drunkeness & drawing a sword on a commissioned officer. Broke jail Dec. 1862 and escaped."

HOWARD, Thomas J.     Co. H, 26TN
    Born c1838, TN. Farm laborer res. house hold J. C. Roberts in Long Savannah. Enl. July 8, 1861, Knoxville. Married Frances E.; died Oct. 13, 1861. [TP4193]

HOWARD, Thomas J.     Co. C, 16TN Bn.
    Born March 3, 1845 in Rhea Co., the son of the Rev. Robert Tate and Penelope Majors Howard, he enl. Jan. 9, 1862 in Co. L, 36TN at Chattanooga and transferred to Co. L, 35TN. Enl. Mar. 3, 1862 in Co. C, 16TN Cav., Rucker's Legion. Captured Black's Ford in Roane Co. and imprisoned Camp Chase. Deserted March 15, 1865 at Salisbury, NC; fair complexion, dark hair, blue eyes, 5'10" tall; took USA oath April 17, 1865. Married (1872) Frances E. Brown. Moved to

Chattanooga from Roane in 1868, becoming jailer, then Chief of Police in 1889. Supported by wife keeping boarders in 1902 and soon thereafter listed as lunatic in Lyon's Asylum in Knoxville where he died Aug. 8, 1905 in Buried in CSA Cem. Brother was R.H. Howard. [TWP, 286; NBFM2; TP4193]

HOWARD, William     Co. G, 8GA Bn.
    Born Greenville Dist., SC, 1839. Enl. Oct., 1861. Wounded at Chickamauga. To TN, 1907. Res. Sale Creek, 1910. In 1910 applied from HC for admission to TN Soldiers Home. [SAACH; 1910HC]

HOWARD, William A.     Co. H, 26TN
    Age 34 in 1861, he enl. Sept. 5, 1861, Knoxville. Honorably disch. Dec. 6, 1861.

HOWSER, John M.     Co. I, 5TN Cav.
    Married (1865) Margaret Fore. Died 1893 in HC. [TWP 455]

HOWSER, Polk W.   - Co. B, 1TN Cav. (Carter's)
    Enl. Aug. 7, 1861, Cleveland.

HUDDLESTON, Leroy     Co. A, 4TN Cav.

HUDDLESTON, William H.     Co. A, 4TN Cav.

HUDGINS, 1Lt. John D.     Co. D, 37TN
    He enl. Sept. 1, 1861, at Knoxville and was severely wounded at Chickamauga. Before the war, Hudgins was a barkeeper in Chattanooga. He was born about 1830.

HUDLOW, Michael K.
    Born 1849, GA. Res. 1910 in household of son on Ryan St. Retired farmer. [1910HC]

HUFSTEDLER (HUFFSTULLER), William W.  Barry's Btry.
    Enl. April 4, 1863 at Pollard, AL as substitute for W. A. Anderson; paroled May 11, 1865 at Meridian, MS. [NBFM1]

HUGGINS, Hasting Young     2Lt., GA Inf.
    1832-1863. Buried CSA Cem.

HUGHES (HUES), A. F.     Co. K, 43TN
    Enl. Oct. 17, 1861 at Ooltewah; captured at Vicksburg, July 4, 1863 and paroled; captured Newburn, VA, April 12, 1865; dark complexion, dark hair, blue eyes, and 5'10" tall.

HUGHES, A. W.     Co. G, 26TN; 2d Co. K,
               1CSA (GA)

Enl. July 12, 1861, Knoxville. Captured Fort Donelson, Feb. 16, 1862 and imprisoned at Camp Douglas. Detailed in Govt. Blacksmith shop, Jan. 25-June 30, 1863. Absent sick Sept. 15, 1864. Paroled at Greensboro, NC, May 1, 1865.

HUGHES (HUES), B. H. (M.?)     Co. K, 43TN
Enl. Dec. 8, 1862 at Ooltewah; captured at Vicksburg, July 4, 1863 and paroled.

HUGHES (HUES), Carter     Co. K, 43TN
Enl. June 10, 1862 at Ooltewah; captured at Vicksburg, July 4, 1863 and paroled.

HUGHES (HUES), Hardy     Co. K, 43TN
Enl. Dec. 31, 1861 at Pikeville, TN; deserted Feb. 20, 1862 at Knoxville.

HUGHES, Hutson B.     Co. K, 43TN
Born May 18, 1829 in Franklin Co., GA, he was a farmer in Catoosa Co. before enlisting; captured at Bunker Hill, VA, July 14, 1864; imprisoned at Camp Chase, then moved to Point Lookout, MD. Returned to Catoosa before moving to Ooltewah where, in 1904, he was blind, destitute. "I earn nothing." Died 1905. [TP 1843]

HUGHES, J. Crittenden
Inmate of Old Soldiers home in Nashville, 1902. [NBFM3]

HUGHES, Joseph
Enl. May 15, 1863 at Allisonia. Captured Manchester June 27, 1863.

HUGHES (HUES), S. [H.] P.     Co. K, 43TN
Enl. July 1, 1862 at Ooltewah; captured at Baker's Creek, May 16, 1863; imprisoned at Camp Douglas; died at Camp Douglas, June 30, 1863 and buried in National Cem. [Brooks, p. 111]

HUGHES, Capt. William     Co. F, 35TN
W.L. Hughes d. Sept. 4, 1897 in Denison, TX. Long time res. of Cleveland. [CT Sept. 1897]

HULL, J. M.     Co. I, 19TN
Mortally wounded and died at Corinth. [Worsham, p. 200]

HULSEY (HULCY), Beriah (Bryant)     Barry's Btry.
Enl. April 4, 1862 at Chattanooga; captured Sept. 2, 1864 in Atlanta; imprisoned at Camp Douglas, IL; 5'9" tall, gray eyes, fair complexion, and light hair.

HULSEY, Jesse H.     Co. D, 37TN

Enl. Sept. 1, 1861 at Knox.; deserted Nov. 14, 1863 at Missionary Ridge; took USA oath Dec. 9, 1863; dark complexion; black hair.; black eyes; and 5'5" tall.

HULSEY, John T.     Barry's Btry..
Born 1830 in TN. Farm laborer in Chattanooga with wife Jane. Enl. April 4, 1862 at Chattanooga; teamster; killed at Spanish Fort. [MSR does not mention death]

HUMPHRIES, Henry Jefferson "Jeff" Co. K, 43TN
Born Spartanburg, S.C. 1843, son of Joe Syre and Amanda Milvinia Bridges Humphries, and was farmer when war broke out. Enl. Oct. 17, 1861 at Ooltewah; captured at Vicksburg, July 4, 1863 and paroled; wounded (compound fracture of right thigh) and captured Aug. 21, 1864 at (Leestown) Winchester, VA; hospitalized at US Genl. Hospital, Baltimore, MD. June, 1865, imprisoned at Ft. McHenry, Md. After war tried tanning business, then farming. Baptist. Res. James Co., 1904, 1910 with wife Mary E. (m. 1872) and at McDonald, TN in 1920. [CVQ; TP1843; 1910 James Co.]

HUNT, Anderson     Co. D, 37TN
Born 1834 in TN. Miller at Soddy with wife Elizabeth. Enl. Sept. 1, 1861 at Germantown, TN. Deserted Oct. 31, 1861.

HUNT, R. H.     ANV
Wife was Molly E. Died Oct. 9, 1912, age 74, and buried Forest Hills Cem. [CT Oct. 10, 1912]

HUNT, William Armstrong 3d Lt.     Co. D, 37th TN Inf.
Born May 15, 1823, he came to Chattanooga in 1858. Enl. Sept. 1, 1861, at Knoxville. He was discharged at Corinth, MS, on May 15, 1862, because of ill health. Before the war, he had a farm near Chattanooga. A native of GA, he was born c1825. His wives were Sarah E. (born in May 15, 1823 at Dahlonega, GA; died 1882) and Mahala. Presbyterian. After the war, he was in the hotel business. Died Dec. 31, 1899 and buried at Citizens Cem. [CT Jan. 2, 1900; CTS]

HUNTER, James     Co. B, 10GA
Born c1838 in Rabun Co., GA. Married Jan. 28, 1849 at age 21 Lettissia Towery in Rabun. Wounded and captured at Cedar Run, Oct. 19, 1864 and imprisoned at Point Lookout. Res. of Alton Park in 1904. [TP6000]

HUNTER, James Alexander (Albert)     Thos. Polk Edmundson's GA Cav. Bn. (3CSA Cav.)
Born Harrison Nov. 26, 1847. Enl. Oct., 1864.

Captured Ooltewah, Jan., 1864; command disbanded before surrender of Army of Tennessee and served as guerillas. JAH accused of being spy. At skirmish at Conasauga River where Edmundson was killed, Apr. 1865. Returned to Harrison after war and farmed. Methodist. Married (1883 in HC) Sophronia Jackson. Died April 16, 1928 at home in Hixson. [TWP, 265; CT April, 17, 1928; TP 16,120; 1910HC]

HUNTER, Pleasant Eaves        Co. I, 5TN Cav.
        Born March 1844, Meigs Co., son of John Hunter (1815-1891) who had a 350-acre farm on TN River, Meigs Co. His mother was Katherine Eaves, daughter of Thomas Eaves, who lived at Decatur, TN. Thomas Eaves was a soldier in the Revolution. He brought his family from SC to TN. The Eaves family was Irish. Wounded at Munfordville in Oct., 1862, Hunter also saw action at Chickamauga, Resaca, and New Hope Church. He was discharged at Charlotte, NC, on May 12, 1865. Married (Mar. 12, 1869) Harriet B. Whiteside in Meigs Co. Pleasant Hunter lived the last years of his life in north Chattanooga Salesman. Died April 26, 1928 and buried Hunter's Bluff Cem., Meigs Co. [NBFM2,7; 1910HC]

HUNTER, Thomas H. -  Co. G, 2TN (Robinson's)
                [TP 1441]

HUNTER, William W.        Co. F, 35TN
        Born in Meigs Co., TN in 1826, he became a farmer in HC where he enl. on Dec. 2, 1862. Dark complexion, dark hair, dark eyes, 5'8" tall; captured at Missionary Ridge and imprisoned at Rock Island where he remained until March, 1865. [RI ledger]

HUSKEY, Francis    - Co. D, 4th (12th) GA Cav.
        He enl. Oct. 4, 1862 under Capt. William J. Rogers. He was later reported sick and deemed not physically fit for duty.

HUTCHESON, Capt. Joseph Chappell    21VA; Co. E, 14VA
        Born near Boydton, VA, May 18, 1842. Grad. Randolph-Macon College. Studied law at Univ. of VA and began practice in Anderson, TX. Moved to Houston, 1874. Elected Texas House, 1880, U.S. Congress, 1893-97. Died at his summer home on Walden's Ridge, May 25, 1924. Buried Glenwood Cem., Houston.

HUTCHINSON, John
        Born 1839, GA. African-American. In 1910 he was boarding on W. 13th St. No occupation. [1910HC]

HUTSON, Reuben        Co. G, 26TN; 2d Co. K,

1CSA (GA)
        Enl. Aug. 28, 1861, Knoxville. Deserted at Knoxville, Nov. 5, 1862.

HUTTON, Cornelius Marion        Chaplain and staff officer, 36AL
        Married Laura. [TWP 10,526]


# I

INGRAM, James Aaron        Co. I, 22MS
        Born c1826 Nahoba Co., MS. Enl., 1861. "We were beaten & quit & went home." Farmer after war. April 21, 1932 applied from HC for admission to TN Soldiers Home.

INGRAM, John A.        Co. G, 26TN; 2d Co. K,
                1CSA(GA)
        Enl. July 8, 1861 in Co. G, 26TN at Knoxville; captured at Fort Donelson, Feb. 16, 1862; imprisoned at Camp Douglas, Chicago. Exchanged and joined 2d Co. K, 1CSA(GA). Killed at Chickamauga.

IRVIN, George W.        Co. F, 35TN
        Born in TN and a farmer in HC, he enl. Nov. 24, 1862 at Chattanooga. Brown eyes, dark hair, fair complexion, and 5'6" tall.

IVEY, James C.        Co. H, 4TN Cav.; Co. B, 5TN Cavalry Bn.
        Born April 1840, near Chattanooga, son of John and Nancy. Enl. Aug. 11, 1861, at Chattanooga. Wounded slightly at Murfreesboro and again just after Perryville by a Bush-Whacker. "Captured twice but escaped both times through the assistance of some of my comrades capturing my captors, one time killing one of them and capturing the others." Elected 1Sgt. Aug., 1862. In battles of Fishing Creek, Shiloh, Perryville, Murfreesboro, Chickamauga, Missionary Ridge, Atlanta Campaign, Bentonville. Surr. April 26, 1865. Res., 1911, Princeton, TX. [Yeary, Rems. of Boys in Gray, pp. 373-74]

IVEY, William O.        Co. B, 5TN Cav.
        Enl. Aug. 11, 1861 at Chattanooga.


# J

JACKSON, Sgt. A. G.   Co. G, 26TN; 2d Co. I,
1CSA (GA)
    Born c1829. Enl. July 8, 1861 in 26TN;
captured at Fort Donelson, Feb. 16, 1862 and
imprisoned   Camp Douglas; when exchanged he
transferred to 1GA CSA; reduced to pvt., June 1, 1863;
Feb. 1, 1864 transferred to Clark's Independent Cav.
Company.

JACKSON, Daniel C.   Co. D, 37TN; Co. H, 4TN
Cav.
    Born 1831 in TN. Farm laborer in Harrison
with three children born in AR. Enl. Sept. 1, 1861 at
Knoxville. Disch. July 5, 1862, disability, but appears to
have joined dismounted cavalry. [1860HC]

JACKSON, Henry Clay   Co. B, 1TN
    Born Feb. 12, 1838. Enl. May, 1861 in
Nashville. Captured in VA and imprisoned at Fort
Delaware 18 months. Contractor who came to
Chattanooga about 1884. Built St. Peter & Paul and
Centenary churches, 1st National Bank, and Shipp
Hotel. Died June 5, 1892 in Chattanooga and buried
Murfreesboro. [CT June 6, 1892; NBFM2,7]

JACKSON, 1st Lt. James P. T.      Co. I, 19TN
    Born 1838 in TN, prob. son of Asahel and
Maranda. Farmer at Harrison with wife Rebecca. Enl.
May 25, 1861, in Knoxville in Co. B and transferred to
Co. I, July 17, 1862.  Promoted to sgt.

JACKSON, Nimrod      Co. A, 19TN
    Born 1816 in TN. 1860 res. Chattanooga with
wife Rebecca and six children. Enl. May 20, 1861,
Knoxville. Teamster. Disch. by May, 1863. [1860HC]

JACKSON, Peter H.
    Born 1843, in VA. 1910 res. Southern St. with
wife Ellen N. whom he married (2d wife) 1886.
Railroad watchman. [1910HC]

JACKSON, Robert M.      Co. B, 2AL Cav. Bn.
    Born Marion Co., 1829. Enl. 1863. Res.
Chattanooga 1905 "very old and destitute." [TP 6700]

JACKSON, Sam      Co. H, 4TN Cav.
    Wounded at Chickamauga "for life."

JACKSON, Shadrack      Co. H, 26TN; Barry's Btry.
    Age 47 in 1861, he enl. July 8, 1861 in Co. H,
26TN at Knoxville; left sick at Cumberland City, TN,
Feb. 12, 1862; enl. May 31, 1862 in Barry's Btry. at
Chattanooga; his duty was making oil for harness;
deserted and took USA oath, Feb., 1864. [Brown's

Diary]

JACKSON, Wiley T.      Co. D, 37TN
    Born 1845 in TN, son of Nimrod and Rebecca
of Chattanooga. Enl. Sept. 1, 1861 at Knoxville. Sent
from Corinth to hospital, May 5, 1862. Disch. Nov. 24,
1862. Took USA oath, Jan. 5, 1864 in Chattanooga; 5'5"
tall, black hair, brown eyes, dark complexion.

JACKSON, William W.  36GA
    Born Maury Co., GA. 1Lt. and Adjutant, Oct.
16, 1863. Captured Vicksburg, July 4, 1864 and paroled.
Captured Nashville Dec. 16, 1864 and imprisoned
Johnson's Island. To Chattanooga where he became
brakeman on Western & Atlantic and later in wholesale
grocery business in firm of Jackson & Trigg. Died Jan.
1905 in sanitarium in Tuscaloosa, AL.

JACOBS, S. Y.
    Born 1846, in TN. Res. 1910, with wife
Varlinchia, on Whiteside St. Riverboat keeper. [1910HC]

JACOWAY, William Usery      Co. G, 3GA Cav
    Born Aug. 16, 1845 in Franklin Co., TN.
Married Mollie Shook on 19 Dec. 1871 in Winchester,
TN. She was born 29 Dec. 1850 in winchester, TN and
died 7 Aug. 1832 in Fort Payne, AL. Counsel for
Southern Railroad. Christian Church. Long time resident
of Trenton, GA, but "spent most of later years in
Chattanooga" Died March 8, 1944 in Chattanooga and
buried in Trenton. [Chattanooga Free Press, March 9,
1944; NBFM10]

JAMES, Adam      Co. H, 26TN
    Enl. July 8, 1861 at Knoxville; captured at Fort
Donelson, Feb. 16, 1862; imprisoned at Camp Douglas,
IL, where he died July 21, 1862.

JAMES, Monroe Hatch      Co. D, 61NC
    Born 1832; died April, 1918.

JAMES, 2Lt. Richard P.      Co. A, 19TN
    Born March 11, 1844. Ill with pneumonia in
Jan. 1862, he recovered and re-enl. May 10, 1862 at
Corinth. Promoted to Orderly Sgt. He was ill again in
June, 1864, then was captured at Franklin, TN, on Dec.
17, 1864 after suffering a gunshot wound. He was sent to
Louisville, KY, from Nashville and then to Ft. Delaware.
He was in a hospital in Richmond, VA, in March, 1865,
with a fractured right leg. He signed the USA Oath of
Allegiance on June 2, 1865. Prior to the war, he was a
tinner's apprentice, living at the home of John A. Lee in
Chattanooga. Died Feb. 19, 1910. [Worsham, p. 118; CV
19:174]

JAMES, William A.    Co. H, 26TN; 2d Co. I,
1CSA (GA); Co. F, 39GA
Prior to the war, he had a farm at Limestone north of Harrison where he lived with his wife, Milly, and daughter, Mary T. He was born c1834, son of William. He enl. July 8, 1861. He was captured at Fort Donelson on Feb. 16, 1862, and was held a prisoner at Camp Douglas, IL. Absent, sick at Chattanooga, April 30, 1863; deserted from hospital, June 12, 1863; captured at Vicksburg, paroled, then deserted Dec. 10, 1863.

JAMISON, J. T.        Co. A, 3MO
Born Mar. 17, 1831 in Calloway Co., MO. Enl. June, 1861. Rose from Orderly Sgt. to Lt. Col. Real estate agent in Chattanooga. Moved to KY. [NBFM2,7]

JARNAGIN, Cpl. Albert L.     Barry's Btry.
Brother of Mrs. T. H. McCallie; enl. Feb. 9, 1862 at Memphis; captured Jonesboro, Sept. 3, 1864; imprisoned Camp Douglas, IL; 5'8" tall, dark eyes, light complexion, dark hair.

JARNAGIN, Sgt. Gustavus Henry "Gus"     Barry's Btry.
Born at Athens, TN, April 9, 1844, son of Spencer Jarnagin, US Senator. Gus Jarnagin received an appointment to the USNA but resigned to enlist Oct. 4, 1862, at Knoxville. He was paroled May 11, 1865, at Meridian, MS. He clerked briefly for prosperous Chattanooga businessman Joseph Ruohs following his war service. Later, he and John T. Staff had a grocery at the corner of Seventh and Market and in 1893 Jarnigan married Irene Virginia Ruohs, daughter of his former employer. He died April 24, 1914 at his home on Vine Street and was buried in Forest Hills Cemetery. [CT April 25, 1914; TWP, 10,805; 1890VetCensus]

JARNAGIN, Pleasant D.    Co. G, 26TN; Co. F, 39GA
Enl. July 8, 1861, in Knoxville. Left sick at Bowling Green, Jan. 23, 1862. Captured Atlanta, July 22, 1864 and imprisoned Camp Chase, OH.

JARNAGIN, Maj. R. A.    Co. E, 19TN
Appointed asst. commissary Sept. 11, 1861, he was killed at the battle at Murfreesboro on Dec. 31, 1862. [Lindsley, Mil. Annals of AofT]

JAY, Louis E.   Co. E, 59GA (Andersonville Guards)
Born 1848, in GA. Carpenter in Chattanooga, 1910, Joined NBF Camp. March 1910 Louis and wife Lula moved to Tampa. [NBFM4; CT March 2, 1910; 1910HC]

JEFFREYS, Alexander       Co. K, 43 TN
Enl. Oct. 17, 1861, at Ooltewah. He was captured at Vicksburg on July 4, 1863, and paroled. Before the war, he was living at Soddy as a farm laborer with Sarah Coleman. His age on the 1860 census is given as 15.

JENKINS, Allen      Co. A, 5th (McKenzie's) TN Cav.
Enl. Aug. 24, 1861 at Camp Cumming. Age 37 on March 11, 1864 roll. Captured June 20, 1864 in HC. Took USA oath July 16, 1864 and "went north of Ohio River."

JENKINS, Ephraim       Co. A, 23GA
Born 1844, Lincoln Co., NC. Enl. Aug. 31, 1861. ANV: Seven Pines, Malvern Hill, Chancellorsville. Transf. Jan., 1864, to ordnance dept. in Etowah, GA. Paroled Columbus, GA, Apr., 1865. To TN 1881. Res. Chattanooga, 1907. 1910 res. household. of grandson Love Lowrey. [TP8819; 1910HC]

JENKINS, Thomas John
His second wife was Georgia Anna. [CT June 7, 1908]

JENKINS, Lt. W. C.        Co. L, 35TN; Co. B, 3GA Reserves
Battle of Murfreesboro; transferred to Co. B, 3GA Reserves; absent without leave Aug. 15, 1863. Buried Yellow Springs, Poe Road, Walden's Ridge via Daisy.

JENNINGS, Ephraim    23GA [TP 8819]

JENNINGS, John Henry        Co. H, 19AL
Born Walker Co., GA 17 Nov. 1842. Enl. Aug. 1861. Shiloh, Murfreesboro (wounded), Chickamauga, Missionary Ridge, Franklin, Nashville, Bentonville. Paroled Salisbury, NC. To TN, 1877. Married Emily Elrod on 14 Feb. 1861 in Chattanooga. She was born 25 Apr. 1846 in Chattanooga and died 12 Sept. 1909 in Chattanooga also. Passenger agent for NC&St.L RR; member of Chattanooga Fire Dept.; 1910 undertaker, res. house hold of son-in-law Wm. K. Garmany. Died 2 Jan. 1917 in Montgomery, AL and buried in Forest Hills Cemetery. 75 years old. [CT Jan. 17, 1917; FHR; TP 8607; 1910HC]

JENNINGS, W. H.
Born Nov. 17, 1842 in Walker Co., GA. Enl. Aug., 1861. Wounded in Battle of Murfreesboro. Paroled May, 1865 at Salisbury, NC. Merchant in Chattanooga. [NBFM2]

JOHNS, Z. L.        Co. L, 36TN
Enl. Jan. 9, 1862 at Chattanooga.

JOHNSON, A. J.          Co. B, 1TN Cav. (Carter's)

JOHNSON, Abraham Malone
        Served the Confederacy during the war in the railroad department. His father, Col. Ephraim Malone Johnson of Hall County, GA, had opposed secession, but he supported his three sons who joined the southern army. Born in Gainesville, GA Jan. 31, 1830, Johnson had come to Chattanooga in 1851 and established himself as a tinner and mail agent. He became superintendent of the Wills Valley Railroad which he continued to manage during the Civil War until Chattanooga was evacuated. He afterwards operated on the Macon and Brunswick line. Near the end of the war, he oversaw repairs of the Atlanta and West Point and GA railroads.
        It was written of Johnson long after the war that he was "an ardent supporter from first to last of the Southern Confederacy, believed in the doctrine of state rights and a strict construction of the Federal Constitution, which involved the rights of property in the South, the real cause of the war, and now that 40 years have passed is of the same opinion still, and under like circumstances would do the same as he did in 1861."
        After the war, having "lost house and possessions," he became a bank cashier, then became involved in the operation of a rolling mill. He also was president of the Lookout Water Company and Chattanooga Medicine Company (which evenually would become Chattem Corporation), and led in the development of the Chattanooga suburb of St. Elmo. He also founded Forest Hills Cemetery. He married Thankful Whiteside, daughter of Col. James A. Whiteside. Mason. Episcopalian (left land for Thankful Parish). He died at his res. in St. Elmo April 21, 1903 and is buried in Forest Hills Cemetery. [CT, April 22, 1903; Forest Hills Cemetery; Hist. of St. Paul's, p. 170; 1860HC.]

JOHNSON, C.          Co. K, 43TN
        Enl. July 31, 1863 at Ooltewah; captured at Vicksburg, July 4, 1863 and paroled.

JOHNSON, Sgt. Campbell          Co. K, 43TN
        Enl. Oct. 12, 1861 at Ooltewah; discharged Nov. 1, 1862; paroled.

JOHNSON, Elias Presnel     Co. F, 5SC or Co. B, 13SC
        Married Mary Elizabeth; Sarah Lou. [TWP 2401, 828]

JOHNSON, Henry, Sr.
        Born c1845, VA. Farmer, 1910 in HC with wife Burnettie. [1910HC]

JOHNSON, Sgt. J. G.     2nd Co. K, 1st CSA Cav.
        Enl. July 14, 1862 in HC. Deserted at Shelbyville, TN, Feb. 14, 1863.

JOHNSON, J. G.          Co. G, 2GA Cav.
        Born Hall Co., GA, 1849. Enl. 1865. To TN 1912 and res. Alton Park, 1916. [TP 15,053]

JOHNSON, James M.     Co. H, 4TN Cav.

JOHNSON, James M.     Co. K, 43TN
        Enl. Dec. 1, 1861, at Ooltewah. Captured at Vicksburg, July 4, 1863. Before the war, he had a farm at Long Savannah. He and his wife, Mary, were from NC. They were born there c1829. They moved to HC from NC c1860.

JOHNSON, John Nettleton     Co. C, 1KY Cav. Bn.
        Born Bedford Co., VA, Aug. 18, 1847, he moved to Bristol as a youth and attended Emory and Henry. Attempted to enlist, riding almost 200 miles into western VA, but was sent home for being too young. He ran away at least twice again but was sent back by authorities or intercepted by his father. Finally he succeeded in joining Co. C, 1KY Cav. Bn. and was in the fights at Cynthiana, KY and the raid across the TN River at Paducah. After fighting with Morgan, Johnson fought with Forrest and was wounded at Harrisburg. After war made home in Savannah, GA. Lawyer. Episcopal. Married (1882) Lucy Herndon Botts. To Chattanooga 1912, then appointed Pres. CSA Pension Board and moved to Nashville where he died Feb. 4, 1931 and was buried in Mt. Olivet Cem. [NBFM2,8]

JOHNSON, Lewis          Co. B, 1TN Cav. (Carter's)
        Born 1822 in TN. Carpenter. Married Mary. Res. of Birchwood, 1860. [1860HC]

JOHNSON, Martin     2nd Co. K, 1st CSA Cav.
        Enl. July 14, 1862 in HC. Deserted Sept. 1, 1863.

JOHNSON, Oscar Bowman
        Born Penfield, GA and served in a GA regiment. Married Martha E. McLaurin of Jackson, MS. Patrolman, then Sgt. in Chattanooga Police Force, serving 25 years. Episcopalian. Died July 1, 1912 at home on East 10th and buried Forest Hills Cemetery.

JOHNSON, Stephen     Co. K, 43TN
        Enl. Oct. 12, 1862 at Ooltewah; captured at Vicksburg, July 4, 1863 and paroled.

JOHNSON, Thomas H.     Co. K, 4GA Cav.
        Born HC, Nov. 6, 1839. Fort Donelson,

Chickamauga, Siege of Knoxville. Took USA oath, Jan., 1864. "My health was bad. I saw nothing but defeat." Res. household. of son Samuel H. in James Co, 1910. Res. Ooltewah, 1919. [TP 15,415; 1910 James Co.]

JOHNSON, Thomas     Co. F, 35TN
     Born in Bledsoe Co., TN in 1832, he was a miller at Harrison when he enl., Oct. 1, 1862. He became ill Jan. 11, 1863 and died in Chattanooga March 31, 1863. [Worsham, p. 8; 1860HC]

JOHNSON, Lt. V. Q.     Co. A, 19TN
     He was appointed adj. of the 19TN Infantry on Sept. 1, 1861, after earlier being 1Lt. in Co. A. In February, 1862, he was home sick on furlough. Prior to the war, he was a clerk in Chattanooga with a personal estate of $20,000. A native of VA, he was born about 1829. His wife was Jane E.

JOHNSON, W. D.     Co. L, 36TN
     Enl. Jan. 9, 1862 at Chattanooga.

JOHNSON, William     Co. B, 1TN Cav. (Carter's)
     Enl. Aug. 7, 1861, Cleveland.

JOHNSON, William A.     Co. K, 43TN
     Born c1845 in TN, son of William and Mary A. Johnson. Enl. Oct. 17, 1861 at Ooltewah; captured at Vicksburg, July 4, 1863 and paroled.

JOHNSON, Zack     Co. K, 43TN
     Enl. Nov. 10, 1861 at Ooltewah; captured at Vicksburg, July 4, 1863 and paroled.

JOHNSTON, Ambrose     2nd Co. K, 1st CSA Cav.
     Enl. July 14, 1862 in HC. Deserted Sept. 12, 1863.

JOLLY, 2nd Lt. James W., Jr.     Co. B, 66 GA; Wooford's Cav.
     Born Forsyth Co., GA, 1840. Enl. 1862. Lookout Mtn., Missionary Ridge, Atlanta Camp. Paroled Kingston, GA, May, 1865. To TN, 1892. Married (1904) Sarah "Sally" Williams. Died 1909 in HC. [TWP, 292; TP 11,262]

JONES, A. G.     Co. K, 4AL
     Born GA. Enl. 1861. Contractor in Chattanooga c1895. [NBFM2]

JONES, Ambrose     Co. B, 5TN Cav.
     Enl. Aug. 11, 1861.

JONES, B. A. J.     Co. H, 26TN

Enl. July 8, 1861, Knoxville. Mortally wounded Fort Donelson, Feb. 13, 1862 and died Feb. 23, 1862.

JONES, Benjamin F.     2nd Co. K, 1st CSA Cav.
     Enl. Sept. 24, 1862 in HC. Detailed by Maj. Gen. Sam Jones at Chattanooga. Deserted Dec. 28, 1863 at Charleston, TN, and took oath Jan. 11, 1864. Res of HC. Fair complexion, light hair, gray eyes, and 5'4" tall.

JONES, Elias P.     Co. H, 35TN; Co. H, 4TN Cav. (Starnes)
     Born April 7, 1842 in Graysville, GA. Enl. Sept. 1, 1861 at Dunlap, TN. Captured twice and was in Little Wills Valley at time of surrender. Married (1865) Mary Elizabeth Farmer. Occupation butcher. Died 1909 at res. on Duncan Ave. in Chattanooga on Feb. 12, 1909. Buried in Forest Hills Cemetery. [FHR; TWP, p. 67; NBFM2; TP8289]

JONES, Francis M.     Co. F, 35TN
     Born in Bledsoe Co., TN, in 1830, he farmed in HC until enlisting at Varnell Station; captured at Missionary Ridge, he took the USA oath Dec. 16, 1863. Blue eyes, dark hair, florid complexion, 5'8" tall.

JONES, George Washington     Co. H, 26TN; 2d Co. I, 1CSA (GA) F&S
     Grad. Medical Univ. of Nashville, 1860. Enl. Aug. 6, 1861, Knoxville. Prom. Asst. Surg., Sept. 8, 1861. Elected 2Lt, Jan. 29, 1863. In arrest undergoing sentence Genl Court Martial to be suspended from pay and command for two months, Aug. 31, 1863. Detailed as Acting Asst. Surgeon, June 17, 1864. Acting Asst. Surg., 66GA, July 1, 1864. Paroled Greensboro, May 1, 1865.

JONES, Henry Hall     Co. D, 4GA Cav.
     Born Aug. 25, 1844 in Bienville Parish, LA, of GA parents, he enl. June, 1864 at LaGrange. Wounded Sept. 19, 1864 at Battle of Winchester and hospitalized at Lynchburg. Res. of Chattanooga, 1909. 1910 boarding on Market St. Collector for roofing co. [NBFM2,7; 1910HC]

JONES, James
     Born Knox Co. and married (1883) Emma Bates. Died 1928 in HC. [TWP, 270]

JONES, Sgt. James H.     Co. H, 4TN Cav.
     Born Dec. 19, 1842 in Wilson Co., TN. Enl. May 15, 1861 in Co. H., 4TN Cav. Afterwards served in McClung's Btry. and with John H. Morgan. Captured at Greenville Sept. 4, 1864 and released May, 1865. Butcher and sometime salesman in Chattanooga. Left Chattanooga in late 1890's for Galveston, Tex. where he

and his wife were killed in great storm, Sept. 8, 1900. Bodies never recovered. [NBFM2,3]

JONES, James W. "Jim"    Co F, 2SC; Co. B, 5TN Cav.; Co. A, 1TN Cav. (Carter's)
Born Abbeville Dist., SC, Dec., 1846. Enl. Aug. 11, 1861. Became commissary sgt. and later disch. because of disability. Married Aley Cleveland (1883, Loudon Co.). Res. 1910 Miller Ave. Died Oct. 27, 1910 in East Chattanooga and buried CSA Cem. [TWP 3674; 1860HC; 1910HC]

JONES, Joshua    Co. A, 1Cav. (Carter's)
Born c. 1835 in TN. 1860 res. in household of Rachael Eldridge. [1860HC]

JONES, William
Born 1843, NC. Res. 1910 in Soddy with wife S. E. Manager of office building. [1910HC]

JONES, William Thomas    Co. A, 38AL
Born Greenville, SC, and married (1893) Martha Ayers. Contractor in Chattanooga after war. Died Nov. 22, 1914, age 72, and buried CSA Cem. [CT Nov. 23, 1914; TWP, 280]

JORDAN (JORDON), James
Born c1848 in Bradley Co. and married (1896) Lizzie Vandergriff. Farmer in HC. [1910HC]

JUDD, Amos Wilson    Dykes Co., Fla. Lt. Arty.
Born Watertown, CT in 1846, he moved with his family to Winchester, TN in 1859. He began his service in Nashville in the Ordnance Dept., turning out 136 million gun caps until transferred to Atlanta in early 1862. He continued to manufacture caps and powder until June, 1863, when he joined Gamble's FL Btry. He later guarded prisoners at Andersonville, GA and Salisbury, NC.
After receiving his parole in Tallahassee, he attended Union Univ. (TN), practiced photography at Valparaiso and Indianapolis, IN, then moved to Chattanooga in 1877 and established a photography business. "Dean of the photography profession in Chattanooga." Episcopalian. Married (1894) Ida Eakin. Died April 27, 1929 in Chattanooga [TWP, 269; CT April, 27, 1929; Hist. St. Paul's, 173-74; NBFM6]

JULIAN, William Isom    Co. A, 5TN Cav.
Son of Marsena R. Julian, a Methodist circuit rider, and Malinda Crowder Julian who lived at Tyner. Enl. Aug. 24, 1861 at Camp Cummings by J. W. Gillespie for 12 months in White's Co. Age 25 on Mar. 11, 1864 roll. Present on rolls (though sometimes listed in Co. F, 1TN Cav.) through March, 1864. Detailed by

order of Gen. Humes in East TN, June 30-Dec. 31, 1864. Serving on detached duty as scout in North GA when captured Feb. 26, 1865 in Murray Co. "A guerilla and bushwhacker." Took USA oath Mar. 11, 1865 in Chattanooga as deserter. Married Elizabeth Craighead, April 26, 1865. His second marriage was to Bettie J. Farris, Oct. 24, 1867 in Catoosa Co. GA. He died Aug. 10, 1898 and was buried in Julian Cem., Graysville, GA. [TWP 219; Eliz. Manley, Julians and Allied Families]

JUSTICE, Joseph    Co. K, 43TN
Enl. Oct. 17, 1861 at Ooltewah. Captured at Vicksburg, July 4, 1863. Paroled.

JUSTICE, William M.    Co. F, 35TN
Born in Calhoun Co., GA, in 1841, he was working as a railroad laborer in Chattanooga when he enl. on Oct. 14, 1862. He was hospitalized much of 1863-64. He had blue eyes, dark hair and a fair complexion.

# K

KANESTER (KANASTER), Alex    Co. G, 26TN; 2d Co. K, 1CSA (GA)
Enl. Aug. 28, 1861, Knoxville. Sick in hospital, Nashville, Aug. 28-29, 1861. Captured Fort Donelson, Feb. 16, 1862 and imprisoned Camp Morton. Absent on furlough, June 30, 1863. Deserted in Whitfield Co., GA.

KAYLOR, Daniel Pringle    Chattanooga Home Guards
A leading Chattanooga businessman before the war, he served in the Home Guards because of a physical disability. Born in New York City in 1825, he was the son of George Kaylor and Mary Pringle. In 1852, he moved to Crawfish Springs, GA, and from there to Chattanooga, where he had a distillery and flour mill. He married Sarah Whitfield McBryde in 1846. His second wife was Eliza Cordelia Hagan Walling. He died in Chattanooga in 1898.

KAYLOR, Harry    Co. H, 2TN Cav. (Ashby's)
One of the sons of Daniel Kaylor, the Chattanooga businessman. Enl. Aug. 14, 1864 in Griffin, GA. Paroled April, 1865. After the war operated Kaylor Hall and the Kaylor Distillery. May be Wm. Kaylor, 11yrs., bn. NY in household of Daniel P., 1860.

KEEF, Alexander    Co. D, 37TN
Born 1847 in TN, son of Jonathan and Nancy of

Chattanooga. Enl. greatly underage Sept. 1, 1861 at Knoxville, but "sent home by order of Col. White, Nov. 11, 1861.

KEEF, Henry          Co. D, 37TN
    Res. McAlester, OK, 1912.

KEEF, Jesse          Co. D, 37TN

KEEF, William Dale "Daily"     23TN; Co. D, 37TN
    Born Dec. 25, 1845 in HC and enl.  Sept. 1, 1861 at Knoxville. He caught measles which settled in his lungs, and he was disch. Nov. 4, 1862. Resident of Chattanooga for 30 years. Married (1870) Amanda Cruze. Died at his home in Hill City July 29, 1906 and buried in White Oak Cem. [CT July 30-31, 1906; TWP, p. 68; TP6478]

KEENER, James D.     Co. B, 43TN
    Born c1820. Enl. June, 1862, Sulphur Springs.

KEISER (KEZER, KEZEIR), Frederich
    Enl. Jan. 9, 1862 in Co. L, 36TN at Chattanooga; transferred to Co. F, 35TN; disch. April, 1863 as "non conscript."

KEISTER, Henley Crocket   Moreland's Co., VA
                          Local Defense Force
    Born 1845 in Newport, VA and married (1874) Sarah Angeline Stanfield. Died 1890 in HC. [TWP, 304]

KEITH, Asa          Co. G, 26TN; Co. D, 37TN
    Born 1797 in Jackson Co., GA. Farmer at Chattanooga with wife Eliza. Enl. July 8, 1861, Knoxville. Disch. because of age but re-enl. April 24, 1863 at Chattanooga. Hospitalized that summer and died in Catoosa Hospital of chronic hepititis in June, 1864. 5'6" tall, dark complexion, black eyes, and black hair.

KEITH, John Bailey     Co. F, 3CSA Cav.
    Born May 6, 1845 in Murray Co., GA he married (1860) Mary Constance Terry, Oct. 20, 1866 in Murray. Surrendered with unit in Kingston in 1865. Died in HC. [TWP 2650]

KEITH, M. L.
    Died prior to 1915. His wife, Kate, was 77yrs. when she died in Chattanooga and was buried in Pleasant Valley. [CT June 21, 1915]

KELLER, Isaac          Co. D, 36GA
    Born April 20, 1833 in Greenville Dist., SC, he

enl. in March, 1862. He was wounded at New Hope Church and at Jackson, MS. During the latter battle a shell burst near him paralyzing him for eight days and he never recovered fully from its effects. Paroled May, 1865 at Kingston, GA. He came to TN in 1878 and was res. in Chattanooga in 1908. [TP 6462]

KELLEY (KELLY), G. F. M.       Co. H, 26TN
    Born 1841. Enl. July 8, 1861 at Knoxville; died Oct. 8, 1861.

KELLEY, George W.          Co. H, 26TN; 2d Co. I, 1CSA (GA)
    Born c1838, in TN. Enl. July 8, 1861, Knoxville. Wounded in arm at Fort Donelson, Feb. 15, 1862 and sent off. Transferred from Bradshaw's Co., Dec. 15, 1862. Appt. Sgt. April 30, 1863. St. Mary's Hospital, Dalton, May 9, 1863. Farmer. Res. 1910 on Shallowford Rd. with wife Manda L. Died June 11, 1918 at home and buried in Concord Cem. [1910HC; CT June 12, 1912]

KELLY, Ike
    Died at age 75 on April 21, 1908 at his home on Cowart St. Buried Forest Hills Cemetery. [CT April 22, 1908]

KELLY, John          Barry's Btry
    Lost on retreat in Feb. [Brown's Diary]

KELLY, Miles          Co. D, 4th (12th) GA Cav.
    Enl. Oct. 4, 1862, under Capt. William J. Rogers. Absent Oct. 18, 1862. Born in Ireland about 1832, he was a day laborer living with his wife, Bridget, at Chattanooga prior to the war. Also enl. Jan. 10, 1863. Winston's Lt. Arty. On detached service to Mobile, April 28, 1863. Took USA oath at Chattanooga and said he had been conscripted. Paroled April, 28, 1865.

KELLEY (KELLY), William A.    Co. D, 19TN; Co. H, Cons. 3TN
    Born on 6 Mar. 1839  and was raised near Dayton in Rhea Co., he was wounded trying to carry his captain off the field at Chickamauga. He married Eliza Ann Singleton on 27 Oct. 1870 in Rhea Co., TN. He was a mail carrier for a time in Rhea County in the early 1900s. Died of pneumonia Dec. 9, 1904 and is buired in the first Shaver Cem. in Rhea Co. [CT Dec. 23, 1904]

KELTNER, Thomas W.     Co. A, 19GA; Co. B, 6CSA Cav. Bn.
    Born Hamburg, SC, 1842. Enl. June 11, 1861. Second Manassas, Seven Days, Petersburg. Captured Nov. 12, 1864 in Owen Co., KY and imp. Camp Douglas. 1910 res. in Ridgedale. July 7, 1920 entered

Soldiers Home. [TP 12,045]

KENNEDY, D. N.
        Tax collector in CSA Chattanooga. [WF]

KENNEDY, Capt. Daniel Allen        Co. A, 19TN
        Born c1840. Enl. May 20, 1861, elected 2Lt, May 20, 1861 and became Capt. in May of 1862. He was stationed with the unit at Corinth, MS, spending part of this time in the hospital. He was captured by Federal troops on Dec. 16, 1864. Kennedy was transferred to the prison in Louisville, KY, and from there to Johnson's Island in OH.
        Dark complexion, eyes and hair, and stood 5'8 tall. His father was Allen Kennedy, a pioneer at Ross's Landing, and his mother was Margaret Hackett. His brothers were Dr. William E., John and Mark. After the war, Daniel was a druggist on Market St. at Chattanooga. He died in 1876. [CT Jan. 18, 1912]

KENNEDY, Capt. John Hackett        Co. A, 19TN
        Son of Ross's Landing pioneer Allen Kennedy and younger brother of Daniel A., John, and Daniel Kennedy operated a wholesale drug store on Market St. JHK was promoted to Sgt., then Captain. Wounded in right thigh, July 22, 1864, Battle of Atlanta. Captured at Macon. Afterwards in Ocmulgee Hospital, Macon. Returned to Chattanooga and died here in 1870.

KENNER, William H.        Co. A, 2TN Cav. Bn.
        Born Sept. 26, 1835 in Marion Co. TN. Enl. May 10, 1861. Wounded at Fishing Creek. Paroled Apr., 1865 in NC. Merchant in Chattanooga but moved away. [NBFM2]

KENT, Wiley S.        Co. D, 37TN
        Born 1835 in TN. Farm laborer at Harrison. [1860HC]

KERNS, Burton        Co. H, 33GA
        Born Lumpkin Co., GA, 1840. Enl. early 1861. Chancellorsville (wounded), Fredericksburg, Gettysburg, Spotsylvania CH, Petersburg. To TN c1880. Res. Soddy, 1908. [TP 9948]

KERR, Jesse M., Jr.        Barry's Btry.
        Enl. Feb. 12, 1863 at Pollard, AL; hospitalized May 31, 1863 in Jackson, MS.

KERR, James M.        Barry's Btry.
        Enl. Oct. 4, 1862 at Knoxville; wounded in head at Spanish Fort, April 7, 1865.

KESTERSON, John C.        Co. A, 19TN
        He was among those enrolled by Col. F. M. Walker at Cumberland Gap, VA, in August, 1861. Kesterson was with the unit at Corinth, MS, and then at Shelbyville, TN In July of 1863, he was detailed to cut logs at Chattanooga. On Sept. 10, he deserted by coming into the Union lines and taking the USA Oath of Allegiance. He was sent to Louisville, KY, for release there. John, born 8 Nov. 1844, was a son of Abel and Margaret Cook Kesterson. The Kestersons had come down the river to Chattanooga from Claiborne Co., TN, in the mid-1850s. After the war, John Kesterson lived for a time at Moccasin Bend, but he moved to the Indian territory in OK when his daughter was small. He married Harriet Lewis of Polk Co., and their only child was the daughter Margaret. He died 14 Dec. 1915. [UDC1 pg 234]

KEY, B. P.        9TN Cav., Co. E, 14TN Cav.
        Enl. in 9TN Cav, Jan. 7, 1863. Charter member NBF Camp, 1885-96. Physician in Chattanooga. [NBFM2]

KEY, Lt. Col. David McKendree
        A prominent Chattanooga attorney and political leader when the Civil War broke out. After TN joined the Confederacy, he had an active role in the organization of troops and was appointed adjutant-general on the staff of Gen. William R. Caswell. In June 1861, he assisted in organizing 43TN Infantry, of which he was Lt. Col. Took part in the KY campaign, the retreat through Cumberland Gap, and the action around Vicksburg. There he suffered a wound to the thigh and was captured. He was exchanged and, after the battle at Chickamauga, he reorganized his regiment at Decatur, GA. He went with Longstreet into VA, but his health failed, and he was unable to complete the campaign. Key was born in Greene Co., TN, in 1824, son of John Key, a farmer and minister. He studied at Hiwassee College and moved to Chattanooga in 1853. After the war, Key resumed his law practice at Chattanooga. In 1875, after the death of former President Andrew Johnson, he was appointed his successor in the U.S. Senate. He retained this post until 1877 when he was appointed postmaster general by President Rutherford B. Hayes. In 1880, he was named as Federal judge, a position he held until 1896. He was married in 1857 to Elizabeth Lenoir, and they had seven children. The Key home was at Fourth and Chestnut streets. [GHT, 956]

KEY, Lucius Eugene        Co. I, 13GA
        Born July 9, 1838 in Henry Co., GA. Enl. in Griffin, GA, April 8, 1861. Fought with ANV. Wounded Chancellorsville, Wilderness and Petersburg. Paroled at Appomattox Courthouse. Carpenter in Chattanooga, also Chattanooga Sewer and Pipe, for more than 20 years. Died March 15, 1915 in North Chattanooga and buried

CSA Cem. [NBFM2,9]

KEY, Lt. Summerfield Armitage
He was 28 years old in April, 1861 when he enl. as a private in the 19TN Infantry. Two months later, he was transferred to 43rd Infantry and appointed adjutant. He was in the KY and MS campaigns, including the siege of Vicksburg. He was with Longstreet in East TN and accompanied Early through MD and in the Shenandoah Valley campaign. Capt. J. N. Aiken of Co. K, 43TN reported that at the cavalry fight at Darksville, VA, late in the war, when "our brigade was pitted against five times its number, it is but justice to state that if it had not been for the coolness and bravery of Adjt. S. A. Key, who was acting as chief of staff [adjutant], our entire command would have been surrounded and captured. On all occasions he proved himself to be a cool-headed, brave, efficient officer, and to-day has the highest respect and affection of every survivor of the command." He was with the escort of Jefferson Davis until the latter's capture in GA.
The younger brother of David Key, Summerfield was born in Monroe Co., TN, Oct. 14, 1835. Attended Hiwassee College, Carson-Newman College, and then studied law. He was a leading attorney and he was chancellor for two years. In 1871, Summerfield Key married Mary Divine, daughter of John L. and Elizabeth Williams Divine. Represented HC in TN Gen'l Assembly, 1877-79. He died in Chattanooga, June 14, 1891 and was buried in Forest Hills Cem. [FHR; BDTA, 2:494-95]

KIDD, W. H.          Co. E, 6AL
Born in NY state. Enl. June 6, 1861. RR Car builder in Chattanooga c1895. [NBFM2]

KILGORE, J. J.    Co. G, 26TN; 2d Co. K,
                         1CSA (GA); Co. F, 39GA
Enl. Aug. 28, 1861, Knoxville. Left sick at Clarksville, Feb. 11, 1862. In 39GA Dec. 31, 1862-Feb. 28, 1863; as CSA deserter, went into Fed. lines at Sale Creek, Oct. 18, 1863, where he took USA oath and was released to remain north of the Ohio. [Henderson, 304]

KILGORE, Robert D.      Co. H, 26TN; 2d Co. I,
                                   1CSA (GA)
Born c1842. Enl. July 8, 1861, Knoxville. Captured at Fort Donelson, Feb. 16, 1862 and imprisoned at Camp Douglas. Deserted at Kennesaw Mtn., July 2, 1864.

KILLIAN, Billy          Co. C, 3TN Cav. Bn.
Son of William and Elizabeth who farmed in the Salem community 1860, and brother of Henry. [Roark, Hardtack and Hardship]

KILLIAN, George Washington          Co. B, 1TN Cav. (Carter's)
Born 1845 in TN, son of William and Elizabeth of Birchwood. Enl. Aug. 7, 1861, Cleveland.

KILLIAN, Henry
Son of William and Elizabeth; who farmed in the Salem community and brother of Billy and George. Married (1853) and moved to Arkansas. Fought in CSA, returned to Ark. and moved to Texas in 1878. Married second time (1897) Sarah Elizabeth Roark, sister of James A. [Roark, Hardtack and Hardship]

KIMBALL, LeVert      Garrrity's AL Btry.
Born in Mobile Sept. 24, 1845. Was college student and contrary to father's advice enl. at Fort Barrancas. Served five weeks in cav. and then transferred to Garrrity's Btry. Participated in all battles from Shiloh to Nashville. Wounded at Murfreesboro and imprisoned at Springfield, IL. Exchanged and fought at Mobile, surrendering at Cuba Station in May, 1865. Lawyer in Chattanooga Member of NBF Camp. Died in Chattanooga Nov. 28, 1892 and buried in CSA Cem. [1890VetCensus; NBFM2]

KIMBROUGH, Capt. William Bradley      Co. A,
                                                         21GA
Born at Rocky Hollow, Jefferson Co., TN, May 29, 1833. Enl. June 6, 1861 at Cumberland Gap, TN. Merchant in Chattanooga c1895. Member NBF Camp, 1896. [NBFM2; 1890VetCensus]

KINCHELOE (See KINZALOW)

KING, A. W.          Barry's Btry.
Enl. Sept. 30, 1862 in Chattanooga.

KING, Alfred Columbus      Co. B, 1TN Cav. (Carter's)
Son of the Rev. Alfred and Susan Matthews King of Ooltewah. Enl. at Cleveland, Aug. 7, 1861. At Bristol Oct., 1864 waiting on the sick including his older brother, Wm. H. King.

KING, Fielding S.      Co. B, 1TN Cav. (Carter's)
Born c1842, son of the Rev. Alfred and Susan Matthews King of Ooltewah.

KING, Herbert Lewis      Co. B, 1TN Cav. (Carter's)
Born 1839, son of the Rev. Alfred and Susan Matthews King. Enl. Aug. 7, 1861, Cleveland. Captured Sept. 2, 1864 Martinsburg, VA as member of Vaughn's Brigade by Gen. Wm. W. Averell and imprisoned Fort Delaware where he died of small pox Feb. 17, 1865 and was buried on Jersey shore. 5'10 1/2" tall, grey eyes, and brown hair.

94 CONFEDERATE SOLDIERS OF HAMILTON COUNTY, TENNESSEE

\* \* \* \* \* \* \* \* \* \* \* \* \* \* \* \* \* \* \* \* \* \* \* \* \* \* \* \* \* \* \* \* \* \* \* \* \* \* \* \* \* \* \* \* \* \* \* \* \* \* \* \* \* \* \* \* \* \* \* \* \* \* \* \* \* \* \* \* \* \* \* \* \* \* \* \* \* \* \* \* \* \* \* \* \* \* \* \* \* \*

KING, Maj. Horace Watson          61TN
Born 25 Jan. 1829 in Athens, TN son of William Carrol and Mary Guy Branley King. Asst. QM, 61TN. On staff of John C. Breckinridge and Chief QM on staff of Gen. Sam Jones, Feb. 6, 1863. Paroled 22 Nat 1865. Lived some time in Atlanta and in Washington, DC. Died 15 Feb. 1884 in Chattanooga and buried in Citizens Cem. [CTS]

KING, Major John B.        Co. C. 1TN Cav. (Carter's)
After joining the company formed by Capt. William Snow of Snow Hill, he quickly rose through the ranks. Initially he was a 1st. Lt. in Co. B, 1TN Cav. after enlisting in Cleveland and being mustered in at Knoxville in August of 1861. He later rose to the rank of Mjor. He was killed June 6, 1864 at the Battle of Piedmont, VA.
King had a farm at Snow Hill prior to the war, residing with his wife, Susan. He was born about 1833. His father was Alfred King, who also farmed at Snow Hill.

KING, Sgt. John C.        Co. F, 35TN
Born in Newberry District, SC, in 1833, he became a merchant in Chattanooga where he enl. Oct. 4, 1862. He deserted Nov. 25, 1863 near Ooltewah and took the USA oath Dec. 11, 1863. Gray eyes, dark hair, fair complexion, 5'10" tall.

KING, Thomas        Clark's Independent Cav. Co.
Enl. Aug. 18, 1863. Deserted Sept. 10, 1863 at Loudon, TN.

KING, Thomas J.        Co. H, 4TN Cav.

KING, William H.        Co. B, 1TN Cav. (Carter's)
Born c1829, son of the Rev. Alfred and Susan Matthews King of Ooltewah. He was deputy sheriff prior to war. Enl. Nov. 14, 1862. Wounded at Morristown, TN, and in October 1864 was in hospital at Bristol, TN. Lived with his parents after war in Houston Co., GA. and still unmarried at age 39 in 1870.

KINGTON (KINTON), G. W.        Co. G, 26TN
Enl. July 8, 1861, Knoxville. Prom. to Sgt. Captured Fort Donelson, Feb. 16, 1862 and imprisoned Camp Douglas.

KINMAN, Cpl. Elisha W.        Co. A, 19TN; Co. H, Cons. 3TN
Born Dec. 8, 1820 in Roane Co., TN. A veteran of the Mexican War, he enl. at Knoxville, then re-enl. at Chattanooga on July 31, 1863. He was hospitalized that fall and was carried on the rolls as still hospitalized in June, 1864. On roll of 3TN in April,

1865 in NC. Fisherman in Chattanooga, drawing Mex. War pension. Wife Mary A. Died in Chattanooga April 19, 1901 and buried CSA Cem. [NBFM2,7; 1890VetCensus]

KINZALOW (KINCHALOE), William L.        Co. A, 62TN
Born McMinn Co., c1831 and married to Elizabeth McCarty in Chattanooga Enl. Sept. 20, 1862. Captured Vicksburg. Died near Walden's Ridge, 1898. [TWP 1982]

KIRKLIN, Allen J.        Co. A, 19TN
Son of Elisha Kirklen who was formerly of Bledsoe Co. and had bought farm at foot of Lookout Mountain in what would become St. Elmo. AJK had married Laura Vanstory just prior to war. Enl. Aug. 6, 1863. Listed sick at home and died during war.

KIRKPATRICK, James T.        Co. I, 1GA State Troops
Born Blount Co., TN, Dec. 22, 1839. Atlanta Campaign, Jonesboro (wounded). Paroled May 11, 1865 at Atlanta. 6'2 1/2" tall, auburn hair, blue eyes. To TN, 1906. 1909 res. Mitchell Ave., Chattanooga. [TP 11,423]

KIRKSEY, George W.
Born Fulton Co., GA. Married (1869) in MO Julia Gaines. Died in HC. [TWP, p. 171]

KIRKWOOD, R. M.        Clark's Indep. Cav. Co.
Enl. April 5, 1861 Marion, AR. Deserted Nov. 25, 1863 near Chattanooga.

KLOTZ, John P.        Co. A, 4TN Cav. Bn.
A native of Prussia, he was a shoemaker at Chattanooga prior to the start of the war. He lived with Jacob Kunz, another European immigrant. Disch. overage Sept. 15, 1862. Returned to Chattanooga after war.

KNIGHT, Alexander        Co. H, 37TN
Born 1833 in KY. Married Mary. Farm laborer in Harrison who enl. Sept. 17, 1861, Knoxville. Reduced to ranks from 4th Sgt. by court-martial, July, 1863. Deserted Sept. 9, 1863 and took USA oath, Sept. 23, 1863. Fair complexion, sandy hair, blue eyes, and 5'6" tall. Enl. in 11KY (USA).

KNIGHT, George W.        Co. I, 19TN
Born c1837, son of Jacob and Rebecca Knight of Harrison. Enl. May 20, 1861, Knoxville and arrived Cumberland Gap, Aug. 15, 1861. Wounded Chickamauga, Sept. 20, 1863 and captured Nov. 29, 1863 at Harrison. Imprisoned at Rock Island where he stated he was "opposed to the rebellion and tired of

fighting for it." Took USA oath, May 21, 1865.

KNIGHT, James D.          Co. D, 35TN
          Born c1824 in KY. Farm laborer in house hold of Alexander Knight, 1860. [1860HC]

KNIGHT, Sgt. James H.          Co. K, 43TN
          Enl. Oct. 17, 1861 at Ooltewah.

KNIGHT, Meredith          Co. H, 37TN; Co. H, 4TN
          Cav.
          Born 1844 in TN, son of Jacob and Rebecca. Res. Harrison with parents when he enl. Sept. 1, 1861, Knoxville. Prom. to Cpl., May 1862. Under arrest since Jan. 10, 1863. Deserted Sept., 1863 near Ringgold, took USA oath and enl. in 11KY Cav. (USA). Dark complexion, black hair, brown eyes, and 6'1 1/2" tall. Signed name Marit Night. [1860HC]

KNOX, 1st Lt. Henry H.          Co. A, 62MS
          Born 16 July 1840, in Bradley Co. TN. To Chattanooga in 1870's. Married Emma Knox. Res. 1910 Fort Wood Place in household son-in-law George M. Smart who had married his daughter Emma. Died June 18, 1910, age 70, and buried Citizens Cem. [CT June 19, 1910; 1910HC; UDC2 pgs 308]

KRAFT, Conrad          Co. A, 4TN Cav. Bn.
          He was a cabinetmaker, residing with Jacob Kunz prior to the war. He was originally from Wurttemberg, Germany. Captured April, 12, 1863 at Camp Dick Robinson and imprisoned at Louisville, but released April 23, 1863. Died 1866.

KRIES (KRICE, KREISE), Sgt. George W.          Co. H, 2TN Cav. (Ashby's)
          Born 1841 in Germany. Day laborer in Chattanooga, 1860, in household of A. Cook. He had his horse shot on Nov. 7, 1861. He placed its value at $250. Absent sick during part of war but present at surrender April, 1865.

KREIGNER, 3rd Lt. Joseph Q.          Co. F, 21MS
          Infantry
          He joined his brother, Louis Kreigner, at Chattanooga, then went to MS to go into the harness business. He was living there when the war broke out. He fought under Capt. Jerry Robins, who later lived on Lookout Mountain. Joseph Kreigner was killed at Sharpsburg, VA.
          The Kreigners were from Teplitz, Germany. Joseph accompanied his brother to America on an extended bridal tour beginning in 1849. They reached NY in early 1850, and later went to Charleston, SC, then Atlanta, and on to Chattanooga. They decided to remain at Chattanooga because the mountainous region reminded them of their homeland on the border between Bohemia and Saxony. They settled permanently at Chattanooga in early 1852. [CT Nov. 3, 1900]

KREWS --see CREWS

# L

LACEWELL, William L.          Co. G, 37TN
          Born 1846, in Cleveland, TN. Res. 1910 with wife Mary Elizabeth Hayes (m. 1870) on 20th St. Mail carrier. [1910HC;UDC2, pg 309]

LAMB, Meredith          Co. A, 4TN Cav. Bn.
          Born about 1827 in GA. He was a carpenter at Chattanooga prior to the war. Hospitalized July 1862. Disch. overage Sept. 15, 1862.

LANCE, J. J.          Co. L, 11TN Cav.
          Served under Forrest. Died Jan. 9, 1920, age 85, and buried in McMinnville, TN. [CT Jan. 10, 1920]

LANDIS, Charles Frederick          Co. H, 12TN
          Born Reedsville, PA, June 19, 1840, he enl. at Trenton, TN, April, 1861 in Co. H, 12th TN Vol Inf.. Captured at Selma, April 2, 1865. Mason. Married Clara Elizabeth Delano in 18 April 1865. She was born 17 June 1846 and died 22 Aug. 1926 in Chattanooga. Insurance solicitor, 1910. Died at his home on Bailey Ave. Aug. 14, 1924 and buried in Forest Hills Cem. [NBFM2; CT Aug. 15, 1924; 1910HC; UDC1 pg 241]

LANE, Joseph M.          Co. B, Phillips GA Legion
          Born Bradley Co., 1841. Enl. Aug. 16, 1861; Second Manassas, Sharpsburg, Gettysburg, Wilderness. Wife was Amanda. To TN 1893. Res. East Chattanooga, 1913. [TP14,042]

LANGFORD, William   Clark's Independent Cav. Co.
          Enl. Aug. 31, 1862 at Chattanooga; deserted Nov. 25, 1863 near Chattanooga.

LANGFORD, William          Co. H, 2TN Cav. (Ashby's)
          Killed in action, Aug. 31, 1862. [Lindsley]

LANGSTON, Cpl. William          Co. D, 37TN
          Enl. Sept. 1, 1861 at Knoxville; died May 10, 1862 in a Confederate hospital.

LANKFORD, Martin Van Buren          Co. G, 1SC Arty
          Born May 3, 1835 in Rutherford Co., NC. Enl.

Feb. 22, 1862. Captured March 10, 1865 and imprisoned Point Lookout, MD. To TN 1906 and res. Chattanooga; 1910, retired clergyman res. on Beech St. [1910HC; TP12,352]

LANKFORD, William      Co. A, 4TN Cav. Bn.
Born c1828, he was a farm laborer with two young sons in Chattanooga, 1860. Enl. June 17, 1861 at Knoxville. Killed in action Aug. 31, 1862.

LARD, John W.      Co. H, 2TN Cav. (Ashby's); 26TN; 2nd Co. I, 1CSA (GA)
Enl. Feb. 15, 1863 in Ringgold, GA. On daily duty as horseler for Maj. Gordon, Aug. 31, 1863. Signed USA oath, Jan. 4, 1864. Resid. HC. Dark complexion, black hair, grey eyes, and 5'8" tall.

LASATER, Benjamin
Born 1843, TN of TN parents. 1910 res. James Co. with wife Elizabeth J. (m. 1868). [1910 James Co.]

LATHAM, William
Born 1846, TN. Res. West 13th St. with wife Sarah (m. 1865) and running a boarding house.

LATIMER, James Howard      Co. H, 49GA
Born Dec. 24, 1843 in Culverton, GA, son of William and Tabitha Wilson Latimer. Left Mercer Univ. as junior to enl., June, 1863, as Sgt. Fought at Seven Pines, Antietam, Gettysburg, and Cold Harbor. Wounded at capture of Manassas Junction. Married Anne Winnefred Huston (1845-1880) in 1867. Lived in AL; moved to Sequatchie Valley, 1874, where he farmed and taught school in Jasper. To TX in 1898 and taught school ten years at Lubbock. 1910 back to TN, living in Nashville until 1920, then Chattanooga. Baptist. Died July 11, 1935 in Chattanooga and buried CSA Cem. [CT July 12, 1935; UDC2 pg 314]

LATIMORE, Col. J. H.      Co. F, 49GA
Enl. Augusta, GA, Aug. 12, 1862; paroled April 9, 1865 at Appomattox. Involved with CSA railroads. Took Pres. Davis and cabinet part of the way on their flight from Richmond into GA, April, 1865. Died July 11, 1935. [NBFM4]

LATTNER, Thomas Jefferson      Co. I, 19TN
He walked for several months at the war's end before he was reunited with his family in TN. He had enl. at Knoxville in May, 1861. Lattner had been a commission merchant on the riverfront at Chattanooga, and his business experience was put to use as a commissary sergeant. Wounded near the war's end and spent time in a hospital at Meridian, MS. Joined Consolid. 3TN, Apr. 9, 1865. He was among those who surrendered and were paroled at Greensboro, N.C., in May, 1865. Lattner had fair complexion, dark hair, blue eyes and stood 5'10" tall.
The Lattners lived at Newberry, SC, when he was born Oct. 19, 1822. But they moved to a plantation near Carnesville, GA. His father was Dr. John Valentine Lattner. T.J. Lattner settled at Chattanooga in the early 1850s and purchased the old home of Jane Henderson on First St. This house was used by Gen. U.S. Grant as his headquarters. T.J. Lattner resumed his business career in Chattanooga and died here March 26, 1884. His wife was Josephine J. They are buried at Citizens Cem. [CTS]

LATTY, Fleming      Co. F, 35TN
Born in Dade Co., GA in 1825, he was a farmer in HC who enl. at Chattanooga on Nov. 15, 1862. Disch. at Tullahoma, TN Feb. 20, 1863 for physical disability. Grey eyes, dark hair, fair complexion, and 5'10" tall.

LAUDERDALE, 2Lt. James (Jim)      Barry's Btry.
Enl. May 15, 1862 at Chattanooga.

LAUDERDALE, Maj. John
Quartermaster, A.P. Stewart's Corps, Aug., 1864. [Elliott, Stewart]

LAUDERDALE, 1Lt. John F.      Co. A, 2TN Cav. (Ashby's)
Enl. Aug. 10, 1861 at Cleveland, TN; captured Jan. 1864 in Murray Co., GA; imprisoned Fort Delaware; res. of Bradley Co., TN; light complexion; dark hair; blue eyes, and 5'11" tall.

LAVENDER, Sgt. William Robert      Co. E, 2GA Cav.
Born Henry Co., GA, Nov. 2, 1816. Wounded at Murfreesboro and Atlanta. He was made Sergeant at the beginning of the war under Gen. N.B. Forrest. He was wounded in the Battle of Atlanta and carried a ball in his shoulder until his death. He fought in the Battles of Chickamauga, Above the Clouds, Murfreesboro, Shiloh and other battles. He contracted rheumatism from exposure, which finally resulted in total blindness. Methodist. Mason. Married (1848) Elizabeth Edmondson. Long-time resident of McMinn Co. Died in Chattanooga April 20, 1901 and buried Forest Hills Cem. [FHR; NBFM2; CT April 21, 1901]

LAWING, Dan      Barry's Btry.
Deserted near Demopolis, Feb. 1864. [Brown Diary]

LAWING, William      Barry's Btry.
Deserted near Demopolis, Feb. 1864. [Brown Diary]

LAWLESS, Rufus Jefferson    Co. H, 55AL
Born Dec. 25, 1838, Jackson Co., AL, in 1835, his old home was Woodville, AL. Champion's Hill, Vicksburg, Atlanta Camp. Shocked by shell at Peachtree Creek, captured and imprisoned Camp Douglas, IL until May, 1865. Wife was Mary Jane Wann born October 1845 in Jackson Co., AL, married 14 Sept. 1866 in Jackson Co., AL. They came to TN, 1895. Res. in Chattanooga, 1910. She died 5 Dec 1905 in Hamilton Co., TN and he died July 10, 1916, age 81, at his res. on Read Ave. and was buried in Woodville, AL. [CT July 11, 1916; CSA Patriot Index, 3:138; TP11,771; 1910HC; UDC2 pg 315.]

LAWRENCE, Lewis H.    Co. B, 33NC
Born Edgecombe Co., NC, July 27, 1839. Enl. Apr. 1861; Seven Days, Chancellorsville (wounded), Petersburg (captured and imprisoned Johnson's Island). Wife was Carrie C. To TN 1910. Res. on Bailey Ave., 1913. [TP14,260]

LAWS, Guilford Cathey    Co. C 17th TN Inf.,
and 10/11TN Cav.
Married Martha E. [TWP2493]

LAWSON, Edward A.    36TN; Co. K, 43TN
Enl. Dec. 12, 1861; had transferred from 36TN; captured at Vicksburg, July 4, 1863.

LAWSON, ELIAS    2nd Co. K, 1st CSA Cav.
Enl. Sept. 21, 1862 in HC. Paroled May 3, 1865 at Charlotte, NC.

LAWSON, Sgt. R. C. - Co. I, 5TN Cav. (McKenzie's)
Born McMinn Co., TN, Jan. 8, 1836. Enl. Dec. 10, 1861. Disch. at Charlotte, NC, 1865. Res. East Chattanooga, 1907. Res. Rodgers St., 1910. [TP9388; 1910HC]

LEACH, Sgt. Maj. Christian Shultz "Shutty"    Co. D, 13KY Cav.
Born June 25, 1842 in Mason Co., KY. Enl. Dec. 1862 in 2KY and afterwards served in 13 Cav. Captured near Maysville, KY, May 7, 1863 and exch. Jan. 6, 1865. Paroled at Mt. Sterling, KY May 1, 1865 as Maj., 13 Cav. Clerk in Chattanooga Died in New Orleans March 20, 1914 and buried in Maysville, KY. [NBFM7,9]

LEADAM (LEADIM), A. S.    Clark's Independent Cav. Co.
Enl. Aug. 31, 1863 at Knoxville. Courier for Gen. Buckner, then QM duty.

LEADAM (LEADIM), F.    Clark's Independent

Cav. Co.
Enl. Aug. 10, 1863 at Knoxville. Absent, on detached service.

LECROIX (LECROY, LEACROY), Andrew M.    Co. G, 26TN; 2d Co. K, 1CSA (GA)
Born c1844, TN. Enl. July 8, 1861 at Knoxville; captured at Fort Donelson, Feb. 16, 1862 and imprisoned Camp Morton, IN. Exch. and joined 1CSA (GA). Married Paralee E. 1910 HC census lists him as Union vet, however.

LECROIX (LECROY), Samuel D.    Barry's Btry.
Enl. May 12, 1862 at Chattanooga

LECROIX (LECROY), Thomas H.
Enl. Oct. 5, 1861 at Bowling Green, KY; died Jan. 30, 1862 at Bowling Green where he had been ill since the day he enl.; wife was Julia Ann.

LECROIX (LECROY, LEACROY), William M.    Barry's Btry.
Enl. May 12, 1862 at Chattanooga; sent to hospital Sept. 25, 1862 from Palmetto, GA.

LEDFORD, Thomas    2nd Co. K, 1st CSA Cav
Enl. April 30, 1863 at Martin Mills, TN. Left sick near Decatur, captured and imprisoned in Alton, IL.

LEE, Clark    1CSA (GA)
Black soldier born near Ringgold, GA, n.d. Slave of Jim Lee. Joined 1CSA "about three weeks before the battle of Chickamauga." Captured Nashville, Dec. 1864. To TN c1871. Res. 1812 Whiteside, Chattanooga, 1921. [TP#107]

LEE, Clem    2nd Co. K, 1st CSA Cav.
Enl. June 30, 1863 in HC. Deserted July 25, 1863.

LEE, J. U.    1TN lt. Arty. McClung's Btry.
Born in 1848 in Loudon, TN; became a dentist in Chattanooga and President of the TN Dental Assoc. He died in Chattanooga March 26, 1884. [CTS; NBFM2]

LEE, James    Co. B, 1TN Cav. (Carter's)
Born c1828. Enl. Aug. 7, 1861, at Cleveland. He had a close call on Dec. 30, 1862, when his horse was killed in action. He was later paid $200 for the loss of his horse. Captured at Piedmont, VA, on June 5, 1864. He was sent to Camp Morton prison in IN in June of 1864. The following March 3 he died of "hospital gangrene." He was buried in grave 1485 at Green Lawn Cemetery at Camp Morton. Lee was a railroad laborer living at Harrison with his wife, Susan, and their four children

prior to the war. [1860HC]

LEE, James S.          Co. D, 37TN
        Enl. Sept. 1, 1861 at Knoxville. Disch. underage Nov. 4, 1862 at Knoxville; Re-enl. May 15, 1863 at Chattanooga.

LEE, John
        Born 1836, in TN. Res. 1910 on White Oak Rd. in household. of son-in-law Joseph A. Sanders. [1910HC]

LEE, John A. S., Sr.
        Born Sept. 8, 1826 in Greenville, TN. To Chattanooga c1850 and employed in tin and house furnishings business. "Not in the Confederate army, yet he did a great deal of work that was valuable to the Confederate Government." "Invented a hand-carding cotton machine and other articles for the Confederate Army." Exemption from service by President Davis. Following war he returned to Chattanooga and became "expert mechanic" and did coppersmith work for the AL and Great Southern RR. Methodist. Mason. Died March 18, 1905 at res. on Boyce St. and buried Forest Hills Cemetery. [NBFM4; CT Mar. 19, 1905]

LEE, Robert          Co. D, 37TN
        Born about 1831 in HC. Enl. Sept. 1, 1861 at Knoxville. Wounded at Fishing Creek, KY and disch. July 2, 1862 for disability. Substitute who "illegally returned to duty," April 25, 1863; deserted Aug. 28, 1863 at Tyner Station; took USA oath Sept. 13, 1863. Afterwards transferred to cav. and "at solicitation of Maj. Tankersley" returned to Co. D, 37TN and remained with it till end of war. Fisherman in Chattanooga, 1891. [TP1188]

LEE, Samuel          Co. D, 37TN
        Age 22 in 1861; enl. Sept. 1, 1861 at Knoxville; absent, sick in hospital, May 8, 1862; deserted Sept. 7, 1863 near Ooltewah; took USA oath.

LEE, Teral (Terry)          Co. D, 37TN
        Born c1837. Enl. Sept. 1, 1861 at Knoxville. Teamster. On rolls till captured Missionary Ridge, Nov. 25, 1863. Imprisoned Rock Island; took USA oath April 2, 1864; light complexion, brown hair, black eyes, 5'8" tall.

LEE, William P.          Co. D, 37TN
        Age 19 in 1861: Enl. Sept. 1, 1861 at Knoxville; Wounded June 21, 1864 at Kennesaw Mtn. and hospitalized.

LEE, William W.          Co. F, 39GA

Enl. 1862. Captured Vicksburg. 4th Sgt., April 25, 1864. Captured Alpine, GA, Oct. 19, 1864 and evidently imprisoned Nashville where he took USA oath on April 22, 1865. Served 2 years in 39GA, fighting at Missionary Ridge. Methodist. Died Oct. 10, 1918 in Chattanooga and buried Forest Hills Cemetery. [CT Oct. 11, 1918; 1890VetCensus]

LEIGH, J. G.
        Brother of John W. Manager of Chattanooga Times. Died in TX.

LEIGH, John Wesley          Co. C, 8GA
        Born Oct. 18, 1832 in Hertford, NC. Moved to GA in early life. To Chattanooga soon after war and founded law firm of Leigh and Yarnell. Grain merchant then elected judge of County court, c1895. Member, NBF Camp, 1895. Died June 15, 1910 and buried CSA Cem. [CT June 16, 1910; TP9554]

LEMMONS, Enoch M.          Co. H, 37TN
        Born c1850, TN. Wife Annie (m. 1904). Grocery merchant in St. Elmo, 1910. Died March 1, 1915 at his home in Dry Valley and buried in Missionary Ridge Cem. [CT Mar. 3, 1915]

LENOIR, Cpl. H. A.          1st Co. H, 26TN; 2d Co. I, 1CSA (GA)
        Enl. July 8, 1861 in Knoxville, TN. Tranferred to 1CSA, Nov. 8, 1862. Wounded on picket duty Sept. 3, 1864 and died following day at Catoosa Hospital, Griffin, GA.

LENOIR, William H.          Co. I, 26TN
        Died in service Dec., 1861.

LEVI, George
        Born c1814. Farmer at Harrison with wife Martha. CSA and res. of HC. Related to Vandergriff and Kell families. [Wormsley info]

LEVI, Jasper Newton          Co. A, 4th TN Cav. Bn. (Ragsdale's)
        He was a farmer at Harrison prior to joining the Lookout Rangers, Aug. 1, 1861, at Knoxville. Sick in hospital July 15, 1862. Captured Stone's River, Dec. 31, 1862. Imprisoned Camp Douglas, IL and exchanged. Detailed as teamster Aug. 10, 1863. Paroled April 1865. Born in 1836 in Anderson Co., TN, he was the son of William M. and Anna Levi. Married Nancy McCullough in 1867. Died 1902 in HC [JW, Levi family; TWP, 225; TP3786]

LEWALLEN, C. W.          Co. A, 2TN Cav. (Ashby's)
        Age 21 in 1863; enl. Jan. 9, 1863. Killed in

action June 5, 1864.

LEWIS, Archibald Newton    4TN Cav. (McLemore's)
Born March 19, 1842 in Marion Co., TN. Enl. Oct., 1864. Captured Dade Co., GA, Feb., 1865 and imprisoned at Chattanooga. Lived in GA, 1869-79 before returning to TN. Married Margaret Ann. [TP12,197; TWP 4068]

LEWIS, J. C.          Co. L, 36 TN
Born c1833. Enl. Jan. 9, 1862, at Chattanooga Prior to the war, he was living on a farm at Harrison with his mother, Catherine Lewis.

LEWIS, James          5TN Cav.
Born McMinn Co. Several months a courier for Gen. Wheeler. Died July 2, 1920 in Chattanooga and buried in Athens, TN. Farmer. Baptist. Lived in Chattanooga about seven years. [CT July 3, 1920; NBFM10]

LEWIS, James          Co. I, 3AL Cav.
1846-1919. Buried CSA Cem.

LEWIS, James H.          Co. H, 26TN; Barry's Btry.
Enl. July 8, 1861, Knoxville. Captured Fort Donelson, Feb. 16, 1862 and imprisoned Camp Douglas. After exchange was honorably disch. Oct. 13, 1862. Re-enl. May 14, 1864 at Rome, GA; paroled May 11, 1865. in Meridian, MS.

LEWIS, Joab          Co. K, 43TN
Enl. Dec. 2, 1861 at Ooltewah; deserted Aug. 5, 1862.

LEWIS, M. J.          Co. L, 36TN
Enl. Jan. 9, 1862 at Chattanooga.

LEWIS, Peter E.    Co. H, 2TN Cav. (Ashby's) Co. A, 4TN Cav. Bn.
Prior to the war, he was a brick mason in Chattanooga. A native of VA, he was born c1827. His wife was Harriet Lewis. His father, Peter Lewis, was also a brick mason and VA native who lived with his son in Chattanooga in his latter years. Enl. June 17, 1861 at Knoxville. Disch. overage Sept. 15, 1862.

LEWIS, W. J.    Co. E, 40GA
[NBFM4]

LEWIS, William
"Free black" who "forged manacles for Yankee prisoners in the old jail on Market St." [WF]

LIGHT, Cpl. Samuel B.    Co. D, 4th (12th) GA Cav.
Born April 15, 1843, in GA., son of Michael P. Light and Rhoda Ellis, who lived in Lookout Valley. Enl. Oct. 1862. Missionary Ridge. Wounded at Triune Station. Captured and took USA oath May 9, 1864. He had a light complexion, brown hair, blue eyes, and was 5'7" tall. After the war he married (1859) Lavinia Cummings, and they lived on a farm on the side of Lookout Mountain opposite Moccasin Bend. Lived near Chattanooga all his life. Died in Wauhatchie, Jan. 31, 1925 and buried Forest Hills Cemetery. [JW, Light Family; TP 13,330; CT Feb. 1-2, 1925; 1910HC]

LIGHT, William          Co. B, 5TN Cav.
Born c1838, he was one of the sons of Michael Light and Rhoda Ellis of Lookout Valley. Enl. Aug. 11, 1861, at Chattanooga. Wounded at Morrison's Depot. Died in prison at Rock Island, IL, in 1864. It was at the Light mill where the Union crossing of Lookout Creek was made at the start of the Battle Above the Clouds. This is at the present-day Reflection Riding.

LIGHT, 2Lt. William Hamilton    Co. D, 2VA
Born Jan 7, 1830 in Martinsburg, VA. Enl. at Harper's Ferry April 18, 1861. Fought in "nearly every important battle except when wounded." (Wounded at First Manassas and at Kernstown). Promoted to 2Lt. after Fredericksburg. To Chattanooga and served as member of Police force, 1878-1909. Member NBF Camp, 1895. Died May 19, 1912 at res. on West 6th St. and buried Forest Hills Cemetery. [FHR; CT May 20, 1912; NBFM2]

LIGHTSEY, Henry          Co. F, 11SC
1901 res. HC. [TP3541]

LILLY, George G.          Co. E, 4AL Cav. (Russell's)
Born June 24, 1849 in Larkinville, AL. Entered CSA cavalry under Forrest at age 14. Married (1868) Annis Rutledge. Living in AL until he came to Chattanooga in 1882 and became a wholesale grocer. Member NBF Camp, 1895. Died May 16, 1914 and buried Forest Hills Cemetery. [CT Oct. 10, 1910; May 17, 1914; TP 12,666]

LINCOLN, James H.          Co. B, 43TN
Born June 26, 1839 in White Co., TN. Enl. in 1863. Wounded at Strasburg. Dentist on Lookout Mtn. Died June 8, 1899 as result of fall from roof of his house. "He was a fine artist, a cousin of Abraham Lincoln whom he much resembled in his features. A kind Christian gentleman." Buried at Forest Hills Cem. Wife or dau. probably Charity Emma (1851-1879) buried in Citizens Cem. [FHR; NBFM2,7]

LINDER, R. B. William          Clark's Independent

Cav. Co.
Enl. March 20, 1864 Calhoun, GA.

LINDERMAN, C.          Co. A, 4TN Cav. BN.
Born c1824. Enl. June 17, 1861 at Knoxville. Absent sick July, 1862. Disch. overage Sept. 15, 1862.

LINDSAY, John          41TN
Born Aug. 4, 1843 in Fayetteville, TN. Member of 41TN at Chickamauga and Missionary Ridge. Died June 9, 1917 in St. Elmo and buried in Fayetteville. [CT June 10, 1917]

LINER, Andrew Jackson          Co. H, 43TN
Born McMinn Co., TN, April 28, 1845. Enl. Feb. 16, 1863. Captured Vicksburg, paroled, and took USA oath, March 19, 1864 at Chattanooga. Res. East Lake, 1923. [TP 9253]

LIONS, Lindsay
African-American, born 1842, GA. Res. 1910 on Hunter St. with wife Celia. No occupation listed. [1910HC]

LIVELY, B. Wiley          Co. G, 26TN
Enl. July 8, 1861, Knoxville. Detached for division teamster. Left sick Russelville, KY, Feb. 9, 1862.

LIVELY, Emory M.  Co. G, 7AL; Co. H,
3CSA Cav.
Born Aug. 29, 1846, Jackson Co., AL, his father, Ab Lively, moved the family to Jackson Co., AL. E.M. Lively enl. at Ringgold, Ga., in 1861, then re-enl. April 17, 1862 in Jackson Co. His first action was seen at Santa Rosa Island at Fort Pickens, FL. He fought at Bridgeport, Battle Creek, Fort Donelson, Unionville, Triune, Liberty, Snow Hill and Smithville. Lively was in a hospital for three months with smallpox. Captured at McMinnville, TN1 July 1863, after he was sent with dispatches from Gen. John Morgan to Gen. Braxton Bragg. Imprisoned Fort Delaware in June, 1863 and released 14 June 1865. He entered the war at 142 pounds and was down to 60 pounds by the time he was released from prison July, 1865. Res. Oct., 1899, 1910 on Lookout Mountain, TN; wife Paralee Nunley born 26 May 1853 in Jackson Co., AL; merchant [TCVQ; TP 10,828; 1910 HC]

LIVELY, Capt. Jackson D.          "Marsh Blues", Co. I, 19TN

LIVELY, James R.  2GA, 3GA Bn.; 64VA Cav.
Born April 25, 1842 in Harris Co., TX. Enl. in Columbus, GA, April 16, 1861 in Columbus Guards,

2GA, then 3GA Bn. (37GA). Wounded in right groin at Franklin and was captured. Paroled at High Point, NC, April 26, 1865 with rank of Capt. Agent and telegraph operator in Chattanooga in 1904. [NBFM2; TP 8630]

LIVELY, William E.          Co. I, 19TN

LOCKE, 1Lt. Adoniram J.          Co. B, 1TN Cav.
(Carter's)
Born 1832 in TN, son of Jesse and Agnes Locke of Ooltewah. Farmer. Enl. Aug. 7, 1861, Cleveland. Captured Piedmont, June 5, 1864. Exchanged and hospitalized Wayside Hospital in Richmond, VA, Mar. 1865.

LOCKE, Cpl. Jonathan N.          Co. B, 1TN Cav.
(Carter's).
Born 1830 in SC. Farmer at Harrison with wife Almirah and three children. At Chickamauga and was captured shortly thereafter near his home area of Harrison, Sept. 20, 1863 and imprisoned at Camp Douglas. He told Union authorities he had been loyal, but was forced into the Confederate ranks. He said he desired to take the oath of allegiance. He was released on May 13, 1865. He seems to have been demoted to private. Locke was 6'4", fair complexion, black hair and black eyes. [1860HC]

LOCKE, John M.          Co. K, 43TN

LOCKETT, Eli F.          Co. D, 2TN Cav. Bn.
Born June 23, 1844 in Sumner Co., TN. Enl. as bugler Sept. 1861. Captured Harrisburg, MS July 14, 1864. Solicitor and salesman in Chattanooga. Died in Chattanooga March 18, 1891 and buried CSA Cem. [NBFM2,4,7]

LOCKMAN, Capt. Isaac Newton     Howell's Btry. GA. Light Arty.
Born 1846, Hall Co., GA, he enl. in the fall of 1862 at Gainesville, GA. He was in fighting at Jackson, MS, Chickamauga and Missionary Ridge. He was wounded in August, 1864 at Jonesboro when his leg was broken but he returned to his unit within 60 days. He was married in 1900 to Lulah Cox. A Baptist, he died at age 84 at his res. on 7th Ave. in East Lake, on Feb. 21, 1930. He was buried at New Liberty Church. [TWP 291; CT Feb. 22, 1930; TP 16,495]

LODOR, [----]
Buried in CSA Cem. [NBFM3]

LOGAN, Joab Drewry          23GA; Co. B, 6GA Cav.
Born Sept, 1839 in Union Co., GA. Enl July 10, 1861 in Union Co. in 23GA and afterwards in Co. B,

6GA Cav. Paroled May 12, 1865. Married (1874) Mary Louisa Barnett. Res. Chattanooga where employed as a "machine hand." "Remains found in the ruins of his watch house at Wheland's Foundry about 6 AM Friday, Jan. 17, 1908, when the fire company went there to put out the fire." Buried Forest Hills Cemetery. [TWP, p. 89; NBFM2]

LOMMACK, James        Co. A, 5th (McKenzie's) TN Cav.
        He enl. Feb. 10, 1863 at Knoxville. Captured Aug. 1, 1863 at Irvine, KY. Age 20 on March 11, 1864 roll. At Fort Delaware, Feb. 27, 1865 for exchange. Paroled May 3, 1865 at Charlotte, NC.

LOMINICK, (or Lominack) James A.        Co. B, 4TN Cav.
        Before the war, he lived with his parents, P.R. and Melvina Lominick, on a farm near Chattanooga. He was born about 1843. [1860HC]

LOMINICK, William
        Born c1838 in TN, son of David Lommack. [1860 HC]

LONDON, John    Co. E, 5TN Cav. (McKenzie's)
        Born 1838, in GA. 1910 farmer in James Co. with wife Zana (m. 1903). Mason. Baptist preacher. Died at res. in Appison, Dec. 16, 1923. [1910 James Co.; CT Dec. 18, 1923]

LONDON, Martin Van Buren        Co. E, 5TN Cav.
        Born Murray Co., GA and married (1866) Caroline Whittle. Died in James Co. [TWP 1539]

LONG, James Cozby        CSN
        Born Dec. 2, 1844, son of John Pomfret and Eliza Smith Long, he resigned from the U.S. Naval Academy to join the Confederate Navy, participating in a number of naval fights:  a member of the crew of Curlew, the Merrimac at Hampton Roads, and the Plymouth. At the close of the war, he served as a blockade runner. After the war, he attempted a life as an engineer and surveyor in Chattanooga, but relocated to Mussel Shoals, AL, then Birmingham. He married (1872) Frances Walker. Died Chicago, May 26, 1910. [CT Oct. 12, 1890; GHT, 964; NBFM4]

LONG, John Pomfret
        Born in Knoxville Nov. 25, 1807, son of William and Jane Bennett Long. He moved to Ross's Landing as a pioneer settler April 18, 1836 and was one of the three commissioners who laid out the town of Chattanooga. Until the Civil War, he practiced law and was a merchant. He was appointed provost marshal of

Chattanooga by Gen. J. P. McGown and he served until the Federal occupation. At the approach of the Union army, he went south to prepare a place for his family. Mrs. Long and her sons, John P. Long Jr., Milo Smith Long, and Marcus B. Long, with their servant, Aunt Clary, and her daughters, were still in town at the time of the battle of Chickamauga. They were living on South Market St. where the Chattanooga Choo-Choo is now located. They had to flee just before their frame house was demolished in the turmoil of the aftermath of the Union loss at Chickamauga. Mrs. Long and her children endured the siege, while staying at the home of her brother, Dr. Milo Smith, on the side of Cameron Hill. She once made a personal appeal for food to Gen. James A. Garfield, the future president. He gave her part of his own food--a piece of hardtack and a piece of white meat. A native of Knoxville, John P. Long was Chattanooga's first postmaster and was city recorder. The Longs lived at West Seventh and Cedar after the war. John P. Long lived in Chattanooga until his death in 1889. Eliza Smith Long died in 1900. [CTS; GHT, 961-64]

LONG, John Pomfret Jr.        Co. A, 19TN
        Born March 4, 1847, he was in Chattanooga with his mother, Eliza Smith Long, at the time of Chickamauga. Joined the Confederate forces (May 5, 1864), although he was barely old enough to enlist. At the battle of Atlanta, July 22, 1864, he had a foot blown off. Rheumatism developed in his other leg so that it was useless to him. He died March 1, 1880, at age 33 of heart disease at his parents' home in Chattanooga. [GHT, p. 965]

LORENZEN, Sgt. Auguste A.        Co. G, Crescent Regt. of New Orleans - Louisiana Inf.
        Born 23 Nov. 1840 in Hensburg, Duchy of Schleswig Holstein, Germany. Enl. Mar. 8, 1862 in New Orleans. Captured Shiloh and imprisoned at Camp Douglas. Exch. and joined Co. L, Consolidated LA Vol. Inf. Captured Laforche, LA Oct 27, 1862 and put aboard a prison ship. Exch. Feb. 23, 1863. Wounded in left groin at Mansfield, LA, April, 1864. He married Anais Des Essarte on 7 May 1867. They came to Chattanooga in 1883. Here through 1900. Occup. bookkeeper. Moved to Norfolk, VA. Died March 4, 1901 and buried CSA Cem. [Booth, 2:793; NBFM2,7; UDC2 pg 327.]

LOUDENBER, Frank W.        Co. A, 2GA
        Born Girard, AL, 1849. Enl. 1864, but disch. underage. Rejoined army and surr. at Appomattox. Paroled Aug. 9, 1865. Married Minnie Ingersol Baird. Died March 18, 1905 in Chattanooga. [TWP 7389]

LOVE, James Cozby
        Born in HC. NBF Camp. 1888 living in IL and

died in Chicago, May 26, 1910. [NBFM2]

LOVE, Jesse R.
        Born 1837, TN Res. 1910, Poplar St. with wife Margarita (married 1877). Died there June 30, 1910 and buried Emory Gap. [1910HC; CT July 1, 1910]

LOVEJOY, 3rd Lt. John        Co. I, 19TN

LOVEJOY, 2Lt. William H.        Co. I, 19TN
        He enl. in the spring of 1861 and went from Knoxville to Cumberland Gap, VA where he was taken ill in early Sept., 1863 and left there. When the Union soldiers arrived, he was taken prisoner. Sent to Johnson's Island and released upon taking the oath of allegiance on June 12, 1865. He was then 26 and was 5'8" tall with blue eyes.

LOVELADY, Charles W.        Co. B, 1TN Cav. (Carter's)
        Enl. Aug. 7, 1861 at Cleveland. Res. HC. He took the oath of allegiance on June 3, 1865. Lovelady was 5'5" with a sandy complexion, dark hair and blue eyes.

LOW, Thomas        Co. D, 19TN
        Born 1839 in TN; married Mary H.; farm laborer in household of J.W. Watkins at Ooltewah in 1860. [1860 HC Census]

LOWE, Powell H.        Co. B, 36TN, Co. K, 43TN
        Enl. Dec. 12, 1861 at Ooltewah as transfer from 36TN; deserted Aug. 3, 1862. Baptist. Died Sept. 7, 1920, 78yrs.old, in Ooltewah. [CT Sept. 8, 1920]

LOWE, Samuel Brunswick
        Born about 1828 in Bethel, Fairfield, CT, son of John G. and Naoma Lowe. He built the first iron mill in Chattanooga and attempted to manufacture cannon, bridge iron, and armor plates for ships until he was forced to relocate to Selma, AL. He returned to Chattanooga after the war, operated a foundry and served as a manufacturer's representative. He also founded Chattanooga Paint Co. Presbyterian. His wife was Elsie Elida Tucker whom he married in 1880. Died April 13, 1891 and buried in Forest Hills Cem. [CTS; FHR; NBFM7]

LOWE, Wiley K.        Co. F, 35TN
        Born in HC in 1842, he lived on the family farm near Chattanooga until enl. on Sept. 5, 1862. He deserted at Chattanooga on Nov. 10, 1862. His parents were M.A. and Rhoda Lowe. He had blue eyes, light hair, fair complexion, and was 5'10" tall.

LOWREY, Benjamin C.
        Born 1840 in GA, he married (1867) Eliza Simpter. Died HC. [TWP, p. 78]

LOWREY, John Samuel        Co. C, 3VA
        Born April 6, 1844 in Fredericksburg, VA. After joining a heavy artillery unit he transf. to Co. C, 3VA. Res. in St. Elmo and was "valued" employee (machinist) of City Water Co. Married first to Elizabeth Ann Martin on 20 October 1872. She was born 22 July 1850 and died 6 Sept. 1891. He married a second time to Georgia born 27 Jan. 1874 in Harralson Co., GA. John died at res. at corner of Georgia Ave, and 4th St., July 17, 1911 and buried Forest Hills Cemetery. [1910HC; CT July 18-20, 1911; NBFM2; FHR; UDC1 pg 257, UDC2 pg. 328.]

LOWRY, Mark        Co. G, 26TN
        Enl. July 8, 1861, Knoxville. Detailed as nurse to Nashville, TN, Oct. 2, 1861.

LUCAS, John        Co. D, 37TN
        Born in GA c1819. Enl. Sept. 1, 1861, Knoxville. Disch. Nov. 24, 1862 overage.

LUCAS, Cpl. L. R.        Co. D, 5TX; Co. I, 4TN Cav.
        Born Scott Co., MO, Nov. 24, 1839. Enl. Aug. 1861. Wounded Red Bird Creek, KY and imprisoned Fort Delaware 14 months. Wife was Sarah J. Res. 1909 in Chattanooga. [TP 14,849]

LUKEROY, Samuel        Barry's Btry.

LUKEROY, William "Will"        Barry's Btry.
        Born c1830 in SC, prob. son of Dorcas, he was living in Chattanooga when the war broke out. His wife, Elizabeth, was also from SC.

LUMPKIN, Thomas J.        Co. H, 48AL
        Born Jan. 7, 1839 MD. Died Nov. 4, 1916 at New England City, TN. [NBFM7]

LUNTSFORD, Benjamin F.        Co. D, 37TN
        Enl. Dec. 1, 1861, Knoxville. On rolls through Oct. 1863.

LUSK, Elijah Rogers        Co. L, 36TN; Co. L, 35TN
        Born 1843 in TN, son of Nancy. Enl. Jan. 9, 1862, at Chattanooga; transf. to 35TN; teamster with ordnance train.

LUSK, James M.        Co. L, 36TN; Co. L, 35 TN
        Born about 1842, he was living on a farm near Chattanooga with his mother, Nancy before the war. Enl. Jan. 9, 1862, at Chattanooga. He was the company

drummer.

LUSK, Monroe R.          Co. F, 35TN
        Born in 1837 in HC, he was living on a farm near Chattanooga with his mother, Nancy Lusk before the war. Enl. on Oct. 1, 1862. He deserted Sept. 6, 1863, at Chattanooga

LUTHER, Albert W.
        Born 1846, NC. 1910 res. household of son-in-law John F. Parris, James Co. with wife (m. 1866). [1910James Co.]

LUTTRELL, Jacob G.     Co. B, 1TN Cav. (Carter's);
                2nd Co. K, 1st CSA Cav.
        Born 1845 in TN. Farmer at Long Savannah, son of C.D. and Isabella. Enl. Aug. 7, 1861 in 1TN Cav. Joined 1CSA Cav. Sept. 10, 1862 in HC. Deserted at Shelbyville, TN, Jan. 23, 1863, but hospitalized at Raleigh, NC, June 1864.

LUTTRELL, 2Lt. James D.          Co. B, 1TN Cav. (Carter's)
        Born c1833. Farmer at Long Savannah. Enl. Aug. 7, 1861, Cleveland, joining his younger brother, Joseph A. [1860HC]

LUTTRELL, Joseph A.          Co. B, 1TN Cav. (Carter's)
        Born c1838, he enl. Aug. 7, 1861, Cleveland. He was killed near Dalton, GA, in 1864. Before the war, his family had a farm at Limestone north of Harrison. His parents were C.D. and Isabella Luttrell.

LUTTRELL, 2nd Lt. Lewis  Co. B, 1TN Cav. (Carter's)
        Enl. Aug. 7, 1861, Cleveland.

LUTTRELL, Louis          2nd Co. K, 1st CSA Cav.
        Enl. July 14, 1862 in HC. Hospitalized July, 1863. Paroled May 3, 1865 at Charlotte, NC.

LUTTRELL, William G.          Co. I, 5TN Cav.
        Born 1842 in TN. Farmer at Long Savannah, son of C.D. and Isabella.

LYERLEY, Sgt. Charles Abner     Co. A, 1MS
        Born 29 March 1847 in Clark Co., MS. Enl. Apr. 1864 in 1MS. After war became merchant in Enterprise, MS until 1867, then moved to New Orleans where he entered the wholesale dry goods business. In 1884 relocated in Jackson, MS, then moved to Chattanooga in 1887 and organized Chattanooga National Bank. Became treasurer, O.B. Andrews Co; vice president Summerville Cotton Mills, and director of AL Great Southern Railroad and TN Power Co.

among a multitude of business interests. Member NBF Camp, 1895. Daughter was Mrs. Z.C. Patten, Jr. Died Aug. 9, 1925, in Chattanooga and buried Forest Hills Cem. [CT Aug. 10, 1925; NBFM2]

LYLE, Jefferson Young          Co. C, 24AL
        Born Augusta, GA, 11 Dec. 1836 in Paulding Co., GA. Married 3 Nov. 1859 Sarah Jane West in Pickens Co., AL. She was born 13 Dec. 1842 in Pickens Co., AL and died 8 March 1926 in Chattanooga. Enl. 1862. Fought at Corinth, Farmingston, Chickamauga and Missionary Ridge. Paroled Augusta, GA, May 1, 1865. To TN, 1881. Lyle died Oct. 31, 1923, age 87, at res. on Dodds Ave. and buried CSA Cem. [TWP, 228; CT Nov. 1, 1923; TP 15,481; UDC2 pg 330.]

LYLE, 2nd Lt. John     Clark's Independent Cav. Co.
        Enl. Aug. 31, 1862 at Chattanooga; absent without leave May 14, 1863.

LYLE, William G.          Co. F, 35TN
        Born 1830 in Spartanburg, SC, he was a coal miner in HC when he enl. on Oct. 11, 1862; detailed to work on Nashville and Chattanooga RR, April, 1863. Apparently resident of St. Elmo where he died Jan. 14, 1899. Buried Hooker's Station. [CT Jan. 15, 1899]

LYMAN, W. B.          Co. B, 1TN Cav. (Carter's)
        Enl. Aug. 7, 1861, Cleveland.

LYON, [first name not given]
        Captured at Ooltewah, Jan., 1864 and accused of being spy (may be William Lyon, 30 in 1860, lived at Snow Hill with wife Susannah, only Lyon in county in 1860).

LYONS, JAMES A.          Co. E, 19TN Inf.
        Born July 3, 1845 in Knox Co., TN son of Daniel and Sybella Lonas Lyons and enl. at Shelbyville May 15, 1863. Wounded July 22, 1864 at Atlanta. Paroled at Greensboro, NC, May 1, 1865. Shortly after becoming a Methodist minister he married first to Margaret Lenoir on 6 March 1884. In 1891 they moved to Texas on account her health. She died at Center point, Texas in 1892. Married secondly, Jean Buchanan 17 April 1901. She was born 31 July 1856 in Saltville, VA and died 1 June 1943 in Keywood, VA. Minister, M. E. Church South living in St. Elmo c1905. [NBFM2; Holston Conf Journal 1929, 1943.]

# M

MABRY, Thomas M.   Co. K, 4GA Reserves

Died at age 67 on Feb. 20, 1908 at residence on Harrison Ave. Buried in Sugar Valley, GA.

MADDEN, John W.     Co. D, Phillips GA Legion; 23GA Cav. Bn. (4GA Cav.)
Born Lawrence, SC, 1841. 1903 res. of Hill City. [TP5349]

MAHONEY, John Thomas
Born 1852 in Lawrenceburg, IN and married (1882) Rose Elizabeth Bradley. Died 1929 in HC. [TWP, 307]

MAJORS, John W.   Co. K, 43TN
Enl. Oct. 17, 1861 at Ooltewah; captured at Baker's Creek, May 16, 1863 and paroled.

MALCOMB, Charles N.    Barry's Btry.
Enl. May 24, 1862 at Chattanooga; paroled May 11, 1865. in Meridian, MS.

MALLOY, James   Co. H, 2GA
Born in SC, 1820. Veteran of three wars: he lived in TN when this country was inhabited by Indians. Shortly before the Indians were moved west, he served in several campaigns against troublesome tribes, and was detailed a representative of the govt. to accompany them when surviving members of the race were sent to reservations beyond the Mississippi. He remained there in Indian wars several years. Mexican War veteran; enl. in Co. H, 2GA in 1861     . Carpenter in Chattanooga. Member NBF Camp, 1896. Died Mar. 3, 1912 and buried Cloud Springs. [NBFM2; CT March 4, 1912]

MALLOY, John   Co. B, Phillips GA Legion
Farmer in Rossville, 1889. Member NBF Camp, 1896. Died at his res. in Rossville, Feb., 1909 and buried Chickamauga, GA. [NBFM7]

MANN, James M.   Co. B, 5TN Cav.
A Georgia native, he was a Chattanooga merchant prior to the war. His wife, Mary, was also from Georgia.

MANNING, Alexander Frederick  Co. H, 8GA
Born Richmond, VA, Oct. 18, 1842, his family moved to Rome, GA in 1849. Great grandson of Rev. War Gen. W. H. Manning. Enl. May 13, 1861 at Rome. Discharged five times because of medical reasons: measles and tuberculosis. Merchant and Methodist minister in Chattanooga after war. Married Sallie K. Loeman on 6 July 1869 in Rome, GA. Died at res. on Walnut St., June 9, 1926. Joint funeral at Alton Methodist Church with his friend Martin M. Fry. [NBFM2,7;CT June 10, 1926] and buried CSA Cem.

[NBFM Feb. 7, 1910; UDC 2 pg 336]

MANNING, Amos Smith    Co. F, 34GA
Born Warren Co., TN, 1827. Enl. May, 1862. Captured Vicksburg. No record found after paroled. To TN, 1899, from Dade Co., GA. Res. of Sale Creek, 1908, "broken in health." [TP10,687]

MANNING, Dennis J.   Co. B, 14GA State Guards
A citizen of Cobb Co., GA and younger brother of John W. Manning, enl. at Marietta, GA. He came to Chattanooga in 1883 and worked as a contractor and builder. He also served as policeman and justice of the peace. He married Florence Baxter. [NBFM2]

MANNING, Orderly Sgt. John W.  Co. L, 3AR; Co. B, 14GA
A citizen of Cobb Co., GA, enl. in an Arkansas regiment, then transferred into Phillips GA Legion in which he served with the Army of Northern VA from the Seven Days battles to Appomattox, during which time he was wounded three times. He was paroled at Appomattox.

MANSFIELD, Isaac C.   Co. A, 6AL
Born Fort Valley, GA March 23, 1840. Enl. at Lumpkin GA in Stewart Grays, afterwards trans. to 6AL. After the war he came to Chattanooga and resided on Lookout Mountain. Grain merchant in 1890. He was a Presbyterian and a member of NBF Camp. Wife Sarah K. Pres. Steven Food Co., 1910. Died on Lookout Mtn. Feb. 24, 1913 and buried Forest Hills Cemetery. [CT Feb. 25, 1913; FHR; NBFM2;1910HC]

MAPLES, Henry     Co. B, 36TN; Co. K, 43TN
Transferred Dec. 12, 1861 into Co. K, 43TN at Ooltewah from 36TN; deserted.

MAPLES, W. J.   Barry's Btry.
Deserted June-July, 1864. [Brown Diary].

MARSH, Charles Wesley     Lee Light Arty
Born Aug. 17, 1843 in Campbell Co. VA. Enl. June 7, 1861 in Lee Light Artillery (Capt. Charles I. Raine). Captured Spotsylvania Court House in May, 1864. Pattern maker in Chattanooga. Married (1872) Amanda Huey. Died at his home on E. 4th St. May 29, 1922 and bur. Forest Hills Cemetery. [NBFM2,7; TWP, 221]

MARSH, Edwin
A prominent merchant at Chattanooga prior to the war, he supplied uniforms and completely equipped the company organized by Francis Marion Walker. It was first called the "Marsh Blues" in his honor. It was

mustered into service as Co. I of the 19th TN Infantry. Marsh was born at Chatham Co., NC, in 1824, the son of Spencer Marsh. The family moved to Covington, GA, when Edwin Marsh was eight. In Chattanooga, he and William Adolphus Moore operated the Moore and Marsh dry goods and grocery business. This firm stayed open as long as possible, but the partners finally had to flee to Georgia. Edwin Marsh went directly to Atlanta, where he bought an interest in the <u>Southern Confederate</u> newspaper. After the war, he and Moore were reunited in Atlanta. In 1864, they opened "the first and largest wholesale dry goods house in Atlanta."

MARTIN, Alfred Douglas Cpl. Co. K, 43TN; 2nd Co. K, 1st CSA Cav.
Born Sept. 1, 1844, in TN, son of Russell M. and Mary Rogers Martin. Enl. Feb. 1, 1862 at Ooltewah; enl. Sept. 20, 1862 in HC in 2CSA Cav.; captured at Vicksburg, July 4, 1863 and paroled; fair complexion, dark hair, gray eyes, 5'10" tall. Detailed May, 1864 as messenger for division QM. Paroled May 3, 1865 at Charlotte, NC. Married Virginia Ann Dill Ramsey and later Maggie Ivey. In 1870 he was living in Ooltewah with wife Martha. Lived in Atlanta after war and died there at CSA Soldiers home, May 19, 1925. Had 14 children.

MARTIN, E. H. Co. D, 60GA
Born in Whitfield Co., GA. Enl. 1861. Wounded 2nd Manassas and Fredricksburg. Captured Sept. 14, 1864 and imprisoned at Johnson's Island. To TN c1885. Leg amputated in 1901 as result of war wounds. Res. Ooltewah, James Co. [TP3726]

MARTIN, Elisha Russell (Rogers?) 2nd Co. K, 1CSA Cav.
Born 26 June 1840, son of Russell Martin and Mary Rogers, he was named for his grandfather, Elisha Rogers. Enl. Sept. 20, 1862 in HC and served four years under cavalry leader Joe Wheeler. He was sent on secret mission behind Federal lines and reported captured. After the war, he was a leading Democrat and was active in the Cumberland Presbyterian Church. He married Catherine Eliza Rogers and had five sons and five daughters. The family home was on Dry Valley Road in Red Bank. He died March 28, 1900, and was buried in Memorial Park in White Oak. [CT March 29, 1900]

MARTIN, Fletcher Burr Co. H, 11TN Cav.
Born April 1, 1847 in Warren Co., TN, son of Jesse Martin who also fought for the CSA. Enl. at McMinnville and served under Gen. Dibbrell to the last days of the war, escorting President Davis through Georgia. He was paroled at Washington, GA May 10, 1865. In banking business in Tullahoma and came to Chattanooga about 1911. Died at his home on Oak St. Jan. 23, 1920 and buried Tullahoma. [NBFM2; CT Jan. 29, 1920]

MARTIN, Sgt. George A. Co. K, 43TN
Born Anderson Co., TN in 1837, he was a farmer who enl. Oct. 17, 1861 at Ooletwah; discharged Nov. 12, 1862.

MARTIN, George Washington Co. D, 37TN
Enl. Sept. 16, 1862 at Whitesides; had enl. previously June 24, 1861 at Jackson, TN with Gen. W. H. Carroll; transferred from dismounted cav., July 22, 1863; paroled May 1, 1865 at Greensboro, NC.

MARTIN, Henry Neal
Born Woodville, MS, Oct. 10, 1844, son of Dr. Henry Martin. Grad of VMI. Enl. April, 1861. 2Lt. AADC, staff of Earl Van Dorn, then promoted for gallantry at Baker's Creek to Capt., AAG, on staff of Stephen D. Lee, 1863-1864. Practiced law in Jackson, MS until 1867, then moved to Vicksburg and became a merchant. Then relocated in New Orleans where he was a cotton factor. Mason. To Chattanooga in 1887 and became a real estate agent. Died in Phila., PA, July 11, 1890 and buried New Orleans. [CRUTE, CSA staff, 118; NBFM2, 2, 7]

MARTIN, Isaac Co. K, 43TN
Enl. Oct. 17, 1861 at Ooltewah; died March 25, 1863. [Lindsley, 528]

MARTIN, James M. Co. K, 43TN
Born and raised in Meigs County. Enl. Nov. 10, 1862 at Ooltewah; captured at Vicksburg, July 4, 1863 and paroled; fair complexion, dark hair, blue eyes, and 6' tall. Chattanooga Times shows a J. M. Martin born and raised in Meigs who moved to Chattanooga in 1886; Presbyterian; died May 2, 1897 in Chattanooga, 71 years, buried Beason's Cem. [CT May 2, 1897]

MARTIN, James Madison Co. K, 43TN
Born Oct. 4, 1841, Charleston, TN. Enl. Nov. 10, 1862 at Ooltewah; captured at Vicksburg, July 4, 1863 and paroled; fair complexion, dark hair, blue eyes; 6' tall. Married 4 April 1867 in Hamilton County to Minerva Joanna Coulter. She was born 23 Feb. 1845 in Coulterville, TN and died 4 July 1895 in Hamilton County. He died April 2, 1892, HC. [UDC3 pg 151]

MARTIN, John A. Co. K, 43TN
Born 1833 in Cocke Co., he was a farmer who enl. Oct. 17, 1861 at Ooltewah. Injured shoulder and captured at Vicksburg, July 4, 1863 and paroled; again

captured at Bunker Hill, VA, July 14, 1864; imprisoned at Camp Chase; fair complexion, blue eyes, light hair, 5' 10" tall. Res. Marion Co., 1900.

MARTIN, John S.  9GA Arty. Bn.

Born May 6, 1843 in Madison, GA. Enl. Jan., 1862 in 9GA Arty. Bn. Wounded Chickamauga. To Chattanooga in early 1870's and became grocer and grain merchant. Married Kate Kilpatrick. Methodist. Member NBF Camp, 1895-96. Died May 6, 1912 on his birthday at his res on E. 8th and buried Forest Hills Cem. [FHR; NBFM2. CT May 7, Nov. 1912]

MARTIN, L. G. "Gould"  Co. F, A, 5TN Cav.

Born 5 Jan. 1841 in Hamilton Co.  Enl. Aug. 24, 1861, Camp Cummings. Age 24 on March 11, 1864 roll. Present on rolls through 1864. Detached by order of Gen. Hume in June, 1864 for service in East TN. Living in HC in 1910. Died Aug. 14, 1913 at Shepherd, TN and buried in Concord Cem.; 72 years. [CSR; Pension Application #12869 for service in 5th (McKenzie's) TN Cav. [CT Jan. 2, 1910, Aug. 15, 1913; TP12879]

MARTIN, Sgt. Richard     Co. F, 35TN; Co. H, 4TN Cav.

Born in 1834 in Warren Co., Tenn., he was farming in HC when he enl. on Oct. 1, 1862. He is listed as a deserter in September 1863, but returned to duty as a calvaryman, receiving "3 Sabre wounds on head" at Charleston, TN. His father, Tavise Martin, was from NC, and his mother, Cynthia Martin, from VA. 1870 at Wauhatchie.

MARTIN, Washington Coanane

Died in Federal prison camp in Jackson, MS and buried there. Married Matilda.

MARTIN, William     Co. F, 35TN

Enl. Oct. 5, 1862 at Chattanooga; detailed to work on Nashville and Chattanooga RR, April 8, 1863. Pay stopped while on this detail. Deserted Dec. 1863 at Tunnel Hill, GA.

MARTIN, William Augustine  Co. K, 1AL Cav.

Born in Madison, GA, May 18, 1839, son of John Bryan Martin, he was a Montgomery, AL businessman who enl. in the Montgomery Mounted Rifles early in 1861. Served at Pensacola, then in the fighting around Corinth, MS, Martin was severely wounded, crippling him for life. In 1866 he moved to Chattanooga and with his brothers built up a wholesale grain business. Married Elmira Smith. He married (1877) Alice Gillespie and died April 29, 1887 and was buried at Forest Hills Cemetery. [CTS; FHR; NBF

Minutes; Hale, TN, 8:2457-58]

MARYE, Lawrence Slaughter  -  Staff Officer
"Hampden Artillery"

Born at Fredericksburg, VA c.1825, son of John Lawrence Slaughter and Ann Maria Burton Marye. Attended Hampton-Sidney College and Univ. of VA. Practiced law in Richmond, VA. Served in 1861 as lieutenant in Hampden Arty.; Captain of ordnance under W. W. Loring, and later for Jubal Early and John S. Williams. In 1864, he became Inspector of Ordnance under John C. Pemberton. Lived in Shelby County, TN before coming to Chattanooga in 1872. Practiced law here until 1877 when he moved to Lynchburg, VA and became editor of the Virginian. Represented Hamilton County in TN Gen'l Assembly, 1875-77. Died after 1881. [BDTA, 2:607; Crute, CSA Staff Officers.]

MASSENGALE, David L.(C.)  Co. F, 19TN

Born 1824 in TN. 1860 farmer at Chat-tanooga with wife Susan and 8 children. [1860HC]

MASSENGALE, George Pierce  Co. I, 19TN

Born c1844. Although only 17, he followed his older brothers into the Confederate service, enl. in Co. A, Oct. 20, 1861, Cumberland Gap. At Corinth became Sgt. in QM Dept. and was wounded in the fighting at Chickamauga, falling at his father's farm. He was left among the dead, but survived. CSA: "having been recommended for position of Adjutant of Whitfield's Texas Legion Cav., will report to officer commanding Whitfield's Legion."

MASSENGALE, Henry White

A former mayor of Chattanooga, he was exempt from war service, but he was an enthusiastic supporter of the Southern cause. He gave a large amount of gold for Confederate bonds at the first offering. Three of his sons, Henry White Massengale, Thomas Massengale, and George Pierce Massengale, served with the Confederate forces. His daughter, Laura Massengale, gave the presentation speech at the Central Hotel at Fifth and Market when the company organized by William Ragsdale marched away to war. Born at Wrightsboro, GA, in 1808, he married Rebecca Lowe in 1832. She was descended from a prominent Virginia family. The Massengales moved to Chattanooga and built a brick house south of town. This house was later purchased by John A. Lee when the Massengales moved to a farm by Chickamauga Creek in Walker Co., GA. The Massengales were slave owners and had a large vineyard.

MASSENGALE, Major Henry White Jr.

Born 1835 in GA, son of Henry White and Rebecca Lowe Massengale. He was an officer with the

19th TN.

MASSENGALE (MASSINGALE), J. T.   Co. H, 4TN Cav. (Ashby's);
    Wounded in battle of Murfreesboro; with 2TN at Tunnel Hill, GA, March 12, 1864; transferred to Co. F, 5TN Cav. Bn.

MASSENGALE, Thomas
    The son of former Chattanooga mayor Henry White Massengale, he was quick to join the Southern army.

MASSENGALE, William       Co. H, 4TN Cav. (Ashby's)
    Married (Aug. 10, 1861) Martha C. Davis. Killed during Wheeler's 1864 raid.

MASSEY, James S.   Barry's Btry.
    Enl. Sept. 24, 1862 at Chattanooga; paroled May 11, 1865 in Meridian, MS.

MASSEY, T. L.   Barry's Btry.

MASTELLA (MASTELLER, MASTELLET), M. D. Co. G, 4GA
    Born Cherokee Co. GA, 1847. Enl. May 20, 1864 at Atlanta. Paroled May 20, 1865 at Montgomery, AL. 1904 res., Apison, James Co. [TP3980]

MASTELLA (MASTELLER, MASTELLET), W. P. Co. G, 4TN

MASTON, Cpl. Samuel D.   Co. D, 37TN
    Age 50 in 1861; enl. June 24, 1861 at Knoxville; discharged Aug. 15, 1862.

MATHIS (MATHES), Obediah    Co. K, 43TN
    Enl. Oct. 17, 1861 at Ooltewah; deserted March 2, 1862.

MATHIS, William B.   Co. H, 26TN; 2d Co. I, 1CSA
                (GA)
    Born c1844. Enl. Aug. 6, 1861, Knoxville. Captured Fort Donelson, Feb. 16, 1862 and imprisoned Camp Douglas. Sick in hosp., Atlanta, Aug. 31, 1863. Bell Hosp., Nov. 1, 1863; absent without leave, Jan. 1-13, 1864. Deserted near Atlanta, Aug. 13, 1864.

MATLOCK, Christopher       Chattanooga Home Guards

MATTELL, Jacob   Co. I, 19TN
    A shoe cobbler, he was born in Sardinia c1822. Married Frederica Schneitman and came to Chattanooga with the Schneitmans. Enl. May 20, 1861, Knoxville. Went home sick on furlough and was disch. May 27, 1862.

MAURICE, M.       Barry's Btry.
    Died at Pollard, March 6, 1863. [Lindsley].

MAXWELL, Albert   Co. K, 43TN
    Born 1836 in HC, son of William and Elizabeth Maxwell, who were from NC. Prior to the war, he lived on a farm at Zion Hill south of Ooltewah. Enl. Nov. 10, 1862, at Ooltewah; slightly wounded at Mossy Creek, TN, and was captured at Vicksburg, July 4, 1863, and paroled. He married in James Co. Caroline Gray and died in James County.[TWP, p. 153; TP6394]

MAXWELL, Hiram L.   Co. B, 36TN; Co. K, 43TN
    Enl. Dec. 10, 1861 at Ooltewah; transferred from 36TN; died at Vicksburg, July 1, 1863. [Lindsley, 528]

MAXWELL, Holder       Barry's Btry.
    Enl. Oct. 1, 1862. at Knoxville; captured 7 July [?] 1864 in Hamilton Co., TN [Brown's Diary]; took USA oath; 5'11"tall; dark complexion; dark hair.; and dark eyes.

MAXWELL, Cpl. James M.   Co. L, 36TN
    Enl. Jan. 9, 1862 at Chattanooga.

MAXWELL, Cpl. John   Co. K, 43TN
    He enl. along with his older brother, Albert Maxwell, at Ooltewah on Nov. 10, 1862. Like his brother, he was captured at Vicksburg on July 4, 1863, and was paroled. His parents were William and Elizabeth Maxwell. Res. Ooltewah, 1870, wife Narcissus.

MAXWELL, M. C. (C. M.)   Co. G, 26TN
    Enl. July 8, 1861 at Knoxville, died at a hospital in Nashville Nov. 15, 1861.

MAYBERRY (MABRY), Arch   Co. K, 43TN
    Enl. Dec. 12, 1861 at Ooltewah, having transferred from 36TN; captured at Vicksburg, July 4, 1863; paroled.

MAYBERRY (MABRY), Stephen H.   Co. K, 43TN
    Enl. July 1, 1862 at Ooltewah; captured at Vicksburg, July 4, 1863; florid complexion, dark hair, hazel eyes, 5'10" tall.

MAYES, Noble Irven
    Born Sweetwater, TN, May 6, 1846 and enl. 1862 in Lynchburg, VA in CS Military Express Service and served in that capacity in VA until the war ended.

1867-82, practiced law in Sweetwater; 1884-1913, real estate in Chattanooga. Presbyterian. Died at res. on 4th St, July 21, 1926 and buried Forest Hills Cem. [NBFM2,8]

MEDLOCK, Cpl. John V.    Co. F, 35TN
Born 1843 in Knox County, TN; farmer in HC when enl. Jan. 9, 1862; black eyes, dark hair, dark complexion, 5'5" tall.

MEE, William    Co. K, 19TN
Born 1830 in NC. Wife Martha, bn. NC. Farm laborer at Harrison, 1860. Had recently moved to HC from NC. Enl. June 4. 1861, Knoxville. Wounded at Adamsville, GA, May 17, 1864. Paroled Apr. 26, 1865. [1860HC]

MEEHAN, Capt. James    CSN
Born Covington, KY. Engaged in railroading before the war. "During the war he was in Cuba as foreman of extensive machine shops. From there he went to Vera Cruz, Mexico where he filled a responsible executive railway position." Returned to US in 1865 and continued in the railroad business. Came to Chattanooga in 1879 as superintendent of motive power for the Alabama Great Southern. In 1889 he founded Ross-Meehan Foundry in Chattanooga "A typical Irish-American, a gentleman of ready wit, of most engaging manner, and of most remarkable mechanical and business abilities." Meehan married Eleanor Childs. Died Feb. 28, 1908 in Hyde Park, OH, near Cincinnati.

MELTON, Andrew J.    Co. I, 19TN
Enl. May 20, 1861 in Knoxville, though from Walker Co., GA. He died in March, 1862 at Corinth. [Worsham, p. 49]

MELTON, George Washington    Co. K, 27AL
Born HC July 14, 1835. Enl. Jan. 8, 1862. Married P. J. (1860). Res. 1906 in Blackfox, Bradley Co. where he died July 12, 1909. [TP 8,249; TWP 2820]

MERRIMAN, Wiley    Co. K, 4TN Cav. (Murray's)
Born 1839 in TN, son of Margaret. Farm laborer.

METCALF, Francis M.    Co. C, 19AL
Born in AL. Wounded at Murfreesboro, Glasgow, KY, and Kennesaw Mountain. To HC in 1884. Res. 1899 in Ridgedale where he was unable to work.[TP1906]

MICKEY, John H.

[NBFM3]

MIDDLETON, Capt. Hugh Montgomery  Co. H, 39GA
Born Aug. 20, 1835 near Cunningham, Forsyth Co., GA, son of Capt. John and Matilda Middleton. Moved with parents to Chattooga Co. in 1838, and married (1861) Mary A. Carter. Both his wife and her mother were held prisoners for 18 days in Chattanooga, after being arrested at their home in Summerville, GA. They were charged with withholding information concerning the where abouts of Wood's men. Mrs. Middleton was also in camp at Vicksburg during the siege. Helped organize and became 3Lt of Co. H, 39GA. Prom. to captain in 1864. Fought at Champions Hill, Bridgeport, AL, Vicksburg, and Missionary Ridge Captured Feb. 22, 1864 at Summerville and imp. at Fort Delaware. After war returned to Summerville, then moved to Louisville KY. Relocated in Chattanooga in 1890. Member of County Court. Presby. NBF Camp, 1894. Mason. Died March 28, 1903 at res. on McCallie Ave. and buried Citizens Cem. [TWP, p. 101; CT March 30, 1903; NBFM6; UDC1 pg 290]

MILLER, Burris R.    Co. F, 2TN
Born March 12, 1843 in Rutherford Co., NC. Enl. April 21, 1861. Transferred to Polk's Brig., PRC Div. Wounded at Richmond, KY and Chickamauga. Captured at Peachtree Creek and sent to Camp Douglas and Point Lookout, MD, and held till June, 1865. He came to Chattanooga "soon after the war." Married Laura Eugenia Palmer in Shelby Co. in 1885. Employed by Miller Bros. since 1895. Methodist. Died at res. on Georgia Ave., May 4, 1904 and buried CSA Cem. [CT May 5, 1904; TWP, 313; NBFM2; UDC1 pg 291]

MILLER, C. P.    Co. H, 26TN
Born c1821. Enl. July 8, 1861, Knoxville. Captured Fort Donelson, Feb. 16, 1862 and imprisoned Camp Morton, IN. Left in Chattanooga Oct. 5, 1862.

MILLER, Thomas    Barry's Btry.
Enl. April 26, 1862 at Chattanooga; deserted at Chattanooga April 31,[sic] 1862.

MILLER, Thomas Anderson    Co. K, 43TN
Born 1836 in Roane Co. Enl. Nov. 10, 1862 at Ooltewah; wounded in knee by minie ball and captured at Vicksburg, July 4, 1863 and paroled. Returned to Bradley Co. in 1865, left in 1869, but returned about 1880. Married (1887) Rhoda or Matilda Shannon. Lead removed from his wound in 1890 but he continued to suffer until his death. Res. Hill City in 1903. [TWP, p. 115; TP5731]

MILLIGAN, Alexander

Veteran of Mexican and Civil Wars. Friend of Gov. Bate. [NBFM4]

MILLIROUS, Jackson    Co. D, 60GA
Enl. April 18, 1861. Real estate agent in Chattanooga, 1887. [NBFM2]

MILLS, Charles H.
Born c1826 in MD. Colonel, CSA. Wife was Sallie E. Wholesale and retail merchant Chattanooga in 1870. Buried Forest Hills Cemetery. [CT July 31, 1916]

MILLS, John W.    26TN; 3TN (Vaughan's)
Born June 17, 1828 in Bedford Co., VA of VA parents. Enl. Aug., 1861. Badly injured at Lick Creek, Greene Co., TN. To Chattanooga from Knoxville in 1874. By 1901 was unemployed carpenter. 1910 boarding Whiteside St. with wife Lucille (m. 1866). Buried Forest Hills Cemetery. [TP3253; 1910HC]

MILTON, Harvey Oliver    Co. F, 44AL; 15AL
Born Edgefield Dist., SC, Nov. 28, 1832. Enl. June 1862 in Co. F, 44AL. Seven Days. Became asst. surgeon and served at Texas Hosp. in Richmond for 11 months. Assigned to 15AL. After Chickamauga occup. in examining conscripts. "While having charge of a Confederate conscript camp in Macon he met and married Miss Sarah Fort, sister of Col. Tom and Miss Kate Fort of Chattanooga." Sarah was born 23 Dec. 1843 in Baldwin Co. They moved to Chattanooga after war and lived here until 1894. Physician in Chattanooga ca 1890. On Chickamauga and Chattanooga National Park Committee. Died Nov. 7, 1906 in Knoxville and buried Forest Hills Cemetery. [FHR; CT Nov. 8-9, 1906; NBFM2]

MINIARD, Thomas R.
Enl. Jan. 9, 1862, in Co. L, 36TN at Chattanooga; transferred to Co. L, 35TN. Absent without leave since Aug. 16, 1863.

MINNIS, John A.    Co. H, 4TN Cav.; 8TN Cav.
Born 1813, Franklin Co., NC. Married Catherine Abrams. Practiced law in White Co. before moving to Chattanooga where he also practiced. Member of Genl. Assembly, 1847-49 and represented HC in TN Senate, 1859-61. Resettled at Memphis just before the war. Enl. 8TN Cav., Oct. 20, 1862, Tullahoma and became regimental adjutant same day. Captured in Sumner Co., March 11, 1863 and imp. Louisville and Johnson's Island until exchanged Feb. 24, 1865. After war, returned to Memphis, then came back to Chattanooga before relocating in Greenville, AL, 1867. To Montgomery, AL, 1869, becoming Atty.

for Middle Dist. of AL, 1870-74; City Judge of Montgomery, 1874-80. Died Aug., 1886.

MITCHELL, ---(1)---    Barry's Btry.
Deserted, Brown's Diary.

MITCHELL, ---(2)---    Barry's Btry.
Deserted, Brown's Diary.

MITCHELL, A. T.  Co. F, 16Tn
Member NBF Camp, 1895. Died July 7, 1920. Buried CSA Cem. [NBFM2]

MITCHELL, Adam R.    Co. H, 2TN Cav.(Ashby's)
Born c1830. 1870, carpenter in Chattanooga, wife Sarah A. Buried CSA Cem.

MITCHELL, Charles  Co. F, MS Vols.

MITCHELL, E.    Barry's Btry.
Deserted. [Brown's Diary].

MITCHELL, Flavius J.    5TN Cav.
Took the USA oath of allegiance on February 13, 1864. He had a florid complexion, light hair, blue eyes and was 5'8" tall.

MITCHELL, James
This may be the J.C. Mitchell who was 26 in 1860 with wife Nancy J. at Ooltewah).

MITCHELL, John    Co. F, 35TN
Born 1831 in Claiborne, TN, he was a Chattanooga merchant when he enl. Jan. 1, 1863. Blue eyes, dark hair, fair complexion, and 6'1" tall.

MITCHELL, John
This may be John Mitchell with wife Elizabeth who was barkeeper at Chattanooga in 1860.

MITCHELL, O. K.    Co. H, 4TN Cav.
Wounded at Murfreesboro, Jan. 1, 1863.

MITCHELL, R. C.  Co. A, 5th (McKenzie's) TN Cav.
He enl. Aug. 29, 1861 at Camp Cumming. Captured at Wallace's Crossroads, Sept., 1862. Paroled May 3, 1865 at Charlotte, NC.

MITCHELL, Thomas A.    Co. F, 35Tn
Born in 1840 in Hall County, GA, he was a farmer in HC when he enl. Jan. 1, 1863. He deserted Aug. 21, 1863, at Graysville, AL. He had gray eyes, light hair, a fair complexion, and stood 5'10" tall. His father apparently died before the war. His mother was Jane Mitchell.

MITCHELL, Capt. Thomas R.    Co. F, 35TN
        Born in 1834 in White Co., TN, he was a lawyer in Chattanooga when he enl. Oct. 1, 1862. The young lawyer "recruited forty-two men for his 'Mountain Rifles,' which became Company F." Mitchell became AIG on the staff of Brig. Gen. Lucius E. Polk, Oct. 7, 1863. Killed by Federal troops near Shelbyville, TN, 9 Dec., 1864 while on furlough visiting his wife and infant daughter.. Brown eyes, dark hair, a light complexion and 6' tall. Wife was Mary E. Mitchell. [WF; UDC1 pg 294]

MONDS, Capt. A. M.    Co. L, 36TN, Co. L, 35TN
        Enl. Jan. 9, 1862, in Co. L, 36TN at Chattanooga; transferred to Co. L, 35TN. [Jennie (1852-1873) and Walter (1889-1915) buried in Citizens Cem.]

MONTAGUE, John R.    Co. I, 19TN
        Enl. May 20, 1861 at Knoxville, then to Cumberland Gap, VA. Montague was a carpenter and a mechanic. He was killed at Shiloh on April 7, 1862. He was originally from Vermont.

MONTGOMERY, Capt. David Nelson    Co. B, 1TN Cav. (Carter's)
        Successor to John A. Teenor as captain. Captured at Piedmont, VA, on June 5, 1864. He was sent to Camp Morton, then to Johnson's Island on June 20, 1864. He was released on May 19. After the war, he resided at Talladega, AL. Prior to the conflict, he lived at Harrison with his wife, Mary J. The Montgomerys were from NC. He was born c1829.

MONTGOMERY, Sgt. George W.    Co. B, 1TN Cav. (Carter's)
        Captured June 5, 1864, at Piedmont, VA, he was received on the James River for exchange on March 23, 1865 and paroled on March 28. He went to a hospital at Richmond for treatment of smallpox. Before the war, he lived with his parents, George and Sarah Montgomery, on a farm at Snow Hill. The elder George Montgomery was a native of KY. George W. Montgomery was born about 1841. Res. in OK in 1912.

MONTGOMERY, Lt. Col. John George Morgan
        5TN Cav.(McKenzie's).
        Born 12 Dec. 1833 in Auburn, NY and came to Chattanooga in 1856, but moved to Cleveland in 1858, where he engaged in the grocery business. Enl. Feb. 15, 1862, Cleveland and elected Capt. same day. Elected major, May 24, 1862. He was part of Gen. Wheeler's raid through TN at Farmington and he was in command of the regiment. In less than 30 minutes, the 5th TN had 70 men killed and wounded. Col.

Montgomery had his horse shot from under him and he was dangerously wounded at Lylton, GA. He was badly wounded in the last battle at Bentonville, NC. On the 29th of April 1865, he was paroled in the hospital in Charlotte, NC. He married Mary E. Wheeler on 24 Jan. 1855. After they war he moved to Smithville, Lee Co., GA. Died June 15, 1914 in Cartersville, GA.[CT 6.17.04]

MONTGOMERY, Joseph E. Co. A, 16TN Cav. Bn.
        Born March 29, 1846 in Roane Co., son of Alexander Montgomery. After war farmed in Roane and OK before coming to Chattanooga in 1889. Methodist. Married Jennie Whittenburg. Buried Chattanooga Memorial Park. [CT July 21, 1937; 1910HC]

MONTGOMERY, Matthew Houston Co. B, 1TN Cav. (Carter's)
        Born 1844 in HC of TN parents. Enl. July, 1862. Paroled May, 1865 near Talladega, AL. Married (1900 HC) Susan Elizabeth Mahan. Farmer in James Co., 1910. Died April 24, 1920, age 76, at home near Ooltewah and buried Montgomery Fam. Cem. [TWP, 300; TP3253; CT April 25, 1920; 1910 James Co.]

MONTGOMERY, W. F.    Co. F, 39GA
        Born Forsyth Co., GA in 1838. Pvt., March 4, 1862. Captured Vicksburg. Wounded Bridgeport, AL. Deserted Dec. 10, 1863. 1901 res. HC. [TP3676; Henderson, 305]

MOORE, Alexander Fitzgerald
        Born 1835 in HC and married (1864) Elizabeth Hightower. Died 1911 in HC. [TWP, 252]

MOORE, Orderly Sgt. Alexander N. (M.)  Barry's Btry.
        Enl. April 25, 1862 at Chattanooga. Disabled in Knoxville in early part of war and transferred to Post Office Dept.

MOORE, Lt. Col. Beriah Frazier    19TN
        Born c1838 in TN, son of Antipas and Rebecca Frazier Moore. A promising young attorney, res. in 1860 in household of Tom Crutchfield, he was a bachelor, "a large, handsome man of austere countenance." He led one of the two large companies out of Chattanooga in 1861 (the "Marsh Blues"). A member of Co. A, 19TN, he had risen to 2Lt. and then Lt. Col. He was at Shiloh, Corinth and in the fighting around Vicksburg as well as Murfreesboro and Baton Rouge before moving on to Chattanooga where he was killed at Missionary Ridge. His body was moved to the Frazier cemetery in Rhea County. [Worsham, p. 101; 1860HC; CT Oct. 4, 1906]

MOORE, Erasmus D.  Asst. Surgeon, Barry's Btry.

MOORE, Hewlitt S.   Chaplain
Born 1829 in SC, he was pastor of the First Baptist Church at Chattanooga from 1857 until the outbreak of the war, when he volunteered as chaplain in one of the first Confederate regiments that was formed. After the war, he settled on a farm at Chickamauga Station. He resided there except for a few years when he was pastor of a church at Ringgold, Ga. He died March 6, 1902, leaving a widow and seven children. [CT March 7, 1902]

MOORE, J. L.   Co. K, 43TN
Born c1830, he and wife Nancy had a farm at Harrison before the war. Enl. Oct. 10, 1862, at Ooltewah. Captured at Vicksburg on July 6, 1863, and paroled. [1860HC]

MOORE, J. W.   Co. A, 34AL
Born Russell Co., AL, 1846. Atlanta Camp. Deserted at Rutledge, TN and took USA oath at Knoxville, Oct., 1864, although claimed he was at Franklin, captured and imprisoned Camp Douglas. To TN, 1916. Res. Rossville, TN, 1917. [TP 15,245]

MOORE, James
Born 1840, in TN, of TN parents. Laborer in foundry, 1910. Boarder on Carter St. African-American. [1910HC]

MOORE, John   Co. A, 19TN
Captured at Missionary Ridge; brother of Col. B. F. Moore. [Worsham, pp. 101, 204.]

MOORE, Lemuel J.   Co. B, Wm. Walker's Bn.,
Thomas' Legion
Born c1842, Monroe Co., TN; res. Cherokee Co., GA; Dec. 20, 1842. Enl. Thomas' Legion of Indians and Highlanders which was organized at Knoxville, Sept., 1862. Present through Aug. 1862; absent without leave Nov.-Dec. 1862; present Jan. 1863-Feb. 1864. Captured at Battle of Piedmont, June 5, 1864 and imp. Camp Morton, IN until May, 1865. 1st Sgt. Res. Chattanooga, 1907. [TP9019]

MOORE, Nicholas Gibbs   Co. I, 19TN
Born 12 Dec. 1844 in Rhea Co. TN, son of Antipas and Rebecca. He was wounded at Missionary Ridge, while his brother, Beriah Frazier Moore, was killed nearby. He had been enl. at Chattanooga on Oct. 3, 1862, by William Spears. Moore was captured at Graysville, GA, on June 12, 1864. He was sent to Louisville, Ky., and then on to Rock Island, IL. Afterwards, he rejoined the army and was hospitalized at Richmond, VA in March of 1863. He surrendered at Asheville, NC on May 6, 1865. He was 6' tall with blue

eyes. He married amanda Jane Elder in 1868 in Dayton. She was born 30 Aug. 1847 in Meigs Co. And died 22 April 1920 in Dayton.   He died 15 Aug. 1921 in Rockwood, TN. [CSR; RI ledger; 1860HC; UDC2 pg 380]

MOORE, Richard
Born c1847, GA. Res. in household of son-in-law Fred Nelson on White Oak Rd., 1910. Laborer. African-American.

MOORE, Robert
Born c1835 in HC, he married (1858) Julia Ann Davis. He died 1909 in HC. [TWP, p. 87]

MOORE, W. H.   Co. K, 43TN
Born c1835, he had a farm at Harrison with his wife, Isabella, before the war. Enl. Oct. 10, 1862, at Ooltewah and deserted Nov. 8, 1862. [1860HC]

MOORE, William A.   2nd Co. K, 1st CSA Cav.
Born and raised in HC, he was engaged in the mercantile and milling business in Mt. Airy before enlisting Sept. 24, 1862. As a member of Morgan's Cavalry, he fought in ten engagements and was sent on secret mission behind Federal lines and supposedly captured. He married 1) Menerva Myers and 2) Rosa Blalock. Baptist. He died Sept. 1, 1917 in Dunlap, TN and was buried in Rankin Cem. [CT Sept. 2, 1917]

MOORE, William L.   Co. B, 19TN
Captured at Cleveland, TN, Nov. 24, 1863 and imprisoned at Rock Island. Enl. in USN and sent to rendezvous Jan. 28, 1864. [RI ledger]

MORELAND, John A.(E.)   Co. G, 26TN; Barry's Btry.
Born Jan. 21, 1842 in Jackson Co., AL. Res. 1860 in household of D.C. Hamill in Chattanooga Enl. July 8, 1861; sick at Bowling Green, KY, Jan. 23, 1862. Captured at Fort Donelson. After exchange, transferred May 15, 1862 to Barry's Btry. at Chattanooga; fought at Jackson, MS; Resaca, New Hope Church, Peachtree Creek, Atlanta, Jonesboro, Spanish Fort. Paroled May 11, 1865 at Meridian, MS. Carpenter in N. Rossville, TN., 1907. [NBFM2, TP 9314; 1860HC]

MORELAND, John H.   2nd Co. D, 26TN; 1CSA (GA)
Enl. Feb. 18, 1863 in Ringgold, GA. Sent to General Hospital, Chattanooga, Aug. 9, 1863. Captured at Lafayette, GA, Dec. 22, 1863 and imprisoned at Rock Island. USA oath July 27, 1864. Res. of HC. He had fair complexion, brown hair, blue eyes, and was 5'6" tall.

MORELAND, Ransom   Co. F, 35TN
Born 1826 in Buncombe Co., NC, he was a

farmer in HC when he enl.; deserted at Chickamauga, Sept. 20, 1863; brown eyes, light hair, dark complexion, and 5'4" tall.

MORELAND, Cpl. Thomas Jefferson  Barry's Btry.
Born 20 May 1839 in Monroe Co. TN. Enl. Oct. 3, 1862. at Knox.; promoted to Cpl.; paroled May 11, 1865 at Meridian, MS. He married Mary Powell who was born in Alabama and died in Sept 1879 in Cloverdale, GA. Farmer. Res. 1888, Rossville, GA; member NBF, 2/08. He died Sept. 1918 in Walker Co., GA. [NBFM2,4; UDC2 pg 382]

MORELAND, William J.   2nd Co. D, 26TN; 2d. D, 1CSA (GA)
Born in Gilmer Co., GA. Enl. Aug. 18, 1862, Fort Gaines, AL. Disch. at Mobile on surgeon's certificate of disability, Feb. 10, 1863. Farmer. He had dark complexion, black eyes, auburn hair and was 5' tall.

MORGAN, A. J. Co. A, 1GA
Res. 1910 in HC. [TP11, 859 (J. H. Smith's)]

MORGAN, Isaac C., Sr.
Of Cumberland Co., TN, he was a surgeon in Bragg's army. Res. in Chattanooga. Constable in 14th Civil Dist. [NBFM2]

MORGAN, Isaac C., Jr. Co. C, 35TN
Res. Chattanooga. Constable in 14th Civil Dist. [NBFM2]

MORGAN, J. T.   Thomas' Brigade, Hill's Division, ANV
1845-1882. Buried CSA Cem.

MORGAN, James M.   Co. H, 4TN Cav.
Died in prison.

MORGAN, Joseph R.  Co. D, 37TN
Born c1836. Enl. Sept. 1, 1861, Knoxville. Wounded at Perryville, Oct. 8, 1862, wounded again at Vineville. hospitalized in Chattanooga Prom. to 5th Sgt., Feb. 15, 1863. Prom. 1st Sgt. Died of wounds at Empire Hosp. near Macon, Oct. 3, 1864. Killed in battle (Lindsley).

MORGAN, Silas Marion  Co. G, 3TN
Born 1840 in McMinn Co. Enl. May 7, 1861. Married (1867) Mahala Givens. Res. 1870 in McMinn Co.  Moved to HC and was living in Falling Water, 1900, crippled with rheumatism and supported "by the labor of my wife and two youngest children." Died 1908 in HC. [NBF2; TWP, p. 53; TP2444]

MORRIS (MORRISSEY, MORRISON), John   Barry's Btry.
Enl. March 16, 1863 at Chattanooga as substitute; captured July 17, 1863 near Jackson, MS; died of pneumonia Feb. 16, 1864 as POW, Camp Morton, IN; bur. Green Lawn Cem., Camp Morton.

MORRIS, Joseph    Co. H, 2TN Cav. (Ashby's)
Killed Aug. 31, 1862. (Lindsley).

MORRIS, Kittrell H.  Co. F, 10GA
[NBFM1]

MORRIS, Luther A.   Co. B, 35MS
Born Perry Co., AL, Sept. 21, 1845. Enl. winter, 1863. Atlanta Camp., Ordnance Dept. and captured at Ft. Blakely, Apr. 9, 1865 and imprisoned Ship Island. To TN, 1883. Res. of East Chattanooga 40 yrs. Pastor Taylor St. Baptist Church. Died Feb. 9, 1924 in Chattanooga and buried Forest Hills Cemetery.[TP 10,737; 1910HC; CT Feb. 10, 1924]

MORRIS, Rufus Monroe    Co. A, 36GA Inf.
Born July 14, 1848 in Gordon Co. GA. Enl. Jan. 15, 1862 in Co. A, 36GA. Captured at Vicksburg and imprisoned Camp Morton. To Chattanooga about 1893. Newspaper publisher, farming interests in North GA and AL, merchant, real estate, and member of HC court. Baptist, Mason.   He married Margaret Catherine Dowling on 7 Feb. 1869 in Ringgold, GA.  She was born 30 July 1848 in Augusta, GA and died 27 Jan. 1888 in Ringgold. He was a member of the Nathan Bedford Forrest Camp.  He died Dec. 11, 1927 in Chattanooga and buried Forest Hills Cem. [NBFM2,8,10; CT Dec. 12, 1927; UDC1 pg 302.]

MORRIS, Sgt. Wilburn           Co. H, 7TN
Born Lebanon, TN, Oct. 19, 1836, he moved to Chattanooga early, becoming a "pioneer" settler. Enl. May 20, 1861 at Lebanon, TN. He was severely wounded at Seven Pines and served the remainder of the war in the Treasury Dept. Paroled Washington, GA, May 1865. He came to Chattanooga in 1874 and was a merchant, remaining until 1879 when he became involved in timber and real estate business in East Tennessee. Returned to Chattanooga at his retirement and died here Jan. 17, 1911 and was buried at Forest Hills Cem. Married Miss Darden of Knoxville and after her death m. (1880) Mrs. W. G. Anderson (Lou Hoskins). Baptist. Res. Lansing St. [CT Jan. 18, 1911; FHR; 1910HC; NBFM2; TP6781]

MORRISON, E. J.  Co. D, 5TN; Co. D, 35TN
Born Warren Co., TN, 1842. Enl. Sept. 6, 1861. Shiloh, Richmond, KY, Perryville, Murfreesboro, Chickamauga; paroled Washington Co., GA, May,

1865. Res. East Lake, 1906. [TP8541]

MORRISON, George W.  Co. I, 26TN
        Born March, 1840, TN. Res. with wife Lucinda 1910 in Soddy where he was coal miner. Died May 3, 1910. [CT May 4, 1910]

MORTON, S. M.  Co. K, 3d State AL Inf.
        1843-1914. Buried CSA Cem.

MORTON, Wesley  Co. A, 4TN Cav.
        Enl. June 17, 1861 at Knoxville. Prom. cpl., May 27, 1862. Captured at Big Hill, near Lancaster, Ky., July 31, 1863 and imprisoned Camp Chase and Fort Delaware. Exch. Feb. 27, 1865.

MOSES, Frank A.  Sgt., F&S, 63rd TN
        Enl. Co. D, May 13, 1862, age 18. Absent sick, then detailed as Color Sgt. Prom. to Sgt. Dec. 7, 1863. Sick in hospital, Charlottesville, Jan. 16, 1864., having gotten sick on furlough. Wounded Drewry's Bluff, May 16, 1864. Treated Wayside Hosp., Richmond, for gunshot wound to left arm. Prom. to Ensign, Aug. 18, 1864. Exch. Feb. 27, 1865. Surrendered at Appomattox, April 9, 1865. He married Lizzie Mitchell who was born 12 Nov. 1847 in Hawkings Col., TN. Died and buried in Knoxville, 1922. [NBFM7; UDC1 pg 304]

MOSS, William R.  Co. B, 5TN Cav.
        Born about 1828 in SC, he was a carpenter at Chattanooga prior to the war and afterward. His wife, Mary, was a native of VA. He enl. Aug. 11, 1861, at Chattanooga

MOSTELLER, William D.
        Born 1848, GA. Res. of Chattanooga, 1905. Farmer, James Co., 1910 with wife Mary A. (m. 1904) and six young children. [NBFM7; 1910 James Co.]

MOTLEY, James  Co. D, 37TN
        Enl. Sept. 16, 1862 at Whitesides; tranferred to dismounted cavalry, July 22, 1863; wounded at Chickamauga and again Feb. 24, 1864; detailed to drive cattle, Sept. 1, 1864; paroled May 1, 1865 at Greensboro, NC.

MOUNCE (MAUNZ, MONTZE), Frederick (Fritz) Barry's Btry.
        Enl. Aug. 30, 1862 at Knoxille; paroled May 11, 1865; res. Stevenson, AL.

MOUNTCASTLE, 2Lt. Theo  Co. K, 43TN
        Enl. Feb. 26, 1862 at Ooltewah; captured at Vicksburg, July 4, 1863 and paroled; again captured at Morristown, TN, Oct. 28, 1864; imprisoned at Johnson's Island. Born in TN, he was 32 years old in 1865; mother in 1865 living in IL. Declared himself a resident of Cleveland, TN. Dark complexion, dark hair, hazel eyes, 6' tall.

MURDOCK, J. T.  Co. G, 26TN; 2d Co. K, 1CSA (GA)
        Enl. July 8, 1861, Knoxville. Sick in hosp., Bowling Green. Disch. Oct. 13, 1862.; enl. Dec. 14, 1862, Mobile. Killed at Jonesboro, Aug. 31, 1864.

MURPHY, Horatio L.  Co. A, 4TN
        He was a blacksmith prior to the war, residing near William Ragsdale, his unit captain. He was a native of SC, and his wife, Caroline, was from GA. Enl. June 17, 1861 at Knoxville. Sick in Chattanooga Nov. 1861 and April 1862. Had a requision for forage at Chattanooga, Sept. 30-Oct. 9, 1862.

MYERS, Frederick N.  Co. I, 19TN
        Born c1835. Farm laborer in Chattanooga in 1860 with wife Nancy. They were from GA. Enl. May 20, 1861 in Knoxville. Deserted 1863, then "returned from desertion" Nov. 1, 1863. Captured near Atlanta, July 22, 1864. Imp. Camp Chase, Aug. 1, 1864, where he died of pneumonia Feb. 15, 1865. Grave 1/2 mi. south of Camp Chase.

MYERS, J. M.  Co. H, 26TN
        Born c1840. Enl. July 8, 1861. Mortally wounded, Fort Donelson, Feb. 15, 1862.

MYERS, 2Lt. Louis William  2d Co. I, 26TN; Clark's Independent Cav. Co.; 2d Co. I, 1CSA (GA)
        Enl. July 14, 1861 in Knoxville. Left sick in Nashville, 1861. Joined Clark's Cav. Co. Aug. 31, 1862 at Chattanooga; captured June 27, 1863, Manchester, TN and imprisoned Camp Chase.

MYNATT, George W.  Barry's Btry.

# Mc

McAFEE (MCABEY), Thomas Wesley  Co. A, 63GA
        Born in Ashville, NC, 1845. Enl. Jan. 7, 1863. Atlanta Campaign. Surr. at Greensboro, May 1, 1865. To TN, 1884. Railroader, bookkeeper in Chattanooga c1890. Married (1870) Martha Elizabeth Eddleman. Died July 7, 1920 in Chattanooga, age 75, and buried Forest Hills Cemetery. [CT July 8, 1920; TWP, 212; NBFM2,7; TP14483; 1910HC]

McAMIS, James P.
        Born 1845, TN. Res. 1910 in James Co. with wife Eliza. [1910James Co.]

McARDLE, Bernard "Barney"    Co. I, 19TN
        Enl. May 20, 1861, Knoxville. Surgeon's disch. July 1861. Re-enlisted April 9, 1863, Chattanooga, as substitute for A.C. Ladd. Deserted and captured near Chattanooga, Sept. 10, 1863. Sent to Louisville where he took USA oath agreeing to stay north of Ohio River.

McBEE, William H.    Co. K, 43TN
        Enl. Oct. 17, 1861 at Ooltewah; captured at Vicksburg, July 4, 1863.

McBRIDE, James    Co. G, 11TN
        Born March 14,1818, Ireland. Enl. May 7, 1861 and served till disch. overage, 1862, but returned unofficially and fought at Murfreesboro and Chickamauga. Laborer after war. Res. of Chattanooga, 1900, when he applied for admission to TN Soldiers Home.

McCALL, James Price    8GA
        Born in Camden, NY, Oct. 5, 1836. He emigrated to Augusta, GA at the age of 17, then to Greensboro, GA, where he became prosperous in general merchanise and banking. In 1861, he enl. in 8GA and was wounded at 1st Manassas. Later he was wounded again, captured and imprisoned at Point Lookout. He returned to Greensboro after the war, but moved to Chattanooga in 1880 where he entered the wholesale dry goods business. He died in Chattanooga Jan. 27, 1907. His wife was Claudia Wingfield Weaver.

McCALLIE, John    Co. C, 1TN Cav. (Carter's)
        Born c1828 in TN, son of Archibald. Farmer at Birchwood with wife Amanda. [1860HC]

McCALLIE, the Rev. Thomas Hooke
        Exec. Committee, Soldiers Relief Society at Chattanooga, Aug. 29, 1862.

McCALLISTER, D.    Co. B, 2TN Cav. Bn.
        Living in James Co. in 1902.

McCAN (see McCAW)

McCARLY, W. H.
        Born 1841, TN. Widower, res. household of son L. H. on Back Valley Rd.

McCAW (McCALL, McCANN), David    Co. K, 43TN
        Enl. July 31, 1863 at Ooltewah; captured Oct. 28, 1864 in Jefferson Co., TN; imprisoned at Camp Douglas; res. Monroe Co., TN; fair complexion, brown hair, hazel eyes, 5'9" tall.

McCAW, John H.    Co. H, 37TN
        Born 1843. Enl. Sept. 1, 1861, Ooltewah. Deserted at Chattanooga, Aug. 29, 1862.

McCAW (McCALL, McCANN, McCAN), John M.    Co. K, 43TN
        Enl. Oct. 17, 1861 at Ooltewah; died Feb. 14, 1863 at Vicksburg. [Lindsley, 528]

McCAW (McCALL, McCANN, McCAN), William    Co. K, 43TN
        Enl. Feb. 19, 1862 at Ooltewah; died Feb. 11, 1863 at Vicksburg. [Lindsley, 528]

McCLATCHEY, William M.    Co. B, 2KY Cav.
        Served with Gen. John Hunt Morgan. Died June 4, 1908 at his home near Chickamauga, GA. [1890VetCensus; CT 5 June 1908]

McCLATCHEY, William Penn    Co. B, Georgia Cadets
        Born McMinn Co., Feb. 16, 1847, son of Wiley Jarratt and Minerva Lear Rowles McClatchey. Educated at GA Military Institute and Emory College, Oxford, GA. Served in bn. of cadets and later as member of Texas Rangers. Atlanta Campaign and Hood's Tenn campaign. Captured as he fled seeking to reach Trans-Miss. army. To Chattanooga, 1887. Lawyer. Recorder for city judge. Married (1880) Julia E. Allen, who reported that "as a little girl she regularly visited the Confederate soldiers at the Marietta, GA hospital, helping as best she could." and res. Bluff View St., 1910. 1Lt. NBF Camp, 1894-96. Died July 6, 1920 at his home on 2nd St. and buried Forest Hills Cemetery. [FHR; CT July 7, 1920; TP15451; 1910HC; UDC1 pg 273]

McCLUNG, Frank Armstrong    Co. C, 4AL Cav.
        Born Madison Co., Ala., Dec. 11, 1843. Cadet at LaGrange Military Academy, 1860-61, then left to become pvt. in 4AL Cav. in which he served throughout the war. Employed by US Railway Mail Service, 1882-1897, then established himself in business in Chattanooga. Living on Missionary Ridge at time of death, Feb. 9, 1905. Buried in Huntsville in his old Confederate blanket.[Wyeth, Hist. of LaGrange Mil. Acad, pp.146-47; CT 01 Feb. 1905.]

McCOLLUM, Joab Lafayette    Co. D, 6 AL
        Born May 10, 1842, son of Joab McCollum and Sarah Wood, he grew up in Dade County, GA and was a friend of John B. Gordon who organized the Raccoon Roughs (Co. D., 6AL Inf.). McCollum enl. in Brown's unit in Montgomery, AL, April 25, 1861 and served throughout

the war with this company. He was wounded at the battle of Seven Pines, VA, then served as a nurse in the hospital at Danville, VA in summer, 1862. He was later wounded at Chancellorsville, Spottsylvania and Petersburg. Some of his wounds to the head and limbs were severe. Captured April 2, 1865 at Petersburg and imp. at City Point.

He married Bettie Ann Holmes, a native of Whitesburg, Ala., on April 19, 1866. McCollum became a prominent railroad agent for the Alabama and Chattanooga Railroad and later the Nashville, Chattanooga and St. Louis Railroad. He was assigned to Chattanooga in the latter part of 1874 as train master and later became agent. The McCollums moved to Atlanta in 1890. He appears to have served as an ordained Presbyterian minister in Nashville about 1905. He died in Atlanta, Dec. 10, 1926 and was buried in Forest Hills Cem. [CSR; GHT, pp.970-71; CT Dec. 11, 1926;NBFM8]

McCONNELL, Capt. Thomas M.    26TN
Born Jan. 1831 in Grainger Co., he became a merchant in Ringgold. Married Mary M. Donohoo (from Chattanooga) in Bentonville, AR, then they returned to Ringgold. Helped organize 26TN. Captured at Fort Donelson. Following exchange at Vicksburg in Sept. 1862, he was not reelected at reorganization, so he joined staff of Gen. John C. Vaughn as AIG and rose to major. McConnell was badly injured at Winchester, VA. After war returned to East TN and became a drummer for a NY wholesale house. Then he and his cousin T. C. McConnell opened a general store and later a flour mill in Ringgold, GA. To Chattanooga in 1875. Practiced law. Appointed (1876) HC Clerk and Master, he served until he became chancellor in 1891, a post he held until his death. He twice sought the governorship of Tennessee. Died here Jan. 30, 1915 and buried in Forest Hills Cemetery. His elegant home on Fifth Street was restored in the 1990's by the Lyndhurst Foundation. [CTJan.31.1915;Jan. 19, 1916; NFP, Sept. 10, 1995; FHR; NBFM2,7]

McCORD, Henry  2nd Co. K, 1CSA Cav.
Enl. July 14, 1862 in HC. Deserted at Shelbyville, TN, Dec. 28, 1862.

McCORD, James  2nd Co. K, 1CSA Cav.
Born c1844 in GA, son of Henry and Lucy McCord. Enl. July 14, 1862 in HC. Deserted at Shelbyville, TN, Dec. 28, 1862. [1860HC]

McCORKLE, Dr. D. V.  Co. A, 4TN Cav. Bn.
(2TN Cav.)
Captured in Battle of Somerset, KY; In prison at Johnson's Island.

McCORKLE, Dr. W. A. Surgeon, 2TN Cav. (Ashby's)
He was later Brigade Surgeon. His daughter Jennie says that her father's three brothers were all in the Confederate service. [UDC1 pg 275]

McCORMACK, James    Co. B, 1TN Cav. (Carter's).
Enl. Aug. 7, 1861, Cleveland. Captured at Lovejoy Station on Nov. 16, 1864. Imprisoned at Point Lookout, MD, he was exchanged Feb. 14, 1865. Before the war, he lived on the farm of his parents, William F. and Sarah McCormack, at Birchwood. The McCormacks were from NC. He was born c1845. [1860HC]

McCORMACK, 2Lt. Robert T.    Co. B, 1TN Cav. (Carter's)
Born 1834 in HC, son of William F. and Sarah McCormack. Before the war, he farmed at Birchwood with his wife, Sarah. Enl. March 1, 1861. Wounded by shell at Missionary Ridge resulting in loss of one eye. Indicted for treason at Knoxville. "Fellows kept shooting at McCormack and he at them even after the close of the war," reported Franz Gardenhire. 1902 res. of Long Savannah. [TP5290, 4276; 1860HC]

McCRARY, Joel    Co. A, 5th (McKenzie's) TN Cav.
He enl. May 1, 1862 at Kingston. Age 24 on March 11, 1864 roll. Paroled May 3, 1865 at Charlotte, NC.

McDANIEL, William C.   Co. H, 26TN; 1CSA Inf.
Born c1841. Enl. July 8, 1861, Knoxville. Captured Fort Donelson, Feb. 16, 1862 and imprisoned Camp Douglas.

McDERMOTT, 1Lt. John McG.   Co. H, 19TN; Co. C, Cons. 3TN
1Lt. of Co. C, Cons. 3TN. Steamboat captain in Chattanooga, 1889. Married Penelope Fielding (1830-1875). Member, NBF Camp, 1894-96.

McDONALD, George Lafayette   2nd Co. K, 1st CSA Cav.
He enl. Sept. 22, 1862 in HC. Paroled May 3, 1865 in Charlotte, NC. Before the war, he lived at Ooltewah on the farm of his mother, Nancy McDonald, who was from Virginia. He was born about 1844.

McDONALD, W. H.   2nd Co. K, 1st CSA Cav.
He enl. Sept. 22, 1862 in HC. Killed in action in Perry Co., TN, May 8, 1863.

McDONALD, Wiley P.    Co. F, 35TN
Born 1825, McMinn Co. Family moved to HC when he was boy and Indians were still in vicinity. Enl. Jan. 5, 1863. Captured at Missionary Ridge; took USA

oath Dec. 21, 1863; fair complexion, light hair, brown eyes, and 6' tall. Cumberland Presbyterian. Boarder in household of George P. Will, James Co., 1910. Died Nov. 19, 1911 in Chattanooga and buried McDonald Cem. [1910HC; CT Nov. 21, 1911]

McDONALD, William C. Co. I, 26TN; 2d Co. I, 1CSA (GA)
Born Nov. 20, 1840 in HC and enl. at Crawfish Springs, GA, July 4, 1861. Captured at Fort Donelson and exchanged Sept. 1862. Detailed as wagoner for brigade baggage wagon, Aug. 31, 1864. "Was badly wounded by a minie ball striking him in the side, going through his body, glancing his backbone while he was going up the first line of Federal breastworks at Franklin." Not able to return to duty. Farmer. [NBFM2]

McDONOUGH, James    Co. H, 4TN Cav.
At Morrison's Depot, he was badly wounded in the arm and it had to be amputated. Before the war, he lived on a farm at Zion Hill south of Ooltewah. His parents were Andrew and Sarah McDonough, natives of NC.

McDUNNER, J.    Co. K, 43TN
Enl. Oct. 12, 1862 at Ooltewah; deserted Nov. 4, 1862.

McELWEE, Capt. W. E.  Co. I, 26TN
Buried at Oak Grove Cem. in Rockwood, TN. Born 16 April 1835 and died 6 October 1929 married Martha Jane Brown. He was the grandson of James McElwee, a veteran of King's Mountain during the Revolutionary War.

McFARLAND, Lt. Chappel    19TN
Killed at Missionary Ridge in sight of his parents' home.

McFARLAND, Capt. C. D.    Co. G, 26TN;
2d Co. K, 1CSA
Age 45 in 1862, he enl. July 8, 1861 at Knoxville; captured at Fort Donelson, Feb. 16, 1862; imprisoned Johnson's Island, then Camp Chase; exchanged Nov. 8, 1862; 5'9" tall, red hair, and blue eyes.
In GA on recruiting service July 3, 1863. Promoted to 1st Lt. Aug. 27, 1863. Missing since Missionary Ridge.

McFARLAND, C. M.    Co. G, 26TN
Enl. July 8, 1861. Detailed as nurse at Bowling Green, KY; captured at Fort Donelson, Feb. 16, 1862, imprisoned at Camp Morton, IN. Elected 2Lt Oct. 13, 1862. Promoted to 1st Lt. Aug. 27, 1863. Missing since

Missionary Ridge.

McFARLAND, J. Anderson    Co. D., 12GA
Born Oct. 10, 1847 in Sequatchie, TN. Enl. in Co. D., 12GA Militia June, 1864. Res. in 1901 was Rossville, but died in Chattanooga Feb. 4, 1925 and bur. Forest Hills Cemetery. [NBFM2]

McFARLAND, John Buie    2d Co. K, 26TN; 2dCo. K, 1CSA (GA)
Enl. Nov. 11, 1862 at Chattanooga. On detached service Marietta, GA, July 20, 1863-Feb. 29, 1864. Severely wounded at Atlanta, July 22, 1864. Paroled at Thomasville, GA, May 15, 1865.

McFERRIN, Chaplain John P.  2TN (Robison's)
Born Williamson Co., TN. Enl. Apr. 1861. Methodist minister in Chattanooga, 1889.  Chaplin, NBF Camp, 1894-96. Moved to Louisville in 1896. [NBFM2,3]

McGARR, Owen    Louisiana Guards Battalion
Born 1836, Westmoreland Co., PA. Enl. Jan 7, 1864 in NC. Paroled 14 Apr, 1865 at Lynchburg, VA. Lawyer in Chattanooga Diplomatic service in Ecuador. Deeply involved in Cuban affairs prior to Spanish American War. NBF Camp. Catholic. Died at res. on High St., Jan. 14, 1906 and buried at Mt. Olivet. [CT 17 Jan. 1906; [NBFM2]

McGAUGHY, C. O.
Buried Forest Hills Cemetery. [FHR]

McGEE (McGHEE), J. M.  Co. A (H), 19TN
Killed at Murfreesboro, Dec. 31, 1862. [Mil. Annals of TN]

McGHEE, Daniel
Born 1847, TN, of TN parents. 1910 farmer in James Co. with wife Virginia (m 1890). [1890 James Co.]

McGHEE, Sgt. John    Co. K, 43TN
Born c1841 and a farmer at Zion Hill near Ooltewah, he was one of the sons of A.H. and Elizabeth Bryant McGhee to join the 43TN on Oct. 20, 1861, at Ooltewah. The brothers were present during early skirmishing at Chattanooga in 1862. Sgt. John McGhee was captured at Vicksburg, July 4, 1863. A.H. McGhee was a native of Granger Co., TN. The McGhees had 250 acres and a log six-room home. A. H. McGhee was a farmer and justice of the peace. He died several years before the war. His wife Elizabeth was from NC.

McGHEE, Orville    Co. K, 43TN

Born about 1829, he was a farmer in Ooltewah prior to the war and the oldest of the McGhee brothers, enl. Dec. 22, 1862 at Ooltewah. He was captured at Vicksburg, July 4, 1863. Prior to the war, he and his wife, Penelope, were living by his mother, Elizabeth Bryant McGhee, in the Zion Hill section of HC.

McGHEE, Samuel    Co. K, 43TN
Born 1846, he enl. with his older brothers Oct. 20 (Dec. 28?), 1861, at Ooltewah. He was captured at Vicksburg, July 4, 1863, and discharged at Christianburg, VA. Married (1892) Virginia W. Pierce. Presbyterian. Died May 19, 1927, age 83, at home in Apison where he had resided many yrs. Buried in Plowman's Cem. [TWP, 272; TP 7375; CT May 20, 1927; TCVQ]

McGHEE, William B.    Co. K of the 43TN
Born about 1833, he was another of the McGhee brothers enlisting at Ooltewah on Oct. 20, 1861. He was captured at Vicksburg on July 4, 1863. He and his wife, Sarah of NC, lived at Tyner prior to the start of the war.

McGILL, Charles  Co. D, 4th (12th) Georgia Cav.
Enl. Oct. 4, 1862 and died 18 Feb. 1863 at a camp in TN. He was a farm laborer living with his wife, Penelope, in Lookout Valley before the war.

McGILL (MAGILL), Walter Milton    Co. H, 4TN Cav.
Born 1841 in TN, son of W.M. and Isabella McGill of Chattanooga. Killed at Murfreesboro, Jan. 1, 1863. [1860HC]

McGRIFF (MCGRIFFIN), Jefferson (Jeff)    Barry's Btry.
Enl. April 4, 1862 at Chattanooga; teamster.

McGOWINGS, Robert C.
Born c1843 in Va. of Scottish parents. Res. in St. Elmo with wife Lillie (m. 1906). Shoe repairman. [1910HC]

McGUIRE, Reid    Co. F, 35TN
Enl. Nov. 1863 at Chattanooga; captured at Battle of Murfreesboro.

McJURKIN [McJUNKIN], Davis  Co. F, 19Tn
Enlisting at Loudon, he died on March 25, 1863, at Bell Hospital at Rome, GA from pneumonia. The effects he left were two suits of clothes and a pocketbook containing 10 cents.

McKAIG, Francis  Co. F, 34GA

Born Dade Co. and married (1874 in Bedford Co.) Elizabeth. Died 1901 in HC. [TWP, 218]

McKEEHAN, Cpl. A. H.    Co. B, 1TN Cav. (Carter's)
Enl. Aug. 7, 1861 at Cleveland. Present June, 1862.

McKEEHAN, Haywood Alexander
Born in Monroe Co., he married (1852 in HC) Mary C. Sylar. He died 1892 in Shelby Co. [TWP]

McKEEHAN, JAMES    2nd Co. K, 1st CSA Cav.; Co. B, 1TN Cav. (Carter's)
Enl. June 14, 1862 in HC, then joined 1TN Cav. Sick Bristol Hospital in October of 1864.

McKENZIE, B. F.  Co. L, 35TN
Enl. Jan. 9, 1862 in Chattanooga. Wounded at Chickamauga.

McKENZIE, William Morrison    Co. I, 5TN Cav.
Born 1846 in McMinn Co. and married (Meigs Co.) Sarah Fine Hudson. Baptist. Long time citizen of Athens although most of family lived in Chattanooga. Died Dec. 13, 1918 in St. Elmo and buried in Athens. [TWP, 202]

McKIBBENS, James  Co. D, 37TN
Born 1844. Enl. Sept. 1, 1861, Germantown, TN. Disch. Nov. 4, 1862, Knoxville, underage.

McKIBBON, Hugh A.  Co. I, 19TN
Born c1816 in Ireland, he was schoolteacher at Harrison with wife Sarah, also from Ireland. Enl. May 20, 1861, Knoxville. Surg. disch. July 1861.

McKINNEY, Cpl. John Vardaman    Co. G, 1TN (Turney's)
Born Dec. 4, 1841 in Fayetteville, TN where he enl. April, 1861: wounded Seven Pines. Captured Gettysburg. Released March 2, 1865. Res. Fayetteville until moving to Chattanooga in 1901. Employed by Chattanooga Bakery. Died at res. in East Lake, Nov. 22, 1923 and bur. Forest Hills Cem. [NBFM2]

McKINNEY, Patrick A.
Born c1827 in GA. 1870 retail grocer, wife Martha A.

McKINNEY, William    Co. A, 19TN
Enl. at Cumberland, KY, on Oct. 26, 1861. He died at Corinth, MS, April-May, 1862. Prior to the war, McKinney was a day laborer residing with the jailer, John Swaim. He was a native of SC. [Worsham, p. 48]

McKINZIE (McKINSEY), B. F.   Co. L, 36TN; Co. L, 35TN

Enl. Jan. 9, 1862 at Chattanooga; fought at Murfreesboro; wounded in hand at Chickamauga.

McLEMORE, William H.   Co. A, 1TN

Born 1845 in Tenn. From Tullahoma and the son of Sterling Jackson McLemore, he enl. in spring, 1861 in 1TN, then, following the 1862 reorganization, re-enl. in McClung's Battery, becoming sergeant and acting lieutenant. Fought at Fishing Creek, Shiloh, Vicksburg, Baton Rouge, then in East TN and southwest VA. In Battle of Greeneville and advance on Knoxville. Captured in fight at Morristown and not released until June, 1865. After the war, he worked in merchandising and the lumber business, then was appointed postmaster of Tullahoma. He came to Chattanooga where he served many years as clerk in the Read House. Episcopalian. Died Jan. 29, 1912, age 69, in Chattanooga and buried Forest Hills Cemetery.[1910HC]

McMAHON, John

Served in CSA cav. Res., 1920 in HC. [TP14,889]

McMAHON, Thomas   Co. B, 19th GA

Born May, 1820 in Mohal Parish, County Leftrian, Ireland, he emigrated to NY in 1845, then came to Chattanooga in 1852 where he prospered as a stonecutter. Enl. 1861: Bull Run, the Peninsula Campaign, Malvern Hill, Chantilly, the Wilderness, Cold Harbor, Fredericksburg, Spotsylvania, and Bentonville. He returned to Chattanooga where he died Feb. 25, 1901. [CT 26 Feb. 1901]

McMILLIN, Christopher [Clint] C.   Co. E, 4AL

Son of D. C. McMIllin. Memphis and Charleston RR. [NBFM7]

McMILLIN, G. H.   Co. I, 5th (McKenzie's) TN Cav.

Enl. July 19, 1862 at Shiloh. Age 18 on March 11, 1864. Captured Sept. 9, 1863 at Cumberland Gap. Was conscript and "wishes to take oath and remain in the north," but not released from prison until May 17, 1865 at Camp Douglas, IL.

McMILLIN, Thomas Paris   Co. A, 2TN Cav. Bn.

Born Feb. 20, 1844 in Chattanooga, son of D. C. McMillin and brother of Christopher C., David C. and W. W. Employed by E. TN and GA RR. Enl. at Cleveland, TN, 1861. After war returned to RR work: Alabama and Chattanooga and later N. C. & St. L. Methodist. Died in Atlanta, Oct. 14, 1930 and buried Forest Hills Cemetery. [NBFM6]

McMURRY, Christopher Columbus   Co. H, 15NC; 7Bn., NC Cav.

Born April 28, 1840 in Alamance Co., NC. Enl. at Graham, NC in Co. H, 15NC. Also served in Co. F, 2NC Bn. Wounded at Dam #1, Warick Creek near Yorktown, April 16, 1862. Joined Co. E, 7Bn., NC Cav on July 15, 1862. He transferred to Co. D, 6th Bn., NC Cav., Aug. 3, 1863 and was present through Nov., 1864 and "served against Sherman in 1865." Paroled as 2Lt. April 29, 1865 in Chattam Co., NC. Married (1865) Laura Taylor. To Chattanooga in 1898. Res. on 11th St. in 1901 and worked as a tinner. Died at his home on Missionary Ridge Oct. 27, 1918 and was buried in Citizens Cem. [CT 28 Oct. 1918; TWP, 201; NBFM2; Manarin, NC Soldiers]

McMURRY, Francis Goulding   Co. B, 23AL

Born Muscogee Co., GA, Feb. 27, 1842, son of a Presbyterian minister. First cousin of B. L. Goulding. Enl. summer, 1861 in Macon Co., AL in company which his father was captain. Vicksburg, Atlanta Campaign. Wife was Emma Alexander. To Chattanooga in 1905. Died at res. on Tucker St., Feb. 23, 1925 and buried CSA Cem. [1910HC;NBFM7; TP 13,139; CT Feb. 24, 1925]

McNABB, Aaron S.   Co. D, 37TN

Born 1843 in GA, son of Nancy. Day laborer in Chattanooga who enl. March 18, 1863 in Catoosa Co., GA. Captured Missionary Ridge, Nov. 25, 1863 and imprisoned Rock Island.

McNABB, Nathaniel Pinckney   Co. D, 36TN

Born 24 Feb. 1839, son of Alford W. and Susannah Ramsey McNabb who went from Carter County to Bradley County, TN. He was training to be a doctor when the war broke out. Enlisted at Cleveland Dec. 17, 1861 in Capt. John N. Dunn's Co. D. He was a doctor at Georgetown for several years after the war, then moved to Big Spring in Meigs County. Postmaster at Big Spring and helped incorporate the Big Spring Academy. Owned dry goods stores at Big Spring and Lamontville and a livery stable in Dayton. Married in 1867 to Mary Anna Matilda Soloman. He died 21 March 1918 and is buried at Beta Cem., Meigs County.[JW McNabb Family; CT March, 1919]

McNELLY, Patrick   Co. D, 4th (12th) Georgia Cav.

Born in Ireland about 1835. He farmed near Chattanooga until enl. Oct. 4, 1862. Captured at Missionary Ridge, Nov. 25, 1863 and sent to Louisville, Ky., where he was discharged on Dec. 8, 1863. [1860HC]

McNULTY, Peter Cutting   Co. B, Charleston German Arty.

Born 1847 Georgetown, SC and enl. there. After

war to Rome, GA where he lived until coming to Chattanooga in 1886 and opening a clothing store which he operated many years. Married (1874) Elizabeth B. Samuel. Baptist. Died Oct. 8, 1922 and buried in Rome. [TWP, 288; 1910HC; CT Oct. 9, 1922]

McPHERSON, Edgar P.   Co. F, 19NC
Born March 1, 1843 in Cheraw Dist., SC. Was student at time he enl. at Laurel Hill, NC, May 18, 1861. Present throughout until captured Spotsylvania Courthouse, May 12, 1864 and imprisoned Point Lookout, MD until transferred to Elmira, NY where he remained until paroled June 21, 1865. Living in Hill City. Died "in extreme poverty," April, 1896 (perhaps Feb. 23, 1906) and buried in Forest Hills Cem. [NBFM2; FHR; NBFM2; NC Regts. 6:373]

McREE, Lt. Robert Clark, Jr.   Co H, 4TN Cav.
(McLemore's)
Born 9 Aug. 1837 in TN. 1860 reading law under John L. Hopkins and res. in Hopkins household. He died 4 Dec. 1922 in Soddy, Tn. Married Mary Anderson. Charter member of NBF Camp, 1885. [UDC2 pg 365]

McROBERTS, Reuben M. Co. D, 37TN
Enl. Jan. 1, 1862, Knoxville. Prom. to 2d Sgt., Feb. 7, 1864. Captured on picket duty, July 20, 1864. near Atlanta and imprisoned Point Lookout.

McROY, Anderson   Co. D, 37TN
Enl. Jan. 28, 1863, Chattanooga. Absent sick from July 8, 1863. Deserted from hospital in Chattanooga and dropped from roll.

McROY, J. C.   Co. D, 37TN
Enl. 28 Jan. 1863, Chattanooga Conscript. Deserted from Catoosa Springs, 29 Jan. 1863.

McROY, Thomas J.   Co. D, 37TN
Enl. 28 Jan. 1863, Chattanooga Conscript. Deserted from Catoosa Springs, 29 Jan. 1863.

# N

NABORS, B. F.   Co. D, 4GA Cav.
James Simpson went as his substitute.

NABORS, Sgt. William H.   Co. D, 4GA Cav.
He enl. Oct. 4, 1862, at Chattanooga. He was reported absent without leave and supposed to be in the enemy lines on April 30, 1863.

NAGLE, David  Co. F, 35TN
Born c1818. Enl. Sept. 20, 1862, Chattanooga Wounded Chickamauga, Sept. 20, 1863 and hospitalized. Had returned by Jan. 1864.

NAIL, J. K.   Co. K, 43TN
Died in hospital in Loudon, TN during war.

NAIL, Lt. Nicholas Pope   Co. A, 19TN
Born 22 April 1822 in Bledsoe Co., son of John and Fannie Nail. He grew up in the Sequatchie Valley near Pikeville but had lived in Bradley County prior to coming to Chattanooga in 1853. His first wife was Susan, and his second wife was Georgie Anna Kemper of Giles Co. whom he married in 1856. He was a tinner by trade.

He took part in the campaigning in eastern KY under Gen. Zollicoffer in 1861 and in the Battle of Fishing Creek, where his regiment opened the battle by attacking a superior force. Originally a wagon master, Nail won a commission as 2nd Lt. and participated in the battles of Shiloh and those around Corinth in the late spring of 1862. In the battle of Baton Rouge, 5 Aug. 1862, he was shot through the spine and the left forearm. When the surgeon was unable to remove the ball. Nail had to submit his resignation and was replaced by another Hamilton Countian, Richard P. James. After he returned home to Missionary Ridge, he was arrested by Federal authorities, accused by a neighbor who said he was harboring Rebel spies in his home. He was sent to Nashville to prison but released. His home on Missionary Ridge was occupied by General Bragg who warned the Nail family to flee just prior to the Missionary Ridge fighting. The family refuged to Columbus, GA.

Nail had a stove and tinware business on lower Market Street after the war and served as city marshal. A charter member of the Walnut Street Christian Church, he survived until March 3, 1901. He was bothered by the pain of his war injuries and he had lost his eyesight and was an invalid at the time of his death.
[CSA Mil. Hist. 10:641-42; Worsham, p. 185; CT Jan. 19, 1917; JW Nail Family; TP 16, 176; 1860HC; UDC1 pg 308]

NAIL, William Stanford   Co. A, 5GA
Born in 1849 at Cleveland, Tenn., he was the son of Nicholas Pope Nail and his first wife, Susan. At age 16, he enl. the last year of the war after his family had refugeed to Columbus, GA. He was in the engagements in and around Atlanta and at Macon. He was at Savannah six weeks, then was captured and paroled in May 1865.

He returned to Chattanooga and married Mollie Gray in 1871. They resided at 1022 Peachtree St. in Ridgedale. He was a deputy sheriff in 1917 when he accidentally was shot in the foot and it had to be amputated. [JW Nail family, TP 16,176;1910HC]

NAPIER, William   Co. H, 37TN

NASSAUER, Lewis (Lee)   Co. K, 1TN (Field's)
Born March 4, 1839 in Germany. To TN. in 1857. Enl. May 2, 1861 in Pulaski, TN. Wounded in head at Cheat Mtn. Merchant in Chattanooga, 1904. [NBFM2; TP6231]

NATION, William Walker "Bill" Co. C, 16SC
Cav. Bn.
Born Spartanburg, SC, 1845. Enl. 1864. Paroled Kingston, GA, May 1865. To TN, 1902. Res. Chattanooga, 1910. [TP12,126]

NATIONS, J. A.   Co. G, 26TN; 2d Co. K,
1CSA (GA)
Enl. July 8, 1861. Knoxville. Sick in Cumberland City, Feb. 12, 1862. Detached to Sappers and Miners, May 19, 1863.

NATIONS, J. N.   Co. G, 26TN; 2d Co. K, 1CSA (GA)
Enl. Aug. 28, 1861. Knoxville. Sick in Cumberland City, Feb. 12, 1862. Detached to Sappers and Miners, May 19, 1863.

NAVE, Isaac   Co. K, 61TN MI
Born c1833, TN. Railroad boss at Zion Hill with wife Susan. [1860HC]

NAVE, William R.  Clark's Independent Cav. Co.
Born 1839 in TN, son of James and Martha of Chickamauga, TN.

NEAL, James R.   Co. K, 43TN
Enl. Oct. 17, 1861 at Ooltewah. Died March 28, 1862 in hospital at Loudon, TN. [Lindsley, 528; Aiken 1886:528]

NEAL, Ralph J. Sgt.  Co. E, 20TN
1903 in HC. [TP4995]

NELMS, 1st Lt. John W.   Co. D, 37th TN;
Co. A, 10KY Cav.
Born in McDonough, GA, June 19, 1838, he was the son of Allenson Nelms and Frances Melvina Williams. The family moved to Texas when he was an infant, then Henry Co., TN. He married (Dec. 1860) Emma Marlin in Nashville, and they resided in Chattanooga where he worked for the RR. He raised Co. D, but refused to serve as its captain. He fought at Fishing Creek, Shiloh and Corinth and then was discharged May 5, 1862. He raised another company, Co. A, 10th Kentucky Cavalry, and served under Gen.

John Hunt Morgan, participating in Morgan's last raid and the fights at Mount Sterling and Cynthiana. He left TN and settled in Campbell Co., GA which he represented in the legislature, then became "keeper" of the state penitentiary, then U.S. marshal for N. GA. He also served as mayor of West End, GA, county commissioner and sheriff of Fulton County. He married his second wife, Lillie Lee, in 1881. [Evans, CSA 8:881-883]

NELSON, David W.   Co. B, 1TN Cav. (Carter's).
Before the war, he lived with his parents, John and Rebecca Nelson, on a farm at Long Savannah. The Nelsons were from NC. David was born about 1842. He was assigned as a teamster, receiving pay of 25 cents per day.

NELSON, M. A.   Co. B, 11TN
Born Sept. 22, 1838 in Bedford Co., TN. Enl. May 12, 1861 and rose from Pvt. to 1st Sgt. Wounded at Jonesboro and Franklin. Saloon keeper in Chattanooga, 1890. Moved to Nashville, 1891. [NBFM2]

NETTER, Patrick   Co. A, 4TN Cav.; Co. F, 35TN
Enl. 35TN Oct. 21, 1862, Knoxville. Died in hospital in Chattanooga, Jan. 15, 1863.

NEVILLE, Benjamin Franklin   Co. A, 1TN;
4TN Cav.
Born Jan 19, 1844 in Franklin Co., TN. Enl. at Pelham May 10, 1861 in 1TN ANV. Also served in 4TN Cav. Wounded at Fort Donelson; captured near Resaca, GA and imprisoned Camp Douglas. Released May 17, 1865. Railroader and real estate in Chattanooga. Methodist. Died Nov. 24, 1925 in Dalhart, TX and buried there. [NBFM2,8]

NEWELL, Capt. J. D. S.  Co. C, 4LA Cav.; Bondurant's Co., 15LA
Enl. Aug. 29, 1861 in R.C. Woods 14LA Cav. Bn. "Distinguished officer" who fought at Manassas, Shiloh, Mansfield and Pleasant Hill. He died c1895. His wife, Nannie C. was born Nov. 2, 1844 in Clarksville, TN and died in Chattanooga July 18, 1915; buried in Vicksburg, MS. [CT July 19,1915]

NEWMAN, 1st Sgt. Thomas W. "Slade"  Co. F, 35TN
Born Feb. 26, 1825 in Knox Co., he was a merchant at Chattanooga until he enl. Nov. 19, 1862. Paroled Greensboro, May 1, 1865. Blue eyes, dark hair, fair complexion, and 5'10'. His wife was Phoebe. 1870 dry goods merchant in Chattanooga. Resided St. Elmo, 1891. NBF Camp. Died Dec. 25, 1915 at his home on Pearl St. and buried CSA Cem. [CT Dec. 26, 1915; NBFM 2,7]

NEWMAN, Sgt. - 1st Lt. William T.    Co. H, 2TN Cav. (Ashby's)
        Born June 23, 1843 in Knoxville, he was the son of Henry B. Newman. By 1860 young Newman was a law clerk in Chattanooga living in the household of lawyer John A. Minnis. When TN seceded Newman first joined the Lookout Rangers, then transferred to Co. H, 2TN Cav. in which he rose to 2nd Lt. Fought at Fishing Creek, Perryville, Murfreesboro and in Pegram's Kentucky raid in which he was wounded and captured. Imp. Camp Chase and Johnson's Island. After his exchange, Newman fought at Chickamauga, Wheeler's Tennessee raid and the Atlanta campaign, losing his arm in the battle of Jonesboro, July 30, 1864. After the war, he returned to Knoxville, then moved to Atlanta to resume the study of law. He became city attorney for Atlanta in 1871 and in 1886 was appointed federal judge for N. GA. He married Fanny Alexander Percy. [Evans, CSA, 8:888-889]

NEWTON, Judson J.    Co. K, 43TN
        Born 1846 in McMinn Co., he enl. Oct. 17, 1861 at Ooltewah; captured at Vicksburg, July 4, 1863; paroled and discharged Sept. 21, 1863 for being under age. Dark complexion, black hair, black eyes, and 5'10" tall.

NICHOL, J. W.
        Captain of cavalry, CSA. Former Chattanooga Died at 76 yrs. in Murfreesboro, TN, Sept. 14, 1915. [CT Sept. 15, 1915]

NICHOLDSON, B. A.
        [NBFM1]

NICHOLS, Jasper N.    Co. K, 4GA Cav. (Avery's)
        Born in Catoosa Co., GA in 1844. Enl. Oct. 25, 1862. Listed as having deserted Aug. 17, 1864, but claimed he had become ill in July, 1864 and was confined at hospitals until end of war. To TN about 1875. In 1906 residing at Apison, James Co. Farmer in James, 1910 with wife Mary J. (m. 1869). [TP8060]

NICHOLS, J. S.
        Resided near Parker's Gap. Methodist. Mason. Died March, 1916, age 70, and buried West View Cem. [CT March 15, 1916]

NICHOLS, Jack
        Born 1828, Ark. 1910 res. household of niece Maggie Carter on Curtiss St.

NICHOLSON, James V. (R.?)    Co. K, 43TN
        Enl. Oct. 17, 1861 at Ooltewah; deserted March 3, 1862.

NICKOLL, Isaac D.
        Died Nov. 1, 1906 in Ridgedale, 67 years old. Buried Christiana, TN.

NIGHT, 3rd Lt. Meritt    Co. H, 37TN
        Born 1844; enl. Sept. 1, 1861 at Knoxville; under arrest Jan. 10, 1863-April, 1863; deserted Sept. 9, 1863. Took USA oath Sept. 23, 1863; enl. in 11KY Cav., USA; dark complexion, blond hair; brown eyes; and 6'1 ½ tall."

NISBET, Col. James Cooper
        Born Macon, GA, Sept. 26, 1839, he lived many years in Trenton, GA. Col. 66GA Inf. and Capt. 21 GA. Nisbet was wounded at Cold Harbor and at Sharpsburg. Captured Atlanta, July 22, 1864, imprisoned Johnson's Island, and not paroled until Sept. 1865. See Nisbet's Memoirs, Four Years on the Firing Line. He married Mary E. Young and later (1882) Louise W. Bailey, a "well known author of adventure stories," who attended Christ Church. Also married Jennie Cooper (died 1918). JCN to Chattanooga 1905 and worked in office of Acme Kitch. Furniture Co. Presbyterian. He died at his residence in Chattanooga May 20, 1917 and was buried in CSA Cem. [CT May 21, 1917; Louise's obit-CT May 24, 1918; TWP, p. 193; NBFM2; TP13,194]

NIX, Capt. Joe John    Co. B, 31AL Inf.
        Born in Wetumpka, AL, July 24, 1839. Married (1863) Maggie C. Wisdom in HC. Died Jan. 16, 1900, Fort Payne, AL and buried in Citizens Cemetery.

NOLAN, Robert
        [NBFM4]

NOLAND, Dr. James F.    Co. K, 5SC Cav.
        Born Union Dist., SC, 1837. Enl. 1861; paroled Greensboro, NC, April 26, 1865. Married Ione Sadler (Oct. 1865). To TN in 1898. Died Feb. 17, 1907 in Rossville (P.O. Rossville but res. in HC) and buried CSA Cem., Chattanooga. [CT Feb. 27, 1907; TP7308]

NOONE, John J.    Fisher's Arty. Co.
        Born c1842 in Ireland. Married Mary S. Soon after the war employed by N & C Railroad as engineer and remained one until his death, April 8, 1914 at his home on West 14th. Buried Mt. Olivet. [CT April 9, 1914]

NORMAN, Dr. J. W.
        Res. 1913 in Denver, CO. [TP 14,159]

NORMAN, John    Co. I, 19TN
        Born Oct. 16, 1843 in HC, son of Joshua and Nancy, who came from NC to HC in late 1830's. Res.

1860 in household of J.H. Todd. Enl. Apr. 1861 in Walker Co., GA. Disch. July 23, 1862, underage. Enl. again July 10, 1863, Chattanooga. Wounded at Kennesaw Mountain by piece of shell which disabled him for remainder of war and from which he suffered until death. Illiterate. Married (1869) Rhoda J. Brown and died Oct. 29, 1905, HC; buried Concord Baptist Church. [TWP, p. 24; TP2517]

NORMAN, W. J.     Co. D, 4GA Cav.
        Enl. Oct. 4, 1862, at Chattanooga.

NORMAN, William    Co. I, 19TN
        Son of Joshua and Nancy of HC and older brother of John. Enl. May 20, 1861, Knoxville. Deserted, then "returned from desertion," April 15, 1863. Captured at Chickamauga, Sept. 20, 1863 and sent to Louisville, where he took USA oath, Oct. 14, 1863 and enl. in 11KY Cav. (USA). Married Elizabeth Cogburn and they lived in Tyner.

NORMAN, Sgt. William C. (J.?)    Co. K, 43TN
        He enl. Oct. 17, 1861, at Ooltewah. He died April 3, 1862, in Knoxville [Brooks gives death date as March 4, 1862]. Before the war, he and his wife, Sarah J., had a farm at Limestone north of Harrison. His parents were Henry and Judith Norman, who were from NC. William Norman was born about 1838. [Lindsley, 528]

NORMENT, Sgt. William Thomas    1st Co.,
                Washington Artillery of New Orleans
        Born Nov. 23, 1838 in Rapides, LA and res. of Shreveport. Enl. May 26, 1861, 1WA. Captured at Appomatox Apr. 9, 1865 as Sgt. Paroled at Jackson, MS in May, 1865. He relocated in Chattanooga, becoming a bookkeeper and a member of NBF Camp. Died here June 26, 1890, having been nursed by J. N. Payne, "both having belonged to the Washington Artillery." Buried CSA Cem. [NBFM2]

NORTON, John Columbus    Co. B, 39GA
        Born Whitfield Co., GA, Mch. 28, 1842. After war was Ordinary of Whitfield; then moved to Atlanta and worked with IRS, then to Dalton and finally to Chattanooga in 1903. Bookkeeper, wholesale tobacco, 1910. Married Annie Sarah Wert (1877). Died in Chattanooga Oct. 27, 1918 and buried West View Cem. [1910HC; CT Oct. 27, 1918]

NUNLEY, Cpl. H. J.    Co. L, 36TN
        Enl. Jan. 9, 1862, at Chattanooga.

# O

OAKMAN, Robert Harper    Co. D, 2GA; 26GA
        Born on family estate "Longstaple," 1827, three miles from Barnwell, SC. Married Emily Rebecca Hagood (1862, Augusta, GA). ANV, then with Army of Tennessee as asst. Surgeon. Atlanta Campaign. Resigned because of illness and returned home "a shadow of the man he once was." As Sherman's army approached, refugeed with two family slaves. Dr. Oakman moved to Chattanooga after war and died here in 1884. [TWP 5919]

O'BRIAN, John    Co. F, 35TN
        Enl. Oct. 4, 1862; served as clerk at Brig. Gen. Lucius E. Polk's headquarters; captured at Franklin, Nov. 30, 1864 and imprisoned at Point Lookout, MD.

O'CONNER, John    Co. D, 37TN
        Born 1844 in Canada, son of John and Hanorah. Bar keeper at Chattanooga when enl. Sept. 1, 1861, Knoxville. Prom. 2nd Cpl. May, 1862. Disch. Nov. 4, 1862 underage.

OGLE (OGLES), George    Co. D, 37TN
        Enl. Sept. 16, 1862 at Whitesides; transferred to dismounted cav. July 22, 1863; deserted Oct. 19, 1863 at Missionary Ridge.

OGLE, James    Co. H, 37TN
        Born 1841; enlisted Oct. 14, 1861 at Ooltewah; deserted Sept. 21, 1863; fair complexion, dark hair, gray eyes, and 5'6" tall. Took USA oath Dec. 9, 1863.

OGLE, Cpl. John    Co. H, 37TN
        Before the war, he was a day laborer at Chattanooga, residing with his wife, Rebecca. He was born about 1837. Enl. Nov. 20, 1862, at Chattanooga. Deserted Sept. 21, 1863, captured Nov. 28, 1863 and imprisoned at Rock Island, IL. He enl. in the USN and was sent to rendezvous May 23, 1864. [1860 HC; RI ledger]

OGLE, Laurence    Co. H, 37TN
        Born 1846, HC. Res Chattanooga 1860. Enl. Nov. 17, 1861 at Knoxville; conscript; 5'5" tall, black hair, blue eyes, and fair complexion.

OGLE, Like    Co. H, 37TN
        Born DeKalb Co., AL; enl. Nov. 18, 1861 at Chattanooga; died Feb. 28, 1862 at Carthage, TN.

OLDHAM, David    Co. E, 3TN Cav. Bn.

************************************************************************

Born Meigs Co., 1845. Enl. Aug. 5, 1861. Fought at Fishing Creek. Res. Chattanooga, 1907. [TP8728]

OLIVER, Isaac    Co. B, 5TN Cav.

Born c1836, son of Wesley and Elizabeth Oliver. Enl. Aug. 11, 1861, at Chattanoooga. Lived before and after war at Harrison, wife Sarah E.

OLIVER, James    Co. B, 5TN Cav.

Born about 1840, he was a day laborer at Chattanooga prior to the war. He enl. on Aug. 11, 1861, at Chattanooga

OLIVER, John

Born c1842, son of Wesley and Elizabeth Oliver.

O'NEAL, David    Co. H, 2TN Cav. (Ashby's)

He was among those losing his horse in the retreat from Fishing Creek in KY. He served the army as a butcher. Detached by Gen. Ledbetter as asst. in Commissary Dept. at Chattanooga. Absent sick July 1862. Absent without leave after March 1, 1864. 5'10" tall with red hair.

O'NEAL, Phillip Sherrill    Co. E, 3CSA Cav.

Born Madison, GA, July 7, 1836. Enl. in Cleveland, TN in 1861. Twice married. 2) Annie McBride. Had lived in HC since 1875. Baptist. Died Oct. 19, 1920, 84 yrs, at home in Jersey (community within present city limits of Chattanooga; 7 miles east of downtown near Lake Hills). and buried in Tyner Cem. [CT Oct. 20, 1920; NBFM2; TP7849]

O'NEAL, Zachariah    Co. D, 37TN

Enl. Nov. 18, 1861 at Knoxville; deserted Oct. 26, 1863 at Missionary Ridge; took USA oath Nov. 25, 1863; fair complexion, sandy hair, blue eyes, and 6' tall.

ONLEY, Edward W.    Co. G, 3TN Mounted Inf.
(Lillard's)

Born 1840 in Bradley Co., he married (1861 in McMinn Co.) Malissa D. Randolph and died 1892 in HC. [TWP, p. 18]

O'REAR, Sims Kelley    Co. D, 17TN

Born Winchester, TN, Nov. 25, 1846, son of Ben and Margaret Sublet O'Rear. Conductor and engineer with NC&St.L RR, since 1860. Also alderman in Chattanooga. Married (1886) Alice Handman; married (1898) Fannie Dempsey. Died at his home, Brelsford Heights, North Chattanooga, Dec. 28, 1927 buried Forest Hills Cem.

ORR, Aquilla Q.    Co. F, 3TN Mounted Inf. (Lillard's)

Born Sweetwater, TN, 1837 of Virginia parents. Enl. 1861. Wounded Vicksburg and again in hip at Cumberland, OH, during Morgan's raid. To Chattanooga in 1899. Died Nov. 11, 1912, age 71, and buried Forest Hills Cemetery. [CT 12 Nov. 1912 ; TP9024; 1910HC]

OSBORN, Cpl. John    Clark's Independent Cav. Co.
Enl. Aug. 31, 1862 at Chattanooga

OSBORNE, Capt. --------

Commanded Osborne's Scouts; killed in action.

OSBORNE, Lt. Hill    Co. H, 36TN

O'SHIELDS, John    Clark's Independent Cav. Co.
Enl. Aug. 31, 1862 at Chattanooga.

OSLLING, Eric

Born 1843, TN. Res. 1910 on Elizabeth Ave. with wife Mary. Carpenter. Died July 9, 1913 and buried Forest Hills Cemetery. [1910HC; CT July 10, 1913]

OSMENT, Joseph S.    Co. A, 2TN Cav. Bn.

Born in Davis Co., NC. Enl. May 10, 1861 in Cleveland. Forage master. After battle of Murfreesboro, he was captured. His health broke, and he was transferred to Commissary Dept. Surrendered at Macon, GA. Physician and traveling insurance agent living in Chattanooga c1890.Married Mary L. Bates. Died Aug. 12, 1909 in Birmingham and buried in Forest Hills Cemetery. Brother-in-law of Creed F. Bates. [FHR; NBFM2]

OTT, William Anderson    Capt., Co. F, 23TN

Born Dec. 27, 1838 in Rutherford Co., TN, he enl. in the spring of 1861 in Co. F, 23TN. After the regiment's reorganization he became Captain of Co. H. Badly wounded at Perryville and captured, remained imprisoned until April, 1863. Wounded again at Chickamauga and resigned his commission because of disability and was hospitalized for most of the remainder of the war. Living in Hill City in 1902. Died at home on Boyleston St. May 7, 1919 and buried CSA Cem. [NBFM2; TP14192; 1910HC]

OVERBY, Nicholas    Co. G, 1GA Cav.
[NBFM1]

OWENBEY, Jonathan W.    Co. C, 1GA State Troops

Born June 29, 1825 in White Co., GA and represented Catoosa Co. in GA Legislature. Married Cassie Nixon in Milledgeville July 3, 1859. Enl. April, 1864. Newspaper carrier in Chattanooga; res. on 8th St. NBF Camp. Died in Chattanooga June 17, 1904 and buried Liberty Church graveyard near Grayville, GA. [CT June 18, 1904; NBFM2,4; TP5035]

OWENS, 2nd Lt. George W.    Co. H;, 26TN; 2d Co. I, 1CSA (GA)
     Born c1830 in SC. 5'9" tall, light hair, and blue eyes. Enl. July 8, 1861, Knoxville. Elected 2nd Lt., Nov. 19, 1861. Captured Fort Donelson, Feb. 16, 1862 and imprisoned Johnson's Island and Camp Chase. Exch. and sent to Vicksburg for exchange. Resigned on surgeon's certificate (weakness of eyes), Jan 14, 1863. Remained at home 15 months and then conscripted. Captured in Walker Co., Oct. 18, 1864 and forwarded to Louisville, Nov. 21, 1864. Disch. to Johnson's Island, Nov. 28, 1864.

OWENS, Jesse    Co. D, 1CSA (GA)
     Born July 12, 1838 in Campbell Co., TN. Enl. Sept. 1861 in Ringgold, GA. in Co. I, 27GA, afterwards Co. D, 1CSA. Became cpl. Wounded at Kennesaw Mountain, June 18, 1864. Died April 4, 1915 in East Lake and buried Graysville, GA. [CT April 5, 1915; NBFM2; TP6232]

OWINGS, William L.     Co. H, 26TN; 2d Co. I, 1CSA (GA)
     Born c1819, SC. Day laborer at Chattanooga with wife M. E., and seven children. Enl. Aug. 6, 1861, Knoxville. Sick in hosp. and left sick at Russellville, KY, Feb. 9, 1862. In Howard's Cav., Dec. 31, 1862. Disch. from 1CSA having joined another command.

OYLER, George Washington    Co. H, 21GA
     Born DeKalb Co., GA. Enl. July 16, 1861. ANV: Second Manassas, Sharpsburg, Chancellorsville, Gettysburg, Plymouth, NC. Captured at Winchester, Sept. 19, 1864 and imprisoned Point Lookout. Married (1871) Sarah C. Davis. To TN in 1893. Living in Retro in 1896. Died in HC. [TWP, p. 63; TP7912]

# P

PACHETT, John    Co. H, 4TN Cav.
     Killed in Wheeler's Raid, 1864

PACK, Jeremiah "Jerry"    Co. D, 1CSA (GA)
     Born Catoosa Co., GA, 1845. Fought at Jonesboro. "Badly injured by innoculation from vaccination" and hospitalized at Macon. His home for

many years was Catoosa Co., GA. Married Margaret. To TN Nov. 1910. He worked in Chattanooga as a railroad crossing watchman and died here Feb. 8, 1918. Buried Boynton, GA. [CT Feb. 9, 1918; TP14282]

PADGETT, Hicks    Co. I, 50NC
     Born 1839 in Rutherford Co., NC, he married (1860) Caroline Pintuff. He died 1894 in HC. [TWP, p. 84]

PADGETT, Joshua    Co. D, 37TN
     Born 1835. Enl. Ooltewah, 1 Sept. 1861. Deserted Chattanooga Nov. 5, 1862.

PALMER, Albion W.  Co. E, 31GA; Surgeon 17GA
     Born at Washington, GA, May 5, 1845, son of John T. Palmer. He joined Co. E, 31GA in 1863 at Orange Court House, VA and served in the regimental band. As a staff member, he served Gens. John B. Gordon and C. A. Evans and took part in the battles of the Wilderness, Spotslyvania, Cold Harbor, Early's Maryland and Shenandoah campaigns, and the defense of Petersburg. After the war, he entered the Univ. of TN and studied dentistry. He practiced in Chattanooga and acted as instructor in dentistry in various colleges. Married (1) Elizabeth Barbour [born 9 Nov. 1856], (2) Elizabeth A. Brause. Life ins. agent, 1910. Asst. Surgeon, NBF Camp, 1894. Died Jan. 17, 1918 in Chattanooga and buried in CSA Cem. [CTJan. 18, 1918; GHT, p. 977; NBFM2; TP15096; 1910HC]

PALMER, Mrs. Ella
     Born in NC and spent girlhood in Hiawatha, GA. Her husband fought in Mexican War. Citizen of Chattanooga during Civil War. Served as matron and "organized the hospital corps of the Army of TN and remained at its head during the Civil War. She discovered a valuable soda mine in Lake County, CO and immediately began studying and became known as an expert on ores. Moved to CO about 1889 and died in Boulder, CO Nov. 7, 1909. Daughter was Mrs. Charles Hart of Chattanooga. [CT Nov. 9, 1909]

PALMER, William W.  Co. E, 31GA, 3GA Cav.
     Born Washington, GA, Jan. 13, 1843. Clerk in Chattanooga, 1887, died Aug. 30, 1912 at his home on East 9th St. and buried Forest Hills Cem. Wife was Annie M. [CT Aug. 31, 1912; NBFM1,7; 1910HC]

PARK, 4th Sgt. Lunsford Yandell    Co. F, 39GA
     Enl. July 10, 1861. Fought at Baker's Creek, Champion Hill and Vicksburg. Captured and exchanged. Later fought at Missionary Ridge. A clerk in Chattanooga in 1887, he is shown as a RR man in 1901. [applications for NBF Camp]

PARKER, Benjamin    Barry's Btry.
        Born c1830 in GA. Enl. April 4, 1862 at Chattanooga; deserted Feb. 7, 1863 from guard house in Canton, MS [Brown's Diary]. Res. 1870 in Chattanooga, wife was Martha E.

PARKER, George Press    Barry's Btry.
        Born Aug. 15, 1843 in McMinn Co. Enl. July 21, 1862 at Chattanooga as substitute for Robert McCormack; captured April 4, 1865 by 1st Brig., 2 Cav. Div., USA. Carpenter and odd jobs in Soddy, 1910. [TP8192; 1910HC]

PARKER, H. L.    Gen. J. P. McCown's Escort
        Flagman, Nashville & Chattanooga RR, 1888. Died June 14, 1892. [NBFM1]

PARKER, Hiram P.  Co. F, 7TN
        Born Wilson Co., TN, 1839. Enl. 1861. 1903 res. Chattanooga. Died Oct. 3, 1910, age 71, at home in East Lake;  buried CSA Cem. [TP5384; CT Oct. 4, 1910]

PARKER, J. L.  Co. G, 36TN
        Born c1833, day laborer living in Chattanooga with wife Elizabeth, 1860.

PARKER, James H (G.)  Co. I, 7KY
        Born in Fulton Co., KY. Enl. July 1861. Surr. with Forrest at close of war. Fish and oyster business in Chattanooga 1896. [NBFM2]

PARKER, 1st Sgt. John Henegar    Barry's Btry.
        Born Cleveland, TN, Jan. (June) 4, 1839, son of George T. and Teressa Thornberry Parker. Educ. at old Oak Grove Academy and Bradley Co. Public Schools. Enl. Oct 2, 1861, Knoxville; QM Sgt.; surrendered at Citronelle, AL and paroled Meridian, May 11, 1865. Married 15 April 1873 Mary Kezie Smith [b. 4 Jun. 1839 in Cleveland, TN and d. 2 Mar 1895 in Chattanooga, TN]. Moved from Cleveland where he was asst. cashier to Chattanooga in 1893 where he was a clerk. Died March 2, 1895. [NBFM7; CSA Patriot; UDC3 pg 175]

PARKER, Joseph  Co. A, 5TN Cav.
        Res. of HC. Enl. Aug. 24, 1861 at Camp Cummings. Age 30 on March 11, 1864 roll. Present on rolls through 1864. Captured at Wallace's Crossroads, July 15, 1862. Paroled at Cumberland Gap, July 23, 1862. Detailed as brigade teamster, Sept. 20, 1862. Captured April 23, 1863.

PARKER, Joseph Peler "Joe"  Co. D, 1CSA (GA)
        Born 1840 in Monroe Co., TN. Moved from

Ooltewah in 1859 to Ringgold, GA where he was clerk in dry goods store. Enl. 1861. During battles on Mobile Bay in charge of telegraph and signals at Fort Blakely. Paroled at Meridian, MS. Could not safely return to his father's home in East TN so he located in Butler Co., AL where he remained for two years before returning to TN. Res. 1906 in Ooltewah. Atty. at Law in James, 1910. Died April 6, 1917. [TP8559; 1910 James Co.]

PARKER, Lorenzo D.        Co. I, 19TN
        Enlisting at Knoxville, he went with the troops to Cumberland Gap, VA, where he died on Feb. 24, 1862 of typhoid. Lorenzo Parker was one of the many children of Allen Parker of Lookout Valley. He was born in 1844. [Worsham, p. 49: died from sickness at Corinth, April-May, 1862.]

PARKER, Patrick  Co. A, 47AL
        Born Jan. 9, 1841 in Walton Co., GA, son of Luke Parker. Enl. May 1861. Wounded at Chickamauga, Sept. 20, and later at Petersburg. To TN c1885. In 1901 listed as Chattanooga res., a peddler without property. "The old man will not beg and tries to make himself independent." Methodist. Died May 7, 1923 at home in East Lake and buried in CSA Cem. [CT May 8, 1923; TP3240; TCVQ].

PARKER, Robert    Co. H, 4TN Cav.

PARKER, Tandy M.  Co. I, 19TN
        Born 1842 in TN, son of Allen and Dovey, he joined his brother, Lorenzo, in Co. I, and also went to Cumberland Gap, VA. Died Feb. 12, 1862 of typhoid pneumonia.

PARKER, William    Co. D, 4GA Cav.
        Born 1829 in GA. Farm laborer in Chattanooga with wife Lucinda. Enl. Oct. 4, 1862, at Chattanooga. He began another enlistment at Kingston on Nov. 1, 1862. [1860HC]

PARKES, Lt. Thomas  Co. H, 20TN
        Born April 16, 1840 in Williamson Co., he was the son of Thomas and Elizabeth Field Parkes. He married S. E. Smith of Nashville. After the war, he was a cotton commission merchant at Nashville and opened the Daisy Coal Mines on lands that his father had purchased thirty years before the Civil War. [GHT, pp. 980-81]

PARKERSON (PARKINSON), 2Lt William C. (M.?)
                Co. K, 43TN
        Born in Alabama c1826, son of Peter and Rebecca Parkerson. His mother was from VA. Prior to the war, he had a farm at Ooltewah with his wife, Mary

A. Enl. Oct. 17, 1861, at Ooltewah.

PARKS, John M.    Co. F, 3d Mounted Inf.
        Born Coker Creek, Monroe Co., TN, 1834.
Enl. Apr. 1861. First Manassas, Vicksburg. Captured
Black River, May 17, 1863 and imprisoned Point
Lookout. Res. Chattanooga, 1908. [TP 10, 025]

PARMETER, Cpl. W. H.    Clark's Independent Cav.
Co.
        Enl. Aug. 31, 1862 at Chattanooga; captured
June 27, 1863 at Manchester.

PARRISH, J. B. M.    Co. H, 26TN
        Born c1842. Enl. July 8, 1861., Knoxville. Left
sick in hospital, Nashville, Nov. 1861.

PARRISH, Thomas J.
        Born 1846, Bunceton, MO. 1910 res. Cedar St.
with wife Jennie (m. 1874). Physician. To Chattanooga
c1899. Died April 24, 1911 at his home on Oak St.
[1910HC]

PARROTT, John V.    Co. I, 63TN
        Born Oct. 3, 1841, in Cocke Co., TN. Enl. Oct.
1, 1862. Res. Chattanooga in 1905. [TP7382]

PARTIN, George A.    Co. H, 26TN
        Enl. 6 Aug. 1861 at Knoxville. Died in
Nashville, Jan. 28, 1862. Wife was Sarah A.

PARTON (PARTAIN), John B.    Barry's Btry.
        Enl. Feb. 1, 1863 at Knoxville; paroled May
11, 1865 at Meridian, MS. Wounded at Spanish Fort.

PARTON, Robert    Co. B, 59TN
        Born 1830 in Buncombe Co., NC. Enl. 1861.
Captured Vicksburg and paroled. Married (1870)
Susan. To East Lake, Dec. 1905. Illiterate. Unemployed
1910. [TP7981; 1910HV]

PARTON, Wilson    4TN Cav.

PASLEY, William M.    Barry's Btry.
        Enl. May 14, 1862 at Chattanooga.

PATTERSON, A. J.
        [NBFM1]

PATTERSON, Jacob Alfred Newton  Co. C, 2TN Cav.
        Born June 17, 1838, son of Lewis and Mary
Young Pearson Patterson and brother of James Lewis
and William Douglas Patterson, J.A.N. Patteron was a
farmer and a teacher at the Sale Creek Academy. He
married (1860) Elizabeth Samantha Coulter, who died

in 1877, and Margaret H. Wallace (1879). School teacher
a number of years. In 1885 he opened a general store in
Sale Creek. He became a leader in the Democratic Party
and was a Presbyterian elder for sixty years. Mason. Died
Nov. 6, 1927, age 90, at his home in Sale Creek within
half a mile of his birthplace. Buried in family cemetery
at Sale Creek. [1910HC; GHT, p. 981; CT Nov. 7.27]

PATTERSON, James    Co. B, 1TN Cav. (Carter's)
        A native of England, he was a stone cutter
living in Chattanooga when the war broke out. He had
gone south in December of 1856 and arrived in HC on
Oct. 11, 1860. He enl. Aug. 7, 1861, at Cleveland. He
later claimed he had been forced into the Confederate
forces after being told he would be imprisoned if he did
not join. He fought in a battle at Somerset, KY., and was
on duty with the regimental surgeon. He was discharged
on Aug. 6, 1863, on account of his age. When Grant's
forces reached Chattanooga, Patterson gave himself up to
the provost marshal. He was sent to Nashville and on to
Louisville, KY. Patterson took the oath of allegiance after
going into custody. He was transferred to the Myrtle
Street Prison in St. Louis, MO, arriving there on Jan. 2,
1863. Patterson was held for a year at the St. Louis
prison, then was released in January of 1864 on condition
that he stay north of the Ohio River. Patterson had a dark
complexion, dark eyes, black hair, and stood 5'10" tall.

PATTERSON, James Lewis  Co. D, 1TN Cav. (Carter's)
        Born in 1843, he was a son of Lewis and Mary
Young Pearson Patterson of Sale Creek. Enl. March 25,
1862, at Knoxville. He was captured Jan. 27, 1864, at
Dandridge, Tenn., and was imprisoned at Camp Chase,
then at Rock Island. He had a dark complexion, light
hair, gray eyes, and was 5'11" tall. He married Eleanor
Wadsworth.

PATTERSON, L. A.
        Born 1845, TN, son of Lewis and Mary P.
Patterson. Res. 1910 in household. of his brother Jacob;
farm laborer. [1910HC]

PATTERSON, William Douglas    Co. D, 1TN Cav.
        Born in 1840, he was also son of Lewis and
Mary Young Pearson Patterson of Sale Creek. Enl. Sept.
16, 1861, at Knoxville. He was first married to Katherine
Thatcher, and his second wife was Eliza. He had a fair
complexion, dark hair, blue eyes, and stood 5'9" tall. He
died in 1895.

PATTILLO, S. D.    Co. D, 4GA Reserves
        Born 1847 in Cobb Co., GA. Paroled at Albany,
GA in May, 1865. Carpenter in Ridgedale, 1890.
[NBFM2]

PAUL, Franc M.          Newspaper publisher
Born in 1832 in Wadesboro, NC. Paul was a pioneer newspaperman. Before the war he worked on the staff of Brownlow's Whig, during the war he published the Chattanooga Daily Rebel using the old offices of the Chattanooga Advertiser at Sixth and Market. It was produced for circulation in the army and to Southern adherents. The first issues were run off on an old hand press, but later a power press was secured from Rome, Ga. After the office was shelled, he was able to move his equipment south on the Western and Atlantic Railroad. Paul had been clerk of the Senate in the Thirty-Third Tennessee General Assembly when he was directed by Gov. Isham Harris to move the state archives from Nashville to Chattanooga. After arriving here by a circuitous route, he decided to set up the Daily Rebel. Paul later returned to Chattanooga to become publisher of the Chattanooga Daily Dispatch in 1877. He also was the state printer. Paul left Chattanooga and returned to Nashville where he served as state printer. He died in Nashville in 1898. [JW, Chattanooga Story; CT April 28, 1898]

PAUL, Wylie B.   31TN
Born Knox Co., 1836. Farmer near Riceville before the war. Baptist. Enl. March, 1862. 1903 res. of Sherman Heights. Died April 22, 1914 and buried at Riceville. [CT April 23.14; TP5295]

PAYNE, Sgt. E. C., Jr.   1st Co., Washington
Artl. of New Orleans
Shown as member of above battery in 1862 and discharged before end of war by order of Secretary of War. Member of NBF Camp. Died in Chattanooga in 1890.

PAYNE, J. W.
Born 1841 in IN, he married (1870) Emeline Malone. Died May 6, 1917 at res. on Manning St. and buried Chattanooga Memorial Park in White Oak Cem. [TWP, p. 192; CT 7 May 17]

PAYNE, John Newton    1st Co., Washington
Artl. of New Orleans
Born May 13, 1839 at Versailles in Woodford Co., KY. Age 22 and married when he enl. May 26, 1861 in New Orleans. Transferred to Byrnes Bn., Morgan's Cav., March 14, 1864, and was with Morgan when he was killed. Married (1869) Lisette Walker. Disch. April 4, 1865 at Appomattox. Died in Chattanooga, Feb. 5, 1892 and buried CSA Cem. [TWP, p. 76; Booth, 3:88; NBFM2; NBFM1,7; CSA Patriot]

PAYNE, Lemuel S.   Co. B, 5GA; Co. D, 1CSA (GA)
Born 1848 in GA. Enl. May 1, 1862, Ringgold,

GA. Sick in quarters, Oct. 31, 1862. Present Aug. 31, 1863. Married (1869 in HC) Elizabeth Jane James. Res. 1910 in Soddy. Died 1911 in HC. [TWP, p. 109; TP11937]

PAYNE, Lindsay    Co. C, 40MS
Born Dec. 17, 1833 in Hall Co., GA. Served in KY unit, then enl. May, 1862 at Goodman's Station, MS. Captured at Vicksburg. Paroled July 10, 1863. To Chattanooga in 1873 and became a clerk in confectionary. Member NBF Camp, 1895. Mason. Res. in household of son on Palmetto St., 1910. Died Jan. 3, 1913 in Hill City and buried Cartersville, GA. [CT Jan. 4, 1913; NBFM2; 1890VetCensus; TP11114; 1910HC]

PAYNE, William    Clark's Independent Cav. Co.
Enl. July 10, 1863 at Chattanooga; deserted Nov. 25, 1863 near Chattanooga.

PAYNE, Capt. William C.   Co. I, 28TN
Born Aug. 9, 1831 in Smith Co., TN, son of John and Eunice Chambers Payne. He was educated at Irving College, Warren Co., TN and at Cumberland Univ. at Lebanon, TN where he obtained his degree in law in 1855. After a year in the west, he returned to TN and began his practice in White Co., being elected attorney-general for the 16th Circuit in 1858. He enl. as a private in the 28TN, and fought at Fishing Creek. After an absence due to illness, he joined the 4TN Cav. in Feb. 1863. He was captured and imprisoned at Alton, IL until his exchange in Aug., 1863. He became a staff officer under Gen. George G. Dibrell and fought at Chickamauga, Charleston, Philadelphia, Knoxville and Clinch River until the fall of 1864 when he was again captured. He moved to Chattanooga in Nov. 1866 and returned to the practice of law. He married (1855) Mary Joliffe Bruce. Presbyterian. Died Nov. 9, 1919 and buried in Forest Hills Cemetery. [FHR; GHT, pp. 979-80; NBFM2]

PAYNE, William Henry    Co. B, 1GA Bn.;
Co. G, Phillips Legion
Born Oct. 30, 1838 in Marietta, GA. Joined CSA in 1861 at Pensacola. Later enl. in Phillips Legion. Paroled Apr. 26, 1865 as 1Lt. After war lived in Ringgold and married on 11 May 1882 Flora Brownlow. To Chattanooga in 1889 and went into law practice. After several years of bad health, W. H. Payne died at his home on Douglas St. Oct. 20, 1910 and was buried in Forest Hills Cem. [TWP, p. 131; FHR; CT Oct. 21, 1910; NBFM2]

PAYNE, Cpl. William P.    Co. F, 35TN
Born 1845 in Walker Co., GA, he was a farmer in HC when he enl. Oct. 30, 1862; deserted at Salisbury,

NC, March 15, 1865; gray eyes, dark hair, dark complexion, and was 5'6" tall; took USA oath April, 1865 and released at Chattanooga. 1910 machinist. Res. Cowart St. with wife Sarah (m. 1867). 1912 in Soddy. [CSR; TP 11,937 (L.S. Payne's application)]

PEAK, C. Standifer    3CSA Cav.
        Born in Meigs Co. Aug. 25, 1839, he was the son of Jacob and Mary Jones Peak and early in life entered the steamboat business, marrying Maggie Doss, the daughter of a steamboat owner. During the war, he was operating two Confederate steamers on the Tennessee River and also fought with N. B. Forrest, being "dangerously wounded" at the Battle of Philadelphia. Following the war, he operated a steamer on the Mississippi, then in the 1870s, he entered the grain and warehouse business and the 1880's engaged in the lumber business in E. TN. He married (2) Virginia Lee Watters in 1896. Peak died March 8, 1905 at his res. in Highland Park and was buried Forest Hills Cem. [CT, March 9, 1905; TWP, 265; FHR; Wilson, Peak Family]

PEARSON, James M. D.    Co. L, 36TN; Co. L, 35TN
        Enl. Jan. 9, 1862, in Co. L, 36TN at Chattanooga; transferred to Co. L, 35TN; deserted 6 May 1862.

PEEPLES, William Oscar    Co. F, 3CSA Cav.
        Born Apr. 26, 1846 in Gordon Co., GA, son of Drewry Murrah and Mary Francis Collier Peeples. Enl. in Murray Co., GA Apr. 15, 1864. Atlanta Campaign. Served in N. GA. and became 1Lt of Co. E in Btn. raised by Edmundson. Surrendered at Kingston, GA. Paroled May 12, 1865. Married (1869 in HC) Rachel Ellen Tankesley. Merchant in Chattanooga. Charter member of NBF Camp, 1885. Died Feb. 16, 1907 at Graysville, GA and buried Forest Hills Cemetery. [FHR; TWP, 218; CT Feb. 18, 1907; NBFM2]

PENDLETON, Hugh T.    Co. A, Tredegar Btry.;
                    Richmond Howitzers
        Died at res. on High St., May 1, 1901 and buried CSA Cem. [NBFM,7]

PENDLEY, Hezekiah    Co. L, 36TN; Co. L, 35TN
        Enl. Jan. 9, 1862, in Co. L, 36TN at Chattanooga; transferred to Co. L, 35TN; discharged May 1, 1863 as "non conscript."

PENDLY, Joel C.    Co. L, 35TN; Latrobe's Btry.
        Enl. Jan. 9, 1862; transferred to Latrobe's Battery, May 1, 1862.

PENDLEY, Sgt. John M.    Co. L, 36TN;

Co. L, 35th TN
        Enl. Jan. 9, 1862, in Co. L, 36TN at Chattanooga; transferred to Co. L, 35th TN. Fought at Murfreesboro.

PENLAND, James H.    Barry's Btry.
        Enl. July 2, 1862 at Chattanooga.

PENLAND, Lorenzo D.    Barry's Btry.
        Enl. May 29, 1862 at Chattanooga; lost on retreat in Feb. [Brown's Diary]

PENNINGTON, James    Co. I, 19TN
        Born in SC, 1816. Enl. Nov. 24, 1862. Shot through left hand at Murfreesboro, Dec. 31, 1862. Hospital guard, Camp Direction Hospital, Chattanooga, Apr., 1863. 1903 res. of HC. [TP5024]

PENNY, George Washington    Co. D, 37TN
        Age 18 in 1861; enl. Sept. 1, 1861 at Knoxville; killed Nov. 27, 1861.

PENNY, Joseph L.    Co. H, 37TN
        Enl. Sept. 1, 1861, Knoxville. Prom. 3d Sgt. May 15, 1862. Deserted Nov. 5, 1862 at Chattanooga

PENNY, Martin    1TN Cav. (Carter's)
        Born c1836 in TN, son of Elizabeth. Res. 1860 in Birchwood. [1860HC]

PENNY, Monroe    Barry's Btry.
        Born c1839. Enl. April 4, 1862 at Chattanooga; $50 bonus; deserted Sept. 1, 1864 at Atlanta. Res. 1870 at Harrison, wife Catherine. [1860HC]

PERKINS, Robert R.    Co. H, 2GA
        Born 1835 in Monroe Co. Enl. April 20, 1861. Measles and sunstroke (20-40 days incapacitated). Captured Buchanan, VA, March, 1865. To TN about 1890. 1905 in Avondale. Died Dec. 3, 1908. Wife was Mary M. [NBFM7]

PERKINS, 1Lt. William H.    Co. H, 26TN; 63TN
        Age 20 in 1861, he enl. June 27, 1861 at Knoxville; captured at Fort Donelson, Feb. 16, 1862; imprisoned at Camp Morton, IN but escaped April 23, 1862; elected 2Lt., Oct. 13, 1862; detailed to Conscript Bureau summer and fall, 1863; cmdg. Co. H, Oct. 17, 1863; paroled May 1, 1865 at Greensboro, NC. Reported by Lindsley to have died May 7, 1862 [see Wm. M. Perkins].

PERKINS, William M.    Co. H, 26TN
        Born c1836. Enl. July 8, 1861, Knoxville. Captured Fort Donelson, Feb. 16, 1862 and imprisoned

Camp Douglas where he died, May 7, 1862.

PERRIGEN, George W.   Co. I, 19TN
        Enl. May 20, 1861, Knoxville. At Corinth. Hospitalized then deserted. Took USA oath, Sept. 10, 1863 and released by Fed. authorities at Nashville.

PERRY, Henry J.   Co. D, 6GA State Troops
        Born Marion Co., GA, 1847. Enl. July, 1864 in P. J. Phillips "Brigade." Fought at Griswoldville. Res. 1915 on Lansing St. in Chattanooga. Wife was Mattie (Martha). Married 1869. "Bench man" in coffin factory. [TP 14,617; 1910HC]

PERRY, Holdman   4AL Cav.
        Res. 1870 in Franklin Co., TN. Well known CW veteran and merchant of Chattanooga Died Dec. 10, 1925, age 85, and buried Chattanooga Memorial Cem. [CT Dec. 12, 1925; TP15670]

PERRY, Richard   Co. H, 4TN Cav.; Co. B, 5TN Cav.
        Born c1839, he was a farm laborer living near Moccasin Bend prior to the start of the war. His wife was Viney. He enl. on Aug. 11, 1861 in Chattanooga.

PERRY, William A.   Co. D, 4GA Cav.
        He enl. Oct. 4, 1862, at Chattanooga. He was detailed on a pontoon bridge at Kelly's Ferry on Dec. 5, 1862, and remained at this duty through June of 1863. He was captured near Fort Gates on April 1, 1864. He was sent from near Jacksonville to Fort LaFayette in New York Harbor, where he arrived May 17, 1864. He was moved to Fort Delaware in Delaware. On March 21, 1865, he was furloughed from a hospital at Opelika, Ala.

PETER, Pvt.   Co. D, 37TN
        "Servant Boy of R.M. Tankesley."

PETTY, George W. Essman   Co. B, 3VA Reserves
        Born Appomattox Co., VA, 1846. To TN in 1852 with father and returned to VA in 1857. Enl. April 16, 1864. Fought at Lineburg, VA and Roanoke Station Paroled May 1865 at Campbell Court House. To TN from VA in 1868; in TX, 1917-19. [TP15,303]

PETTYJOHN, Sgt. Enoch   Co. K, 6GA Cav.
        Born 1818 in Jackson Co., AL. Married (1853) Jane Newman. Died 1895 in HC. Res. Wauhatchie, 1870, wife Lucinda J. [TWP, p. 65]

PFEIL, Sgt. Auguste   Co. C, 6LA
        Born in Germany, he was single, working as a mechanic, a resident of Washington, LA at the time of his enlistment, June 4, 1861, at Camp Moore, LA.

ANV. Promoted to Sgt. July 7, 1862. Discharged 1863 on surgeon's certificate because of gunshot wound received at Chantilly. Member NBF Camp, 1896. Res. of Chattanooga c1890, carpenter. Moved from Chattanooga in Oct., 1898 because of health of daughter. Reported in "destitute circumstances in Richmond, VA., Dec. 1914. [Booth, 3:128; NBFM2,4]

PHEDFORD, J. P.   Co. G, 1GA
        Died March 8, 1916, age 70, at daughter's home in Blue Springs, GA and buried Pea Vine Cem. [CT 9 March 1916]

PHELAN, Capt. John
        Born in Marion, AL, Nov. 22, 1841, he enrolled at the State University at Tuscaloosa in 1859. When the war broke out he quickly became Orderly Sgt. of the Warrior Guards which would become the well-known Fowler's-Phelan's Battery of the Army of Tennessee. After the war Phelan was admitted to the bar and practiced in Moulton, AL until he moved to Courtland where he became a partner with Gen. Joseph Wheeler. Phelan relocated to Chattanooga in 1877 remaining until 1885 when he settled in Birmingham. He died in Birmingham Feb. 10, 1890.

PHILLIPS, E. S.   Co. G, 26TN; 2d Co. K, 1CSA(GA)
        Enl. July 12, 1861 at Knoxville; captured at Fort Donelson, Feb. 16, 1862; imprisoned at Camp Douglas. At home, sick furlough, Bradley Co., Dec. 31, 1862-Feb. 28, 1863. Present Aug. 31, 1863.

PHILLIPS, F. B.   Co. H, 26TN
        Born c1839. Enl. July 8, 1861. Captured Fort Donelson, Feb. 16, 1862 and imprisoned Camp Douglas where he died May 21, 1862.

PHILIPS, James W.   Co. L, 26TN; Co. L, 35TN
        Enl. Jan. 9, 1862, in Co. L, 26TN at Chattanooga; transferred to Co. L, 35TN; captured Aug. 7, 1863 at Stevenson, AL.

PHILLIPS, John   Co. D, 4GA Cav.
        Enl. Oct. 4, 1862, at Chattanooga. He was reported absent without leave on Dec. 12, 1862.

PHILLIPS, John W.   Co. K, 43TN
        Born 1842 in Greenville, SC, he was a farmer who enl. April 17, 1862 at Ooltewah; discharged Sept. 8, 1862; dark complexion, dark hair, blue eyes, and 5'11" tall.

PHILLIPS, Samuel K.   Co. I, 40GA
        Born in Washington City (on the MD side), Oct. 7, 1833. Raised and educated in MD. Enl. 1861 in Big

Shanty, GA in 40GA. Disch. because of defective hearing. Rejoined in Knoxville, disch. again and then joined QM. Captured at Vicksburg. Joined Capt. Gabbett's Div. of Nitre and Mining Bureau as chief clerk at Rome. Became accountant in Chattanooga after war. Poet who was published locally and in other veteran periodicals. Historian, NBF Camp, 1894. "Was sent to Soldiers' Home near Nashville" where he died Nov. 15, 1902 and was buried. [NBFM2]

PHILLIPS, William Alfred    Co. G, 6GA
        Born Grayson Co., VA, 1848. Enl. Sept., 1864 in Co. G, 6GA Cav. Injured when thrown from horse. Paroled May, 1865 at Kingston, GA. Moved to TN in 1875 and married (1893 in James Co.) Eliza A. Scott. Res. Howardsville, James Co. in 1905 and died there in 1909. [TWP, p. 187; TP7353]

PHILLIPS, William E.    Co. H, 26TN
        Age 23 in 1861, he enl. July 14, 1861 at Knoxville; killed at Fort Donelson, Feb. 15, 1862.

PHILLIPS, William T.    Co. G, 26TN
        Enl. Aug. 28, 1861 at Knoxville; captured at Fort Donelson, imprisoned at Camp Douglas where he died July 1, 1862.

PHILLIPS, William Theodore    Co. G, 26Tn; 2dCo. K, 1CSA (GA)
        Born 1843, Greenville Dist., SC of SC parents. Enl. Aug. 28, 1861, Knoxville. Absent, sick in hospital, April 7, 1863. Married (1865 in HC) Cynthia Jane Rogers. His brother was G. W. Phillips of Logan Co., AR. 1910 farmer in James Co. with wife Cynthia. Baptist. Died Nov. 27, 1921 and buried in Cleveland. [TWP, 237; 1910 James Co.; CT Nov. 28, 1921]

PICKARD, Lt. John A.    Co. H., 1TN;
                Co. H, 34TN (4CSA)
        Born Savannah, GA, March 28, 1840, he was in Maury County, TN, and had just gotten his law license when the war broke out. Enl. May 1, 1861, at Nashville and sent to Camp Cheatham in Robertson Co. His unit was involved in skirmishing in western VA, then was sent to Corinth, MS. He was in fighting at Shiloh, Murfreesboro, Chickamauga, Missionary Ridge and was wounded at Resaca, GA (lost left eye). He rejoined his unit at Kennesaw Mountain, but was sent back to the hospital. He was back with his unit at Jonesboro and went with them to Tuscumbia, AL. He joined the staff of Gen. Benjamin H. Hill, serving to the end of the war. He surrendered where he had enl., at Nashville May 15, 1865. After the war, he was in the lumber business, but his business was hit hard by the Panic of 1893. He lived his latter years at Chattanooga.

Real estate agent, 1910, sick at Newell's, 1913. [NBFM4; TP 12,511; TCVQ]

PICKETT, James M.    Co. H, 4TN Cav.
        "Eye shot out on Cumberland Mountain 1863." Killed at Cumberland Mountain, 1864.

PITTS, John    Co. D, 4GA Cav.
        He enl. Aug. 6, 1863, at Chattanooga.

PLATT, Robert Baxter    Co. H, 1MS Cav. Reserves
        Born Evergreen, AL, Jan. 21, 1846, he enl. Feb., 1863, at Quitman, MS. Fought at Holly Springs and Tupelo. Paroled Meridian, May 13, 1865. Married 1) Lucy Andrews Jones (1874), 2) Hannah Eliza Prescott (1890). Cross-tie contractor for L&N RR. To Chattanooga in 1906, having lived previously in Evergreen, Collierville and Memphis, TN. Methodist. Died March 29, 1934 and buried CSA Cem. [CT 30 March 1934; NBFM8; 1910HC]

PLEMONS, John L.    Co. F, 60GA
        Born NC in 1835, "youngest of a large family of boys." Married Sarah E. Isbell. Res. 1870 Bradley Co. Died 1913 in HC. [TWP, p. 172]

PLUMMER, Charles    Co. D, 4GA Cav.
        A school teacher who was born in Ireland about 1832, he enl. Oct. 4, 1862, at Chattanooga. He was detached for service at a saltpetre cave on Oct. 27, 1862.

PLUMMER, Sgt. Jerry    Clark's Independent Cav. Co.
        Enl. Aug. 31, 1862 at Chattanooga; deserted Nov. 15, 1863 at Ringgold, GA.

PLUMMER, M.    Clark's Independent Cav. Co.
        Enl. Aug. 31, 1862 at Chattanooga; deserted Dec. 1, 1863 in East TN.

POE, Adam W., Jr.
        He married Mary J. Crutchfield, daughter of Wm. Crutchfield on 20 June 1876. She died Dec. 7, 1915. Their home was in St. Elmo and she was active in the UDC.

POE, Hasten
        A pioneer settler at the section that became Daisy, he gave aid to the Confederate cause. It was at his tavern home that the first courts were held for HC in 1819. A Virginia native, his wife was Celia. He remained at home during the war, although Union soldiers took over his dwelling. He was stripped of much of his property because of his Southern sympathies. He died in 1878.

POE, Hasten H.   Jackson's Cav. Co.
        Born Nov. 24, 1845, son of Samuel P. and Mary Bryant Poe, and grandson of pioneer settler Hasten Poe, he fought for the Confederacy. He married (1878) Ruth Champion. Cumberland Presbyterian. [GHT, p. 983-84]

POE, Jesse Henry    Co. F, 35TN
        Born in 1838 in McMinn County, he was a son of John Poe and Rebecca Hinkle. He enl. Dec. 8, 1862, but he deserted Aug. 31, 1863, at Gardenhire's Ferry. He took the oath of allegiance on Sept. 29, 1863. He had brown eyes, dark hair, a dark complexion, and was 6' tall.

POE, John Lindsay   4GA Cav.; Co. F, 35TN
        Born in 1840 in McMinn Co., he was another of the sons of John Poe to fight for the Confederacy. He enl. Feb. 9, 1862 in 4GA Cav., captured and was imprisoned at Rock Island, IL. Paroled and joined, Dec. 8, 1862, Co. F of the 35TN. He deserted near Chattanooga on Sept. 13, 1863 and took the oath of allegiance on Sept. 29, 1863. Railroader in Chattanooga. c1890. 1903 res. of Chattanooga [TP5152]

POE, Larkin Haskew    Co. K, 4GA Cav.
        Born 1835, McMinn Co., son of John Poe and Rebecca Hinkle. Married Sarah Brotherton, daughter of George and Mary Carter Brotherton. The battle of Chickamauga was fought around the Poe and Brotherton homeplaces which LHP "disliked to visit and made his home elsewhere." John Poe died near the close of the war, and Rebecca Hinkle Poe died in 1878. Larkin Poe later lived at Apison. Presbyterian. Farmer and JP for 23 yrs. in James Co., 1910 with wife Sarah (m. 1860). Died in Apison, Jan. 14, 1929 and buried Plowman's Cem. [1910 James Co.; CT Jan. 15, 1929]

POE, William H.   Co. K, 43TN
        The eldest son of the pioneer Hasten Poe, he enl. Oct. 17, 1861, at Ooltewah. He was captured at Vicksburg on July 4, 1863.

POGUE, George Washington    Co. A, 19TN
        Born 1844, SC, son of William. Family had lived in Alabama prior to moving to Chattanooga Enl. May 20, 1861, Knoxville and reenlisted Aug. 1, 1863. [1860HC]

POLLARD, John W.    Co. F, 2TN
        Born March 4, 1830 in Bledsoe Co. and enl. at Pikeville, July, 1861. Served until surrender. Never wounded nor captured. 1899: doing gardening and odd jobs in Hill City for $0.25 a day. Died April 9, 1902 and buried Burk Cem. [TP2394;NBFM7]

POLLARD, William A.    Co. B, 1TN Cav. (Carter's)
        Captured near Knoxville on Sept. 22, 1863, he was sent to Camp Morton. He was sent via the Baltimore and Ohio Railroad to Point Lookout, MD, and was exchanged March 15, 1865. He was taken to a hospital at Richmond. Before the war, he lived on the farm of his parents, Winston and Clarinda Pollard, at Ooltewah. William A. Pollard was born about 1844. Res. Ooltewah, 1870, wife Rebecca.

PONDER, M.        Co. K, 43TN
        Enl. April 17, 1862 at Ooltewah; transferred from 36TN.

POOLE, Lorenzo Dow   Co. G, 26TN
        Enl. Aug. 28, 1861, Knoxville. Captured Fort Donelson, Feb. 16, 1862 and imp. Camp Morton, IN. Dark complexion, dark hair, grey eyes, and 6' tall. Res. Cass Co., GA. Took USA oath, June 10, 1864, agreeing to stay north of Ohio River.

POPE, Alexis Dowin    Co. H, 3AL Cav. Cpl.
        Born 1840 in Prattville, AL, he married (1877 in HC) Anna Thornton Bryan.

POPE, Cpl. James Thomas    Barry's Battery
        Born c1843, he enl. May 9, 1862, at Chattanooga. He was paroled May 11, 1865, at Meridian, MS Prior to the war, he resided with his father, A.F. Pope, at Chattanooga. His father was from AL. James T. Pope was a carpenter. Died March 8, 1932, age 85, at res on Martin Rd. Married Della. Buried in Chattanooga Memorial Park. [CT March 9, 1932]

POPE, John Townson
        Born 1846 in Bledsoe Co., he married (1879) Cordelia Frances Songer. Died 1932 in HC. [TWP, 298]

POPE, Cpl. Levand M.(W., N.) "Van", "Lee" Co. F,
                2TN Cav. (Ashby's)
        Born April 10, 1844 near Pikeville, son of Jerome and Mary Pope. Enl. May 24, 1862 (also Oct. 1, 1864 at Lancaster, KY); captured Farmington, MS; imprisoned at Camp Morton, IN, also Point Lookout, MD; again captured Dec. 1862 and Aug. 1, 1863; captured near Shelbyville, TN, Oct. 7, 1863; paroled; also imprisoned at Camp Chase; surrendered in Washington, GA; one of President Davis guards to that point. He married Penelope Johnson in 1871 at Mt. Airy, TN [Bledsoe County]. She was born in Pikeville in 1847 and died 1917 in Wildwood, GA. At close of war emigrated to Calif. until about 1870, "then came back to Chattanooga." Later made his home at Wildwood, GA.

Farming, stock raising. Died April 19, 1937 and buried in Hooker Cem., Dade Co. [UDC2 pg 430]

POPE, Ross
    Born 1846, NC. Res. 1910 with wife Sarah (m. 1865) in household of son-in-law Augustus G. Thomas. [1910HC]

POPE, Thomas W.     Co. K, 43TN
    Died in hospital in Loudon, TN during war.

PORTER, James Sterling
    Born 1839 in White Plains, AL, he married (1871) Lucy Ann Tanner.

PORTER, Thomas W.     Co. K, 43TN
    Enl. Dec. 2, 1861 at Ooltewah; died March 27, 1862 in hospital in Loudon, TN. [Lindsley, 528]

POSEY, Lewis   Co. F, 35TN
    Born 1840 in HC, he was a laborer here and married (Jan. 30, 1861) Susan Powell. Enl. Dec. 21, 1861; died in hospital at Tullahoma June 22, 1863; black eyes, black hair, fair complexion, and 5'9" tall.

POSEY, Winchester     Co. D, 37TN
    Enl. Feb. 14, 1862 at Chattanooga; conscript; deserted Feb. 15, 1862.

POSEY, Young   Co. G, 36TN
    Born 1832 in GA. Farm laborer at Ooltewah, 1860. Wife S. [1860 HC Census]

POTTER, Andrew J. "Andy"     Co. B, 1TN Cav. (Carter's)
    A blacksmith before the war, he lived at Birchwood with his wife, Artimisia. He was born in KY about 1833. Regt. blacksmith, 1863-64. [1860HC]

POTTER, Silas     Co. B, 1TN Cav. (Carter's)
    Enl. Aug. 7, 1861, Cleveland. Killed at Blue Springs, TN, Sept. 1863.

POTTER, Thomas C.     Co. H, 63TN
    Born Feb. 1, 1828 in McMinn Co. Enl. fall, 1861. Chickamauga. Eye injured in battle of Richmond. Captured at Petersburg. Res. of Sherman Heights in 1905. Res. in TN all his life.

POTTS, Calvin J.   Co. B, 46NC
    [NBFM1]

POTTS, Edward W.     Co. F, 39GA
    Born Knox Co., TN. Enl. March 1862. Surr. Greensboro, NC, April 26, 1865. Carpenter in

Chattanooga c1890. [NBFM2]

POWELL, Benjamin Thomas     Co. G, 60GA
Surgeon
    Born April 14, 1846, Dooley Co., GA, son of Silas and Jane Hodges Powell. Conscript, enlisting Dec. 1862 at Savannah. Second Manassas (wounded), Fredericksburg, Chancellorsville (wounded). Crippled at Cold Harbor. En route home, he crossed the Oconee River on a mule, but fell off after reaching the other side. Word reached his family, and they came for him and brought him home in a wagon. Lived in Macon, GA, Dallas, TX before coming to Chattanooga where he lived 36 years. In butcher trade, but "blind and crippled" by 1915. Died at res. on McCallie Ave., July 1, 1927 and bur. Forest Hills Cem. [NBFM7; TCVQ; CT July. 2,3, 1927; 1890VetCensus]

POWELL, Henry Clay     Barry's Battery
    Born Jan. 19, 1847, he enl. May 4, 1864 at Griffin, GA., joining his older brother, S. F. Powell. He was paroled May 11, 1865, in Meridian, MS. Upon parole, he gave his address as Griffin, GA. Before the war, he had lived in Chattanooga. His parents were Irby and Jemmia Powell, natives of NC, who moved to AL and on to Chattanooga. Irby Powell was a merchant who in 1873 died and left a large estate for his four children, which also included Cicero A. and Adeline. The Powells resided at 616 Georgia Ave. Henry Clay Powell died on July 12, 1893 at Thomasville, GA, of derangement of the liver and was buried Forest Hills Cem. [CT Aug. 8, 1898; 1860 HC Census; NBFM2]

POWELL, Capt. John Dudley     Co. A, 19TN
    Born and raised in HC, he was a veteran of the Mexican War and a commission merchant at Chattanooga before the war. Absent on Jan. 19, 1862 on sick leave. Not re-elected captain and succeeded by Daniel Allen Kennedy. Dropped May, 1862. John Dudley Powell d. Sept. 18, 1897 in Huntsville, AL, of typhoid. Attache[sic] of Ala. Hosiery Co. [CT Sept. 19, 1897]

POWELL, John W.
    Born 1837, GA, of GA parents. 1910 farmer, res. James Co. with two grown daughters and their children. [1910 James Co.]

POWELL, Sidney F.     Barry's Battery
    Born Mar. 5, 1843 in Randolph Co., AL, the son of Irby and Jemmia Powell. He enl. Oct. 6, 1862, at Knoxville and served throughout the war. Both he and his younger brother, Henry Clay Powell, returned home "without a scratch." Both served "with bravery and gallantry." Sidney F. Powell was paroled May 11, 1865, at Meridian, MS.

After the war, he went to Vinings, GA where he married Miss Randall of an old Georgia family. She died in 1883 of consumption. They had no children. He operated a grocery and cotton business in Atlanta before returning to Chattanooga. Here he and his brothers ran H.C. Powell and Co. grocery at 1201 Whiteside (South Broad) St. The firm was dissolved in early 1898. Sidney Powell then set up a business at Lytle, Ga., serving regular soldiers who were training for the Spanish-American War. He died Aug. 7, 1898, after eating too-ripe peaches and was buried at Forest Hills Cemetery. [CT Aug. 8, 1898; FHR; NBFM2]

POWERS, James  Co. A, 19TN
He enl. at Knoxville and was killed by Thomas Stevens in December, 1861, although reported to have been killed at Shiloh.

PRACHARD, Henry R.  Co. F, 35TN
Born 1838 in Edgefield District, SC, he farmed in HC at the time he enl. on Sept. 5, 1862. Gray eyes, dark hair, fair complexion, and 5'10" tall; deserted at Chattanooga Jan. 22, 1863.

PRESLEY, William  Van Der Corput (Cherokee) Battery, 3GA Arty. Bn.
Born 1824 in Campbell Co., GA. Captured June, 1864 and imprisoned at Jeffersonville, IN. Took USA oath July 16, 1864. Res. of Chattanooga in 1903 with personal and real property valued at $25. Earned subsistence by selling matches. [TP5748]

PRICE, J. W.  Co. H, 26TN
Enl. July 8, 1861 in Knoxville. Detailed as wagoner at Bowling Green, Nov. 1861.

PRICE, Orderly Sgt. James Lott  Cutt's Btry.
Born Aug. 12, 1844 in Stewart Co., GA, he received his education at the Georgia Military Academy, and from there he enl. in Co. A, Sumter Flying Artillery Bn. (Cutt's). He soon transferred to Co. B and became Orderly Sgt. He fought at Dranesville, Yorktown, Seven Days, South Mountain and Sharpsburg. For meritorous work at Fredericksburg, he was brevetted 2LT by Gen. R. E. Lee. He fought at Gettysburg, Petersburg and was captured making his way to NC following Appomatox. He married Eunice Rylander in 1863 in GA. After the war he returned to GA, but emigrated to Chattanooga in 1885 to become engaged in mining and real estate. Member, NBF Camp, 1894. He died at his home in St. Elmo Nov. 24, 1906 and was buried in CSA Cem. [CT Nov. 25, 1906; UDC2 pg 435]

PRICE, Samuel V.  Co. H, 26TN; 1CSA

Born c1840. Enl. Aug. 6, 1861. Detached as hospital steward, Dec. 7, 1861. Left sick Bowling Green, Jan. 13, 1862.

PRIDE, Thomas W.  Co. H, 2TN Cav. (Ashby's)
Prom. Lt. May 24, 1862. Captured in Ky. Exchanged Aug. 25, 1862. He later resigned.

PRIGMORE, John  Co. L, 36TN; Co. L, 35TN
Enl. Jan. 9, 1862 at Chattanooga; re-enl. Jan. 9, 1863 in Chattanooga. Absent without leave since July 20, 1863.

PRINCE, William
Born 1844, GA. Res. 1910 on W. 24th with wife C.N. Wagon driver. [1910HC]

PRITCHETT, Edward W.  Musician, Co. I, 1TN (Field's)
Born Murfreesboro, TN, 1846. Enl. April 21, 1861 at Murfreesboro as drummer boy, then became infantryman. Carpenter who died in Chattanooga Oct. 13, 1893 and buried CSA Cem. [NBFM2; NBFM1,7]

PRYOR, James S.  Co. D, 37TN
Age 17 in 1861, he enl. Sept. 1, 1861, at Knoxville. He took the USA oath of Jan. 2, 1865. Before the war, he lived with his mother, Eliza Pryor, at Chattanooga. He was a day laborer and her occupation was housewifery. He had a fair complexion, light hair, blue eyes, and was 5'8" tall.

PURSLEY, Thomas L.  (probably Co. D, 33TN)
Married (Aug. 3, 1861) Rosanna B. Robertson. Well known 74 year-old Confederate who lived in HC "the greater part of his life." He died April 17, 1904 at his home in East Lake and was buried in the McFarland Cem. [CT April 18, 1904]

PURYEAR, William M.  Co. H, 26TN; 1CSA
Born c1834. Enl. July 8, 1861, Knoxville. Captured Fort Donelson, Feb. 16, 1862. and imprisoned Camp Douglas.

PYATT/PYOTT, Henry C.  Co. B, 43TN
Born Rhea Co., July 8, 1844 son of Edward and Margaret Pyott. Brothers were Samuel A. and Stephen C. Enl. summer, 1862. Port Gibson, Baker's Creek, Vicksburg. Paroled, sick, did not return to army. Wife was Alice. Res. 1915, St. Elmo. [TP14,608]

PYOTT, 3rd Lt. John E.  Co. B, 43TN
Born 19 Dec. 1838, son of Edward and Margaret Pyott. "A man of considerable wealth, owning large tracts of land in Rhea, Meigs and McMinn

counties. He was a school teacher in 1860 and 1870. Resided on West 6th St. Died Nov. 1, 1904 in Chattanooga and buried in Spring City Cem. Served as Asst. Surgeon, 19TN. [NBFM4; Lindsley, pp. 375, 380]

PYRON, Sgt. Maj. John Bell       Co. H, 11th TN Cav.
       Born May 16, 1843 in Shreveport, LA of parents who were native Tennesseans but living temporarily in LA. The family moved to Nashville in 1848. JBP enl. at Manchester, TN in 1862. Captured July 5, 1864. Paroled May 9, 1865 as sgt. major. To Chattanooga in 1871 and entered mercantile business. Married (Sept. 18, 1876 Mary Ruohs. 1901 travelling salesman in Chattanooga. Died March 2, 1906 in Chattanooga and buried in Citizens Cem. [CT March 3, 1906; NBFM2]]

# Q

QUALLS, H. J.       2nd Co. K, 1CSA Cav.
       Enl. Sept. 24, 1862 in HC. Deserted Sept. 21, 1863.

QUALLS, J. M.       2nd Co. K, 1CSA Cav.
       Enl. Sept. 24, 1862 in HC Deserted Sept. 21, 1863.

QUALLS, Jesse       Co. L, 35TN
       Enl. July 10, 1862 at Tyner Station. Deserted Aug. 10, 1863 at Tyner's.

QUEEN, C. P.
       Exec. Committee, Soldiers Relief Society at Chattanooga, Aug. 29, 1862.

# R

RADFORD, William, Jr.       Co. B, 1CSA Cav.

RAGAN, A. C.
       Died at age 63 on Jan. 15, 1908 and buried Forest Hills Cemetery. [CTJan. 16, 1908]

RAGON, Capt. Alfred Jackson       Co. F, 35TN; Co. A, 5TN Cav.
       Born 1834 in Monroe Co., TN, son of Absalom and Jane Hixson Ragon. He was a farmer in HC when he enl. Oct. 1, 1862 in 35TN; resigned commission March 25, 1863; later in 5TN Cav.; gray eyes, black hair, fair complexion, 5'9" tall. Married Anne E. Hartsell. Died Nov. 1, 1889. [JWilson Ragon family]

RAGON, Capt. Eli Cleveland       Co. A, 60 Mil. (AR)
       Born 1826, son of Absalom and Jane Hixson Ragon. Married Nancy Rogers, and they moved to Logan Co., AR about 1850. Died in 1878 and buried in old Ragon Cem. at Morrison Bluff.

RAGON, Jesse M.       Co. F, 35TN
       Born c1835, Monroe Co., TN, son of Absalom and Jane Hixson Ragon. Enl. Oct. 1, 1862. Prom. to 1Lt., but resigned March 25, 1863.

RAGSDALE, Benjamin Franklin       Barry's Battery
       Born in Athens, TN, in 1836, he was the son of Benajmin and Mary Ann Ragsdale. He came to Chattanooga about 1866 as agent for the East Tennessee, Virginia and Georgia Railroad. He married Sally Ewing McMillin. The B.F. Ragsdales were afflicted during the Yellow Fever epidemic of 1878 at Chattanooga, Ragsdale dying on Nov. 28. His wife and mother also died in the epidemic but his three children, Minnie, Emma and Benjamin, survived.

RAGSDALE, David Baxter       Co. F, 35TN
       Born about 1828 in Rhea County, TN, son of David S. and Cynthia Churchwell Ragsdale. He lived for a time in New York and set up a New York Store in Chattanooga. Married Eugenia Howard (1857). Enl. Oct. 1, 1862 at Chattanooga. He was wounded and was hospitalized in Way Hospital in Meridian, MS, January, 1863. Unfit for further infantry service, he hired a substitute, Peter Cain and apparently joined the QM Dept. Leading Chattanooga citizens petitioned that Ragsdale be put in charge of procuring supplies in Middle TN: R. B. Brabson, J. P. Millis, D. S. Gillespie, William L. Rogers, William A. Moore, Milo Smith (mayor), Tom K. Wornacut, and J. L. Edwards. Ragsdale had gray eyes, dark hair, fair complexion, and was 6'2" tall. After the war, Ragsdale returned to Chattanooga and operated the Hamilton House hotel at 535 Market St. He won a term as county trustee in 1878. After his wife died about 1889, he moved to Knoxville to live with one of his sons. He died at the home of his nephew, Joseph G. Ragsdale, at 106 Oak St. Buried Citizens. Cem.

RAGSDALE, Lt. Thomas Hoyle       Co. A, 4TN Cav.
       Born c1839, he was the son of David S. Ragsdale and Cynthia Churchwell of Rhea County. Enl. June 17, 1861, at Knoxville in the company formed at Chattanooga by his brother, William Ragsdale. The

company was reorganized as Co. H, 2TN Cav. Captured near Lancaster, KY, on July 31, 1863. Imp. Camp Chase, Camp Douglas. Believed to have died in prison.

RAGSDALE, Capt. William F.    Co. A 4TN Cav.
Recruited a company of his fellow citizens to fight for the Confederacy--Co. A of the 4TN Cav. in the battalion of Lt. Col. B. M. Branner. After the company assembled at Knoxville, Ragsdale was directed "to proceed to Nashville to obtain the arms necessary for his company and return with as little delay as possible." Ragsdale and his brother, David B. Ragsdale, were prominent merchants in early Chattanooga. W.F. Ragsdale also operated the Central Hotel at Fifth and Market. His parents were David and Cynthia Ragsdale of Rhea Co. W. F. Ragsdale married Sarah Garwood and built a mansion for her at the foot of Cameron Hill. This handsome white-columned home on Pine Street had passed to the Kennedy family by the time the war started. It was occupied by generals from both armies. Ragsdale and his brother, James M. Ragsdale, had earlier fought in the Mexican War. W. F. Ragsdale lost much of his holdings during the war. He died Jan. 1, 1873 in Chattanooga, age 53 and was buried at Citizens Cem. [HC Register of Deaths; UDC1 pg 348]

RAINES, Robert A.    36TN; Co. K, 43TN
Served in 36TN then enl. March 16, 1862, at Ooltewah in 43TN. He was captured at Vicksburg on July 4, 1863. Before the war, he lived on a farm at Ooltewah. His parents, J.S. and Mary Raines, were natives of GA. He was born c1839.

RAINES, William    Co. K, 50 NC
Born Dec. 2, 1823, Buncombe Co., NC and was farmer in Polk Co., NC prior to war. Enl. Apr. 1862. Served in Army of Northern Virginia & Army of Tennessee. Hospital at Wilmington, March 8, 1864 with chronic rheumatism. Returned to duty, March 21, 1864. Hosp. at Charlotte, Feb. 6, 1865 with ulcers. Returned to duty, Feb. 9, 1865. Paroled Greensboro, May 1, 1865. Day laborer in Chattanooga, 1900, destitute. Living here and in Kensington. [NBFM3; Soldiers home Application]

RAINES, Sgt. William M.    36TN; Co. K, 43TN
Born in 1836, he enl. March 19, 1862, at Ooltewah in Co. K of the 43rd TN Infantry after having transferred from the 36th TN Infantry. He was captured at Vicksburg on July 4, 1863. After being paroled, he was again captured at Martinsburg, Va., on Sept. 2, 1864. Prior to the war, he lived on a farm at Ooltewah with his wife, Phebe. He was one of the sons of J.S. and Mary Raines.

RAND, Vincent Lockhart
Born 1849 Whitfield Co., GA. Married (1930 in HC) Margaret Ocoa Ayers. Died at res. on 8th St., Feb. 13, 1912 and buried Boynton, GA. [TWP, 312; CT Feb. 14, 1912]

RANDAL, George Washington    Co. D, 37TN
Age 20 in 1861; enl. Sept. 1, 1861 as a conscript; paroled at Glasgow, KY July 10, 1862; sick at Catoosa Springs, March 10, 1863; sick summer of 1863 and sent to hospital; deserted Sept. 12, 1863; took USA oath Oct., 1863; light complexion, dark hair; blue eyes, and 5'11" tall.

RANDOLPH, Tip    Co. D, 4GA Cav.
He is reported with the unit in Nov. and Dec. of 1863, but was left on the march in Georgia sick.

RANKIN, David Byron  Co. B, 21TN Cav. (Carter's);
Wheeler's Scouts
Born in Marion Co., TN Mar. 2, 1845. Merchant in Cleveland for long time. Enl. N. B. Collin's Co., Wheeler's Cav. (scout) in 1863, and served throughout war. "Played poker & won $2,500 in Confederate money just before surrender in N.C. Greensboro." Married Lettie Bennett (1867). To Chattanooga c1882 and shown as a clerk in 1887. Died at Red Bank, Oct. 2, 1903 and buried in Red Bank Cemetery. [NBFM2]

RAPER (ROPER), H. H.    Co. K, 43TN
Enl. Nov. 10, 1862 at Ooltewah; captured at Vicksburg, July 4, 1863.

RAPER (ROPER), 2Lt. Jacob R.    Co. K, 43TN
Born in 1832 in TN, he was a farmer at Ooltewah who Enl. Nov. 10, 1862 at Ooltewah; captured at Vicksburg, July 4, 1863; paroled; again captured at Morristown, TN, Oct. 28, 1864 and imprisoned at Johnson's Island; blue eyes, dark hair, dark complexion, 5'9" tall.

RAPER (ROPER), John P.    Co. K, 43TN &
Co. B 1TN Cav. (Carter's)
Enl. Feb. 1, 1862 at Ooltewah; captured at Vicksburg, July 4, 1863.

RAWLINGS, James N. "Jim"    Co. A, 19TN; QM
Born Oct. 14, 1835, HC, son of Asahel Rawlings and apparently was the grandson of Rezin M. Rawlings. Served in the quartermaster dept. during the war. Maj. Bromfield Ridley wrote of him: "Captain Jim Rawlings is the Chevalier Bayard [of our company]. He wears the heaviest mustache, the longest beard, and rides

the best saddle-horse in the company. He hails from Chattanooga, Tennessee, was clerk in Lauderdale's department for several years, and one of the best book-keepers in America. It is doubtful whether the Captain is more careful of himself or of his horse, Jeff." After the war, JNR was an accountant for the Roane Iron Company at Chattanooga. Inmate TN Confed. Soldiers' Home, Nov. 17, 1902 and died there Oct. 31, 1904. [CT Nov. 1, 1904; TCSH; Ridley, Battles and Sketches, p. 476; TN Soldiers home Application]

RAWLINGS, 2Lt. John Goodwin   Co. I, 36TN
Born at Jasper, Tenn., 1841, son of Daniel Ritchie Rawlings and Martha Goodwin. The Rawlings family came to Chattanooga in April, 1852 when John was ten. He joined the Confederate army, but his regiment, the 36th TN Infantry, disbanded after 12 months' service. He then joined the medical department, serving at a hospital in Augusta, GA. John G. Rawlings married Annie Moore soon after the war and in 1904 married Dora Crutchfield. He was a druggist in St. Elmo. He was alderman in 1872 for the Second Ward. He died Dec. 23, 1924. [1910HC; TWP, 289]

RAWLINGS, Rezin M.
Born at Ross's Landing in 1835, he was a son of Asahel Rawlings and apparently was the grandson of Rezin Monroe Rawlings. In 1859, he married Hattie Ingersoll, a cousin of Robert G. Ingersoll, the orator and lawyer who was colonel of an IL cavalry regiment during the war. It was said of Rezin M. Rawlings, "A Confederate throughout, he served with distinction in the war." He was living in East Lake when he died of blood poisoning in 1897. Buried Forest Hills Cemetery.

RAY, James   Co. B 1TN Cav. (Carter'st)
He was born about 1836. Prior to the war, he was a farm laborer for Richard Taliaferro in Limestone north of Harrison. Horse was killed by enemy on March 30, 1863.

RAYL, George Washington   Co. K, 43TN
Born c1835. Enl. Dec. 1, 1861 at Ooltewah; discharged May 11, 1862. Res. 1870 in Ooltewah, wife Lydia.

RAYNES, G.L.   Co. D, 4GA Cav.
He enl. Oct. 4, 1862, at Chattanooga as a substitute for Alexander Anderson.  He deserted in April, 1863.

READ, Green B.   Co. A, 16AL
Killed on East TN, VA & GA Railroad near Citico Furnace, Aug. 11, 1891. Buried CSA Cem. [NBFM7]

READ, Surgeon John Thomas   16TN
Born Dec. 2, 1825 in Rutherford Co., TN son of son of Sion Spencer and Hardinia Jefferson Spencer. Sion was the Chief of Staff for Andrew Jackson. John Thomas lived in McMinnville before volunteering for the Civil War.  During this war he broke his leg which was improperly set, so broke it over again and reset it himself.  Served during the Mexican War also. Upon his return he studied medicine at Jefferson College in Philadelphia.  He practiced in Warren and Marion counties before becoming surgeon of the 16TN. After the war he practiced medicine and operated a hotel in McMinnville. He founded the Read House in Chattanooga, Jan. 1, 1872 with his wife Laurena Caroline Rankin He died in Chattanooga 3 Jan. 1900.. [Tenn.: A History 1673-1932 vol. 3 pg 133.]

REAGAN (RAGON), A. J.       Co. A, 5TN Cav (McKenzie's)
Enl. Aug. 24, 1861 at Camp Cumming. Elected 1Lt., May 24, 1862. Promoted to Capt., Dec. 17, 1862. Age 27 on March 11, 1864 roll. Paroled May 3, 1865 at Charlotte, NC.

REARIDEN, James J.   Barry's Btry.
Enl. Sept. 20, 1862, at Chattanooga; deserted Jan. 10, 1862.

REAVLEY, John L.   Co. K, 43TN
Born 1827 in TN. Before the war, he had a farm with his wife, Elizabeth J. Finley, at Sale Creek. He enl. Oct. 10, 1862, at Ooltewah and was captured July 4, 1863, at Vicksburg. Died in HC. [TWP, 318]

RECTOR, George   Co. H (Lookout Rangers)
2TN Cav. (Ashby's)
He was killed in action on Nov. 27 (or Nov. 17), 1863, when he was 16, but muster roll states: enl. June 17, 1861. at Knoxville. Arrested there May 25, 1862. Sick at hosp. Nov. 29, 1864. Took USA oath, March 30, 1865 at Chattanooga.

REDMAN, Uriah   Co. D, 4GA Cav.
He enl. Aug. 15, 1863, at Chattanooga. Captured near Chattanooga less than a month later on Sept. 11, 1863. Sent to Louisville where he took the oath of allegiance. He then joined the 11KY Cavalry, USA. He had a dark complexion, brown hair, blue eyes, and was 5'7" tall. Born about 1822, he farmed at Chattanooga prior to the war. His wife was Margaret.

REED, Orderly Sgt. John G.   Co. K, 43TN
Born in 1839 in Jefferson Co., TN, he was a carpenter who enl. Oct. 17, 1861 at Ooltewah; fair complexion, gray eyes, light hair, 5'10" tall. Res. 1870 in

Harrison, wife Mary J.

REED [REID], Martin VanBuren    Co. A, 62TN
                Vaughn's Brigade; 29TN
        Born July 21, 1841 in Polk Co., TN. Enl. Oct.,
1862. Served in 29TN last year of war. Wounded
Kennesaw Mountain, May 27, 1864 and was at home on
wounded furlough when war ended. Res. Chattanooga
where he was in partnership with a man named Green.
The store was on Market Street and Martin had a house
on 9th Street in 1889 and owned a ferry at Moccasin
Bend. He moved back to Spring City after 1889 where
he died  stroke, March 4, 1907. Buried in the Spring
City Cemetery with his third wife Susan B. [NBFM2,7;
*Rhea County, A Story* pg 349-350.]

REED, Thomas D.    Co. C, 13MS
        Born 19 Nov. 1840 in Pickens Co., AL. Enl.
May 12, 1861 as 2Lt. Served in ANV. Released Apr. 9,
1865. Became druggist in Chattanooga

REEVES, Cpl. C. B.    34GA
        Born Feb 20, 1846 in Cherokee, GA. Enl. Oct
15, 1864. Wounded at Jonesboro. Captured at Nashville,
Dec. 1864 and paroled May 12, 1865. Carpenter in
Chattanooga. [NBFM2]

REID, 2Lt. Charles L.    2Lt., Co. G, 26TN;
                2d Co. K, 1CSA(GA)
        Enl. July 8, 1861 in Co. G, 26TN at Knoxville;
captured at Fort Donelson, Feb. 16, 1862; imprisoned at
Johnson's Island; exchanged fall, 1862. Joined 2d Co.
K, 1CSA (GA). Cmdg. 2d Co. K at Chickamauga.

REINHART,    Co. B, 1TN Cav. (Carter's)
        Killed in battle at Piedmont, VA, June 5, 1864.

REMNY, M.    Barry's Btry
        Captured on retreat from Atlanta, Sept. 10,
1864. [Brown Diary]

RENFRO, James Coxe    Co. E, 12TN Cav. Bn.
(Day's)
        Born Grainger Co., TN, Dec. 24, 1842. Enl.
Nov. 1862. Murfreesboro, Chickamauga. Married Laura
Swaggerly on 8 Aug. 1875 in Knox Co., TN. She was
born 21 Sept. 1860 in Knox Co. and died 17 March
1940 in Knoxville. Merchant and baker in Knoxville.
Res. of Chattanooga, 1927 and died here Oct. 14, 1929
in Knoxville.[TP 15,246; UDC2 pg 445]

RENSHAW, John Allen   Co. C, 18TN
        Born Aug. 14, 1836 in Rutherford Co., TN.

Married (1859) Samantha C. Myers. Died March 4, 1911
at res. on Dodson Ave. and buried in Murfreesboro.
[TWP, p. 136; CT March 5, 1911]

REYNAND, Capt. A. G.
        A personal acquaintance of Nathan Bedford
Forrest, he joined the Confederate service at Memphis.
Reynand was "a great favorite" of Forrest's and became
a captain of scouts for him.   "When there was a
dangerous piece of work to be done, he was always
picked to do it." He was wounded several times,
including a shot near the ear that damaged his hearing.
He was taken prisoner and kept at Little Rock, AR for
eight months.
        Reynand was born on the island of Martinique,
his father having an adjoining plantation to that of
Empress Josephine. His parents moved to Cuba when he
was quite small. Then they moved to Paris, France. He
was educated in the finest military schools of Toulouse,
a Paris suburb. He left France at age 18 to go to the
United States. After the war, Reynand was a bookkeeper.
He lived in Chattanooga for 22 years, serving as manager
for Vetter and Co. beer business and as bookkeeper for
Gibson and Lee and then W.O. Peeples. He was also in
the coal business. He was living at Chickamauga, GA,
when he died May 5, 1902, at the age of 68. He was
raised a Catholic and joined no other church, but he was
buried at the Baptist Cem. in Chickamauga. [CT May 8,
1902]

REYNOLDS, Alexander   Co. D, 4GA Cav.
        Born March 19, 1832. Enl. March 1, 1863, at
Chattanooga, receiving a $50 bounty. He was reported
absent sick on July 3, 1863. Died Sept. 9, 1883 and
buried Forest Hills Cemetery. [Lusk, FH]

RHEA, James    Co. K, 1CSA Cav.
        Along with his younger brother, Thomas, he
joined Co. K of the 1TN Cavalry. He was killed in action
near Chattanooga in 1863. Before the war, he lived at
Harrison on his parents' farm. They were John and
Elizabeth Rhea. His mother was from Virginia. He was
born about 1842. [1860HC]

RHEA, James A.   2nd Co. K, 1st CSA Cav.
        Enl. July 14, 1862 in HC "Deserted."

RHEA, Thomas (replaces Thomas Ray)   Co. L, 36TN
        Enl. Jan. 9, 1862 at Chattanooga He was the son
of John and Elizabeth Rhea. He was born c1843.

RHEA, William   1Sgt.   Co. B, 1TN Cav. (Carter's).
        Enl. Aug. 7, 1861, at Cleveland, TN. Captured
March 30, 1863, at Somerset, KY and imprisoned at City
Point, VA. He was exchanged and captured again June

5, 1864, at Piedmont, Va. Before the war, he was a farm laborer living at Harrison with his wife, Nancy. He had a dark complexion, black hair, blue eyes and stood just over five feet tall. He was born c1836.

RHEA, William M.    2nd Co. K, 1st CSA Cav.
Enl. July 14, 1862 in HC. Hospitalized in Chattanooga. Deserted Jan. 12, 1864.

RHODES, J. H.  Co. L, 35TN
Enl. July 10, 1862 at Tyner Station. Deserted Aug. 10, 1863 at Tyner's.

RHODES, Richard L.    Co. H, 3GA Cav.
Born Walker Co., GA. Enl. May, 1862 in Co. H, 3GA. Captured and imprisoned at Rock Island. Carpenter in Chattanooga c1893. In 1896 reported "in a deplorable condition, and his family in a destitute condition." Died Sept. 28, 1896 and buried at Soldiers Home, Nashville. [NBFM2,7]

RICE, Jesse C.  Co. E, 3TN Cav.
Born 1825, TN. 1903 res. of Chattanooga. Wife was Frances A. Res. 1910 was household of daughter Lethia Cawood. Worked in cement plant. [TP5266; 1910HC]

RICE, John L.  Co. I, 5TN Cav.
Born c1837 in TN, son of Lewis of Long Savannah.

RICH (Ritch), Isaac  Co. A, 19TN
Born c1840 in Prussia. Clerk in Chattanooga for merchant J. S. Litteaur. Enl. May 20, 1861, Knoxville.

RICHARDS, Joseph J.    Co. A, 26TN
Born in 1834 son of Curtis and Edith Maynard Richards. Enl. in Meigs County. Married Elizabeth Smith 30 June 1853 in Meigs Co., TN. Member of NBF Camp in 1885. Farmer. In financial distress. [NBFM2]

RICHARDSON, Foster R.  Co. D, 37TN
Born 1829, SC. Enl. Sept. 1, 1861, Knoxville. Detailed as mechanic, July 22. Tupelo, MS, to work Briarfield Arsenal, Columbus by order Gen. Hardee. In 1863-64 working in CSA armory, Macon.

RICHARDSON, Jonathan    Co. H, 26TN; 2d Co. I, 1CSA (GA)
Enl. July 8, 1861. Knoxville. Sick in hospital, Nashville, 1861. Absent in Co. E, 39GA, Dec. 31, 1862. Joined 1CSA by transfer, March 2, 1863.

RICHEY, Charles A.      Co. D, 37TN
Enl. Sept. 1, 1861 at Knoxville; regimental drummer; wounded by a falling tree at Catoosa Springs, March 25, 1863 and left at hospital. Deserted Aug. 1, 1863 at Catoosa Springs; took USA oath Dec. 24, 1863; fair complexion, light hair, blue eyes, and 5'5" tall.

RICHEY (RITCHIE), Cpl. David L.    Barry's Btry.
Enl. March 16, 1863 at Knoxville; paroled May 11, 1865 at Meridian, MS. [Brown's Diary]

RIDDLE, A. M. C.  Co. A, 19TN
Enl. May 20, 1861 in Knoxville. Died during war. No details.

RIDDLE, Cpl. Robert L.    Co. F, 35TN
Born 1832 in Moore Co., NC, he was a blacksmith in Chattanooga when he enl., Dec. 21, 1862; detached as brigade blacksmith, July 10, 1863; deserted Sept. 6, 1863 in Chattanooga; blue eyes, dark hair, dark complexion, 5'5" tall; took USA oath.

RIDDLE, Wesley    Co. F, 35TN
Born in 1840 in Warren Co., TN, son of Brittain and Jane Riddle, NC natives. He was a blacksmith in Chattanooga at the time he enl., Dec. 21, 1862; black eyes, dark hair, dark complexion, 5'3" tall. Res. Chattanooga, 1870 and a blacksmith.

RILEY, Michael (Mike)   Barry's Btry.
Enl. Sept. 24, 1862 at Chattanooga as substit. for P. H. Watkins; surrendered at Augusta, GA, May 4, 1865.

RILEY, Shepherd W.  Co. I, 19TN
Enl. May 20, 1861 in Knoxville. Died in Jackson, MS, July-Sept., 1862, and buried there.

RINEHART, Gifford C.
Born 1832, TN, of TN parents. 1910 res. James Co. with wife Lula E. Smith (m. 1887). [1910 James Co.]

RISTINE, John S.  Huwald's Btry.
Born Lexington, VA. enl. Jan. 7, 1862. Merchant in Chattanooga, 1887. Moved away by 1893 and died in Knoxville. [NBFM2,7]

RITCHEY, D. L.  2nd Co. K, 1st CSA Cav.
Enl. Sept. 1, 1862 in HC. "Deserted."

RITCHEY, J. A. T.    2nd Co. K, 1st CSA Cav.
Enl. Aug. 25, 1862 in HC. Deserted Sept. 12, 1863 near Harrison, TN. Took USA oath.

RITCHEY, John Tate  Co. K, 1CSA (GA)

Born 1840 in Warren Co., TN. Enl. Aug. 25, 1862; Fort Donelson, Linden. Deserted Sept. 27, 1863 and released at Nashville, Oct. 23, 1863 upon taking USA oath. Married (1881 in HC) Hattie Robertson. Died July 24, 1921 at res. on Campbell St. and buried White Oak Cem. [TWP, 220; CT July 25, 1921]

RITCHEY, Robert    2nd Co. K, 1st CSA Cav.
Enl. Sept. 1, 1862 in HC. Captured in Ooltewah Valley, Sept. 20, 1863. Took USA oath.

RITCHEY, Cpl. William    2nd Co. K, 1st CSA Cav.
Enl. July 14, 1862 in HC. Deserted Shelbyville, TN, Dec. 10, 1862. Took USA oath.

ROARK, James A.  Co. C, 3TN Cav. Bn.;
Co. B, 1TN Cav. (Carter's)
Born Feb. 15, 1840, on Grasshopper Creek, HC, a son of Joseph Roark and Juda Carr, pioneer settlers at Birchwood. He enl. Sept. 17, 1861, at Cleveland. James Roark married America Jane McGill. He died in 1905 in Texas. and he and his wife are buried at Rehoboth Church Cem. at Arlington, TX. [Roark, Hardtack and Hardship; 1860HC]

ROARK, James W.    Co. C, 7TN
He broke his back while in service and remained disabled the rest of his life. He was born in 1835, a son of John Roark and Margaret Gross. He is said to have crawled to the grave of his younger brother, William Roark, at Nicholasville, KY, to plant a tree in his memory. He was offered a pension, but refused it. A bachelor, he died in 1905.

ROARK, John Wesley   Co. C, 3TN Cav. Bn.;
Co. B, 1TN Cav. (Carter's)
Born Aug. 15, 1841, on Grasshopper Creek, HC, a son of Joseph Roark and Juda Carr. He enl. Sept. 17, 1861, at Cleveland. He married Permelia Conner, sister of Jim Conner. [Roark, Hardtack and Hardship; 1860HC]

ROARK, Joseph    Barry's Battery.
He was a son of James Roark and Jerusha Blythe. Born about 1842 in TN, he married Elizabeth Smith. [1860HC]

ROARK, William
He died of measles at Nicholasville, Ky., while serving in the Confederate forces. He was born c1840 and was the son of John Roark and Margaret Gross.

ROARK, William Marion   Co. C, 3TN Cav. Bn.;
Co. B, 1TN Cav. (Carter's)
Born 15 Sept. 1843 in Birchwood, he joined the 1TN Cavalry along with his older brothers, James and John Roark. He was a son of Joseph and Juda Carr. He married in Birchwood Virginia Ann Conner in 1878. She was born 2 March 1852 and died 27 Oct. 1934. He died Dec. 8, 1923 and was buried at Bald Hill Cem. in HC. [TWP, 295; UDC2 pg 452]

ROBBS, Aaron B.    Co. D, 4GA Cav.
Born c1842, he lived in Lookout Valley with his mother, Mary Robbs, his two younger sisters, and two younger brothers until marriage, July 6, 1861 to Eliza Baker. Enl. Oct. 4, 1862, at Chattanooga. Captured by Sherman's forces near Moore's Bridge, GA, on July 13, 1864, he was sent to Nashville, then Louisville, arriving July 26, 1864. He arrived at Camp Douglas, IL, on July 26, 1864.

ROBERSON, C. P. "Chris"    Co. G, 24GA
Born Nov. 2, 1845 in Clarksville, GA, he enl. Aug. 13, 1861 when he was fifteen years and seven months old. Fought in thirty battles with the ANV and was wounded five times. Captured at Front Royal and sent to Elmira where he was imprisoned 8 mo. Surr. at Appomatox. He came to Chattanooga in 1872. Roberson at one time was a partner of John T. Wilder as grocery dealers. Married Miss Waterhouse in Chattanooga Farmer in Chattanooga Died April 25, 1903 and buried CSA Cem. [CT, May 19, 1897, April 26, 1903; NBFM2]

ROBERSON, B. H.    Co. K, 43TN
Enl. Oct. 17, 1861 at Ooltewah; transferred from 36TN; deserted Dec. 18, 1862.

ROBERSON, James M.    Co. K, 43TN
Enl. Dec. 28, 1861 at Ooltewah; captured at Baker's Creek, May 16, 1863.

ROBESON, Littleberry Polk.    Co. K, 43TN
Born 9 Nov. 1844 in McMinn Co. Enl. Nov. 10, 1862 at Ooltewah. Elbow blown out of joint at West Point, MS; captured at Vicksburg, July 4, 1863. Recaptured at Dallas, TN by Federals after discharge as POW at Vicksburg. Married Margaret Elizabeth Long 18 Dec. 1867. She was born 2 July 1846 in Marion Co., TN and died 26 April 1914 in Ooltewah. Res. of Ooltewah, James Co. in 1903 He died 24 April 1908 and is buried in the Sylar Cem. [TP5973]

ROBERTS, Augustus M.    Barry's Btry.
Born Nov. 29, 1838 in Atlanta. Deserted. His wife's name was Minnie. FH has wife Zellis M. He died Sept. 28, 1909 in Chattanooga and was buried in Forest Hills Cemetery. [CT Sept. 29 1909; Brown's Diary; Lusk, FH]

ROBERTS, Edward Gunning    Co. I & D, 16SC
Born Jan. 28, 1843 in Greenville, SC, son of William Taylor and Julia DeBernier Gunning Roberts. Enl. there Jan., 1862. Became officer and capt. of Co. I, 16SC. Wounded Jonesboro and Franklin (hip and head). Elicited remark by Gen. Cheatham who found him on field at Franklin munching bread while blood poured from hole in his head. Wife Margaret Ellen (m. 1871); To Chattanooga in 1886, employed by Frierson and Scott, real estate firm, died June 25, 1934 at res. in St. Elmo and buried Forest Hills Cemetery. [1910HCFHR; CT 26 June 1934; TP15335; NBFM8]

ROBERTS, Capt. Edward R. Co. I, 16SC
Born Jan. 28, 1843 in Greenville Co., SC. Enl. at Greenville, Jan. 1862 in Co. A, 16SC, then became captain, Co. I, 16SC. Wounded at Atlanta, July 22, 1864 and again at Franklin. [NBM2]

ROBERTS, Cpl. Francis Marion    Barry's Btry.
Enl. May 7, 1862 at Chattanooga; died Sept. Oct. 1863 in hospital in Newton, MS.

ROBERTS, James A. Co. K, 43TN
Enl. Oct. 17, 1861 at Ooltewah; deserted Nov. 10, 1862.

ROBERTS, James K. Co. G, 26TN
Son of William Roberts, he enl. July 8, 1861; left sick at Russelville, KY, Feb. 9, 1862; died March 1, 1862.

ROBERTS, James M. Barry's Btry.
Enl. May 31, 1862 in Barry's Btry. at Chattanooga; tranferred from Co. G, 26TN; captured Spanish Fort, April 8, 1865; imprisoned Ship Island, MS.

ROBERTS, John    Co. H, 37TN
Enl. Nov. 16, 1861 at Chattanooga; died at General Hospital, Knoxville, Dec. 21, 1861.

ROBERTS, John C.    Lookout Regt. TN Art.
Born 1 June 1835, son of Thomas and Sarah J. Kennedy Roberts of Rossville. TN. Enl. in 1862 in the Lookout Arterilly and saw action in Alabama and Mississippi as well as the Atlanta Campaign, captured at Jonesboro, Sept. 1, 1864 [verified by Brown Diary], 5'9" tall, gray eyesm, dark hair, and dark complexion. He served on the County Court of Hamilton and for some years as a member of the School Board. Methodist. 1910 res. Dodds Ave. with 2d wife, an English woman he had married in 1906. [1910HC; *Tennessee - A History* pg 89]

ROBERTS, John T.    Co. K, 43TN
Enl. Oct. 17, 1861 at Ooltewah; detached to hospital in Knoxville, March 1, 1862; captured at Vicksburg, July 4, 1863; took USA oath Dec. 23, 1863; dark complexion, brown hair, black eyes, 5'9" tall.

ROBERTS, Sgt. Joseph Phillips    Co. L, 36TN
Born 1843 in Loudon Co. Enl. Jan. 9, 1862, at Chattanooga; became hospital nurse in Dalton, Cartersville and at St. Mary's Hospital in LaGrange; dark complexion, dark hair, brown eyes, 5'6" tall. He married (1866 in HC) Isabella Reed and died 1881 in Fla. [TWP, p. 14]

ROBERTS, Posey    Barry's Btry.
Enl. Oct. 4, 1862 at Chattanooga; detached Feb. 1863, to Commissary duty in Pollard, AL; left in hospital in Mobile when battery surrendered.

ROBERTS, R. Wesley    Barry's Btry.
Enl. May 14, 1862 at Chattanooga; deserted Feb. 25, 1864 at Demopolis, AL; took oath to USA; 5'6 ½" tall, light hair, fair complexion, and hazel eyes. Desertion at Demopolis, substantiated by Brown's Diary.

ROBERTS, T. J.    Provost Guard (MS)

ROBERTS, T. M.    Co. G, 3CSA (TN) Cav.
Born McMinn Co., 1843. Murfreesboro, Chattanooga, Knoxville, Atlanta Campaign. Res. 1911 in Hill City. [TP12, 396]

ROBERTS, William B.
Born 1838, he married (1860) Elizabeth B. Harrison and died 1905 in HC. [TWP, p. 181]

ROBERTSON, Christianburg P.    Co. G, 24GA
Born Jan. 26, 1846, Habersham Co., GA. Enl. Aug. 13, 1861. Wounded four times: Crompton's Gap, MD; Front Royal, VA, Chaffin's Bluff, VA; Fredericksburg. Captured Deep Bottom, VA, Aug. 19, 1864 and imprisoned Elmira, NY, but escaped before exchanged. Merchant in Chattanooga, 1900 when applied for admission from HC to TN Soldiers Home.

ROBERTSON, Zachariah    Co. D, 37TN
Enl. March 18, 1863 at Chattanooga; captured May 26, 1863 at Chattanooga and imprisoned at Rock Island, IL, where he died of typhoid and was buried (grave #1106).

ROCK, R. L.
Charter member of NBF Camp, 1885.

RODDY, James 2nd Lt. (Adjutant)    Co. B, 1TN Cav.

(Carter's)

Prior to the war, he was a lawyer who resided at Harrison. Born about 1817, he was a son of John and Elizabeth Lane Roddy, who had moved to HC from Meigs Co. about 1840. John Roddy was a son of Col. James Roddye, a Revolutionary soldier and political leader in early East TN. James Roddy married Mary Jane Luttrell on Christmas Day of 1845. After her death in 1852, he married her sister, Sarah E. Luttrell. He enl. Aug. 7, 1861, at Cleveland. Again enl. July 14, 1862 in HC in 2nd Co., 1st CSA Cav. March, 1863 absent sick on surgeon's certificate. Resigned April, 1864, too ill to perform his duties. Transferred to Co. F, 39GA, April 1, 1864. Dark complexion, black hair, hazel eyes, and 5'10" tall. After the war, he lived at Rome, GA, then at Macon. [JWilson Roddy family; 1860HC]

RODDY, Sydna Caroline McDonald (Mrs. T. H.) Rhea County Girls Company

Born July 26, 1848 near Dayton, TN the daughter of Bryant R. and Elizabeth [Brown] McDonald and sister of "Capt. Molly" (Mrs. Mary E. McDonald Sawyer). "Once the whole group of women were arrested by Union army officers on charge of furnishing relief to the Confederates, brought to Chattanooga on a boat and marched to Gen. Steadman's headquarters. Gen. Steadman promptly released the young women." Died March 22, 1917 in Chattanooga and buried in Ooltewah. [CT April 23, 1917]

RODDY, Thomas H.    B Co., 43TN

Born c1830, son of Elizabeth. Doctor in Ooltewah. Married Sydna McDonald 13 Dec. 1876. [1860 HC]

RODGERS, J. J.    2nd Co. K, 1st CSA Cav.

Enl. July 14, 1862 in HC. Hospitalized in Chattanooga. Deserted June 21, 1863.

RODGERS, J. M.    2nd Co. K, 1st CSA Cav.

Enl. Sept. 19, 1862 in HC. Deserted June 21, 1863. He died 1890 in HC. [TWP, p. 85.]

RODGERS, J. N.    2nd Co. K, 1st CSA Cav.

Enl. July 14, 1862 in HC. Deserted Dec. 28, 1862 in Shelbyville, TN.

RODGERS, James Madison    Co. G, 43TN

Born Monroe Co., TN, Jan. 6, 1836. Married (1857) Rachel Fannie Young. Tenant farmer in McMinn Co. when he enl. Spring, 1861 at Charleston, TN. Returned to McMinn after war. Res. in East Chattanooga, 1908. Died Feb. 11, 1920 at home on Palmetto and buried Forest Hills Cem. [NBFM7; TP10228]

RODGERS, 1st Sgt. Jerry    2nd Co. K, 1st CSA Cav.

Enl. Sept. 12, 1862 in HC. Deserted Jan. 10, 1864.

ROE, Gayle

Born Charleston Dist., SC. Wounded eleven times. Married (1885 in Dade Co.) Mary L. Lowe. Res. of Soddy fifty years. Died Nov. 18, 1920, age 87, at his home. [TWP, 226; CT Nov. 20, 1920]

ROE, Isaac T.    Barry's Btry.

Enl. July 14, 1862 at Chattanooga

ROE, James M.    Barry's Btry.

Enl. July 12, 1864 at Atlanta; paroled May 11, 1865 at Meridian, MS; res. Cherokee Co., AL.

ROE, Samuel B.    50th GA

Born 1844, he was living on Market St. in Chattanooga when he died Oct. 19, 1902, at the age of 58. Buried CSA Cem. [CT Oct. 19, 1902]

ROGERS, Enoch    Co. I, 43TN

Born c1844 and living at Long Savannah with parents, William (blacksmith and native of GA) and Sarah, prior to war. Enl. Nov. 13, 1861, Charleston. On sick furlough, then listed as deserter, Aug. 6, 1862.

ROGERS, Sgt. Howell N.    Co. F, 39TN Mtd. Inf. (Lillard's)

Born 1834, Buncombe Co. NC on French Broad near Ashville. Enl. March, 1862: Perryville and Chickamauga. Captured Sept. 13, 1863 in Cleveland and took USA oath following day. To TN 1869. House carpenter, 1910, James Co. with wife Harriet M. (m 1860). Worked at E. I. Dupont powder mill till May 1, 1911. Res. Ooltewah. [TP 13,712; 1910James Co.; CT 22 June 1915]

ROGERS, J. N.    Barry's Btry.

Enl. June 2, 1862 at Chattanooga; paroled May 11, 1865 in Meridian, MS.

ROGERS, J. W.    Co. D, 4GA Cav.

Enl. Oct. 4, 1862, at Chattanooga.

ROGERS, Lt. James C.    Co. D, 4GA Cav.

Born April 11, 1834 in HC, he was a son of George W. Rogers and Catherine Jackson. He married (1854) Mary W. Smith and was a farmer and blacksmith until he joined the Confederate Army. He fought at Chickamauga and elsewhere and rose to Orderly Sgt. and 2nd Lt. He returned home in 1864 and was "forced into service in the regular army of the United States." After the war he farmed and worked as a blacksmith. He married his second wife in 1867, Lydia Barker. [GHT, p. 989; *Goodspeed's History of Hamilton County*, p. 989]

ROGERS, James M.
Born 1828, Va. Presbyterian. Married Martha L. House carpenter. Died Feb. 11, 1920, age 82, at res. on Palmetto and buried Forest Hills Cem. [CT Feb. 12, 1920]

ROGERS, James Madison   Co. F, 1GA Regulars
Born Culpepper, VA, 1841. Married (1857) Rachel F. Enl. March 4, 1861. ANV: Second Manassas, Seven Days. On detached service in QM Dept. in FL. Paroled in 1865. Carpenter, prison guard. Died Nov. 13, 1909. [TP9131]

ROGERS, Jeremiah   Co. L, 36TN; Co. L, 35TN
He was born c1830, son of William and Elizabeth Rogers, who lived at Ooltewah. Enl. Jan. 9, 1862, at Chattanooga.

ROGERS, John B.   Co. D, 4GA Cav.; Co. D, 37TN
He enl. Oct. 4, 1862, at Chattanooga. Then enl. June 10, 1863, Beech Grove, TN in 37TN. Deserted July 9, 1863; took USA oath of allegiance, May 9, 1864. He had a light complexion, brown hair, blue eyes and stood 6'1" tall.

ROGERS, Jonathan   Co. I, 43TN
Born c1843 and living at Long Savannah with parents, William (blacksmith and native of GA) and Sarah, prior to war. Enl. Nov. 13, 1861, Charleston. AWOL, spring, 1862.

ROGERS, Joseph Madison   Co. A, 4TN Cav.
Born 1838 in VA, enl. March 4, 1861 at Cartersville, GA in Co. F, 1GA. Paroled in Apr. 1865, never wounded nor captured. Farmer at Chattanooga. Presbyterian. Died Feb. 11, 1920, age 82, at res. on Palmetto St. and buried Forest Hills Cemetery. [FHR; CT Feb. 12, 1920; NBFM2,3,7]

ROGERS, W. H. H.   Co. G, 9GA
Born Calhoun, TN, Feb. 13, 1840 and lived in McMinn Co. the greater part of his life until coming to Chattanooga c1896. Fought in the Army of Northern Virginia and was twice wounded. Baptist. Member NBF Camp, 1895. Died July 15, 1916 at res. on Wilson St. in Avondale and buried Forest Hills Cem. [CT July 16, 1916; TP5297]

ROGERS, W. T.   "Uncle Billy"
School teacher before the war. Passenger agent with Nashville & Chattanooga RR for 40 years. NBF Camp. Left Chattanooga in 1880's and opened passenger office in Knoxville, then moved to Atlanta. Died Feb. 24, 1918 in Atlanta. [CT Feb. 25, 1918; NBFM2]

ROGERS, William A.   Co. D, 4GA Cav.
He enl. Oct. 4, 1862, at Chattanooga. After being captured near Summerville, GA, on May 10, 1864, he was sent to Nashville, then Louisville and on to Alton, IL, later that month. He was at Tallahassee, FL, in May of 1865, then he was paroled at Thomasville, GA.

ROGERS, Capt. William Jefferson   Co. B, 4GA Mounted Inf.
In the Mexican War, he was captain of the Fourth Company, Fourth Regiment, of Tennessee Volunteers. In October, 1862, he organized Co. D, 4GA Cav. This unit, part of Avery's Regiment, was recruited in Lookout Valley. Beginning in Jan. 1863, he was part of Gen. Alfred Iverson's Brigade, Allen's Division, Wheeler's Corps, Army of Tennessee.
Born in 1820, he was the son of the pioneer HC settler William Rogers. W. J. Rogers was a deputy sheriff and then county clerk for HC. A bachelor, he was known as "crippled or limping Bill Rogers." He died near Jonesborough, GA, in the summer of 1866.

ROLLINS, James V.
Buried Forest Hills Cemetery. [FHR]

ROOK, William
Born 1843, TN of TN parents. 1910 res. James Co. with wife Virginia A. (m. 1880). [1910 James Co.]

ROPER, 2Lt. Jacob R.   Co. K, 43TN
Born c1837. Enl. Oct. 17, 1861, Ooltewah. 2Lt., May 10, 1862. Captured Vicksburg, July 4, 1863, then paroled. Rejoined unit and recaptured at Morristown, Oct. 28, 1864. Sent to Chattanooga, then Louisville. Imprisoned at Johnson's Island until May 25, 1865.

ROSE, Jeremiah M. A. "Jerry"   Co. L, 36TN;
        Co. H, 35TN
Born HC, April 25, 1845 and prior to war lived on a farm at Soddy with his parents, Emannuel and Jane Rose. Brother of John W. Conscripted Jan. 9, 1862, at Chattanooga, but claimed his musket hit by cannon ball at Murfreesboro, injuring his chest. Disch. at Wartrace, May 1, 1863. Res. Hill City, 1915. [TP14,617; 1860HC]

ROSE, Cpl. John W. (F.)   Co. L, 35TN;
        Co. C, 5TN Cav.
Born c1820. Enl. Jan. 9, 1862 at Chattanooga. Fought at Murfreesboro. Absent without leave since July 1, 1863. 1870 farm laborer at Long Savannah, wife

Arabell. Res. 1915, Chattanooga. Brother of Jerry Rose. [TP14,617]

ROUTH, Capt. Andrew S.  CSA Cav. (Wood's Regt), 1st Co. A
Born 1848. Died at his home in Trion, GA, Dec. 23, 1919. [CT Dec. 20, 1930] --also A. S. Routh, 3LA Cav. (Harrison's), Co. A.

ROUTH, Francis M.    Co. K, 43TN
Born c1820. Enl. Dec. 17, 1861 at Ooltewah; transferred from 36TN; captured at Vicksburg, July 4, 1863; took USA oath Jan. 3, 1864. 1870 res. Bradley Co.

ROUTH, 1st Sgt. J. C.    Co. K, 43TN
Enl. Dec. 17, 1861 at Ooltewah; transferred from 36TN; captured at Vicksburg, July 4, 1863; paroled; wounded (compound fracture of femur) and captured Sept. 19, 1864 at Winchester, VA.

ROUTH, Lafayette K.
Born 1837, TN. Res. 1910 in household of uncle Joseph P. Parker in James Co. [1910 James Co.]

ROUTH, W. J.  Co. K, 43TN
Enl. Nov. 15, 1862 at Ooltewah; died at Vicksburg, May 20, 1863. [Lindsley, 528]

ROWE, Sgt. Benjamin F.  Co. A, 19TN
Born c1845. Enl. May 20, 1861, Knoxville. Prom. to Sgt. Slightly wounded at Murfreesboro, Dec. 31, 1862. and sent home. Given 30 day furlough, May 15, 1863. Captured at Missionary Ridge, Nov. 25, 1863 and imp. Rock Island. Applied to US Navy but rejected.

ROWE, Charles  Co. I, 19TN
Born 1844 in TN, son of Solomon and Martha. Enl. May 20, 1861, Knoxville. Absent sick in hospital by July, 1863 and ceased to belong to company. [1860HC]

ROWE, Sgt. James O.  Co. I, 19TN
Born 1839 in TN, son of Solomon and Martha. Enl. May 20, 1861, Knoxville. Rose to sgt. Teamster. Absent sick March, 1863. Captured near Chickamauga, GA, Sept. 19, 1863 and imprisoned Camp Douglas. Released April 5, 1865 upon taking oath. [1860HC]

ROWE, Sgt., Lewis    Co. A, 19TN
Enl. May 20, 1861, Knoxville. Prom. to color sgt. Nov. 1, 1862. He left a destitute widow and a family of small children when he was killed Jan. 2, 1863. He survived the fierce fighting at Shiloh and Murfreesboro where he was slightly wounded, but died in a railroad accident en route home from Murfreesboro. A native of Wayne Co., Ky., he had blue eyes, brown hair, dark complexion and stood 6 feet tall. He had risen to a sergeant's rank in John D. Powell's company. Rowe was 26. His older brother, Solomon, had a farm at Chattanooga
Rowe's widow, Sarah, wrote the Confederate authorities, saying she was "in want of money with a large family of small children and no way to maintain them but only by my own labor." She pointed out that produce was fetching "enormous prices and it makes it quite difficult for me to get sufficient food for my family." She was awarded $61.19.

ROWE, Cpl. Madison  Co. I, 19TN
Born 1841 in TN, son of Solomon and Martha. Enl. May 20. 1861, Knoxville. Promoted to Cpl., May 20, 1862. [1860HC]

ROWE, Robert    Co. H, 2TN Cav. (Ashby's)
Born 1839 Roane Co., TN. Farm laborer in Chattanooga, 1860, with wife Mary. Enl. June 17, 1861, Knoxville. Sick at Chattanooga, May 21, 1862. Section foreman in Chattanooga c1890. [NBFM2; 1860HC]

ROWLES, W. R.
Born Cleveland, TN c1849. Enl. Feb. 1865 in AL State Reserves. Insurance Agent in Chattanooga c1896. Died Sept. 28, 1928. [NBFM2,7]

RUBLE, J. A.    Barry's Btry.
Enl. June 2, 1862 at Chattanooga; deserted Sept. 19, 1862.

RUSSELL, Capt. Milton    Co. C, 4GA BN, 60GA
Born June 13,1837 in Camden Co., GA, son of Henry Richard Russell and Caroline Hardee, he became a farmer before the war. He enl. in Co. C, 4GA BN and was elected 1st Lt. He fought near Savannah and was at Hilton Head at the time of the capture of Fort Walker. In June, 1862, as a member of the 60GA, he saw action in Jackson's Valley Campaign, Seven Days, Cedar Mountain, and Second Manassas. He fell ill and could not serve until after Sharpsburg, at which time he was promoted to Capt. He commanded his company at Fredericksburg, Chancellorsville and Gettysburg. He fought in the great battles of 1864 until being severely wounded and losing his arm at Winchester, Sept. 19, 1864. He was captured and taken to Point Lookout, MD, Old Capitol Prison and Fort Delaware, not being released until June, 1865. Upon the end of the war he became a teacher, then was elected judge of the ordinary court of Camden Co., an office he held 16 years. He moved to Chattanooga in 1885 and became a member of the County Council. Treasurer, NBF Camp, 1894. Died Dec.

4, 1903 and buried Forest Hills Cemetery. [CT Dec. 4, 1903; FHR; NBFM7; UDC1]

RUSTON, Hiram H.  Co. D, 37TN
Born 1845 in TN, son of John and Elizabeth of Ooltewah. Laborer. Enl. Sept. 1, 1861, Knoxville. Disch. Nov. 24, 1862, underage. Black eyes, black hair, and 5'6" tall. [1860 HC census]

RUSTON, J. J.  Co. D, 37TN
Probably Jefferson, bro. of Hiram, age 17 in 1860.

RUTH (see Routh)

RUTHERFORD, Preston    Co. E, 25TN
Born c1826, he was farm laborer living south of Ooltewah with wife Elizabeth when he enl. Nov. 25, 1861, Monticello, KY. Last paid Feb. 28, 1862. Listed as sick at home and then as deserter in Nov. 1862. Res. of Bradley Co., 1870.

RUTLEDGE, William Watkin  Co. A, 6TN
Born 1837 (1846) in Brownsville, TN, he married (1882) Claudia Catherine Nolen. Moved to Chattanooga in 1893. He died April 19, 1918 on Signal Mtn. and buried Forest Hills Cem. [TWP, 298; CT April 20, 1918]

RYALL, Lemuel (Lem, Lamb)  Co. H, 4TN Cav.;
Co. B, 5TN Cav.
Born 1822 in Ireland, he was a farmer near Chattanooga. His wife was Mary Jane Simpson. He enl. Aug. 11, 1861, at Chattanooga. He was discharged after a year of service. Died July 30, 1894 and buried Concord Baptist Cem. [JW, Ryall Family; 1860HC]

RYALL, Thomas C.  Co. F, 41TN
Born c1844, Shelbyville, TN. Res., 1910, household of Abbie H. Estes on McCallie Ave. Owned home on Lookout Mtn. and in Auburndale, FL. Died at daugher's home, Vancouver Barracks, Vancouver, WA in 1927. [1910HC; CT Feb. 26, 1927]

# S

SAFFER, George   Chattanooga Home Guards
Born c1834 in Bavaria, Ger. Married (Mar. 31,1861) Mary B. J. Kuhn. Wife Rosa (1870HC) was from Ohio. 1870 occup. cooper in Chattanooga.

SAMPLES, 1Lt. James G.   Co. F, 35TN

Born in 1837 in Bradley County, TN, he was a merchant res. in house hold of George Curry in 1860. Enl. in HC, Oct. 1, 1862. Seriously wounded at Chickamauga, he was left at home to recuperate and "moved north about 1st of Dec. 1863." Dropped June 2, 1864. Gray eyes, sandy hair, fair complexion, and 5'11" tall. Took USA oath. [1860HC]

SAMPLY, Martin V.  Co. F, 35TN
Born 1842 in TN, son of William and Mary.

SANDELS, John
Born Apr. 21, 1810 in Ireland, Sandels emigrated to Ohio where he became an Episcopal priest. He was a professor at Kenyon College and taught at the Columbia (TN) Female Institute. In 1853 he became a missionary at Chattanooga and organized St. Paul's Church. After serving as a chaplain in the Confederate Army, Sandels served churches in Arkansas and Louisiana where he died Oct. 10, 1874.

SANDY, Lt. F. H.    2TN Cav. (Ashby's)
Captured Sept. 9, 1863; imprisoned at Johnson's Island.

SARTIN, John T.  2nd Co. K, 1st CSA Cav.
Born NC 1831. 1860 res. in household of W. M. Shropshire at Ooltewah. Enl. Sept. 24, 1862 in HC. Deserted Sept. 15, 1863 at Linden, TN. Residence listed in HC. Light complexion, light hair, blue eyes, and 5', 8" tall. [1860 HC]

SAVAGE, Jesse L.  Co. I, 19TN
Born c1843, he was living in Chattanooga with his parents, Warren and Bartheny Savage. Enl. May 20, 1861, Knoxville. Deserted in May, 1862.

SAWYER, Aaron Madison
(an Aaron Matthew Sawyer was younger brother to Jefferson Elgin Sawyer.  He married Elizabeth Guthrie)

SAWYER, Jefferson Elgin  Co. F, 35TN
Born December 25, 1821 and died in May 16, 1905, buried in the Chattanooga Memorial Park Cemetery in White Oak. Enl. July 31, 1863, at Cleveland. Two months later, he was present when the fierce fighting began at Chickamauga. Records show he "deserted" on the second day of the battle on Sept. 20. His brother, Eli T. Sawyer, was a first lieutenant and adjutant with the Sixth Mounted Infantry of the Union Army. He was the son of George Washington Sawyer and Mary Thurman. He was married first to Elizabeth Stringer, then secondly to Mary Jane Henninger and then thirdly to Mary E. McDonald. [See Below]

The Sawyers moved at an early date from Bledsoe County to Dallas in Hamilton County. Jefferson E. Sawyer had a farm at White Oak, where Chattanooga Memorial Park was later established. He also had property on Walden's Ridge above Falling Water. Here he operated a mountaintop resort known as the Sawyer Hotel until it burned. This community on the mountain is now known as Sawyer. Jefferson E. Sawyer died May 15, 1905. [JW Sawyer family; CT May 16, 1995]

SAWYER, Capt. Mary E. McDonald - Rhea Co. Girls Company
Born May 18, 1834 in Rhea Co. the daughter of Bryant R. and Elizabeth (Brown) McDonald. She was the Captain of the Girls Company along with her sister Sydna Caroline McDonald Roddy [see her entry]. The Girls unit was captured in Rhea County and taken to Chattanooga for trial where General Steadman released the girls and made them all walk home without escort or guards. Mary married Jefferson Elgin Sawyer and is buried in the Butram Cemetery in Rhea County having died December 14, 1914.

SCHNEIDER, Frederick          Home Guards
Born at Baden, Germany, in 1823, he arrived in New Orleans in 1848 and came to Chattanooga in 1851. He was an expert cabinetmaker. He and his wife had five children. At the time of his death on March 16, 1900, he was living with his daughter, Mrs. Mary Noll, at 322 E. Eighth St. [CT March 17, 1900]

SCOGGINS, James McDonald   Co. B, 36TN
Born Bradley County, July 7, 1835. Enl. Dec. 1861 and fought at Cumberland Gap and Fishing Creek. Discharged because of measles and later in war served as trackman on East TN & GA railroad. Methodist. Res. 1908 in Highland Park. Died April 6, 1909 in Chattanooga. [CT April 7, 1909]

SCOTT, Bartley W.   Co. B, 1TN Cav. (Carter's)
Born about 1825, he was a farmer at Snow Hill when the war started. Enl. Aug. 7, 1861, at Cleveland and served as a farrier. He deserted at Bristol, TN, on March 7, 1865. Fair complexion, light hair, blue eyes, and 6'2" tall.

SCOTT, Charles   Co. F, 35TN
Born 1837 in Washington Co., TN, he was a HC farmer when he enl. Oct. 1, 1862 at Chattanooga; serving as hospital nurse, Feb. 10, 1863; deserted at Chattanooga, Feb. 1863; gray eyes, dark hair, dark complexion, and 5'10" tall.

SCOTT, J. K. P.   Co. K, 43TN
Enl. Dec. 17, 1861 at Ooltewah; transferred

from 36TN; discharged Dec. 13, 1863.

SCOTT, James M.   Co. D, 37TN
Age 47 in 1861; enl. Sept. 1, 1861, at Knoxville; became ill March 20, 1862 and sent to Chattanooga where he died Aug. 20, 1862.

SCOTT, M. S.   Co. F. 8GA Bn.
Born Spartanburg, SC. Enl. 1861 in Co. F GA Bn. under Gen. Lawton at Savannah. Later moved to Mississippi, then back to Army of Tennessee.

SCOTT, Milo W.   Barry's Btry.
Born c1835, he was a clerk in Chattanooga when the war broke out. He resided with the Thomas J. Lattners at the time of the 1860 census. Married (May 14, 1861) Mary Ann Doyl. Enl. July 28, 1862 at Chattanooga; captured Spanish Fort, April 8, 1865; imprisoned at Ship Island, MS.

SCOTT, Saumel Joseph   7GA
Born Greene Co. GA, Nov. 17, 1844. Stationed Mobile. Fought in Atlanta Campaign (rec. shell wound), Franklin and Nashville. Married (Dec. 23, 1869) Mary Virginia Elizabeth Kemp. Worked for Western and Atlantic RR. 1882 settled in HC, seven miles east of Missionary Ridge in sight of Mackie Schoolhouse. 1888 opened merchandise business, Chickamauga, TN. Tyner Methodist Church. Died Dec. 12, 1925 at res in Chickamauga, TN and buried in Concord Cem. [TWP, 239; CT Dec. 13, 1925; TP6526, 15390; Robert Sparks Walker Papers]

SCOTT, Samuel Joseph   Co. F, 1GA Reg.
Born Newton Co., GA., son of William and Rosannah Hollingsworth Scott. Enl. Dec. 1862 at Powder Springs, GA., to Fort Gaines, AL was in battles at Resaca, New Hope Church, Kennesaw, Peachtree Creek and Atlanta (wounded). Also in fighting at Jonesboro, Franklin, and Nashville. He was a butcher after the war and moved to Chattanooga in 1890. [TCVQ]

SCOTT, Sterling   Co. K, 43TN
Born about 1836, he enl. Oct. 17, 1861, at Ooltewah. He was absent on sick furlough from the fall, 1861 through April, 1862. Prior to the war, he had a farm at Long Savannah north of Ooltewah.

SCOTT, Thomas A.   Co. K, 43TN
Enl. Dec. 17, 1861 at Ooltewah; captured at Vicksburg, July 4, 1863; paroled; again captured at Cleveland, TN, Dec. 15, 1863; imprisoned at Rock Island Barracks and released Oct. 18, 1864. [CSR; RI ledger]

SCOTT, Sgt. T. J.   2nd Co. K, 1st CSA Cav.

Enl. July 14, 1862 in HC. Captured at Linden, TN, Jan. 12, 1864. Imprisoned at Alton, IL.

SCRIBNER (SCRIVENER), James Henry   Co. C, Walker's Bn., Thomas Legion
Born Blount Co. TN, March 4, 1844. Enl. 1861 in Maryville, but went on leave with measles. Re-enl. Sept. 29, 1862. Present through Oct. 1862; AWOL July 15, 1863 - Apr. 7, 1864, but claimed he was engaged in "hauling of supplies." Married (1876) Mary Fuller. Res. 1915 in Soddy. Died June 27, 1931 in HC. [TWP, 289; TP14815; 1910HC]

SCROGGINS, G. W.     Clark's Independent Cav. Co.
Enl. Aug. 31, 1862 at Chattanooga.

SCROGGINS, James McDonald     Co. B, 36TN
Enl. Cleveland, but not found in 1860HC.

SCRUGGS, Alfred T.   Co. E, 4TN Cav. (McLemore's)
Born Bedford Co., TN Sept. 24, 1834. Served under Forrest and Wheeler. To Chattanooga in 1905. Died May 20, 1912 and buried Forest Hills Cemetery. [CT May 21, 1912]

SCRUGGS, Barlow O.  Co. H, Holcombe Legion (7SC Cav.)
Died January 15, 1889 and is buried in the Concord Baptist Church Cemetery.

SCRUGGS, Drury Dobbins   Co. C, 4SC State Troops
Born June 23, 1848 in Spartanburg, SC, enl. there, Sept. 1864. Lived in TX before coming to Chattanooga, 1899. 1910 res. Elizabeth Ave. with wife Harriet. Baptist. Dairy farmer, died April 16, 1927 at res. on Mitchell Ave. Buried Concord Baptist Church Cem. [NBFM7; 1910HC; CT Apr. 17, 1927]

SEAGERS, James  Co. K, 43TN
Born 1818 in Franklin Co., GA, he was a farmer and "ditcher" living at Harrison when the war started. He enl. Oct. 17, 1861, at Ooltewah and soon was detached to the general hospital at Loudon, TN, and was discharged due to a disability on July 19, 1862. His wife was Jane. He had a dark complexion, dark eyes, dark hair and was 5'10" tall. [1860HC]

SEAGLE, William E.  Co. F, 35TN
Born 1843 in TN, son of John and Nancy Seagle of Ooltewah. [1860HC]

SEAGLE, William E.  Co. F, 35TN
Born 1831 in VA. Farm laborer; wife Eliza and three children. [1860HC]

SEALE, Reuben Harrison   Co. E, 11TH SC
Born Greenville, AL in 1834. Married Eliza M. Hughes (1857), in Greenville, AL. Captured Petersburg, June 24, 1864 and imprisoned at Point Lookout six months. Family moved to TN, 1893 and became res. of Ooltewah, James Co., doing "pick-up jobs" at 50 cents a day. Died May 29, 1909 in Chattanooga. [CT May 30, 1909; TP3541; TWP 3220]

SEARCY, Shadrick   Co. I, 46GA
Black soldier, born March 1, 1846, Talbot Co., GA. Slave of Dr. John Searcy who became body servant for his sons James (killed at Franklin) and Kitchen (killed near Rome, 1865). After war he was for 40 years an employee of Central of GA RR. To TN, 1903. Received pension with support of NBF Camp. Died May 11, 1937 and buried in CSA Cem., "first Negro, it is believed, to be buried there." [TP#235; undated CT clipping in NBFM6]

SEGARS, James     2nd Co. K, 1st CSA Cav.
Enl. Aug. 20, 1862 in HC. Deserted at Shelbyville, TN, Dec. 10, 1862.

SEIGLER (SIGLER, SIEGLER), 1Lt. Samuel W.   Co. K, 43TN
Enl. Oct. 17, 1861 at Ooltewah; resigned Dec. 4, 1862.

SELCER (SELTSER), William H.   2nd Co. K, 1st CSA Cav.
Enl. Sept. 23, 1862 in HC. Paroled May 3, 1865 at Charlotte, NC.

SELF, F. T.   Clark's Independent Cav. Co.
Enl. Aug. 31, 1862 at Chattanooga; deserted Nov. 25, 1863 near Chattanooga.

SELF, M. P.   Clark's Independent Cav. Co.
Enl. July 18, 1863 at Chattanooga; deserted Nov. 25, 1863 near Chattanooga.

SEVERIN, Adam     Co. H, 2TN Cav. (Ashby's)
He left his 45-acre grape vineyard at Harrison to join Capt. William Ragsdale. A native of Germany, he was born Dec. 10, 1826 and made his way to Chattanooga in 1859 where he grew fruit trees and grape vines to make wine. His orchard and arbors were destroyed by the war, but he replanted and offered the public "Concord" and "Hive Seedling." His wife, Louisa, was also from Germany. "Probably no man was known to a larger group of Chattanoogans." Absent at Chattanooga by order Gen. Smith. Disch. overage, Sept 15, 1862. [CT, Dec. 5, 1903; 1860HC]

SEVIER, Elbert Franklin   Co. I, 26TN
        Born in Kingston, Roane Co., Feb. 5, 1841, son of Garry and Mary Caroline Brown Sevier, he was a direct descendant of Gov. John Sevier and was related to the James family, with whom he stayed when first coming to Chattanooga He was also the nephew of another Elbert F. Sevier, a Methodist minister who married Eliza James. He was a student at Von Aldehoff's Institute on Lookout Mountain when he enl. Oct. 1, 1862, at Knoxville in Co. I, 26th Tennessee Infantry. He was wounded by a spent cannonball at Murfreesboro, and spent months in a hospital in Chattanooga where he was captured by the Federals and paroled. After war attended college, then came to Chattanooga and became bookkeeper at Watkins Hardware Co., then a director of the Chattanooga Gas Light Co. (1871-76). Later he was in the insurance business, and served as the treasurer of the Chamber of Commerce. He married Bettie Taylor, and they lived at the corner of Georgia Avenue and Vine Street. Episcopalian. He died in sanitarium in Cincinnati, OH, Oct. 11, 1905 and was buried in Chattanooga at Forest Hills Cemetery. [CT, Oct. 13-14, 1905; FHR; NBFM2; Hist. St. Paul's, 172-73]

SEXTON, Blackburn        Co. D, 4GA Cav.
        He is listed as only 11 years old in the 1860 census, but he enl. in the Confederate forces on Aug. 1, 1863. He took the USA oath of allegiance the following May 9. He had a light complexion, brown hair, blue eyes and was 5'7" tall. His parents were Joseph and Lorraine Sexton.

SEXTON, John          Co. D, 4GA Cav.
        Born about 1843, his parents were Joseph and Lorraine Sexton. Enl. Oct. 4, 1862, at Chattanooga. Records show him returning to the ranks at Camp Millville on Feb. 12, 1863. Became 2nd Sgt.

SHADDOCK, Elisha   Co. H, 26TN; 2d Co. I, 1CSA (GA)
        Born 1840. Enl. July 8, 1861, Knoxville. Captured Fort Donelson, Feb. 16, 1862. and imprisoned Camp Douglas. Deserted at Tunnel Hill, April 19, 1863. Present June 30, 1863. Deserted at Chattanooga, Aug. 24, 1863. Captured at Cooper's Gap, Sept. 12, 1863. Released at Nashville upon taking USA oath.

SHALER, James Riddle  Lt. Col. 1MO
        Born Dec. 23, 1830 in Allegheny Co., PA. Merchant in St. Louis who enl. 1860 in Minute Men, then 1MO Inf. with rank of Maj.; Adjt, D. M. Frost's Brigade. Col, 31AR. Briefly commanded combined 7th/9th Divisions in early 1862. Maj and AAG to Adj. Gen. Lt. Col and AAG on staffs of Genls. Price,

Magruder and E.K. Smith. Colonel, AIG, on staff of Sterling Price, Aug. 29, 1864. Discharged and released 1865. Lt. Col. at end of war and AAG. Episcopalian. RR supt. in Chattanooga in 1893. Later Panama RR. Left Chattanooga in 1896. Died Sept. 7, 1910 at Ocean City, NJ and buried in Bellefontaine Cem., St. L. MO. [Crute, CSA staff officers; NBFM2; CT Sept. 11, 1910]

SHANKLIN (SHANKLES), Thomas      Co. F, 35TN
        Lindsley-died April, 1862; killed in action.

SHANNON, H.  Co. D, 37TN
        Born 1837 in TN. Farm laborer at Harrison with wife Ora Ann and three children. Enl. March 3, 1863, Chattanooga as conscript. Deserted March 29, 1863. [1860HC]

SHARP, E. P.    Co. K, 43TN
        Enl. Oct. 17, 1861 at Ooltewah; captured at Vicksburg, July 4, 1863.

SHARP, Elisha F.    Co. A, 26TN; Co. I, 3d Mtd.
                Inf. (Lillard's)
        Born 5 Jan. 1842 in TN, son of Elisha and Ellender Huff Sharp. Enl. at Decatur, TN, May 13, 1861 in 26TN. Promoted to Lt. Jan. 5, 1864. Resigned Oct. 5, 1864. Deserted Jan. 14, 1865 and took USA oath. Rept. Meigs, James and Rhea counties in TN General Assembly, 1883-85. Married (1870) Mary J. Peak. He died 12 Oct.1898 and both he and his wife are buried in the Sharp Cem. in Meigs Co. TN. [BDTA, 2:806]

SHARPE, Gabriel Marion    Co. F, 35TN
        Born 1830 in Hawkins Co., TN. Married (1850 in HC) Catherine Flora. He was a farmer in HC when he enl. Oct. 4, 1862; detached to guard bridge down river from Chattanooga at Kelly's Ferry, Nov. 10, 1862. To Miners and Sappers, May 13, 1863. AWOL, Sept. 7, 1863. Blue eyes, dark hair, dark complexion, and 5'7" tall. Res. Wauhatchie, 1870. [TWP, 302]

SHARP, James M.
        Born 1830, TN. Res. 1910 with wife Catherine on River Road. Farmer. [1910HC]

SHARPE, James W.   Co. A, 19TN
        Born Hawkins Co., TN, 1839. 1860 farm laborer in household of J.K. Denton at Chattanooga. Married 1) Amelia Ann, and 2) Elizabeth J.. Enl. July 22, 1861, Cumberland Gap. At Corinth, May, 1862. Res. 1911 in Valdeau, HC, TN.

SHARP, Leonard Japhet "Jabe"      3d TN Inf.
        Born in McMinn County, Jan. 11, 1845, he was the son of Elisha Sharp, a large landowner and

slaveholder who was killed during the Civil War. His mother was Eleanor Huff. His grandfathers, William Sharp and John Huff, fought in the Revolution. Enl. in 26TN and later 3TN, fighting under John C. Vaughn at Bull Run, Tazewell, Cumberland Gap, Chick-amauga, Lookout Mountain and other encounters. His brother, Elisha F. Sharp, was also in CSA, but deserted near the end of the war. LJS came to Chattanooga in 1870 and was in the grocery business before opening a successful livery and mortuary. Baptist and active in Democratic politics. Married Nellie Gillespie in 1875. They resided on East Sixth Street and had a summer home at Mabbit Spring on Walden's Ridge. LJS died March 1, 1917 and was buried Forest Hills Cem. [JW Sharp family; CT March 2, 1917, Hale and Merritt Vol. VII, pp. 2,056 and 2,149; 1910HC]

SHAW, James W.   2d Co. D, 26TN; 2d Co. D, 1CSA (GA)
      Enl. July 8, 1861 in Knoxville. Captured at Missionary Ridge, Nov. 26, 1863 and imprisoned Rock Island. Took USA oath of allegiance, Oct. 11, 1864. Res. HC Fair complexion auburn hair, blue eyes, and 5'4" tall.

SHELLY, George W.   2nd Co. K, 1st CSA Cav.
      Born 1840 in TN, son of West and Priscilla Shelly of Harrison. Enl. Sept. 24, 1862 in HC. Captured near Chattanooga, Dec. 26, 1863. Took USA oath, Jan. 6, 1864. Res. in HC Fair complexion, light hair, gray eyes, and 5' 9" tall.

SHELLY, Cp. James   2nd Co. K, 1st CSA Cav.
      Born 1836 in TN, son of West and Priscilla Shelly of Harrison. Enl. Sept. 24, 1862 in HC. Promoted to 3rd Cpl. Aug. 31, 1863. Left sick on march from Oxford to Dalton, Feb. 12, 1864. Sent to hospital in Atlanta, June 22, 1864. Died in hospital in Macon, GA, July 11, 1864.

SHELLY, John   2nd Co. K, 1st CSA Cav.
      Born 1843 in TN, son of West and Priscilla Shelly of Harrison. Enl. Sept. 23, 1862 in HC. Sick in hospital in Chattanooga. "Deserted."

SHELLY, William C.   Co. K, 43TN
      Born c1838, son of West and Priscilla Shelly. Before the war he resided on a farm near the Tennessee River north of Missionary Ridge. Enl. 17 Oct. 1861, at Ooltewah. He deserted 3 Aug. 1862.

SHELTON, Erasmus Archer   Co. C 3rd NC Junior Reserve
      Born 9 May 1846 in Tazewell Co., VA, the son of Samuel F. Shelton, a Methodist Minister. Married Lydia J. Umberger 21 Jan. 1868 in Wythe Co., VA. He died 10 Jun 1925 in Graysville, and is buried Citizens Cem. [UDC1 pg 386]

SHELTON, H. W.   3CSA Cav.

SHELTON, Richard Elijah   Surgeon, 1TN Cav. (Carter's)
      Born c1839, he was a physician living at Sale Creek before the war.

SHELTON, Woodly T.   Co. K, 4TN Cav. (McLemore's)
      Born Feb. 18, 1834 in Jackson Co., AL. Enl. Oct. 5, 1862. Paroled May 21, 1865. Married twice, first to Elizabeth Young on 27 Jan. 1859 in Jackson Co., AL [she died 20 June 1880] and secondly to Amanda who was born in Sequatchie Co., TN. To Chattanooga 1876, wholesale grocer. Merchant in Chattanooga, 1891. Moved to Bradley Co. Died near Rossville, Feb. 28, 1902. Buried Forest Hills Cemetery. [FHR; NBFM2;CT 1 March 1902; UDC1; UDC2]

SHEPHERD, Lewis   Co. A, 5TN Cav.
      Born March 7, 1846 in Hickory Valley, Hamilton County, Shepherd was the son of Lewis Shepherd Sr., a planter and politician who moved to Hamilton County from Newberry, SC. A student at Von Aldehoff's Academy when he enl., Lewis, Jr. was assigned to duty in East Tennessee guarding bridges and repressing bushwhackers. Then he went on the Kentucky campaign and was in the fighting at Fishing Creek. He was involved in several skirmishes under Wheeler and was in the rear guard on the retreat from Kentucky. At Chickamauga, he fought under Forrest and was with the unit that captured the Cloud Springs Federal hospital. He was with Gen. Wheeler in his famous raid through Tennessee, but he was later made prisoner and sent to Camp Morton, IN where he remained a year. He was exchanged Feb. 1865 and joined the 16TN Cav. Bn. in southwest Virginia. After Lee's surrender, he marched under John C. Vaughn to Charlotte, NC. He was with Jefferson Davis and his cabinet as a cavalry escort until they were disbanded at Washington, GA.
      Lewis Shepherd Jr. was a leading attorney at Chattanooga after the war, representing a number of railroad lines. Became widely known for his spirited defense of a Melungeon. Also represented HC in TN General Assembly, 1877-79, 1890-91. Married (1876) Lilah Pope. Shepherd was a Baptist and published his memoirs not long before his death May 14, 1917 in Chattanooga. He was buried Forest Hills Cemetery. [CT Jan. 2, 1910, May 15,1917; FHR; BDTA, 2:812-14; NBFM7]

SHEPHERD, T. Pope

[NBFM4]

SHIPMAN, John   Co. C, 1TN Cav. (Carter's)
Born c1836, son of William, of Long Savannah. Wife was Margaret. [1860HC]

SHIPP, John Thomas   Co. C, 4TN Cav.
Born Aug. 4, 1846 in Rutherford Co., TN. Enl. Aug., 1864; wounded 1865 at Branchville, SC (left leg amputated). Day laborer and "attends engine and boiler for Mountain City Stove Co." Res. 1910 with wife Mary on Curtiss St. Died Dec. 24, 1920 in Chattanooga and buried Forest Hills Cem. [CT Dec. 25 & 27, 1920; TP310; 1910HC]

SHIPP, Capt. Joseph Franklin   Co. G 4GA
Born Jasper Co., GA, Feb. 23, 1845. He was first assigned to duty along Hampton Road, later served in the battles fought around Richmond, at the battle of Malvern Hill, Shipp was dangerously wounded. Soon after he was promoted to captain and continued as such throughout the war. He married Lillie Estella Eckles on 12 Aug. 1866 at Social Circle, GA. She was born 7 Jan. 1850 at Social circle and died 25 Oct. 1828 at Chattanooga, TN. He became a cotton ginner and merchant before moving to Chattanooga in 1874 where he manufactured pumps. He re-enl. during the Spanish American War and served as a quartermaster. He became HC tax assessor in 1900 and sheriff in 1904. Died at res. on Shipp St., Sept. 18, 1925 and buried Forest Hills Cemetery. [NBFM7; UDC1 pg 338; UDC2 pg 480]

SHIRLEY, 3rd Sgt. James Brown   2nd Co. K, 1st CSA Cav.
Born c1837 at Savannah Creek near Ooltewah, he was named for the Indian chief James Brown who resided at Ooltewah by his parents, Thomas and Julia Ann Shirley. 1860 farmer in Ooltewah. Enl. July 14, 1862 in HC. Captured at Linden, TN May 12, 1863 and exchanged June 12, 1863. Hospitalized at Thomaston, GA, Oct. 1863. Graduated from Tennessee Medical College and became a doctor. He married Mary Achsah Andrews of Thomaston, GA. He died in 1924.

SHOEMAKER, 2Lt. William C.   Co. A, 4TN Cav. Bn. (Branner's); Co. K, 36TN; Co. K, 2TN Cav. (Ashby's)
Born c1837 in VA, the son of William L. Shoemaker of VA. Left his father's prosperous farm at Harrison to enlist. He was transferred on Jan. 9, 1862, to Co. K, 36TN. He also served as a sgt., Co. K, 2TN Cav. (Ashby's). He was paroled at Charlotte, NC, on May 3, 1865. [1860HC]

SHOOK, Harvey M.   Co. H, 37TN

Enl. May 7, 1862, at Corinth, MS. He deserted at Chattanooga on Aug. 28, 1863. He took the USA oath of allegiance on Dec. 9, 1863. Before the war he lived on a farm at Harrison with his mother, Margaret Shook. He was born c1839. He had a dark complexion, dark hair, brown eyes and was 5'8" tall. [1860HC]

SHOOK, William L.   Co. F, 42TN
Born c1834 and living at Harrison prior to war with wife Margaret. Enl. Nov. 2, 1861, Camp Cheatham. Prom. to Sgt. Captured at Fort Donelson, Feb. 16, 1862 and imprisoned Camp Douglas. Exch. Vicksburg.

SHOOPMAN, Alexander Co. G, 26TN; 2d Co. K, 1CSA (GA)
Born 1834 in TN. Farm laborer in Harrison, 1860, with wife Harriet. Enl. July 8, 1861, Knoxville. Due 3CSA Cav. pay to Nov. 17, 1862. Captured at Nashville, Dec. 16, 1864 and imprisoned Camp Douglas, Dec. 1864-June 20, 1865. [1860HC]

SHOOPMAN, John   Co. H, 2TN Cav. (Ashby's)
Born 1842 in GA. Farm laborer in 1860 in household of his brother, Alexander.

SHROPSHIRE, John Doak   2nd Co. K, 1st CSA Cav.
Born in 1837, he was a son of John Jackson Shropshire. Enl. July 14, 1862 in HC. Later listed on the roll of deserters and was admitted within the lines of the Department of the Cumberland. He was transferred from Nashville to Louisville, KY, where he arrived Dec. 13, 1863. He took the oath of allegiance and was released upon agreement he would stay north of the Ohio River for at least six months. "Exchanged for R. M. Underwood." He had dark complexion, brown hair, black eyes, and was 5'10" tall. Married Rebecca King.

SHULL, Sgt. Franklin Tate   Co. A, 2TN Cav. Bn.
Born July 5, 1844 in Roane Co., TN, he enl. Oct. 1, 1861 at Loudon. Fishing Creek, Perryville, Murfreesboro, Chickamauga, Missionary Ridge, Atlanta Campaign. Severely wounded at New Hope Church and leg amputated Nov. 1864. Spent remainder of war in FL and Selma, AL. Res. in East Chattanooga, 1908. Died in Tallahassee, FL, Dec. 22, 1911. Obit. states he was buried in NC. [CT Jan. 2, 1912; TP10367]

SHULL, William   Co. B, 5TN Cav.
He was killed in action on Dec. 1, 1861. Before the war, he was a farm laborer near Chattanooga, living with his wife, Octavia. Born c1836. His father was William Shull, who was also a farm laborer. [1860HC]

SIDEBOTTOM, Capt. Augustus William  Co. A, 5TN
Born Dec. 28, 1836 in Stewart Co., TN, he

became a merchant in Henry Co., TN, before enlisting early in 1861 in Co. A, 5TN. He fought at Island No. 10, Shiloh and Perryville. After the Kentucky Campaign he was promoted to 2Lt and to acting Captain following Murfreesboro, Chickamauga and Missionary Ridge. He was severely wounded at Resaca "by a piece of shell striking him in the forehead, leaving a mark which was plainly visible during the remainder of his life," but rejoined his regiment in time for New Hope Church and Kennesaw Mountain. He was captured at the battle of Atlanta and imprisoned at Johnson's Island until June, 1865. He settled in Evansville, IN, then was a traveling salesman with his home in Paris, TN. He came to Chattanooga in 1886 and engaged in real estate work and became a bank director. Married (1857) Julia A. Bunch (born 19 March 1834). Died Feb. 20, 1908 at his home on Chamberlain Ave. and buried Forest Hills Cem. [CT Feb. 21-22, 1908; Dec. 11, 1911; FHR; NBFM2; UDC1 pg 390].

SIEGER (see SEIGLER, SIGLER)

SIGGERS, James      Co. K, 43TN
Born in 1818 in Franklin County, GA, he was a farmer who enl. Oct. 17, 1861 at Ooltewah; detached to general hospital, Loudon, TN discharged because of disability, July 19, 1862; dark complexion, dark eyes, dark hair, and 5'10" tall.

SIMMONS, Jordan B.      2nd Co. K, 1st CSA Cav.
Enl. Sept. 12, 1862 in HC. Captured near Chickamauga, Nov. 28, 1863. Imprisoned at Rock Island, IL. Released Oct. 27, 1863. Took USA oath Oct. 27, 1864. Residence listed as Catoosa Co., GA. Dark hair, dark complexion, black eyes, and 5', 8" tall, 47 years old. [CSR; RI ledger]

SIMPSON, James      Co. D, 4GA Cav.
He enl. Oct. 4, 1862, at Chattanooga as a substitute for B. F. Nabors.

SIMPSON, R. A.      Russell's Bn., Pendleton's Mtd. Inf.
Enl. Feb. 1864. Res. 1901 in Chattanooga but moved to Memphis. [NBFM3,7]

SIMPSON, William Watkins
Born Norfolk, VA, Nov. 29, 1844. He moved to Chattanooga in 1870 and in 1894 moved to Wheeling, WV. Mason. Married Marion Corbin. Died Sept. 6, 1910 in Cincinnati and buried in Forest Hills Cem. [CT Sept 7, 1910]

SIMS, George William      Co. K, 43TN
He enl. Oct. 17, 1861, at Ooltewah and was

captured at Vicksburg on July 4, 1863. Before the war, he was a farm laborer living at Ooltewah with his family on the farm of Alexander McDaniel. He was born in Georgia about 1842. His father, J.B. Sims, was from South Carolina, while his mother, Margaret Sims, was from North Carolina. [1860 HC Census]

SIMS, Jeremiah "Jerry " Myers      Co. G, 39GA
Born in Gilman Co., GA, son of William R. and Bicie Woods Sims. He enl. at Dalton, Ga. on Nov. 18, 1864, at age 15. He was in fighting at Resaca, LaFayette and Atlanta. He walked to Ellijay, GA after being paroled at Greensboro, NC, May 1865. He was married at James County in 1907 to Sarah Isabell Davis. Res. 1918 in Harrison. Died 1930 in HC buried in McDonald Cem. [TWP 283; TCVQ; TP 15,382]

SIMS, Little Page
Married (1869) in HC Margaret Sivley. Died HC. Descendant, Bruce Benton.

SIMS, William H. H.      Co. K, 43TN; Barry's Btry.
Enl. Oct. 17, 1861 in Co. K, 43TN at Ooltewah; transferred to Barry's Battery, May 9, 1862 at Chattanooga; deserted Sept. 1, 1864 at Atlanta; Brown Diary says Sims captured on retreat from Atlanta Sept. 10, 1864; took USA oath, Nov. 26, 1864; dark complexion, dark hair, gray eyes, and 5'9" tall.

SIMS, William W.
Born 1840 in TN. Farmer at St. Elmo, 1910 with wife Myra (m. 1865) in household of son Fletcher T. [1910 HC]

SINNETT, Richard  Co. H, 2TN Cav.; Co. L, 36TN
Enl. June 17, 1861 at Knoxville, then re-enl. Jan. 9, 1862, in 26TN at Chattanooga.

SIVELY, J. Absalom B. S., Sr. "Ab"      Co. H, 2TN (Ashby's) Cav.
Born Jan. 16, 1827 in HC, son of Daniel. Enl. in 4TN Inf. during Mexican War. Enl. in Chattanooga May 15, 1861, as 2Lt. Re-enl. Sept. 22, 1862 in HC in 2nd Co. K, 1st CSA Cav. Afterwards served in 2TN. Paroled May 20, 1865 in Charlotte, NC. Farmer in East End. Baptist. Had eight children by Mary Lyon and nine by Mary Milliken. Postmaster at King's Point and member of County Court. Died at res., Jan. 16, 1912, in East Chattanooga and buried King's Point Cem. [NBFM2; CT Jan. 17, 1912]

SIVLEY, 2nd Lt. Absalom B. S., Jr.      Co. H, 2TN Cav. (Ashby's)
He was one of the sons of Absalom Sivley and

Rebecca Canterbury, who lived at King's Point. Enl. June 17, 1861, Knoxville. Left service May 26, 1862 but re-enlist. Nov. 29, 1862 at Chattanooga. Prom. lieut. Listed absent without leave Feb. 12, 1864. Buried in King's Point Cem., HC.

SIVLEY, Daniel H.    Co. H, 4TN Cav. (Ashby's)
Born 1830, son of Absalom and Rebecca Canterbury Sively of King's Point. He had earlier been a lieutenant of Lawson Guthrie's first company of volunteers organized in East Tennessee for the Mexican War. He saw service at Buena Vista and was in the storming of Mexico City. He suffered no wounds in either war. While in the Confederate army, he was crossing the Cumberland Mountains and his company became surrounded by a large detachment of Federal troops in the darkness. Preparing to surrender, he caught sight of a regiment of Confederates coming up on the Federals from behind. He pointed out the gray-clad soldiers to the Union major saying, "You are my prisoners now, Major." After the battle of Fishing Creek, DHS came into possession of a fine racing horse formerly owned by Lewis Shepperd, Sr. En route back to Chattanooga, he was able to swim the rivers, though other horses faltered. DHS was one of the first to arrive in Chattanooga and break the news of the Mill Springs disaster and the death of Gen. Felix Zollicoffer. DHS and his wife, Mary, had seven children. He died on 16 Jan. 1912 and was buried in the family cemetery at King's Point. [1860HC]

SIVLEY, Sgt. Daniel, Jr.    Co. D, 4GA Cav.
Born 1836 in TN, son of Daniel and Margaret, he was farmer at Chattanooga. Enl. Oct. 4, 1862 and was promoted to sergeant on March 26, 1863. He was later listed as absent without leave. While he was away, Yankee soldiers harassed his wife, Caroline, by firing their rifles over the Sivley homeplace at Mountain Creek. Later, Federal soldiers came to the house to get her only hog, which was all the food she had except for some buried sweet potatoes. She grabbed an axe and threatened to attack the first soldier who touched the hog. A Federal officer then ordered the soldiers to leave her alone. [JW Sivley family; 1860HC]

SIVLEY, 3rd Lt. George Washington    Co. D, 37TN
Enl. Sept. 1, 1861, at Knoxville and was wounded at Perryville on Oct. 8, 1862. On Nov. 10, 1862, he "did in company with two other officers and several citizens go to a house of ill fame and there get drunk. . . was engaged in a riot in which loaded and empty pistols and brickbats, etc. were used until suppressed by police." He resigned May 15, 1863. Col. Moses White reported that Sivley "is not only worthless as an officer, but is a positive nuisance in the regiment."

Born about 1821 the son of Daniel Sivley and Elizabeth McGuire. He married Sarah Boswell, a native of Kentucky. Sivley lived in Chattanooga after the war and was a hauler of wood. He worked for the firm of Baldwin and Williams. Died April 4, 1873 in HC, age 51. [HC Register of Deaths]

SIVLEY, PETER    2nd Co. K, 1st CSA Cav.
Born 1815 in TN, son of Absalom of King's Point. Farmer in Harrison in 1860 with wife Rutha Sively (his cousin). Enl. Aug. 15, 1862 in HC. Paroled May 3, 1865 in Charlotte, NC. Died 1867.

SIVLEY, Ransom Henry    Co. K, 43TN
Enl. 17 Oct. 1861, at Ooltewah. He deserted Feb. 1, 1862 and joined Co. G, 5th TN Cav. (USA). Co. G was commanded by Wm. J. Clift. Commissioned 1Lt. Oct. 4, 1862 and released from service at Pulaski, TN, Aug. 14, 1865. RHS was one of the sons of Absalom Sivley of King's Point. He was born about 1837. [1860HC]

SIVELY, Thomas Jefferson    Co. H, 37TN
Born 1830 in TN. Farmer at Harrison with wife Eliza. Enl. Sept. 17, 1861, Knoxville. Captured, sick during KY Campaign. Paroled. Rejoined regt., but deserted Sept. 11, 1863 near Chattanooga, took USA oath and enlisted in Co. F, 12TN Cav. (USA) becoming a Cpl., June 2, 1864, wounded Aug. 19, 1864. Promoted to Sgt. Oct. 1, 1864.

SIVLEY, William M.    Co. H, 2TN Cav. (Ashby's)
Born 1843 in TN, son of Peter and Ruth. Enl. June 17, 1861, Knoxville. Captured Aug. 31, 1862 in Ky. Exch. Sept. 1, 1862. Re-captured. near Chattanooga Sept. 12, 1863. Sent to Nashville and was to be released upon taking USA oath. [1860HC]

SKELTON, Thomas B.    Co. C., 3AL
Born 1843 in Jackson Co., AL, he married Martha Jane Shankles and died Feb. 15, 1911, age 67, at res. on Long Street; buried Forest Hills Cem. Pipemaker renting home on Long St. Resident of Chattanooga 13 years. [TWP, p. 121; CT Feb. 16, 1911; 1910HC]

SKILES, C.    Co. D, 37TN
Enl Jan. 28, 1863, Chattanooga. Conscript. Deserted from Catoosa Springs, Jan. 29, 1863.

SKINNER, Temple R. "Temp"
Born c1837 in AL, he was living in Chattanooga with his wife Mary. A printer, he was among those helping put out the Chattanooga _Daily Rebel._ Described by writer Henry Wiltse as "good-natured, happy-go-lucky."

SKIPPER, James W.     Co. D, 4GA Cav.

Listed absent without leave late October 1863 and was supposed to be in the hands of the enemy. The Federals reported him captured in Lookout Valley on Oct. 29, 1863 and sent to Louisville "for exchange." He arrived at Louisville on Nov. 8, 1863 and was forwarded to Camp Morton at Indianapolis and was in the USA Pest (Smallpox) Hospital at Indianapolis in January, 1865. He was released May 23, 1865. The Chattanooga resident had a dark complexion, black hair, blue eyes, and was 5'9" tall.

SLIGER, Cpl. Joseph LaFayette     Co. D, 43TN

Born McMinn Co., 1839. Enl. at Decatur, TN, 1861. Captured at Vicksburg. Paroled and went home. Married Sarah Brock (1866, McMinn Co.). Living in North Chattanooga in 1920, "according to comrade John Hart of Athens, TN." Died in North Chattanooga, Jan. 7, 1922. [TWP 8197]

SLOAN, A. N.

Citizen of Chattanooga in 1915. [CT April 5, 1915]

SLOAN, Robert Fidelio     Co. E, 3TN

Born Polk County, TN, Aug. 5, 1830. In mercantile business at Ocoee. Enl. in 3rd TN and served in VA, then became adjutant of 5th TN Cav. Crippled by his horse in spring, 1863 and never fully recovered. Gen. E. Kirby Smith detached him for office duty on his staff when he came out of the hospital. Surrendered at Macon, May 25, 1865. Married Annie Stuart on 12 Aug. 1869. In 1887, Robert moved to southern California to see if a change of climate would improve his health. In 1890, he returned to Tennessee and located in Chattanooga where he died on 8 May 1909 at "Elizabeth Flats", leaving a widow and three sons, and is buried Forest Hills Cem. [CT May 9, 1909; FHR; NBFM2, 7; Allen, *Reminiscences*, pg 23]

SLOAN, Dr. Rudolphus A. Capt., Major, Lt. Col, Col. in Fuller's Rangers - 2nd TN.

Born Norfolk, VA, Dec. 13, 1830. Methodist preacher, then went to Nashville to study medicine, practicing in Pikeville. Enl. in CSA as pvt., but soon made surgeon. Settled in Charleston, TN and Calhoun, GA before coming to Chattanooga in 1886. Married (1866) Margaret L. Died May 28, 1912 at residence on Houston St. and buried Forest Hills Cemetery. [CT 12 May 1912; 1910HC; UDC2 pg 487]

SLOVER, Albert M.     Barry's Battery

Enl. Oct. 17, 1862 at Knoxville. He was captured at the Spanish Fort on April 8, 1865, and imprisoned at Ship Island, MS. His older brother,

James, was also in Barry's Battery. Before the war, the Slovers resided at Sale Creek on the farm of their parents, Alfred and Cynthia Slover. Albert Slover was born about 1838. 1870 res. Long Savannah, wife Nancy A.

SLOVER, James E.     Barry's Battery

He enl. Oct. 17, 1862 at Knoxville. He was captured along with his younger brother, Albert Slover, at Spanish Fort on April 8, 1865, and imprisoned at Ship Island, MS. His parents were Alfred and Cynthia Slover of Sale Creek. He was born about 1836. 1870 a laborer on his parents farm in Long Savannah.

SMALLEY, Phillip     Co. D, 4GA Cav.

He enl. Oct. 4, 1862, at Chattanooga. He was listed as absent sick, then was reported as having deserted to the enemy lines at Bridgeport, Ala., on Nov. 1, 1863. He was taken by the Federals in November 1863 to Louisville. He took the oath of allegiance and was released north of the Ohio River. He had a dark complexion, dark hair, gray eyes, and was 5'4" tall. He was living before the war in the vicinity of Moccasin Bend with his wife, Phebe. A farm laborer, he was born about 1837. The Smalleys were originally from North Carolina.

SMARTT, James Polk     Co. C., 16TN

Born Sept. 11, 1844 at Smartt (Warren Co.), TN, son of George Madison and Ann Waterhouse Smartt, he attended Hannah Highland College in Warren County and represented Warren Co. in the TN legislature before joining the Confederate army in the fall of 1862. He fought at Murfreesboro, Chickamauga, Missionary Ridge, the Atlanta campaign, Hood's Tennessee Campaign and Bentonville. He was paroled at Greensboro, NC in May, 1865. Following the war he completed his education and taught a year in the Hannah Highland College. He engaged in the wholesale hat business at Nashville and then, beginning in 1875, in Chattanooga. He became head of Smartt Brothers & Co., wholesale dealers in boots and shoes, then the mercantile house of Smartt and Oehmig. He was director and vice-president of Third National Bank and director of the Chattanooga Savings Bank. Active in veterans affairs, Smartt became volunteer historian of Chickamauga-Chattanooga National Military Park. He died in Chattanooga 9 Sept. 1914 and was buried in Citizens Cem. His wife was Rowena Kennedy.[GHT, p. 995; CT Sept. 10-11, 1914]

SMITH, A. J. 2nd Co. K, 1st CSA Cav.

Born 1830 in TN, son of John. Farmer at Soddy with wife Caroline and two children. Enl. March 7, 1862 in Camp Casey, KY. Deserted Dec. 28, 1862 at

Shelbyville, TN. [1860HC]

SMITH, A. P.
Born June 6, 1842 in Wilkes Co., GA, he served on the staff of Gen. D. H. Hill during the war. Afterwards he entered the milling business at Dalton, then relocated at Augusta, then Atlanta and became a fireman, then conductor on the Western and Atlantic RR and the N C & St. L. He came to Chattanooga as depot master for the Southern RR. NBF Camp. Died Oct. 25, 1906 at his home in Highland Park and buried in Forest Hills Cemetery. [CT Oct. 26-27, 1906]

SMITH, Albert        Co. K, 43TN
Enl. Oct. 17, 1861 at Ooltewah; captured at Vicksburg, July 4, 1863; again captured Oct. 28, 1864 in Jefferson County, TN; imprisoned at Louisville, then Camp Douglas. Released June 17, 1865. Dark complexion, light hair, blue eyes, and 5'9" tall.

SMITH, Alexander        Co. B, 1TN Cav.(Carter's)
Born c1821 in TN. Farm laborer at Birchwood in 1860. Wife Amanda. He was ill in the hospital in the summer of 1862. He was taken prisoner at Staunton, Va., on June 8, 1864. [1860HC]

SMITH, Augustus A.    Co. H, 4TN Cav.
Wounded at Winchester, TN, 1862. "Of Hill City. Sick and in distress," Sept. 1901. [NBFM3]

SMITH, Col. Baxter    7TN Cav. Bn.; 4TN Cav.
Born March 10, 1832 in Davidson Co., son of Dr. Edmond Byars and Sally Baxter Smith. Prominent lawyer and Know-Nothing political leader in Nashville prior to the war in which he became a well known cavalry leader under Forrest and Wheeler. After war resumed practice in Nashville, partner with Ed Baxter. Representing Davidson County in TN Senate, 1879-81. Moved to Chattanooga in 1910 and became Secty of Chickamauga Park Commission. Married (1856, Sumner Co.) Bettie Guild. Presbyterian. Died June 25, 1919 in hospital at Fort Oglethorpe, GA and buried in Mt. Olivet Cem., Nashville. [TWP, 220; CT June 26, 1919]

SMITH, Elbert S.    Co. B, 3AL
Born April, 1831 in Knox Co. Enl. Apr., 1863. Captured just before Chickamauga while carrying a dispatch. Officially carried as having deserted 25 Sept. 1863. Res. 1908 in Sale Creek. [TP6101]

SMITH, Eli T.    Co. F, 35TN
Born 1832 in HC, he farmed at Harrison with wife Lydia until enlisting Oct. 4, 1862; killed at Chickamauga Sept. 20, 1863; dark eyes, dark hair, dark

complexion, 5'11" tall. [1860HC]

SMITH, Felix Grundy
Born Union Co., GA in 1842. CSA. Became a Congregationalist minister. Died in Chattanooga Dec. 6, 1915 and buried at Sunnyside. [CT Dec. 7, 1915]

SMITH, Francis Marion "Frank"   Co. B, 3TN
(Vaughn's)
Born April 18, 1844 in Knox Co., son of James Monroe and Cynthia Lee Gambell Smith. Boyhood spent in Blount Co. Enl. Apr. 19, 1861. First Manassas. Was transferred to scout duty under Col. Osborne. Also served in 19TN. Paroled Washington, GA, May 9, 1865. Married (1862 in Knox Co.) Anne Nott who was born 16 June 1844 in Newark, OH and died 14 Nov. 1924 in Chattanooga, TN. Taught in public schools throughout TN and became supt. of Jackson, TN schools. Appointed state school supt. by Gov. Robert L. Taylor and reappointed by Gov. Turney. Became professor at Univ. of TN at Knoxville, then joined Butler school book company. Retired to farm in Harrison. Mason. Methodist. Res. 1917 on Bailey Ave. Died Feb. 1, 1921 in HC and buried at Concord Cem. [TWP, 214; CT Feb. 2, 1921; TP15192]

SMITH, George W.    Co. K, 43TN
Enl. Oct. 17, 1861 at Ooltewah; captured at Vicksburg, July 4, 1863; paroled; enl. in 4TN Cav. Killed in action at Pulaski, TN.

SMITH, Sgt. Hendrix    51TN or 59TN
Born 18 Dec. 1842. Farmer in James Co. died June 2, 1922 and buried Concord Baptist Church Cem. [CTT 3 June 1922, info from descendants at Chattanooga CWRT]

SMITH, Henry    1TN Cav.
Took the USA oath of allegiance on February 11, 1864. He had a dark complexion, dark hair, hazel eyes, and was 5' 5" tall.

SMITH, Isaac N.    Co. B, 1TN Cav. (Carter's)
Before the war, he lived on a farm at Limestone near Ooltewah. His parents were Thomas D. and Dolly Smith. Thomas D. Smith was a native of NC. Isaac Smith was born about 1842. Enl. Aug. 7, 1861 in Cleveland.

[Smiths: some of these may be same :  J.A., A. J., Jackson, John Augustine, Albert and Alexander may be same person.]

SMITH, J. A.    Co. B, 5TN Cav.
Enl. Aug. 11, 1861, at Chattanooga.

SMITH, J. A.    Co. B, 4TN Cav.
    Enl. April 10, 1862; captured July 1, 1863 and paroled July 25, 1863, having taken USA oath of allegiance. Buried CSA Cem.

SMITH, J. C.    Co. A, 5th (McKenzie's) TN Cav.
    He enl. Aug. 24, 1861 at Camp Cumming, by J. W. Gillespie for 12 months in White's Company. "In North Carolina during the closing weeks of the war, the company was in a skirmish near Darlington. J. C. Smith of Company A was riding a small mule. The Yankees had formed some 300 years across a swamp from the railroad. As the company moved into this cut, the Yankees fired a volley, striking Smith's mule in the head and a nearby horse in the breast. Both fell clocking the road." [Allen's *Reminiscences* pg 90] Age 33 on March 11, 1864 roll. Paroled May 3, 1865 at Charlotte, NC.

SMITH, J. H.    Co. A, 1GA
    Born Feb. 16, 1833 in Monroe Co., TN. Enl. May 12, 1862. Disch. Sept. 1863 because of health and returned home. Moved to TN, 1887. Res. 1910 Mitchell Ave., Chattanooga. [TP 11,859

SMITH, J. H.    Washington Rifles, 1GA
    Born Apr. 9, 1835 in Houston Co., GA. Enl. in GA in Washington Rifles, 1GA. Afterwards served in 21 Bn Cav, 7Regt., Cav., Hampton Legion. Wounded twice in pursuit of Butler while making his raid to Lynchburg, VA. Captured near Beverly, VA and released in 1861. Disch. April, 1865. Res. in Ridgedale, TN, occup. coal dealer. [NBFM2]

SMITH, J. M.    Co. H, 4TN Cav.
    Killed in action Dec. 12, 1862.

SMITH, J. T.    5TN Cav. (McKenzie's); 4GA Cav.
    Born 1841 Whitfield Co., GA. Bull's Gap, Chickamauga. To TN 1893, and living in Whorley in 1905. [TP7090]

SMITH, Jackson "Jack"    Co. H, 4TN Cav.; Co. B, 5TN Cav.
    Enl. Aug. 11, 1861. Killed at Battle of Murfreesboro, Dec. 31, 1862.

SMITH, James
    Born 1841, TN of parents born in TN. 1910 laborer in James Co. with wife Callis Jenkins. [1910 James Co.]

SMITH, James    Co. F, 49TN
    "Evidently colonel" [1890 Vet Census]

SMITH, James David
    Born 1833, Lincoln Co., Tenn., of SC parents. Res. 1910 East End Ave. Died March 5, 1916 in Chattanooga and buried Winchester, Tenn. [1910HC; CT June 6, 1916]

SMITH, John    Clark's Independent Cav. Co.
    Enl. Aug. 31, 1862 at Chattanooga; deserted Dec. 22, 1863 at Morristown, TN.

SMITH, John A.
    Born 1839, TN of TN parents. 1910 res. James Co. with wife Martha E. (m. 1866).

Smith, Lt. Col John A.    Co. K, 36TN
    Company commander, then elected Lt. Col. of the regiment.

SMITH, John Augustus "Gus"    Co. H, 4TN Cav.
    Born March, 1838 in Jackson Co., AL. Enl. 1861. Wounded at Pulaski and captured at Brentwood in 1863 but escaped. Paroled at Raleigh. Resided in Hill City where he died May 8, 1903 and was buried White Oak Cem. [NBFM4; TP3636]

SMITH, Sgt. John C. I.    Co. C, 3TN Cav. Bn.; Co. B, 1TN Cav. (Carter's),
    Born 1838 in Bledsoe Co. He was captured at Piedmont, Va., on June 5, 1864 and sent to Camp Morton, then via the Baltimore and Ohio Railroad to Point Lookout, MD. Exchanged March 15, 1865. He married (1865 in HC) Martha A. Bean. Res. 1903 in Birchwood (James Co.) where he died in 1910. [TWP, p. 91; TP5905]

SMITH, John H.    Co. C, 5TN Cav. (McKenzie's)
    Born Feb. 19, 1840 in Campbell Co. Enl. Nov. 1863. Atlanta Campaign, Franklin, Nashville. Life long res. of TN, he married (1867) Bettie Burgess. Res. in East Lake in 1905 and died 1917 in Howardsville, James Co. [TWP, p. 191; TP7382]

SMITH, Sgt. John P.    Co. F, 35TN
    Born 1837 in Lumpkin County, GA, he was a laborer in Chattanooga at the time he enl., Oct. 4, 1862. Detailed as teamster. Promoted to 4th Sgt. Paroled at Greensboro, NC, May 1, 1865.

SMITH, John Tyler    Wm Brown's Cav.
    Born Rutherford Co., NC, 1841. Disabled Dec. 1862, rheumatism. Wife was Sarah Jane. To TN c1895. Res. Chattanooga, 1919. [TP 15,398]

SMITH, John W.    Co. K, 43TN
    Born 1818 in Anderson District, SC, he enl.

Dec. 15, 1861 at Ooltewah; discharged July 22, 1862 because of disability; fair complexion, gray eyes, black hair, and 6'1 1/2" tall.

SMITH, John W.        Co. B (D), 1TN Cav. (Carter's)
        He was captured at Jacksboro, TN, on Aug. 27, 1863. He was held at Camp Nelson, KY, then he arrived at Louisville on Sept. 5, 1863. He went to Camp Chase, OH, and on to Rock Island, IL. He died there on March 1, 1864, from diarrhea. He was buried in Grave 676 south of the prison barracks. [RI ledger]

SMITH, Joseph A.    Co. A, 36TN
        Born McMinn Co., TN in 1846. Enl. Dec. 11, 1861. Fought at Cumberland Gap and latter part of war with QM Dept. Paroled at Meridian, MS. To TN 1898. [TP14,159]

SMITH, Leander B.  Co. G, 26TN; 2d Co. K,
                            1CSA Cav.; Co. F, 39GA
        Enl. as pvt. in 26TN, Aug. 28, 1861. Trans. to 1CSA Cav., Nov. 8, 1862; to 39GA, 1863. Captured Baker's Creek, May 16, 1863. Exch. 2nd Lt., June 10, 1864. Surr. Greensboro, April 26, 1865.

SMITH, Dr. Milo
        Served as surgeon when wounded Confederates brought into Chattanooga from battles of Fort Donelson, Murfreesboro and Missionary Ridge.

SMITH, Nathaniel Henry  Co. D 1st TN Cav.
        Enl. 6 Aug 1861 in Capt. Gass' Co. 3rd Corp. Capt. Darius Waterhouse's Co. Married Elizabeth [?] prior to 1850 and he died sometime between 1880 and 1900. [TWP1602; V.C. Allen pgs 6, 37]

SMITH, Pleasant F.    Co. K, 43TN
        Enl. Oct. 17, 1861 at Ooltewah; captured at Vicksburg, July 4, 1863.

SMITH, R. A.  Co. L, 35TN
        Enl. Oct. 13, 1863 in Chattanooga. Sick at Ringgold Hosp.

SMITH, Richard S.      1TN Cav. (Carter's)
        He was taken prisoner on Sept. 11, 1863. He was received at Cumberland Gap, TN, after which he agreed to take the oath of allegiance. He had a fair complexion, light hair, black eyes, and was 5' 7" tall.

SMITH, Robert C.    Co. B, 1TN Cav. (Carter's)
        He was a teamster, receiving 25 cents a day. He took the oath of allegiance on June 12, 1865, at Charleston, WV. He was then 25 with a dark complexion, blue eyes, dark hair, and 5'10" tall.

SMITH, Sterling Tried    Surgeon, 36TN; Co. H, 26TN
        Born Long Savannah April 11, 1839, son of Maj. Peyton Fauntleroy and Nancy Welch Smith. Attended Georgetown Academy. Married Amy L. Matthews (1856). Enl. July 8, 1861, Knoxville. Left sick, Bowling Green, Jan. 23, 1862. Sequatchie Valley doctor for 56 years. Died May 21, 1916 at Dunlap. [CT May 25, 1916; Donnelly, James Co.]

SMITH, W. H.       Co. B, 1TN Cav. (Carter's)
        He was sent home sick.

SMITH, Wayne S.   Co. H, 2TN Cav. (Ashby's)
        Enl. June 17, 1861. Knoxville. Detached as engineer. Captured Aug. 31, 1862 in Ky. and exch. Sept. 4, 1862. Re-enl. Chattanooga, Jan. 25, 1863.

SMITH, William A.   Co. L, 36TN, Co. L. 35TN
        Enl. Jan. 9, 1862 at Chattanooga. Enl. Jan. 8, 1863 in Co. L, 35TN. Sick at hospital, Aug. 31, 1863.

SMITH, William Rutledge
        Married Ann Eliza. [TWP4159]

SMITH, William Spotswood
        Medical Director under Gen. Stout

SNEED, Gilbert H.      Co. F, 1GA Heavy Arty
                            22nd Bat., GA Art.
        Born June 6, 1846 in Wilkes Co., GA. Enl. Apr. 12, 1862. Captured Fort Pulaski, April 1862, released Nov., 1862. Next served in W. R. Pritchard's heavy btry. being promoted to Sgt. Major, 22GA Arty. Bn. Paroled May, 1865. Married Freddie G. born 22 Feb.1874 who was a member of the UDC, A.P. Stewart Chapter. Hotel man on Carter St. in Chattanooga last 35 years. Died Aug. 2, 1912 at home on Carter St. and buried Forest Hills Cemetery. [FHR; NBFM2; 1910HC; CT Aug. 5, 1912]

SNIDER, James H.  Co. H, 3TN Cav.
        Born c1842 in TN. Served under Gen. Wheeler. Both feet severely frozen and caused Snider to remain an invalid many years. Died June 22, 1912, on Walden's Ridge and buried in Athens, TN. [CT June 23, 1912; 1910HC]

SNIDER, 2Lt. S. W.   Co. K, 43TN
        At Camp Ramsey, Athens, TN, Nov. 1, 1861 as 2nd Lt.

SNODGRASS, Charles L.    Co. H, 26TN; 2d Co. I, 1CSA (GA)
        Born c1840. Enl. 8 July 1861, Knoxville. Captured Fort Donelson, Feb. 16, 1862 and imprisoned

Camp Douglas. Left at Chattanooga sick, Oct. 5, 1862. Deserted and took USA oath, Dec. 24, 1863. Res. Walker Co., GA.

SNOW, George Washington     Co. B, 1TN Cav. (Carter's)

A son of Capt. William Snow, he served in his father's company. He enl. Aug. 7, 1861, at Cleveland. Snow is also shown as a member of the 2nd Co. K, 1st CSA Cavalry, which he joined in HC Sept. 12, 1862. His CSR shows he "deserted" at Shelbyville, Dec. 10, 1862. He was captured at Piedmont, VA, on June 5, 1864. Snow was imprisoned at Camp Morton, IN, then was shipped via the Baltimore and Ohio Railroad to Point Lookout, MD, for exchange. He was paroled at Talladega, AL, on June 20, 1865. Snow was living at Snow Hill with his wife, J. Snow, and daughter, Amanda. They left the area along with other family members just after the war.

SNOW, Capt. William   Co. B, 1TN (Carter's)

He was 52 when the war started, but he was a staunch Confederate and he formed neighboring farmers into Co. B of the 1TN Cav. (Carter's) at Cleveland, TN, enlisting Aug. 7, 1861. Snow resigned from the army on May 12, 1862 "in consequence of ill health." He is said to have afterwards formed "Snow's Scouts."

Born 1809 in NC, he was the son of Thomas Snow and Elizabeth Hale Curroughs. Thomas Snow died in 1818, but Elizabeth Hale Curroughs was living at Snow Hill in HC when she died in 1860 at the age of 80. William Snow married Emily Monger in Knox County in 1832 and Mary Waller in Roane Co. in 1835. He was in HC prior to 1840 and had a large farm in the section that came to be known as Snow Hill. Meeting hostility from neighbors after the war, he left Hamilton County in 1865 and died at Tiptonville, TN, 1876. [Chattanooga Bi-C. Library Clipping file]

SNYDER, William M.     3CSA Cav.

Born Decatur, TN, Aug. 1852, and enl. 1864 in 3CSA Cav. Dentist in Spring City before coming to Chattanooga where he died Feb. 22, 1936 and was buried in Spring City Cem. next to his wife, Olivia A.. Baptist. Mason. [CT 23 Feb. 1936]

SPECKLE, Edward   Co. H, 2TN Cav. (Ashby's)

Born c1832,  was a butcher at Chattanooga prior to and after the war. He was from France and his wife, Christiana, from Wurtemburg, Germany. A gray mare was shot from under him at Rowena, KY, on 27 Nov. 1861. He reported the mare's value at $250. Sick at Chattanooga, July 5, 1862. Deserted July 9, 1862.

SPENCER, James

Detailed by CSA to superintend mines at Tennessee Island, AL.

SPENCER, Webb   Co. A, 2TN Cav. Bn.

Died in prison 9 Aug. 1864.

SPICER, Benjamin F.     Co. K, 43TN

Enl. Oct. 17, 1861 at Ooltewah; captured at Vicksburg, July 4, 1863.

SPILLER, Lt. Col. Collins C.  Co. B, 5TN Cav. Bn.;
Co. H, 4TN Cav. (Murray's)

Prior to the war, Spiller was a prosperous farmer in HC. His worth in 1860 is listed at $25,000. He and his wife, Sarah, were natives of VA. Enl. Aug. 11, 1861 at Chattanooga. In the Kentucky campaign, Capt. Spiller was detached by Gen. George B. Crittenden for scouting duty near the mouth of Yellow Creek. It is said of Capt. Spiller during the Confederate loss at Fishing Creek that "due to his skill and energy may be attributed in a great measure the safety of that division of the army." The company lost all its wagons in that battle that occurred Jan. 19, 1862. Afterwards, Capt. Spiller plead with Confederate authorities for replacements, saying "the only wagon we have is broken down." Later, he was promoted to lieutenant colonel. July 13, 1862 in Forrest's attack on Murfreesboro, "our beloved young Captain [Spiller], while leading a charge, was killed." [Yeary, Rems of Boys in Gray, pp. 373-74]

SPRADLING, Andrew A.   Co. L, 36TN; Co. L, 35TN

Born about 1833, he and his wife, Jane, had a farm at Soddy prior to the war. Enl. Jan. 9, 1862 at Chattanooga. He fought at Murfreesboro. [1860HC]

SPRADLING, Robert   Co. I, 19TN

1903 res. of Chattanooga.

SPRAY, Thomas M.     Co. F, 35TN

Apr. 29, 1861, 1Lt. Chattanooga Home Guard.

SPRINGER, William Franklin   Co. H, 45AL.

Born 1837, Lafayette, AL. Enl. Jan. 1862. Atlanta Camp. Wounded Jonesboro and Franklin and imprisoned Camp Chase at end of war. Employee of U.S. Pipe and Foundry; Policeman in Chattanooga c1893. Wife (2) Martha A. Married 1868. Died in Jacksonville, FL. [TP12983; 1910HC]

SPRINGFIELD, E. C. Co. B, Hillyer's Railroad Bn.

Born Greenville, SC, 1833. With Georgia State Road (W & A) in Macon when workers organized into a battalion and were sent to meet Stoneman's raid, 1864. Fought at Griswoldville. To TN in 1879. [TP9065]

SPRINGFIELD, Ord. Sgt. Hiram Jackson "Jack"
Co. D, 25AL
Born Sept. 15, 1841, Murray Co., GA, son of Solomon Langston and Catherine Bradley Springfield. Moved to Alabama after war and took active part in Republican Party, becoming state legislator from St. Clair County. To HC when Grant was president and settled at Tyner's Station. Owned there H. J. Springfield & Bro. merchandising. Served 3 terms as sheriff. County Court. Married (1) Mary C. Masteller (1861), Joicey L. Simpson (1866), Mary E. Franklin. Died Apr. 1, 1906 and buried Forest Hills Cemetery.

SPRINGFIELD, 4Lt. John S. Barry's Btry.
1Lt., HC Home Guard, May 3, 1861; enl. May 15, 1862 at Chattanooga.

STAFFORD, Daniel Co. D, 37TN
Enl. Sept. 1, 1861, Knoxville. Detached as orderly to Gen. Marmaduke, Aug. 24, 1862.

STAFFORD, Frederick McKee 4MS
Born Jan. 24, 1842 in Tuscaloosa, AL. Received military training at VMI and entered CSA with Corps of Cadets. Stationed in Richmond three months then sent to Columbus, KY, as drill master of 4MS. Became adjutant of 4th MS and captured at Fort Donelson and imprisoned seven months. When exchanged became AAG on Pemberton's staff at Vicksburg. Again captured and when exchanged sent to Gen. Johnston at Dalton who assigned him as staff officer for Gen. C. H. Stevens of SC. Also on staff of W. H. Jackson. Wounded at Franklin and returned home till war over. Married Alice M. Rix on June 16, 1872 in Keokuak, IA. She was born 6 June 1845. In 1890 they moved to Chattanooga where Stafford engaged in banking and bond business. He died in Chattanooga Dec. 9, 1920 and was buried in Forest Hills Cem. [FHR; CT Dec. 10, 1920]

STAFFORD, J. Henry Co. D, 37TN
Born 1845 in GA. Enl. Sept. 1, 1861, Knoxville. Disch. Nov. 24, 1862.

STAFFORD, James Brennan Co. A, 8GA
From Spartanburg, SC. Married Sarah Hammonds (1848, Rome, GA). Enl. at Rome, GA, 1862. ANV. Severely wounded but returned after recovery. Captured at Wilderness, May 6, 1864 and imprisoned at Elmira, NY. Paroled March 2, 1865. Moved to Chattanooga, 1890, and died here May 1, 1900. [TWP2872]

STANDIFER, Leroy Co. K, 43TN
Enl. Dec. 15, 1861 at Ooltewah; killed during one of shellings of Chattanooga, June 8, 1862; [2nd source: Mortally wounded at Murfreesboro, Jan. 1, 1863; died in Nashville soon after]; body brought to HC and buried in family cemetery of his father, William Standifer, Sr., two miles from Silverdale. Mother was Mary Moore. Cousin of Leonidas Standifer who was also son of a William. [JW, Feb. 25, 1895; Lindsley, 528; Z.]

STANDIFER, Luke Leonidas Co. F, 2TN Cav. (Ashby's)
Born Bledsoe Co. May 9, 1842, he enl. July 8, 1861 in Pikeville in Tulloss Rangers. Perryville, Murfreesboro. Captured at Big Hill, KY, July 30, 1863; imprisoned at Camp Chase and Fort Delaware. Exchanged and surrendered at Morgantown, NC. Resided since the war in TN and TX. Died May 6, 1931 at King's Pond and buried Mt. Airy Cem. [NBFM2]

STANDIFER, Samuel Co. H, 37TN
Born 1845, son of Leroy and Mary of Zion Hill. Enl. Oct. 4, 1862, Morristown. Sick in hosp. and deserted from there May 15, 1863.

STANDIFER, W. L. Co. F, 2TN Cav. (Ashby's)
Enl. July 6, 1861 at Knoxville.

STANDIFER, William Isaac
Born, probably in VA, in 1801, son of James and Patsy Standifer of Bledsoe Co. Graduate of Blount College. He was past fighting age, but he was an adherent of the Confederacy. He was visiting with Samuel Williams at the time of the escape of James Andrews of the Andrews Raiders. Standifer helped in his capture. Afterwards, he was a wanted man. He was able to escape from town when friends loaded him in a rowboat with food and put him off in the night at the old wharf at the foot of Market Street. He had first come to Chattanooga in 1837 when it was still Ross's Landing. William I. Standifer was pvt. in the Seminole War (Lauderdale's Regt.), and he raised a company (1st TN, 2nd Brigade) to fight in the Mexican War. Mason. Father of CSA Pvt. Leroy Standifer who was killed June 7-8, 1862 at Chattanooga. [BDTA, 1:692-93]

STANFIELD, JAMES W. Co. K, 34AL.
Born Jan. 28, 1839 in Heard Co., GA. Captured at Missionary Ridge, Nov. 25, 1863 and imprisoned at Rock Island where he remained until May, 1865. Living in St. Elmo in 1902. [RI ledger]

STANFIELD, R. H. Co. F, 39GA
Born 1834 in Troup Co., GA. Shoemaker in Ooltewah, 1860. Wife, Mary J. Enl. June, 1862. Shoemaker in Chattanooga c1893. [1860 HC Census]

STANLEY, Allen R.   Co. F, 59AL
        Born Aug. 17, 1837 Robeson Co., NC. Enl. April 7, 1862. Peddler in Chattanooga, c1905. [TP6925]

STANLEY, John T.   Co. I, 13GA Cav.
        Born 1846 in Gwinett Co., GA. Gunshot wound broke his right arm at Morristown, TN, Oct. 28, 1864. Captured and imprisoned at Camp Douglas, IL. Residing in Hill City in 1903, but moved to Chavies, AL shortly there after. [TP5683]

STANSELL, W. S.   Co. B, 18GA
        Enl. March 13, 1862 at Tunnel Hill, GA. Car inspector, W&A in Chattanooga, 1890. [NBFM1]

STEEL (STEELE), Isaac   Barry's Btry.
        Enl. May 29, 1862 at Chattanooga; paroled May 11, 1865 at Meridian, MS.; res. DeKalb Co., AL

STEEL, John B.   Co. F, 2KY
        Buried CSA Cem.

STEEL (STEELE), Cpl. Levi   Barry's Btry.
        Enl. July 14, 1862 at Chattanooga; deserted March 10, 1864; took USA oath March 19, 1864; Res. Jackson Co., AL; 5'5" tall, brown hair; dark complexion, and gray eyes

STEEN, Samuel   Hillyer's Railroad Battalion
        Born White Co., TN, 1837. With Govt. Railroad (W&A) when mobilized as infantry battalion to meet Stoneman's raid. Fought at Griswoldville. Paroled at Atlanta at end of war. To TN, 1892. Res. in TN near Rossville, 1907. [TP8886]

STEGALL, Robert Blackwell   Co. K, 14GA
        Born June 15, 1842, Cartersville, Bartow Co., GA, son of Emsly and Sarah Lachen Stegal. Schoolmaster who enl. May 1, 1862 and fought with ANV. Wounded June 26, 1863. RR business after war in Columbus, GA--brakeman, conductor, yardmaster with W&A. To Chattanooga in 1879 and lived on McFarland Gap Rd. 50 years. Married 1) Mary Jefferson, 2) Bessie Lowry. Baptist. NBF Camp. Died April 18, 1935 in Rossville, GA and buried Forest Hills Cemetery. [CT March 2, 1910, April 18, 1935; NBFM6; TCVQ]

STEPHENS, James (Jackson) "Jack"   Co. D, 39GA; Co. A, 19TN
        Born Trenton, GA, 1832. Baker's Creek, siege of Vicksburg. Paroled at Vicksburg, sent home, never exchanged. Res. Jackson Co., AL, 1899. To TN, 1909. Res. Ridgedale Station. Married (in HC) Eva Harner.

Died June 17, 1926 in Chattanooga, "age 105," and buried CSA Cem. [TWP, 263; CT June 18, 1926]

STEPHENS, N. Henry   Co. F, 2SC Rifles
        Born Aug. 10, 1845, Anderson Co., SC. Enl. Aug. 1863. Wounded at Fort Harrison, Oct. 1864. Paroled at Appomattox. To TN 1883. Res. Ridgedale, 1909. Groceryman. Res. on Douglas St. with wife Georgia. Married 1870. [TP11329; 1910HC]

STEPHENSON, A. B.   Co. G, 26TN
        Enl. Aug. 28, 1861, Knoxville. Sick in hospital, Cumberland City, TN, Feb.

STEPHENSON, Samuel F.   Co. G, 26TN; 2d Co. K, 1CSA (GA)
        Enl. Aug. 28, 1861, Knoxville. Captured Fort Donelson, Feb. 16, 1862 and imprisoned Camp Morton. Sick in hospital, Jackson, MS, Sept. 26, 1862. Deserted at Dalton, Feb. 14, 1864 and took USA oath. Res. Jackson Co., AL.

STEVENSON, Benjamin F.   Co. D, 4GA Cav.
        Born Whitfield Co., GA. Enl. Dec. 1861: Shiloh, Chickamauga, Knoxville, Atlanta Campaign. Deserted July 5, 1864 at Atlanta. Carpenter. Res. Chattanooga 1912. [TP 13,451]

STEWART, Alexander Harvey   Co. B, 6GA
        Born Rising Fawn, GA, Dec. 31, 1840. Enl. at Trenton, May 20, 1861. Wounded 1863 at Fort Sumter and again by bushwacker. Married Theresa Wood (1877). Moved to Chattanooga April, 1910 and res. on Cherry St. Indigent, left arm atrophied from shoulder to elbow. Lived later years in St. Elmo where he died April 16, 1919. [TP3232]

STEWART, Lt. Gen. Alexander Peter
        Known to his soldiers as "Old Straight," he lived in Chattanooga for a number of years after the war. A statue to his memory was erected at the grounds of the HC Courthouse. It was unveiled April 22, 1913, as a gift of the A. P. Stewart Chapter of the United Daughters of the Confederacy. The sculptor was Mollie Kavanaugh. One of the speakers, Lapsley G. Walker, referred to Gen. Stewart as "a man with no guile in his heart, but with the courage of a lion."
        Born in 1821, he taught mathematics at West Point and resigned in 1845 to teach at Cumberland University and the University of Nashville. With the outbreak of the war, he was commissioned a major and commanded artillery at Columbus, Ky. His appointment as brigadier general came Nov. 8, 1861. He led a Brigade at Shiloh and in the Kentucky campaign. He fought not only at Perryville, but Stones River, the battles around

Chattanooga and throughout the Atlanta campaign, rising to division command. He was promoted major general on June 5, 1863, then, after the death of Gen. Leonidas Polk, was named lieutenant general on June 23, 1864. He commanded the Army of Tennessee in North Carolina at the time of the surrender. Following the war, he again taught at Cumberland University and was in the insurance business. He also served as chancellor of the University of Mississippi. He was a park commissioner of Chickamauga and Chattanooga National Military Park. He died Aug. 30, 1908 in Biloxi, MS and is buried in St. Louis.

STEWART, Charles    Co. K, 43TN
        Enl. Oct. 17, 1861 at Ooltewah; died Dec. 1, 1861 at hospital in Knoxville. [Lindsley, 528]

STEWART, George Henry    23Bn. GA Home Guards
        To Chattanooga 1911. Res. 4217 Dodds Ave. Died Jan. 26, 1937 and buried Greenwood Cem. [CT Jan. 27, 1937]

STEWART, Henry
        Member NBF Camp, April, 1907; connected with Chattanooga Evening News.

STEWART, James    2nd Co. K, 1st CSA Cav.
        Enl. in HC Sept. 12, 1862. He deserted June 21, 1863.

STEWART, James A.    2nd Co. K, 1st CSA Cav.
        Enl. in HC Sept. 19, 1862. He was killed in action at Dover (Fort Donelson) Feb. 3, 1863.

STEWART, John H.    26TN; 2d Co. K, 1CSA (GA)
        Born c1841. Enl. Aug. 28, 1861 in Knoxville. Captured Dec. 16, 1864 at Nashville and imprisoned at Camp Douglas. Enl. 5USA Vols, April 18, 1865. 1870 res. Bradley Co. [Henderson1:113]

STEWART, Robert C.    Co. F, 35th TN
        Enl. Jan. 1, 1863 in Co. F, 35TN at Chattanooga; captured at Ingoe's Ferry, Nov. 26, 1863 and imprisoned at Rock Island. Enl. in USN and sent to rendezvous Jan. 25, 1864. [CSR; RI ledger]

STEWART, William K.    Co. L, 36th TN; Co. L, 35TN
        Enl. Jan. 9, 1862, in Co. L, 36TN at Chattanooga; transferred to Co. F, 35TN; fought at Murfreesboro; wounded in hand at Chickamauga.

STIFF, John C.
        Born in Dallas, TN, Dec. 15, 1839, he spent his younger life in Lafayette, GA. After serving in the CSA he located in Chattanooga in 1865 and became a partner of G. H. Jarnigan in a mercantile business. He died at his home on Lookout Mt. March 14, 1894. [CTS] [CSA photo in CTS]

STINGELL, R. H.    Co. C, 21VA.
        Born 6 Dec. 1840 in Lee Co., VA. Enl. March 25, 1862 in Wytheville, VA in an artillery company, then in 21VA. Captured at Moorefield, VA and imprisoned at Camp Chase. Blacksmith in East Chattanooga in 1900. [NBF Camp applications]

STOKES, Lowe H.
        Born 1854, Ga., of SC parents. Blacksmith, 1910, boarding on Market St. [1910HC]

STONE, Francis Irvine    Oglethorpe Arty, 12 GA Bn.
        Born June 6, 1844 near Decatur, DeKalb Co., GA. Enl. April, 1862 in Augusta, GA in 12GA Bn., then Oglethorpe Btry. Served summer, 1862 in front of Buell above Chattanooga & in an independent command above Knoxville. Fall, 1862 transf. to Savannah, remaining 18 months till regt. transf. to Johnston's army in spring, 1864. Participated in all battles of Atlanta Campaign and Hood's TN Campaign. Made color-bearer for last six months of war and wounded three times in charge on breastworks at Bentonville as Oglethorpes served as infantry. Manufacturer and commission merchant in Chattanooga who moved to Atlanta in 1897. Died June 22, 1920, in Auburndale, FL. Resident of Chattanooga almost 20 years. [CT June 26, 1920; NBFM2]

STONE, Spencer Clark    Co. F, 2nd TN Cav. (Ashby's)
        Born Sept. 21, 1825 in Delphi, TN, the son of Gen. William N. Stone, he was a successful lawyer in Sequatchie County before the war. He raised a cavalry company known as the Tulloss Rangers (Co. F, 2nd TN Cav.). He lived in Chattanooga during the 1870's then moved to Ocala, FL where he died in December, 1905. [CT Dec. 19, 1905]

STONE, William F.    Co. B, 5TN Cav.
        Born in Virginia about 1815, he was a farmer at Ooltewah prior to the start of the war and enl. on Aug. 11, 1861. He was a farrier for the unit. Stone was arrested on Dec. 8, 1861, for shooting a prisoner taken in a skirmish near Somerset, Ky. Wounded at Fishing Creek, KY.

STOPHEL, David    Co. H, 26TN; 63TN
        Born c1837. Enl. Oct. 1, 1862, Zollicoffer. Wounded on picket June 29, 1864 and died July 17, 1864 at hospital, Forsyth, GA.

STOUT, Charles    Co. A, 4TN Cav.
        Captured in battle of Somerset, KY; imprisoned

at Johnson's Island.

STOUT, Thomas Edmond   CSN
        Born in Nashville, TN, Jan. 24, 1849. Enl. 3 Feb. 1865 in Richmond, VA and was appt. midshipman, CSN. Aboard CSS Patrick Henry. Served as part of naval brigade as guard of Treasury Dept. and Pres. Davis on retreat from Richmond. Command disbanded at Washington GA and paroled at Atlanta. To TN, March, 1907. Southern Express agent in Chattanooga Died Aug. 31, 1920 in Atlanta and buried there. [CT Sept. 1, 1920; NBFM2; TP15373]

STRADLEY, W. W.   Co. G, 26TN; 2d Co. K,
                  1CSA (GA)
        Enl. July 8, 1861, Knoxville. Sick in hospital, Cumberland City, Feb. 1862. Absent in Howard's Bn., AL Cav., Dec. 31, 1862.

STRATTON, John M.     Co. F, 35TN

        Died April, 1863 [Lindsley]; Killed in action [Z]

STREAKER, J. E.   4TN Cav. Bn. (Ragsdale's)
        Res. HC, 1908 [TP 10,470]

STRICKLAND, George W.     Co. E, 19AL
        Born Cherokee Co., GA, 1836. Enl. Aug., 1861. Disch. June, 1862, disability. To TN, 1867. Res. Sale Creek, 1907, 1910. [TP9218; 1910HC]

STROTHER, George E.   Co. A, 19TN; Co. H,
                      Cons. 3TN
        Enl. June, 1861. He was at Yandell Hospital at Columbus, MS, in May, 1862. From there he was sent to a hospital in Atlanta. Joined Co. H, Cons. 3TN, Apr. 9, 1865. Paroled at Greensboro, N.C., May 1, 1865.

STUART, Nathan
        Died on double quick march to Nashville (there is a Nathaniel Stewert, age 21, in 1860 census).

STUART, Thomas A.   Co. G, 26TN
        Enl. 28 Aug. 1861, Knoxville. Died 27 Nov. 1861 at hospital, Bowling Green.

STUART, W. A.   Co. G, 26TN;
                2d Co. K, 1CSA (GA)
        Enl. Aug. 28, 1861, Knoxville. Absent in 36GA.

STURGIL, Robert Henry   Oliver's Btry.; Co. C,
                        21VA Cav.
        Born Dec. 6, 1840 in Lee Co., VA, son of

William and Sarah Osborn Sturgil. Boyhood in KY and NC. Enl. at Abington, VA in spring of 1861 in J. M. Oliver's Btry. and sent to Wytheville and was in small battle near there. Later in Co. C, 21 VA Cav. Fought at Piedmont, Lynchburg, second battle of Winchester and Frederick City. Captured Moorefield, VA, Aug. 7, 1864 imprisoned Camp Chase. Released March, 1865 in Nashville and "nearly beat to death by a mob of Yankees that didn't like my uniform." Married Mary Ann McKendrie Smith (1870). Blacksmith and in railroad construction work for 19 years. Moved to East Chattanooga, 1898. Res. VA and TN and employed by Chattanooga Implement Co. until 1919. Also U. S. deputy marshal six years. Baptist. Died Nov. 24, 1937 at home on Searle St. and buried CSA Cem. [NBFM3; CT Nov. 25, 1937; TP10375; TCVQ; 1910HC]

SU--SON, R. H.
        Born Jan. 1, 1850 in Spartanburg Dist., SC. Enl. in Pendleton, SC, Feb., 1864 in Pendleton Co. Mounted Inf., Russell's Bn. Engaged in guarding mountain passes along the lines of SC and E. TN. "After Johnston's surrender I with several others under Lt. Bartlett struck out for Trans Miss. Dept until finding all hope gone, we returned to our homes." [NBFM2]

SUBLETT, Capt. David L.   Co. E, 4TX
        Born 1837 in Sublettsville, Powhatan Co., VA. Graduated VMI, 1858. Served as Lt. in US Army in Texas until war began when resigned and became Lt. and ADC to Gen. J. B. Hood, 1862. He served as ordnance officer with Hood in 1863-1864 and chief of ordnance for S.D. Lee with rank of colonel. After war joined US Engineers and came to TN in 1877 to build improvements on the Tennessee River near Knoxville. From 1880-1887 designing and building locks and dams on the Kentucky River. To Chattanooga in 1887 where he entered real estate business (Sublett and Carson). Once again entered US Engineer service as assistant to Capt. G.W. Goethals. Returned to Chattanooga as civil engineer. Member NBF Camp, 1895. Died at his home in Highland Park, March 24, 1896, and was buried at St. Luke's Church, Sublettsville, VA. Married Mattie Owen in 1871. [CT March 25, 1896; NBFM2]

SUDDATH, Sgt. Frank K.   Co. A, 4TN Cav.
        Born c1835, he was a clerk for the merchant A.D. Taylor before the war. Enl. June 17, 1861, Knoxville. Disch. June 23, 1862 and sick at home. Re-enl. and captured Sept. 1, 1862. near Clinton, at Lenoir Station. Imprisoned Johnson's Island. Released June 12, 1865. Res. listed as Talbottom, GA. He was living at Savoy, Texas in 1909. [Name also spelled Suddreth in some records.]

SULLINS, David   Chaplain, 19TN
Born near Athens, McMinn Co., TN, 23 July 1827, son of Nathan and Rebecca Mitchell Sullins. Attended Emory & Henry College. Became Methodist preacher and held pastorates at Jonesboro (1852-54), Centenary Church in Chattanooga, 1857. Married 3 May 1855. Ann Rebecca Blair. Chaplain for 19TN and QM for brigade; and later QM for Breckinridge's Div. Fishing Creek, Shiloh, Baton Rouge. Resigned from army and refugeed to Jonesboro, TN and Wytheville, VA. In Bristol, TN, 1868-80 as head of Sulllins College. Became president of Emory and Henry. Died 19 Feb. 1918 in Birmingham, AL. [NBFM1]

SULLY, John J.
Lived in Chattanooga 48 years, during which time he was engaged in tailoring. Died June 15, 1920, age 85, in Nashville. [CT June 17, 1920]

SUMMERS, Cpl. George P.   Co. F, 35TN
Born in 1836 in Iredell County, NC, he was a laborer in HC when he enl. Oct. 20, 1862. Severely wounded at Chickamauga, he was sent home to recuperate and was captured; took USA oath Dec. 11, 1863; blue eyes, sandy hair, fair complexion, 5'8" tall.

SUTTON, James Montraville   Co. B, 6GA
Born near Trenton, GA, Aug. 24, 1841. Enl. July 1861 at Yorktown, VA. Wounded at Drewry's Bluff, May 1864. A fellow soldier, H. H. Moreland, said, "We were all on our knees in front of the enemy. A ball entered the inside of his leg just below the knee and came out the ankle. The bone was shattered and muscle was hanging out. I think it was the ugliest wound I ever saw. He was sent home and was crippled." Returned to Trenton after war and became county office holder. To Chattanooga in 1878 where he became an agent for Memphis and Charleston RR. Married Mary Elizabeth "Mollie" Carmichael. Died Aug. 4, 1899 at res. on E. 8th St. and buried in Trenton. [NBFM2,7; TWP5206; CT Aug. 5, 1899]

SUTTON, Uriah R.   Co. B, 5TN Cav.
Born 1839 in HC, son of Isaac and Elizabeth Sutton. They had a farm at Harrison. His father died at the start of the war. Uriah Sutton enl. at Chattanooga on Aug. 11, 1861. He died Feb. 18, 1862. Sutton had never married. He had yellow eyes, light hair, a light complexion, and was six feet tall.

SWAFFORD, A.
Born 1834, TN. 1910 res. Rossville Rd with wife Sarah whom he married in 1860 four grown daughters, and grandchildren. [1910HC]

SWAFFORD, George   Co. L, 36TN; Co. L, 35TN
He enl. 9 Jan. 1862, at Chattanooga. He fought at Murfreesboro. He deserted Sept. 10, 1863, at Tyner's Station. Before the war, he lived on the farm of Sampson Ballard at Harrison. He was born c1843. 1870 farmer at Harrison. [1860HC]

SWAN, J. L.   Barry's Battery
Robert J. Woody enl. Oct. 14, 1862 in Barry's Btry. at Knoxville as substitute for J. L. Swan.

SWEENEY, George W.   14MS
Black soldier. [TP#129]

SWEETS, Isaac J.   Barry's Btry.
Deserted. [Brown's Diary]

SWENNY, F.   Barry's Battery

SWETT (SWEAT), John   Co. G, 21GA
Born Aug. 28, 1834 in Fulton Co., GA. Enl. April, 1861. Served in ANV under Stonewall Jackson. Wounded twice. Paroled May 8, 1865. Became watchman in Chattanooga Died Dec. 24, 1896 and buried CSA Cem. [NBFM2, 7]

SWICK, Henry M.   Co. E, 4GA Cav.
(Avery's Squadron, GA Dragoons)
Born c1833, Staunton, Augusta Co., VA. He and three of his brothers came to Chattanooga before the war. They were painters. HMS and wife Mary Ann Lowery were members of 1st Presbyterian Church, but they moved to Dalton where he enl. May 15, 1862. HMS and Mary Ann were married in 1857 in Dalton, GA. She was born 1841 in Dalton and died 1915 in Chattanooga. Sick in the Dalton hospital, Nov. 1863 but rejoined his unit. Mason. Returned to Chattanooga and res. at 512 W. 7th St. He died Nov. 10, 1915 in Chattanooga and was buried in Dalton. [CT Nov. 12, 1915; JW, Swick Family]

SWICK, Micajah T.   Co. F, 35TN
Born in Staunton, VA. To Chattanooga with his 3 brothers: H.M., D. P. and William L. Swick. Married (Jan. 15, 1861) in Chattanooga to Lizzie P. Fyffe. Enl. Oct. 5, 1862. He had hazel eyes, black hair, a dark complexion, and was six feet tall. Became contractor after war. Oldest member of 1st Presbyterian at his death, Aug. 28, 1911. [CT Aug. 29, 1911; JW Swick Fam.]

SWIFT, R. B.   Co. G, 1MS
Born 1843 in Noxubee Co., MS. Enl. at Macon, MS, May 1861 in 1MS., then Co. G, 1MS Cav. Paroled May 1865. Clerk in Chattanooga in 1893. [NBFM2]

SWISHER, Sgt. Elbert W.   Co. K, 43TN

Born c1834 AL, son of H. R. and Elizabeth Swisher, natives of Alabama. Prior to the war, the Swishers lived at Zion Hill south of Ooltewah. HRW was a farmer and minister. Enl. along with his younger brother, James H. Swisher, on Oct. 17, 1861, at Ooltewah. Both were captured at Vicksburg on July 4, 1863. Paroled Washington, GA, May, 1865. 1870 res. near Red Clay, GA, wife Martha. 1870 res. next to Samuel R., 60 years, school-teacher. Res. Apison, TN where he died Sept. 30, 1906. [TP8079]

SWISHER, Sgt. James Henegar    Co. K, 43TN
Born Jan. 27, 1835 in McMinn Co., son of H.R. and Elizabeth Swisher, he lived all his life in Tennessee. Before the war, he lived at Zion Hill south of Ooltewah. He enl. Oct. 17, 1861, at Ooltewah. He was captured at Vicksburg on July 4, 1863. After being paroled, he was again captured on Sept. 4, 1864, in Green County, TN but, exchanged. Res. in Apison, James Co. in 1904

SYLAR, Sgt. Houston H.    Co. B, 1TN Cav.
(Carter's); 2nd Co. K, 1st CSA Cav.
Born Jan. 16, 1835 in Roane Co., son of Peter H. (from VA) and Sarah Syler (from SC). Farmer at Ooltewah, 1860 with wife Sarah A. Enl. in HC July 14, 1862. He deserted at Shelbyville, Feb. 14, 1863. 1870 res. of HC with wife Martha A. at Ooltewah near his parents. 1891 unemployed but still living in Ooltewah, now in James Co. [TP494]

# T

TABLER, J. H.    Wise's Legion
Born Wytheville, VA. Enl. May, 1861. Railroader in Chattanooga, 1888. Moved to Paducah, KY in 1902 and died there July 20, 1902. [NBFM2,7]

TALIAFERRO, George D.
Born 1841 in HC, he enl. in Co. A, 5TN Cav. Served also in Co. B, 2TN Cav.; also Osborne's Scouts for Gen. Longstreet. After the war, he was arraigned for treason but the charges were dropped. He succeeded in organizing the Acme Kitchen Furniture Co. and was a director of the American Textile and Woolen Co. He married Margaret Queener. He died Aug. 19, 1914 at his home in East Chattanooga and was buried in Forest Hills Cemetery. [CT Aug. 20-22, 1914]

TALIAFFERRO, George W.    Co. B, 1TN Cav. (Carter's).
Born 1843, Tenn. 1910 Res. with wife (2) Eliza J. on 2d St.

TALIAFERRO, J.    Co. K, 43TN

TALIAFFERRO, Richard J.    Co. B, 1TN Cav. (Carter's)
A bugler with Co. B, he deserted at Bristol, TN, on April 4, 1865, and took the oath of allegiance on April 15, 1865. Fair complected with light hair and blue eyes, and was 5'8" tall. Before the war, he lived at Limestone near Ooltewah with wife, Martha J. Born c1836, his residence in 1865 is listed as Blount Co.

TALIAFERRO, Wiley Franklin    Co. D, 60GA;
Co. I, 1GA State Troops;  Co. A, 34GA
Born Feb. 8, 1845 in Surry Co., NC. Enl. at Dalton, GA, Sept. 19, 1861 in Co. D, 60GA. Disch. May, 1862 and re-enl. Disch. again from Co. I, 1GA State in May 1863 from Co. A, 34GA. Wounded 3 times at Battle of Missionary Ridge and imprisoned at Rock Island. Res. Sherman Hts, occup. farmer and dairyman. Married Susie Pollen 8 Feb. 1870 in Rome, GA and she died 1889 in Dalton, GA. His second wife was Jemima G.  Baptist. Died Dec. 27, 1916 at residence in East Chattanooga and buried Greenwood Cem. [CT Dec. 29, 1916; NBFM2; TP12254; 1910HC; UDC2 pg 519]

TALLANT (TALENT, TALLENT), David H.    Co. K, 43TN
Born 1837 in TN. Farmer at Ooltewah who enl. Nov. 15, 1861, at Ooltewah. He was captured at Vicksburg on July 4, 1863, and took the oath of allegiance, Dec. 11, 1863. Wife was A. C.  Fair complexion, brown hair, black eyes, 6' tall. [1860 HC.]

TALLANT, James    2nd Co. K, 1st CSA Cav.
Born 1842 in TN, son of Enoch and Catharine Tallant. Enl. Sept. 23, 1862 in HC Captured near Charleston, TN, Dec. 28, 1863. Imprisoned Rock Island, IL. Exch. Jan. 17, 1864. [1860 HC]

TALLANT, John  Co. B, 1TN Cav. (Carter's)

TALLANT, Richard  2nd Co. K, 1st CSA Cav.
Enl. in HC Sept. 23, 1862. He was captured Linden, TN, May 12, 1863 and exch. June 12, 1863.

TALLEY, Benjamin D.  Co. H, 1TN Cav. (Carter's)
Born 1838 in TN, son of Robert and Rachel of Ooltewah.

TALLY, Floyd    Co. A, 5TN Cav. (McKenzie's)
Born GA, 1836, son of Stephen and Eliza Talley. To HC from Gordon Co. GA before war with half-brothers Wm. B. and Berry. 1860 farm laborer in household of J. B. Peters in Ooltewah. Enl. Aug. 24 at Camp Cummings. By end of Feb., 1863, had been mounted 164 days and due $50 bounty. Listed as AWOL

1864. Married Nancy Jane Shull, 1870. She died 1896. Res. 1910 in household of son-in-law Mike Stewart. He died 1912 and was buried Concord Baptist Church Cem. [1910HC]

TALLY, William B.    Co. B, 1TN Cav. (Carter's)
        Born 1818, Laurens Co., SC, son of Stephen and Polly Pool Talley. Family moved to Gordon Co., GA, 1832, and he and two brothers moved to HC c1856. Talley Rd. in Brainerd was named for family and old home still stands at 4212 Howell Rd. Served in Creek War and assisted in Indian removal. His horse was killed by the enemy Dec. 30, 1862. Carpenter in Chattanooga before and after war. [1860,1870 HC Census]

TANKESLEY, Major Rufus Miller    Co. D, 37TN
        Born June 10, 1836 in Dandridge, TN, son of Reuben and Sarah Emmeline Miller Tankesley, he moved to Chattanooga with his parents in 1852 and worked as a clerk. He was known as a Union man prior to the war, however he enl. in Co. D, 37TN. He became ill in Aug. 1862 and was furloughed to the CSA Army Hospital at Catoosa Springs near Ringgold, GA. though he almost died, he recovered after four months and was given command of the Catoosa Springs facility. He ended his tenure at the hospital on April 30, 1863, and rejoined his unit. At Chickamauga, he rallied on troops after the company's lieutenant colonel was struck down. He fought at Missionary Ridge and throughout the Atlanta campaign. On Dec. 1, 1863, he was promoted to major. At Jonesboro, GA, he was wounded in the side and hospitalized two months. He returned to fight at Franklin and Nashville and was at the final surrender in North Carolina.
        Afterwards, Rufus returned to Chattanooga and was general agent for the Southern Express Co. He also served as constable and was Circuit Court clerk. He was in the grocery business, real estate and had a medicine company. His wife was Addie R. Fouts. He died April 18, 1905 in Chattanooga [CT, 19 April 1905; Robin Rudd, "City's Rufus Tankesley Survived Civil War Hardship"]

TANNER, John Q.    Co. A, 18GA
        Born in Campbell Co. GA, 23 June 1840. Enl. at McDonald, GA, June 1861. Served in ANV in Wofford's Brigade, Hood's Div. Fought at Seven Pines and Gettysburg. Wounded at Wilderness. Captured at Sailor's Creek. Merchant in Chattanooga Baptist. Died Dec. 17, 1912, at home on Kirby Ave. and buried Forest Hills Cemetery. [CT 18 Dec. 1912; NBFM2; FHR; TP9356]

TANNER, L. H.    Co. A, 18GA

        Born Aug. 18, 1832 in Walton, GA. Enl. at Big Shanty, GA June 11, 1861. ANV. Captured at Cedar Run, VA, Oct. 18, 1864. Res. of Chattanooga in 1895. Merchant and member of Board of Health. Died March 15, 1910 in Stockton, CA and buried Forest Hills Cemetery. [FHR; NBFM2; CT22 Mar. 1910]

TARVER, Benjamin Marcus    Co. E, Phillips GA Legion
        Born June 20, 1846 in Twiggs Co., GA, he enl. Sept. 1864, in Macon and served in VA. In fighting at White Oak swamp. He was paroled at Greensboro, NC, May 2, 1865. Lived in GA and TN after war. His wife Eliza V. was born 7 Jan 1851 in Baldwin Co., GA. Real Estate. Baptist. Died Oct. 20, 1928 in Selma, AL and buried Forest Hills Cemetery. [NBFM2,8; TP 16,371; UDC1 pg 418]

TARWATER, James M.    Co. D, 37TN
        Enl. Sept. 1, 1861, at Knoxville. Captured near Franklin on Dec. 17, 1864, and imprisoned Camp Douglas, Ill. Before the war, he lived with his father, David Tarwater, a farm laborer near Chattanooga. He was born about 1844. He had a dark complexion, dark hair, hazel eyes, and was 5'7" tall.

TARWATER, William    Co. D, 37TN
        Born 1842 in TN, son of David. Enl. Nov. 2, 1861, Knoxville. Trans. to Pioneer Service June 26, 1862. Captured on picket at Big Shanty, June 1, 1864 and imprisoned Rock Island. Gave res. to USA as Knoxville. [1860HC]

TATE, Elisha    Co. I, 26TN    3d Lt.

TATE, Perryman M.    Barry's Btry.
        Enl. Jan. 19, 1863 at Chattanooga; daily duty was making oil for harness; captured Spanish Fort, April 8, 1865; imprisoned Ship Island, MS. [there is a 53-year-old Perryman Tate, farm laborer born in SC, at Tynerville in 1860 HC census]

TAYLOR, A. C.    7TN Cav. Bn. (Lt. Col. James D. Bennett)
        Buried CSA Cem.

TAYLOR, Capt. Alfred D.    Co. F, 19TN
        A prominent merchant at Chattanooga for many years prior to the start of the war, he was appointed Sept. 11, 1861, assistant quartermaster and served in the campaign in Mississippi, then was with the unit as it returned to Tennessee. He was elected captain in October, 1864 when the troops were at Eatonton, GA.
        Taylor was known as "Doctor" and he may have been a medical doctor, perhaps a regimental assistant

surgeon. He married Catherine Glass, daughter of John Glass. She died at the start of the war. Dr. Taylor resumed business in Chattanooga after the war. He also served as city treasurer and tax collector.

TAYLOR, E. B.
Born Fayetteville, TN. Died Dec. 1914, age 84, and buried in Fayetteville. [CT Dec. 13, 1914]

TAYLOR, J. H.    Co. D, 37TN
Enl. 1 Dec. 1861, Knoxville. Listed as deserter, Jan. 5, 1863,

TAYLOR, James    Co. A, 5th TN Cav. (McKenzie's)
Enl. Aug. 24, 1861, Camp Cumming. Age 34 on March 11, 1864 roll. Deserted Feb. 24, 1864. Took USA oath at Chattanooga, Feb. 26, 1864.

TAYLOR, Lt. John R.    Co. F, 35Tn
He "served gallantly from the beginning to the end of the war and was never wounded." He enl. in the "volunteer regiment headed by Col. Hill, which later became part of Bragg's army." He took part in the invasion of Kentucky and fought at Cumberland Gap and Chickamauga. He defended Missionary Ridge and was in the Georgia campaign. Taylor was "still wearing the gray when Richmond fell." Born Nov. 20, 1821, in Rutherford Co., NC, he lived on his father's farm and walked a long distance to a log schoolhouse. He made his way to Chattanooga in 1844 and followed the carpenter trade. He resided with the family of Dr. Joseph Reeves and married into that family in 1850. He and his wife had no children, and she died in 1889. After the war, Taylor was in the insurance business, living at 521 Lookout St. He died Jan. 28, 1900 and was buried CSA Cem. [CT Jan. 29, 1900; TP1790; NBFM7]

TAYLOR, Thomas Daniel    Co. C, Walker's Bn., Thomas NC Legion.
Born June 9, 1844 in Grainger Co., TN and res. Blount Co.; enl. Sept. 29, 1862, Maryville, TN. Captured at Piedmont, VA, June 5, 1864; imprisoned Camp Morton, IN; tranferred to Point Lookout, MD where exchanged Feb. 28, 1865 and finally paroled June 26, 1865. After war, became a tinsmith and grocery clerk at Chattanooga Married Julia Ames. Died in FL after 1906. Buried CSA Cem. [NBFM2; TP8320]

TAYLOR, W. L.    Co. A, 1TN Cav. (Carter's)
Born Monroe Co., TN, Feb. 17, 1843; cousin of R. L. Taylor. In fight at Big Creek Gap had to wade across creek in ice and snow and developed rheumatism which ended his service. "Too fleshy and large to serve as a soldier. Became "Minister of the Gospel," 1877. Wife was Gertrude. Res. Ooltewah, 1916. [TP15,102]

TEENOR, 1Lt. John A.    Co. B, 1TN Cav. (Carter's).
Born 1836 in TN. He was on sick furlough in October, 1864. His younger brother, Jacob Teenor, married a daughter of the company captain, William Snow. The Teenors were sons of Eliza Teenor, who had a farm at Long Savannah.

TEMPLE, Sgt. Charles    Co. K, 43TN
He enl. Oct. 17, 1861, at Ooltewah. His father, Daniel Temple, was a farmer at Harrison and was also superintendent of the Asylum for the Poor. The Temples were originally from North Carolina. Charles Temple was born about 1837.

TEMPLETON, A.
Born 1820. Clergyman. Exec. Committee, Soldiers Relief Society at Chattanooga, Aug. 29, 1861. Wife was Mahala. [1860HC]

TEMPLETON, Burl    Co. L, 35TN
Enl. Jan. 9, 1862 in Chattanooga. Last paid by Capt. Brown, Oct. 31, 1863.

TEMPLETON, John C.    Co. A, 19TN
He fought at Missionary Ridge and the Atlanta Campaign, but was killed July 22, 1864, at the Battle of Atlanta. [Worsham, 129]

TERRELL, Sgt. Cicero W.    Co. F, 16GA; Co. G, 42GA
Born Jan. 1, 1834 in Walton Co., GA. Enl. at Monroe, GA, Feb. 1, 1862. Perryville. Captured at Vicksburg, imprisoned Camp Morton, and parolled. Wounded four times: Atlanta Campaign, Nashville, Kingston (NC) and Bentonville. To Chattanooga, July 1873 as lineman for Western Union Teleg. Co. In Chattanooga, 1900. Married (1875) Margaret. Christian Church. Died at res. on Cherry St., Dec. 19, 1928 and was buried Forest Hills Cem. [NBFM2,8; TP12851; 1910HC]

TERRELL, William Alexander    Co. F, 3VA Cav.
Born 1844, Henrico Co., VA, son of William Alexander and Clarasy Dickinson Terrell. His mother was daughter of William Dickinson of Goochland Co. W. A. Terrell was living in Goochland Co. when he enl. in New Kent Co. in Co. F, 3VA Cav. in June, 1863. He participated in "all the raids, battles, skirmishes, and campaigns of his regiment" until Spotsylvania Court House when he was wounded and captured. He was hospitalized in Washington, then imprisoned at the Old Capitol prison and Elmira, NY. After his release at the time of surrender he returned to VA and became a merchant in Powhatan Co. until 1890 when he moved to Chattanooga and became an insurance agent. On Chattanooga City Council for 9th Ward in 1905 and was

in Tenn. Genl. Assembly. 1911-1913. Democrat. Episcopalian. Married (2) Mary A., 1870. Died at his home on Chamberlain Ave. on 25 Jan. 1923 and was buried Forest Hills Cemetery. [NBFM2; TP15,316; TCVQ; CT Jan. 26, 1923; Biog Directory of TN Gen'l Assembly,

TERRY, Charles A.     Co. I, 19TN
         Enl. at Knoxville and proceeded to Camp Cumberland Gap, Va. He died in Vicksburg, Aug. 1861. [Worsham, 201.]

TERRY, Capt. F. B.   Co. A, 17TN
         Born Oct. 19, 1839 in Bedford Co., TN, son of R. H. and Elizabeth Terry. Enl. May 16, 1861 at Estill Springs. Elected captain May 16, 1862. Wounded Chickamauga. Became ADC for B.R. Johnson. Captured May 16, 1864 near Petersburg, VA. Paroled at Fort Delaware, May 16, 1865. Married Martha Landess (1868). Died at East Lake Aug. 20, 1919 and buried at Griffin, GA. [NBFM2; TP10124; CT 21 Aug. 1919]

TERRY, John   Co. F, 4TN Cav. Bn. (Branner's)
         Black soldier, born 1826, Bledsoe Co., slave of Scott Terry of Bledsoe, and was waiter at Panter Hotel in Pikeville. Served with Terry's grandson, Maj. John M. Bridgeman. "I was with General Zollicoffer who was Kild at Fishing Creek." CT article (and photo) about Terry when he was 105 (1931). Res. 10th St., Chattanooga, 1930. Died August, 1935. James A. Tulloss of Bledsoe gave the men commanded by Capt. John N. Bridgeman their uniforms and they in turn named their unit ("Tulloss Rangers") for him. They received at Big Creek Gap their flag from Miss Finley who accompanied Mr. Tulloss. [TN CSA Pension Applications; TP#255; NBFM10]

THACKER, James     Co. D, 4GA Cav.
         He was the youngest of three brothers who joined the same company on Oct. 4, 1862. The brothers deserted on May 6, 1863, and were captured at Cowan, TN, on July 23, 1863. He was sent as a prisoner to Louisville, Ky. The son of Joel and Eda Thacker, he was born about 1841. The Thackers lived in Lookout Valley at the start of the war.

THACKER, Solomon     Co. D, 4GA Cav.
         Born 1836 in TN, son of Joel and Eda. Promoted to sergeant, but he resigned that post prior to deserting and being captured at Cowan, TN, on July 23, 1863. He took the USA oath of allegiance. He was born about 1836.

THACKER, William     Co. D, 4GA Cav.
         Born 1839 in TN, son of Joel and Eda.

Promoted to corporal, but resigned that post prior to deserting and being captured at Cowan, TN on July 23, 1863. 1870 res. Wauhathie, wife Lucy. Died May 7, 1914, age 77, at home on Campbell St. and buried Forest Hills Cemetery. [CT May 8, 1914]

THATCH, Samuel G.     Co. G, 26TN; 2d Co. K, 1CSA (GA)
         Enl. July 8, 1861, Knoxville. Detached to company of Miners and Sappers, Nov. 12, 1861 (CSA Engineeers), Co. A, Pioneer Bn. for work on TN River at Chattanooga.

THOMAS, A. J.     Co. D, 37TN
         Born 1825 in TN. Res. Harrison with wife Louiza. Enl. March 27, 1863, Chattanooga. Conscripted. Deserted Catoosa Springs, March 29, 1863.

THOMAS, Archer D.     Barry's Btry.
         He and his brother, David D., joined Barry's Battery at Chattanooga on May 15, 1862. They were sons of William Adam Thomas, a native of Wales who arrived in Chattanooga about 1848. The mother was Mary Williams. Archer Thomas became sick during the war and was hospitalized for a lengthy period at Greenville, AL. He returned to action in early 1864, but in September at Atlanta he deserted and took the oath of allegiance on Oct. 26, 1864. He had hazel eyes, light hair, a light complexion, and was 5'6" tall. After the war, he resided in Walker Co., GA. He died in 1915 at the age of 74.

THOMAS, Arthur Reece
         Born in Wales, Feb. 4, 1845, one of the sons of William Adam Thomas, he joined the Watts Cadets, an Alabama infantry unit, when he was 19. The Watts Cadets were organized at Montgomery, AL. He was later transf. to a cavalry unit. Finally he was paroled by Federal forces and returned to Chattanooga. He and his brother, I. W. Thomas, opened a general store on Market Street in 1867. A. R. Thomas served as a second ward alderman at Chattanooga, was on the school board.,and was secretary of the city park commission. After I.W. Thomas moved to Oregon, A.R. Thomas became proprietor of the Natural Bridge Hotel on Lookout Mountain. He later resided at St. Elmo and was its first mayor. He was also president of the South Chattanooga Business League. Methodist. Mason. His residence was at 4202 St. Elmo Ave. He was married and divorced. He was living with his niece, Mrs. W.S. Weatherford, on Kelley Street in Chattanooga when he died March 14, 1935 at the age of 90 and was buried Forest Hills Cem. [CT March 15.35; NBFM7]

THOMAS, Benjamin F.     Co. I, 3TN (Vaughn's)

Born 1842 in AL and brought to TN as child. Enl. 1861. Paroled Washington, GA, May, 1865. Married (1865) Evaline Price. Res. 1907 in East Chattanooga. 1910 farm laborer. [TP9538; 1910HC]

THOMAS, Cpl. David Dyer    Barry's Btry.
Another of the sons of William Adam Thomas, he enl. May 15, 1862, at Chattanooga. He was wounded in the fighting at Resaca and was captured at Spanish Fort, April 8, 1865. Imprisoned at Ship Island, MS. After the war, he lived at Dry Valley in Walker County, GA, and at Mountain Junction at the south end of St. Elmo. He married Sarah Caroline Williams. Their sons were Randolph William, A., Lawrence, David W., and George. The family had a grocery store on Whiteside (South Broad) Street and resided nearby at 1203 Whiteside.

THOMAS, Iltid W.    2d Co. K, 26TN; 1CSA(GA)
Born in Wales in 1839, son of William A. Thomas, he emigrated to the US in 1849 and settled at Blowing Springs. He enl. July 8, 1861 in Co. G, 26TN at Knoxville. Captured at Fort Donelson, Feb. 16, 1862 and imprisoned at Camp Douglas. Evidently exchanged, he won promotions to cpl., Feb. 28, 1863, and sgt., Sept. 16, 1864. Thomas participated in the battles of Murfreesboro, Lookout Mountain, Chickamauga, Missionary Ridge, Ringgold, Tunnel Hill, Rocky Face, and Atlanta. He was wounded in the latter struggle. At the battle of Franklin, all Thomas' company except 12 were shot down. He took charge of the remaining soldiers and charged the third line of the enemy's breastworks. A ball went through his left arm, shattering the bone. It passed into his body and lodged against the spinal column. This leaden missile was never removed. Captured in this battle, Thomas was hospitalized at Nashville and later imp. at Camp Chase, OH, then Point Lookout, MD. He was released June 5, 1865.
After the war, he operated a store on Market Street with his brother, A. R. Thomas. In 1876, I. W. Thomas moved to Medford, OR, where he accumulated a large estate. His wife was Catherine Anderson, daughter of Congressman Josiah Anderson of Sequatchie Valley, who had been killed at the start of the war. Catherine Anderson Thomas died in OR in 1902. Thomas married a second time in 1906. He died in OR in Jan. 1916. [JWilson Thomas Family, CNews Jan. 29, 1916]

THOMAS, John    Co. H, 1TN Cav.
Born Cumberland Co., TN, 1816, he was wounded at Murfreesboro. In 1891, John was living near Sale Creek where he had supported himself by fishing and truck farming since the war. [TP598]

THOMAS, John Jenkins    Barry's Battery
He enl. along with his brothers in 1862, but resigned after 10 months due to ill health. He was one of the sons of William Adam Thomas. He married Elizabeth Jane Willis, sister of the wife of his brother, David Dyer Thomas. After her death, he married another Willis sister, Georgia Anna. John Jenkins Thomas and his first wife are buried in unmarked graves in the old McFarland Cem. about two miles south of the Rossville, GA Post Office. [United Daughters of the Confederacy application of Mrs. W.S. Weatherford; JW Thomas Family]

THOMAS, L. M.    Co. F, 3TN Mtd. Inf.
Captured Vicksburg. [TP10,686]

THOMAS, Thomas Lafayette  Co. B, 31GA
Born Muscogee Co., GA. Enl. Oct. 5, 1861, and was in battles around Richmond, 1863. At Columbus, GA, 1864, he was wounded in left hip. "The top of his hip joint was gone and he could only hobble around with the aid of a cane" afterward. Married (1866) Adaline Bird and died in Chattanooga, Easter Sunday, 1904. [TWP, 4780]

THOMAS, N. C.    Co. C, Phillips Legion, GA Inf.
Born Aug. 5, 1837, Habersham Co., GA. Second Manassas (wounded), Gettysburg, Chickamauga, Knoxville, Wilderness. Captured Andersonville, GA, May 3, 1865 and paroled. Returned home to Clarksville, GA. To TN 1880. Wife was Rebecca. Carried the mail in North Chattanooga many years. In 1911 res. Signal Mountain, where he died Sept. 11, 1925 and was buried Chattanooga Memorial Park. [TP 13,150; CT Sept. 12, 1925]

THOMAS, Nicolis G.    Co. A, 2KY Cav.
Born Dec. 9, 1845 in Montgomery Co., TN. Enl. in north AL, Sept. 1864. Paroled May 12, 1865 at Washington, GA. Married (1869) Mildred Amelia Gilmer. Physican. Res. Appison, James Co. where he died Nov. 8, 1909. Buried Clarksville, TN. [CT Nov. 9, 1909; TWP, p. 196; NBFM2]]

THOMPSON, David    Co. H, 4TN Cav.
Died "at home near the suck 1862."

THOMPSON, Eriah [Enid]    Co. G, 4AL
Born in Rhea Co. Enl. Sept., 1862. Res. Chattanooga Farmer, but had moved away by 1893. [NBFM2,7]

THOMPSON, Frank Blevins  5TN Cav.
Born March 14, 1847, Blount Co., TN. To Chattanooga, 1868. Employed by govt. in TN River work. On commisson which built county bridge across

CONFEDERATE SOLDIERS OF HAMILTON COUNTY, TENNESSEE

the Tennessee, member of County Court, and for several years manager of Chattanooga Co., Ltd. Married (1869) Josephine Gurley. Mason. Died at home in Hill City, Aug. 17, 1903 and buried White Oak Cem. [CT Aug. 18, 1903]

THOMPSON, George W.     Co. B, 8GA Bn.;
          Co. F, 39GA
        Born Apr. 17, 1842, Cass Co., GA. Enl. 6 July 1861. Wounded Secessionville, Kennesaw Mountain., Franklin. Paroled at Salisbury, NC, Apr., 1865. Carpenter in Chattanooga, 1887 but unable to work because of dent in skull and palsied walk from wounds. Died at residence, on Montgomery Ave., Aug. 29, 1906. [CT 30 Aug. 1906; NBFM2; TP4062; 1890Vet Census]

THOMPSON, H. W.     2d Co. K, 1CSA (GA)
        Enl. Nov. 11, 1862, Chattanooga. Prom. Sgt. Killed at Peachtree Creek, July 20, 1864.

THOMPSON, Henry B.     Co. G, 3AL
        Born 1833, Chester Dist., SC, he enl. 1862. At Second Manassas, Fredericksburg, Chancellorsville (was wounded in jaw), and Gettysburg (wounded in head). To TN in 1884 and 1909 res. Shepherd, "old and needy and very infirm." Res. Bird's Mill Rd., 1910. [TP10769; 1910HC]

THOMPSON, Isaac     Co. K, 43TN
        Enl. Oct. 17, 1861 at Ooltewah; deserted Aug. 1, 1862.

THOMPSON, J. W.     Co. B, 1TN Cav.
        He was captured Sept. 23, 1864, at Strasburg, Va. and taken to Point Lookout, MD. He was exchanged on Feb. 17, 1865, at Camp Lee near Richmond.

THOMPSON, Joseph     Co. I, 19TN
        Born c1836 in TN. At outbreak of the war was a day laborer living at Chattanooga with his wife, Lucinda. Enl. May 20, 1861 in Knoxville. He was named to the Roll of Honor for his conspicious bravery at the battle of Murfreesboro. Yet, when he was severly wounded and taken prisoner at Chickamauga, he told Union authorities that he had enl. with the rebels "through false means." At Camp Douglas, IL, he claimed to have been loyal and took the oath of allegiance, and enl. in 6th U.S. Volunteers. [1860HC]

THOMPSON, Joseph M.     Co. B, 39NC
        Born Macon Co., NC, 1841. Enl. Buncombe Co., age 19. At Chickamauga, musket ball hit his rifle and shattered it wounding him severely in face and chin. Deserted May 12, 1864 and cited as having piloted Federal Officers who were escaping from imprisonment

in NC. To TN very soon after war and res. in Chattanooga, 1905. [TP7726; NC Troops, 10:128]

THOMPSON, Newcomb Frierson     Forrest's Escort
        Born Dec. 25, 1844 in Bedford Co., TN and enl. at Shelbyville about June 1863. Paroled at Gainesville, AL, June 10, 1865. Res. Walnut St. in 1888. [NBFM2]

THOMPSON, William H.     Co. C, 51VA
        Born Franklin Co., VA, 1844. Enl. July 1861. Winchester, New Market (wounded). Imp. Fort Delaware, released July 1865. [TP11,068]

THORN, Edward D.     Co. B, 8GA BN.
        Born near Spartanburg, SC, 18 Aug. 1845, son of Robert Thorn. Enl. about Christmas, 1861. The unit remained in Charleston until May, 1863 when it went to MS to fight at Jackson. Subsequently he took part in the Atlanta Campaign, Franklin and Nashville. He surrendered at Kingston, GA and soon moved to Chattanooga where he became a grocer in Ridgedale. Member of NBF Camp, 1895. He married Candis Wofford in 1854 in Calhoun, GA. He died June 11, 1911 at Boynton, GA and was buried in CSA Cem. She died in June 1918 in Chattanooga. [CT June 12, 1911; NBFM2; CSA Mil. Hist., pp. 748-49]

THORNBROUGH, Allen M.
        Presbyterian. Died July 31, 1916, age 77, and buried Silverdale. [CT 2 Aug. 1916]

THORNTON, John W.     Co. B, 3VA
        Enl. April 1863; color bearer. After war was bookkeeper for Betterton, Ford & Co. and officer in Lookout Iron Co. Member of NBF Camp, 1885. Moved away prior to 1893 and died Cape Girardeau, MO. [NBFM1,2,7]

THRAILKILL, Sgt. Isaac P.     Co. B, 36GA (Broyles)
        Born c1839, GA. Res, 1910 household of grandson James Johnson.[1910HC]

THRASHER, Jesse Scaife     Co. K, 7GA; Co. A, 64GA
        Born Jan. 27, 1845, Fulton Co., GA, at old Adam Poole place, several miles from Atlanta, son of J. J. Thrasher and Margaret Bethuel. Contracted pneumonia following battle of First Manassas and discharged. Returned home and organized Co. A, 64GA, becoming 2Lt., and sent to Fla. Wounded in battle of Olustee. To Petersburg and promoted to Captain following Battle of Crater. Cmdg. regt. in closing days of war. Married (Oct. 8, 1876, Gainesville, GA) Lilly James Wilkes. To TN, 1894. Baptist preacher. Manufacturer of germ killer in HC, 1910. Res. Hill City but moved to Atlanta where he died June 22, 1927. His son Wilkes

became Hamilton County judge. [NBFM2,7; TP9817; TWP10598; 1910HC; CT June 23, 1927]

THURMAN, Cpl. John B.    Co. D, 4th (12th) GA Cav.
        Born Feb. 9, 1845 on a farm where South St. Elmo was later located, his family was living in a log cabin on Missionary Ridge in Nov. 1863 which became Bragg's headquarters. Enl. Nov. 15, 1863. Fought at Missionary Ridge and in the Atlanta campaign. After the battle of Jonesboro, his company was sent to MS to bring a drove of cattle to Hood's army at Tuscumbia, AL. He surrendered at Kingston, GA, on May 12, 1865. He married (1871 in HC) Margaret Jane Hamill. A son of Elijah Thurman and Minerva Rice, he had an older brother Monroe Rawlings Thurman who fought with the Union. After the war, JBT had a farm south of Ooltewah. He was a member of the St. Elmo Methodist Episcopal Church South. When he died on Feb. 27, 1933, he was buried in the Thurman family plot at St. Elmo. [JW Thurman Family; CT Feb. 28, 1933; TWP, 305; TCVQ; CSA Mil. Hist. 750-51]

TIDWELL, Capt. William M.    Co. B, 6GA
        Born March 7, 1832. Married Georgia Anne. Died June 5, 1890 in Chattanooga and buried in Citizens Cem. [TWP3477]

TILLERY, Richard C.    Co. H, 2TN Cav. (Ashby's)
        Enl. June 17, 1861, Knoxville. Transf. to 26TN. Captured Somerset, Ky., March 30, 1863 and sent to City Point, VA for exch. Sept. 13, 1863.

TIMMONS, William    Co. A, 4TN Cav. Bn.
                    (Branner's); Co. D, 4GA Cav.
        Born 1837 in HC, son of Matthew and Rosannah Timmons, who had emigrated from Ireland. The family lived at Tynerville before the war. Enl. Oct. 4, 1862. Joined 4GA Cav. after Fishing Creek disaster. Chickamauga, Missionary Ridge. 1910 res with wife Martha J. (m. 1870) on Roanoke St. Worked at odd jobs. Died Feb. 8, 1924 on W. 38th St. and bured in Ooltewah Cem. [TP10,470; 1910HC; CT 9 Feb.1924]

TINKER, Henderson "Henry"    Co. H, 21GA; Barry's Btry.
        Enl. July 30, 1862 at Chattanooga; paroled May 11, 1865 at Meridian, MS; res. Trenton, GA.

TIPPS, Barny M.    Co. D, 37TN
        Enl. Sept. 1, 1861, Knoxville. Made Drum Major, Oct. 10, 1861. Also served as 4th and 5th Sgts.

TIPPS, Drummer W. P.    Co. L, 36TN
        Enl. Jan. 9, 1862 at Chattanooga; chief musician; paroled May 1, 1865 at Greensboro, NC.

TIPTON, Andrew H.    Co. E, 3CSA (GA) Cav.
        Born Walker Co., GA, 1845. Enl. early 1863: Philadelphia, TN (wounded), Catlett's Gap, GA. Captured near Lafayette, GA during Atlanta Campaign and imprisoned Chattanooga. Wife was Lizzie. To TN 1889. Pension disallowed because no record found. 1913 in Chattanooga. [TP 13,882]

TIPTON, George Washington    Co. C, 60GA
        Born Walker Co., GA, 1841. Enl. Sept. 19, 1861. Antietam, Fredericksburg, Gettysburg, and Petersburg (wounded). Imprisoned at Chattanooga; released Apr., 1865. To TN from TX 1914. Sometime carpenter. Wife was Mattie Kleason. 1916 res. East Lake. [TP 15, 039]

TITTLE, George Washington    Co. F., 34GA
        Born April 30, 1846 in Dade. Res. Wauhatchie, HC. Enl. at Lick Skillet near Atlanta, July 9, 1864. Wounded in siege of Atlanta by cannon ball which broke his left hip. Paroled near Greensboro, NC April 27, 1865. Married Mary Elizabeth. Died at Wauhatchie, Feb. 21, 1904 and buried in Wauhatchie. [NBFM2]

TODD, Charles M.    Co. E, 1AL Cav. (Wheeler's Escort)
        Born June 16, 1839 in Laurens Co., SC. Enl. June 13, 1861 at Huntsville. Wounded at Munfordville, KY. Captured at Shelbyville, TN in 1864. Paroled at Kingston, GA. One time sheriff of Rhea Co. and postmaster of Dayton, TN from Jan. 1885 - May 1886. Married first 11 June 1874 to Angeline Paine, a member of the Rhea Co. Girls Company, and second Mary Fuller June 22, 1895 in Meigs Co. NBF Camp. Salesman; res. Chamberlain Ave. Died in North Chattanooga June 27, 1915 and buried CSA Cem. [NBFM7]

TODD, James M.    Co. G, 10SC
        Buried CSA Cem.

TODD, Lemuel M.    Co. G, 10SC
        Buried CSA Cem.

TODD, Samuel C.    Barry's Btry.
        Born c1840, he enl. Sept. 23, 1862, at Chattanooga. Suffered loss of fingers on his left hand due to a gunshot wound that occured before October, 1863. He was paroled May 25, 1865, at Selma, Ala. His parents, J. H. and Mary Todd, Virginia natives, farmed in the vicinity of Lookout Mountain. [1860HC]

TOLER, Joseph Marion "Joe"    Co. A, 25VA Bn.; Co. E, 4VA
        Born Hanover Co., VA, Sept. 25, 1843. Enl. March 1861 and re-enl. Jan. 1864. Wounded and

captured Fort Harrison, Sept. 29, 1864 and imprisoned Point Lookout where exchanged Nov. 15, 1864. To TN, 1872. Carpenter in Chattanooga, 1891. Member NBF Camp, 1895-96. Res. E. 8th St. Married Katherine Engledow. Died July 12, 1918 on visit to Richmond, VA. Buried Forest Hills Cemetery. [FHR; CT July 13,1918; NBFM2]

TOLLEY, Capt. William P. , Co. E, 1TN (Turney's) [NBFM4]
Willilam P. Tolley served in Peter Turney's Vol. 1st TN and later joined Gen. Forrest in his Cavalry units. [UDC1 pg 429]

TOMMEY, James W.   Co. F, 35TN
Born in Ireland, he was a laborer in Hamilton Co. who enl. Oct. 1, 1862 at Chattanooga. Captured April 20, 1865 in Macon, GA; gray eyes, dark hair, dark complexion, and 5'6" tall.

TORBITT, S. M. B.   2nd Co. K, 1st CSA Cav.
Enl. Sept. 23, 1862 in HC. Became teamster at brigade headquarters.

TOWNSEND, R. M   Co. D, 4GA Bn.
Born July 31, 1843 in Gordon Co., GA. Enl. in 1861. Paroled Apr. 12, 1865. Market gardener in Chattanooga, 1890. [NBFM2]

TOWRY, Henry M.   2nd Co. K, 1CSA Cav. (GA)
Born c1837, son of John and Nancy Towry. Enl. Sept. 23, 1862 in HC. "Deserted." Enl. Feb. 12, 1863, at Chattanooga, by J. L. Hopkins in Co. A, 5TN Cav. Age 25 on March 11, 1864 roll. Deserted Feb. 25, 1864 and took USA oath following day in Chattanooga.

TOWRY, John K.  2nd Co. K, 1st CSA Cav.
Born c1844 in TN, son of George Towry. Enl. Sept. 23, 1862 in HC. Died March 1, 1863 near Shelbyville, TN. He was unmarried at time of death. [CSR]

TRAMELL (TRAMEL, TRAMBELL, TRAMILE), Thomas
Enl. Jan. 9, 1862, in Co. L, 36TN at Chattanooga; transferred to Co. L, 35TN; fought at Murfreesboro.

TRAVIS, Joseph V.   Co. H, 2TN Cav. (Ashby's)
Born c1837, he was a carpenter's apprentice, 1861, in Chattanooga with wife Josephine. Enl. June 17, 1861, Knoxville. Wounded in action, Aug. 31, 1862, and died of wounds.

TREW, Thomas J.   Co. B, 1TN Cav. (Carter's)

Born in McMinn Co., TN in 1844; enl. at Knoxville; captured at Vicksburg July 4, 1863; wounded, disabled; fair complexion, light hair; gray eyes, and 5'11" tall. Reported KIA, Somerset, KY, 1862. Res. 1870, McMinn Co.

TRIGG, Orderly Sgt. Guy S.   Co. G, 22VA Cav.
Born Wythe Co., VA, Oct. 7, 1845. Enl. 1862 in Wytheville, VA. Real Estate agent in Chattanooga, 1887. Methodist. Died April 1, 1920 at res. on Georgia Ave. and buried Forest Hills Cem. [FHR; CT April 2.20; NBFM1; TP14762]

TROUSDALE, James Henry  Co. E, 7TN Cav. Bn.
Born Maury Co., TN. Married (1884 in Maury) Alice Eugenia Lentz. Died 1925 or 1926 in HC. [TWP, 317]

TRUEHEART, William A.   Co. A, 46VA
Born Richmond, VA, Dec. 19, 1834. Enl. in Richmond, May 10, 1861. Came to Chattanooga in 1887. Saddler. Left Chattanooga in 1897 for Fairburn, GA, then to Buford, GA, then to Paducah, KY where he died July 20, 1902. Buried Buford, GA. [NBFM3,7;CT July 21, 1902]

TRUNDLE, Robert T.   4GA Cav.
Born c1845. Died June 9, 1917 at 72 yrs. near Ringgold and buried Bethel Cem.

TRUHART, W. A.   Co. A, 46VA
Born in Hanover Co. VA. Enl. May 10, 1861. Honeymaker.   Member NBF Camp, 1896. Lived at 427 High St. Died July 20, 1902 in Paducah, KY and buried Buford, GA.[NBFM2]

TRUSSELL, Eli   Co. L, 35TN
Enl. Jan. 9, 1862, in Co. L, 36TN at Chattanooga; transferred to Co. L, 35TN; fought at Murfreesboro; sent home sick, Jan. 15, 1863, and "has since died."

TRY, M. M.   3TN; 2TN Cav. (Ashby's)
Born Linnville, TN, Aug. 19, 1844. Surrendered with Ashby's Cav. at Charlotte, NC, April, 1865.

TSCHUDY, Matthias  Co. I, 19TN
Born 1833 in Switzerland. Railroad laborer res. in Chattanooga with wife Mary and infant dau.[1860HC]

TUCKER, George Livingston   Barry's Btry.
Born Apr. 24, 1831, son of Joseph and Mary Isbell Tucker. Married (July 15, 1863) Minerva McKamy Frazier, a member of the Rhea Co. Girls Company. She was born 12 Dec. 1844 in Rhea Co. and died 14 Feb.

1870 in Rhea Co. Enl. Feb. 2, 1864 at Decatur, GA; paroled May 11, 1865 at Meridian, MS; res-Newnan, GA. George served in the Battles of Murfreesboro, Chickamauga, and Atlanta. Died Dec. 14, 1878 when killed by a laborer as they were killing hogs in the winter of 1878, and both are buried in the Mynatt (Old Washington) Cem., Rhea Co. [UDC1 pg 433; UDC2 pg 537]

TUCKER, Gustavus Adolpus Rose
Born Feb. 16, 1828, Amherst Co., VA. Univ. of VA. and Jefferson Medical College, Philadelphia. Practiced medicine 30 yrs. Wife was Sally Brown Coleman of Amherst Co. Collector for Times, 1910, and had been for 31 yrs. Died Feb. 10, 1911 in Hill City and buried Forest Hills Cem. [1910HC; Lusk; CT Feb. 10, 1911]

TUCKER, J. L.     Co. E, 13GA
Born in Randolph Co., GA. Enl. May 16, 1862. Paroled at Appamattox. Bookkeeper in Chattanooga, 1888. Member NBF Camp, 1896. [NBFM2]

TUCKER, William H. "Bill" Co. C, 60GA
Born Walker Co., GA, c1835. Enl. Sept. 1861: Hilton Head, Seven Days, Fredericksburg, Gettysburg, Winchester, Mine Run, VA (wounded). Took USA oath, April 19, 1864. Wife was Elizabeth. To TN 1903. 1910 res. household of son on Rossville Rd. [TP 13,852; 1910HC]

TURNER, Albert J.     Co. K, 43TN
Although he was only 15 at the time of the 1860 census, he enl. Dec. 1, 1861, at Ooltewah. He was captured at Vicksburg on July 4, 1863. His parents were William and Charlotte Turner. William Turner was a farm laborer residing at Harrison prior to the war. He was a native of SC. The family moved to HC from GA. [1860HC]

TYE, John     Barry's Btry.
Born c1842 in TN. Enl. Oct. 1, 1862. at Knoxville; deserted Sept. 1, 1864; captured Sept. 10, 1864 on retreat from Atlanta [- Brown Diary]; took USA oath Oct. 26, 1864; 5'7" tall, blue eyes, light hair, and light complexion.

TYE, William M.     Barry's Btry.
Enl. Oct. 1, 1862 at Knoxville; bugler; deserted Sept. 1, 1864 at Atlanta. Captured Sept. 10, 1864 on retreat from Atlanta [Brown Diary]; took USA oath Oct. 26, 1864; 5'9" tall, blue eyes, light complexion., and light hair.

TYLER, William Thaddeus   Co. E, 16MS
Born Tylertown, Pike Co., MS, Nov. 23, 1838. Enl. in Quitman Guards and fought in the ANV from Bull Run to Appomatox, holding ranks including commissary sgt. and captain. To Chattanooga in early 1880's. Manager of Magic Food Co. Member NBF Camp, 1895. Baptist. Married (1869) Miss Mary Elizabeth Quin. Moved to Chattanooga in 1887. Died Dec. 17, 1918 and buried Forest Hills Cem. [FHR; CT Dec. 18, 1918; TWP10,113]

TYMES, A.     Co. H, 2TN Cav. (Ashby's)
Res. Harrison. Enl. Dec. 31, 1863, Chattanooga. Paroled Apr. 1865.

TYMES (TYMS), George Washington     Co. H, 2TN Cav. (Ashby's)
Enl. June 11, 1861 at Chattanooga. Captured July 31, 1863. Big Hill near Lancaster, KY and imprisoned Camp Chase and Fort Delaware. At Chimborago Hospital Oct. 1864, suffering from chronic diarrhea. Given passport to Macon, GA.

TYMES, James     Co. H, 2TN Cav. (Ashby's)
Enl. June 17, 1861, Knoxville. At Floyd House and Ocmulgee Hosp., Macon, suffering from syphillis, 9, 1863. Sick in hosp. at Augusta, GA, Dec. 4, 1864.

TYNE (see FINE)

TYNER, James Sevier     Co. I, 19TN
Born Feb. 15, 1847 in HC, he was only 15 years old when he enl. in May, 1861. The authorities later found out, and he was discharged July 23, 1862, as being "underage." While with the army, he was a private and was a musician. Following the war he "took up steam-boating" in Nashville where he died July 4, 1935. He married (1902) Georgia Hunter. [TCWVQ 5:2085; Pension applications #13750, 10876; TWP, 310]

TYNER, Capt. John S.
He organized the Second Co. K, 1CSA Cav., was an engineer living at Harrison at the start of the war. He was born c1827 and grew up in Macon, GA, the son of Reuben Jackson, a veteran of the Indian Wars, and Obedience Tyner. He was the grandson of Dempsey Tyner, a Revolutionary War veteran. 1860 census shows wife "S.C." and two sons.
Commanded Co. B, Bradshaw's Squadron, Oct. 7, 1862. Actually it was an independent command stationed at Chattanooga that fall. Enl. for duration in HC, July 14, 1863. Several months after organizing his command Tyner applied to Gen. Beauregard for an engineering position at Charleston or to "dismount his command", and bring them to Charleston to man a

battery. His application was supported by Col. Alfred Colquitt, commanding 6th Georgia, who stated, Tyner "comes with the highest recommendations as an Engineer and a man of integrity and influence.".

Apparently unsuccessful, Tyner remained in the west and fought at Shiloh, Corinth, Perryville, and Chickamauga. June 30, 1864 he and his command were detached as "Tyner's Sappers and Miners," becoming in effect the engineering department of Wheeler's Cavalry Corps by Oct. 31, 1864 he was on leave in Troup County, GA, then was assigned to special duty with Gen. J. B. Hood during the invasion of Tennessee, Nov. 1864. He was paroled at Gainesville, AL on May 12, 1865. [CSR; Chattanooga Bi-C. Library Clipping file; 1860HC; see also Hunter Nicholson, major and Asst. Chief, Conscript Barracks, personal papers, March 14, 1863, in NARS]

TYNER, William     Co. D, 4GA Cav.
He enl. Oct. 4, 1862, but was listed as absent wihout leave the following Feb. 1 and as a deserter in Sept., 1863.

# U

UNDERWOOD, A. B.   2nd Co. K, 1st CSA Cav.
Enl. in HC July 14, 1862. He deserted at Shelbyville, Feb. 14, 1863.

UNDERWOOD, E. R.   Barry's Btry.
Enl. May 13, 1862 at Chattanooga; died Sept. 18, 1863 in hospital in Lauderdale Springs, MS.

UNDERWOOD, R. M.   2nd Co. K, 1st CSA Cav.
Enl. in HC July 14, 1862. He deserted at Shelbyville, Feb. 14, 1863.

UNDERWOOD, Wallace
Buried CSA Cem.

USREY, John L.   Co. A, 19TN
Born c1840 in Guntersville, AL, he came to Chattanooga after the war and served ten years on the police force. 1870 res. Chickamauga Station. Married Emmeline. Died May 31, 1918 at home in East Lake; buried in King's Point Cem. [CT June 1, 1918]

# V

VANCE, D. B.   Co. A, 18TN; Co. B, 4TN Cav.
Born Feb. 20, 1845 in Wilson Co., TN. Enl. at Nashville May 16, 1861. Captured at Fort Donelson. After exchange in Sept. 1862, served in Co. B, 4TN Cav. County Court Clerk, Cannon Co. Married (1868) Elizabeth Brewer. Attended Southern Baptist Seminary, Louisville. In 1900 minister in Missionary Baptist Church. To Bell Buckle, c1908, but returned to Chattanooga c1910. Res. on Marble St. Died June 20, 1921 and buried Bell Buckle, TN. [NBFM2,7; CT June 21, 1921]

VAN DYKE, Maj. William Deaderick   Co. A,
59TN Mounted Inf.
Born Oct.1, 1836 in Athens, TN, the son of Chancellor Thomas Nixon Van Dyke, William received his education at Maryville College and began the practice of law. He enl. June 1861 and became regt. commissary late that year; also acted as brig. commissary for Gen. J. C. Vaughn and div. commissary for Gen. B. F. Cheatham. When he returned home after the war, he found that his father had been imprisoned and his mother banished north of the Ohio. After joining them at Quincy, IL, he returned to TN in March 1866, and made his home in Chattanooga. He became a partner in the law firm of Van Dyke, Cooke and Van Dyke and served as president of the Iron, Coal and Manufacturing Assoc. He supervised the construction of the Hamilton County Courthouse, jail, and orphan asylum. He died in Chattanooga, Aug. 1, 1883. His wife was Anna Mary Deaderick. [CTS; CSA Mil. Hist., 10:764-65]

VAN EPPS, George C.   Co. A, Co. E, 19TN
He went to a Federal prison after being captured and wounded at Franklin, TN, on Dec. 18, 1864. He was a son of the Chattanooga merchant A. C. Van Epps. His mother, Caroline Howard, was originally from Columbus, GA. The Van Epps family had a handsome frame home at 302 Walnut St. that was used as officers' quarters during the war.

VAN EPPS, Howard 19th TN Reg. Hamilton Grays
Born in Eufala, AL on 21 Dec 1847, the son of Amos C. Van Epps, a native of New York and soldier of the Mexican war. As a young man, Amos came south to Columbus, GA. He and his wife Caroline came to Chattanooga early in their marriage to set up a merchants store. In 1864, Howard joined the Hamilton Grays at age 16. He served in Atlanta campaign, participating in the great battles of July 22 and of Jonesboro. He was afterward on detached duty to Mississippi and at Egypt Station in January 1865, he was severely wounded in the head. While recovering, the war ended and he returned home to study law. He moved to Atlanta and became a Judge there. [Evans. Confederate

Mil. History (Expanded Edition) 7:1019]

**VARNELL, Francis Marion   2nd Co. K, 1CSA Cav.**
He enl. Sept. 20, 1862, in HC. Paroled May 3, 1865, at Charlotte, NC. Born in 1830, he was one of the sons of William M. Varnell and Margaret Nelson of Tyner. He married Margaret Whittle. Francis Marion Varnell died Nov. 14, 1900. [1860HC; CSA Mil. Hist., 10:767-68]

**VARNELL, Glasgow W.    Co. F, 35TN Inf.**
Born 1828, McMinn Co., "Glass" first fought with the Confederates, then he joined the Union, enlisting with Co. F, 6TN MI on Oct. 24, 1864. Before the war, he lived with his parents, William M. and Margaret (Nelson) Varnell, at Tyner. He had blue eyes, light hair, a fair complexion, and 5'7" tall. He married Elizabeth Hughes. Died Mar. 25, 1909 in Chattanooga and buried in Varnell Cem. [JW Varnell Family; CT, Mar. 26, 1909]

**VARNELL, Josiah   Co. F, 35TN Inf.**
Born Sevierville, TN, June 8, 1823, he was one of the sons of William M. and Margaret (Nelson) Varnell. Before the war he was a farmer at Ooltewah, living with his wife, Caroline Shropshire. He enl. Jan. 16, 1862, at Chattanooga and was shot through the body at Chickamauga, Sept. 20, 1863, and remained hospitalized nearly two years. Following the war he was an invalid and in 1901 is reported in Ooltewah, James Co., where "he putters around a little." [Donnelly, James Co.; JW Varnell Family; TP494].

**VARNELL, Richard Nelson    Co. A, 5TN Cav. (McKenzie's)**
Born about 1825, he was one of the sons of William M. and Margaret (Nelson) Varnell, who lived at Tyner. He married Sally Morris. Enl. Jan. 14, 1863, at Knoxville. Later that year, he was reported ill since April 30. [JW Varnell Family]

**VARNELL, William Columbus    2nd Co. K, 1TN Cav.**
Born in 1837, he was also a son of William M. and Margaret (Nelson) Varnell of Tyner. He married Sarah E. Miller and lived until 1892. Enl. July 14, 1862, in HC and deserted Nov. 28, 1863. [JW Varnell Family]

**VARNELL, William E.   Co. B, Phillips GA Legion**
Born Oct. 10, 1844, Whitfield Co., GA. Enl. Aug. 1861. Gettysburg (wounded), Cold Harbor. Paroled Kingston, GA, May 1865. Methodist. Mason. To TN 1885. Res. Chattanooga, 1909, 1913. Died Chattanooga Jan 6, 1927. [CTJan.7,1927(listed in error as Barnell)

**VARNELL, William Riley    Co. F, 35TN Inf.**
Born 1835, he was a son of James and Lavinia (Nelson) Varnell of Tyner. Enl. Oct. 19, 1861, at Knoxville, and began another enlistment Jan. 16, 1863, at Chattanooga. His unit was camped at Tyner's Station near his home in mid-July, 1863. Wounded at Chickamauga and taken to his home to recuperate. He married Sarah Moore. He died April 26, 1896. [JW Varnell Family]

**VARNELL, Zachariah Nelson    Co. A, 5TN Cav. (McKenzie's)**
Born c1825, he was also a the son of James and Lavinia (Nelson) Varnell of Tyner. He married Hulda Smith. Enl. Feb. 12, 1863, at Knoxville. He fought throughout the war and was paroled on April 26, 1865 at Charlotte, NC, May 3, 1865. [JW Varnell Family]

**VAUGHN, LaFayette   E Co., 4TN Cav. Bn.**
Enl. Oct 4, 1861 at Cumberland Ford, KY. Sent home sick Oct. 27, 1861. Returned to Cumberland Ford by Jan. 1862.

**VEAL, Thomas C.   Arty., Hampton's Legion; Co. F, 3CSA Engineers**
Born at Columbia, SC, Jan. 4, 1829. Enl. May 10, 1861 at Columbia. Fought at Mechanicsville, Cold Harbor and Savage Station (where his horse was killed and he was wounded), Fredericksburg, Brandy Station, Sharpsburg and Second Manassas. Commanded Co. F, 4CSA Engineers and went to Charleston (Battery Wagner, Fort Moultrie). In charge of fortifications of Edisto River. Thence to Cheraw. During Battle of Bentonville ordered to take charge of engineer train. To pontoon duty in NC. Architect and Civil Engineer in Chattanooga. Member NBF Camp, 1896. Res. in 1901 in Columbia. "He has moved away many years ago." [NBFM2]

**VENABLE, T. W.   Co. I, 10GA**
Born in Forsyth GA, Aug. 21, 1837. Enl. Sept. 1, 1861, then served in Co. I, 1GA Cav. Captured at Adairsville, GA, May 24, 1864. Paroled and released July 1865. 1901 Res. Highland Park. His wife E. M. Venable, born 11 July 1847 was a member of the A.P. Stewart UDC. Died Dec. 7, 1910 at home on Chester St. and buried Forest Hills Cemetery. [FHR; CT Dec. 8, 1910; NBFM2; TP11458; UDC1 pg 440]

**VEST, Robert F.   Co. E, 5TN Cav. (McKenzie's)**
Born in TN so of Francis & Elizabeth (Davis) Vest of NC. Enl. in Co. E, 5TN Cav. Carpenter in Chattanooga, 1888. Married Susan Elizabeth Willis.

Died at res. on Read Ave. Dec. 13, 1900 and buried Forest Hills Cem. [NBFM2,7]

VICK, John    Co. F, 35TN
Born 1823 in Bledsoe Co., TN and was a farmer in HC until he enl. Nov. 21, 1862 at Chattanooga; died Apr. 20, 1863 at Tullahoma, TN; blue eyes, dark hair, dark complexion, 5'9" tall. His wife was Susan.

VINEYARD (VINYARD), Noah H.    Co. A, 4TN Cav.; Co. D, 37TN
Noah was born VA c1815. His wife, Caroline, was from GA. He was a plasterer at Chattanooga. Enl. June 17, 1861, Knoxville. Detached QM Dept., July 1, 1862. Disch. overage, Sept. 15, 1862. Evidently re-enl., serving as substitute for A. J. Wisdom. Vineyard was sick at Chattanooga in July 1863, and he was captured at Gordon's Mills in GA on Sept. 15, 1863. Died Oct. 21, 1863.

VINSON, Bartlett C.    Co. K, 43TN
Enl. Oct. 17, 1861, at Ooltewah. Deserted June 5, 1862. He then entered the Union army, serving with Co. B, 5TN Cav. (USA). His brother, James A. Vinson, also was in the Federal forces, serving with Co. K, 5TN Inf. (USA). The Vinsons were sons of Anderson A. Vinson and Sophia Moon. The Vinsons were in Cocke Co., then Roane Co., before coming to HC c1835. Another brother, Charles Washington Vinson, was a county official who remained at his post during the war. Bartlett Vinson was born in 1839. After the war, he moved to Texas. He died at Trenton, TX, 1919. [1860HC]

VINSON, W. H.
Died Dec. 7, 1912, age 88, at Waukesha, WI. [NBFM1;CTDec.12,1912]

# W

WADSWORTH, William W.    1MS Lt. Arty
1890VetCensus]

WAKEFIELD, William Peyton    Co. D, 39GA    Sgt.
Born 1838 in Smith Co. 4th Sgt., Mar. 4, 1862. Captured Vicksburg, July 4, 1863; paroled and captured Port Hudson, July 9, 1863. Married (1866 in Dade Co.) Jennie M. Steadman. 1910 railroad watchman; res. 14th St. with wife. Died 1912 in HC. [TWP, p. 136;

1910HC]

WALKER, A.    Clark's Independent Cav. Co.
Enl. Aug. 31, 1862 at Chattanooga; transferred Jan. 30, 1864 to 1GA CSA.

WALKER, Clement L.    Co. G, 23AR
Born Tensas Parish, LA. Enl. June 20, 1862 in 23AR and later in 2Lt. in Bn. of Engineers. Merchant in Chattanooga, 1888; lawyer, 1899. Died here Feb. 23, 1896 and buried CSA Cem. [NBFM2]

WALKER, Brig. Gen. Francis Marion, was commissioned brigadier general the day before he was killed while leading his regiment at Atlanta. He had quickly risen through the ranks after joining Co. I, 19TN. In July, 1861, he "was carelessly handling or shaking a box of caps in his hand when they exploded, . . . cutting his hand in several places." He re-enl. at Corinth in May, 1862 for two years. He was a lieutenant colonel by the time of Shiloh and won praise for the leadership and skill he displayed. He was also in the hottest of the fighting at Murfreesboro.. He was 37 years old when he died, his body was returned to Chattanooga for burial.
Walker was born Nov. 12, 1827 in Paris, KY, son of John and Tabitha Taylor Walker. He taught school in East Tennessee before participating in the Mexican War as a lieutenant, 5TN Infantry. After the war he attended Transylvania University and upon graduation began the practice of law in Rogersville, TN, then in Chattanooga in 1854. He married Margaret K. Walker [no relation] in Sept. 1853 in Rogersville He served as alderman and attorney general. Walker provided conspicuous service on several occasions most notably at Kennesaw Mountain. [UDC2 pg 550]

WALKER, G. M.    4MO Cav.
Born 1847 in Lookout Valley, he was son of Harvey and Sarah Walker and moved to Arkansas in 1856. In 1863 he joined the Confederate Army and fought at Arkansas Post, Jenkinson Ferry, Poison Spring, and participated in a raid through north Arkansas and south Missouri. He fought the latter part of the war in the Indian Territory. Afterwards he emigrated to Honduras with fellow ex-Confederates, returning to Texas in late 1865. He came to Chattanooga in 1866, then was off to Louisville, McMinnville before settling here about 1870. He married (1871) Margaret Hackwarth and M. M. Clift (1882). Mason. Presbyterian. [GHT, p. 1007-08]

WALKER, J. A.    Co. L, 36TN
Enl. Jan. 9, 1862 at Chattanooga Died Sept 20, 1916 and buried Whitwell.[NBFM7]

WALKER, J. F.

Wealthy planter in TX who retired and came to Lookout Mountain in 1890 to establish hotel "Southern Home." He died on Lookout Mountain Feb. 23, 1892 and was buried in CSA Cem. 55 years old. Methodist. [CTFeb. 24, 1892]

WALKER, J. M.   Co. H, 31AL
        1909 res. HC. [TP11,481]

WALKER, 1st Lt. John T.   Co. K,
                Palmetto Sharpshooters
        Born 1842 in SC and enrolled at S. C. College when war began. Served in Sparta Rifles, Co. K, Palmetto Sharpshooters, for entire war. Wounded in right leg at Wilderness and in right lung at Sharpsburg. Married Margaret Jones, born 18 Dec. 1843. Formerly a res. of Gainesville, Tex. Methodist. Member NBF Camp, 1895. Died Feb. 25, 1896 on Lookout Mountain. and buried CSA Cem.[NBFM2; CT Feb. 25.96]

WALKER, Joseph   Co. F, 35TN
        Enl. Dec. 17, 1862 at Chattanooga; died May 27, 1863.

WALKER, O. P.      Clark's Independent Cav. Co.
        Enl. Aug. 31, 1862 at Chattanooga.

WALKER, Capt. Thomas H.      Co. I, 19TN
        When the war broke out, he was reading law under Francis M. Walker. Elected 1Lt. May 20, 1861. Only recently married to the Chattanooga belle Ann Kennedy, he was killed at Shiloh. His body was brought back to Chattanooga for burial at the Citizens Cem. He was the son of a Rogersville, TN. Doctor (MCCD).

WALKER, William   Co. D, 37TN
        Born 1843. Enl. Sept. 1, 1861, Knoxville. Deserted Camp Direction, Chattanooga, May 26, 1863

WALKER, Sgt. William P.
        Enl. Jan. 9, 1862, in Co. L, 36TN at Chattanooga; transferred to Co. L, 35TN; fought at Murfreesboro; deserted Oct. 1, 1863 at Chickamauga Station.

WALL, Perry A.   Co. K, 5SC
        Born Oct. 18, 1844 in Spartanburg, SC, he was son of J. and S. L. Jackson Wall. He enl. in 1864 and fought till its conclusion. Afterwards he attended school and farmed. Then he began school teaching, coming to Soddy in the late 1870s, then made his home in Sale Creek. He taught school 40 years in HC. Also farmed. Married (1875) Sarah "Sallie" Copeland. Mason. Presbyterian. Died April 28, 1925, age 80, and buried in Sale Creek. [GHT, pp. 1006-07; TWP, 236; TP14083;

CT April 29, 1925; 1910HC]]

WALLACE, Henry    Barry's Battery.
        Born in Virginia, 1831. Married (Dec. 18, 1856) Sarah Jane Roberts. He farmed in the vicinity of Lookout Mountain prior to enlisting Sept. 16, 1862, at Chattanooga He was paroled May 11, 1865, at Meridian, MS. Married Sarah Jane. Died Aug. 21, 1897 in Rossville. [TWP; TP #1938; 1860HC]

WALLACE, Isaac Abraham      Co. L, 36TN; Co. L, 35TN
        Born Dec. 19, 1841 in HC, son of Mary Anderson and the Rev. Benjamin Wallace, Presbyterian minister who lived at Soddy. Before the war, Isaac A. had a farm at Harrison with his wife, Rhoda A. Enl. Jan. 9, 1862, in Col. J. W. Clift's company and fought at Murfreesboro and Chickamauga (where he was wounded). Company rolls show he "deserted" Jan. 10, 1864 at Tunnel Hill. Married (1867 in HC) Nancy K. McDonald, granddaughter of staunch Unionist William Clift. He accumulated considerable property at Soddy and had a fine farm there, then moved to New Mexico and Texas to try to reclaim his health, then he resided in Highland Park. He returned to Soddy in 1909 and died there on April 14, 1911. [JW Wallace Family; CT April 15, 1911; TWP, p. 121; TP10,227; 1910HC]

WALLACE, Lt. James Anderson      Co. D, 19TN
        He was born Aug. 27, 1836, the son of Rev. Benjamin Wallace, the pastor at Soddy Presbyterian Church. He was educated by his father, then began the study of law at 20 under Judge Thomas N. Frazier. Just after he was admitted to the bar as a lawyer, the war broke out and he joined Capt. Warner E. Colville's Co. D, 19TN, being elected 2Lt. May 29, 1861 and serving as "a drill master." He was with the 19th Tennessee until suffering a severe wound in the thigh at Shiloh. He remained with the army although unfit for combat. Wallace was captured at Knoxville on June 6, 1865, and sent to Chattanooga and then to Louisville, KY. He was released upon taking the oath of allegiance. He had a fair complexion, light hair and blue eyes and stood five feet, nine inches, tall. He married (1870) Fannie Bell Darnall, born 29 Set. 1839. After the war, he practiced law in Rhea County for a year, then was a partner with fellow Confederate Moses H. Clift at Chattanooga for two years.
        Wallace decided to become a minister so he attended college at Maryville where he studied under Dr. Dabney of Stonewall Jackson's staff. For many years he resided in Highland Park and was pastor of the Presbyterian church there. He suffered paralysis "on the same side as his Shiloh wound" and died July 9, 1900, while visiting his brother at Bristol, TN. He was buried

at Soddy. His son, James, was also a minister, pastoring a congregation in Alabama. [CT July 11 Oct. 1900; TP #2584; MCCD; Goodspeed, p. 1006 lists J. Albert Wallace, bro of Isaac A., "is one of the leading educators of Sullivan County. He is president of King's College at Bristol, where Isaac A.'s oldest son is attending school."

WALLEN, Hugh    Barry's Btry.; Cook's Cav. Co.
        Enl. May 14, 1862 in Barry's Btry. at Chattanooga; tranferred to Capt. Cook's Cav. Co.

WALLER, Sgt. Manly B.    2nd Co. K, 1st CSA Cav.
        Born c1831, son of George and Martha. Res. 1860 in Chattanooga with wife Nancy. Enl. Sept. 20, 1862 in HC. "Sent as a secret scout into enemy's lines in January, 1864. Stayed." Listed as deserter. 1870 railroad carpenter in HC. [1860,1850HC]

WALSTON, Cpl. Seth    Clark's Independent Cav. Co.
        Enl. Aug. 31, 1862 at Chattanooga; deserted Feb. 25, 1864 near Dalton, GA.

WARD, Charles E.
        He was born in Baltimore March 18, 1816, and before the Civil War came to Chattanooga where he was associated with Adams Express Company. "A man of wealth at outbreak of the Civil War," he espoused the Confederate cause and invested his means in bonds of the new government." He lost everything and lived the remainder of his life impoverished. Died in Chattanooga Sept. 1, 1901. [CT Sept. 2, 1901]

WARD, E. G.    Co. K, 43TN
        Enl. Oct. 17, 1861 at Ooltewah; captured at Vicksburg, July 4, 1863; paroled; again captured Oct. 28, 1863 in HC; imprisoned at Camp Morton, IN where he died Nov. 25, 1863 of congestion of the lungs. Buried at Green Lawn Cem.

WARD, James Raulston
        Born 1830 in Rutherford Co., TN. Married (1866) Nancy S. Vaughan and died April 28, 1901, age 71, at res. in Hill City and buried in Bell Buckle, TN. [TWP, p. 194; CT April 30.1901]

WARE, Samuel    Co. C, 1GA CSA Inf. Bn.
        Born Feb. 4, 1846 in Walker Co., GA. Enl. fall, 1864 on crew of gunboat Raleigh and after boat abandoned joined the infantry. Paroled Greensboro, NC, May 1, 1865. To TN in 1906 and died in Chattanooga, Sept. 14, 1909. [TP 8709]

WARLICK, Noah Franklin
        Born Oct. 16, 1845 in AL. Took part in Battle

of Atlanta and battles in that vicinity. Baptist. Carpenter who res. on E. 8th St. with wife Margaret M. Hancock. Charter member of Central Baptist Church. Deacon. Died at home 1010 East 8th St., April 11, 1922 and buried Forest Hills Cem. [1910HC; Lusk, FH; CT 12 Apr. 1922]

WARNER, James Cartwright
        Born Gallatin, TN, Aug. 20, 1830, son of Jacob L. and Elizabeth Cartwright. Married (1852, Nashville) Mary Thomas Williams. Moved to Nashville in 1847 and in 1853 to Chattanooga to enter the hardware business. Mayor of Chattanooga, 1861. Represented HC in TN Assembly (Confederate), 1861-63. Relocated in Nashville where he became president of Tennessee Coal, Iron and Railroad Co. Pioneered in pig iron manufacture at Tracy City, Rising Fawn, GA, and South Pittsburg and Chattanooga. Episcopalian. Mason. Died July 21, 1895 in Nashville and buried at Mt. Olivet. [BDTA, 2:951]

WARNER, Joseph Henry    Co. A, 19TN
        Born in Sumner Co., Sept. 5, 1842, he was the son of Jacob and Elizabeth J. Cartwright. Warner came to Chattanooga in 1856 from Gallatin in Sumner County, and entered the hardware business with his older brother, James C. Warner. Warner was slightly wounded at Murfreesboro on Dec. 31, 1862. He was captured at Ringgold, GA, the following November, then imprisoned at Rock Island, IL where he was released upon "taking of the oath," Sept. 27, 1864. He went to Iowa and returned to TN in late 1865, working in Nashville. He came back to Chattanooga in Dec. 1866 and again entered the hardware business. He helped found the first public transportation system - mules up and down Market Street which grew into the Streetcar Company. He served as a city commissioner and was an organizer of the Third National Bank. Also, he owned a fleet of Tennessee River steamboats, including the *J. C. Warner*. Warner Park of the city is named for him. He married (1867) Alice G. Hord [born 5 Feb 1844], who was from Murfreesboro. They built a brick mansion on Vine Street in the Fort Wood section of the city. Buried Forest Hills Cemetery. [FHR; Worsham, p. 217; RI ledger; CT Jan. 13, 1908; GHT, pp. 1008-09; Warner, "Personal Glimpses"]

WARNICK, Edward A.    Barry's Btry.
        Enl. May 11, 1862 at Chattanooga; captured Spanish Fort, April 8, 1865; imprisoned at Ship Island, MS.

WARREN, James P.    Co. D, 4GA Cav.
        He enl. Oct. 4, 1862. Before the war he had a farm near Moccasin Bend with his wife, Sarah. Born about 1831, he was apparently a son of William and

Hannah Warren.

WARREN, Ord. Sgt. John Randolph     Co. E, 12GA
Born Greene Co., TN, Dec. 25, 1836. Enl. April, 1861. To Chattanooga TN c1891. Moulder in foundry by trade. Married (1867, Columbus, GA) Louisa Virginia Blankenship. Res. St. Elmo. Died Nov. 10, 1916. [TWP#6614; TP 13,033; 1910HC]

WARREN, 4th Cpl. Reubin     Co. H, 4TN Cav.
Enl. Aug. 11, 1861 at Chattanooga.

WARREN, Thomas V.     Co. K, 4AL
Born Feb. 27, 1839 in Larkinsville, AL. Enl. April 27, 1861 in Larkinsville. Fought at 1st Manassas, Fredericksburg, Hanover Junction, Gettysburg and many smaller battles. Wounded in right jaw near Cold Harbor, 6 May 1864. Transf. with regt. to Army of Tenn. with Longstreet and returned with him to VA. With Gen. Joe Johnston at the end but did not surrender until met a fleet of gunboats at Bellefont. Long time resident of Chattanooga where he was a carpenter and a member of NBF Camp, 1895. Res. in household of Thos. Henderson, 1910. Died Jan. 18, 1920 in Nashville and buried there. [CT Jan. 18, 1920; NBFM2,7; TP 6896; Applic. for TN Soldiers' Home; 1910HC]

WARREN, 4th Cpl. William T.     Co. H, 4TN Cav.
Born 1841 in TN, son of William and Hannah. Enl. Aug. 11, 1861 at Chattanooga. Wounded at Murfreesboro, Dec. 31, 1862.

WATERHOUSE, Silas (Cyrus)     Barry's Btry.
Res., Calhoun Co., GA. Enl. April 4, 1862. at Chattanooga; hearing impaired by shell that brushed past his face at Resaca; paroled May 11, 1865 in Meridian, MS; 1903 res. Ridgedale. [TP 5333]

WATERS, C. N.     Co. C, 40GA
Born Jan. 10, 1838 in Habersham Co., GA. Enl. March 4, 1861 at Rome. Wounded at Chickasaw Bayou, Dec. 29, 1862 and wounded again in the head. Captured and imprisoned at Camp Morton, IN. Exchanged Feb. 1865. 1900 res. Whorley, HC; indigent. [TP 2630]

WATERS, G. W.     -
[NBFM1,3]

WATKINS, Jacob     Co. D, 4GA Cav.
Married Betsey J. Davis (Dec. 21, 1859, HC). Enl. Oct. 4, 1862. He was captured at Chattanooga on Oct. 27, 1863, and sent to Nashville, then to Louisville and on to Camp Morton, IN. A resident of Chattanooga, he had a dark complexion, black hair and eyes and was 5'6" tall. [HC Marriage Books]

WATKINS, John W.     Co. L, 36TN; Co. L, 35TN
Enl. Jan. 9, 1862. He fought at Murfreesboro, then deserted Jan. 24, 1864, at Tunnel Hill, GA. Before the war, he was a farm laborer at Ooltewah. He was born about 1837. His wife was Elizabeth A. 1870 res. Harrison.

WATKINS, Kimsey     2d Co. I, 1CSA (GA)
Enl. Aug. 7, 1863, Chattanooga. Wounded at Chickamauga, Sept. 20, 1863. Absent on furlough, June 30, 1864. Deserted at Kennesaw Mtn., July 2, 1864.

WATKINS, Peter     Co. H, 26TN; 2d Co. I, 1CSA (GA)
Born c1842. Enl. July 14, 1861, Knoxville. Captured Fort Donelson and imprisoned Camp Douglas. Exch. Aiken's Landing, Nov. 10, 1862. Wounded at Chickamauga "and sent to rear and I have ascertained since that he was serving in the cavalry." Deserted at Kennesaw Mtn., July 2, 1864.

WATKINS, Capt. Richard Levens "Dick"     Barry's Btry.
He was "a strong believer in the cause of the Southland, and when Tennessee called her sons to arms, he was among the first to respond, organizing and securing equipment for a battery of artillery, which went into service March 1, 1861." Robert L. Barry was placed in command of this "Lookout" unit which first saw action when Chattanooga was threatened in the spring of 1862. He took a gun to Shellmound and skirmished with the Union troops that were trying to make their way to Chattanooga. Then his entire battery was ordered back to Chattanooga and stationed on Cameron Hill. For two days they had a brisk artillery fight with Union forces under Gen. John Wilder on Stringer's Ridge. Watkins and his unit were able to force the Federal forces back to the base of Walden's Ridge.
The Lookout Battery (Barry's Battery) was in Mississippi during the Vicksburg campaign and fought at Jackson in July, 1863. It later moved to Georgia and was engaged in the fighting at Resaca and points south to Atlanta. Watkins "was in command much of the time and won distinction as an artillery offier. He was never absent from his battery a single day, and in all its engagements was in the thickest of the fight." He commanded Barry's Battery at Peachtree Creek, July 20, 1864 and at Spanish Fort at Mobile (April, 1865) after he and his battery were sent to the fort in small boats. He had just reached the fort when he was wounded in seven places by an exploding shell. Only about 50 men in his command escaped the Federal assault uninjured, and they had to swim eight miles to safety. The Lookout Battery surrendered at Meridian, MS on May 16, 1865, and

Watkins made his way home on crutches, walking much of the way.

He was born Jan. 29, 1836 in Jefferson County, and the family was left in dire straits after his father died when he was nine months old. "Deprived of the advantages of an education," he was employed in Knoxville at the age of ten, before he and two of his brothers made their way to Chattanooga in 1854 and set up what was said to be the largest hardware store in the state. After the war, he was again prominent in business and real estate in Chattanooga. He was a leader in the development of the Lookout Inn on Lookout Mountain and a railroad up the mountain. He was an original stockholder in the Roane Iron Company, director of several banks, and mayor of Lookout Mountain. He married Helen Whiteside, a daughter of Col. James A. Whiteside. NBF Camp, 1894-96. Died Dec. 24, 1895 and buried Forest Hills Cem. [CTS; FHR; NBFM7]

WATKINS, Lt. Robert    26TN
2Lt., HC Home Guard, organized at Chickamauga, April 29, 1861.

WATKINS, Thomas    Co. B, 5TN Cav. Bn.;
Co. H, 4TN Cav.
Died near Chattanooga Oct. 1862.

WATTERSON, Henry (1840-1921)
Editor of Chattanooga *Daily Rebel*, 1863; became celebrated political journalist, politican, and lecturer.

WATTS, H. E.   Co. C, 21-22TN Cav.
[NBFM4]

WATTS, John C.   Co. D, 37TN
Born 1844. Enl. Sept. 1, 1861, Knoxville. Sick at Shelbyville, Dec. 7, 1862. Re-enl. May 1862. Hospital Dalton with gonorrhea, Dec., 1862. Also arrested for stealing and jailed. Slightly wounded Chickamauga. Captured on picket at Big Shanty, June 10, 1864 and imprisoned Rock Island. Gave res. as Whitfield, GA. Took USA oath, Oct. 18, 1864. 5'7" tall, black hair, hazel eyes, with fair complexion.

WEATHERFORD, Silas S.    Co. G, 5TN Cav.;
Co. G, 35TN
Born Aug. 3, 1844 in Mecklenburg Co., VA and came to TN in 1850. Enl. Sept. 6, 1861 at McMinnville. Wounded in head at Shiloh. Chickamauga, Perryville, Murfreesboro, Missionary Ridge, Franklin, Bentonville. Paroled as sgt. at Greensboro, NC Apr. 26, 1865. He came to Chattanooga from Coal Creek in 1916. NBF Camp. Died Feb. 18, 1918 in Chattanooga and buried Citizens

Cem. [CT 19 Feb. 1918; NBFM2,7; TP 6726]

WEATHERLY [Weatherby], Jonas    Co. G, 26TN;
2d Co. K, 1CSA(GA)
Enl. July 8, 1861, 26TN, at Knoxville; captured at Fort Donelson, Feb. 16, 1862 and imprisoned at Camp Douglas. Present Aug. 31, 1863. Killed at Chickamauga.

WEATHERLY, Samuel    Co. G, 26TN;
2nd Co. K, 1CSA(GA)
Born about 1842, he enl. July 8, 1861 in Co. G, 26TN at Knoxville. Captured at Fort Donelson; imprisoned at Camp Douglas. Light complexion, dark hair, gray (blue) eyes, and 6' tall. Deserted and captured in Catoosa County (his residence) June 24, 1864 and took USA oath of allegiance. He worked 36 years as an employee of the NC&St.L Railroad. Sam Weatherly died March 18, 1909 and is buried in Confederate Cem. [CT 19 Mar. 1909]

WEBB, William    Co. B, 1st TN Cav. (Carter's)
Born c. 1843 in TN, son of Meredith and Elizabeth Webb of Birchwood. [1860HC]

WEBSTER, John William    Co. H, 2TN Cav. (Ashby's)
Born June 28, 1845 in Philadelphia, PA, son of foundryman Thomas Webster, he enl. in 2TN Cav. at Griffin GA in summer of 1863. Serving with Ashby's brigade, he was in the thick of fighting in numerous battles, but was never wounded. He had moved to Chattanooga in 1856 and was 18 when he enlisted. Father was foundry man Thomas Webster. After the war, J.W. Webster started out as a machinist. He ran the first engine on the "dummy line' belonging to his brother-in-law, Charles James, in 1886. Later, he was an engineer for the Chattanooga Southern Railroad. He was also an official of the Chattanooga Railway and Light Company. At age 61, he took a position as a streetcar conductor. Known affectionately as "Daddy Webster," he was given a Confederate uniform by the streetcar workers. He was buried in this suit of gray in Forest Hills Cemetery when he died Jan. 7, 1918. His wife was Susie McCarver, who wrote a history of Chattanooga. [CT Jan. 8, 1918; FHR; NBFM2; TP 12,828]

WEBSTER, Thomas
Born at Weather Oak Hill, near Birmingham, England, June 28, 1818, he was taken by his father at age nine to see the locomotive of George Stephenson. The boy was thrilled and decided to become an engineer. At age 12 he became an engineer's apprentice and served as such for four years. He emigrated to the United States and entered the business of supplying machine plants across the South. He came to Chattanooga in 1857 and established a foundry. Leader in Home Guard "Vigilance

Committee," 1861. "At the outbreak of the war he joined with Maj. D.[sic] R. Rains and planned and built a powder mill at Augusta, Georgia," remaining there until the conclusion of the war.

Webster returned to Chattanooga in 1865 but lost his foundry and machine shop to fire in 1866. As chief mechanical engineer he built the English Company's shops at South Pittsburg and later superintended construction of the three first furnaces in Birmingham. He returned to Chattanooga from Birmingham and became "the prime mover for the initial water plant built in this city by the Hazlehurst Company." Mason. 1st Presbyterian. Married (1844) Kate Rhodes of Philadelphia. Died at his home on McCallie Ave. Oct. 25, 1908 and buried Forest Hills Cemetery. [CT 26 Oct. 1908]

WEBSTER, William W.   Co. H, 2TN Cav. (Ashby's)
Enl. Aug. 14, 1864, Griffen, GA. Paroled April 1865. Address Chattanooga.

WEIR, J. L.
Enl. Jan. 9, 1862, in Co. L, 36TN at Chattanooga; transferred to Co. L, 35TN; fought at Murfreesboro; deserted Sept. 19, 1863 at Chickamauga.

WEIR, John Bradford   Co. A, 4TN Cav.; Co. D, 2nd TN Cav. (Ashby's)
Born Bradley Co., Feb. 17, 1845, he enl. 8 Dec., 1862, and served throughout the war. Twice wounded: in right side (when Sherman crossed the Chattahoochee) and in thigh by shells at Wadesboro, NC. After war attended Univ. of VA. Married Mary Cleage. Lived and worked in Boston, New York, Baltimore, Washington, D.C. before moving to Chattanooga in 1920 where he became a civil engineer residing (1924) on Vine St. US Coastal Geodetic Survey, 1871-89. Died 20 April 1936 and buried Athens, TN. [NBFM2,7; CT 21 April 1936; TP 15706]

WELCH, Gideon   Co. I, 43TN
Born 1841 in TN. Farmer at Ooltewah. Married Rebecca A. [1860 HC Census]

WELCH, James   2nd Co. K, 1st CSA Cav.
Enl. Sept. 1, 1862 in HC. Sent to hospital at Rome, GA by brigade surgeon. Captured near Chickamauga, Sept. 18, 1863 and imprisoned at Camp Douglas, IL where he died of small pox May 5, 1864. Buried at Camp Douglas.

WELCH, Leander   Co. I, 19TN
Enl. Aug. 12, 1861, fought at Cumberland Gap, then died in the Battle of Fishing Creek in Kentucky, Jan. 19, 1862.

WELCH (WALSH), Michael "Mike"   Co. D, 37TN
Enl. Jan. 20, 1863 Chattanooga. Substitute for G.W. Haskel. Sent to hosp., 16 Dec. 1863. Prom. to 4th Sgt., Sept. 1, 1864. Res. Memphis, TN. 5'5 ½" tall, light hair, blue eyes, and fair complexion.

WELLBORN, A. J.   Co. H, 26TN; 2d Co. I, 1CSA (GA)
Enl. 16 Sept. 1861, Knoxville. Captured Fort. Donelson, 16 Feb. 1862 and imprisoned Camp Douglas. Exchanged and left at Chattanooga 5 Oct. 1862. AOL, 29 Feb. 1864.

WELLONS (WILLONS), C. M.   Capt. Co. A, 22TN
Married (1894 in HC) Maria Louisa Acree and died 1916 in Hardeman Co. [TWP, p. 179]

WELLS, B. F.   39GA (Capt. Anderson's Co.)
Died March 15, 1914 at home in Woodlawn Park, age 73, and buried CSA Cem. [CT March 16, 1914]

WELLS, James   Co H, 4th TN Cav.
The son of Ross's Landing pioneer Moses Wells, he fought with the Confederate forces. Afterwards, he returned to his wife, Matilda Teed Kesterson whom he married 1 Oct. 1859 in HC, and their daughter, Susan Hannah. However, he was accused by the Reconstruction government of killing a man in Arkansas to take his horse during the war. Wells was placed in prison at the brick building at Fourth and Market. He claimed he was innocent, but felt he had little chance of proving it given the climate of the times. He escaped one night, came home and got some money, and paddled a canoe up the Tennessee River. No one knew his whereabouts for many years, and his grieving wife died. His daughter was raised by her aunt, Elizabeth Kesterson Mitchell. Jim Wells later returned to Chattanooga for a short time with his second wife, Sarah Ann. He had apparently married her in Alabama.

WELLS, Matthew   Co. D, 37TN
Enl. Jan. 24, 1863, Catoosa Springs. Prom. to Sgt., Jan. 1, 1864. Deserted at Dalton, Jan. 14, 1864.

WELLS, Thomas P.   Co. B, Phillips GA Legion
Born Dalton, GA May 8, 1845. Enl. in Dalton, July 1, 1861. Served fall and winter, 1861 under Gen. J. B. Floyd in western VA. Participated in all the battles of ANV: Second Manassas, South Mountain, Shaprsburg, Fredericksburg, Chancellorsville, Gettysburg, Wilderness, Spotslyvania Court House, Cold Harbor. Captured and recaptured at South Mountain within an hour. Wounded slightly at Fredericksburg and

Gettysburg. Became 2nd Sgt. of company. Res. Chattanooga, occupation as bookkeeper. Adjutant, NBF Camp, 1894-96. Moved to southern Missouri in Aug. 1898. Died at Sea Breeze, FL, Jan 12, 1908. Buried at Rome, GA. [CT Jan. 14.08; NBFM2,3]

WELLS, Maj. W. H.
Brother of T. P. Lived in Chattanooga. Chief Engineer of Southern RR. [CT 14 Jan. 1908]

WELLS, William Bryant
Born June 8, 1838 in Habersham Co., GA, he was the son of John and Mary Stewart Wells. He had just begun the study of medicine when the war broke out and he became surgeon of Gist's Brigade, Walker's Division. After the war he entered Atlanta Medical College and graduated in 1866. He practiced in GA until 1886 when he came to Chattanooga. Mason. Baptist. Married M. E. Pope of GA in 1867. Baptist. Member of NBF Camp who died in Chattanooga Dec. 16, 1890. Buried Forest Hills Cem. [FHR; GHT, p. 1011]

WEST, J. L.    Co. D, 37TN
Died May 11, 1862 (Lindsley).

WEST, Joel (Joseph) P.    Barry's Btry.
Enl. July 14, 1862 at Chattanooga; deserted. [Brown's Diary]

WEST, Willis Ridley    Co. B, 1GA
Born July 28, 1842 in Cobb Co., GA. Enl. 1861 at Monterrey, VA. Also served in pistol factory in "arsenal battalion" in Columbus, GA. Married (1890 in HC) Lucinda Bowers. To TN 1886. Died Feb. 28, 1916 at res. in East Lake and bur Forest Hills Cem. [TWP, p. 178; CT 29 Feb. 1916; TP 13,016]

WETMORE, Maj. William H.    36TN
Served as First Sgt., then was elected major, but he was never commissioned. He later saw duty in charge of a Conscript Camp of Instruction.

WHALEN, James K. P.    Co. H, 1 E.T. Cav. (Carter's)
Born June, 1845 in Jefferson Co. and raised there. Enl. at Dandridge, TN about Aug. 1, 1863. Captured at or near Mossy Creek, March 27, 1864 and imprisoned at Camp Morton until June 12, 1865. About one year after war, he left TN and went to KY and stayed two years before moving to IL and eventually back to TN. Res. Sherman Heights. Occupation of carpenter and peddling papers in 1903, "broken down in health." 1910 res. 5th Ave. with wife Mary. [NBFM2; TP5388; 1910HC]

WHITE, James    Co. D, 4GA Cav.
Enl. Oct. 4, 1862 and captured at Missionary Ridge on Nov. 25, 1863.

WHITE, James A.    Co. I, 8TN Cav.
Born Meigs Co., April 23, 1828. Enl. Oct. 1, 1862 at Pikeville. Shot through chin and right arm at Parker's Crossroads. Returned to home in Bledsoe Co. after war but had lost use of right arm. In 1903 res. of Hill City. [TP3854]

WHITE, James C.    Co. A, 4TN Cav.
Served as a farrier. He became sick and was furloughed, then he resigned on Nov. 15, 1861. He was on the Kentucky campaign and lost his horse at Beech Grove.

WHITE, James M. Co. I, 5TN Cav. (McKenzie's)
Born Washington Co., TN. Enl. July 19, 1862. Company blacksmith. Deserted Nov. 23, 1863. Res. 1905 in Birchwood. [TP7546]

WHITE, Lt. Col. John Fletcher    Co. A, 5th TN Cav.
Born in Rogersville, Hawkins County, TN, Feb. 18, 1824, he was the son of the Rev. George White and Sarah Snodgrass. He married Martha Faw, a native of Switzerland, and they had 12 children. After serving in the Mexican War, White, at age 21, was elected to represent Hawkins County in the Tennessee Legislature, 1847-1849. He read law, moved to Chattanooga in 1850, and settled near the section later known as Shepherd. He was appointed as the first county judge of HC when the office was established in 1856. The office was abolished two years later.
Fletcher White organized a Confederate cavalry company (Bird's Rangers) at his own expense and served as its captain prior to being elected lieutenant-colonel of the 1st TN Cav. Jan. 7, 1862. White was captured at a skirmish at Big Creek Gap, TN, March 14, 1862 and sent to Louisville, then to Camp Chase, OH, in early April. He finally was sent to Fort Warren in Boston Harbor. The prominent Chattanooga attorney and former state legislator was able to gain a parole from the Secretary of War. He was released May 24, 1862, and allowed to return to his home near Tyner. White sought unsuccessfully to gain permission from Confederate authorities to organize his former company or raise two new volunteer companies. He also wrote President Jefferson Davis asking that he be appointed as an appraiser of property impressed by the army. He was again rebuffed, although he complained he had been "reduced to the lowest rung of the ladder." Finally, he rejoined his former company, which was then headed by A. J. Ragon, at Knoxville on March 11, 1864. But he soon decided to load up his family in some "broken-down

wagons pulled by discarded army mules" and head for Florida. He settled at Live Oak and served with the Provisional Army until the end of the war.

In Florida, he was a Criminal Court judge in Suwanee County, state's attorney, then Circuit Court judge for three terms. He was an active Methodist layman, serving as Sunday School supt. 45 years. He died at Live Oak, FL, on Aug. 14, 1901. [Hamer Vol. III, p 112; GHT, p. 1012; JW White Family; Biog. Souvenir of GA and FL, pp. 835-36; Goodspeed, History of Tennessee, p. 1012.]

WHITE, Lt. William W.     Co. D, 4GA Cav.
Enl. Oct. 4, 1862, and deserted in early December the following year. He was held at Chattanooga, where he took the oath of allegiance to the Union on Sept. 10, 1863. Historian Zella Armstrong says White "was charged with desertion to the enemy, court martialed, convicted and executed in Chattanooga. Many people, however, who knew him well protested and believed that he was innocent. W. J. Gillespie, orderly Sergeant of Co. B, believed in Lieut. White's loyalty and frequently made the statement in the years that followed the war." [Zella Armstrong, Hamilton County Confederate Soldiers]

WHITECOTTON, Harrison (Harry)     Barry's Btry.
Enl. April 4, 1862 at Chattanooga; paroled May 11, 1865 in Meridian, MS.

WHITECOTTON, Isaac M.     Co. H, 4TN Cav.
Born c1831 in AL. He was wounded four times. Before the war, he was a day laborer at Chattanooga. In 1870 he was a farmer in Chattanooga, wife Sarah E.

WHITEHEAD, Isaac Thomas
Born 1842 in Bledsoe Co. Married (1865) Mary E. Carney. Died 1879 in HC. [TWP, p. 65]

WHITESIDE, Foster
Born Jan. 24, 1836. Brother of Hugh Whiteside. Leader in Home Guard "Vigilance Committee," 1861. Married Sarah Miranda Harris. Died June 21, 1897, Morristown, TN. where he resided. [CT June 22, 1897]

WHITESIDE, Harriet Leonora Straw (Mrs. James A.)
Born May 3, 1824 Virginia, governess who married (1844) James A. Whiteside. Expelled from occupied Chattanooga, 1864, by Sherman and imprisoned Louisville. Died Feb. 19, 1903.

WHITESIDE, James L.     Co. B, 1TN
Born at "the old Whiteside homestead" on

Cedar St., April 17, 1845, son of Col. James A. and Harriet Straw Whiteside, he enl. at Nashville in Co. B, 1TN. He participated in the Cheat Mountain Campaign under Gen. R. E. Lee and the Bath and Romney campaign under Gen. T. J. Jackson. He became ill in Virginia and his father went there to bring him home. The rigors of the trip, however, led to the death of JLW's father in Nov., 1861. The 1TN returned and fought at Shiloh, the Kentucky Campaign, Murfreesboro, Chickamauga, Missionary Ridge, the Atlanta Campaign, and Hood's Tennessee Campaign. After the war JLW was engaged in railroading in Chattanooga, serving as conductor on the broad-gauge Lookout Mountain railroad and agent of the Incline No. 2 railway. His wife was Mary (Mollie) Tidwell. Died July 6, 1912 at his home on McCallie Ave. and buried Forest Hills Cem.[CT July 7, July 9, 1912]

WHITESIDE, John B.     [CSA?]
Born Oct. 28, 1829 in Pikeville, TN; married 1 Jan 1851 Adelaide L. Hooke born 17 Jan 1832 in Washington, Rhea Co., TN. In Chattanooga, he was a Civil Engineer and is credited with drawing the first map of the city. He died May Nov. 1874, HC. [HC Register of Deaths]

WHITFIELD, Gordon W.     Co. E, 1AL Cav.
(Wheeler's Escort)
Born in GA, Feb. 1, 1844. Wounded Elk River, New Hope Church. Married (Aug. 20, 1904, Soddy) Sarah Harden Sisson and living at Soddy in 1906 where he was stable man for Soddy Coal Co. Died Sept. 10, 1916 at Chattanooga. [TWP, p. 186; NBFM2; TP 4880; 1910HC]

WHITLOCK, James A. Co. B, 1TN Cav. (Carter's)
Born 1845 in GA. 1860 living in household of of Jesse and Agnes Locke at Ooltewah. [1860 HC Census]

WHITSITT, William Jimos Co. A, 154 Sr. Inf.
Born 7 Oct 1831 in Rockingham Co., NC married Harriett Willis. Enlisted 28 July 1863 at Ringgold, GA, served to the end of the war. He is listed as Captain in Co. B 1st Reg. GA Inf. paroled Kingston, GA 12 May 1854.Died and buried in Ringgold, GA. [NBFM1,7; UDC2 pg 572]

WHITTEN, James  36TN; Co. K, 43TN
Enl. Dec. 17, 1861 at Ooltewah; transferred from 36TN; captured at Vicksburg, July 4, 1863.

WHITTENBERG, William Wesley
Married Mary Ann Stout on 3 Jan. 1840 in Rhea Co. He was the son of John and Sarah (Lotspeich)

Whittenburg. He was on the 1850 and 1860 Rhea Co. Census. From a listing of member of May 1862, there is a Wm. Whittenburg joint Capt. Darwin's Co. C, 16th TN Batt., Neal's Cav. He died between 1860 and 1870. [TP768]

WHITTLE, Archimides "Ark"  Co. G, 26TN;
2d Co. K, 1CSA (GA)
Born Bradley Co., Feb. 15, 1842. Enl. 28 Aug. 1861, Knoxville. Captured Fort Donelson, 16 Feb. 1862 and imprisoned Camp Morton. Detached to Miners and Sappers, May 19, 1863. Died Dayton, TN, April 8, 1929 and buried Mt. Vernon Church. [CT 9 Apr 1929]

WIDEMAN, John P. (F.),  Co. A, 19TN
He was discharged from the army on Nov. 26, 1862, and died at Chattanooga in Oct. 1863. [Worsham, 98]

WIEHART, P. R.  8GA
[TP 15,797]

WILDS, Lt. Darlan A.  Co. H, 19TN

WILDS, Sgt. George B.  Co. C, 7KY
Born at Carroll County, MS, in 1846, he was a lineal descendant of Lawrence Washington, grandfather of George Washington. Enl. Sept. 15, 1861, at Mayfield, KY and fought at Shiloh, Baton Rouge and Corinth. He was made a sergeant March 1, 1864, and was mounted under Gen. Forrest. He was with him at Paducah, KY, and Harrisburg, MS. His unit surrendered at Citronelle, AL, on May 4, 1865, and he was paroled May 19, 1865, at Grenada, MS. An attorney, he moved to Chattanooga in 1928 when he was offered a house there. He was living at Clarksville, TN, when he died July 18, 1936. [TP 16,626]

WILEY (WILY), Cpl. James M.  Co. L, 36TN;
Co. L, 35TN
Born c1831 in TN. Married Elizabeth. Laborer. Enl. Jan. 9, 1862, at Chattanooga; transferred to 35TN. [1860HC]

WILEY, William E.  Co. L, 36th TN
Born about 1835 in AL. Before the war, he was a railroad agent at Chattanooga living with his mother, Lucinda. Married Laura A. Carey (Sept. 17, 1859 in HC). Enl. Jan. 9, 1862, at Chattanooga. [1860HC; HC Marriage Book]

WILHOITE, Phillip Rainey  Co. D, 8GA
Born July 10, 1841 in Merriwether Co., GA. Enl. Feb. 1864 at Strawberry Plains, TN. Army of Northern Virginia. Wounded Reams Station. Wilderness, Cold Harbor. Paroled at Appomattox. To Shelbyville, TN after war and was married in 1877 to Letitia Cannon. Many years "prominent grain dealer in Chattanooga" Lived in St. Elmo (1910). Methodist. Living in Miami, FL in 1931 and died there March 2, 1937. [NBFM2; CT May 3, 1931; CT March 3, 1937; 1910HC]

WILKERSON, William M. (N.?)  Co. H, 21GA
Born Dade Co., GA, Jan. 1, 1845. Enl. July 18, 1861. Winchester, Pt. Republic, Cold Harbor, Cedar Mountain. Wounded twice at Manassas and Feb. 1, 1864 at New Berne, NC. Surr. Orange Co., VA, 1865. To TN, 1905. Wife was Josie. Res. 1909 East Lake. Died May 20, 1914 and buried CSA Cem. [TP 11,538;CT May 21, 1914]

WILKINS, Drury Dobbins  26TN
Born Cleveland Co., NC, March 18, 1834, son of blacksmith Anderson Smith and Lavina (Warlick) Wilkins who came from Rutherford and Cleveland counties, NC and were early settlers of East Brainerd and organizers of Concord Baptist Church. Before the war, he lived on his father's farm at Chickamauga near Tyner and was engaged in railroading with Gray, Dent & Co., working on the Illinois Central. Orderly Sgt., HC Home Guard, April 29, 1861. Enl. in Brant's Battalion, 1861, serving under Col. Jarrett Dent before being detailed in 1862 to QM Dept where he mined salt for CSA until close of war. Married (April 9, 1861) Mary "Mollie" Eskridge whom he met while working on the railroad at Duck Hill, MS. Took his family and their possessions from MS in a wagon to East Brainerd after the war with Mollie going the 200 miles on horseback. They returned to Duck Hill in fall, 1865 and DW became an extensive plantation owner and cotton farmer. He also operated a mercantile firm. 1870 res. near parents with wife Mary R. of MS. Died 1906.

WILKINS, Sgt. Luther Rice  2nd Co. K, 1st CSA Cav.
Born 1837, son of Anderson Smith and Lavina Warlick Wilkins Enl. July 14, 1862 in HC Killed in action at Fort Donelson, Feb. 3, 1862.

WILKINS, Thomas  Clark's Independent Cav. Co.
Enl. July 18, 1863 at Chattanooga; deserted Feb. 25, 1862 near Dalton, GA.

WILKINS, William Woodson  2Lt. Co. E, 60GA
Born c1835, son of Anderson Smith and Lavina Warlick Wilkins. Attorney, Spring Place, GA. Enl. Sept. 19, 1861 in Bartow Avengers. Died Sept. 5, 1862.

WILKINSON, William M.  Co. H, 21GA
Born Jan. 1, 1845 in Dade Co., GA. Enl. at

Rising Fawn, July 1861. Wounded at Bachelor's Creek in Eastern NC, Feb. 1, 1864. Res. East Lake in 1888. Died at res. in Rossville May 20, 1914 and buried CSA Cem. [CT May 21, 1914; NBFM2]

WILLETT, Edward D.    Co. G, 1LA
Born KY. and was clerk in New Orleans when war broke out. Enl. May, 1861 in Co. G, 1LA Vol., Nichol's Brig. Commanded regt. at Chancellorsville "up to Gettysburg." Promoted to major in 1864. Severely wounded in the Wilderness, May 5, 1864. Paroled at Meridian, MS, May, 1865. Res. Chattanooga. Died at his summer home near New Orleans several years ago. Death not known here. [NBFM2]

WILLIAMS, Adolphus N.
Born 1841 in Smith Co., married (1872) Cassandra C. Reeves, and died 1922 in HC. [TWP, p. 113]

WILLIAMS, Alonzo G.    Co. H, 4TN Cav.
A son of the pioneer Samuel Williams, he died during the Kentucky campaign in 1862. He was listed as age 14 at the time of the 1860 census.

WILLIAMS, Sgt. Andrew Alexander (Andy)    Co. K. 43TN
Born in Blount County, March 19, 1833 and came to HC in 1835. Brother of John L. Williams. Was small boy when group of citizens met at the old schoolhouse on Georgia Ave. and changed name from Ross' Landing to Chattanooga. Wagon master in Knoxville in 1861, then joined Co. K, 43TN, Oct. 17, 1861, at Ooltewah when the regt. was organized and served throughout war becoming commissary sgt. He was appointed sergeant Sept. 1, 1862. He was captured at Vicksburg on July 4, 1863. After being paroled and rejoining the Confederate forces, he surrendered on May 5, 1865, at Asheville, NC. He married (1872 in HC) Elizabeth Hamill.
His father, James Williams, was a pioneer Ross's Landing settler who first visited the landing in 1835. He built a hut on a bald knob east of town and planted an orchard there. This was later known as Orchard Knob. As a young man, Andy Williams worked for the Crutchfields in their brickyard at Chattanooga. A schoolteacher and farmer, he had a dark complexion, dark hair, hazel eyes, and was 5'9 ½" tall. He lived with the Bush family. His sister, Sarah Williams, had married James Bush. In his latter years, he lived in Rhea County, but res. Poplar St., 1910. Died Aug. 14, 1913 in HC and was buried White Oak Cem. He was an uncle of N. P. Nail and brother of John Williams. [TWP, p. 144; CT Aug. 15, 1913; NBFM2; 1910HC]

WILLIAMS, Henry    Co L, 4GA Cav.; 12GA Cav.
Born Meriweather Co., GA, 1845. Enl. Dec. 12, 1862: Chickamauga, Atlanta Campaign, opposed Stoneman's Raid. Offical records show "sent to wagon train" c. Nov. 19, 1863 and no later record. To TN, 1867. Wife was Elizabeth L. Res. 1917 in St. Elmo. Died June 9, 1919 at home in St. Elmo and bur. Forest Hills Cem. [TP 15,231;CT June 10, 1919]

WILLIAMS, James
Born in Grainger Co., TN, about 1814, son of Ethelred and Mary Copeland Williams, he owned a line of steamboats plying the Tennessee River from Knoxville to Decatur. He located in Chattanooga because of river location and with his brother William established Chattanooga's first bank as well as Tennessee River Mining, Manufacturing, and Navigation Co. Given a silver service by citizens of Chattanooga "for his contribution to development of river." He was well-known by President James Buchanan and was offered a cabinet post. Instead he became Minister to Turkey. When war broke out he remained abroad, selling Confederate bonds in London and throughout Europe. He also wrote pieces in London papers in support of CSA. He was author of The Model Republic, but found himself unwelcome in his native country. He married Lucy Graham. Died at Gratz, Austria in 1869 and buried there. [BDTA, 1:793-94]

WILLIAMS, James M.    Co. H, 4TN Cav.
He was another of the sons of Samuel Williams who died during the war. On Oct. 8, 1862, he fell in a charge at Perryville, KY. He was shot off his horse and then mortally wounded by cannon shot after he remounted. He was born about 1840.

WILLIAMS, James W. D.    Co. K, 31TN
Born Monroe Co., TN, 1841. Enl. Feb. 1862. Vicksburg. Captured, paroled but did not return to army. 1909 res. St. Elmo. Died Jan. 4, 1911 on Lookout Mtn. and buried in Knoxville. [TP 11,296; CT Jan. 5, 1911]

WILLIAMS, John Henry    Purcell's Btry; Co. H, 46VA
Born June 18, 1843 at Norfolk, VA. Served in Purcell's Btry, Field's Brigade, A. P. Hill's Div. Re-enl. in Charleston, SC in Co. H, 46VA. Paroled at Appomatox as Cpl. To Chattanooga, 1887. Res. College St., Chattanooga. US Cast Iron and Foundry. Married in HC Tillie Wickman. Died Nov. 23, 1921 in HC and buried at Forest Hills Cemetery. [FHR; TWP, 229; NBFM2; TP 12,829; CT Nov. 24, 1921]

WILLIAMS, John L.  Co. C, 5TN Cav. (McKenzie's)
Born c1840, son of James Williams who came

to HC, 1835, and settled section that became Orchard Knob. Enl. 1 Nov. 1861., Decatur, TN, and detailed as courier for Gen. Reynolds, July 1, 1862. Captured July 9, 1862, Big Hill, KY. Imprisoned Camp Chase, then Camp Douglas, arriving in August 1863. Paroled Feb. 24, 1865. After war farmed in Meigs Co. and died there Sept. 7, 1914 and buried Old Pisgah Cem. [JW Williams Family; CT 9 Sept. 1914]

WILLIAMS, Madison     Co. F, 35TN

The eldest son of the pioneer Samuel Williams, he was born in HC in 1835. He was a farmer and trader before the war. He enl. Oct. 21, 1862, at Chattanooga. His wife was Jennie Cowart, daughter of John Cowart. He had gray eyes, dark hair, a dark complexion, and was 5'6" tall. He resided in North Chattanooga after the war.

WILLIAMS, Robert L.          Co. C, 5TN Cav.
(McKenzie's)

He enl. Nov. 29, 1861, at Decatur. Age 19 at time of enlistment. Reduced to ranks from Cpl., July 23, 1862. Captured March 11, 1864 at Tunnel Hill. Paroled, not having been exchanged, May 3, 1865 at Charlotte, NC.

WILLIAMS, Samuel

This pioneer Hamilton County settler was past the age for active service, but he served as a guide to Generals Nathan Bedford Forrest and Joseph Wheeler. He was a Whig who opposed secession, but he and his sons cast their lot with the Confederacy. Williams was living along the Tennessee River near Williams Island when James Andrews made his escape from Swaim's Jail at Chattanooga. Andrews was the leader of the celebrated Andrews Raiders, who had captured the railway engine The General and tried to sabotage railroad tracks south of Chattanooga Andrews swam over to Williams Island, where he was apprehended by Williams. Andrews had dinner with the Williams family before he was turned back over to Confederate authorities and was later hanged. Williams had to flee after his home was occupied by Federal soldiers. He stayed under a rock on a nearby hillside and would sometimes visit his wife. For his role in the capture of Andrews, he was still in jeopardy even after the war ended. His wife was finally able to gain a pardon for him after she went to Washington and entreated President Andrew Johnson in his behalf. Due to the war, the Williams holdings shrank from several thousand acres to the home place and a few hundred acres. He lived until 1898 when he was 91.

WILLIAMS, Dr. W. L.

Lived in North Alabama but enl. in HC.

WILLIAMS, William     Barry's Btry.

Born 1835 in TN. Railroad worker, res. Chattanooga, 1860 with wife Mary. Killed at Spanish Fort, 1865. [1860HC]

WILLIAMS, William (may be the railroad laborer at Chattanooga in 1860 census, age 25 with wife Mary. There is also a William Williams who was a carpenter living at Birchwood age 45 with wife Caroline)

WILLINGHAM, John Wesley     Co. A, 1GA

Born Lincolnton, Wilkes Co., GA, March 24, 1846. Enl. July 20, 1864 at Augusta, GA. At battle of Peachtree Creek; fell ill just before Atlanta fell and was captured and sent to Camp Douglas where he remained until June, 1865. Married Susan A. Smith in 1863. After the war, was in mercantile business in Huntsville. Married (2) Alice Ann McBroom (1881). About 1882 they moved to Chattanooga. Methodist. Merchant. Died Oct. 20, 1909 at home on Oak St. and buried in Forest Hills Cem. [FHR; TWP, 214; CT Oct. 21, 1909; NBFM2]

WILLINGHAM, William A.

Born Beaufort Co., SC 6 July 1837, son of Thomas and Phoebe S. Lawton Willingham, he married (1859) Emillie F. Dews. He enl. in 1862 and served one year. Immediately after the war he emigrated to GA where he engaged in the lumber business in Forsyth, before coming to Chattanooga and establishing a general lumber business in 1885. Mason. Baptist. [GHT, p. 1015]

WILLINGHAM, Winborn Joseph   Hampton Legion

Born Jan. 25, 1844 in Lawtonville (Beaufort Co.), SC, son of Thomas Willingham, joined the Hampton Legion in 1861 and fought at First Manassas, Yorktown, Williamsburg, Seven Pines, and the Seven Days. He transferred to the 2GA Cav. became ill and was discharged, then re-enl. in an independent company on the coast of SC. Following the war he planted cotton until 1870, engaged in business at Macon, GA until 1876 when he moved to Atlanta to enter the lumber trade. In 1886 he settled in Chattanooga where he dealt in real estate and established the Willingham Lumber Co. Sgt. Maj., NBF Camp, 1894. Baptist. He died at daughter's home in Eufaula, AL, July 28, 1926. His wife was Florence Baynard. [CSA Mil. Hist., 10:878; CT July 30, 1926]

WILLIS, 2nd Lt. George T.  Co. G, 26TN;
          2d Co. K, 1CSA (GA)

Age 27 in 1861, he enl. July 8, 1861 in Co. G, 26TN at Knoxville; captured at Fort Donelson, Feb. 16, 1862; imprisoned at Camp Chase, OH, then Johnson's Island; dark hair, blue eyes, and 5'10" tall. Elected captain Oct. 13, 1862. Cashiered Aug. 27, 1863 at Chattanooga.

WILLIS, John B.   Co. G, 26TN; 2d Co. K, 1CSA (GA)
Enl. July 8, 1861 in Co. G, 26TN at Knoxville; captured at Fort Donelson, Feb. 16, 1862; imprisoned at Camp Morton, IN. Died in Walker Co., GA, Nov. 3, 1862.

WILSON, George W.   Co. B, 1CSA
Born 1842 in Ringgold, GA. Enl. Oct., 1864. Wounded Florence, AL, fall, 1864. 1902 living near Graysville in James Co. [TP 4343]

WILSON, J. M. D.   Co. K, 8TN
Born March 9, 1837 in York District, SC, he enl. at Camp Harris, Franklin Co., TN, May 15, 1861, and served in western VA and Charleston, SC. He was severely wounded at Franklin, Nov. 30, 1864. He held the rank of first Sgt. of his company at the time of surrender in NC. Residing Chattanooga, 1909. Moved to OK. [NBFM2,4,7]

WILSON, James A.   Co. G, 26TN; 2d Co. K, 1CSA (GA);3CSA Cav. (Howard's Ala. Bn.)
Born c1843, son of Elizabeth. Res. 1860 at Limestone. Enl. Aug. 28, 1861, Knoxville. Left sick at Cumberland City, Feb. 12, 1862. In Howard's Bn., Dec. 31, 1862-Feb. 28, 1863.

WILSON, John B.   Co. G, 26 TN
Enl. July 8, 1861 at Knoxville; captured at Fort Donelson, Feb. 16, 1862; imprisoned at Camp Morton, IN.

WILSON, Joseph H.   Co. K, 43TN
Enl. Oct. 17, 1861 at Ooltewah; captured at Vicksburg, July 4, 1863.

WILSON, Leroy Halsey   Co. D, 4AL Cav.
Born Sept. 30, 1845 in Huntsville, AL and spent early life as pharmacist there, coming to Chattanooga in 1886. Co. C, 4AL Cav. Covered Hood's retreat from TN and paroled at Greensboro, AL. Episcopalian. Res. Huntsville, 1866-1886. Married (1872) Ellen S. Ward. Druggist in Chattanooga, 1888. Died Feb. 12, 1933 in Chattanooga and buried in Huntsville. [TWP, 305; CT Feb. 13, 1933; NBFM1; TP 16,103]

WILSON, Samuel   Co. B, 19TN
Born c. 1830. Farm laborer with wife Linne and three children. [1860HC]

WILSON, Samuel C.   1SC Cav. (Edgefield Rangers)

Born April 16, 1848 in Richmond Co., GA. Served as vol. courier for Genls. P.M.B. Young, B. D. Fry, S. R. Gist and W. D. Smith. [NBFM2]

WILSON, William H. H.   Co. G, 26TN; 2d Co. K, 1CSA (GA)
Born about 1842 in Hawkins Co., TN, he was a farmer who enl. in Co. G, 26TN July 12, 1861 in Knoxville. Captured at Fort Donelson, Feb. 16, 1862 and imprisoned at Camp Chase. On sick furlough, Bradley Co., TN, Dec. 31, 1862. Discharged June 8, 1863: "has not been fit for military duty during the last fourteen months owing to a dropsical affliction produced by the exposure at the fight at Fort Donelson."

WILSON (WILLSON), William M.   Barry's Btry.
Born 1830 in Scotland. Immigrated to U. S., 1846. Enl. May 14, 1862 at Chattanooga; deserted May 12, 1863 at Pollard, AL. Res. 1910 east of Missionary Ridge along Ringgold Rd. with wife Nancy. Laborer doing odd jobs.

WILSON, William Moore   Co. B, 43TN
Born Nov. 1, 1831 in HC. Enl. Oct. 16, 1861 at Sulphur Springs, Rhea Co in Capt. Cawood's Co. Prom. to 1st Lt., May 10, 1862; captured, Aug. 5, 1863. Among those surrendering May 8, 1865, at Washington, GA, while with escort for Jefferson Davis. Married Amanda M. Brown (1871, Roane Co.). Died in Rhea Co., Dec. 27, 1909. [TWP9713; Allen 1995:7-8]

WINFREY, C.   2d Co. I, 1CSA (GA)
"Pay due as cavalryman for self and horse from Sept. 1, 1862 to Dec. 15, 1862 and as infantryman from that date. Transferred from Bradshaw's Cavalry by order of General Bragg." Absent in hospital at Chattanooga, June 30, 1863. On daily duty guarding a vineyard in Chattanooga, Aug. 31, 1863.

WINFREY, Sanford   Co. G, 26TN; 2d Co. K, 1CSA (GA)
Enl. 8 July 1861, Knoxville. Captured Fort Donelson, Feb. 16, 1862 and imprisoned Camp Morton. Florid complexion, brown hair, blue eyes, 6' tall. AOL Dec. 31, 1863. Took USA oath, Dec. 11, 1863. Enl. 10TN Cav. (USA)

WINN, C. Z.   Co. K, 43TN
Enl. Oct. 10, 1861 at Ooltewah; deserted Oct. 10, 1862.

WINN, R. R.   Co. G, 26TN
Enl. 8 July 1861, Knoxville.

WINSETT, William R.   Co.(B) C, 1TN Cav. (Carter's)

Enl. Sept. 7, 1861 at Cleveland, TN; captured Oct. 21, 1863 in Rhea Co., TN; imprisoned at Camp Morton, then to Fort Delaware March 19, 1864; killed in battle of Murfreesboro, Dec. 31,1862

WISDOM, Abner J. "Ab"
He was in the supply department for the Confederate forces until captured and imprisoned at Nashville. His wife went there and was able to gain his release upon the condition that he would not again aid the Confederacy. Wisdom was born in Floyd Co., GA, Aug. 26, 1826, the son of Jesse Wisdom and Elizabeth Griffin. He married Fannie Glass in 1842 in Arkansas. After her death, he married Perlenna Parolee Clowdis. Moving to Chattanooga in 1852, he worked at a livery stable until the war began. Destitute at the conclusion of the war, he borrowed money to purchase one carload of mules and they became the basis for a successful livery and undertaking establishment. He was also a contractor and active in the early streetcar operations. He resided on Houston Street. A member of Centenary Methodist, he died Jan. 15, 1897 in Chattanooga and is buried in Forest Hills Cem.[CT Jan. 16, 1897]

WISE, James
[NBFM3]

WISHOPT (?), Jacob    Barry's Btry.
Wounded at battle of Atlanta.

WITHAM, Alexander "Andy" 43TN
Born March 19, 1833, he was brought to Chattanooga in 1835. He served as a wagon master, then became commissary Sgt. for 43TN. He left Chattanooga after war and returned to Meigs Co. for a few years, then came to Chattanooga once again, dying here Aug. 14, 1913 buried in White Oak Cem. His wife was Lizzie Hammil. [CT Aug. 15, 1913]

WITT, _____    Co. A, 19TN;
Died in Knoxville during war

WITT, Colonel Allen Rufus  10AR
Born 17 Aug. 1830, HC, oldest son of Jesse Witt (1808-1881) and Sarah Rogers (1808-1845). In 1842 family moved to AR, settling on Little Red River near Quitman. Allen was only one of the children to receive an education, attending Arkansas College in Fayetteville. As a young man, he went on a cattle drive to CA, and in 1857, elected state land commissioner. Married Henrietta C. Miller and had five children.
In July, 1861, at Springfield, AR, chosen to be Captain of Co. A ("Quitman Rifles"), 10AR. Fall 1861; 10AR to Camp Beauregard, KY where many became ill

and died; 31 Dec. 1861 10AR to Bowling Green, then to Shiloh where Co. A suffered 84 casualties including ARW who was wounded. May 1862 ARW elected colonel of 10AR. Vicksburg, attempt by Breckinridge to capture Baton Rouge, being posted for a time at Ponchatoula before joining garrison at Port Hudson.
During first major assault on Port Hudson on May 27, 1863, Allen was captured along with 50 of his men. Eventually taken north to be confined at Fort Delaware, but on 10 June 1863, he was one of 70 CSA officers who escaped from the US steam transport *Maple Leaf*, and made their way to Richmond. From there, he travelled to AR. By the time he arrived, the enl. men of his regt. at Port Hudson had been surrendered and paroled and had returned to the state.
Allen reorganized 10AR as 10AR Cav., and throughout most of 1864, regt. scouted and raided in northern AR. In fall, 1864, they joined S. Price during his last raid into MO. Winter, 1864 regt. continued to harass Union forces in northern AR until eventually dispersed by Col. Abraham H. Ryan's 3AR Cav. (USA) based in Lewisburg.
May 1865, Gen. M. Jeff Thompson, cmdg. Northern Subdistrict of AR, negotiated surrender of command. 10AR surrendered and was paroled at Jacksonport, AR, 5 June 1865.
After war, Allen elected to AR Senate, representing Van Buren and Izard Cos. until disqualified by Congressional Reconstruction Acts. With the return of the Democrats to power, Allen was elected (1874) to constitutional convention representing Van Buren. On 27 April 1901 he was awarded UDC cross of honor. By the time of his death in 1903, Allen had been named Brig. Genl. of Militia.

WITT, Charles 10AR
Born 1835 in HC, 3d son of Jesse Witt and Sarah Rogers. Though of military age, no record of his having joined CSA until 1864 when he became member of 10AR Cav. commanded by his brother. Aug. 12, 1864, he was captured near Quitman, AR by members of 3d AR Cav. (USA) and imprisoned at Alton, IL, where he died, probably of smallpox, Dec. 10, 1864.

WITT, Daniel A.   Co. H, 37TN

WITT, James   Co. K, 43TN
Born c1829, TN, son of John P. and Celia Witt of Chattanooga. Enl. April 1, 1862 at Ooltewah; discharged June 23, 1862. 1870 at Long Savannah, wife Catherine. [1860HC].

WITT, Jeremiah  10AR
Born 1833, HC, 2d son of Jesse Witt and Sarah Rogers. In 1842 family moved to Van Buren Co., AR,

and 10 yrs later Jeremiah m. Zerelda Jane Garner. With three children at home, did not enlist in 10AR with his brothers in July, 1861, but indications are that he went with the regt. when it left state that fall. One muster roll indicates Jeremiah enl. in 10AR at Corinth, two days after Shiloh to avoid being drafted by new conscript law. Fought at Vicksburg, Ponchatoula, LA, under M. Jeff Thompson, Port Hudson (where he was captured and paroled). Returned to Quitman, AR. In fall, 1864 accompanied 10AR on Price's last raid into MO. The regiment shared in the hardships and casualties at Pilot Knob, Westport, and Mine Creek. As Price's army returned to AR, Jeremiah joined another regt which proceeded to Marshall, TX. He later said of the end of the war, "at Marshall, Texas . . . we (our company) laid down our arms, and [as] there was no officer present with authority to issue discharges, we went home." Returned to farming near Quitman, AR, finally moving to Temple, OK, where he died in 1926 having fathered 13 children.

WITT, Jesse L.   Co. D, 37TN
    Born 1835 in TN, son of Charles and Jane of Sale Creek. Enl. Sept. 1, 1861, Knoxville. Sent to Nashville hospital as nurse. "Has since died." Feb. 20, 1862.

WITT, John Gibson  Co. A, 10AR
    Born 22 Mch. 1838 in HC, 4th son of Jesse Witt and Sarah Rogers. In 1842 family moved to Van Buren, AR, settling near Quitman. Enl. July 1861 with brother Milton in "Quitman Rifles," Co. A, 10AR which his brother A. Rufus commanded. JGW promoted to sgt. Fought at Shiloh, Corinth, Vicksburg, Ponchatoula, LA. 16 Sept. 1862 at latter place repulsed attack by Maj. George Strong and sev. companies of 12th Maine and 26th Mass. May 1863 to Port Hudson which was beseiged and surrendered 8 July 1863. Enlisted men paroled and went home (including John, Milton and Jeremiah), probably thinking war was over for them. When they arrived in AR, however, their older brother Allen Rufus (who had been captured early in the fighting at Port Hudson and had escaped) was there reorganizing 10AR as a mounted regt. Likely John served during 1864-65 with his brothers in 10AR Cav. After war he returned to home near Quitman where he died 4 Sept. 1893 survived by wife and six children. [JWitt to ed., Sept. 4, 1998]

WITT, Milton  Co. A, 10AR
    Born 1839, the youngest surviving son of Jesse Witt and Sarah Rogers. Enl. 15July 1861 Co. A, 10AR at Springfield, AR. Milton eventually prom. to Sgt. Shiloh, Corinth, southern LA before being ordered to Port Hudson where it was captured 8 July 63. Upon

surrender, Milton paroled 9 July 63 and returned with his brothers John and Jeremiah to AR. Milton killed in an ambush "by Jayhawkers" near his home at Quitman during fall, 1863, whereupon neighbors attacked his assailants in the resulting "Battle of Quitman." Not known whether Milton left descendants.

WITT, Rufus    Co. L, 35TN
    Enl. Jan. 9, 1862, Chattanooga. AWOL, July 16, 1862.

WITT, Samuel A. (T.)    Barry's Btry.
    Enl. April 4, 1862. at Chattanooga; captured at Spanish Fort 1865; paroled May 11, 1865 at Meridian, MS; res. Morrisville, Calhoun Co., AL. [might be son of John P. and Celia Witt of Chattanooga] [1860HC]

WITT, Silas    Co. K, 43TN
    Born c1835. Enl. April 1, 1862 at Ooltewah; captured at Vicksburg, July 4, 1863. 1870 res. Long Savannah, wife Martha J.

WOFFORD, Mark J.   Barry's Battery
    He enl. along with his younger brother, Merrick H. Wofford, on May 12, 1862 at Chattanooga. He was an artificer. He was captured at the Spanish Fort on April 8, 1865, and paroled May 11, 1865, at Meridian, MS. Before the war, he was a carpenter at Chickamauga near Tyner. The Woffords were from SC. He was born about 1828, NC. His wife, Nancy J., was from GA. Died June 21, 1912 in Chattanooga, age 84, and buried Concord Cem. [CT June 22, 1912; TP 3959; 1860HC; 1910HC]

WOLFF, G. W.    Drummer, 36TN; Co. F, 35TN
    1901 living in Ooltewah. [TP494]

WOLFE (WOLFF), Jeremiah M.   Co. F, 35TN
    Born Bradley County, 1831, son of George W. and Elizabeth of Ooltewah. He farmed in HC until he enl. Sept. 20, 1862 at Chattanooga; blue eyes, "Dove" hair, fair complexion, 5'11" tall. Died, age 81, Feb. 4, 1922 at home on East 35th St. Buried in Ooltewah [CT Feb. 5, 1922; 1860HC.]

WOMACK, _____    Barry's Btry.

WOOD, E. J.   Co. K, 43TN
    ' Enl. Oct. 17, 1861 at Ooltewah; captured at Vicksburg, July 4, 1863.

WOOD, Luke   Co. E, 31GA
    Born Dawson Co., GA and married (1867, Pickens Co., GA) Mary E. Monroe. Enl. 1862: Roanoke Island, Gettysburg, Wilderness, Spotsylvania (wounded); also wounded at Little Washington, VA. Surr.

Appomattox Courthouse, April, 1865. To TN, 1881. 1911, res. E. Main St. where he died Jan. 10, 1928 and was buried in CSA Cem. Mary E. died 1952.[TWP, 254; TP 12,727; CT Jan. 11, 1928]

WOOD, M. E.  Morgan's Cav.
Black soldier, born July 1, 1848, HC, slave of John Taliaferro. Res. Cornelia St., 1927. [TP#222]

WOOD, Samuel T.   Barry's Btry.
Enl. Oct. 3, 1862 at Chattanooga. Wounded in battle of Atlanta; hospitalized in Lumpkin Hospital, Cuthbert, GA.

WOODALL, Josiah   Co. I, 19TN
Married (Jan. 12, 1861) Mary Jane Davis. He was captured in the Battle of Fishing Creek (Mill Springs), KY, on Jan. 19, 1862. He was in the fighting at Logan's Crossroads. Woodall was imprisoned at Camp Chase, OH. An exchange was arranged and he was on his way to Vicksburg, when he died. [Reported killed in battle of Atlanta, 1864, but was captured. [See G. T. Willis biog.]

WOODS, 1st Sgt.& 1st Lt. Andrew J.  Co. D, 37TN
Enl. Sept. 1, 1861, Knoxville. Commanding. company, summer, 1862. Resigned Feb. 11, 1863. Blacksmith.

WOODS, R. R.   Co. G, 26TN
Enl. 8 July 1861, Knoxville. Left sick at Russellville, Ky., Feb. 9, 1862.

WOODS, W. P.  Co. L, 35TN
Enl. Jan. 7, 1862 in Chattanooga

WOODWARD, Richard Henry   Co. F, 3VA
Local Defense force
Born Nov. 28, 1845 in Richmond, VA. Spent 4 yrs in ANV. To Chattanooga in 1870 and was timber inspector for Alabama and Chattanooga Rail Road, then formed Woodward and Morrison, the Woodward Lumber Co. Married Louisa Emma Corbin. Deacon in Baptist church. Charter member of NBF Camp, 1885. Res. Oak St. Died June 20, 1917 and buried Forest Hills Cem. [NBFM2,7; 1890VetCensus; CT June 21, 1917]

WOODY (WOODIE), Robert J.   Barry's Btry.
Enl. Oct. 14, 1862 at Knoxville as substitute for J. L. Swan; captured Kennesaw Mtn. July 3, 1864; deserted 7 June, 1864 [Brown's Diary]; imprisoned at Camp Douglas, IL.

WOOTEN, Andrew J.   Co. K, 6GA Cav.
Born Chatooga Co., GA, Oct. 11, 1845. Enl.

July 27, 1863. Wounded Dandridge, TN. Surrendered at Kingston, GA, May 12, 1865. Wife was M.E. "Gets mail in Rossville but lives over line in Tennessee." (1906). [TP8506]

WOOTEN, William Dow   Co. I, 1GA Cav.
Born 1845, Dalongea, GA. Enl. spring, 1862 near Cartersville, GA. Surr. near Greensboro, May, 1865. Married (Dec. 13, 1866, Cass Station, GA) Arrie Elizabeth Grogan. Lived at Cleveland, TN 20 years. Died Sept. 14, 1905, at Ooltewah. [TP#6962]

WORD, Dr. F. L.
[NBFM4]

WRIGHT, James M.  1LT  Co. D, 19TN
Born Forsythe Co., NC Dec. 30, 1840 and brought to Rhea Co., TN about 1846. Wounded at Resaca, minie ball hit above left ear resultling in deafness. In 1902 res. Coulterville (HC). 1910 res Soddy with wife Sarah. Farmer. Died 6 Dec. (year unknown). [TP 3855; 1910HC]

WRIGHT, Joseph Fulton     Co. G, 28VA
Born Bedford Co., VA, Jan. 8, 1833. Enl. Apr. 1862 at Orange Court House, VA. Army of Northern Virginia. Captured at Harper's Farm three days before surrender and imprisoned at Johnson's Island until June 1865. After war settled in Knoxville, then came to Chattanooga in 1871 and established first brickyard in the city. Married (1868) Frances J. "Fannie" Wells. Methodist. Member NBF Camp, 1895. Died March 4, 1908 at res. on Georgia Ave. and buried Forest Hills Cem. [FHR; CT March 5, 1908; NBFM2]

WRIGHT, Thomas   Co. A (E), 19TN
He was wounded at Murfreesboro, Dec. 31, 1862, and again at Chickamauga, Sept. 19. He lay on the field "as dead" until the next morning when he was "picked up and taken to the hospital." Wounded three times, once in the right side and twice in the breast during the course of the war. [Worsham, 92]

WRIGHT, William     Co. H, 26TN
Recognized for conspicious bravery at Murfreesboro, Dec. 31, 1862, by having name inscribed on the Roll of Honor.

WUNDER, John    Co. H, 4TN Cav.

WYATT, John   Co. L, 35TN
Enl. Jan. 9, 1862. Died in a hospital in Chattanooga May 10, 1862.

WYLDE, Capt. William

Born at sea Aug. 10, 1810. Died Oct. 27, 1887 in Chattanooga and buried Citizens Cem.

WYLEY, W. S.  2nd Co. K, 1st CSA Cav.
Enl. Oct. 31, 1862 in HC. Sent to hospital at Rome, GA by brigade surgeon, March 1863. Died May 16, 1863 in Dalton, GA of typhoid.

WYNN, George W.    Co. B, 1TN Cav. (Carter's)
Enl. Aug. 7, 1861 at Cleveland.

# Y

YARBROUGH, A. D.  Co. C, 52GA
Born White Co., GA, Feb. 13 1841 and was a long time resident of Catoosa Co., GA, and before his death in East Lake. Baptist. He died on Feb. 11, 1913 and buried at Boynton. [CTFeb. 12, 1913]

YARBROUGH, George M.    Co. F, 3GA Reserves
Born Oct. 28, 1849 at Abbeville, SC, son of John Yarbrough, he enl. in late 1863 in Co. F, 3GA Reserves and was assigned to guard duty at Andersonville. In the fall of 1864 his unit was ordered to the SC coast where they fought at Honey Hill. On April 16, 1865, he fought at Columbus, GA and was captured but escaped. He was paroled at Macon later that month. After the war he became a merchant at Columbus, GA, but moved to Chattanooga in 1887 and engaged in the wholesale business. He married Ella Johnston. Died Feb. 8, 1892 (1902?) and buried Forest Hills Cem. [FHR; NBFM2,7; CSA Mil. Hist., 10:802-03.]

YARRINGTON, Thomas L.  Co. D, 3AL
Born Marion, AL. Enl. at Union Springs, AL, Apr. 27, 1861. Fought at South Mountain, Bethsada Church near Richmond, Chancellorsville, 1st and 2nd Wilderness, Cedar Run, Winchester, Gettysburg. From the Rapidan to Richmond, siege of Petersburg. From High Bridge to Appamattox. Wounded at Boonesboro Gap (South Mtn.). Surrendered and paroled April 9, 1865. Res. East Lake, occup. RR clerk. Member NBF Camp, 1895. Died in county hospital of cancer June 12, 1899 after being returned from soldiers' home in Nashville. Buried CSA Cem. [NBFM2,7; CT June 14, 1899]

YODER, Marcus A.    Barry's Btry.
Enl. Feb. 1, 1863 at Knoxville; wounded Oct. 1864 (eye destroyed); paroled May 11, 1865 in Meridian, MS; res. - Lincoln Co., NC. 1870 res.

Jeffeson Co., TN.

YOUNG, Isaac Franklin   Co. H, 6AL
Born March 13, 1844 in Merriwether Co., GA. Enl. April 17, 1861 at Opelika, AL; wounded Sharpsburg (elbow broken) and so disabled that unfit for further duty. Married Sarah Pickett, Dec. 15, 1863. Couple lived at Opelika for some years, then moved to Chattanooga. Peddler and farmer "with no property" in HC, 1899; operating grocery store in 1910; was living at res. of Walter Cummings in Wauhatchie at death, Aug. 23, 1920. Buried CSA Cem. [TP7551; 1910HC; CT Aug. 24, 1920; NBFM2;TP697]

YOUNG, J. R.  Co. H, 26TN
Enl. July 8, 1861, Knoxville. Killed at Fort Donelson, Feb. 15, 1862. Married Mary A.

YOUNG, James P.  Co. I, 1TN (Turney's)
Born Oct. 1, 1844, Franklin Co., TN. Enl. at Winchester, Nov. 3, 1862. Wounded and captured at Gettysburg. Carpenter in Chattanooga in 1888. In NBF Camp in 1904. [NBFM2]

YOUNG [YOUNGER], John W.    Co. D, 7AL
Born Sept. 20, 1833 in Caldwell Co., KY, he was a printer and editor in Huntsville when he enl. March 26, 1861. Afterwards served in Co. I, 4AL. Wounded four times: Gaines's Mill (twice), Antietam and Gettysburg where he lost three fingers of his right hand. He served on the staff of the brigade commissary and as a hospital clerk until the surrender, Apr. 9, 1865. 1890 res. in Chattanooga. Occup. printer and editor. [NBFM2; Coles, Huntsville to Appomattox, pp. 80, 110, 204, 264n]

YOUNGBLOOD, 1st Sgt. William Henry  Co. F, 35MS
Born May 25, 1828 in Bibb Co., AL. Enl. June 1, 1861 at Columbus, MS. Corinth, Vicksburg (captured), Atlanta Campaign, Franklin, Nashville (captured) Released from Camp Douglas June 20, 1865. Married Lucy Kyle. To TN 1908. Died in Chattanooga March 24, 1916 and buried Forest Hills Cemetery. [FHR; NBFM2; TP 14,206; CT March 25, 1916]

# Z

ZORN, William G.        Co. K, 5GA; Co. B, 2GA Sharpshooters
Born April 3, 1842 in Upton Co., GA. Enl. April 11, 1861 Thomaston, GA. Served at Pensacola and

under E. Kirby Smith at fight at Cumberland Gap. Captured at Bardstown, KY, imprisoned at Louisville, but exchanged and fought in battles of Murfreesboro, Chickamauga, Atlanta. Wounded at Marietta and disabled for field service. Switched to Commissary Dept. and assigned to govt. bakery where he had his left hand crushed between two rollers of dough maker. Paroled at Macon in June 1865 and came to Chattanooga the following month. Carpenter in Chattanooga, 1889; wife (1) Hammia (2) Martha J.; res. in Hill City, 1912. Died Feb. 28, 1918 and buried White Oak Cem. [NBFM2,7; TP10,174; 1910HC; CTMarch 1, 1918]

\*\*\*\*\*\*\*\*\*\*\*\*\*\*\*\*\*\*\*\*\*\*

\*\*\*\*\*\*\*\*\*\*\*\*\*\*\*\*\*\*\*\*\*\*\*\*\*\*\*\*\*\*\*\*\*\*\*\*\*\*\*\*\*\*\*\*\*\*\*\*\*\*\*\*\*\*\*\*\*\*\*\*\*\*\*\*\*\*\*\*\*\*\*\*

ABERCROMBIE, A.    1st Co. H, 26TN;
            2d Co. I, 1CSA (GA)   Cpl.
    Enl. 8 July 1861, Knoxville. Transf. to 1CSA,
8 Nov. 1862. Deserted at Owen's Ford, GA, 16 Sept.
1863. Took USA oath at Nashville and released 17 Oct.
1863.

ACREE, Franklin   1st Co. H, 26TN;
            2d Co. I, 1CSA (GA)
    Enl. 1 July 1861, Knoxville. Transf. 8 Nov.
1862. Killed at Peachtree Creek, July 20, 1864.

ADAMS, J. W.    Co. K, 43TN
    Killed at Vicksburg, June 7, 1863.

ADAMS, Thomas   Co. L, 35TN
    Age 23 in 1862; enl. Dec. 11, 1862 at Tyner's.

ADAMS, William J.   Co. K, 43TN
    Enl. Feb. 1, 1862 at Ooltewah; killed at
Vicksburg, June 7, 1863.

AIKEN, John    Co. K, 43TN
    Enl. July 13, 1862 at Ooltewah; discharged
Nov. 1, 1862.

AIKEN, John W.    Co. H, 4TN Cav.
    Died in prison, 1864.

AIKEN, Thomas    Co. K, 43TN
    Enl. July 1, 1862 at Ooltewah; captured at
Vicksburg, July 4, 1863; died at Vicksburg July 11,
1863. [Lindsley, 528]

ALFORD, Wilburn
    Enl. 15 Dec. 1862 in Co. L, 36TN at
Chattanooga; transferred to Company L, 35th Tennessee
Infantry.

ALLEN, Thomas A.
    Wife was Sarah E. [TWP336]

ALLISON, James J.    Co. A, 4TN Cav. Bn.

ALLISON, J. M.

ALLRED, Henry   2d Co. I, 1CSA (GA)
    Enl. 1 Jan. 1864., Ft. Gaines. AWOL, 20 May
1864-30 June 1864; Deserted near Marietta, 1 July 1864.

ANDERSON, George    Co. L, 36TN
    Enl. Jan. 9, 1862 at Chattanooga

ANDERSON, George W. H.    Co. B, 1GA
    2Sgt, 3.18.61; Elected 2Lt. 9.30.61; Disch. by
expiration of term of service, 3.18.62.

ANDERSON, James Madison    4TN Cav.;
            Co. K, 43TN?
    He was the son of Josiah McN. and Nancy
Lamb Anderson. His first cousin of exactly the same
name served in the Federal army and was killed in the
battle of Pulaski. from Bledsoe County.

ANDERSON, Lt. Col. Josiah McNair
    Bn. 29 Nov. 1807 in Pikeville, TN; Killed 8
Nov. 1861 near Whitwell, TN; buried on his farm near
Dunlap, TN; wife-Nancy Lamb. [Biog. Dir. of Congress]

ANDERSON, Seymour
    Enrolling officer; captured; imprisoned Rock
Island.

ANDERSON, W. A.

ANDERSON, W. P.   Co. L, 35TN
    Age 18 in December, 1862; enl. at Jasper.

ANDERSON,, William    Clark's Indep. Cav. Co.
    Enl. 20 June 1863 at Allisonia. On rolls Apr.
1864.

ANDREWS, James   Co. F, 5TN Cav.(McKenzie's)
    Took the oath of allegiance and was released at
Nashville on January 7, 1864. He had fair complexion,
light hair, blue eyes and stood almost six feet tall.

ANDREWS, Samuel   Co. L, 36TN
    Enl. Jan. 9, 1862 at Chattanooga.

ANGLEY, J. A.    2d Co. K, 1st CSA Cav.
    Enl. Aug. 15, 1862 in Hamilton Co. "Deserted."

ANSLEY, F. J.   2d Co. I, 1CSA Inf.
    3d Cpl., July, 8 1861. Tranf. to 1CSA, Nov. 8,
1862; Aug. 31, 1864 roll shows him present.

ARNOLD, Francis Fieldon
    Blacksmith, Jackson's Cav. Co. Married
Almedia Fredora. TWP6421]

ASHLEY, William Clinton
    Married Louisa Evaline. [TWP5306]

ATKINS, Tom   Co. K, 3TN (Vaughan's)
    Capt. Vicksburg and paroled. "Absent without
leave," Sept. 1863.

AUSTIN, Joseph   Co. D, 37TN
    Enl. Sept. 1, 1861, Knoxville. Re-enlisted May
9, 1862. Deserted Sept. 7, 1863 at Ooltewah. Took USA
oath and paroled Mar. 27, 1864. Light complexion, light
hair, gray eyes, and was 5'11" tall.

\* \* \* \* \* \* \* \* \* \* \* \* \* \* \* \* \* \* \* \* \* \* \* \* \* \* \* \* \* \* \* \* \* \* \* \* \* \* \* \* \* \* \* \* \* \* \* \* \* \* \* \* \* \* \* \* \* \* \*

AUTRY, MARK L. Racoon Roughs, 6AL
Enl. May 11, 1861 at Clifton AL. Died July 17, 1861 in Charlottesville, VA of typhoid pneumonia.

AUTRY (Awtry, Aughtrey, Anthony), Raiford E.(Rayford, Ralph) Cpl. Age 19 in 1861, he enl. July 14, 1861 in Co. H, 26TN at Knoxville; Transferred to 2nd Co. I, 1 GA CSA Regulars, Nov. 8, 1862; Enl. July 7, 1862 in Barry's Btry; Deserted Sept. 2, 1864 near Atlanta [Brown Diary - captured Sept. 10, 1864 on retreat from Atlanta and enl. in US Army]; enl. March 24, 1865 in Co. E, 6th US Vol. Inf. at Camp Douglas, IL. Mustered out Oct. 10, 1866 as 1st Sgt.

AWLS, Bill Co. H, 4TN Cav.
Killed 1864.

### B

BABER, Leonard B. Co. G, 26TN; Barry's Btry.; 2d Co. K, 1CSA (GA)
Enl. July 8, 1861, Knoxville in 26TN; left sick at Cumberland City, TN, Feb. 12, 1862; transf. June 3, 1862 to Barry's Btry. Disch. Oct. 4, 1862 on account of expiration of term of service. Enl. Feb. 2, 1863, Ringgold. Captured July 22, 1864. and imp. Camp Chase. Exch. Feb. 65 and hosp. Jackson Hosp., Richmond.

BAKER, George Co. L, 36TN; Co. L, 35TN
Enl. Jan. 9, 1862 at Chattanooga; transf. 35TN.

BALDWIN, Chesley Co. A, 19TN
Enl. Aug. 23, 1861. Discharged because of disability but evidently re-enl. He was with the troops near Shelbyville in May 1863, wounded and captured at Chickamauga. [CSR]

BALDWIN, William H. Co. B, 1TN Cav. (Carter's)
Born c1824 and was pvt. in Mex. War. (1847) Living in Meigs Co., 1850. Enl. Aug. 7, 1861, Cleveland. Not in Meigs 1860 Census and no marriage record found for him there.

BALLARD, James. K. (R.)
Enl. Jan. 9, 1862 in Co. L, 36TN at Chattanooga; transferred to Co. L, 35th Tennessee Infantry; captured near Chattanooga, Sept. 11, 1863; took USA oath Sept. 21, 1863.

BALL, George D. Barry's Btry.
Enl. as substitute in Knoxville. Residence was Chattanooga; Paroled in Chattanooga May 6, 1865; 5 feet 9 inches tall, hazel eyes, and light hair.

BALLARD, 3Lt. William H. (K.)
Enl. Jan. 9, 1862 in Co. L, 36TN at Chattanooga; transf. to 35TN; captured near Chattanooga, Sept. 11, 1863; took USA oath Sept. 24, 1863.

BALLEW, Sgt. JOHN Co. H, 4TN Cav.;
2nd Co. K, 1st CSA Cav.
Enl. Aug. 11, 1861 in 5TN; Enl. again, Sept. 23, 1862, in Hamilton Co. in 1CSA Cav. Captured Nov. 30, 1863 at Ringgold, GA. Imprisoned at Rock Island, IL, where he died Feb. 23, 1864 and was buried. [CSR; RI Ledger]

BALLEW, John W. Co. G, 26TN
Enl. July 8, 1861 at Knoxville; captured at Fort Donelson, Feb. 16, 1862; imprisoned at Camp Chase, OH, where he died April 4, 1862.

BALLEW, Zebulon Co. H, 4TN Cav.

BANGER, Thomas H. Co. I, 19TN
Born c1841, DeKalb Co., AL. Enl. 5.20.61, Knoxville. Wounded at Shiloh, 4.7.62. Rec'd disability disch. at Chattanooga, Apr. 3, 1863.

BARBER, Jefferson Co. H, 4TN Cav.

BARLOW, John Co. H, 4TN Cav.
Killed Aug. 31, 1863

BARNES, Hiram Co. K, 43TN
Enl. Oct. 17, 1861 at Ooltewah, TN

BARNES, Joel 1st Co. H, 26TN; 2d Co. I, 1CSA (GA)
Enl. 8.6.61., Knoxville. Absent, left at Graysville, Oct. 5, 1862. Disch. term of service expired, Feb. 18, 1863.

BARNETT, James R. Co. K, 43TN
Born in Murray Co., GA, he was an 18 years old clerk when he enl., Oct. 17, 1861 at Ooltewah. Discharged Nov. 5, 1862; fair complexion, gray eyes, sandy hair, and 5'3" tall.

BASS (BOSS), H. J. Co. H, 26TN
Enl. July 8, 1861 at Knoxville; died in Nashville probably in December, 1861.

BASSHAM, Martin L. Co. L, 35TN
Born c1845. Enl. Jan. 7, 1862., Chattanooga. Wounded in leg at Murfreesboro, Dec. 31, 1862. At Tyner's Station with his unit, July 1863. Prom. 4th Cpl., Oct. 15, 1863. Captured near Atlanta, July 22, 1864 and imp. Camp Chase. Took USA oath and enl. Mar. 20, 1865, Chicago.

BATES, Miller McAfee

# APPENDIX 1
## INDIVIDUALS REMOVED FROM THE ROSTER

✳✳✳✳✳✳✳✳✳✳✳✳✳✳✳✳✳✳✳✳✳✳✳✳✳✳✳✳✳✳✳✳✳✳✳✳✳✳✳✳✳✳✳✳✳✳✳✳✳✳✳✳✳✳✳✳✳✳✳✳✳✳✳✳

Married Lucinda Alice. [TWP9506]

BAYLESS, 1Lt. B. J.    4TN Cav; 2TN Cav.
Buried Athens Cem.

BAYLISS (BALIS), R. B.    Co. K, 43TN
Enl. Dec. 11, 1862 at Ooltewah; captured at Vicksburg, July 4, 1863; died in hospital in Charlottesville, VA, Aug. 21, 1864 due to wound to right arm.

BEAN, Sgt. Jacob    Co. K, 43TN
Enl. Dec. 1, 1861 at Ooltewah.

BECK, L. M.    Co. L, 36TN; 35TN
Enl. Jan. 9, 1862, Chattanooga; transf. to 35TN; fought at Murfreesboro.

BELK, John W.    Co. A, 4TN Cav. Bn.

BELL, John W.    Co. K, 43TN

BELL, 3d Sgt. Pleasant M.    Co. B, 5TN Cav.
Enl. Aug. 11, 1861 and died in Knoxville a month later from disease contracted while on duty.

BENNETT, F. R. H.    Co. A, 2TN Cav.
Killed in action 11.11.1861

BENNETT, Henry L.    Clark's Independent Cav. Co.
Enl. Aug. 31, 1862, Chattanooga On rolls through Apr. 1864. Deserted Sept. 11, 1863. Took USA oath and "gone to work in Q M Dept. at Stevenson."

BENNETT, Jesse    Co. K, 43TN
Enl. Dec. 22, 1862 at Ooltewah; captured at Vicksburg, July 4, 1863.

BENNETT, (Dr.) John E.    Co. G, 26TN
Enl. July 8, 1861 at Knoxville; captured Feb. 16, 1862 at Fort Donelson; imprisoned at Camp Douglas (Chicago) where he became an hospital steward.

BENNETT, William S.    Co. G, 26TN
Enl. July 8, 1861 at Knoxville; captured; imp. Camp Douglas (Chicago) and exchanged; killed in action June 22, 1864.

BESHEARS (BESHERS), J. C. Co. C,
1st TN Cav. (Carter's)

BESHEARS, John    Co. A, 36TN

BESHEARS (BESHERS), Robert R. Co. L, 35TN
Age 15 in 1862; enl. Feb. 23, 1863 near Tullahoma, TN.

BETTIS, Daniel T.    Co. H, 1TN Cav. (Carter's);
Co. C, 39TN Mtd. Inf.

BETTIS, Duke K. Co. I, 39TN Mtd. Inf.

BIDDLE, A. M.    Co. A, 19TN
Died in Knoxville early in war. [Worsham, 198, 207.]

BIRD (BYRD), George    Chattanooga in Barry's Btry.
Enl. Apr. 4, 1862 at Chattanooga; Paroled May 11, 1865 in Meridian, MS.

BIRD (BEARD), Perry Co. I, 26TN
Enl. July 22, 1861, Roane Co. Captured Fort Donelson, Feb. 16, 1862; imp. Camp Morton, IN. Died April 2, 1862 of typhoid fever.

BISPLINGHOFF, Pvt. Herman
He was a bugler for William Ragsdale's Company A of the Fourth Tennessee Cavalry. Later, he transferred to Company H of the First Tennessee Cavalry before he was discharged on Sept. 17, 1862. He was a brother of Chattanoogan Henry Bisplinghoff and of Augustus Bisplinghoff, who also fought for the Confederacy.

BLACKABEE (BLACKERLY), ROBERT
Enl. July 14, 1862 in Hamilton Co. Captured Sept. 11, 1863 near Stevenson, AL. Took USA oath and enl. in 11th KY Cav. (USA).

BLACKBURN, Jesse    Co. A, 2TN Cav. (Ashby's)
Enl. Oct. 1, 1861 at Loudon, TN; captured July 30, 1863 at Big Hill, KY; imprisoned at Camp Chase, then Fort Delaware; died at Fort Donelson March 31, 1864; buried on New Jersey shore opposite prison.

BLACKBURN, Maj. J. H.            5TN Cav.

BLACKWELL, R.
1TN Cav; died in Knoxville 2.15.1862

BLAIR, George W.    Co. K, 43TN
Enl. Dec. 8, 1862 at Ooltewah; took USA oath June 20, 1864; light complexion, brown hair, blue eyes, and 5'10" tall; residence was Catoosa Co., GA.

BLAIR, "Hu" C.    Co. K, 43TN
Enl. Oct. 17, 1861 Ooltewah, TN; captured at Vicksburg, July 4, 1863.

BLAKELY, Alex M. Co. H, 4TN Cav.

BLAKELY, William    Co. H, 4TN Cav.

BLANKINSHIP, John Co. A, 2TN Cav. (Ashby's)

# INDIVIDUALS REMOVED FROM THE ROSTER

\*\*\*\*\*\*\*\*\*\*\*\*\*\*\*\*\*\*\*\*\*\*\*\*\*\*\*\*\*\*\*\*\*\*\*\*\*\*\*\*\*\*\*\*\*\*\*\*\*\*\*\*\*\*\*\*\*\*\*\*\*\*\*\*\*\*\*\*\*\*\*\*\*\*\*\*\*

Enl. Nov. 10, 1862 at Kingston, TN; captured Manchester, TN, June 27, 1863 and again at Big Hill, KY, July 30, 1863; imprisoned at Fort Delaware where he died of small pox May 8, 1864; buried on New Jersey shore opposite prison.

BLANSITT, G. H.    2TN Cav BN
        Wounded at Wallace's Cross Road, July 12, 1862.

BLAYLOCK, Samuel    Clark's Independent Cav. Co.
        Enl. Aug. 31, 1862 at Chattanooga; captured June 27, 1863 at Manchester, TN.

BOLEN, William  Co. K, 43TN
        Enl. Jan. 15, 1862 at Ooltewah, TN.

BOOKER, [not found]    Barry's Btry

BOOKOUT, Silas B.    Co. A, 19TN
        Enl. at Whitesville, Ga. He was hospitalized for chronic diarrhea in September, 1863 at Macon, Ga. until discharge in May, 1864. Mortally wounded in Battle of Atlanta, July 22, 1864. [CSR; Worsham, 129]

BOOKOUT, Wade    Barry's Btry.
        Enl. July 23, 1862 at Chattanooga. Hospitalized in Canton, MS Nov. 5, 1863; to hospital in Jackson, MS Feb. 16, 1864. He died there of chronic diarrhea on July 5, 1864.

BOOTHE, Joel A. (H.)    Barry's Btry.
        Enl. 7.14.62 at Chattanooga. Rec'd $50.00 bounty for enlistment; deserted. [Brown's diary]

BORDEN, Wheeler  Co. K, 43TN
        Died Dec. 3, 1861.

BOSSHAM, M. L.    Co. L, 36TN
        Enl. Jan. 9, 1862 at Chattanooga.

BOWEN, Marion
        Married Rachel L. [TWP3449]

BOWERS, Henry  Clark's Independent Cav. Co.
        Enl. May 3, 1862 at Richmond, VA; deserted Feb. 15, 1864 in East TN.

BOZEMAN, Crawford W.        Barry's Btry
        In Knoxville prior to war. Wounded at Jackson, MS; Captured at Spanish Fort. In Franklin Co., TN, 1870.

BROCK, Richard Emerson  1Sgt., Co. E, 42NC
        Married Mary Ann. [TWP6391]

BROWN, Leroy  Co. A, 4TN Cav. Bn.

BRYAN, William Duncan
        Married Margaret Emma. [TWP10,987]

BRYANT, Samuel

BURKES, Capt. H. H.    Co. K, 4GA Cav

BURNETT, James  Co. H, 4TN Cav.
        Killed near Cedar Town, GA, 1864.

BURTON, Christopher  Co. G, 26TN
        Died at Camp Morton, IN, June 23, 1863.

## C

CAMPBELL, George W.

CANTRELL, Rufus  Co. H, 4TN Cav.

CARRUTH, William H.    Co. E, 7TN Cav.
        Wife was Elizabeth Victoria. [TWP8655]

CARTER, Sgt. Chesley C.    Co. F, 3TN (Vaughan's);
        Co. B, 59MS.

CARTER, Henegar C.  Co. H, 4TN Cav.

CARTER, John        Co. D, 4th (12th) Georgia Cav.
        Enl. Oct. 4, 1862.

CARTER, Todd
        Killed at Franklin

CARTER, William  Co. H, 4TN Cav.

CARVILE, William Z.    Co. H, 1TN Cav. (Carter's);
        Co. G, Walker's Bn., Thomas Legion
        Born c1832 in Jefferson Co., TN. Enl. Sept. 24, 1862; hospitalized Petersburg May 30-June 23, 1863 with debilitas (paroled prisoner).

CAUTHON, William A.
        Wife was Emily Margaret. [TWP9773]

CENTER, J. S. W.  Co. I, 26TN
        Died Camp Morton, IN, Aug. 30, 1863

CENTER, John    Co. A, 4TN Cav.

CENTERS, Morgan  Co. A, 19TN
        Died Camp Morton, IN, June 9, 1865

CHILCUT, J. A.  Co. L, 36TN
        Enl. Jan. 9, 1862 at Chattanooga.

# APPENDIX 1
## INDIVIDUALS REMOVED FROM THE ROSTER

\*\*\*\*\*\*\*\*\*\*\*\*\*\*\*\*\*\*\*\*\*\*\*\*\*\*\*\*\*\*\*\*\*\*\*\*\*\*\*\*\*\*\*\*\*\*\*\*\*\*\*\*\*\*\*\*\*\*\*\*\*\*\*

CHILDRESS, P. F.   Co. H, 26TN
Enl. July 8, 1861, Knoxville. Sent home sick, Aug. 1861.

CHILDRESS, R. A.   Co. H, 26TN
Enl. Aug. 6, 1861, Knoxville. Honorably disch. Dec. 6, 1861

CHILDRESS, Thomas A.   Co. A, 19TN
Enl. May 20, 1861, Knoxville. Deserted near Chattanooga Sept. 1863 and sent to Louisville.

CHISHOLM,
Barry's Btry. - Brown Diary. [perhaps J. C. Chisum of Polk's Btry., TN Lt. Arty.,

CLAMPETT, George W.
Wife was Martha J. [TWP3655]

COGHORN, GEORGE A.   Co. H, 37TN
He died Jan. 24, 1862.

COLLUM, John Basil
Wife was Frances Malinda. [TWP9548]

COOK, William A.   Co. A, 19TN
Died at Camp Morton, IN, Jan. 26, 1865

COUCH, George Washington
Wife was Nancy Ann [TWP9941]

COULTER, R. W.

COZBY, Lt. W. M.   4TN Cav.

CRAWFORD, William Henry
Wife was Julia F. [TWP3929]

CRETSINGER, Jacob R.   Co. G, 26TN
Died at Camp Morton Feb. 1, 1865.

CREW, Joseph   Co. A, 4TN Cav.

CREW, Lambert J.   Co. A, 4TN Cav.

CREWE, Ben S.   4TN Cav

CROCKETT, Edward R.   Co. A, 20TN

CULPEPPER, D. H.
Killed on picket duty, Jan. 1862.

CUTTEN, Peter E.
Wife was Sophrania. [TWP4749]

## D

DAFFRON (DAFRON, DOFRON), Capt.   Co. L, 35TN
Enl. Jan. 9, 1862 at Chattanooga.

DAFFRON (DAFRON, DOFRON), Joel   Co. G, 26TN
Enl. July 8, 1861 at Knoxville; died in hospital at Bowling Green, KY, Nov. 15, 1861.

DAFFRON (DAFRON, DOFRON), Rice   Co. L, 35TN
Enl. Sept. 23, 1862 at Jasper, TN; fought at Murfreesboro.

DAFFRON (DAFRON, DOFRON), William
Co. L, 35TN  Capt.
Enl. Jan. 9, 1862 at Chattanooga.

DAVENPORT, Luke Levander   Co. D, 37TN
Wife was Syrena Elizabeth. [TWP 6981]

DAVIS, William Galius
Wife was Anna Washington. [TWP5070]

DAY, Lt. Addison C.   Regimental Quarter Master, 43TN
Merchant at Sulphur Springs when he enl. Oct. 16, 1861 at Sulphur Springs (Rhea Springs), TN; captured at Vicksburg, July 4, 1863; killed by Lt. Hopkins, near Lexington, VA Oct. 6, 1864 caused by personal difficulty.

DEAKIN, Samuel B.   47TN

DEAN, George R.   19TN

DENNISON, Peter

DREWETT, James   2nd Co. K, 1st CSA Cav.
Enl. Oct. 22, 1863 in Walker Co., GA.

DUNN, Lt. Col. John N.   Co. D, 36TN
Company commander who was elected Lt. Col. of the regiment in June, 1862, but was never commissioned as such.

DYKE, James D. (L.)   Co. B, 1TN Cav. (Carter's)
Enl. Aug. 7, 1861, Cleveland. Not found in 1860 HC.

## E

EDGEMOND, John   Co. G, 26TN, 2d Co. K, 1CSA (GA)
Enl. July 8, 1861 in Knoxville. Detached to Miners and Sappers as teamster, Dec. 31, 1862.

EDMONDSON, James Henry   Barry's Btry.
Enl. Aug. 25, 1862 at Knox. as substitute; paroled

\*\*\*\*\*\*\*\*\*\*\*\*\*\*\*\*\*\*\*\*\*\*\*\*\*\*\*\*\*\*\*\*\*\*\*\*\*\*\*\*\*\*\*\*\*\*\*\*\*\*\*\*\*\*\*\*\*\*\*\*\*\*

May 11, 1865 at Meridian, MS; Res. Pauling Co., GA.

EDWARDS, Cpl. Willis M.    Co. A, 4TN Cav.

ELISON, R. C.          Co. G, 26TN
        Died at Camp Morton, March 8, 1862.

EPPERSON, James B.   Co. A, 2TN Cav. Bn.
        Res. Bradley Co., 1922.


### F


FALLEN (FALLENT), James

FELTON, John          Co. G, 26TN
        Died at Camp Morton, Feb. 14, 1863.

FISHER, Herman

FISHER, Watson

FORTENBURY, Erastus        Co. A, 4TN Cav.

FRANKLIN, James S.
        Married Martha Rebecca. [TWP10731]

FRAZIER, Nicholas Pope   Co. D, 19TN
        Enl. Oct. 1, 1862, Knoxville. Captured near
Nashville, Dec. 4, 1864 and imp. Camp Douglas, Camp
Chase and Point Lookout. [NBFM3]

FRICKS, Napolian
        Married Elizabeth C. [TWP6575]

FURRY, Thomas     Co. A, 4TN Cav. Bn. (Branner's)


### G


GAD, Andrew          Co. G, 37TN

GADD, Daniel C.       Co. G, 37TN

GADD, J. D.          Co. G, 37TN

GIBSON, James        Co. C, 4TN Cav. Bn.
        Died Oct. 7, 1861.

GILLIAM, Jacob        Co. H, 4TN Cav.
        Died during war.

GILLUM, John J.       Co. H, 4TN Cav.

GLASS, Cpl. Thomas C.   Co. A, 4TN Cav.

GODBY, G. P.     Co. A, 19TN.
        Enl. May 20, 1861, Knoxville. Prom. Sgt. Killed
at Shiloh, Apr. 6, 1862.

GORDAN, Cicero Newton
        Married Mary L. [TWP3425]

GORDON, Cicero N.   Co. H, 26TN; 1CSA (GA)
        Born in Gwinett Co. GA. Enl. July 8, 1861,
Knoxville. Captured Fort Donelson and imp. Camp
Douglas. He had fair complexion, blue eyes, light hair, and
was 5' 9 ½" tall. Disch. Dec. 21, 1862, Choctaw Point,
disability--broken and stiff arm.

GORDON, F. M.     Clark's Independent Cav. Co.   1Lt.
        Enl. Aug. 27, 1861 at Chattanooga.

GORDON, 1Lt. W. L. (H.?)   Co. H, 26TN
        Born in 1830, he enl. July 8, 1861 at Knoxville;
captured at Fort Donelson, Feb. 16, 1862, he was
imprisoned at Johnson's Island until exchanged Nov. 8,
1862; had blue eyes, light hair, and was 5'8" tall.

GORMAN, Peter

GRAHAM, M. V.   Co. L, 36TN
        Enl. Jan. 9, 1862 at Chattanooga; at battle of
Murfreesboro; absent without leave, he was captured by the
enemy and paroled Aug. 7, 1863.

GRANT, Wiley      Co. H, 26TN; 2d Co. I, 1CSA (GA)
        Enl. July 8, 1861 at Knoxville; captured at Fort
Donelson, Feb. 16, 1861 and imprisoned at Camp Douglas.
Present Aug. 31, 1863.

GRAY, William
        Married Frances Josephine. [TWP9791]

GREATHOUSE, H. P.       Clark's Independent Cav. Co.
        Enl. Aug. 27, 1861 at Ellis Co., TX.

GREEN, Henry R.  Co. D, 23TN
        Born Dec. 11, 1836 in Bedford Co. and returned
to Bell Buckle after the war. Although listed as from HC,
it more likely that he remained in Bedford. [TP4687]

GREENLEE, James Augustus
        Married Mary Rebecca. [TWP7911]

GRINDLES, William
        Married Sarah Ann. [TWP4500]


### H


HALLETT, Henry

# APPENDIX 1
## INDIVIDUALS REMOVED FROM THE ROSTER

\*\*\*\*\*\*\*\*\*\*\*\*\*\*\*\*\*\*\*\*\*\*\*\*\*\*\*\*\*\*\*\*\*\*\*\*\*\*\*\*\*\*\*\*\*\*\*\*\*\*\*\*\*\*\*\*\*\*\*\*\*\*\*

Died Feb. 25, 1914 at home in Soddy and buried at the Presbyterian Church in Soddy. [CT Feb. 26, 1914]

HANKS, David          Co. A, 4TN Cav.

HARBISON, J. H. H.          Co. C, 4TN Cav. BN
  Died Oct. 8, 1861.

HARNER, D. W.          Co. A, 1TN Cav. (Carter's)
          Enl. April 15, 1862 at Sulphur Springs, TN; farrier; died Aug. 15, 1862 Rhea Springs, Rhea Co., TN.

HARRIS, Tazewell Polk
          Married Lucy Ann. [TWP 5210

HARRISON, J. N.          Co. G, 26TN
          Enl. July 8, 1861, Knoxville. Left Fort Donelson, Feb. 14, 1862.

HATCH, Lemuel Durant
          Married Willie Adams. [TWP 9538]

HAVRON, 2d Lt. Henry H. [AKA Hodges H.]
          Co. H, 4TN Cav.
          Enl. Aug. 11, 1861 at Chattanooga. Wounded at Chickamauga. Married Rebecca Y. [TWP 3123]

HELMS, Eli - foreman of a cattle drive, Commissary Dept.
          Born Knox Co., Jan. 5, 1820. Enl. 1862. [TP2840] CSA pension application rejected. 1900 res. Cleveland, TN. [TP2840]

HENDERSON, JAMES B.          Co. I, 43TN

HENRY, William Frank
          Married Ophelia. [TWP 11,130]

HICKS, C. W.          Co. C, 4TN Cav.
          Died at Mill Springs, KY, Dec. 23, 1861.

HIGHT, Capt. Frank M.          4TN Cav.

HOLLAND, James          Co. A, 4TN Cav.

HORN, John
          Married Lucy Ann. [TWP 2591]

HOWARD, Joseph          Co. A, 4TN Cav.
          He died in the first year of the war.

HOWELL, John Edward
          Married Sophia Head. [TWP 10,409]

HUFFMASTER, John

HUMBLES, Joseph H.          Co. D, 37TN

HYEMAN, Solomon
          Married Elizabeth Pauline. [TWP 7060]

## J

JACQUET, Father John Chaplain

JENKINS, Capt. LaFayette          LaFayette Scouts

JOHNSON, J. W.          Co. B, 5TN Cav.
          Enl. Aug. 11, 1861.

JOHNSON, Russell C.          Co. C, 4TN Cav.
          Killed at Fincastle, April, 1862.

JONES, Robert

JOURDAN, A. S.          Co. A, 4TN Cav.

## K

KELLEY, Calven
          Married Cordelia A. [TWP 2476]

KING, S. S.

KIRKES, James Washington
          Married Temperance. [TWP 9987]

KIRKLIN, Ephraim W.          Co. M, 4TN Cav.

KIRKLIN, John          Co. H, 4TN Cav.

KIRKPATRICK, David C.
          Quartermaster Department.

## L

LADD, William          Co. H, 4TN Cav.

LAIRD, John W.          Co. A, 4TN Cav. Bn.

LARIMORE, James W.          Co. H, 4TN Cav.

LARIMORE, Theophilis B.          Co. H, 4TN Cav.

LAY, Samson T.          Co. C, 4TN Cav.
          Died Nov. 8, 1861.

LEAHEY, Jeremiah

## APPENDIX 1
## INDIVIDUALS REMOVED FROM THE ROSTER
197

\*\*\*\*\*\*\*\*\*\*\*\*\*\*\*\*\*\*\*\*\*\*\*\*\*\*\*\*\*\*\*\*\*\*\*\*\*\*\*\*\*\*\*\*\*\*\*\*\*\*\*\*\*\*\*\*\*\*\*\*\*\*\*\*\*\*\*\*\*\*\*

Married Licena Carolina [TWP 10,645]

LEVISKERY, Lt. Samuel        Co. G, 47TN

LOADEN, Joseph A.        Co. A, 4TN Cav.

LOCKHART, Andrew J.        Co. H, 4TN Cav.

LOCKHART, George W.        Co. H, 4TN Cav.

LOVE, WILEY B.
        Married Sarah L. [TWP 7546]


### M

MARCUM, Lewis        Co. A, 4TN Cav.

MAYHEW, J. Mike        Co. H, 4TN Cav.

MAYHEW, John        Co. H, 4TN Cav.

MAYHEW, William        Co. H, 4TN Cav.

MILLSAPS, John   Co. G, 26TN; 2d Co. K, 1CSA (GA)
        Enl. July 8, 1861, Knoxville. Sick in hosp.,
Bowling Green, JAN. 1862. Captured Fort Donelson, Feb.
16, 1862 and imprisoned Camp Morton, IN. Deserted Dec.
25, 1863. Res: Walker Co., GA.

MONTGOMERY, Lt. W. S.        Co. B, 1TN Cav.

MORRIS, J. M.   Co. B, 5TN Cav.
        Enl. Aug. 11, 1861.

MORRIS, James M.        Co. H, 4TN Cav.

MORTON, Emsley   Co. B, 1TN Cav. (Carter's)
        Enl. Aug. 7, 1861 at Cleveland.

MURRAY, John        Co. H, 4TN Cav.

MUSGRAVE, Sgt. JAMES W.        Co. B, 1st TN and AL
Cav.
        He was 34 years old. On detached service at
Shellmound per order of Col. Fox.

MUSGROVE, Mathew   Co. L, 35TN
        Enl. March 1, 1863 at Tullahoma. "Wounded at
Battle of Chickamauga and is at home."

MYNATT, P. L.        Co. B, 1TN Cav, (Carter's)
        Regt. Commissary officer.

MYRES, John   Co. L, 36TN
        Enl. Jan. 9, 1862 at Chattanooga.


### Mc

McABEE, A. M.   Co. D, 37TN
        Enl. Jan. 28, 1863 at Chatanooga.; conscript; died
Jan. 29, 1863 at Catoosa Springs.

McABEE, 1st Sgt. George Washington        Co. D, 37TN
        Born c1841. Enl. Sept. 1, 1861 at Knoxville.

McABEE, Hampton H.   Co. D, 37TN
        Born c1837. Enl. Sept. 1, 1861, Knoxville. Prom.
to Sgt.

McBRYER, David        Co. H, 4TN Cav.

McBRYER, Green        Co. H, 4TN Cav.

McCALL, Daniel "Dan"        Co. H, 4TN Cav.

McCALL, John        Co. H, 4TN Cav.
        Wounded at Morrison Station, Aug. 16.1862

McCALLISTER, Alfred A.        Co. H, 4TN Cav.

McCARMACK, Owen        Co. H, 4TN Cav.

McCORCLE, R. P.

McKEEHAN, C. H.   Co. B, 1TN Cav. (Carter's)
        Enl. Aug. 7, 1861 at Cleveland. Bugler.

McLIN, Col. John B.        5TN Cav.

McREE, Brooks

McREE, J. M.   Co. I, 35TN


### N

NASH, James P.   4GA Cav.

NELSON, J. N.   Co. G, 26TN
        Enl. July 61., Knoxville. Left sick in hosp.,
Bowling Green, Jan. 23, 1862.

NEWELL, D. B.

NEWTON, Isaac   Co. D, 37TN
        Born 1842. Enl. Sept. 1, 1861 at Knoxville; Died
June 21, 1862, in Goodwin, MS.

NICHOLS, Capt. Isaac   Co. H, 37TN

198

# APPENDIX 1
## INDIVIDUALS REMOVED FROM THE ROSTER

\*\*\*\*\*\*\*\*\*\*\*\*\*\*\*\*\*\*\*\*\*\*\*\*\*\*\*\*\*\*\*\*\*\*\*\*\*\*\*\*\*\*\*\*\*\*\*\*\*\*\*\*\*\*\*\*\*\*\*\*\*\*\*\*

NOREL, John
    Married Malinda

NORTON, Emsley    Co. B, 1TN Cav.
    Not found in 1860 HC]

### O

O'BRYAN, Peter    Co. H, 2TN Cav.
    Enl. July 8, 1861, Knoxville.

OLIVER, Richard    Co. H, 4TN Cav.

OLIVER, Capt. Samuel    Co. B, Carter's BN

ORR, Arthur

### P

PARKER, QM Sgt. John H.    Barry's Btry.
    Born 4 June 1845 in Cleveland, TN, where he lived before the war. Enl. at Knoxville; served as gunner and afterwards as Sgt. Spanish Fort. Paroled 12 May 1865 at Meridian, MS. Died in Chattanooga in 1895. [NBFM2]

PATTERSON, Edward M. Co. K, 41TN

PATTERSON, William A.    Co. B, 1TN Cav.
    Died Fincastle, TN, March 26.1862.

PAULI, John Co. F, 35TN
    Enl. Oct. 6, 1862 at Chattanooga; died Aug. 27, 1863 at Law Hospital, Dalton, GA.

PETTIGREW, Jasper N.    Co. H, 4TN Cav.

PHELPS, Martin    Co. H, 4TN Cav

PHELPS, Robert    Co. H, 4TN Cav
    Married Elizabeth.

PHELPS, William    Co. H, 4TN Cav

PHILLIPS, Pvt. F. B. (B. F.?)
    Age 22 in 1861, he enlisted July 8, 1861 in Co. H, 26th Tennessee Infantry at Knoxville; captured at Fort Donelson, Feb. 16, 1862, he died in prison at Camp Douglas, May 21, 1862. [A Frank D. Phillips was vet from Harriman, TN who died Dec. 6, 1911. [CT 12.7.11]

PICKARD, John L.    Co. I, 24TN

PICKETT, John    Co. H, 4TN Cav.

PINNEY, George W.    Co. D, 37TN
    Died Nov. 27, 1861.

POOLE, Francis M.    Co. H, 37TN
    Died Oct. 27, 1862.

PUCKETT, W. B.    4TN Cav.

PUCKET, W. R.    Co. L, 36TN
    Enl. Jan. 9, 1862 at Chattanooga.

PUGH, L. J. [L.S.] Co. G, 26TN
    Enl. July 8, 1861, Knoxville. Captured Fort Donelson, Feb. 16, 1862. and imp. Camp Morton.

PURDY, James (Jesse) G.    Co. B, 1TN Cav. (Carter's)
    Enl. Feb. 23, 1863 at Athens. Captured Vicksburg. Exchanged and recaptured Sullivan Co., TN, Dec. 14, 1864. Imp. Camp Chase. Exchanged and hospitalized in Richmond at close of war.

### R

RAMSEY, W. A.    Co. A, 4TN Cav.

RANKIN, Bynum    Co. H, 4TN Cav.

RANKIN, John Co. L, 35TN
    Enl. Oct. 13, 1863 in Chatt.

RANKIN, Orderly Sgt. (2Lt.) William  Co. L, 36TN;
      Co. L 35TN
    Enl. Jan. 9, 1862, at Chattanooga; transferred to 35TN; paroled May 9, 1865 at Calhoun, GA.

RAPE, T. A. Co. G, 26TN; 1CSA
    Enl. July 8, 1861, Knoxville. Captured Fort Donelson, Feb. 16, 1862; imp. Camp Morton.

RAPER, J. P. Co. B, 1TN Cav. (Carter's)
    Enl. Aug. 7, 1861, Cleveland.

RAPER, William    Co. H, 4TN Cav.

RAWLINGS, W. P. Co. D, 37TN
    Born 1818. Enl. Sept. 1, 1861., Knoxville. Disch. Oct. 1, 1861, disability.

RAY, F. M.
    Enl. Jan. 9, 1862 in Co. L, 35TN; transf. to Tatnall's Btry.

RAY, James    Co. B, 1TN Cav. (Carter's)
    Enl. Aug. 7, 1861 at Cleveland.

# APPENDIX 1
## INDIVIDUALS REMOVED FROM THE ROSTER

\*\*\*\*\*\*\*\*\*\*\*\*\*\*\*\*\*\*\*\*\*\*\*\*\*\*\*\*\*\*\*\*\*\*\*\*\*\*\*\*\*\*\*\*\*\*\*\*\*\*\*\*\*\*\*\*\*\*\*\*\*

RAY, Robert  Clark's Independent Cav. Co.
Enl. Aug. 31, 1862 at Chatt.

RHODES, Clark    Co. A, 4TN Cav.

RIDDLE, Pleasant  Co. B, 5TN Cav.

ROACH, S. M.  Co. G, 26TN; 2d Co. K, 1CSA
Enl. July 12, 1861, Knoxville. Left sick at Russellville, KY, Feb. 9, 1862.

ROBERTS, David    Co. B, 1TN Cav.
Killed at Cumberland Mountain, KY, 1864.

ROBERTS, Hiram D.  Co. B, 1TN Cav. (Carter's)
Enl. Aug. 7, 1861 at Cleveland. Died Dec. 31, 1861.

ROBERTS, J. M.  Co. G, 26TN; 1CSA
Born c1836, DeKalb Co., AL; Enl. July 8, 1861, Knoxville. Sick at Bowling Green, Jan. 23, 1862. He was 5'10 1/2 ", gray eyes, black hair, and light complexion

ROBERTS, Perry    Co. A, 5TN Cav.

ROBINS, Francis    Co. L, 36TN
Enl. Jan. 9, 1862 at Chattanooga.

ROGERS, Arthur C.    Co. A, 4TN Cav.

ROGERS, Bartholomew    Co. F, 1AR

ROSS, Thomas   26TN
Captured; in prison at Indianapolis, IN.

### S

SCHMIDT, George - Co. G, 26TN; 2d Co. K, 1CSA (GA)
Enl. July 8, 1861 in Knoxville. Promoted Cpl. May 20, 1863. Killed at Franklin, Nov. 30, 1864. Buried at McGavock Cem.

SEAY, James M. Cpl. Co. A, 19TN

SHADOWIN, Jim    Co. H, 4TN Cav.

SHADOWICK, Peter  Co. A, 2TN Cav. Bn.; Co. A, 5TN Cav. Bn.

SHADWICK, Harvey  B&H Co., 26TN

SHARP, Lewis

SHAW, Charles    Co. I, 19TN

He marched to Cumberland Gap, Va., after enlisting at Knoxville in Aug., 1861. He died the following July at Vicksburg. [Worsham, 201]

SHELL, Tate
Lost his leg in battle

SHELL, William    Co. H, 4TN Cav.
Killed at Mill Springs, KY

SHUFORD, John E.
Married Jessie A.

SHUMATE, Robert  Co. H, 4TN Cav.
Wounded at Perryville

SIMS, Dr. Philander Davis
Born Oct. 22, 1828 in Cookeville, TN, son of Martin Sims. Attended Alpine Instit. where he graduated. Studied medicine at Univ. of Nashville. To Chattanooga 1856. Married (1857) Mary F. Randall. Contract surgeon during occupation of Chatt. He "ministered faithfully and tenderly to many a disabled hero." He tended soldiers who were brought into Chattanooga after Fort Donelson, Murfreesboro and the fighting around Chattanooga. Pres. TN Medical Soc. Mayor of Chattanooga, 1873. Directed efforts during Yellow Fever epidemic. Died Nov. 8, 1920 and buried FH. [CT Jan. 13, 1908; Nov. 9, 1920]

SMALLEY, Joshua    Co. H, 4TN Cav.

SMITH, David Walter  Co. D, 1TN Cav. (Carter's)
Married Lucy Jane. [TWP9346]

SMITH, Frank W.    Osborne's Scouts

SMITH, J. N.    Co. B, 1TN Cav. (Carter's)

SMITH, James Augustine    4TN Cav.

SMITH, John J.    Co. B, 1TN Cav. (Carter's).

SMITH, L. M.  Co. H, 26TN
Died Nashville June 3, 1863[?]

SMITH, Peyton [name crossed through on Z's list]

SMITH, Richard Smith    Co. A, 4TN Cav.

SMITH, William  Co. B, 5TN Cav.
Enl. Aug. 11, 1861.

SMITH, Zach    Co. A, 19TN
Teamster. Missing 6 months without leave, 1865 in Pettigrew General Hospital at Raleigh, NC [residence seems to have been in Estill Springs in Franklin County.]

SOULE, Rufus   Co. A, 4TN Cav.
Died in 1862.

SPRAY, JAMES M.
Died June 15, 1863 (Lindsley)

STEPHENS, J. D.  Co. D, 37TN
Enl. Sept. 1, 1861, Knoxville. Hospitalized Catoosa Springs, GA, April 1, 1863. Deserted from camp near Dalton, Dec. 17, 1863

STUBBS, John Benton
Married Carrie Josephine. [TWP10824]

SULLIVAN, J. M.  Co. D, 37TN
Enl., Sept. 1, 1861, Knoxville.

SUMMER, R. E.  2Lt., Clark's Independent Cav. Co.

SUMPTER, R. B.  Co. H, 2TN Cav.(Ashby's)
Enl. Aug. 8, 1861., Knoxville. AOL Aug. 1, 1862.

SUTTON, Houston   Co. H, 2TN Cav. (Ashby's)
Died in Carthage, TN, 1862.

SWENEY, Bryant  Co. I, 35TN

SWINNEY, Richard H.   Co. F, 35TN; 32TN

SWOPE, David
(1860 census lists a David Swoop with wife, Margaret, at Chattanooga. He was a blacksmith born about 1837)

**T**

TACETT, Alex   Co. H, 4TN Cav.
Died in prison, 1864.

TANNER, B. M.   Phillips GA Cav.

TEAGUE, William C.   Co. A, 4TN Cav.

TEFERTOLER, J.W.   Co. B, 1TN Cav. (Carter's)
He was ill at Bristol in June of 1864.

THOMAS, W. G.

THOMPSON, A. C.  Co. D, 37TN
Enl. Sept. 1, 1861, Knoxville. Sick. Captured Bardtown, KY and paroled.

THOMPSON, Benjamin D.   Co. H, 2TN Cav. (Ashby's)
Enl. June 17, 1861, Knoxville. Detached as asst. purchasing agent, Nov. 20, 1861. In Way Hosp., Meridian,

MS, March 9, 1865.

THOMPSON, J. Matt.   Co. H, 4TN Cav.

THURMAN, John J. L.   Co. D, 37TN
Enl. Sept. 1, 1861 at Knoxville; April 1, 1862 detached to artillery service.

TIBBS, John W.  Co. B, 1TN Cav. (Carter's).
Enl. Aug. 7, 1861. at Cleveland.

TIBBS, William Henry   Member of CSA Congress
Member NBF Camp, 1895.

TOLLEY, Capt. William Polk
A citizen of Lynchburg, Lincoln Co., TN, he enlisted early in 1861 in 1TN and was elected captain. He participated in the early battles in VA from First Manassas to Gaines' Mill where he was so severely wounded in the arm and thigh that he never served in the field again. He married Fredonia Whittaker. [obit: his son Wm M. was important in Chatt., but William Polk may have remained in Lynchburg, Lincoln Co., TN.]  Check NBFM2

TOMBERLIN, James W.   Co. F, 35TN

TUCKER, J. C.

TUCKER, John Samuel
Married Annie. [TWP5777]

TURLEY, 1Lt. John Atlas   C Co., 1TN Cav. (Carter's)
Married Mary Ann. [TWP3842]

**W**

WALLACE, Benjamin

WAMPLER, J. B.
Married Ellen Cecil. [TWP#9064]

WARD, J. H.  Co. B, 1TN Cav. (Carter's)
Killed accidentally during war

WATKINS, Carlow   Co. K, 1TN Cav.
Killed at Murfeesboro, Dec. 31.1862

WATTS, Samuel  Co. A, 19TN
Died in Knoxville during war

WATTS, William J.
Married Anna Harley [TP#7378]

WEATHERS, John H.  Co. H, 26TN
Enl. Sept. June 1861 at Knoxville; Died Nov. 13,

\* \* \* \* \* \* \* \* \* \* \* \* \* \* \* \* \* \* \* \* \* \* \* \* \* \* \* \* \* \* \* \* \* \* \* \* \* \* \* \* \* \* \* \* \* \* \* \* \* \* \* \* \* \* \* \* \* \* \* \* \* \* \* \* \* \*

1861 at Bowling Green, KY.

WELCKER, Judge Albert Gallatin
        z: has him as member of CSA congress, but this is
incorrect.                    [Sketch in z.]

WHEELER, Lt. Henry       Co. A, 5TN Cav.

WHEELER, William Henry
        Married Matilda Catherine [TP#7479]

WHITE, Alfred

WHITE, Martin M.     Co. H, 4TN Cav.
        Dangerously wounded in battle four times.

WHITTLE, William W.   Co. H, 4TN Cav.

WILSON, John Holmes
        Married Louisa Ann [TP#7132, 5240]

WINDER, James B.       Co. H, 4TN Cav.
        Died 1862

WINDER, John    Co. H, 4TN Cav.
        Died Gainsborro, TN, 1862 or 1863.

WOODS, William I.
        Married Louisa Jane [TP#9263]

WORTHINGTON, William
        Married Margaret [TP#2478]


## Y


YOUNG, William   Co. A, 4TN Cav.
        Died May 22, 186- in Coffee County.

YOUNT, James R.    Co. H, 26TN
        Enl. July 8, 1861 at Knoxville. Killed in battle of
Fort Donelson, Feb. 15, 1862; wife was Mary A.

## 1. CAVALRY

Osborne's-Jenkins Scouts
[Capt. Lafayette Jenkins

Snow's Scouts
Capt. Wm. Snow cmdg Co. C, Lt. Col. Wm Brazelton, Jr.'s TN
Cav. Bn, mostly from Hamilton.

Carter's Battalion Mounted Scouts, Company B
[prob. Capt. George W. Carter who cmdg co of cav in 4Tn Cav (Murray's)

J. W. Clark's Independent Cav. Co.
Served as escort for Buckner and Hardee till Miss. Ridge, then as
escort to Gen. Bradley T. Johnson and later Buckner again.

Co. B, 1TN Cav. (James E. Carter's) - Co. C, Wm. Brazelton, Jr.'s
TN Cav. Bn.
Co. H, 2TN Cav. - Co. A ("Lookout Rangers'),
Benj. M. Branner's TN Cav. Bn.

Co. H, 8TN Cav. (Baxter Smith's)

Cav.Co. B. (C.C. Spiller's),
McClellan's TN Cav. Bn.

Co. A, 5TN Cav. - Co. F, "Bird Rangers,"
Roger's East TN Cav.

2d Co. A, 13TN Cav. Bn. (Dibbrell's)
Co. A, 4TN Cav. (Murray's)

Co. I, 5TN Cav.[Capt. Wm. W. Lillard]

Co. K, 1CSA Cav.

Companies B and K, 4GA Cav. (Avery's)

## 2. ARTILLERY

Barry's Battery

## 3. INFANTRY

Companies A and I, 19TN

Companies G and H, 26 TN  which became
2nd Co. K and 2nd Co. I, 1CSA

Companies 3d F, 1st I, 1st K, 35TN (B. J. Hill's)

Companies H and K, 36TN - Co. L, 35TN

Companies D and H, 37TN

Co. K, 43TN

## 4. OTHER

Hamilton County Home Guards

Chattanooga Home Guards

enrollment officers, Tax collectors, doctors, railroad men,
women (Ella Palmer -hospital, mining out West), civilians
helping with commissary, boats

**BIBLIOGRAPHY**

\*\*\*\*\*\*\*\*\*\*\*\*\*\*\*\*\*\*\*\*\*\*\*\*\*\*\*\*\*\*\*\*\*\*\*\*\*\*\*\*\*\*\*\*\*\*\*\*\*\*\*\*\*\*\*\*\*\*\*\*\*\*\*\*\*\*

BIBLIOGRAPHY

PRIMARY SOURCES

Manuscripts

Atlanta, GA
    Atlanta History Center
        Franklin M. Garrett Necrology
    Georgia Department of Archives and History
        Confederate Tennessee Veterans Pension Applications

Chattanooga, TN
    Chattanooga-Hamilton County Bi-Centennial Library
        William C. Brown Diary [Barry's Btry]
        Josephine H. Hooke Diary, 1863-64
        Thomas H. McCallie Diary
        Minute Books, NBF Camp
        Register of Deaths, Hamilton County
        Rudd, Robin. "City's Rufus Tankesley Survived Civil
        War Hardship," unidentified, undated newspaper
            article.
        Milo W. Scott Diary [Barry's Btry]
        UCV applications, NBF Camp

    Forest Hills Cemetery
        Burial Records

    Hamilton County Chancery Court
        Memorial Resolutions by Chattanooga Bar Association

Fort Oglethorpe, Ga.
    Chickamauga and Chattanooga National Military Park
    Warner, J. H. "Personal Glimpses of the Civil War:
        Nineteenth Tennessee."

Nashville, Tenn.
    Tennessee State Library and Archives
        Cheairs Hughes Papers
        Civil War Collection
        Confederate Veterans Questionaires
    Confederate Tennessee Veterans Pension Applications
        Confederate Tennessee Veterans Widows Pension
        Applications
    Soldier's Applications for Admission to Confederate Home

Oklahoma City, Okla.
    Oklahoma Historical Society Archives
        Joe L. Todd. "Confederate Veterans in Oklahoma,
        1912."

Rock Island, Ill.
    Ledger of Inmates, Rock Island Prison

Washington, D. C.
    National Archives
        Army of Tennessee, Surgeons Reports. (M331, Roll
            204) RG 109
        Collection of CSA Records Muster and Pay rolls,
            Box No. 454, RG 109
        Compiled Service Records of Confederate Soldiers
        Who Served in Organizaions from the State
        of Alabama (M266) RG 109
        Compiled Service Records of Confederate Soldiers
        Who Served in Organizaions from the
        State of Georgia (M266) RG 109
        Compiled Service Records of Confederate Soldiers
        Who Served in Organizaions from the
        State of Tennessee (M266) RG 109
        Laminated Muster Rolls, Binder No. 13, RG 109

Collected Works, Letters, Diaries, Memoirs, Reminiscences
    and Unit Histories

Atlanta City Directory, 1871, 1886,

Barry, Robert L. "The Lookout Battery." Confederate Veteran
    30 (Oct., 1922): 385.

Chattanooga City Directory, 1861, 1871, 1881, 1891.

Confederate Veteran

Donnelly, Polly, James County

Guild, George B. A Brief Narrative of the Fourth Tennessee
        Cavalry Regiment, Wheeler's Corps, Army
        of Tennessee. Nashville, 1913.

Lindsley, John Berrien, ed. The Military Annals of Tennessee.
    Nashville, 1896.

McMurry, W. J. History of the Twentieth Regiment Volunteer
        Infantry, C.S.A. Nashville, 1904.

Worsham, William J. The Old Nineteenth Tennessee
        Regiment, C.S.A. Knoxville, 1902.

Newspapers

Chattanooga Free Press
Chattanooga Times

Government Documents

U. S. Government. Census of Catoosa County, Georgia, 1860

------. Censuses of DeKalb Co., Ga., 1870-1900

------. Censuses of Fulton County, Georgia, 1870, 1900

------. Censuses of Hamilton County, Tenn., 1840-1910

------. Census of James County, Tenn., 1880

------. Census of Walker County, Georgia, 1860

------. 1890 Civil War Veterans Census--Tennessee. Evanston,
    Ill., 1978.

------. The War of the Rebellion: A Compilation of the Official
    Records of the Union and Confederate Armies, 128 vols.,
    Washington, D.C., 1880-1901.

\*\*\*\*\*\*\*\*\*\*\*\*\*\*\*\*\*\*\*\*\*\*\*\*\*\*\*\*\*\*\*\*\*\*\*\*\*\*\*\*\*\*\*\*\*\*\*\*\*\*\*\*\*\*\*\*\*\*\*\*\*

## SECONDARY SOURCES

### Books

Adams, Elsie, Mountain Melody or Pioneers of Walden's Ridge. Chattanooga: Andrews Printing Co., 1950.

Allen, Don, Tennessee Prisoners at Camp Morton. Zionsville, Ind., Relative Records, 1996.

Armstrong, Zella. History of Hamilton County and Chattanooga, Tennessee. Chattanooga, 1931

Booth, Andrew B., Comp. Records of Louisiana Confederate Soldiers and Louisiana Confederate Commands. 3 vols. Spartanburg, SC, 1984.

Campbell, Carl E., comp. McKenzie's Fighting Fifth: Questionaires of Veterans of the 5th Tennessee Cavalry Regiment, C.S.A. Chattanooga, 1997.

------. McKenzie's Fighting Fifth: Rosters of the 5th Tennessee Cavalry Regiment, C.S.A. Chattanooga, 1996.

------. McKenzie's Fighting Fifth: Service Records of the 5th Tennessee Cavalry Regiment, C.S.A. Chattanooga, 1997.

Campbell, T. J. Records of Rhea. Dayton, Tenn.: 1940.

Cates, C. Pat, comp. Soldiers Who Served in the 1st Confederate Regiment Georgia Infantry, Army of Tennessee, from Catoosa County and Surrounding Areas. Woodstock, GA, 1993.

Crute, Joseph H., Jr. Units of the Confederate States Army. Midlothian, Va., 1987.

Dennis, Martha N. Confederate Veterans Buried in LaFayette City Cemetery, LaFayette, Georgia. LaFayette, 1994.

Dickey, J. Ralph, and Elizabeth D. Trower. Waller, A Family History.

Douthat, James L. Hamilton County Marriage Books 1-1/12, 1853-1870. Chattanooga, 1986.

------. Roster of Upper East Tennessee Confederate Veterans. Signal Mountain, Tenn., 1997

Estes, Claud. comp. List of Field Officers Regiments and Battalions in the Confederate States of America, 1861-65. Macon, Ga., 1912

Evans, Clement A. ed., Confederate Military History. 12 vols. (expanded edition). Atlanta, 1899.

Foust, Mozette. The Familly of John Foust and Anna Barbara Albrecht and Allied Families. Waco, Tex.: n.p., 1932.

Goodspeed, Weston A., ed. History of Tennessee. Nashville, 1887.

Hale, Will T. A History of Tennessee and Tennesseans. 8 vols. Chicago. 1913.

Henderson, Lillian, comp. Roster of the Confederate Soldiers of Georgia, 1861-1865. Hapeville, 1959-64.

Hewett, Janet B., ed. Roster of Confederate Soldiers, 1861-1865. 16 vols. Wilmington, N.C., 1995-96

Hughes, Buckner L., and Nathaniel C., Jr. Quiet Places: The Burial Sites of Civil War Generals in Tennessee. Knoxville, 1992.

Lindsey, Edwin S. Centennial History of St. Paul's Episcopal Church. Chattanaooga, 1953.

Lindsley, John Berrien, ed. The Military Annals of Tennessee. Nashville, 1896.

Livingood, James W., and Gilbert Govan. The Chattanooga County, 1540-1962: From Tomahawk to TVA. Chapel Hill, 1963.

Livingood, James W. The Chattanooga County: Gateway to History: The Nashville to Atlanta Rail Corridor of the 1860s. Chattanooga, 1995.

------. Hamilton County. Memphis, 1981.

McBride, Robert M., and Daniel M. Robison, eds. Biographical Directory of the Tennessee General Assembly. 4 vols. Nashville, 1975-.

Mickle, William E. Well Known Confederate Veterans and Their War Records. New Orleans, 1915.

Potter, Johnny L. T. N. First Tennessee & Alabama Independent Vidette Cavalry,1863-1864. Chattanooga, 1995.

Roark, John J. Hardtack and Hardship: The Life and Times of Confederate Veteran James A. Roark and His Family. Dallas, Tex., 1996.

Sherrill, Charles A., ed. Tennessee's Confederate Widows and Their Families. Cleveland, Tenn., 1992.

Speer, William S. Sketches of Prominent Tennesseans. Nashville, 1888.

Tennessee Civil War Commission. Tennesseans in the Civil War. 2 vols. Nashville, 1964-65.

United Daughters of the Confederacy, Tennessee Division. Confederate Patriot Index. 3 vols. Nashville: The Division, 1976-96.

Wilson, John. Chattanooga's Story. Chattanooga, 1980.

Wyeth, John A. History of LaGrange Military Academy and the Cadet Corps, 1857-1862. New York: The Drewer Press, 1907.

### Articles or Parts of Books

Livingood, James W. "Chattanooga Under Military Occupation, 1863-        1865." Journal of Southern History 17 (Feb., 1951): 23-47.

Morris, Roy. "That Improbable, Praiseworthy Paper: The

# BIBLIOGRAPHY

\*\*\*\*\*\*\*\*\*\*\*\*\*\*\*\*\*\*\*\*\*\*\*\*\*\*\*\*\*\*\*\*\*\*\*\*\*\*\*\*\*\*\*\*\*\*\*\*\*\*\*\*\*\*\*\*\*\*\*\*\*\*\*\*\*\*

Chattanooga <u>Daily</u> <u>Rebel</u>." <u>Civil</u> <u>War</u> <u>Times</u> <u>Illustrated</u> 23 (Nov., 1984): 16-24.


## Unpublished Studies

Armstrong, Zella. "Hamilton County Confederate Soldiers."

McGehee, Charles S. Wake of the Flood: A Southern City in the Civil War, Chattanooga, 1838-1873." Ph.D. dissertation, University of Virginia, 1985.

Redd, Mrs. William A., "History of Company H, Smith's 4th Tenn. Cavalry"

Weatherbee, F. W., Jr. "Reports, Correspondence and Miscellaneous Records Concerning the 5th Tennessee Cavalry Regiment." 1992.

**-A-**

ABERCROMBIE
A., 190
ABERNATHY
JOHN C., 1
JOHN CLAYTON, 1
NANCY A. BICKNELL, 1
YOUNG L., 1
YOUNG L.B., 1
ABRAMS
CATHERINE, 109
ACREE
DR., 1
FRANKLIN, 190
MARIA LOUISA, 178
ACUFF
MARY ANN, 13
ADAMS
A.R., 1
ASA, 1(3)
CHARLES, 1
ELIZA, 1
ELIZABETH, 1
ELSIE, 205
HAMILTON, 1
J.W., 190
JAMES, 1
SUSAN HIXSON, 1
THOMAS, 190
WILLIAM CHARLES, 1
WILLIAM J., 190
[BLANK], 1
ADCOCK
EDMOND, 1
ELIZABETH, 1
AIKEN
J.N., 93
JASPER NEWTON, 1
JOHN, 190
JOHN W., 190
THOMAS, 1, 190
AIKENS
J.N., 50
ALDEHOFF
HENRY W., 1
RAENA, 1
ALEXANDER
DAVID, 1
EMMA, 118
GIDEON "GID", 1
JAMES M., 2
MARGARET, 2
ROBERT, 2
T.J., 2
WILLIAM M., 2
WILLIAM THOMAS, 2
ALFORD
ALEXANDER W., 2
THOMAS A., 2
WILBURN, 190
ALLEN
ANDREW J., 2
BENTON, 2
DON, 205
ISAAC DAVID, 2
JAMES ALFRED G., 2
JOHN, 2
JOHN BENTON, 2(2)
JULIA E., 114
LOUIS, 2
LUCY FELTZ, 2
PENELOPE JOHNSON, 27
SUSAN ELLEN, 44
THOMAS A., 190
THOMAS BENTON, 3
W.W., 3

ALLISON
ALBERT J., 3(4)
ELIZA A., 3
J.M., 190
JAMES J., 190
JESSE B., 3
JOHN L., 3(3)
MARTHA, 3
W.F., 3
WILLIAM F., 3
WILLIAM P., 3(3)
ALLRED
BLACKSTONE W., 3
HENRY, 190
ALSTON
BEN, 61
AMES
JULIA, 164
AMMONS
WASHINGTON H., 3
ANDERSON
ALEXANDER, 136
ALICE, 79
ALLEN L., 3
CATHERINE, 166
GEORGE, 190
GEORGE W.H., 190
ISAAC W., 3
J.C., 3
JAMES C., 3
JAMES MADISON, 190
JEFFERSON CAMPBELL,
3
JOHN, 3
JOHN C., 3
JOHN HENRY, 4
JOSIAH, 166
JOSIAH McN., 190
JOSIAH McNAIR, 190
LYDIA CRAVENS, 4
MARY, 119
NANCY LAMB, 190
S.B., 29
S.R., 19
SEYMOUR, 190
W.A., 83, 190
W.G., MRS., 112
W.P., 190
W.W., 4
W.W., JR., 4
W.W., SR., MRS., 4
WILLIAM, 190
WILLIAM WALKER, 4
WILLIAM WALKER, JR.,
4
ANDREWS
ANNULET BALL, 4
GARNET, 21
GARNETT, 4
J. GARNETT, 4
JAMES, 157, 183, 190
MARY ACHSAH, 149
PARMELIA R., 4
ROBERT W., 4
SAMUEL, 190
ANGLEY
J.A., 190
ANSLEY
F.J., 190
ARENZ (ARENS)
C.H., 4
ARMISTEAD
ROBERT A., 4
ARMOR
GEORGE W., 4
ROBERT C., 4
ROBERT COWDEN, 4
ARMOUR

JOSEPH T., 4
ARMSTRONG
ADDISON WEAR, 5
JOHN MacMILLAN, 5
MARTIN VAN BUREN, 5
NANCY JANE McMILLAN,

5
WILLIAM CLAYTON, 5
ZELLA, 5, 180, 205,
206
ARNETT
GEORGE W., 5(2)
LUKE, 5, 44
WILLIAM, 5
ARNOLD
FRANCIS FIELDON, 190
ASHBY
HENRY M., 29
HENRY MARSHALL, 5
LUCINDA COCKE, 5
MARSHALL, 5
ASHFORD
ROBERT J., 5
WILLIAM HENRY, 5
ASHLEY
GEORGE REESE, 5
JAMES H., 5
JOSEPH, 5(2)
LOUISA EVALINE, 190
MARY, 5(2)
WILLIAM CLINTON, 190
ATCHLEY
ADA, 5
CALVIN A., 5
DANIEL, 5
JAMES M., 5
MARTHA, 5
ATKINS
TOM, 190
AUSBURN (OSUBURN)
H.M., 6
MARY J., 6
AUSTIN
JAMES R., 6
JOSEPH, 190
LEVI, 6
AUTRY
MARK L., 191
AUTRY
(AWTRY,AUGHTRY,AN
THONY)
RAIFORD
E.(RAYFORD,RALPH)
, 191
AVERELL
WM. W., 93
AVERY
HENRY C., 6
JOHN, 6
LOUISA A., 6
SUSANNAH, 6
AWLS
BILL, 191
AYERS
MARGARET OCOA, 135
MARTHA, 90

**-B-**

BABER
LEONARD B., 191
BABRY
THOMAS MILLIGAN, 6
BACHMAN
JONATHAN, 6
JONATHAN WAVERLEY, 6

BAGGETT
ALIAS, 6
JACKSON, 6
JACKSON A., 6
WILLIAM, 6(2)
BAILEY
C. LEON, 6
E. VOLNEY (VARDELL)
"VOD", 6
JONATHAN, 6
JORDAN, 6
LEON, 56
LOUISE W., 121
MALINDA, 6
MARIA SCOTT (FIELD),
6
MARTHA, 6
THOMAS J., 7
WILLIAM STEWART, 6
BAIRD
EMILINE ANDREWS, 49
LEMUEL MOORE, 7
MARY C., 7
MINNIE INGERSOL, 101
W.T., 7
BAKER
ELIZA, 139
GEORGE, 191
JACOB, 7
NANCY, 7
BALDWIN
CHESLEY, 191
CRISSA, 7(2), 22
ISAAC, 7(2)
ISAAC M., 7(2)
MARY ANN ELIZABETH,
56
WILLIAM, 7
WILLIAM H., 191
WILLIAM L., 7
BALL
GEORGE D., 191
BALLARD
JAMES K., 191
MARY, 19
SARAH BELLE, 38
WILLIAM H. (K.), 191
BALLEAU
MARY, 62
BALLEW
JOHN, 191
JOHN W., 191
THOMAS P., 7
ZEBULON, 191
BANGER
THOMAS H., 191
BANKS
HUGH R., 7
BANKSTON
JOHN HENRY, 7
BARBEE
GEORGE W., 7
MARIA E., 7
BARBER
ALSA, 7(2)
HENRY, 7
JEFFERSON, 191
JOSEPH, 7(2)
BARBOUR
ELIZABETH, 124
BARE
ELIZA J., 31
BAREFIELD
MARY K., 7
WHEELER S., 7
BARKER
LOTTIE, 31
LYDIA, 142

SARAH A., 13
WALTER, 13
BOYDSTON
  ASA CONNER, 13
  CAVANAUGH, 13(2), 14(2)
  GEORGE A., 13
  JAMES MADISON "JIMMY", 13
  JOHN, 13
  MARY ELIZABETH, 37
  POLLY, 13(2)
  POLLY SLAPE, 14(2)
  SARA LEE CONDRY, 13
  WILLIAM, 14
BOYDSTON (BOYDSON)
  THOMAS, 14
BOYLE
  JERE, 33
BOYLES
  JUDY KELLERHALS, 65
  KATHERINE KELLERHALS, 65
BOZEMAN
  CRAWFORD W., 193
BRABSON
  R.B., 134
BRACKEN
  ARCHIE L., 14
BRACKETT
  JOHN, 14
  RUFUS, 14
BRADEN
  O., 14
BRADFORD
  ELIZABETH K., 14
  HENRY, 14
  RACHEL McFARLAND, 14
  TIPTON, 27
  WILLIAM M., 14
BRADLEY
  ANDREW A., 14
  ANDREW ALEXANDER, 14
  NANNIE, 19
  ROSE ELIZABETH, 104
BRADSHAW
  GEORGE H., 14
  J.N., 12
  JOHN D., 14
BRADT
  JULIA, 14
  MORRIS, 14
BRADY
  ARVA M., 15
  BENJAMIN, 14, 15
  JAMES W., 15
  MATILDA, 14, 15
  OWEN R., 15
BRAGG
  BRAXTON, 100
  GEN., 10, 77, 119, 184
BRAMER
  D.B., 15
BRANDON
  PHILLIP A., 15
BRANHAM
  ADELA, 15
  ISHAM R., 15
  JAMES, 15
BRANNER
  B.M., 135
  BENJ. M., 202
BRANSON
  CYNTHIA, 15
  J.R., 15

JOHN, 15
BRANSON (BRONSON)
  JOHN RUFUS, 15
BRAUSE
  ELIZABETH A., 124
BRAYLOR
  GEN., 77
BRAZELTON
  NANCY S., 62
  WM., JR., 202(2)
BRECKINRIDGE
  JOHN C., 19, 94
  STANHOPE PRESTON, 15
BRENNAN
  RICHARD V., 15
BRENT
  N.H., 15
BREWER
  CLARK H., 15
  ELIZABETH, 171
  JAMES M., 15
  JULIETE, 15
BREWSTER
  J.R., 15
BRIDGEMAN
  JOHN M., 165
  JOHN N., 165
BRIDGES
  JOHN F., 15
BRISON
  WILLIAM C., 15
BROCK
  DAVID, 15
  JOHN, 15
  MARY ANN, 193
  RICHARD EMERSON, 193
  SARAH, 152
  YOUNGER, 16
BROOKS
  DAVID, 16
  ELIZA, 16
  GIDEON, 16(2)
  LEVI, 16
  MOSES, 28
  NANCY ARWIN, 28
  PRESTON, 16
  WILLIAM HUSTON, 16
  WINNY, 16(2)
BROTHERTON
  GEORGE, 131
  MARY CARTER, 131
  SARAH, 131
BROWN
  ALEXANDER F., 16
  AMANDA M., 184
  C.N., 17
  CAPT., 164
  CATHERINE, 16
  ELIZABETH E., 16
  ELLA, 16
  ELZANIE, 16
  FRANCES E., 83
  GEORGE E., 16
  GEORGE WASHINGTON, 16
  H.J., 16
  HATTIE, 17
  HIRA [SIC], 16
  J.C., 16
  J.D., 16
  J.W., 16
  JAMES, 16(2), 149
  JAMES B., 16(2)
  JAMES E., 16
  JAMES F., 16
  JAMES G., 17
  JAMES S., 17

JAMES W. (G.D.), 17
  JOHN, 44(2), 45
  JOHN HARDIN, 17
  JOHN J., 17
  JOHN L. "DOC", 17
  JOHN S., 17
  JOSEPH H., 17
  LAFAYETTE, 17
  LEROY, 193
  MARGARET, 16
  MARTHA JANE, 116
  MARTHA W., 17
  MARY ELLA, 34
  MARY K., 16
  MORGAN W., 17
  RHODA J., 16, 122
  RIDLEY S., 17
  S.C., 17
  THOMAS A., 61
  VICTORIA, 61
  WILLIAM A., 17
  WILLIAM C., 17, 204
BROWNING
  CAROLINE, 17
  GEORGE W., 17
  I.J., 17
BROWNLOW
  FLORA, 127
BROYLES
  A. HORTON, 17
  CHARLES E., 17
  SARAH, 17
BRUCE
  MARY JOLIFFE, 127
  WILLIAM M., 17
BRUDER
  J.M., 18
BRUMBY
  EPHRAIM R., 18
  MARY BREVARD, 18
  RICHARD T., 18
BRUMMETT
  JOHN W., 18
BRYAN
  ANNA THORNTON, 131
  DANIEL G., 18
  DANIEL GIDEON, 18
  J.J., 18
  JOSIAH JACKSON, 18(2)
  JOSIAH JACKSON, SR., 18
  MARGARET EMMA, 193
  WILLIAM DUNCAN, 193
BRYANT
  JAMES P., 18
  MARGARET, 18
  SAMUEL, 193
BRYSON
  FLETCHER, 18
  NELLIE J., 70
BUCHANAN
  JAMES, 182
  JEAN, 103
BUCKLAND
  H., 18
  JAMES L., 18
BUCKNER
  GEN., 47, 97
  LEVI, 18
  S.B., 27, 41
BUFF
  JAMES M., 18
  MARY A., 18
BUFORD
  CYRENA, 47
BULLOCK
  CABELL B., 18

BULLON
  JAMES, 18
BUNCH
  BENJAMIN F., 18
  JULIA A., 150
  WILLIAM F., 18
BUNN
  T.H., 19
BURCH
  JOHN CHRISTOPHER, 19
  MORTON NEWMAN, 19
BURG
  CARRIE, 18
BURGESS
  BETTIE, 154
  MARTIN L., 19
  RACHEL, 19
BURGINS
  THOMAS, 19
BURK
  GEORGE W., 19
  J.W., 19
  JAMES A., 19
  MARTHA EMELINE, 41
  MARY, 31
  NANCY, 19(2)
  WILLIAM ALBIE, 19
BURKE
  JOHN F., 19
BURKES
  H.H., 193
BURKHART
  CELIA, 19(3)
  GEORGE W., 19
  GEORGE WASHINGTON, 19(2)
  GEORGE, JR., 19
  LOUISA JANE, 19
BURKHART (BURKHALTER)
  WILLIAM CARROLL, 19
BURKHEART (BURKHEAD)
  WILLIAM, 19
BURKS
  WILLIAM P., 20
BURNETT
  JAMES, 193
  MARY J., 11
BURNS
  ALLEN CROCKETT, 20
  ELEANOR, 20
  GEORGE HENDERSON, 20
  JAMES, 20
  MRS. (LEDBETTER), 20
BURROUGHS
  H.G., 20
  WILLIAM H., 20
BURROUGHS (BURROW)
  NICHOLAS PHILLIP, 20
BURT
  MARY, 20
  MASON, 20
  NASH H., 20
BURTON
  CHRISTOPHER, 193
  MARY ELLEN, 3
  ROBERT, 20
BUSH
  ELLA, 33
  JAMES, 182
  MAHALA, 13
BUSTER
  MARSHALL, 20
  MATILDA, 20

WILLIAM HENRY, 194
CRETSINGER
JACOB R., 194
CREW
BENJAMIN B., 35
JOSEPH, 194
LAMBERT J., 194
PLEASANT, 35
CREWE
BEN S., 194
CREWS
ABRAHAM, 35(4)
DELILA, 35(3)
GEORGE W., 35
REBECCA, 35
CREWS (CRUISE, CRUSE)
WILLIAM M., 35
CREWS (CRUSE)
HENRY R., 35
SOPHRONIA, 35
THOMAS W., 35
CRITTENDEN
GEORGE B., 156
CROCKETT
EDWARD R., 194
EDWARD T., 35
CROFF
R.C., 35
CROFFORD
GEORGE, 35
CROSS
A.L., 35
ABSALOM LOONEY, 35(2)
JENNIE, 35
MARGARET E., 35
ROBERT COLLOP, 35
CROUCH
D.I., 36
HICKMAN H., 36
CROW
CHRISTOPHER COLUMBUS, 36
ELEANOR, 36
FINN M., 36
ISAAC L., 36
JENNIE, 22
MARTHA A., 36
REBECCA, 36(2)
SARAH G., 36
SARAH L., 36
THOMAS, 36
W.P., 36
WILLIAM M., 36
WILLIAM P., 36
CROWE
JAMES R., 36
CRUDUP
DEMPSEY G., 36
CRUISE
J.W., 36
CRUMBLESS
JOHN, 36
CRUMLEY
JOHN, 36
CRUSE
W.M., 35
WILLIAM, 35(2)
WILLIAM M., 35
CRUTCHFIELD
DORA, 136
MARY J., 130
TOM, 110
WILLIAM, 32, 42, 55
WM., 130
CRUTE
JOSEPH H., JR., 205
CRUZE

AMANDA, 91
CUETON
F.A., 36
JAMES, 36
CULPEPPER
D.H., 194
CULVER
JAMES JASPER, 36
LAURA BELLE, 36
CUMMINGS
ELIZABETH, 37(2)
GREENBERRY, 37(2)
GREENBURY, 37
JOHN, 37(2)
LAVINIA, 99
THOMAS, 37
W.F., 37
WALTER, 188
CUNNINGHAM
C.C., 37
CAROLINE, 34
HUGH, 37
MILES C., 37
S.A., 39
WILLIAM M., 37
CUON
CON, 37
CUPP
DOCK, 37
WILLIAM, 37
CURD
RICHARD D., 37
CURRAN
O.S., 37
CURROUGHS
ELIZABETH HALE, 156(2)
CURRY
GEORGE WASHINGTON, 37
JANE GRAY OWEN, 37
ROBERT BROWNLEE, 37
CURTIS
LILLIAN, 63
CUSTER
JAMES M., 37
CUTTEN
PETER E., 194
SOPHRANIA, 194

-D-

DABNEY
DR., 174
DAFFRON (DAFRON, DOFRON)
JOEL, 194
RICE, 194
WILLIAM, 194
[BLANK], 194
DALTON
LEE ANDREW, 37
DANGEY
HARRY, 37
DANIEL
DAVID, 37
J.B., 37
R.P., 37
WILLIAM, 37
DARDEN
MISS, 112
DARNALL
FANNIE BELL, 174
DARR
SAMUEL CURTIS, 38
DARRELL
JOHN A., 38

DARWIN
TENNESSEE WHITE, 64
DAUGHERTY
CYNTHIA A. MADDUX, 51
DAVENPORT
LUKE LEVANDER, 194
SYRENA ELIZABETH, 194
DAVIDSON
JASPER J., 38
SARAH J., 38
DAVIES
DAVID J., 38
DAVIS
ALBERT, 38
ALFRED A., 38
ANNA WASHINGTON, 194
BETSEY J., 176
DAVID, 38
DECATUR, 38
DOLLY D., 17
HARVEY L., 38
HENRY M., 38
HIRAM, 38
J.W., 38
JAMES MACK, 38
JEFFERSON, 20, 39, 55, 93, 148, 179, 184
JEHU R., 39
JERRY, 38
JOHN, 38
JULIA ANN, 58, 111
LUCINDA, 38
M.T., 38
MAHALIE, 38
MARTHA C., 107
MARY, 38
MARY JANE, 187
PRES., 105
ROBIN E., 38
SAMUEL, 38
SARAH C., 124
SARAH ISABELL, 150
SARAH MARTHA, 52
TENNIE, 62
THOMAS PINKNEY, 38
W. SCOTT, 39
WILLIAM GALIUS, 194
WILLIAM M., 39
WILLIAM P., 39
DAWN
FERDINAND F., 39
DAWSON
W.D., 39
DAY
ADDISON C., 194
AMANDA, 39
EDWIN F., 39
EMMA H., 1
GEORGE M., 39
JENNIE A., 33
JOHN, 1, 39
MARY MEE, 39
SAM HOUSTON, 39
DAYTON
LAURA, 47
DEADERICK
ANNA MARY, 171
JAMES W., 39
WILLIAM WALLACE, 39
DEAKIN
SAMUEL B., 194
DEAKINS
ABSOLEUS L. "AB", 39
EDNA, 39

FRANK, 39
J.V., 39
SAMUEL D., 39
WILLIAM ROGERS "FRANK", 39
DEAN
DAISY ROBERTA, 39
GEORGE R., 194
J.R.M., 39
JOHN ROBERT, 39
MARY CLAIR, 39
ROBERT, 39
DEANE
JAMES, 39
DEATON
CHARLES A., 39
REBECCA, 40
DEBARDELEBEN
DANIEL H., 40
ETHEL, 40
DECOSTA
AARON CANADY, 40
DEDMON
JOSEPH, 40
DEFRESE
R.H., 40
DeFRIESE
T.J., 40
DEGALLEFORD
ELIZABETH, 40
JOHN, 40
DELANO
CLARA ELIZABETH, 95
DEMENT
THOMAS J., 40
DEMPSEY
FANNIE, 123
WILLIAM L., 40
DENNIS
JAMES, 40
JOHN, 40
MARTHA N., 205
MATILDA, 40
DENNISON
BARNEY, 40
PETER, 194
DENNY
NANCY, 52
DENT
CHARLES J., 40
JARRETT, 181
JARRETT GRAY, 40(2)
DENTON
ELIZABETH JANE, 55
ISAAC J., 40
JAMES R., 40
MARTHA, 41
WILLIAM L., 41
DEPRISE
R.H., 40
DES ESSARTE
ANAIS, 101
DESHA
ALEXANDER HAMPTON, 41
HAMILTON, 41
HAMPTON, 41
DEVALCOURT
ALEX, 41
DEVIN
CHARLES, 41
DEVOTI
CATHARINE, 41
DUMAM, 41
JOHN C., 41
DEWITT
SAMUEL, 41

LORENZO D., 48
RHODA, 99(2)
SAMUEL M., 48
WILLIAM A., 49
ELLISON
WILLIAM, 49
ELROD
EMILY, 87
ELY
JOHN ALEXANDER, 49
ELZEY
ARNOLD, 4
EMERSON
JAMES W., 49
SARAH, 49
EMORY
JOHN, 49
NANCY, 49(3)
WILLIAM, 49(3)
EMPRESS JOSEPHINE, 137
ENGLEDOW
KATHERINE, 169
EPPERSON
JAMES B., 195
EPPINS
T.P., 49
ERWIN
ANDREW JACKSON, 49
ELLA, 49
GEORGE W., 49
J.B., 49
JAMES C., 49
JAMES L.M., 49
SALINE, 49(2)
WILLIAM, 49(2)
WILLIAM O., 49
ESBY
ALBERT M., 49
ESKRIDGE
MARY "MOLLIE", 181
ESTES
ABBIE H., 144
CLAUD., 205
ETTER
LEONARD L., 49
EUBANKS
EMMA I., 42
EVANS
AUGUSTUS, 49
C.A., 124
CLEMENT A., 205
JAMES, 49
LAN, 49
MARY, 49
MARY ANN SIVLEY, 49
NAN, 49
PETER SOLOMON, 49
EVITT
CHARLES, 49
CHARLES W., 49(2)
NEHEMIAH, 49(2)
REBECCA, 49
WILLIAM, 49(2)
EWELL
RICHARD S., 41
EWING
ALBERT, 50
CALVIN J., 50
EVALINE P., 25
JANE, 50
JOHN, 50
MARY, 50

-F-

FACKLER
CHARLES W., 50
FAIDLEY

ANNIE, 50
ARCH, 50
ARCHIBALD, 50(4)
CHARLES, 50
CHARLES F., 50(2)
CHARLES FENTON, 50
DORA, 50
EDWARD, 50
HENRY, 50
JOSEPH GAILES, 50
ROSANNA YOUNG, 50(2)
ROSE, 50
SUSAN FOTHERGILL, 50
FAIRBANKS
DAVID, 50(2)
NANCY, 50(2)
RICHARD, 50(2)
FALLEN (FALLENT)
JAMES, 195
FARMER
JOHN O., 50
MARY ELIZABETH, 89
SARAH, 50
SHADRICK, 50
FARRIS
BETTIE J., 90
CHARLES AMBROSE
DRISCOLL, 50
CHARLES B., 50
ELIZABETH, 51
ELIZABETH J., 90
HUGH FRANCIS
"FRANK", 50
J.L., 51
JASPER, 51
FAW
MARTHA, 179
FAXON
JOHN WELLINGTON, 51
FEATHERS
ALVIN MARION, 51
NANNIE SALENA, 51
FELKINS
HENRY, 51
LOGAN, 51
MARARITHA, 51
PRESLEY L., 51
WILLIAM L., 51
FELTON
JOHN, 195
FERGUSON
BENJAMIN H., 51
BETTIE M., 51
DORINDA, 51
JAMES A., 51
SAMUEL H., 51
FIELDING
ISAAC N., 51
PENELOPE, 115
THOMAS J., 51
FIELDS
CORNELIUS, 51
JOHN, 51(2)
MARY, 51(3)
RICHARD, 52
WILLIAM, 52
WILLIS, 51(2)
FILBY
R.R., 52
FINE
JOHN A., 52
FINLEY
ELIZABETH J., 136
JOSEPH W., 52
MISS, 165
NAN, 52
WILLIAM, 52
FINNEY

SALLIE, 61
FIRSTE (FOSTER)
W.H., 52
FISCHER
WILLIAM F., 52
FISHER
ANDREW J., 52
HERMAN, 195
IRENEAUS (IRINEUS)
F., 52
WATSON, 195
FITZGERALD
C.B., 52
COLEMAN, 52
MARY, 52(2)
NANCY, 52
NASA, 52(2)
WILLIAM, 30, 52(2)
WOODSON, 52(2)
FLEMING
J.W., 52
WILLIAM WHITE, 52
FLETCHER
J.E. (C.?), 52
FLINN
WILLIAM GRIFFITH, 52
FLINN/FLYNN
BENJAMIN F., 52
FLIPPO
JACKSON, 36
FLORA
EMALINE, 53
JACOB, 53
MARY, 53
THEODORE F.H., 53
WILLIAM, 53
FLORANCE
W.E., 53
FLOYD
J.B., 178
MARY, 12
FLYNN
GEORGE WASHINGTON,

53
RACHAEL, 53
RACHAEL R., 52
FOARD (FORD)
J.H., 53
FORD
BENJAMIN, 53
HETTY, 53
J.H., 53
JAMES H., 53
JAMES H., MRS., 53
JAMES HENRY, 53
JOHN W., 53
MARTIN, 27
MARY, 53
NATHAN C., 53
PENSACOLA HAWLEY, 53

RHODA THOMISON, 53
THOMAS J., 53
WILLIAM B., 53
WILLIAM DANIEL, 53
FORE
MARGARET, 83
FORREST
GEN., 11, 169, 181
N.B., 19, 96, 128
NATHAN B., 59
NATHAN BEDFORD, 137,
183
FORT
GEORGE N., 54
JOHN PORTER, 54
KATE, 109

MARTHA LOW FANNIN,

53
SARAH, 109
TOM, 109
TOMLINSON, 53(2)
FORTENBURY
ERASTUS, 195
FORTNER
WILEY, 54
FORTUNE
JOHN W., 54
FOSTER
A.D., 54
A.H., 54
A.S., 54
A.T., 54
F.G., 54
J.C., 54
J.D., 54
JAMES, 54(2)
JAMES DANIEL, 54
JAMES R., 54
JOHN, 54
JOHN A., 54
JOHN C., 54(2)
MALINDA, 54
MARGARET, 18
FOUST
"POLK", 54, 55
ADDISON TAYLOR, 54
FRANCIS MARION
HAWLEY, 54
JOHN, 54(3)
MATILDA, 54
MATILDA HAWLEY,
54(2)
MOZETTE, 205
NATHAN POLK, 54
WILLIAM HENRY, 55
FOUTS
ADDIE R., 163
JOHN R., 55
O.P., 55
OLIVER PERRY, 55
FOWLER
ELIGA W., 55
J.M., 55
MARY "POLLY", 13
VIRGINIA, 35
FOX
BECKIE, 55
CORNELIUS R., 55
DAVID, 55
JOHN B., 55
MARTHA, 55
FRAKER
WILLIAM M., 55
FRANCIS
ELDRIDGE G., 55
ELIZA JANE, 55
MARY, 55
WILLIAM, 55
FRANCISCO
H.C., 55
MATILDA, 55
FRANK
JENNIE, 2
FRANKLIN
BENNETT J., 55
JAKE, 55
JAMES S., 195
MARTHA REBECCA, 195
MARY, 55
MARY E., 157
SALENA E., 55
FRAZIER
MINERVA McKAMY, 169

NICHOLAS POPE, 195
RUTH CLAWSON, 55
S.J.A., 30
SAMUEL, 55
SAMUEL J.A., 30
SAMUEL JOSIAH ABNER, 55
THOMAS N., 174
FREDORA
ALMEDIA, 190
FREEMAN
DREWRY HUTCHINSON

"HUTCH", 56
JOSEPH, 56
THURSEY, 56(2)
FRENCH
BRYON BROWNLOW, 56
JOHN L.M., 56
JOHN LEE McCARTY, 56
JOSEPH HARRISON, 56
JOSEPH HARVEY, 56(3)
NANCY BENSON, 56(3)
RACHEL A., 38
TIMOTHY ALLEN, 56
FRICKS
ELIZABETH C., 195
FLAVIUS J., 56
JOHN, 56
NAPOLIAN, 195
SARAH DIXON, 56
WILLIAM HENRY
HARRISON, 56
FRIERSON
THOMAS A., 56
FRIST
BILL, 56
J.W., 7(2)
JACOB CHESTER, 56(2)
MARY BALDWIN, 56
ROBERT HARRIS, 56
FRITTS
THOMAS W., 56
FROST
D.M., 147
FRY
B.D., 184
ELIZABETH E., 57
ELIZABETH PECK, 56
GEORGE THOMPSON, 56
HENRY H., 56
HOUSTON GREENBERRY, 57
HUGH LAWSON, 57
MARTIN, 57
MARTIN M., 104
MARTIN MONROE, 57
FRYAR
DELILA, 57
ELIZABETH, 57(3)
JEREMIAH, 57
JEREMIAH "JERRY", 57
JEREMIAH, JR., 57
JOHN, 57(3)
MARY, 57
SEVIER, 57(2)
WILLIAM, 57(2)
FRYAR (FRYOR)
FRANKLIN (FRANK), 57
FUELL
JAMES, 57
FUGATE (FUGATT, FUGITT)

ELIAS, 57
FULET
ELLA, 73
FULLALOVE (FULLILOVE)

J.H., 57
W.E., 57
FULLER
MARY, 146, 168
FULTON
JAMES, 57
JAMES HENDERSON, 57
MARY EPSEY, 57
SARAH M.J.
HENDERSON, 57
WILLIAM DOUGLAS, 57
WILLIAM DOUGLASS, 57
FURRY
THOMAS, 195
FYFFE
LIZZIE P., 161

-G-

GABBERT
OTIS T., 58
W.G., 58
GAD
ANDREW, 195
GADBY
G.P., 58
GADD
DANIEL C., 195
J.D., 195
JOHN, 58
REBECCA, 58
WILLIAM, 58
GAFFNEY
JAMES MATTHEW, 58
GAINES
JOHN HENRY, 58
JULIA, 94
GALLAHER
JOHN F., 58
MAGGIE P., 58
PLEASANT P., 58
GAMBLE
CHARLES P., 64
CHARLES PRESTON, 58(2)
GEORGE WASHINGTON, 58
JOSEPH, 58
MARY L., 58
SAMUEL H., 58
THOMAS J., 58
GAMBLIN
JOSHUA, 58
W.G., 58
GANN
ANDREW, 59
ANDREW "ANDY", 58
DANIEL, 59(2)
JOHN WESLEY, 59
MARY, 58
GANNAWAY
THOMAS COTLETT, 59
GANT
WILLIAM, 59
GARDENHIRE
FRANCIS MARION
"FRANZ", 59
FRANZ, 115
GEORGE W., 59(2)
JAMES T. "JUDGE", 59
LAWRENCE, 30
SARAH, 59
WILLIAM, 59
WILLIAM COLUMBUS, 59
GARDNER
MAUD, 62

GARFIELD
JAMES A., 101
GARMANY
FRANCES, 43
WM. K., 87
GARNER
IRVIN CLARK, 59
JULIA, 59
WILLIAM, 59
WILLIAM H.H., 59
WILLIAM L., 59
ZERELDA JANE, 186
GARRETT
BENJAMIN M., 59
JOHN, 59
JOHN LEANDER, 59
NANCY C., 59
RAPLEY (RALPH), 59
SARAH E., 59
GARWOOD
SARAH, 135
GASKILL
THOS., 60
VARNEY A., 60
GAULT
SAMUEL B., 60
GAUT
WILLIAM, 60(2)
GENNOE
CALVIN, 60
DAVID, 60
GENSEL
MARTHA, 60
N.S., 60
GENTRY
ELLEN JANE, 60
JOHN W., 60
GERALD
JOHN, 60
NANCY, 60
SAMUEL T., 60
GERHEART
GEORGE W., 60
GERMAN
ANDY, 60
GERVIN
E.H., 60
GHOLSON
WILLIAM, 60
GHORMLEY
WILLIAM HENDERSON, 60
GIBBS
CHARLES N., 60
GEORGE W., 60
LEE ANN DIBRELL, 60
GIBSON
DAVID, 60
JAMES, 195
JAMES H., 60
JEREMIAH "JERRY", 61
JOHN C., 61
JORDAN, 61
JOSEPH, 61
JOSEPH W., 61
KEZIAH, 61
LORNIDA, 60
LOU, 61
REBECCA, 60
THOMAS, 61
GIBSON (GIPSON)
H., 60
GIFFORD
ALBERT, 43
GILBERT
CHARLES H., 61
ISAAC N., 61
L.V., 61

STEPHEN M., 61
GILBREATH (GILBRETH)
EVANDER, 61
GILL
MARY A., 81
GILLBRIDE
BARNEY, 61
GILLESPIE
ALICE, 106
ANNA NEILSON, 61
D.S., 134
ELIZA JANE SIMPSON, 61, 62
ELIZABETH
STEPHENSON, 21
GEORGE, 61, 62
GEORGE L., 62
GEORGE L., JR., 61
GEORGE LEWIS, 62
GEORGE S., 61
HANNAH LEUTY, 62
J.W., 90, 154
JAMES F., 61
JAMES WENDELL, 61
JOHN KING, 62
JOHN M., 62
JOSEPH S., 62
JOSEPH STRONG, 62
LIZZIE, 26
MARCUS, 62
MARK, 61
NANCY, 61
NELLIE, 148
ROBERT N., 62
SIDNA, 62
SIDNEY ANN LEUTY, 62
W.J., 180
WILLIAM, 62
WILLIAM A., 62
WILLIAM J., 62
WILLIAM M., 62
WILLIAM N., 61, 62
WILLIAM STANTON, 62
WILLIAM STANTON
LEUTY, 62
GILLIAM
JACOB, 195
GILLUM
JOHN J., 195
GILMER
MILDRED AMELIA, 166
GIRVIN (GIVENS)
EBENEZER H., 62
GIST
S.R., 184
GIVENS
MAHALA, 112
GLADDIS
THOMAS, 62
GLADISH
MARTHA, 63
WILLIAM JAMES, 62(2)
GLASS
CATHERINE, 164
FANNIE, 185
JOHN, 164
JOHN G., 79
SIDNEY A.P., 79
THOMAS C., 195
WILLIAM J., 63
GLOVER
AUGUSTUS C., 63
DANIEL, 63
GRANDERSON F., 63
RICHARD, 63
SAMUEL H., 63
THOMAS, 63
WILLIAM CULFORD, 63

STEVENS
  C.H., 157
  THOMAS, 133
STEVENSON
  BENJAMIN F., 158
  CARTER L., 61
STEVER
  LUCINDA, 55
STEWART
  ALEXANDER HARVEY, 158
  ALEXANDER PETER, 158
  CHARLES, 159
  GEORGE HENRY, 159
  HENRY, 159
  JAMES, 159
  JAMES A., 159
  JOHN H., 159
  MATTIE, 23
  MIKE, 163
  ROBERT C., 159
  WILLIAM K., 159
STEWERT
  NATHANIEL, 160
STIFF
  JOHN C., 159
STINGELL
  R.H., 159
STOKES
  LOWE H., 159
STONE
  FRANCIS IRVINE, 159
  SPENCER CLARK, 159
  WILLIAM F., 159
  WILLIAM N., 159
STOPHEL
  DAVID, 159
STOUT
  CHARLES, 159
  MARY ANN, 180
  S.H., 15
  THOMAS EDMOND, 160
STOWERS
  MARTHA J., 46
STRADLEY
  W.W., 160
STRATTON
  JOHN M., 160
STREAKER
  J.E., 160
STRICKLAND
  GEORGE W., 160
STRINGER
  ELIZABETH, 144
  PENELOPE, 9
  WILLIAM, 9
STRONG
  GEORGE, 186
STROTHER
  GEORGE E., 160
STUART
  ANNIE, 152
  NATHAN, 160
  THOMAS A., 160
  W.A., 160
STUBBS
  CARRIE JOSEPHINE, 200
  JOHN BENTON, 200
STURGIL
  ROBERT HENRY, 160
  SARAH OSBURN, 160
  WILLIAM, 160
SU--SON
  R.H., 160
SUBLETT
  DAVID L., 160
SUDDATH

FRANK K., 160
SULLINS
  DAVID, 161
  NATHAN, 161
  REBECCA MITCHELL, 161
SULLIVAN
  J.M., 200
  MARY, 44
SULLY
  JOHN J., 161
SUMMER
  R.E., 200
SUMMERLIN
  ROXY, 32
  SOPHONIA, 32
SUMMERS
  GEORGE P., 161
SUMPTER
  R.B., 200
SUTTON
  ELIZABETH, 161
  HOUSTON, 200
  ISAAC, 161
  JAMES MONTRAVILLE, 161
  URIAH, 161
  URIAH R., 161
SWAFFORD
  A., 161
  GEORGE, 161
  SARAH, 161
SWAGGERLY
  LAURA, 137
SWAIM
  JOHN, 117
SWAN
  J.L., 161(2), 187
SWEENEY
  GEORGE W., 161
SWEETS
  ISAAC J., 161
SWENEY
  BRYANT, 200
SWENNY
  F., 161
SWETT (SWEAT)
  JOHN, 161
SWICK
  D.P., 161
  H.M., 161
  HENRY M., 161
  MICAJAH T., 161
  WILLIAM L., 161
SWIFT
  R.B., 161
SWINNEY
  RICHARD H., 200
SWISHER
  ELBERT W., 161
  ELIZABETH, 162(2)
  H.R., 162(2)
  JAMES H., 162
  JAMES HENEGAR, 162
  MARTHA, 162
  SAMUEL R., 162
SWOOP
  DAVID, 200
  MARGARET, 200
SWOPE
  DAVID, 200
SYLAR
  HOUSTON H., 162
  MARTHA A., 162
  MARY C., 117
  PETER H., 162
  SARAH, 162
  SARAH A., 162

-T-

TABLER
  J.H., 162
TACETT
  ALEX, 200
TALIAFERRO
  ELIZA J., 162
  GEORGE D., 162
  GEORGE W., 162
  J., 162
  JEMIMA G., 162
  JOHN, 187
  MARTHA J., 162
  RICHARD, 136
  RICHARD J., 162
  WILEY FRANKLIN, 162
TALLANT
  BENJAMIN D., 162
  CATHARINE, 162
  ENOCH, 162
  JAMES, 162
  JOHN, 162
  RACHEL, 162
  RICHARD, 162
  ROBERT, 162
TALLANT (TALENT, TALLENT)
  A.C., 162
  DAVID H., 162
TALLY
  BERRY, 162
  ELIZA, 162
  FLOYD, 162
  POLLY POOL, 163
  STEPHEN, 162, 163
  WILLIAM B., 163
  WM. B., 162
TANKERSLEY
  MAJ., 98
TANKESLEY
  R.M., 129
  RACHEL ELLEN, 128
  REUBEN, 163
  RUFUS, 57, 204
  RUFUS MILLER, 163
  SARAH EMMELINE MILLER, 163
TANKESTLY
  RUBIN, 78
TANNER
  B.M., 200
  JOHN Q., 163
  L.H., 163
  LUCY ANN, 132
TARVER
  BENJAMIN MARCUS, 163
  ELIZA V., 163
TARWATER
  DAVID, 163(2)
  JAMES M., 163
  WILLIAM, 163
TATE
  ELISHA, 163
  MARY GOLDEN, 53
  MARY JANE, 6
  PERRYMAN, 163
  PERRYMAN M., 163
TAYLOR
  A.C., 163
  A.D., 79, 160
  ALFRED D., 163
  BETTIE, 147
  E.B., 164
  GERTRUDE, 164
  J.H., 164
  JAMES, 164

JOHN R., 164
KATIE SEVIER, 65
LAURA, 118
LOUISE, 65(2)
MARY FRANCES, 34
R.L., 164
ROBERT, 65
ROBERT L., 153
THOMAS DANIEL, 164
W.L., 164
TEAGUE
  WILLIAM C., 200
TEENOR
  ELIZA, 164
  JACOB, 164
  JOHN A., 110, 164
  MARY J., 110
TEFERTOLER
  J.W., 200
TEMPLE
  CHARLES, 164(2)
  DANIEL, 164
TEMPLETON
  A., 164
  BURL, 164
  JOHN C., 164
  MAHALA, 164
TERRELL
  CICERO W., 164
  CLARASY DICKINSON, 164
  MARGARET, 164
  W.A., 164
  WILLIAM ALEXANDER, 164(2)
TERRY
  CHARLES A., 165
  ELIZABETH, 165
  F.B., 165
  JOHN, 165
  MARY CONSTANCE, 91
  R.H., 165
  SCOTT, 165
THACKER
  EDA, 165(3)
  JAMES, 165
  JOEL, 165(3)
  LUCY, 165
  SOLOMON, 165
  WILLIAM, 165
THATCH
  SAMUEL G., 165
THATCHER
  KATHERINE, 126
THOMAS
  A., 166
  A.J., 165
  A.R., 165, 166
  ARCHER, 165
  ARCHER D., 165
  ARTHUR REECE, 165
  AUGUSTUS G., 132
  BENJAMIN F., 165
  CATHERINE ANDERSON, 166
  DAVID D., 165
  DAVID DYER, 166(2)
  DAVID W., 166
  GEORGE, 5, 44, 166
  I.W., 165(2), 166
  ILTID W., 166
  JOHN, 166
  JOHN JENKINS, 166(2)
  L.M., 166
  LAWRENCE, 166
  LOUIZA, 165
  N.C., 166

CAROLINE (CALLIE), 67
CLEMENT L., 173
ELIZABETH, 67
F.M., 15, 69, 81, 92
FRANCES, 101
FRANCIS M., 82, 174
FRANCIS MARION, 67, 104, 173
FRANK, 4
G.M., 173
HARVEY, 173
J.A., 173
J.F., 173
J.M., 174
JEMIMA E., 12
JOHN, 173
JOHN T., 174
JOSEPH, 174
LAPSLEY G., 158
LISETTE, 127
LOUISA PENELOPE CAMPBELL, 3
MARGARET K., 173
MARY S., 81
O.P., 174
SARAH, 173
TABITHA TAYLOR, 173
THOMAS H., 174
WILLIAM, 3, 174
WILLIAM P., 174
WALL
J., 174
PERRY A., 174
S.L. JACKSON, 174
WALLACE
BENJAMIN, 174(2), 200
HENRY, 174
ISAAC A., 174, 175
ISAAC ABRAHAM, 174
J. ALBERT, 175
JAMES, 175
JAMES ANDERSON, 174
MARGARET H., 126
MARY ANDERSON, 174
RHODA A., 174
SARAH JANE, 174
WALLEN
HUGH, 175
WALLER
GEORGE, 175
MANLY B., 175
MARTHA, 175
MARY, 156
NANCY, 175
WALLING
ELIZA CORDELIA HAGAN, 90
WALSTON
SETH, 175
WAMPLER
J.B., 200
WANN
MARY JANE, 97
WARD
CHARLES E., 175
E.G., 175
ELLEN S., 184
J.H., 200
JAMES RAULSTON, 175
WARE
SAMUEL, 175
WARLICK
NOAH FRANKLIN, 175
WARNER
ELIZABETH J. CARTWRIGHT, 175

J.H., 5, 204
JACOB L., 175
JAMES C., 175
JAMES CARTWRIGHT, 175
JOSEPH HENRY, 175
WARNICK
EDWARD A., 175
WARNOCK
CAROLINE, 44
WARREN
HANNAH, 176(2)
JAMES P., 175
JOHN RANDOLPH, 176
REUBIN, 176
SARAH, 175
THOMAS V., 176
WILLIAM, 175, 176
WILLIAM T., 176
WASHINGTON
GEORGE, 50, 181
LAWRENCE, 181
WATERHOUSE
DARIUS, 155
MISS, 139
SILAS (CYRUS), 176
WATERS
C.N., 176
G.W., 176
WATKINS
CARLOW, 200
ELIZBETH A., 176
J.W., 102
JACOB, 176
JOHN W., 176
KIMSEY, 176
P.H., 138
PETER, 176
RICHARD L., 5
RICHARD LEVENS "DICK", 176
ROBERT, 177
THOMAS, 177
WATTERS
VIRGINIA LEE, 128
WATTERSON
HENRY, 19, 177
WATTS
H.E., 177
JOHN C., 177
SAMUEL, 200
WILLIAM J., 200
WEACE
JEMIMA, 61
WEATHERBEE
F.W., JR., 206
WEATHERFORD
SILAS S., 177
W.S., MRS., 165, 166
WEATHERLY
SAM, 177
SAMUEL, 177
WEATHERLY (WEATHERBY)

JONAS, 177
WEATHERS
JOHN H., 200
WEAVER
CLAUDIA WINGFIELD, 114
JUDGE, 81
WEBB
ELIZABETH, 177
MEREDITH, 177
WILLIAM, 177
WEBSTER
J.W., 177
JOHN WILLIAM, 177

THOMAS, 177(3)
WILLIAM W., 178
WEIR
J.L., 178
JOHN BRADFORD, 178
WELCH
GIDEON, 178
JAMES, 178
LEANDER, 178
REBECCA A., 178
WELCH (WALSH)
MICHAEL "MIKE", 178
WELCKER
ALBERT GALLATIN, 201
WELLBORN
A.J., 178
WELLONS (WILLONS)
C.M., 178
WELLS
B.F., 178
FRANCES J. "FANNIE", 187
JAMES, 178
JOHN, 179
MARY STEWART, 179
MATILDA TEED KESTERSON, 178
MATTHEW, 178
MOSES, 178
SARAH ANN, 178
SUSAN HANNAH, 178
THOMAS P., 178
W.H., 179
WILLIAM BRYANT, 179
WELSH
JACK D., 64
WERT
ANNIE SARAH, 122
WEST
J.L., 179
JOEL (JOSEPH P.), 179
SARAH JANE, 103
WILLIS RIDLEY, 179
WETMORE
WILLIAM H., 179
WHALEN
JAMES K.P., 179
MARY, 179
WHEELER
GEN., 99, 110, 148, 155
HENRY, 201
JOE, 5, 40, 105
JOSEPH, 129, 183
MARY E., 110
MATILDA CATHERINE, 201
WILLIAM HENRY, 201
WHITE
ALFRED, 201
COL., 91
FLETCHER, 179
GEORGE, 179
JAMES, 179
JAMES A., 179
JAMES C., 179
JAMES M., 179
JANE, 14
JOHN FLETCHER, 179
MARTIN M., 201
MARY ANN, 2
MOSES, 151
SARAH ELIZABETH, 39
SARAH H., 48
THOMAS, 2
WILLIAM W., 180
WHITECOTTON

HARRISON (HARRY), 180
ISAAC M., 180
SARAH E., 180
WHITEHEAD
ISAAC THOMAS, 180
LAURA, 45
WHITESIDE
FOSTER, 180
HARRIET, 60
HARRIET B., 85
HARRIET LEONORA STRAW, 180
HARRIET STRAW, 180
HELEN, 177
HUGH, 180
J.A., 60
JAMES A., 62, 88, 177, 180(2)
JAMES A., MRS., 180
JAMES L., 180
JOHN B., 180
PENELOPE, 62
THANKFUL, 88
WHITFIELD
GORDON W., 180
WHITLOCK
JAMES A., 180
WHITLOW
DELILAH, 10
WHITSITT
WILLIAM JIMOS, 180
WHITTAKER
FREDONIA, 200
WHITTEN
JAMES, 180
WHITTENBERG
WILLIAM WESLEY, 180
WHITTENBURG
JENNIE, 110
JOHN, 180
SARAH (LOTSPEICH), 180
WM., 181
WHITTLE
ARCHIMIDES "ARK", 181
CAROLINE, 101
MARGARET, 172
WILLIAM W., 201
WICKMAN
TILLIE, 182
WIDEMAN
JOHN P. (F.), 181
WIEHART
P.R., 181
WILDER
JOHN, 176
JOHN T., 139
WILDS
DARLAN A., 181
GEORGE B., 181
WILEY
LUCINDA, 181
WILLIAM E., 181
WILEY (WILY)
ELIZABETH, 181
JAMES M., 181
WILHOITE
PHILLIP RAINEY, 181
WILKERSON
JOSIE, 181
WILLIAM M. (N.?), 181
WILKES
LILLY JAMES, 167
WILKEY
THOMAS D., 51

www.ingramcontent.com/pod-product-compliance
Lightning Source LLC
Chambersburg PA
CBHW081433270326
41932CB00019B/3182